FIRE IN AFGHANISTAN 1914–1929

For Arthur

FIRE IN AFGHANISTAN 1914-1929

The First Opening to the West
Undone by Tribal Ferocity Years
Before the Taliban

Rhea Talley Stewart

AN AUTHORS GUILD BACKINPRINT.COM EDITION

Fire in Afghanistan 1914-1929:
The First Opening to the West Undone
by Tribal Ferocity Years Before the Taliban
All Rights Reserved © 1973, 2000 by Rhea Talley Stewart

AN AUTHORS GUILD BACKINPRINT.COM EDITION

Published by iUniverse.com, Inc.

For information address:
iUniverse.com, Inc.
620 North 48th Street, Suite 201
Lincoln, NE 68504-3467
www.iuniverse.com

Originally published by Doubleday & Company
2nd Edition

ISBN: 0-595-09319-1

Printed in the United States of America

"Amanullah has lit a fire that will take us a long time to put out."

Sir George Roos-Keppel, June 4, 1919.

"The ways of the British are inscrutable but they always seem to obtain their own ends without compromising their dignity or their honor."

Mahmud Tarzi, October 28, 1925.

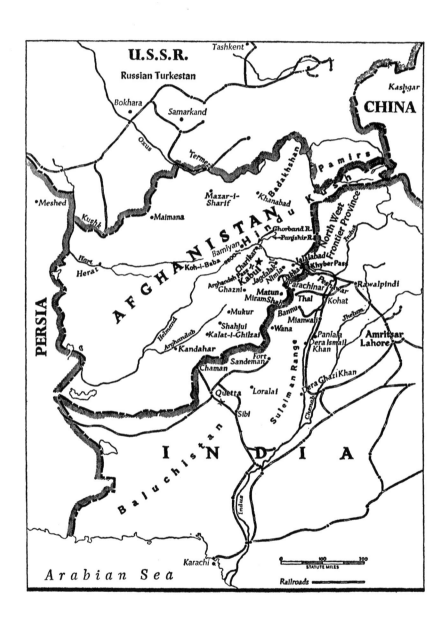

FOREWORD

"Every thing in this book is fact. Every statement, every quoted remark can be documented and, with a few exceptions listed in my chapter notes, all is from primary sources."

So began my foreword to the first edition of this book. I thought this explanation necessary, not only because I had put between quotation marks many words that the dry demands of officialese had put soberly into indirect quotes, but because the story I was telling was so dramatic. I thought I might be suspected of fantasizing, to make things livelier.

Today, as the 21st Century is just beginning, the solid, dependable journalistic sources have told us a great deal about Afghanistan that sounds like an author's imagination run wild…. ragtag bands of tribesmen bringing down a great empire, then quarreling among themselves so that their victory brings the victors only a wasteland, the iron hand of the orphans of that fighting, united behind a religious belief that they distort into denying women the right to a doctor and little boys the right to fly kites, a terror-minded rich man supposedly sending tentacles toward the west. If all that is certified fact, my stories from Afghanistan of the 1920's, which foreshadow all this, should not strike any one as fantastic. Look what happens while we are having breakfast.

The passage of time between editions has given me a second chance that I happily welcome. In the foreword to the first edition, published in 1973, I gave no individual acknowledgement to most of the many Afghans who helped me. I feared to endanger them. Afghan politics have always been volatile, and certain circles suspicious of foreigners. Public friendship with me might have been safe one year, dangerous the next.

Now, however, I may thank especially the Afghan scholar who most supported me, Sayed Qassim Reshtia, a notable historian with connections to the family of King Amanullah, who was a bright, curious teen-ager when the story told in this book ended. Today the distinguished Reshtia lies in a Geneva cemetery and his widow Gololai is a Swiss citizen, and I may say, "Thank you. kind friend." I must thank also A. Hasib Hakimi, the most diligent reader of my first edition, who translated this whole long book into Pushtu, the language of the frontier tribes. This is the third Western book to be thus translated since 1815. The ultimate goal was publication in Pakistan. I saw the manuscript on my last visit to Kabul in 1991., and I hope Mr Hakimi took it with him when, like so many Afghans, he sought refuge from civil war in the Northwest Frontier Province of Pakistan.

The backbone of my research is from the massive archive of the British Empire in London, the Oriental and India Office Collections of the British Library, whose generous assistance I hereby acknowledge. If any one questions the quantity of minutiae in this book, and wonders who would record such details, the answer is that the British Empire did so. Its diplomats were educated, thoughtful men; stationed in a spot so remote that the word "Afghanistanism" meant a fascination with exotic, faraway lands. I suspect that many saved their sanity by enveloping themselves in the smallest details of the world before their eyes, writing it all down., and sending it on to London.

This edition is altered from the first only in this foreword and in the final two pages. Writing in 1973 I had ended on a note of hope and optimism, for I was finishing my manuscript just as Afghan prospects reached their peak. The sad realities of the year 2000 had to intrude. For advice in the preparation of this coda I must thank my friends Thomas Greene, Dr Richard N Frye, Eden Naby and Ann Cottrell Free.

I thank also the Authors Guild, for putting to use a new technology which simplifies publishing by making it possible to print one book at a time, on demand. And let us not forget the creator of this technology, whoever that may be.

Rhea Talley Stewart
Hartford, Connecticut

FIRE IN AFGHANISTAN 1914–1929

CHAPTER 1

The Birth of a King June 2, 1892

Everywhere you go in Afghanistan, you are held in a handful of mountains. As you travel, there always comes a moment when you have rounded the rim of one mountain and suddenly there you are in a sweep of different mountains. The horizon is always close at hand.

So in Afghanistan, for a distant view, men have had to look up. The moon has therefore fascinated Afghans. Today we know what the moon is really like, and it is like Afghanistan. Here is the same unchanging and ungiving surface, marked by peaks and grooves.

In the mountain peaks of Afghanistan, all is brown, gray, lightened in some places by an impersonal sun, in others deepened by the shadows of jagged peaks descending in a relentless ravine.

Gaze over the Valley of Bamiyan, and you face high walls of red rock, once streaked by the tortured upheaval of the earth, and once again distorted by man making honeycombs for monks to live in. The blinded Buddhas carved into the rock, the largest statues in the world, might be giants left over from the same age that twisted the rock, for all they have to do with man.

On the way to Band-i-Amir, there is nothing. The horizon makes a circle around the acres of hard, black soil, speckled with grains of white, which nourish only stones.

Yet when you lower your eyes from the harsh peaks of the Hindu Kush mountains, they are blessed with sudden green, where the water is, and in the wheat fields women in red squat, working toward a harvest.

In the Valley of Bamiyan, not many feet from the Buddhas, a farmer plows with his team of oxen, and from one of those grottoes in the red rocks a twirl of smoke is rising from someone's hearth.

The road to Band-i-Amir is broken by a row of poles carrying a telephone wire beyond the horizon to a man stationed at the sapphire lakes
of Band-i-Amir, and when you get there, he will give you tea.

Man has made his way in Afghanistan, after all.

But geography has not made it easy for him.

Afghanistan owes much of its character to being where it is. It sits
atop Central Asia, and in 1973 it has the Soviet Union on the north,
Iran on the west and south, China on a narrow strip to the northeast,
and on the east and south, Pakistan, which until 1947 was part of the
mass of India ruled by the British.

Conquerors have come. The first was Darius of Persia. In the fourth
century B.C. Alexander the Great came to Bactria, where, three hundred
years earlier, Zoroaster had been born to spread the faith whose followers, the Magi, three hundred years later were to follow a star to Beth-
lehem. Alexander was not a harsh conqueror (he endeared himself
to Afghans by marrying their Princess Roxana when he might have
taken her as concubine) and Darius was actually benevolent. But a
conqueror is always a bogeyman and even today an Afghan child who
does not behave is told, "Clisander will get you." Babur came on his
way to founding the Mogul Empire that would dominate India until
the coming of those new conquerors, the British; Babur loved Kabul
above all places and was buried there. Afghans did their own conquering.
From Ghazni the Idol-Breaker Mahmud kept India sporadically mindful of Afghan power.

Some who came were merchants. There was one main route between
the treasure-filled East and covetous Europe. That route led across
Afghanistan, where it divided southward to the Arabian Sea and westward overland. In the third and fourth centuries A.D. the silk and spice
traders brought Buddhism into Bamiyan. They built the monastery
and carved the giant Buddhas in the cliff. Centuries later, because Mohammed forbade his followers to picture the human form, the Arab
Moslems disfigured all the Buddha faces.

The Arab conquerors left the most enduring residue of all—their
religion. Islam has molded Afghanistan's life to this day, and the constitution of 1964 still affirms that government shall follow the principles of Islam. The Prophet Mohammed preached acceptance of the
will of Allah. This acceptance has given Afghans a special dignity in
the face of their unhelpful landscape and, more recently, in the face of
a technology that has had nothing to say to them.

Two men did damage that has endured to this day. In the thirteenth century, Genghis Khan. In the fifteenth century, Christopher Columbus.

Genghis Khan killed not only every man, woman, and child, but every animal and blade of grass, and lest some person elude him, he made his soldiers wait at the ravaged spot until those in hiding felt safe enough to come outside. Because of Genghis Khan, most ruins in Afghanistan look alike: a few twists that were the mud walls of cities, and that is all.

The lasting harm of Genghis Khan is that he destroyed, along with the people, the irrigation systems they had created. No one was left to replace them. Afghanistan is a dry land; the heavy winter snows must leave enough moisture to last all year. Irrigation means life. The way to Band-i-Amir is dead because once it was irrigated and drained improperly. It turned salt. Of all the places destroyed by Genghis Khan, only Herat, because it is in a fertile valley, really rebuilt itself.

Christopher Columbus sailed west with the intent of replacing Afghanistan as the only route between Asia and Europe. He and Magellan did more than that—they offered Europe a new treasure house. The caravans crossed the Hindu Kush less frequently. Finally Europe did not need them at all. Afghanistan is far less important to a round world than it was to a flat one.

When the sophisticated caravans ceased to bring the news of nations, there was little incentive for people of easier lands to make that hard passage across the mountains. Afghanistan became stagnant. Acceptance of the will of Allah turned into fatalism. Customs hardened. The priests, the mullahs, spoke to Afghans of covering their women's faces, of holy war against the "foreigner" who brought so many disasters, of shunning the books and machines and implements that were strange and therefore not the will of Allah.

The people heard.

Since the world around them held so little of comfort, Afghans drew together toward the human beings they knew. The tribe was the world; the families were the microcosm wherein a face might be recognized. But beyond the jagged horizon, out in the world of state and nation, an Afghan found little to grasp. Beyond his tribe he gave his allegiance nowhere.

Late in the eighteenth century geography began again to alter Afghanistan. Conquest again brought change. This time, instead of one

4

conqueror, there were two—and at two gates. Their conflicts gave Afghanistan safety.

Russia and England were both expanding and the prize was India. Russia coveted India and England had it. Afghanistan stood in the way and therefore was important. The rulers of Afghanistan were wise enough to see that Russia would have walked over her to India, digesting her en route. But England might be satisfied for Afghanistan simply to be there, not necessarily England's, simply not Russia's. Afghanistan played politics and gave England the trump cards.

After two disastrous attempts to occupy Afghanistan, the half loaf with which England contented herself was control of Afghanistan's foreign relations. In return for this control, Great Britain paid an annual cash subsidy to the Amir. Afghans resented this; they resented also that their country was not allowed to deal directly with London but had to go always through the subsidiary, India. Determined to give as little as possible for the subsidy, Afghanistan permitted no official representation of the British Empire within her borders except for a British Agent who had to be an Indian Moslem. He was watched constantly by a spy posing as a tea-seller, who had set up shop across the street from the Agency.

Occasionally the British Empire had something to say to Afghanistan which was too serious for a letter from the Viceroy of India. Then special missions with elaborate arrangements were sent to the Amir. One such mission went in 1893 to Amir Abdur Rahman and negotiated the agreement that settled Afghanistan's eastern boundary with India. This Durand Line was set with no regard for geography or population. It ran between sections of the various tribes that were called Pathans, cutting apart entire families. Since these Pathans cared more for their tribes than for any government, the Durand Line would always be a source of tension.

When Amir Habibullah succeeded his father Abdur Rahman, the British again sent a mission to barter with their subsidy. This time they wanted, in addition to exclusive control of foreign relations, permission to build a railroad into Afghanistan from India. Russia was forcing them to extend Indian railroads by extending her own railway lines in Central Asia. A line into southern Afghanistan would have been far easier to build than rails through the Khyber Pass, that turning, torturous mountain passage in India which led to the Afghan frontier.

Afghanistan behaved with independence and refused to allow the railroad.

But two years later, Afghanistan saw how lightly the world held her opinion when the two giants at her two gates forgot their enmity long enough to sign the Treaty of St. Petersburg. England gained the right to keep Afghanistan under its supervision while Russia took over other areas of Central Asia. No one consulted the peoples thus allotted.

The lack of true independence produced a chafing atmosphere of fierce, frustrated pride. This was the earliest influence on the first son of Ulya Hazrat, chief wife of the about-to-be-Amir Habibullah. This child was born June 2, 1892, in Paghman, a suburb of the capital, Kabul, and after being given a false name to deceive the spirits who might do him harm, he was named Amanullah, which means "The Peace of God."

Amanullah was only the third son of his father, but he had a noble mother, a woman who embodied all the forces that had whipped a group of nomad tribes into a nation. The law of primogeniture was no more honored in Afghanistan than many of its other laws. It was axiomatic that whenever the Afghan throne became vacant, you never could tell.

CHAPTER 2

1914 to 1918

"I desire to inform Your Majesty that a state of war exists in Europe.
Austro-Hungary has declared war on Serbia and Germany has also begun hostilities with France and Russia. As a result, war has also broken
out between Germany and Great Britain, whose interests are vitally
connected with those of France. Under the terms of [our] letter to
the late Amir dated 18th July 1880, which was reaffirmed by Your Majesty in the Dane Treaty of 1905, you agreed to follow unreservedly the
advice of the British Government in regard to your external relations.
In accordance with this agreement, I now advise Your Majesty to remain neutral for the present and to maintain the absolute neutrality
of Afghanistan, to take special precautions to preserve order on both
your frontiers."

The Viceroy of India sent this message to Amir Habibullah on August 8, 1914, announcing the start of World War 1.

Habibullah replied, with thanks for the information, "When the
safety of the Sublime Government of Afghanistan from every kind of
injury and evil intentions of its enemies is assured and no harm comes
to its honor and dignity, and its present state of independence is preserved and maintained, the people of the said Government will, please
God, remain neutral in accordance with your Excellency's friendly advice. Your Excellency may rest assured in this respect."

History would show that the Viceroy was announcing the beginning
of a new world, which would promise a new diplomacy and a new attitude among nations. Not all the promises would be fulfilled, but they
would lead, in Afghanistan, to a new experiment in government. It
would end as it had begun, in conflict and bloodshed.

Amanullah was twenty-two years old. His older half brother, the easy-going Inayatullah, was heir apparent to their father, Amir Habibullah, but the Second Gentleman of the Land was his uncle, Nasrullah, a fanatic Moslem who hated the British so intensely that the Amir had had to restrain him from promoting Holy War against them on the frontier with India.

Amanullah, too, resented the British, but not for their religion. He looked to a future for Afghanistan in the modern world. And British domination was barring the way. Amanullah had never been many miles from Kabul. Except for his father's brief experiment in modern education which had collapsed when the leading teachers were accused of sedition, he had studied only at the military school.

But Amanullah was constantly learning modern ways from his father-in-law, Mahmud Tarzi, who was the only Afghan of his day to adopt a surname. "Tarzi" meant "stylist," and Mahmud Tarzi had made a reputation for perceptive satiric writing while his noble family was in exile in Syria and Turkey during the harsh reign of Amanullah's grandfather. He had suffered much humiliation from British intrigues before he succeeded in accepting the invitation back to Afghanistan of Amir Habibullah, who delighted in his wit and permitted him to establish a newspaper, *Seraj-ul-Akhbar*.

Like all Afghans, Amanullah and Mahmud Tarzi were concerned, in connection with the Great War in Europe, chiefly with Turkey.

Kaiser Wilhelm II had been working to make a friend of Turkey. No other European monarch had deigned to visit Constantinople; Wilhelm did so twice, finding in Sultan Abdul Hamid a soul mate who, like him, felt utter contempt for everyone else in the world. He was photographed on a white horse in Jerusalem and in Turkish uniform wearing a fez.

Haji Wilhelm he called himself. He had no right to the title, which is given only to a Moslem who has performed the Haj, the sacred pilgrimage to Mecca. But if Henry IV of France could say, "Paris is worth a mass," Kaiser Wilhelm could tell himself that India was worth a Haj. The British in the meantime were convinced that he was interested in other Eastern countries only as a steppingstone to their crown of Empire, India. They considered that he was implementing this ambition when he sent officers, arms, munitions, and cheap goods to Turkey.

In Great Britain for many years hardly a public speech had been made in which the word "Turk" was not preceded by the word "unspeakable." As late as July 1914 the Turkish Minister of Marine, Jemal Pasha, went to Paris with good will in his heart for the British and French and asked their aid in regaining the Aegean Islands taken by Italy two years earlier. He was snubbed. In that same month Turkish naval crews were in England preparing to take over two warships that Turkey had ordered built. These ships represented a magnificent and unprecedented cooperation on the part of the humble people of Turkey, for their purchase price of £7,500,000 had been raised by popular subscription and half had been paid over. Now the First Lord of the Admiralty, Winston Churchill, ordered the two ships seized and added to the British Navy. He did not mention reimbursement.

It was only natural that, a few days before the Viceroy announced war to Habibullah, the Turkish Government had made a secret promise to enter the Serbo-Austrian War on the side of Germany if Russia should intervene on the side of England and France.

Turkey was the home of the Caliphate, the supreme seat of the religious authority of all Islam. Its sultan was the Caliph of Islam, whose name was intoned every Friday in every mosque of Afghanistan.

And Amanullah, through Mahmud Tarzi, had emotional ties with a special group of Turks, those who called themselves Young Turks and were attempting to modernize their country and to restore the constitution which had been in abeyance for many years. One of their party, Mustapha Kemal, had been imprisoned for reading such seditious authors as John Stuart Mill. Another author whom the Young Turks read was Mahmud Tarzi, whose unpublished satiric works were circulating underground.

In Afghanistan, Tarzi was editing the country's only newspaper, *Seraj-ul-Akhbar*, and still urging toward modernity, often in the guise of satire. Amir Habibullah tolerated this newspaper for the opportunity it gave to annoy the British whenever that was in his plans. If he recognized some of the satire as being directed at him personally, he never said so. All through Central Asia similar newspapers were being edited by men who, emboldened by the triumph in 1905 of Japan, an Asiatic nation, over Russia, a mostly European nation, were demanding a better place in the world for their countries. "Asia for the Asians" was the motto of *Seraj-ul-Akhbar*, and it was considered that of all the publications of Young Bokharans, Young Khivans, etc., this of the Young Afghans was the best.

Amanullah was a Young Afghan. With his brother Inayatullah, who was director of publications and whose house held the modern printing-press which Amir Habibullah was persuaded to import, Amanullah spent so much time at the newspaper office that he was almost like a member of the staff. It was there that he met Tarzi's daughter, Souraya. Tarzi was modern in his family life as in everything else. Endorsing monogamy, he did not take advantage of the Moslem quota of four wives; although fond of the company of women, he married only the mother of his twenty children. While other Afghan girls were being taught, if at all, only by elderly mullahs who thought the Koran suffi-cient, Tarzi's daughters were having a modern education; the eldest, Kawkab, even served as her father's secretary. Inayatullah married Kaw-kab, with the approval of Amir Habibullah, who admired independence and intelligence in women although his own large harem did not en-courage these qualities. In his teens Amanullah had formed a liaison which was legal, if informal, with one of his mother's ladies-in-waiting, Peri Gul, or Flower Fairy; in 1911 a son, Hiadayatullah, had been born. But when Amanullah married Souraya, he followed Tarzi into mo-nogamy as into so many attitudes; Peri Gul went to live with his mother, Ulya Hazrat. To all purposes Souraya was Amanullah's only wife.

Now, with war bursting forth in Europe, *Seraj-ul-Akhbar* began to call England and Russia "mortal enemies of Islam." It said that the traditional protection granted by the English to Moslems had been transformed into a policy of frank hostility to the Moslem element. England, it said, had begun the war from envy of Germany. All German military resources, or rumors of them, were described by *Seraj-ul-Akhbar* with enthusiasm.

It was the season when nomad tribes were completing their descent from the Afghan hills into the Indian lowlands, and the rumor spread that an attack on India by Afghanistan was imminent, that weapons were camouflaged in the nomad caravans.

On October 26 a German fleet that had been harboring at Constanti-nople, joined by some small Turkish vessels, entered the Black Sea and attacked the Russian ports.

And on November 5 the then Viceroy of India, Lord Hardinge of Penshurst, wrote to Amir Habibullah: "I regret now to have to inform Your Majesty that, owing to the ill-advised, unprovoked and deliberate action of the Ottoman Government, war has broken out between Great Britain and Turkey . . . I am not blind to the fact that ignorant and mischievous persons may attempt to make this war an excuse for raising trouble on falsely called religious grounds."

"Holy War," however, was exactly what the Turks called it, and their cry, "Jehad!" the call to Holy War, was heard throughout Afghanistan. It promised that any Moslem killed fighting would become a Shaheed (martyr) and be assured a place in Paradise.

Nasrullah had been agitating for years to unite his hatred of the British and his love of Islam in a jehad. Mahmud Tarzi would also have fought the British in India, and said so in print. Habibullah, determined to remain neutral, confiscated several issues of the newspaper and threatened to kill Tarzi.

Habibullah wrote to the Viceroy on March 23, 1915, "Even now Your Excellency has pointed out in your letter . . . that the temperate preachings of the mullahs on the frontier and the improvement in the tone of the writings of the *Seraj-ul-Akhbar* are due to my friendly influence . . . I will not, please God, as far as it lies in my power, give preference to the false ideas of ignorant and shortsighted persons, over the interests and welfare of the affairs of my state." Among the "ignorant and shortsighted persons" he was including virtually the entire population of Afghanistan.

Habibullah, in singlehanded determination, held his country in the mold of neutrality that prevented its attacking India. Those who opposed this policy thought that he was ignoring an opportunity sent by Allah himself to be rid of the conquering British. If Afghanistan attacked India, many thousand troops in India would have to be sent to the Afghan frontier, troops that were now boarding ships to go to Europe for the fight against the Central Powers that included the Moslem Turkey. It seemed to many Afghans that Habibullah's neutrality, in operating against Turkey, was operating against all Moslems and, by extension, against Afghanistan itself. The critics were correct in assessing the importance of Habibullah's neutrality. By clever manipulation he gave Great Britain the freedom to employ in Europe the entire Army of India.

Although Habibullah could not "bargain like a shopkeeper," as he once complained, he could bargain like a king, on a grand scale. With the verve of a Central Asian caravan trader who is always willing to try for a higher price, Habibullah kept gazing steadily all this time at a prize that he coveted for his people: freedom from British control.

The Germans also knew the value of his neutrality and began a campaign to alter it. In August 1915 their mission started for Kabul by way of Persia, headed by Oskar Niedermayer and Werner Otto von Hentig and including, as well as Germans and Turks, some Indian revolutionaries. Habibullah, warned of its approach by the British, assured them, "The entry of this party into the territory of the sublime, God-granted Government of Afghanistan will, God willing, have no detrimental effect whatever on the attitude of neutrality of the sublime God-granted Government of Afghanistan." But he had sent for these men and would see what they had in their minds.

Here is how von Hentig described the mission's arrival on the outskirts of Kabul after a twenty-four-day march across the bare mountain ranges of central Afghanistan:

"At about a half hour's distance from the town, the members of the Turkish colony were assembled, recognizable by the national fez. Hearty cheers greeted us. From then on, we had the feeling that we already possessed friends in Kabul, and that we were coming into connection with a part of the world which, if unknown to us, was not entirely so to others. Involuntarily our bearing became solemn, and this was noticeable even in the pace of our horses.

"Suddenly, from a row of poplars, a signal was heard, which was repeated from two more distant posts. Soon there appeared to the left of the road a small body of troops on the march, a company, a squadron and a battery of the famous troops of Kabul. They had always been mentioned to us when, at Herat, we had been unable to conceal our disappointment at the Afghan militia. A loud salaam was, as it appeared, ordered by the officers standing in front, who were Turkish or at least wore Turkish uniforms. Certainly the men did not impress us unfavorably. Followed by them, we marched through the little village, lying sheltered outside the real town, about the walls of the palace of Baber Shah. The people in the streets and on the roofs saluted us with shouts of joy. It may, perhaps, sound arrogant to express the opinion, but we seemed to read distinctly on all faces the hope that, with our arrival, a new day was dawning for the country."

During the following days, von Hentig found more Europeans in Kabul than he had expected. "There were Austrians, prisoners of war, who had escaped from camps in Russian Turkestan and crossed the frontier as best they could. The Amir had received them all kindly. They were getting on as best they could but lived in calm security, waiting for peace. I included them among my men and, together with them, started the practical campaign which I considered would be the most productive of results in Kabul: an active propaganda proving our pre-eminence in culture and civilization.

"One of them, a mason, built the hospital at Kabul according to our hygienic principles of light, air and cleanliness. Another, a Hungarian sculptor, adorned the entrance hall of the hospital with examples of statuary. A decorator embellished the dissecting-room, the little mosque, the authorities' waiting-rooms. The others gave a fresh technical development to manual labor in Kabul by examples of their work. They all quickly won the esteem of the people and took a leading position among them.

"Among the Afghans, we Germans met with much sympathy. For one thing, in spite of our modest pretensions and means, we were good customers in a land so short of money; then, as on principle we bought no English goods, we were able to give the businessmen many a stimulating idea for turning the excellent handmade cotton and other dress materials to account.

"But above all, the people listened eagerly when we told them about the state of affairs in the great world outside, what the war had called forth, and how it would all be likely to end, including the effects on Afghanistan."[1]

Amanullah, hoping to play a greater role in his country than his position in the royal family entitled him to play, was delighted to hear this news of the world, and charmed by the Turkish members of the mission, whose language he could speak somewhat. Von Hentig described him as "a very quiet, intelligent prince." Thirteen years later, in another country, Amanullah would recognize von Hentig's face in a crowd and rush up to embrace him.

An English engineer named Lynch, whom Habibullah had engaged to work in the manufacture of soap, candles and smokeless powder, left for India, where he said that he did not intend to return to Afghanistan "until the Germans left Kabul." He was asked why not.

"Because they are treated like rajahs and we are treated like dogs."

Lynch was asked if the Amir had not always treated him well and paid him handsomely.

"Oh, yes, but these people are treated like rajahs, all of them, Europeans, Moslem deserters from your Indian regiments, and Sikhs, all are treated as if they were Moslems."

He said that he never spoke to the Austro-German party, although he had seen them often in the bazaar. "We passed each other growling like two dogs."

Everyone in Afghanistan, except the Amir, was bitterly hostile to the British, Lynch reported. "Though, mind you, I don't think they'll dare do anything as long as H.M. is alive."

The British countered this on a level in which they were competent indeed: that of class discrimination. Concerning Habibullah's assurances that the German mission would not influence him, the Government of India wired to London, "Nothing could be more satisfactory than his reply. The Amir concludes by referring to my statement that his friendly assurances would be brought to the notice of the King-Emperor, who would warmly appreciate them, and asked to be informed later how His Majesty's appreciation is made manifest. Knowing how very highly Amir values the personal regard of King-Emperor, I made statement referred to in order to make his promises more binding upon him and I now trust latter may be urgently brought to His Majesty's notice. If His Majesty would authorize me to communicate a personal message to the Amir, effect would be most valuable both as gratifying Amir and in strengthening his hand against antagonistic influences that surround him."

A few days later, on September 24, 1915, King George V wrote to Habibullah from Buckingham Palace:

"My dear friend, I have been much gratified to learn from my Viceroy of India how scrupulously and honorably Your Majesty has maintained the attitude of strict neutrality which you guaranteed at the beginning of this war, not only because it is in accordance with Your Majesty's engagements to me, but also because by it you are serving the best interests of Afghanistan and of the Islamic religion.

"I am confident that Your Majesty will continue to preserve unchanged this friendly attitude towards me and my government till victory crowns the arms of the allies, a prospect which daily grows nearer.

"You will thus still further strengthen the friendship I so greatly value, which has united our people since the days of your father, of illustrious memory, and of my revered predecessor, the late Queen Victoria."

In the words of Rudyard Kipling, who understood such nuances, "A throne sent word to a throne."

Habibullah, impatient to receive this letter, delegated a man already on the frontier as messenger. The Sarhang of Dakka went to Landi

Khana in the Khyber Pass accompanied by a company of irregular troops wearing uniforms new for the occasion and carrying a large standard. He arrived two hours ahead of his appointment, for fear the British might bring the letter to the frontier station at Torkham thereby depriving him of his excursion into their territory. To his delighted surprise, a shamiana, or tent, had been put up by Landi Khana stream and refreshments prepared and an honor guard of Khyber Rifles assembled. With ceremony the letter was handed to the Sarhang of Dakka, who had been instructed to carry it to the Amir personally.

Habibullah was standing up when he took King George's letter from the Sarhang, a mark of great honor since he generally sat for such an occasion. He held out his own hand to the Sarhang, who was so overcome with emotion that he did not see it at first. Trying not to weep, the Sarhang described for Habibullah in detail the circumstances of the handing-over at Landi Khana, and then was given seven Lee-Medford rifles for the use of his orderlies.

The Viceroy had told Habibullah that the letter "carries with it some material advantage. His Majesty's Government have been pleased to increase Your Majesty's subsidy by two lakhs [200,000] of rupees a year." That was what Habibullah had meant by asking "how His Majesty's appreciation is made manifest."

The Viceroy awaited Habibullah's thanks. After a month it had not come. "The delay causes us some anxiety," said the Government of India, "and would seem to indicate that antagonistic influences are at work."

From the antagonistic influences a message sent back to Germany, signed by Niedermayer, said, "We were at last received by the Amir in a friendly manner on October 26. The Amir's explanations did not give us much hope. Please send us as soon as possible the Turks for my expedition."

The Turks were crucial and another member of the mission wrote, "I believe it is quite possible to draw Afghanistan into the war if about a thousand Turks with machine guns and my expedition arrive here. Perhaps we shall find it necessary to begin by organizing a coup d'état. Here nothing is ready for war but we are ready to proceed to extremities. It is absolutely necessary gendarmery should accompany my expedition from Isfahan [in Persia] to the frontier, as the roads are held by the enemy. From here, that is to say, from Kabul, we can count on no assistance!"

These letters were never delivered in Germany. The messenger carrying them became frightened and handed them over to the Russian Consul-General in Meshed, Persia, who gave them to his allies, the British, who told their contents to Habibullah, pointing out that a coup d'état would probably include his own death.

From another source pressure was put on Habibullah. A party of Indian revolutionaries, mostly students, formed "The Army of God" and drew up plans for a provisional government of India which would put India under the rule of the Amir of Afghanistan. On arrival in Kabul this party, headed by Maulvi Obeidullah, was put into jail for a fortnight, then released and treated with courtesy. They denounced the Amir as "a religious traitor" but Nasrullah was their friend, and Amanullah showed them so much sympathy that they described him as "an excellent man and a promoter of the jehad."

The Army of God, like the German mission, was undone by a messenger's timidity. Writing out his plans on three squares of yellow silk, Obeidullah gave them for delivery to conspirators in India to an Indian who had worked in the household of a British official. This man had been entrusted with the care of the official's son. In India, apparently with a subconscious urge for self-destruction, he paid a totally unnecessary visit to his employer, who naturally asked where was the son. The reply was evasive. Beating followed; so did a search of the messenger. The silk letters fell into the hands of the British.

On December 11 Habibullah, perturbed and fearful of losing his control over his subjects, summoned the British Agent. This was Hafiz Saifullah, a gentleman who like Nasrullah had learned by heart the entire Koran. Habibullah locked the door before he spoke and his most important words were:

"I am not a double-dealer . . . I mean to stand by the British if I can, but do not judge me by individual acts."

He asked that the British judge him "not from what is current as rumors or the bazaar gossips, but from what actually occurs as an event resulting from my deeds or utterances." He said that any deviation in his past actions, if they did not raise doubt in British minds, would have "secured for me a verdict of infidelity and heresy at the hands of my Moslem subjects or the frontier Moslem tribes."

Public opinion eventually made it necessary for Habibullah to sign a treaty with the German-Turkish mission, but its terms were so stringent that only a victorious Turkey and Germany could have fulfilled them, and in that case a treaty would be useful. He demanded ten million pounds sterling and large quantities of arms and ammunition, telling the mission that war would begin as soon as "20,000 to 100,000 Turks arrived in Afghanistan." He initialed this treaty on January 24, 1916.

Four days later he held a durbar, a ceremonial reception, warning the British in advance not to be disturbed by what might transpire.

Asking the people to gather closely around him because his throat was hurting and he could not talk loudly, Habibullah announced that civil war had broken out in Persia and that an outside force had been asked to enter to keep peace. "This state of things is neither satisfactory nor reasonable, and is utterly destructive of the national life of any nation. Unity in a nation is the only vital force which keeps it alive and strong.

"Without this power a nation must end as in the parable of the three intruders, one of whom was a sayed [a descendant of the Prophet], another a mullah, and the third a commoner, who one morning entered a garden of apricots in order to eat some fruit from the trees. The owner of the garden, when he saw that the intruders outnumbered him, devised a trick to overcome them. He first addressed the commoner, saying, 'This is an estimable sayed sahib, and the other is a mullah sahib; against these there can be no objection whatever, because of their sanctity and reverence; but what business have you to enter my garden and make mischief therein?' The foolish sayed and mullah supported the cause of the owner and helped him to seize the commoner and tie him tightly. Next, using the same process of reasoning, the owner of the garden induced the sayed to help him to fasten up the mullah, and when the sayed was left alone, it was an easy matter for the owner to dispose of him. When all three intruders had thus, one by one, been secured, what the owner did with them may better be imagined than described."

This parable showed, Habibullah said, that there must exist no discord or difference of any kind between the ruler and the ruled, especially on occasions like the present when the conflagration was sky high on all sides.

"Accordingly, I have held this durbar to inform you of what is going on in surrounding countries, because my means of obtaining information are wider than yours, and to forewarn you to be careful to guard against anything you consider destructive in the case of others. I have ordered that similar durbars be held at each and every center of all the provinces and that the people shall be informed by means of a circular [here Habibullah raised his hand to show the circulars he had already printed] which will be sent by trustworthy messengers to be read on my behalf to the people assembled in the durbars, while copies will be issued to each and every delegate and representative, to even representatives of the smallest section of a clan or tribe. I have ordered the highest officials from among members of the royal family to receive in their own quarters delegates and representatives to instruct them fully."

Thereby Habibullah hoped to show to the whole court the clarity of the conflict in the world. The conflict in the court itself was made apparent when Habibullah looked around for the great stacks of circulars he expected to see. His finance officer, the Mustaufi-ul-Mamalik, said that the circulars were still at the press.

This delay seemed suspicious to those who knew of a controversy that had taken place a few days earlier, in the Amir's presence. The Mustaufi-ul-Mamalik, who was a friend of Nasrullah and Inayatullah and a prominent member of the party which hated the British on religious grounds, had said, "Enver Pasha has received a high distinction from the Kaiser, so I expect a similar one from His Majesty the Amir, for whom I am ready to sacrifice my life, my children and my property. I can myself contribute six lakhs of men, fully equipped, from Koh-i-Daman and Kohistan alone; we must help our religion and our coreligionists the Turks, if we claim to be Moslems. If we have made friendship with the British, we must end that friendship now since we have received an appeal through a Mission from our co-religionists the Turks who need us. Otherwise they are lost and their annihilation really means our annihilation because we and the Turks are branches of the same national tree which is rooted on religion alone."

Nasrullah agreed with him. So did Inayatullah.

But disagreement came from another important Afghan, on political rather than religious grounds. This was the Musahib, an official whom Habibullah had brought back from exile in India along with his five sons, one of whom, Nadir, was Commander-in-Chief of the Afghan Army. "This war is no religious war," he said. "Besides, we have experienced no breach of trust in any way from Great Britain, who is a friendly power, and at any rate, we are quite unable to stand against the British alone. Are you going to help the Turks with resources which have to be ordered from India? Take for instance kerosene oil, which is not sufficient even to illuminate properly this one city of Kabul. But I think we can excuse your remarks because you have not been able to go to India and see the British with your own eyes."

Amir Habibullah, returning to the religious question, commented that Islam was based on fidelity to a covenant one had made.

Nasrullah and Inayatullah objected. A whole nation, they said, could not be bound by a contract made by an individual even though the individual was a king; a king should ask the opinion of the people; this was the true meaning of the Koran.

A battle of quotations from Holy Writ, particularly against Nasrullah, who knew the Koran by heart, held no attraction for Habibullah. It was an irate Amir who exclaimed that Nasrullah had better send a man at once to call on the British Agent so that he might be given an ultimatum to leave for India as a preliminary to declaring war against Great Britain. At this outburst, everyone stopped speaking. Habibullah stalked into another room.

Harassed and attacked even in his own family, Habibullah told the Viceroy on the subject of the two lakhs increase in subsidy, "The small compensation is considered as an insult to the honor of Afghanistan." The Viceroy's reply, effusively worded, was a veiled threat of war against Afghanistan by those two rivals now united, Britain and Russia. But the British were worried and one official in the India Office in London mused in a memo: "We had already heard that Ulya Hazrat was strongly pro-British, but she is very much Europeanized and it is doubtful whether her influence amounts to much. Would it be worth while to give her the 'Crown of India' [a decoration] as an encouragement. Perhaps not. The list of wives of Indian chiefs who have it is not very impressive and it might be regarded as another insult."

At the same time, Habibullah asked to be sent forty-four lakhs out of the balance of his subsidy on deposit, which was forty-nine lakhs. "Demand for this large payment is ominous, but Amir may actually require money; he doubtless also wants to have it safe and may be testing our good faith and solvency. In any case we shall of course pay the amount promptly."

Meanwhile the war in Europe was taking on a philosophic coloration. There was talk of a new world when the shooting should stop, of a peace conference that would take into account the wishes of smaller

nations, a prologue to the slogans of "making the world safe for de-
mocracy," "open covenants openly arrived at," "self-determination."
Remembering the Treaty of St. Petersburg and the highhanded ways
of great nations, Habibullah agreed sincerely when his family told him
that, at the least, he should get England's promise that Afghanistan
would be represented at the Peace Conference.

"The demand is, of course, preposterous," the Viceroy, Lord
Chelmsford, wrote to Sir Austen Chamberlain, Secretary of State for
India. "Indeed, we take it that even the strongest political consideration
could not justify us in proposing the admission of the representative of
a petty neutral state to whatever form of peace conference may take
place at the end of the war."

Beset with difficulties within his own nation and his own family, Habibullah remained a stanch ally of Great Britain.

But in 1917 Britain lost another and more important ally; the Tsar
of Russia abdicated on March 15, and the Soviet Government made a
separate peace with Germany and Turkey, releasing all the prisoners
that had been interned in Russian Turkestan and creating a new possibility of danger to the Allies through Afghanistan, since those Austrians and Germans, if unified and disciplined, might converge on
India.

Habibullah sent the Viceroy of India a proposal to make immediate
war on Russia and its new régime. The Viceroy, employing diplomatic
wisdom, did not forward this message to London, where it might not
have been recognized as just a bargaining gambit.[2]

At about the same time Seraj-ul-Akhbar published a cartoon showing
Uncle Sam with his finger to his forehead, pondering a decision. And
in April 1917 the United States made the decision to become an ally
of Britain.

On November 11, 1918, at 11 A.M., the Allies proclaimed a victory
for which Habibullah claimed a large share of credit.

"It is I who have caused India to be swept away of its armies to be
able to fight in France, in Europe and in Egypt," Habibullah had said.
He was right. More than seven hundred thousand Indian soldiers had
gone to fight in Europe, and some of those who fought most bravely
were most closely allied to Afghans by religion and family. Moslems
formed only one-fifth the population of India, yet they had provided
more than one-third the soldiers. Tribes of the two provinces closest to
Afghanistan in geography and tribal ties, the North-West Frontier

Province and the Punjab, which held one-fifth the Moslem population of India, had furnished five-sixths of all Moslem troops.[3]

Like them, Habibullah had paid a price for his support, not in blood but in a weakened position at home, in moral suffering, in the polarization of dissident elements in Afghan society. Exhausted, he was delegating more and more of his regal authority to other people.

To Amanullah and to many others it was evident that the new world of which men were talking everywhere meant a change in the old order even in Afghanistan.

CHAPTER 3

1918 to February 19, 1919

As a young prince, Amanullah liked to put on shabby trousers and long shirt, wrap a slightly soiled turban around his head, toss a worn posteen over his shoulders, and go right into the teahouses where men sat cross-legged on the floor, gossiping. He took along only an aide-de-camp, similarly if reluctantly attired. The flickering light from a dish of oil would be rather dim. If anyone recognized a king's son in a gathering of camel drivers and tinsmiths, no one let it be known.

Later, as Amir, Amanullah was to follow the same pastime. Once in the Hazarajat, in the center of Afghanistan, he asked in a teahouse why there were so many complaints about public officials. Had not the Amir visited their province only last week and instructed the officials to treat his people kindly?

"The visit of the Amir is like a summer rain," he was told. "It is over quickly and one might never know it had been." That was knowledge which would never have been his had he emulated, not Haroun-al-Raschid of the *Thousand and One Nights*, but his father Habibullah.

In winter, when the Amir and his court moved to the warmth of Jalalabad, Amanullah used to remain behind as governor of Kabul. During those months he visited the prisons to see what prominent men his father had jailed, and often he would release them. The releases may have been sometimes whimsical, and based on emotion, but the sentences imposed may have been equally whimsical. Often a prisoner needed food and money to return home; Amanullah supplied that. He also gave food to prisoners who, having no relatives to bring them meals, were dependent on the scanty provisions of the jail. When men from outlying provinces came to Kabul on official business, it was Amanullah who smoothed their way.

He was also a frequent mourner for the dead, assembling with relatives to recite the Fatiha, or the first chapter of the Koran, according to Moslem custom. His mother was credited for pushing him into much of this sociable activity; she had been credited also for suggesting to Amir Habibullah when he succeeded to the throne—and for a while there seemed a chance of Afghanistan's falling into the tumult that generally followed the death of an Amir—that he cement his position with the Army by offering a raise in salary. Amanullah was for a long time her only son, and the instrument through which the ambition of Ulya Hazrat could be fulfilled and her energy could find an outlet.

Amanullah was an attractive prince, of medium height by Afghan standards, round in face and inclined to roundness in figure, with bright black eyes that were never still, hands that constantly punctuated his conversation, and a staccato manner of talking as if he had too much to say to wait for it to come out sedately. By the start of 1919, the name of Amanullah was being spoken with praise all over Afghanistan.

For Amir Habibullah, on the other hand, all the faults of his past years were being remembered and enlarged. While Afghanistan had been tugged in different directions by the forces of the Great War, she had remained in emotional bondage to her distant and difficult ruler. Outside pressure vanished, and now she looked at him and wondered. It was like a marriage that survived years of cataclysm and then fell apart in peace because, as the husband explained, "We never had the chance to know how we felt. It would have been like taking an electrocardiogram during an earthquake."

"He is lucky," men said of their Amir in the bazaar. "He has long since given up the kingdom and said good-bye to it, but the kingdom does not give him up."[1]

They talked about the way he ate a chicken killed by his French cook, who would simply lop off its head. A Moslem, when taking a chicken's life, or when pulling the trigger to shoot at a flying duck, cried out, "Allah akbar!" "God is Great!" To eat flesh killed by a non-Moslem without invoking God's name was to eat something unclean. Habibullah had always eaten this way. He had always worn European clothes. Now men found all this disturbing. When he invited only a few courtiers to dine with him, instead of opening his table to everyone who happened to be around, they said he was stingy.[2]

Especially did the people complain of the time and money Habibullah spent on his hobbies, the chief of which was women. He had one of the East's last large harems; whenever a tribe wished to make him a gift, they knew that a girl would be welcome. No one was ever certain of the population of his harem, but the number of his children was fifty-eight, or approximately one-quarter the number with which legend would credit him.

In the evenings Habibullah would go out horseback riding surrounded by a clutch of wives riding astride in fashionable habits made for them in London by a tailor who kept all their measurements and provided also dresses with high boned collars and leg-of-mutton sleeves. The royal wives, while riding, wore hats from which fell triple folds of veiling. Elsewhere in Kabul women were covering themselves in a sort of slipcover known as a chaderi, falling over the head to the ground, with only a row of crocheting at eye level to permit viewing of the world. In the countryside, where women had to work in the fields, economics decreed custom and a veil over the head sufficed for morality. The royal ladies had freedom to wear brimmed and veiled hats of the type which European ladies used to wear for motoring; in the court they often met men and talked with them; one of Ulya Hazrat's daughters, Nur-us-Seraj, was already catching the eye of one of the Musahib's sons, Hashim.

The people of Afghanistan resented the dresses made in London and brought over the seas so expensively. They resented the European furniture in the palaces, the hours that Amir Habibullah spent in developing photographs and making turnip soup. They resented the delight with which he had announced the victory of Great Britain.

Habibullah was giving them cause to grumble, for he was growing more irascible and irresponsible. The smallest offense would now provoke him to the harshest punishment. The Mustaufi-ul-Mamalik, whom he once had threatened to execute for exploiting the people with his taxation, now became one of his principal advisers, when he would take advice from any one. "He is a wolf," Habibullah had said of this man, "but he is under my hand."[3] It was whispered that Habibullah was taking aphrodisiacs to improve his performances in the harem, and that these were affecting his personality.

Between him and Ulya Hazrat it was no longer the same. Always there had been as much will power as love in their relationship; people suspected that his sessions in her bed had as much of ceremony as of passion. Now all the love disappeared, on both sides, and as with his nation, the two looked upon each other without illusion. She, who had tolerated his affection for other women, so natural in a polygamous society, now found his excesses disgusting. He, who had once spent the night in a summerhouse when banished from her bed and then served her tea with his own hands in reconciliation, now saw only a scold and a domineering shrew.

Toward the end of 1918 one of his four queens, the mother of Inayatullah, died. He married another, and there was speculation as to the effect on Ulya Hazrat's position of this new marriage, for here was a bride of family as noble and influential as hers, not likely to defer to her as the other wives did.

Habibullah was impotent with his new wife.

In Afghanistan there was much casting of spells on newly married couples to prevent sexual relations during the first three days. Some families announced that, in order to prevent a spell by some enemy, they were casting the spell themselves. This was a kind, considerate act toward young bridegrooms, who, confronted with brides they had not seen until the ceremony, were thereby given an excuse for taking it easy until they became adjusted. Habibullah, however, needed no such indulgence.

Affairs of the harem, even such intimate ones, were soon known all over the court, and it was said that Ulya Hazrat had cast a spell on this new marriage. In the light of her immense influence over Habibullah, the sort of dominion that cannot be broken even by distaste, perhaps the whispers were psychologically true. At any rate, Habibullah soon divorced the new bride and sent her back to her family.

But Habibullah had not forgotten his country quite as completely as the Afghans in the bazaars believed. He still had his eye on the reward for which he had kept her neutral against all odds.

Now Afghanistan stood between a strong though weakened India and a Russia whose new government was so busy consolidating itself that no energy seemed to be left for conquest. In fact, Russian Turkestan was something of a buffer itself. Railways had been built there before roads; when a revolt of train workers brought the railways to a stop, communication was difficult and the hold of the Central Government was tenuous. The President of the Turkestan Government could look at an army order signed by Lenin and Trotsky and say, "This order is nothing but a scrap of paper in our eyes. Moscow is so far away that we do what seems right to us."[4]

But force was not to be important in this world after the war. The great powers had said so. Especially had Woodrow Wilson, President of the United States, spoken of self-determination and of respect for the rights of small nations. All over the world these small nations, many of whose names had never come to Wilson's notice, considered that these words applied to themselves.

On January 18, 1919, the Peace Conference opened in Paris. Soon it was besieged by hopeful citizens of small nations, looking for a new kind of international justice, whom an American journalist likened to "the halt and maimed among the nations waiting around the diplomatic pool of Siloam for the miracle of the moving of the waters that never came."[5]

Lord Curzon, Britain's Under Secretary of State, complained of "crowds of people from every land under the sun, Syrians, Zionists, Armenians, Poles, Ukrainians, Chaldeans, everyone who wants to influence the conference. They take rooms in the same hotels as we are, and they dog our footsteps wherever we go."[6]

The Persian delegate finally went home in disgust. A young Indo-Chinese who would later take the name Ho Chi Minh, when refused an audience with any official, went back to his room and wept.[7]

But Habibullah knew nothing of this on February 2, 1919, when, with the same idealistic hope as all the others, he wrote to the Viceroy asking that Afghanistan be represented at the peace conference.

". . . I have considered it necessary and incumbent upon me to write to Your Excellency to say that if the Exalted Government of England can obtain from all the attendants and members of the said conference a written agreement recognizing the absolute liberty, freedom of action and perpetual independence of the Sublime Government of Afghanistan free from future interference, damage or loss, and hand it over to me, well and good; otherwise it will be unavoidable for the representatives of the Sublime Government of Afghanistan to attend the said conference, to put forward and argue all their established rights of liberty, complete freedom of action and settled independence and to obtain, God willing, a written agreement according to their own desire under the signature of the Peace makers there."

Britain owed Afghanistan more than a million rupees, which Habibullah requested nine days later. But this debt to Afghanistan, both moral and financial, was not the only one which the British Empire found herself facing as the war ended. In the spring of 1915 she had promised Constantinople and the Straits to the Tsar of Russia, who made concessions in Persia. Earlier, when she was persuading Italy into the war, she had made certain concessions in Asia Minor which ran counter to even earlier promises to Greece. The Arabs, led by the legendary Lawrence of Arabia, had been induced to aid the Allies by promises of control over the lands they would win from the Turks. France suspected that Britain was not playing fair and intended to keep those lands for herself. Whereupon in 1916 Britain was unfair in a different way and gave France a future share in Lebanon, Syria and Adana. Then Italy raised her demands in Asia Minor, and got them.

With all these chickens coming home to roost, the request of an Amir in far-off Afghanistan seemed remote indeed. Someone, remembering the tears of the Sarhang of Dakka on handing over King George's letter, wondered if another such letter might not be an acceptable reward.

The Viceroy, Lord Chelmsford, would have yielded Afghanistan some measure of self-control, as had been contemplated during the war when this concession appeared needed to maintain Afghan neutrality. But in London the opinion was that putting Afghanistan under any sort of international control "would be opening the door (by however small a crack) to the Foreign Powers and giving them some encouragement to interest themselves in a country from which it has always been our policy rigidly to exclude all foreign influence . . . Circumstances may conceivably arise in which we should have no alternative but direct intervention in order to preserve the peace of our Indian border. We may have to send troops into Afghan territory; to occupy Kandahar, even Kabul . . . and if such circumstances arise, we might find our mandatory position a very embarrassing one."

So on February 19, 1919, the Secretary of State for India, Edwin S. Montagu, approved a draft letter explaining why Afghanistan could not approach the Peace Conference but assuring her that England would once again continue to look after her.

On that day, February 19, Amir Habibullah was in Jalalabad at his winter palace, preparing to go camping and fishing—another of his selfish indulgences, thought most Afghans, who did not know of the moves Habibullah was making on their behalf.

What they did know was that an evil spirit seemed abroad in the land. Something was seething. On the Amir's birthday, when he rode into the Kabul bazaar, a mysterious assassin had taken a shot at him. In the past months Habibullah had included among the things to which, once loved, he now took a perverse dislike, his son Amanullah. As his feelings toward Ulya Hazrat hardened, so did his attitude toward the son she had borne him, the son now so popular and at a time when Habibullah could sense the people turning from himself.

The Mustaufi-ul-Mamalik told Habibullah that Amanullah and Ulya Hazrat were conspiring to murder him. After much whispering and speculating in the bazaars, life went on much as before, but one story was that Nasrullah had interceded to save the lives of Amanullah and Ulya Hazrat.

But Amanullah's days as Governor of Kabul were to be few. Habibullah, who liked to alternate his sons in their positions, remembered his forgettable second son, Hayatullah, who on February 19 started to motor from Jalalabad to replace Amanullah in Kabul. Most of the court had moved with the Amir to Jalalabad, even Ulya Hazrat, who maintained her official position despite the estrangement.

On February 19 Habibullah rode to a pass in Laghman for an overnight outing. Nasrullah and Inayatullah went with him. So did Nadir, the Commander-in-Chief, his brother Shah Wali, and their father and uncle. Another in the party was a young friend of Amanullah named Shuja-ud-Dowleh who was the Amir's Head Chamberlain and who had been beaten in the court at Habibullah's command the previous week for some minor offense.

Tents were pitched beside a stream, and after dinner and prayers everyone except the guard went to sleep in the remote stillness. A cousin of Nadir, Ahmed Shah, was in command of the guard. A twenty-four-year-old colonel, Shah Ali Reza, was the officer of the day.

At three o'clock in the morning someone entered Amir Habibullah's tent and put a bullet into his brain.

CHAPTER 4

February 20, 1919, to April 13, 1919

Afghanistan was never to know who killed Amir Habibullah. He was surrounded by people, both sleeping and waking; in that stillness a revolver shot would alert everyone instantaneously. The wonder was not only that, among all those people, an assassin could approach the Amir's bed, but that, among all those people who must have known something significant, no one told.

Of the first alarms, of the cries and the running-around and bringing of lanterns, nothing was ever known. The second son, Hayatullah, who had gone toward Kabul, was summoned back on his uncle Nasrullah's order; later in the day Nasrullah delegated Shuja-ud-Dowleh to go to Kabul as his intermediary with Amanullah. The others remained in Laghman and in the morning they went to Jalalabad in a procession that looked perfectly normal to any passing farmer who was not so extremely keen as to observe that in one motorcar a reclining figure was his Amir, and that he was dead.

A grave was dug on the golf course, appropriately in a setting of one of Habibullah's hobbies. Later he was to be put into a mausoleum within a garden that became a park for women, and it was said that Habibullah was among the ladies that he loved. The Amir who set so much store on dignity was finding little of it in death.

Before the body was taken to the grave, while the important men of Afghanistan stood around, Nasrullah said that according to Moslem custom the late Amir could not be buried until his successor was chosen. Inayatullah, the eldest son, was standing there, but his unaggressive nature and the ambition of his uncle, Nasrullah, were both well known.

The first man to speak was Ali Ahmed Jan, a big handsome nephew of Ulya Hazrat who had been Habibullah's confidential adviser. The Amir had once told the British Agent to treat him as if he were talking to the Amir himself.

Ali Ahmed took the hand of Nasrullah, kissed it, and cried, "You are our Amir!" Inayatullah did the same; then Hayatullah. So, in turn, did the others, many of whom wondered if this scene had not been arranged in advance.

The news was telephoned to Kabul by one of the two telephone lines in Afghanistan which Habibullah had constructed to keep himself in touch with his capital during holidays. Amanullah was told to remain in Kabul and keep the peace. Nothing was announced to the people of Jalalabad. But suddenly in the early afternoon the bazaar was ordered closed. The British Agent, Hafiz Saifullah, who had moved south with the court, reported, "It was not till about 3 P.M. that it was first whispered to me that His Majesty Amir Habibullah had been shot dead at Laghman that morning, but I had no further news as no one, not even those who knew all about the matter, had the courage to tell me about it, though they clearly looked sad and sighed in a melancholy manner. I purposed going out for a walk to ascertain what was happening, but no sooner was my intention known to the Afghan Guard than the Agency mehmandar [escort] hurriedly appeared and requested me not to go out as, in his own words, 'The times are critical!' "

From Amanullah in Kabul came a telephone message, "What was being done to discover and punish his father's murderer?"

What Nasrullah had done was to announce his own accession to the Viceroy of India, who commented that "he lost even less time than Habibullah on his accession."

The Viceroy drafted a reply in which Nasrullah was called "Your Majesty" and after suitable condolences was told, "I understand clearly from what you say that you mean to abide by [the treaties of Habibullah]." Nasrullah's letter implied no such thing. The Viceroy warned London, "It would be dangerous to hold up our acknowledgment. What we want are a peaceful succession and a friendly Amir. If the former were hanging in the balance, delay might turn the scale. It would almost certainly cost us Nasrullah's friendship."

At the same time the Government of India, fearing war, was taking stock of its military supplies. "Modern mechanical affairs, airplanes, etc., have immensely improved the odds in favor of military forces of organized states as against those of a semi-civilized country like Afghanistan," India assured itself.

From London came the cautious advice: "Our policy in the past has been to recognize Amir who has succeeded in establishing himself . . . I greatly doubt whether we should take action which might turn the scale in [Nasrullah's] favor while, unless the future belies the past, it would certainly not make him friendly to us." The note prepared for Nasrullah offered only condolences on his bereavement, which did not seem to trouble him since he had expressed no grief, and promised recognition after his acceptance by the people of Afghanistan.

But events were progressing faster than letters could be composed and written. On the morning of February 21 a durbar of mourning was held in Jalalabad, with all dignitaries wearing simple dress and no sign of mourning, in according with Moslem custom, which decreed also that there should be no chairs.

Nasrullah entered with Inayatullah beside him in the same role which Nasrullah used to play to Habibullah. When all the audience were seated on the floor, Inayatullah broke the silence with a pledge of allegiance to Nasrullah that closed, "I will serve you loyally and obediently, sir, as I served the late Amir, my father." He spoke so softly that few could hear him.

Also seated on the floor, Nasrullah made an address full of quotations from the Koran. The people held out their hands toward him, palms up, in the Moslem gesture of prayer, and asked Allah to bless him. Then Ali Ahmed led persons, in groups of about a hundred, to Nasrullah for more personal allegiance, and later to sign a document that Nasrullah read in a loud voice, stating that the people and princes were in entire agreement as to electing Sardar Nasrullah as their new Amir of Afghanistan and bound themselves permanently to be submissive to him and loyal to his person and throne. All were ordered to sign.

It was a Friday. In all the mosques of Jalalabad the Khutba, in which the name of the ruler is spoken, was read in the name of Amir Nasrullah.

"Thus this grave event," wrote the British Agent, "full of grief and future possibilities, came to an end officially and ceremonially with praiseworthy calm and tactfulness . . . Some of the faces in the durbar were remarkably cheerful, notably those of Ali Ahmed Jan, and Nadir . . . Others were anxious and wore sad expressions, among them being

Musahiban-i-Khan, the late Amir's uncles, all the ghulambachas [serving boys].

"But real affliction and helplessness was apparent on the faces of the sons of the late Amir, truly representing the hopeless condition of their minds."

Amanullah, in Kabul, was not looking helpless.

News of his father's death reached him when he was almost alone, so far as supporters were concerned. Even his mother was away in Jalalabad. But he did have the Treasury and the arsenal.

Amanullah summoned at once the officials in charge of these two assets, and his grandfather's adviser Abdul Quddus, who was no admirer of Nasrullah, and two elderly sardars. They conferred for three hours. Then Amanullah called a meeting of all civil and military authorities in Kabul and announced that Amir Habibullah had been murdered by Nasrullah, who had proclaimed himself Amir. Nasrullah was a traitor, said Amanullah, and he swore on a naked sword blade to avenge his father's death. Those who heard him took the same oath of vengeance.

Amanullah sent a message to Jalalabad demanding again that the assassin be detected and arrested. On receiving it, Nasrullah hastily consulted with his mullah friends and prepared a deputation to go to Kabul to mollify his nephew.

Ulya Hazrat persuaded him to include her in this group. What she really wanted was transportation to Kabul. On arrival she left the mullahs and went to her son's house.

Already Amanullah had taken a step that Afghans always suspected Ulya Hazrat of suggesting by telephone. He announced that the pay of the Army would be raised by five rupees a month and that all arrears would be paid immediately. Nasrullah had offered a raise of three rupees.

Meanwhile Amanullah was drawing on the treasury and the arsenal of all the good will he had earned while releasing men from prison and helping to mourn the dead. Prominent men of Kabul came to offer allegiance and to swear that Amanullah, not Nasrullah, was the rightful heir to the throne that Inayatullah apparently had relinquished as docilely as he had once given up his horse in a wedding procession.

Now Amanullah sent another message to Jalalabad. The civil and military authorities who were there with Nasrullah had left families behind in Kabul. Amanullah threatened to execute these hostages if the murderer of his father was not arrested.

Thereupon erupted all the outrage that had been seething within the common people and the soldiers since their Amir's murder. Their hostility toward Habibullah vanished with the injustice of his death. All the superficial serenity in Jalalabad, the apparent ease of Nasrullah's accession, existed only among the men of importance. It was evident to the whole city that a crime was being concealed, even rewarded, and this contempt for the Law of the Prophet offended the men in turbans who whispered along the warm, dusty streets. They themselves would be quick to take deadly aim at a man who dared take the life of a kinsman, even a distant relative, and would carry the feud into another generation. Amanullah's cry for revenge was a cry which had sounded in their own homes.

A day earlier the British Agent had sent a message: "Everybody is too afraid to utter his suspicion, as it falls on the strongest family in power, the family of Musahiban, a member of which, Shah Wali, is suspected of abetment. Real murderer yet unknown."

Six days had passed since Habibullah's death. Nasrullah was running out of money. Jalalabad was almost isolated. Amanullah was controlling communications with Kabul and the traffic through the Khyber Pass to India, source of so much supply, was slowed. The British Agent sent to Peshawar news of public and military confusion, of efforts to keep the peace, and a warning of danger.

The soldiers in Kabul had got word through to the soldiers in Jalalabad that Amanullah had raised their pay. Among the shoppers in the bazaar and the soldiers at the guard posts it was Amanullah who was being proclaimed as the rightful Amir.

Friday came again, and Nasrullah, who never missed a Friday service at the mosque, was astounded to hear the Khutba read in the name of Amir Amanullah. The mullah who read it did so under force of arms. The soldiers had moved too quickly even for Nasrullah's religious friends. A few parties of tribesmen tried to get through to Jalalabad to help him but were turned back by the guard.

Nasrullah, having little choice, left the mosque, assembled the leading men, and announced his abdication in favor of Amanullah. He and Inayatullah went by motor to Kabul, where they were put separately under house arrest.

One battalion that had gone to Jalalabad with Habibullah was called

a "harami" battalion, which means "bastard," because of its truculent
and obstreperous nature. The Haramis, who already had set upon Inayatullah demanding why he did not claim his own throne, now encircled Nasrullah all the time he was composing his abdication. They
kept calling to him to point out the murderers. Now they decided for
themselves.

Quickly they seized physically the members of the Musahiban family:
Nadir, his brother Shah Wali, their cousin Ahmed Shah, their father and
uncle. They tugged at these distinguished gentlemen; they fastened
their wrists together. They took them in this humiliating fashion to
Kabul. The Mustaufi-ul-Mamalik, who had been so cruel in his day, was
treated even worse, being teased with bayonets until a clever soldier
jumped on his back and rode him about like a horse, thus making the
humiliation into an amusement.[1]

So Amanullah stood in the great court of the Idgah Mosque in Kabul.
Beside him stood the most highly respected mullah in Afghanistan,
Shah Agha. He was a descendant of the Prophet's companion Omar,
whose descendants carried the title Hazrat.* Because this branch of
the family lived in the Shor Bazaar of Kabul, or Noisy Bazaar, they
were known as the Hazrats of Shor Bazaar. They had learning as well
as ancestry to command prestige.

Because haste seemed important, some of the ceremonial trappings
of a coronation, such as the banner that Amanullah's grandfather had
brought from his long exile in Russia, were omitted this day. The Hazrat
of Shor Bazaar simply took a fine silk turban which had been wrapped
around a Kandahari cap and placed it on Amanullah's head.

He thereby proclaimed Amanullah the Amir of Afghanistan.

Afghanistan's future had won a tug-of-war with her past. Nasrullah
would have abolished all the existing aspects of modernity, which Amanullah ached to enlarge. Nasrullah and his nephew had only one thing
in common: the wish to be free of British control.

On March 3 Amanullah wrote his own letter of accession to the Vice-

* The title "Hazrat" here has nothing to do with Ulya Hazrat. Afghans did not,
at that time, have family names, but a multitude of appellations and titles. Almost
the only Afghan surname which appears in this narrative is Tarzi, which means
"stylist" and indicates the advanced nature of its owner. Such apparent surnames
as Musahiban, applied to Nadir and his family, are merely appellations taken from
their father's title.

roy of India, lamenting that his father had been shot "by the hand of a treacherous, perfidious traitor . . . putting my trust in God I placed on my head the crown of the Amirship of my Government of Afghanistan in the capital of Kabul amid the loud acclamations of the people and troops. And this by the grace of God."

Then Amanullah confounded the British by addressing them as an equal.

"Nor let this remain unknown . . . that our independent and free Government of Afghanistan considers itself ready and prepared at every time and season to conclude, with due regard to every consideration for the requirements of friendship and the like, such agreements and treaties with the mighty government of England as may be useful and serviceable in the way of commercial gains and advantages to our government and yours."

Then a letter from Mahmud Tarzi was received by the Foreign Secretary of India announcing the creation of a Department of State of Afghanistan and his own appointment as the head of it. This letter was numbered 1.

The destination of letter #2 was the neighbor with whom Afghanistan in the past had agreed to have no intercourse, Russia, which was a different Russia from the old. Tarzi's letter #2 to the President of the Russian Republic, dated April 7, hoped for permanent relations with the Bolsheviks. Amanullah also wrote to Russia:

"I seize the opportunity of my accession to announce to the Russian Republic my strong adherence to the principle of equality of all men and peaceful union of all people. Afghanistan has hitherto stood apart from all other nations, but now that Russia has raised the standard of Bolshevism, I hasten to add that she has earned the gratitude of all the world. I hope that the honored President of the Russian Republic will not refuse to accept my friendly greeting."

On the same day he wrote to Japan, America, France, Persia and Turkey identical letters: "This is the first time that I have had the good fortune of sending this friendly letter in the name of the Afghan nation, which is ready to perfect itself, and on behalf of the independent and free government of Afghanistan."

The British did not know of any letters except their own, but on March 11 they could read in the Indian press a proclamation of Amanullah that "The Government of Afghanistan shall be internally and externally independent and free; that is to say, all rights of Government that are possessed by other independent powers of the world shall be possessed in their entirety by Afghanistan."

"It is clear that in his present mood he has no intention of standing in the shoes of his father and grandfather," said the British, while the Foreign Secretary of India, A. Hamilton Grant, mused, "Of course, Inayatullah would be a much more satisfactory Amir than Amanullah, but we cannot interfere."

They delayed replying to Amanullah's letter, and regretted it.

While looking to distant horizons, Amanullah was having troubles close at hand. He began his reign by paying off two debts: he hanged the Mustaufi-ul-Mamalik, who had accused him of treason, and he released from ten years' imprisonment his old schoolmaster, Dr. Abdul Ghani, whose conviction for sedition many Afghans attributed to a conspiracy of mullahs hostile to modern education.

But he did nothing about his father's murder. While he made appointments and established a cabinet with Abdul Quddus as Prime Minister, the Musahiban brothers were without assignments and under arrest. The people, however, had not forgotten; there was trouble in Herat where two of the Musahiban family, Suleiman and Hashim, were Governor and Commander-in-Chief. The troops in Jalalabad were restive because they were asked to take a smaller increase in pay than they had been promised.

On April 13 Amanullah attempted to resolve all this at a durbar which was also a trial. Nasrullah was sentenced to life imprisonment (he would die in prison the following year), and Inayatullah to a sort of house arrest. Nadir, Shah Wali, and the rest of the Musahiban family were declared innocent and set free.

Since a scapegoat was necessary, the young Colonel who had been officer of the guard was declared guilty of dereliction, taken outside and immediately killed by bayonets.

But the people knew that Habibullah's murder had its origin far higher, and they began to wonder if that origin might not be Amanullah.

At the same durbar Amanullah proclaimed the independence of Afghanistan and cried out to the British Agent, "Oh, Ambassador, are you listening?"

He felt that his reign was really beginning at that moment. After many dreams he had the reality. And Mahmud Tarzi looked on in the knowledge that his life's work, for which he had come with much difficulty from Turkey, was succeeding. He had ended the publication of *Seraj-ul-Akhbar*, having achieved its aim of independence, and he was beginning the new career of making that independence work.

For these men it was a historic moment when Amanullah spoke the words "free and independent." And history would accept it as such.

But now most Afghans, the poor men in low places and the workers, were thinking more of the justice that had not been served. "Independence" to them was merely a word; religion and honor were the realities.

What disturbed the British when they heard of this durbar was not the pronouncement of independence, which was not new to them, but the discontent that swirled around Amanullah's failure to avenge his father in a way that the humblest Afghan would have done. Whenever Afghan rulers found themselves in trouble at home, they moved against a common enemy abroad, which was Britain.

In later years a British official was to say that one of the darkest days of the British Empire was April 13, 1919, because of two events. One was Amanullah's exoneration of those linked with the murder. The other dark event took place in India, in the Punjab city of Amritsar, in a public square known as the Jallianwalabagh.

CHAPTER 5

April 13, 1919, to June 3, 1919

The Haj is the pilgrimage to Mecca which every faithful Moslem is
obliged to make at least once in his lifetime. In 1919 the pilgrims were
secretly subsidized by the British Empire.

Everything in India cost more after the war, including the fares
charged by the steamship companies that carried pilgrims from the
ports of India into the Arabian Sea and then into the Red Sea for Jid-
dah, the port from which they made the short, emotional journey overland to Mecca. The Government of India arranged for pilgrims from
India and adjacent countries to be conveyed at the same price as before,
subsidizing the steamship companies up to ten lakhs of rupees.

It was important to the Empire in the spring of 1919 that Moslems be
as content as possible since they were complaining of much and it was
known in the highest councils of Empire that they would have more to
complain of when the peace terms for Turkey were announced. "Should
there be anything in the settlement for which the British Government
can take credit vis-à-vis our Moslems, you will no doubt see that the opportunity is not lost," the Viceroy wrote to the Secretary of State for
India.

Those two gentlemen, the Viceroy Lord Chelmsford and Edwin S.
Montagu, Secretary of State for India, had conferred during the war to
find a formula that would give India more self-government. The results
did not make the people of India happy, although Montagu was sensitive to their feelings and needs to a degree that was remarkable in one
of the British governing group, possibly because he was Jewish and his
people had not inherited the earth but had been wandering over it. He
was capable of writing in his diary:

"However confidently it may be said that the Englishman has succeeded in India, the Englishwoman has been a conspicuous failure. She feels race prejudice far more than the men (so bye the bye do the Indian women) and she has little to do. She cannot do the parson's daughter or the squire's wife among people she does not understand, in districts where she is only allowed to remain a short time. So she degenerates, gets unhealthy and embittered . . . I think the women are at the bottom of it. Our women will not like the Indians and will not try to . . . I believe it is true that the mothers of India are the future heads of real sedition; that the women are almost completely alienated, and that they are powers in their own homes and in affairs generally, and work through the men."[1]

The Montagu-Chelmsford proposals for reforms did not ease tension, and then the Indian Parliament passed the Rowlatt Bills, which provided secret trial without appeal for persons accused of sedition, and in other ways affronted both the Hindu majority and the Moslem minority by abridging what was considered the heritage of British Common Law in Britain, now denied to them. Proponents of the bill kept proclaiming the phrase "law and order," while all over India bonfires of riot began to flicker. Mohandas Gandhi, leader of the All-India Congress, proclaimed April 6 a Day of Humiliation and called for civil disobedience.

The flicker of violence became a blaze. More than most other provinces, the Punjab reacted violently, the land that had sent most men to fight on behalf of these very British against whom they now were fighting. More rewards had been expected there. In Amritsar three bank messengers were burned to death, the luckiest being clubbed senseless in advance. An English woman missionary was severely wounded; a mob destroyed the railway station. The Government of India sent army reinforcements headed by Brigadier-General Reginald Dyer, who on April 13 reported from Amritsar that after some arrests, all was quiet.

Toward sunset that day about six thousand persons were observing a Hindu holy day, trading livestock, and otherwise conducting their business in the Jallianwalabagh, an open space closed in by houses with a few narrow lanes between. Most of them had not heard a proclamation that day forbidding public assemblage. Dyer led his Gurkha troops to a high plateau on one side of the square; to his exasperation the cars carrying his machine guns could not pass through the lane. His men had rifles, however, and on his command with no warning they opened fire.

For ten minutes they kept up a fusillade—1,650 rounds of ammunition. Dyer personally directed the fire to those places where the crowd —or targets, as he called them—were thickest. At the close of those awful ten minutes there were 379 dead and about 1,200 wounded, for whom he did not consider it "his job" to be concerned. He felt like "reducing the town to ashes," he told friends. A few days later he issued an order that all Indians who passed the lane where the woman missionary had been attacked must crawl on all fours, or be flogged publicly.

The Reverend C. F. Andrews of St. Stephen's College, Delhi, wrote to the Viceroy's secretary, "I have read in the press of public whippings in Lahore, that any shopkeeper not opening his shop may be whipped. His Excellency may not be aware that of all the insults and humiliations, this is the one which will rankle most and will never be forgiven." And later that day, after meeting an eyewitness to the whippings, the Reverend Mr. Andrews wrote another letter: "I cannot exactly explain to you wherein the depth of the sentiment lies about this special form of punishment in this country, but I have lived among Indians so long that I have the instinct in me—the loathing, the hatred against the oppressor that it engenders, the sense of shame at the uncovering in public of a person's nakedness—I cannot explain it but it is a universal instinct and cannot be lightly treated.

"I know the provocation of the outrages on Europeans in Amritsar, but this public whipping is being done in cold blood."

Although this letter received no reply, the next day the Viceroy ordered the whippings limited and not publicized. The Lieutenant-Governor of the Punjab, Sir Michael O'Dwyer, to whom the order was addressed, justified himself to the Viceroy, "In Lahore during nine days of martial law only twelve whippings have been inflicted—none within the last fourteen days. All the men whipped were of the badmash [robber] and menial class except one particularly truculent clothseller."

At Amritsar, on April 13, the bitterness between Indian and Briton, conquered and conqueror, reached the point of no return.

Then a long-dead holy man entered the scene, the Moslem Saint Neamatullah, whose odes of prophecy were similar to those of Nostradamus in the Western World. He had predicted that the British would rule India for a hundred years and then would be overcome by the King of the West; the time of this event was pushed forward by the superstitious as each date came without fulfillment. One "Expected One," called the Mahdi, defeated General "Chinese" Gordon in the Sudan in 1885, causing Gladstone's government to fall. As recently as 1915 the odes had been heard again in the bazaars of the East, chiefly on the lips of Indian Moslem soldiers stationed at Cairo, and in 1918 a deputy magistrate in Bihar, told by a holy man that the time was near for an attack on India by the King of the West, obtained furlough and took refuge in a spot he believed immune from attack.

Now there was really a new King of the West and his name was Amanullah.

Late in April, Amanullah called a special durbar and, standing before the notable men of Afghanistan, read letters from India which described with great emotion the massacre of the Jallianwalabagh and other upheavals. As he read, he wept.

"Yes, what tyranny has been practiced on our brethren in India! Not only this, but Baghdad and the holy places have been seized by tyranny. I ask you if you are prepared for Holy War. If so, gird up your loins. The time has come."

The answer rang out, "Ghaza! Jehad! Holy War!"

"I will take no more revenue, but all of you should collect grain for the Holy War. Rich men should buy rifles and ammunition from the arsenal. Poor men will have them issued on security."

Soon the British Agency was surrounded by students of what remained of the Habibia School. "Down with England!" they shouted. Some, whose lessons had not brought them up to date, cried, "Down with Queen Victoria! Down with the East India Company!" The young Afghans had a rallying point at last.

From the frontier close to India there had been coming into Kabul tribesmen who wished to mourn the death of one Amir and say, "Long live the Amir!" Amanullah, following custom, gave each of them some money and a robe of honor, or khillat, a sleeveless, ankle-length cloak which, thrown over the shabbiest of garments, gave its wearer a special dignity as he strode about Kabul. Now these men had a new excitement. Mullahs, who had often been checked from proclaiming Holy War, were unleashed. One of the most prominent, the Chaknawar Mullah, was sent to the Mohmand tribes; others headed for Tirah to raise the Afridis. In the Hadda Mosque near Jalalabad a proclamation describing British cruelty in India was read, and the mullahs all shouted for Holy War. The nomad tribe of Ghilzais, arriving in Afghanistan for the warm months, were sent to the frontier with their camels to transport supplies.

Amanullah, at the center of this, was feeling as much perturbation as excitement. No wave of emotion had swept him into his proclamation; it was a calculated risk. Worried, he wrote a letter to a mullah, now living in India, who had been his spiritual adviser in earlier years, and enclosed it with a gold watch:

"Seated on the throne of learning and knowledge and spiritual guide of the Moslems, commander of the world, Shah Abdul Khair, may you be preserved. The sincerity and friendship which I have cherished for a long time towards that spiritual leader are daily on the increase.

"Now the agitation of my mind and spiritual attraction have induced me to trouble that chief of the learned and spiritual King with this sincere epistle to make haste to beg the prayers of that blessed guide.

"Although I consider your holiness disdainful of worldly ornaments, particularly the use of articles made of gold, yet I venture to send your holiness a watch and compass [for finding the direction of Mecca] by way of the unity of Islam, and as a mark of my yielding unfeigned obedience towards that great, real spiritual King. It is the only sincere desire of this faithful disciple that whenever your holiness happens to look at the watch for determining the time of the five prayers, your holiness may remember this faithful disciple and pray for him . . .

"Your friend and faithful disciple, Amir Amanullah."

What caused the agitation of Amanullah's mind and his need for prayers was his failure to obtain England's recognition of his independence merely by declaring it. On April 15 the Viceroy had finally replied to his letter of March 3, but spoke of "the continuity of relations" on the basis of the treaties with his father and grandfather. Obviously Amanullah had to do something more to make Afghanistan's independence a fact.

Besides there was the restlessness aroused by suspicions that he had connived in his father's murder, either before or after the fact, and the difficulty of meeting his promised increase in the soldiers' pay.

Holy War with England was the solution to all of it.

Amanullah was playing the game of Holy War that his grandfather and father had played; give the people a common enemy and frighten the British. But he took the game many steps further, past words into challenges and proclamations and finally into the movement of troops, whom he regarded as if they were toy soldiers, until finally the soldiers were to show they were human beings and not so easy to handle. He expected that this maneuver, coming at a period of distress for the British Empire in India, would buy his recognition without war. Years later, in another country, this would be known as brinkmanship.

His intelligence reports had exaggerated, not the intensity of the feeling in India, which would be impossible to exaggerate, but the potency of the rebellion. The British, whatever their wounds, had India under control. But they were fearful of the new spirit of brotherhood between Hindus and Moslems, now that those two separate communities had their own unifying common enemy, and they wondered about the loyalty of their native soldiers. "Situation which contains elements of great uncertainty as to future has been disclosed by recent events in India," the Indian Army wired London.

The British were still fighting the Bolsheviks in Central Asia and across the Caspian—or were they? "As to our general policy towards Bolsheviks, I am still rather in the dark," an Indian office official in London, J. E. Shuckburgh, wrote on March 25. "Do we regard them as declared enemies or as people with whom we may eventually be prepared to live in comparative amity? Is our immediate intention to make war on them or somehow or other to settle with them peaceably?" The question was answered in a decision not to hold out any promises of aid against Bolshevism to Central Asians who sought it.

General Wilfred Malleson, who had been leading forces against the Bolsheviks from Meshed, in Western Persia, and had recently had to withdraw from Trans-Caspia, wished to use those forces in Central Asia by threatening Herat, the Afghan city closest to Persia. This maneuver was denied him, but Malleson had an excellent intelligence and underground propaganda machine, and at a moment propitious for the British a rumor arose in Kandahar that the Shiahs, of the Moslem sect that was a minority in Eastern Afghanistan but a majority in Herat, had killed a Sunni boy and thrown his body on a garbage heap. The Sunnis began bloody reprisal; eventually no one was sure whether there had been a dead boy or not. But Malleson's rumormongers told the tale of Sunni attacks throughout Herat, where, as it turned out, Amanullah's jehad against Britain found little support.[2]

Amanullah, meanwhile, had made his own plans with care. In Moscow on April 15 the newspaper *Izvestia* announced Afghanistan's independence. Turning back at the frontier the princely Afghan exile who had set out as emissary from the Soviets to his father, Amanullah sent

And he added, "Khyber will be closed to caravans as long as the situation remains disturbed."

Caravans went down into India on certain days of the week, up into Afghanistan on certain other days. Always on the night before the opening of the Khyber all serais on that side were filled with camels and donkeys protesting under their loads, being relieved of the burdens at nighttime and then loaded again early in the morning for the passage through. On the morning of May 3 the camels and donkeys remained in the serais. Other caravans were coming up behind them.

During the night 150 Afghan soldiers occupied Bagh and a neighboring village called Kafirkot, all of whose residents ran away to Landi Kotal or into the hills. Now it was possible for Afghans to ambush caravans, since they were high above the road. That night also a Shinwari tribesman named Zar Shah appeared with a group of armed men and threatened to fire on the Khyber Rifles who were guarding the caravans.

"This incident may be merely a piece of impudence on the part of Zar Shah," wrote the Chief Commissioner of the North-West Frontier Province at 4 P.M., May 3, "but possibly Zar Shah is acting under orders and incident may be first move in reviving old boundary dispute." The Chief Commissioner was Sir George Roos-Keppel, author of a dictionary of Pushtu, the language of the frontier tribes; he was reported to have said to the man who identified himself as the Amir's envoy, "Which Amir?"

On the night of May 3 Zar Shah's men killed five coolies working on the British waterworks. Zar Shah told everyone around him that General Saleh, who was now back in Jalalabad, had sent him to commence hostilities but that he would do as little as possible until the arrival of Afghan troops. He sent the British officer a lithographed copy of one of Amanullah's denunciatory proclamations.

Roos-Keppel wired to his superiors, "I do not propose to send expeditionary force to Landi Kotal until situation much worse, as movement would have disturbing influence in Peshawar."

The British wanted war so little that they gave Amanullah the chance to disown Zar Shah. By special messenger they sent him on May 4 a message signed by the Viceroy:

"Information has reached me that trouble is being stirred up on the Khyber border by one Zar Shah, a Shinwari of Ningrahar, who has been previously concerned in raids in Peshawar district.

"He has interfered with Khyber Rifles in British territory and impudently states that he has been sent ahead by the General to commence hostilities. Nor is this all. He is parading a proclamation under your seal in which it is declared that great unrest exists in India, that my Government have rewarded the loyalty of our subjects by cruelty and injustice in connection with their religion, honor and modesty and that they are right in rising and creating disturbances.

"Though I am informed that the proclamation bears your seal, I cannot but believe that it is a forgery set in circulation by some enemy of Afghanistan and of yourself. For the misrepresentations of the state of India which it contains are so gross that they could not have been believed by any statesman. It is so palpable that its object is to incite the hot-headed frontier tribes against the British Government (whose power has now been demonstrated by the crushing of the strongest powers in the world) that it could not have been penned by any friend of Afghanistan. It is, in short, so grave a menace to the security of the position which you are now consolidating for yourself after the troubled history of the last few months that it can only be the work of some enemy of yourself who desires to overthrow you . . .

"I request you to issue immediate and stringent orders for the arrest of the said Zar Shah, and to make known along our common frontier that the proclamation distributed . . . by him is an outrageous forgery, based on lying rumors."

That same day the Afghans at Bagh dammed the little stream. Since it provided water for Landi Kotal, and water was a precious commodity in that arid land, the British were thirsty and worried. Their only consolation was their observation that the Colonel in charge of the Afghans seemed very nervous. Also on that day many copies of Zar Shah's proclamation arrived in Peshawar and were distributed by the Afghan Post Office. "Impossible to pretend it is a forgery," said Roos-Keppel.

Amanullah did not accept the opportunity to withdraw. He wrote back to the Viceroy that the arrest of Zar Shah was "inadvisable and difficult at a time when all the people of India have combined against the tyrannical law . . .

"As regards certain sentimental leaflets displayed by Zar Shah, he might have obtained a printed manifesto bearing this friend's royal seal and expressing my Islamic sympathy and human feeling toward mankind and abhorrence of my royal mind of things affecting the fateful religion, freedom and liberty of human beings . . .

"It is a matter of great surprise that the Viceroy wrote a reply to our first letter after great delay and that reply was not such as might have made our heart happy.

"While your government should have recognized our government as one absolutely independent of all governments with all honor and dignity in view of its important political and geographic situation, it is to be regretted thousands of times that it appears from Your Excellency's letter and intentions as if those hopes of ours which we had in a friendly and united government were considered dispersed. The Government of Afghanistan is willing to conclude treaties and have friendly relations with your government. I hope that this friend will use his best and well-meaning endeavors and will to avert this very grave and dangerous state of affairs with great prudence by abolishing tyrannical laws and recognizing absolute independence . . . so that the doors of calamity may not be opened upon the world, for it is right to demand right and not right to shed blood without right in the path of right. I hope confidently that Your Excellency will inform this friend without delay that kind friend will take the necessary steps in this matter.

"For the rest, may the days of friendship endure forever."

But the doors of calamity were already opening. The British refused, in their turn, the opportunity Amanullah offered of accepting Afghanistan's independence.

They designated May 3, 1919, the day when Zar Shah threatened the Khyber Rifles and killed five coolies, as the opening date in what one of their officials would describe as "the tragic absurdity known as the Third Afghan War."

The first British move in the new war was to authorize Roos-Keppel to spend unlimited funds on the tribes on the British side of the frontier, to assure their loyalty. The second was to raid the Afghan Post Office in Peshawar.

Afghanistan did not belong to the International Postal Union. Letters and packages which reached Peshawar from other countries would stop there if the sender had not sent money for Afghan postage or arranged payment by the recipient. From his position at the center of communication the Postmaster, Ghulam Haidar, in early May was distributing Amanullah's leaflets and pamphlets. He was also sending Amanullah information which was often inaccurate, as when he reported that the British were driving empty lorries up and down the Khyber Pass in order to stir up dust and create an illusion of activity. His last letter to Amanullah said, "If after the sealed leaflets have been circulated and three generals have been appointed, the King of Afghanistan refrains from invading India, the Hindus and Moslems here will be very much displeased. It is not expedient to delay the matter and give time to the English to collect troops or beguile the people with their deceitful words and sweet promises."

The Postmaster had returned from a conference at Jalalabad with General Saleh. Here is what, in the opinion of Roos-Keppel, he planned to do:

"I have for some time been convinced that there was a plot in Peshawar for a mob to rise in concert with an Afghan invasion, but the mob, which was liberally supplied with money, was getting beyond control of its organizers and without a cordon we should have had a rising on the night of May 8 and large mobs would have wrecked our wireless stations, mobilizations, godowns [storehouses], treasury, railway, etc. . . . the cry which Afghans would have had if there had been any rioting here that their brothers in blood and religion were being slaughtered would have appealed to Afghans in a way that the misfortunes of strangers like the Sikhs certainly does not."

Peshawar was surrounded by a high wall pierced at intervals by sixteen gates, most of them with heavy doors. Four columns of British soldiers lined up at different points along the railroad track, and at two o'clock in the afternoon on May 8 started out, each designated to close certain gates and accompanied by a civil policeman carrying a slip of paper on which the name of the gate was written in English, Urdu, and Nagri, to keep them from getting lost. This was the hour when most Peshawaris were taking the nap that is customary in hot climates after the noon meal.

Escorted by cavalry, accompanied by hackney carriages and municipal garbage trucks carrying their ammunition and tools, the soldiers advanced dropping off a detachment at each gate. Even at that hour a few men were loitering outside; the soldiers pushed them inside and barricaded the doors. It took eleven minutes to close all sixteen gates and forty-four minutes to barricade them completely and establish guards. Awakening from their naps, the Peshawaris found that they were enclosed and that only certain persons with passes were allowed to leave or enter, and that their supply of water, that necessary ingredient of life even in a city that is not oriental and hot in summer, had been shut off.³

The Afghan Postmaster also took a nap. Visitors awakened him. They came in small groups, all alarmed, all saying, "We have heard that the police are coming to take possession of your arms and put you in the lock-up." Then police messengers arrived from the Deputy Commissioner; the visitors shouted angrily at them and pushed them about, but they managed to deliver their message that the Postmaster should present himself at Kabuli Gate police station with five servants. There the Commissioner rebuked him saying that it was his activities which had brought the British and the Amir to war.

"I am merely a mirza [clerk] of the post office," cried the Postmaster, "how can such a high king listen to my words?"

On May 9 the British bombed the Afghan encampment at Dakka.

In this way the air age came to Afghanistan. No planes had ever before flown over the country. On a few occasions earlier the British had bombed into submission some of their own tribes who were more than ordinarily disobedient. They knew what the effect would be.

To an Afghan in his rim of mountains the world was circumscribed. Everything was known. Death might lurk around the next mountain or upon the ground, but sudden death from the skies was a new disaster for which the Koran had not prepared him.

The first bomb fell in the courtyard of the Sarhaddar's house and injured one of General Saleh's feet. Other bombs destroyed his headquarters camp and killed between twenty and thirty men, both soldiers and tribesmen. It was a terrible hour, with men dying in a new way and cries of horses and camels, who were also wounded and grievously astonished. General Saleh left in a motorcar, telling his second-in-command that he would send reinforcements from Jalalabad. The reinforcements did arrive three days later, and the Afghans fought bravely on the ground but again the attack came from the sky.

The Mohmand and Shinwari tribesmen left the place of destruction, but first they gathered up arms, ammunition, bedding, carpets, many things that the Army had provided for the troops, and took these off into their hills.

"The sample of the Afghan Army that we had to fight in the last few days fought better than I expected," Roos-Keppel wrote to the Viceroy on May 13, "with great bravery and tenacity, but they have no organized

commissariat or transport and are incapable of conducting a campaign
on a large scale.

"A greater danger than the Afghans are the tribes, that they have not
risen against us is extraordinary.

"The greatest danger is the state of Northern India. A large number
of people hate us with such bitterness that they would welcome even
an invasion if they saw a chance of getting rid of us."

Amanullah in Kabul was working all the time. He had turned a large
hall called the Qawmi Bagh into a war office, and he left only at twilight, when he would ride off on horseback wearing his military uniform
with bandoleer, sword and revolver. These days he never wore anything
but military uniform. Since his twilight rides were shared by fifty
soldiers, all armed, it was not necessary to add the sword and revolver
to his uniform, but when Amanullah saw himself in a role, he enacted
it completely. Now he was playing the military leader.

But he was a leader who had not intended to start a war, and he was
perplexed how to handle one.

The news of the bombardment reached him while Mahmud Tarzi
was beginning a conference with the British Agent, Hafiz Saifullah, and
he telephoned in a panic to Tarzi, who hastened to his side for a talk
which resulted in Saifullah and his staff being confined to their quarters
so rigidly that even the little sons of the grooms were not permitted to
play with the street boys. "I know you perfectly well, sir," Tarzi told
Saifullah in his anger. "I have heard of many qualifications of yours
exercised by you in inducing with quotations from the Holy Koran the
late Amir Habibullah from taking the cause of the Turks and the whole
Moslem world; in other words, in the Great War. It was you and your
holy quotations that have brought ruin today to the prestige of Turkey
and through it to that of the whole Moslem world."

To Hafiz Saifullah, whose most valued attribute was his ability to
quote the entire Koran by heart, which had gained him the title Hafiz,
it was distressing to hear that his piety, expressed on behalf of his British masters, had damaged his religion.

That night the Afghans still at Bagh received no reinforcements and
no food. They could not leave because the heavy guns could not be
moved easily; they should have had elephants for this task. In a few
days they and some of their comrades would be going back to Kabul,
and the whole countryside would be hearing that arrangements for food,

transport, and medical attention had been shamefully inadequate at Dakka.

The next morning Roos-Keppel wired, "Desertions have begun from the Khyber Rifles."

Of all the native militia units that gave the British Army a reason to brag of its instinct for working with conquered people, none was more famous in England itself than the Khyber Rifles. But the men of the Rifles were not toy soldiers either; they belonged to families who had kinsmen in Afghanistan, who visited back and forth across the border, and they were as sensitive to the cry "Ghaza! Jehad!" as any other Moslem.

"The Khyber Rifles have behaved very badly," Roos-Keppel reported. "The men at Landi Kotal with British officers did very well but the officers were so occupied with battle fighting in front that they neglected the outposts and did not visit them. Men in outposts had every kind of message sent to them, by intriguers in Peshawar City, that Afghans were winning all over. From deserting as singles men began to desert in large numbers. Have handed outposts to regulars."

And the next day: "I have ordered commandant to disband all [Khyber Rifles]. At Jamrud last night some sniping possibly by deserters from Khyber Rifles. At Landi Kotal and Jamrud yesterday their attitude was sullen or panicky. In Landi Kotal only 100 out of 700 men volunteered to remain and the native officers said they could not be responsible in any way even for these volunteers, as the feeling was thoroughly bad. At Jamrud, on first occasion when men were asked what they wished to do, only 100 out of 500 elected to take their discharge, but when I got down there the number willing to stay had reduced to about 150 and the attitude of these was sullen and curious though they were personally friendly and polite to me. I have come to the conclusion that many of those who volunteered to stay have done so with view to stealing the rifles and deserting so I have directed commandant to disband the whole corps . . .

"From my conversations with maliks [village chiefs] and native officers I am satisfied that there has been recently a conspiracy to undermine their loyalty and that this has been successful. One belief that the men have got into their heads is that we, from fear of an Afridi uprising, wish to reduce the numbers of fighting men and that our object in trying to induce the Khyber Rifles to go forward is to get them into the

firing line and on a convenient occasion to destroy them with a fire
of our own guns."

Of the British soldiers an officer had written earlier that year, "We
dare not give an unpopular order." For four years the fighting men had
lived up to the motto put upon them by a poet who was not fighting
himself: "Theirs but to do or die." Now they had had enough of doing
or dying and if they reasoned why, their own weariness seemed reason
enough. If all the men in India had been demobilized who were entitled
to this release, the Army would have been reduced dangerously, so only
the minimum number, chiefly those who were ill, went home to England;
each man who remained received a bonus and a letter of explanation
and exhortation signed by the commander-in-chief.

When war with Afghanistan broke out, many men were in Bombay
about to board ship for home, including some from Mesopotamia who
were being sent home through India. These were asked if they would
like to volunteer for duty on the Afghan frontier. Their reply was that
jobs were awaiting them in England, and that they would sacrifice those
jobs if they re-enlisted voluntarily. They were willing enough to go to
Afghanistan if the the Army would make this a command so that the
employers in England would not be able to penalize them at a time
when many men were seeking employment. It was agreed.

Then, in an effort to create an image of the sort of patriotism that
had flowered at the start of the Great War, an Army public relations
officer announced to the newspapers that these men had "volunteered."
On the frontier they were more angry at their own superiors than at
the Afghans whom they were fighting, and were worried about their
futures in England. At one point on the railway, before even reaching the frontier, two thousand of these men announced that they were
getting off the train, and pitching tents, and would draw their rations
but would not do anything else and would certainly not travel any
farther west. The other men who passed them, headed for duty on the
Afghan frontier, called them, in honor of their Brigadier, "O'Dowda's
Bolshie Brigade." At Poona, where a large organization was handling
the records on demobilization, the injustice of what they were writing
so aroused the British clerks that they refused to write further and had
to be talked out of staging a riot.[4]

Even among those who went to Afghanistan with good grace, there
was chafing at a sort of restraint they had not encountered in fighting
the European enemy: that of the Political Officer. The British Political

Officer in a tribal area among people who were technically British subjects, however little they realized it, acted almost like a feudal lord of the manor in the most responsible sense. He looked after his people; their unhappiness meant trouble for him, and that imaginary Durand Line dividing Afghanistan from India was so trivial to his tribesmen that an act toward an Afghan would be regarded as an act toward his relatives in India. Long after the departure of the soldiers, the Political Officer would be there inheriting the consequences, and he knew it.

Three times a certain British reconnaissance party found Afghan tribesmen hiding in the dry ditches that had been rushing streams earlier in the year when the snows in the mountains were melting. They examined the Afghans' rifles, saw that they had been fired recently, and handed the men over to the political officer in accordance with their instructions. Inquiring later what had been done, the soldiers were told that these were friendly shepherds who had been released. "As a result we never took any more prisoners," their officer reminisced later.

The same party, riding near an area called Girdi, were stunned by the sight and scent of corpses lying across the road and in the ditches, bodies of English troopers of the King's Dragoon Guards, decomposing in the heat and showing signs of mutilation. The chaplain whom they summoned for a hasty burial service had to stop twice to vomit.

A few days later they were sent again to that area, to Girdi village, which had been occupied but to which the inhabitants would eventually return. The anger at the sight of those corpses still stirred within them. With hand grenades and very thin wire, this party laid booby-traps for the returning villagers, acting secretly because the political officer would have stopped them. On their following visit they saw with satisfaction that the traps had worked. They were fighting their own war, not playing politics.[5]

One man who would have fought earnestly with the British was ex-Amir Yakub. Or so he said when he offered the services of himself and his sons. The British declined this offer from a family who were very anxious to sit on the throne of Afghanistan themselves, and found it wise to omit all mention of it from the public report. The ruling princes of India, from whom they solicited expressions of loyalty, sent in those expressions with added flourishes of indignation against Amanullah. Only one ruler sent a son: the Maharajah of Patiala, whose heir wore in his ears two very large pearls surrounded by diamonds. Although many tribesmen wore a single gold earring, the British soldiers had never seen such jewelry on a man, and if this young man had been wounded, he would have got instant medical attention, for his comrades-in-arms were plotting to take his earrings.[6]

Cholera came to the British camps. War had come so suddenly that there had been no time to inoculate the men in advance, and shots had to be given in the field. There was not enough certified pure water, and in the heat of 114 degrees, with almost no trees to cast a shadow, the men could not resist drinking water from the ditches wherever they could find it. Cholera broke out simultaneously in several areas, and at the height of the epidemic one hospital with three hundred cases ran out of milk. Lime juice, the traditional mainstay of the British fighting man and his guard against scurvy, ran out after the first few days.[7]

And for all their criticism of Afghan transport at Dakka, the British found their own transport problems there. "Heavy casualties were not expected," went the report, "but [the officer] managed to incur them. Two British officers wounded, one with bullet through lung, found no one to meet them on arrival at Murree in a car. Had to hire ponies and find way as best they could."

Another complaint was "to get news from Afghanistan is becoming increasingly difficult as all my messengers are being killed."

The British then attacked Amanullah with one of his own weapons: invective. They prepared a proclamation that copied perfectly the style of his own. Some India Office officials in London objected to disseminating this over the Viceroy's signature, perhaps on the theory that imitation was too sincere a flattery for an enemy king who was not related to their own king. It was not in the British tradition of insulting political repartee. It went:

"O brave and honest people of Afghanistan! When Amir Habibullah was foully murdered, Great Britain was filled with horror and grief, and public mournings were ordered throughout the length and breadth of India. When murmurings arose over Amanullah's action in acquitting some of his father's murderers and condemning others without a trial according to Shariat [Moslem religious law], he sought to stay the murmurings against him by stirring up hostility to Great Britain. He thereby jeopardized the lives and property of the peoples of Afghanistan merely to serve his personal ends and to save his own throne. Nor did he shrink from breaking the ordinance of the Holy Koran which says, 'Surely Allah enjoins the doing of justice and the doing of good to others and the giving to the kindred, and he forbids indecency and evil and rebellion. He admonishes you that you may be mindful. And fulfill the covenant of Allah, when you have made a covenant, and do not break the oaths after making them fast, and you have indeed made Allah a surety for you. Surely Allah knows what you do.' Koran, Sura An-Nahl (The Bee). Will the peoples of Afghanistan allow this inexperienced youth, false to the memory of his martyred father, false to the interests of his country, false to the dictates of the Holy Koran, to bring calamity upon the brave peoples and fair country of Afghanistan? God forbid! Are your traders now to be ruined? Are you and your families to go without the clothes and other necessities and comforts of life which used to be brought from India? Are your camels to be debarred from their winter grazing grounds and perish? It is the one desire of Great Britain to see Afghanistan once again peaceful and prosperous, free and independent, under a wise Amir, as mindful of the welfare of his country and as friendly to Great Britain as Abdur Rahman and Habibullah of blessed memory."

The order went out "The Government of India desire the above in Pushtu and Persian be disseminated by airplane and other means in Afghanistan. Proclamation should be nicely got up, and to mark its authenticity it should bear an imposing seal."

On the same day, Roos-Keppel wired, "We had a terrible misfortune last night when the giant Handley-Paige airplane, which could have bombed Kabul, was wrecked."

Officially the war which began for the British on May 3 began for the Afghans on May 15, when it was announced by Amanullah in Idgah Mosque with a cry, "O my pious brave nation! O my faithful lion-hearted army! . . . the treacherous and deceitful English Government . . . twice shamelessly attacked our beloved country and plunged their filthy claws into the region of the vital parts of our dear country which is the burial ground of our ancestors and the abode of the chastity of our mothers and sisters, and intended to deprive us of our very existence, of the safety of our honor and virtue, of our liberty and happiness, and of our national dignity and nobility . . . may thousands of curses and imprecations be upon the English! After this dropping of bombs without any justification by the unstable airplanes on those who were pursuing the path of the right, it became incumbent on your King to proclaim jehad in the path of God against the perfidious English Government. God is great. God is great. God is great."

The next day the interned British Agent wrote in his diary, "Mobs in different processions, from children to grown-up men, severally and separately went around the city, particularly passing in front of the British Agency building where attempt was also made to start a row with the Agency men peeping at the procession from the upper story, and abuses, curses and spitting exchanged by the Habibia College boys' mob, but the Agency men were recalled to the inside and told not to expose themselves again when processions were passing by the building. The procession cried with the cry of 'God is Great' and had a board inscribed over it abusing the British nation."

At exactly the same time Amanullah was demanding war, his general sent word to the Political Agent of Khyber, "I am ordered to suspend the war (thus unlawfully begun by your side) until the next order. You are accordingly informed that war has been suspended until a final decision has been reached by correspondence between His Afghan Majesty and the Viceroy."

"As this insolent message was so palpably devised to gain time," said the report to London, "the Political Agent was instructed to reply that he was not authorized to answer it and that if Amir wanted peace he should address Viceroy through the General Officer Commanding of Operations."

The Viceroy's personal reaction was "The Afghan trouble has come really as a Godsend. It has diverted public attention from internal matters." The British were learning to play the jehad game too.

The British had sent Amanullah's envoy to India back to him, and the British Agent was notified on May 18 that "owing to the arrival of ghazis and their fiery excitement the peace of the British Agency has become critical," and he was being sent back to India. He insisted on seeing Amanullah first.

"I and the Foreign Minister visited the Amir at Kooti Stor where he was sitting in a council of 50 or 60 men composed either of the city or district representatives or of a few fanatics and misguiders of the so-called Pan-Islamism, the most prominent among whom being Abdul Hadi, the fanatic editor of *Aman-i-Afghan* of Kabul, and also a few Hindus of Kabul. No member of the royal family either young or old and no one from the courtiers of the late reign was visible in the council at that time. And it was clear to me that the rotters present had brought ruin to the fool, passionate, and inexperienced Amir. After exchange of greeting the Amir exclaimed:

" 'British Agent, you remember my durbar speech in which I said that

I would cut the throat (taking his hand to his neck to point out actually what he said) of anybody entering into the limits of Afghanistan with hostile intentions.'

"Here I interrupted him saying that I had come to bid him only a last private good-bye and not discuss any question officially. Hearing this retort he kept silent shamefully.

"A representative of Hazarajat rose from his chair and addressed me: 'I am ready to sacrifice all my Hazara population to the last man over the person and crown of my King!'

"He had scarcely taken his seat than one of the Hindu gentlemen rose up and addressed to me similar remarks and added that being a Moslem I must have stricken to the cause of Islam.

"I told him in reply that true Islam does not teach us blind following but teaches us to discern between right and wrong and listen to reason alone.

"When I finished the Amir extended his hand and bade good-bye saying, 'I hand you over to your own government' and added that 'as Sardar Abdur Rahman Khan was not recognized by your Government as my envoy and was returned alone in dishonor, you will therefore have to go alone in the same way with General Abdul Wakil leaving for Jalalabad in motorcars in a few hours. No servants, no kit, nothing will be allowed as was done with my envoy by your Government, and I do this as a reciprocal reprisal' "

Nadir was approaching Matun in Khost with four battalions, two elephants drawing guns, and twelve thousand tribesmen. He was accompanied by two members of the Hazrat family of Shor Bazaar: the Shah Agha who had put the coronation turban on Amanullah's head, and his brother Sher Agha.

Bombs were falling on Jalalabad but Nadir's advance was the important news on May 19 for he was gathering in the tribesmen with whom he was popular, even the difficult Ghilzais, and the Afghans were making overtures to the tribes of the British side. An Afridi delegation crossed the frontier to a jirga in Jalalabad, but they preserved the British faith in their integrity by saying they went to reconnoiter for the Afghan's weak points in case it was decided to loot their camps.

May 19 was also the day when, from a Turkish port, Mustapha Kemal sailed for Anatolia in the heartland of his country to create there a new life for all his people. Thereafter, when asked his birthday, he would say, "May 19, 1919."

On that day also two emissaries converged on Jalalabad. One was the British Agent Saifullah, who had quoted the Koran again at Mahmud Tarzi when Tarzi had proposed peace terms that included Afghan freedom and the repeal of the offensive Rowlatt Laws in India. Saifullah was on his way back to India. The other emissary, coming in the opposite direction, was the rejected Afghan envoy Abdur Rahman. Amanullah had told them to talk with each other in an attempt to find some understanding between the two governments "to try to stop the coming bloodshed." There was never any hope from their conversations. Although Saifullah saw himself as a guardian of the British Empire, to the British he was an employee who had never been the sort of superspy they would have liked, in whose reports they put little credence—less, as it turned out, than they should have.

Saifullah was aroused from sleep early the next morning by Abdur Rahman, who asked him to write a letter in English to the British officer commanding at Dakka, asking him to stop the bombardment while discussions were held. Abdur Rahman himself would write a letter in Persian.

Bombs were dropped on Jalalabad while they were writing; one exploded under Saifullah's window. The two letters, hastily finished, were handed to three Afghan officers who were told to hasten to Dakka and deliver them at once.

Jalalabad, now having its first experience of the air age, was in a panic. Many people were killed horribly. Some of the survivors, hardly waiting to pack their portable possessions, were hurrying toward Nimla, a nearby spot where the Mogul Emperor Shah Jehan, ruler of India and builder of the Taj Mahal, had created a beautiful garden that was the stopping-place and delight of travelers in that parched land. Somehow a garden seemed more secure from sky-borne death than any other place. The road between Nimla and Jalalabad was clogged with fleeing families, with soldiers returning from Dakka with unhappy tales, and with tribesmen who had gone forth eagerly as ghazis and now were bewildered that their Amir was telling them to desist from jehad. One refugee, riding alone on a weary horse, was a general who, on entering Jalalabad the previous afternoon, had received a salute of seven guns.

Amanullah talked for several hours on the telephone with his generals and envoy, who, like everyone else, had gone to Nimla.

General Mahmud Sami then arrived in Nimla from Kabul, headed toward India, with six Austrian officers who had been interned by the Allies in Russian Turkestan and released by the Bolsheviks, and who were making their way home through Afghanistan. Amanullah liked Mahmud Sami and respected him as a schoolmaster. This worldly officer from Turkey, who had once been assigned in the cosmopolitan society of Berlin, whose mustaches swept so grandly that they seemed more of an escort than an appendage, was a favorite of the royal family. In 1909, in the horrendous days after the discovery of the alleged plot against Habibullah, when the ghulambachas were giving under torture all the names they could think of, the name that caused Ulya Hazrat to stop the recital in disbelief was that of Mahmud Sami.

Now Mahmud Sami and his companions had to stop in Jalalabad. Camels, donkeys, horses, people filled the road so that the car could not get through. He shook hands with Saifullah and apologized for the treatment he had received at Kabul, and for "the Afghan trespass of the border." He said that Amanullah felt General Saleh was chiefly to blame for the war, for occupying that strip of land at Bagh.

"I did not know that things were like that," said Mahmud Sami. "Otherwise I would have intervened. The Amir was badly overpowered by fools like Mahmud Tarzi, Abdul Quddus, and other crazy fanatics."

For about an hour and a half Amanullah talked on the telephone alternately with Mahmud Sami and Abdur Rahman.

In Dakka the Afghan officers delivered the two peace overtures to the Commanding Officer, who thought that the British Agent had written his under compulsion, since military intelligence had been receiving reports that the Amir was at Jalalabad, and they thought this significant. Saifullah did not mention Amanullah's whereabouts in the letter he had written in such haste and fright, although he knew very well that Amanullah was in Kabul at the other end of a telephone line. The Commanding Officer suspected that the soldiers who had brought the message were spies. He permitted only one to return, giving him the verbal message that nothing could be considered until the British Agent was released; if the Amir wished to sue for peace, he should observe protocol by addressing the Viceroy through the officer in command of British forces.

"The discontent with Amanullah's regime in which the present trouble had its origin," wired the Government of India to London, "may be expected to revive and gather strength with demonstration of Amanullah's failure. There is no room for failures in Afghanistan, and good chance (when we occupy Jalalabad) that Afghans will repudiate him and leave way open for a new Amir with whom we shall have no difficulty in treating."

The British were planning to advance to Jalalabad, and were speculating whether they should not also go to Kabul. This seemed to them a gesture that might convince the onlooking rebels in India of British power. Had they moved at once, they would have succeeded at least with Jalalabad. That city was almost deserted except for three hundred wounded and sick soldiers in a cantonment hospital. Three-quarters of the bazaar was destroyed. The neighboring tribes had raided the State Treasury and arsenal. In the hills to which people had fled, and along the roads, the generals and other people of authority were being cursed for losing, although the victor in reality had been the airplane, which no mortal man in Afghanistan had any weapon against. The British Agent Saifullah was returned to Kabul for lack of anything else to do with him.

In Khost, meanwhile, Nadir, who carried with him all the hope of an Afghan military victory, was delaying matters and announcing that he would interview jirgas for several days and then would decide a date for an advance. Nadir stepped warily where Amanullah rushed in.

Kabul was bombed on May 24.

The first airplane ever to fly above its hills, an old Handley-Paige which never could have made the trip without a strong tail wind, appeared at six o'clock in the morning and dropped several bombs. Most Kabulis were just awakening. They ran outside. Some fired their rifles at the deadly thing disappearing in the sky, and a few fired revolvers. As soon as it had vanished, a great humming sound was heard all over the city, the talk of confused people. No sound like it had been heard before in Kabul.

No person was killed, although a few of the royal household's horses were injured. Despite the early hour, Amanullah sent out a military band to play for the alarmed people, and ordered a regiment onto the parade ground. This was not consolation enough; as the day went on, swarms of ghazis trailed in from the frontier fighting, sick with hunger and heat, lamenting that "Ghaza is impossible with the foreigner being high above the sky in airships."

What angered Amanullah most was that on the previous day he had issued orders to all parts of the country and to the whole frontier to cease fighting. It occurred to him that even if the British should stop the war, their message might not get through, and so he, without waiting for reciprocity, put an end to his own fighting. At least, he tried. Peace was more difficult to make than war.

"It is strange," he wrote to his envoy, "that while on the one hand the British Government ask Afghanistan to stop hostilities, on the other hand they sent their airplanes today and, having bombed Kabul capital, went back. It should not be so . . . If this line of action continues, the Afghan nation will never be easily subdued by fighting . . . If the British government do not really want a truce, you should secure a formal letter to this effect from them and send it to me."

All the voices in Kabul that had cried for Holy War now cried that the Amir's Holy War had brought them to ruin. Amanullah, distraught, summoned the leading mullahs, officials, and notables of Kabul. He explained the course of events that had led to war and told them that he had made repeated overtures for peace, but that the British had refused to negotiate.

"If the Afghan people consider me responsible for war and the ruin of Afghanistan," Amanullah said, "I will willingly abdicate and retire to Russia or Bokhara with my family."

He had a servant bring in his infant son, his first by Souraya, and on the child's head he swore the truth of his statements. An Afghan can take no more solemn oath.

The meeting agreed that war had been forced by the British. Mullahs, who had been assigned a few days earlier to accompany the envoys and attempt to restrain the tribes from jehad, again called to Holy War and sent out fatwas (proclamations of the legality and necessity) of jehad to all the tribes.

The next day, May 25, the British wrought their own undoing.

Nadir was still advancing toward the frontier, and they dreaded not his guns, most of which they considered obsolete, nor his soldiers, whom they suspected to be badly trained, but the tribesmen. Many tribes were joining him, and these included tribes who lived close to their own forts. The British soldiers were surrounded by men so troublesome to govern that a few years earlier one group had been sequestered behind a live electrical wire. Especially the Wazirs, to whose hills Nadir was heading, had such slight regard for the British Government that when Lord Curzon had started the system of native militia, he had soon discovered that to station a Wazir regiment in its own home area was like stationing a wolf among other wolves to guard the sheep.

Mullahs were talking to those tribes about jehad, especially a skillful orator known as the Babra mullah, who lived in a cave overhung by ledges which prevented rifle fire from reaching him. When one of these mullahs entered a village to preach, he was accompanied by many men, sometimes thousands and sometimes only hundreds, many already prepared for Holy War with axes, swords, spears, rifles. Drummers kept up a rhythm with curved, double-headed drumsticks until they hypnotized even themselves and fell on the ground. Dancing boys, wearing very full skirts, heavily mascaraed around their eyes, swirled in dance until their skirts were parallel to the rough ground. Above them flew the banners of jehad, both green and black. The mullah wept as he denounced the British Government. His words were usually to the effect that all tribesmen who held employment with that government of unbelievers were lickspittles and liars. His followers must not attend the funerals of any such. All Moslems who served the British were kaffirs, or infidels. They should sever all connections, and if they did so, the British would put down their tails and go. Always the crowd shouted defiance at the British. Sometimes the mullah would go even further and tell his listeners they should not allow any government employee to be buried.

Into this atmosphere Nadir was coming, and he had with him two of Kabul's most persuasive mullahs, the Hazrats of Shor Bazaar. He came by an unexpected route, through area so difficult that the British had assumed no one could pass it accompanied by all those troops and elephants pulling large guns.

As a precaution, orders were given to the British Political Agent in the area Nadir was approaching, the Tochi, that at his discretion he might order forts evacuated.

On the night of May 25 the Political Agent ordered evacuation. The garrison was withdrawn from all posts in Upper Tochi. Nadir led his forces across the border; they found the fort at Spinwam abandoned and moved in, along with many Wazir tribesmen who happily joined the Afghans and pursued the departing British, capturing several prisoners. In other British forts the supplies were burned before evacuation, except in one fort whose commander turned it over to the chief of a small neighboring tribe to guard for him; the chief's neighbors overran the fort and carried off the supplies. At Miranshah the Waziristan militia gave signs that they too were hearing the call of the mullahs, so they were made prisoners in their own fort. Their weapons were being taken away from them when they revolted and escaped by digging a hole through the wall.

Nadir's men came to the fort at Thal and began an attack.

"In one night," lamented Roos-Keppel, "the political situation has changed from 'set-fair' to 'stormy.'" Later he said, "The withdrawal from Tochi posts was an unauthorized and disastrous blunder . . . It is quite heart-breaking." There was no longer any thought of advancing on Jalalabad.

Roos-Keppel expected most of the tribes to rise against the British. They did not.

"Had Nadir been a Skobolev [the Russian General who captured much of Central Asia for the Tsar], he would beyond question have merely masked Thal with a covering force and pushed on a portion with a view to ensuring the upheaval of the Orakzais and Afridis," the Commander-in-Chief of India, General Sir C. C. Munro, was to write. "The object was worth a great risk, and had he appeared at the head of even a few men among the tribesmen, he would have stood a good chance of obtaining his object."

But Nadir remained at Thal to besiege the fort, and the tribes did not rise as wholeheartedly as the British had feared. One reason was that Amanullah's messengers were carrying the word, sent forth before the bombing of Kabul, that fighting should stop.

Then the British had another surprise; the old guns of the Afghans, which they had termed obsolete, performed at Thal better than their own guns. And although two airplanes bombed the Afghans there, they did not prevent their cutting the water supply of the fort on May 27. The Afghans had the upper hand.

Along the frontier men murmured that European powers were all determined to crush Islam, that the British had taken advantage of recent incidents due to the youth and inexperience of Amanullah to annex Afghanistan and tribal territory, turning a deaf ear to Amanullah's petition for peace. Amanullah, who had been first a hero in their conversation and then a villain, now was a victim. They had heard his messengers. They knew that he would give them peace if he could.

Roos-Keppel decided he should do something to counteract this attitude. "I suggest that Ghaus-ud-din [an Ahmadzai Ghilzai interned in Jubbulpore for having lured two exiled sardars into an attempted invasion of Afghanistan] be sent to me for propaganda purposes on the frontier . . . If he plays us false and joins Afghans, it will not matter much."

But the same sort of talk was being heard as far as London. In Parliament the question was asked: Why had the Afghan request for a cessation of hostilities never been published in London officially?

"Our airplanes have done wonderfully," Roos-Keppel was writing, "and have struck terror into the hearts of Afghans and tribesmen. Without them we should by now have been fighting with our backs to the wall instead of advancing." In fact, the British were not advancing at all.

That was the day also when Amanullah sent out a firman to his three generals telling them "to suspend hostilities until the door of discussion and communication is opened."

When Nadir in Thal received this message, he passed the word to the British general opposing him, who was the same Brigadier-General Reginald Dyer who had given the order to fire into the crowd at Amritsar, who was now a hero among most British in India and in England, and would remain so even after a commission appointed six months after the event would forbid his ever serving again in India.

"My guns will answer for me!" bellowed General Dyer. Nadir left the battlefield; the British said he retreated.[8]

But Dyer's superiors were content with the letter they received from Amanullah on May 31, although he did not send back the British Agent, whose return they had called a necessity; they too were now ready to make peace. "Tone of letter is a satisfactory climb-down," went the word from the front. The British also ordered hostilities to cease, and they marked down June 3 as the close of their Third Afghan War, which lasted exactly one month.

Both sides would claim victory in this war. The British were to be outraged when Afghanistan erected a monument to the month's fighting and called it a victory monument, and included a lion in chains. They assumed this was the British lion, although Afghans would point out that the Afghan soldier had always been symbolized by a lion. When a vandal would damage that lion, the Russian Legation would start a rumor that the British Legation had done it, and the British, not suspecting this might be done with tongue in cheek, would become angry again.

It was not yet time for them to learn from their recent, far greater war, its most important lesson: that no one should care who wins a war, what matters is winning the peace.

CHAPTER 6

May 28, 1919, to August 20, 1919

In the Gothic towers of Whitehall, where the British Empire was governed, that Empire ceased to be an abstraction and became a group of men. No one would ever have guessed this, hearing Big Ben chime each hour with such assurance and remembering that even time was time only as certified at the Greenwich Observatory.

But within those buildings men remained men, just as they did on the dry hills adjoining Afghanistan. The men of the India Office received telegrams and letters from the Government of India, they wrote minute papers and scrutinized each other's work and jotted remarks in the margins and sometimes disagreed. Above them was the Secretary of State for India, who in 1919 was the anachronistically sensitive Edwin S. Montagu, and above him was the Foreign Office, where in 1919 the acting Secretary of State for Foreign Affairs was Marquess Curzon of Kedleston, who had once told Amanullah's grandfather to stop scratching his head.

Although Whitehall seemed to bestride its bank of the Thames with the same inevitability that the British Empire bestrode the world, within its walls there was often conflict. Two entities disputed matters having to do with India and, by extension, with Afghanistan: G. of I. (Government of India) and H.M.G. (His Majesty's Government). The individuals involved were of the class that took position for granted, and in their communications they spoke with an ease and grace that could only come from having the same past and the same connotations. Oxford and Cambridge endowed their prose.

Between the men of G. of I. and the men of H.M.G. there was superficially one distinction: £400 per annum for the latter. The British Foreign Service required ancestors who would guarantee this unearned income during the first unpaid years of service. The deeper difference was that the Indian Civil Service, one of the Empire's glories, represented to men of a certain social standing both absolute security and the minimum fate which life might hold for them. To a university senior uncertain or insufficiently focused about his future, his dons suggested the Indian Civil Service.[1] Here was a life which was comfortable except when nature or the fortunes of war intervened, conferred prestige simply from being white of skin among brown skins, and would end decently in England surrounded by souvenirs. Englishmen in India performed conscientiously and with spirit, yet they had the least that a man of their world was likely to settle for.

In their attitude toward Afghanistan, G. of I. tended to act from emotion and H.M.G. to act from reason. This was due not so much to personality as to geography, the path of reason being easy to follow in direct ratio to one's distance from the events.

Lord Curzon, an emotional man, commented on the letter of May 28 with which Amanullah had finally persuaded G. of I. to accept peace: "The Amir's letter struck us as impudent and in the main unashamed, and the latter part of your reply is too anxious for peace."

"What are His Majesty's Government aiming at?" Viceroy Chelmsford wired to Curzon. "Do they really wish for a prolonged Afghan war and what result do they expect from it?"

Curzon replied from the vantage point of his great distance from the hills and passes where men found their stone fortifications too hot in daytime to touch: "My criticism was based on an apprehension that in seeking the peace which we all desired you . . . used language which in our opinion insufficiently conveyed the fact that your attitude was the attitude of the victor."

"God Almighty to a black beetle!" however, was the comment of one of the generals in Peshawar, Sir Arthur Barrett, on reading the Viceroy's terms for Amanullah. This was an expression of admiration for their severity.

After recapitulating the events of the war, and placing the blame for starting it squarely on the Afghans, and quoting letters which Tarzi had written to India asking for loyalty pledges (they had been in the mailbags when the Peshawar Post Office was raided), the Viceroy told Amanullah that he must withdraw his troops to a point twenty miles from the nearest British troops, which would remain where they were but inactive. The British would not drop bombs but their airplanes would fly unmolested. Amanullah must urge tribes on both sides of the frontier to stop fighting.

Finally, the Viceroy would arrange a peace conference at Rawalpindi in India, and would Amanullah please let him know the names of his delegates?

What Amanullah had written to the Viceroy, arousing Lord Curzon's doubt that he was properly chastened, was:

"It is a matter of great regret that the throwing of bombs by zeppelins on London was denounced as a most savage act and the bombardment of places of worship and sacred spots was considered a most abominable operation, while now we see with our own eyes that such operations were a habit which is prevalent among all civilized peoples of the West."

The victors on the frontier were willing to overlook this lecture. Amanullah, though a bit puzzled why this overture for peace had brought results despite the failure of all his others, which began almost at the same time as the war, nonetheless was happy that he had found the formula. The British likewise were content that India had beheld their strength, and it was safe to stop. When they wrote of "prolonged war" it was with dread knowledge of all the difficulties.

Yet even after Nadir's success in Thal they could not feel that peace was properly obtained until two further exchanges of letters with Amanullah had preserved protocol. Then, on the frontier, the eager G. of I. printed Pushto leaflets announcing that the Amir of Afghanistan had formally sued for peace. Throughout the mountains messengers went carrying these. The Afridis, holding a jirga at Bagh to decide whether or not to fight, received some, considered them, and being sophisticated in the ways of war and peace, decided to wait and see.

One Afghan General wrote that although he had ordered the regular troops not to fire a single shot, the British had set loose old resentments by capturing Baldak, and the standard of jehad was up. Around it flocked new people who could not be acquainted immediately with the order to cease firing. More than twelve hundred tribesmen who had deserted from the Zhob militia were roaming the countryside wearing their uniforms and carrying rifles issued by the British. Some were prepared to shoot, others became equally dangerous by spreading wild rumors.

Nadir wrote to the British Political Agent at Waziristan that although the Wazirs and Daurs, two tribes of British India, had ceased hostilities at his order, he would be unable to keep them in hand if the British insisted on demanding fines for their belligerency, and that the result might be to place the situation beyond the control of both governments. "Nadir has transgressed the bounds of diplomatic propriety," said the Agent, continuing the punitive measures.

The real danger to peace was not the proximity of Afghan tribes to the British lines (the distance had been shortened to ten miles) but the British practice of sending over airplanes, which irritated the tribesmen. The British continued to send planes, one of which dropped on the Afghan troops leaflets announcing that the Allies had signed a peace treaty with Germany. The Afghan General, reading about peace being made in a far-off land while he was busy on the spot to the same end, wrote to the Agent asking if he thought this would insure world peace.

This old man, Abdul Quddus, who never kept to the subject at hand, dropped a hint that Amanullah might become the Caliph of Islam in succession to the deposed Sultan of Turkey. This was regarded by the British as a gift of propaganda. "There is no doubt that if this claim made by the Afghan chief minister were known, it would horrify and alienate the great mass of Moslem opinion in India and elsewhere, and cover Afghanistan with derision. It might, I suspect, be useful to let the fact of this claim being made leak cautiously into the Moslem press." This suggestion was marked Most Secret.

Peace was still tenuous, and Amanullah had not formally accepted the peace conference. "We will wait till June 22 for the Amir's acceptance," said G. of I., "and if we do not have it then, we will renew hostilities. The situation is deteriorating."

Amanullah's letter arrived on June 21, promising to send a delegation on July 15. The Viceroy's private secretary, Jack Maffey, who had taken an official position at the front, was delighted. "I am attracted by a vision of peace in two chapters. Chapter 1, 'Caravans and traders as long as you behave yourself.' and 'Stew in your own juice.' Chapter 2: 'Overtures from Amir suppliant.'"

Sir A. Hamilton Grant, the Foreign Secretary of the Government of India, was appointed plenipotentiary to head the British delegation, and he immediately put himself on the unpopular side with a memo suggesting, "If we are to have really satisfactory relations with Afghanistan . . . [they] must be based on real friendliness and mutual trust."

"No one trusts the Afghans and they do not trust one another," Roos-

Keppel reminded him. The Foreign Office memo to Lord Curzon read, "The G. of I.'s . . . plenipotentiary is of a timid disposition . . . It does not seem that we have anything to gain by keeping Amanullah on the throne."

A frontier General, Sir Edward Barrow, called Amanullah "an ill-conditioned young man who has imbibed strong Anglophobe ideas, whereas his older brother Inayatullah is not only Anglophile but leads a well-ordered life, the husband of one wife, and is both sensible and amiable. I saw something of him in 1905 when I thought he was of weakly character, but I am told that he has greatly matured and holds and defends his own opinions, which are favorable to us, so that his advent might be welcome."

Then Englishmen began to think of terms to impose on Afghanistan, much in the spirit of children playing the game of "Wouldn't it be nice . . . ?" and "Why don't we . . . ?" It was suggested in London that Great Britain might simply take over Afghanistan, in a protectorate that, according to the fashion of the times, would have to be "veiled." General Cox objected. "I cannot imagine a less profitable country to 'protect' than Afghanistan . . . A veritable wasp's nest." There was yet another argument against this: "An extension of our control over Afghanistan would be difficult to justify unless it could be shown that we were acting with the full concurrence of the Afghans themselves. Current theories about 'self-determination' and the rights of 'small nationalities' have to be reckoned with." So this plan succumbed to the ghosts of McNaghten and Cavagnari, two Britons who had been murdered in the previous century attempting to establish British rule in Afghanistan, as well as to the living influence of Woodrow Wilson.

"I think we should encourage the Amir to maintain his isolation as the best buffer against Bolshevism," was one proposal. In London a member of H.M.G. agreed that this was not politically a time to take any territory which England had not already claimed. "I wish it were, for we cannot rely on never having a Skobolev on the other side, and if we seriously fight the Bolsheviks (as we probably shall) in the near future, it looks as though we should find one among them to our cost."

G. of I. had proposed a treaty in two parts, first peace and six months later, if Afghanistan behaved well, a treaty of friendship. Jack Maffey exulted, "If the General Staff [of the Army] will wait patiently for chapter 2, they will get the Afghans building a railroad (for them to capture later, of course), they will get their aerial convention [permitting flights over Afghanistan] and everything quite easily. Mention the aerial convention now, and the Afghans will first be scared, and when pressed will say, 'Oh, that will be another 15 lakhs, please.' "

H.M.G. in the person of Lord Curzon, whose family motto was, "Curzon hold what Curzon hath," insisted that continued control of Afghanistan's foreign relations was vital. G. of I. demurred: "In the past year there has been a profound change in political outlook in the Middle East, including Afghanistan . . . If we press the matter, we shall be met either with a flat refusal or with a counter demand that we cannot brush aside . . . If we regain the confidence of the Afghans and get them to turn voluntarily to us in their difficulties, we shall have secured more than we can do by any . . ." and here the Government which ruled many millions of Indians used a phrase that has consoled many a girl who, despairing of marriage, has still longed for some relationship, "a scrap of paper."

Like a maiden yearning for romance but worried about rape, G. of I. awaited the arrival of Amanullah's delegates in Rawalpindi.

"Peace has become difficult and will take a long time," was the sigh in the bazaars of Kabul. "Ghaza!" and "Jehad!" were no longer cried, not even in the vicinity of the British Agency. What had started out with excitement and glory had now become a matter of empty stomachs and empty pockets and a new fear of something unfamiliar, another airplane that might fly above and drop bombs if peace could not be found.

Sugar was costly—"famine rates," said the men as they went from shop to shop—and on the day that the British jubilantly received Amanullah's final letter, the shopkeepers were saying that in a few days there would be no sugar at all. A forty-yard piece of lattha cloth from India cost 120 rupees.

Earlier the well-fed men in the Viceroy's office in Simla had predicted that a closing of the passes to caravans would cause Afghanistan no real disaster, only inconvenience, but in the bazaars and behind the mud walls, it was almost disaster. Having little to sell, the Moslems and Hindus in the bazaar alike lamented the golden period of Amir Habibullah. Yet the harvest was good that year; it was poor in neighboring India and the British imported Australian wheat to avert disaster there.

Amanullah in his palace had to work by the light from local compressed oil, sputtering and dim; the luxury kerosene came from India.

He knew that he was being excused for his youth and inexperience, but that the blame was going to his advisers, chiefly his father-in-law who had pursued this end so long and so publicly. On the road from Jalalabad the British Agent Saifullah had heard from many mouths that "the Foreign Minister has filled the fool head of the Amir with sinister arrogance and false airs and wanted to raise him to the status of the Emperor of Germany in a minute without regard to the capacity and means of a small nation like Afghanistan." Instinctively the critics chose as a comparison a ruler who had been defeated by the British.

The soldiers and the ghazis, trailing in the dust from Dakka and Jalalabad, told tales of incredibly bad management of food supplies; many, they kept saying, had starved. The general at Dakka, Saleh, came home to worse troubles than his bomb-wounded foot. Amanullah and Mahmud Sami blamed him for the defeat. At a military durbar on June 14 Amanullah tried to find the reason for the confused flight from Dakka, and General Saleh was blamed by soldiers who said that when their officers could not make stand, how could they make stand?

By the time elephants came through Kabul, dragging two big anti-quated guns, on the way to reinforcing the frontier in case peace should fail again, people had forgotten the excitement of seeking freedom. Soldiers were whispering, "There is no ghaza in invading a country of others without reason, while no interference or encroachments have first been made by those so invaded into those hearths and homes."

Amanullah continued to act with the freedom he had taken upon himself.

Amanullah's mission to the Russians arrived on June 4, the day after the Armistice with England, in Tashkent, the capital of Russian Turke-stan, most of whose residents were Moslems, who had been leading an unquiet life with a new government that was incredibly unsettled. The Afghan mission was headed by Mohammed Wali, the handsome, self-assured man of thirty-eight who had been trusted by Amanullah's father to handle his secret correspondence. Afghan soldiers in scarlet tunics attended Wali as he stepped from the train into a railroad station decorated in his honor to be greeted by a guard of honor. Fireworks celebrated his arrival. Later, to all this attention was added a gala per-formance at a theater where the boxes were hung with carpets borrowed from the bourgeoisie.[2]

Wali told the Russians that his party was headed for the peace con-ference, and would eventually go to the capitals of the world to announce Afghanistan's independence. He spoke also of mutual aid between Afghanistan and Turkestan, with men being furnished by Afghanistan and arms by Turkestan.

It suited the Bolshevik Government well to recognize Afghanistan. On May 25 Moscow sent out a radio message, in English so that it could be understood by those most closely concerned, recognizing "Amir Amanullah and the independence of Afghanistan and the principle of self-determination for the natives of Central Asia." Then Lenin replied to Amanullah's letter with an enthusiasm that contrasted with the British coolness: "May the aspirations of the Afghan people to follow the Russian example be the best guarantee of strength and independence of the Afghan State." He spoke of "mutual aid against any encroachment of rapacious foreigners."

A few months earlier the Bolsheviks had defeated the White Russians who held the railway north of Tashkent, and now Moscow was able to communicate with Turkestan. Moscow was distressed by the disorder there, the incompetence of the officials and their failure to include Moslems in the government or to placate the Moslems in any way. To correct this situation a party of experienced officials had been sent to Turkestan.[3]

Paul Alexander Bravin was one of these. He was a shrewd, energetic man who had held diplomatic posts under the Tsar in Persia and India, who spoke not only Persian and Hindustani but several dialects of those languages, and whose cleverness was proved by the prestige he had attained in a government that was openly anti-Semitic, in spite of being a Jew. There had been a time when the Bolsheviks suspected him of being a British spy, and upon the authority of a clerk in the Commissariat of Foreign Affairs some papers alleged to involve him as a spy were sent to the Extraordinary Commission to Combat Speculation and Counter-Revolution. Bravin had cleared himself, and now he came to Turkestan with fifty million rubles in Nikolais, the currency of the deposed and murdered Tsar, which would be more valuable than the Turkestan Bolshevik money in seeking aid for the Bolsheviks against the White Russians.

Bravin was named Russia's first Envoy to Afghanistan. On June 13 he and Wali said good-bye to each other. The Afghans headed for Moscow, leaving behind a Consulate at Tashkent, and Bravin started for Kabul. Both had to return.

The Afghans found that Port Alexandrovsk on the Caspian Sea, from which they hoped to sail, had been occupied by the British Royal Navy. Bravin and his party went up the Oxus River by boat, expecting to have a Bokharan military escort on the trip through Bokharan territory, but the Moslem soldiers refused to guard one who did not believe in any God at all, and his steamer went unescorted, towing a barge which held some guns and ammunition. A high cliff overhung the Oxus at one point; as the steamer passed beneath it, rifles were fired down. Two of the crew were killed. The barge caught fire and the ammunition began to explode. Bravin returned to Tashkent about the same time as Wali's mission, and both set out again by different routes.[4]

On the Western frontier of Russia and Afghanistan, Bolsheviks and Afghans were testing each other to see if some cooperation might be possible. Russia's Deputy Commissioner in charge of Soviet relations with Asiatic nations, Karakhan, wired on June 12 to the Turkestan Minister for Foreign Affairs, Bogoyavlenski: "Please reply to Afghan mission regarding the assistance to be given to Afghans in arms and military supplies, that we are ready to render assistance as soon as the railway communication has been re-established. Till then it is desirable to assist them by the means at your disposal. Next week three military experts will be sent to Tashkent for assistance to Bravin and in addition financial help will be sent. For the time being you may ascertain the concrete propositions of the Afghans regarding the desirability of dispatching to the front against Kolchak [a White Russian Admiral opposing the Bolsheviks with the aid of the British] a small detachment of Afghans, in which case we on our part would permit the recruiting among our Moslems in Turkestan for the Afghan Army against the British. Communicate to us the points of the agreement projected by the Afghans but refrain for the time being from signing it."

In the frontier town of Kushk, the Russians were said to be awaiting Amanullah's permission to go into Afghanistan, and Afghans were ready to participate in garrisoning the Kushk post.

But men were going back and forth across the frontier to upset these plans, mostly Turcomans but paid by the British. General Malleson, who employed them, said:

"It became our task to do everything possible to prevent the consummation of Afghan and Bolshevik plans for an offensive and defensive alliance."

The British had broken the code in which the Russians, lacking telegraph between Tashkent and Moscow, were communicating by wireless.

They knew what Tashkent knew as soon as Moscow did. And they set out to create suspicion between Afghanistan and Russia.

"I had some excellent officers speaking numerous languages," said Malleson. "I had agents up to distances of a thousand miles or more, even in the government offices of the Bolsheviks. I had relays of men constantly coming and going in areas which I deemed important. There was hardly a train on the Central Asian railway which had not one of our agents on board, and there was no important railway center which had not two or three men on the spot. Travelers of every sort and description were cross-examined at scores of different places.

"As a preliminary, we laid ourselves to 'queer the pitch' of Bravin.

"In a series of communications which . . . almost invariably circulated freely among the people we desired they should reach, we pointed out to the Afghans that, in view of the notorious faithlessness of the Bolsheviks, they should, before admitting such people to the God-granted kingdom, extract from them suitable pledges. What more suitable than the restitution to Afghanistan of the Panjdeh district filched from them in 1885? And what more agreeable act of justice to the Bolsheviks than such restitution, the Bolsheviks, who never tired of denouncing the iniquitous, land-grabbing imperialism of the former Czarist government?"

Bravin, approached by the Afghans, agreed that this might be arranged and spoke of plebiscites in that area. Four important Afghan mullahs from the Great Mosque at Herat went toward Bokhara to check on the conditions of the plebiscite.

"Having, through numerous agents in both camps, a fairly accurate notion of what was going on, and of how these two interesting parties were seeking how best to take each other in," said General Malleson, "we made it our business to keep each side unofficially informed of the perfidy of the other. The Afghans, about this time, hearing there was a serious and promising anti-Bolshevik rebellion through Ferghana, were gauche enough to send special emissaries there, with letters and presents for the leaders of the insurgents. This information, too, we felt it our duty to bring to the notice of the Bolsheviks."

Late in June a frantic wireless message went from Tashkent to Moscow: "The Afghans have betrayed us." The agents of General Malleson were succeeding.

"An Afghan armed force marched through Kushk without permission and proceeded towards Merv," said the General. "Afghan consuls and agents appeared in every town of Turkestan. Afghan mullahs were everywhere active. As a result of our bringing these matters to Bolshevik notice, there was considerable anxiety. Reinforcements were sent to Kushk. The head of the Bolshevik Turkestan Government went to Merv and Askabad to inquire into Afghan machinations. Afterwards he went to Kushk and was exceedingly annoyed at being insulted by an Afghan officer there. More Bolshevik reinforcements went to Kushk. We informed Herat, who hurriedly sent their reinforcements to the frontier. The Bolsheviks were warned of this, and so the game went on."

Bravin crossed into Afghanistan on July 1 with one hundred and twenty pony loads of ammunition, and an escort of four hundred cavalry of whom only thirty crossed the border with him. A month later he was still in Herat; Amanullah did not intend to jeopardize his peace treaty with Great Britain by letting him come to Kabul.

As his principal delegate to the Peace Conference at Rawalpindi, Amanullah chose his cousin Ali Ahmed, who had been his father's confidential secretary. Ali Ahmed, aged thirty-six, was nine years older than Amanullah and better educated, having been to school in Murree, India, and accompanied Amir Habibullah on his official visit to India. He was the nephew of Ulya Hazrat, to whom his egocentric confidence gave the excitement of a personality she could not dominate. Ali Ahmed could be expected to feel like an older son of Ulya Hazrat and to be permanently surprised that his younger relation had become Amir.

Amanullah, on his part, never forgave Ali Ahmed for having been the first to accept Nasrullah as ruler. With his appointment the gossips of Kabul saw the beginning of a return to favor of the group they called the Jalalabadis, a term normally meaning a resident of Jalalabad but now applied to those who had participated in Nasrullah's brief and localized reign.

Amanullah gave Ali Ahmed authority to conclude a treaty at his own discretion. Any previous Amir of Afghanistan would have kept such authority firmly in his own hands. But he instructed Ali Ahmed that there was one central essential that he must bring back from Rawalpindi, whatever else he sacrificed: Afghanistan's total independence.

Then Amanullah appointed a delegation that upset all the social structure of Afghanistan. Many Hindus lived in Kabul; they sent caravans back and forth to India, and some had skill in treating diseases or mixing medicines. But they were in a minority without a role in public affairs. Now Amanullah appointed a Hindu, Niranjan Das, to his peace delegation. "A most astounding appointment," Grant said when he heard of it, "in a country where Hindus have always been regarded as of no political account." His old teacher whom he had released from prison, India-trained Dr. Abdul Ghani, and a rough-talking soldier named Colonel Ghulam Mohammed were the other delegates.

In mid-July a messenger appeared in the Khyber Pass to give the British this offer, which he said came from Nasrullah:

"I request that peace should not be made with the usurper Amanullah, as I am the rightful sovereign of Afghanistan, having been recognized by the people according to Islam and the sardars of Afghanistan on the death of my brother. The people do not like Amanullah and he is obliged to flee if an advance is made or Kabul bombed.

"I am sure to be released and recognized by the people on the arrival of the British in Kabul and will be ready to enter into a friendly alliance with the British Government like my father and brother and even to surrender Ningrahar as far as Jagdalak and Kandahar and Khost if the British so desire."

Since Nasrullah was unable to deliver these gifts, being a powerless prisoner, the British did not trouble to check the authenticity of the message, which they doubted. Afghans always would believe that it came, not from Nasrullah, but from a group of his followers whom Amanullah discovered at that time to be engaged in a plot to put the pious Nasrullah on the throne after killing the innovator Amanullah. One of the leading conspirators tried to cheat Amanullah out of his punishment by committing suicide; he was unsuccessful in this also, and lived, although without one eye. Amanullah would have liked to pardon this man, whose family had served his; at his trial Amanullah asked him to imagine that he was the ruler; what would he do with a conspirator like himself? "I would put the conspirator to death," replied the man. "If I pardon you, will you try again to kill me?" asked Amanullah. The man said that he would. Amanullah sadly gave the death sentence.

The correspondence under the name of Nasrullah did have an effect on the British, however. One letter warned that Amanullah was anxious to impress the people of India with his concern for their welfare, and for that reason had put the Hindus on his peace delegation. The British did not intend to be second in showing respect for the people of India; they named to their own delegation, as they were planning to do, two Hindu gentlemen heavily laden with British honors.

On July 24 the Afghan delegation went down into India, preceded by attendants who pitched at each stop a large tent for their rest and refreshment. The first stop was a piquet the British called Green Hill because there was nothing green nearby, where 100 riflemen were guarding occupied Dakka. After putting up the tent, the attendants spread its interior with carpets skillfully woven in the intricate mosaic of color and pattern that makes Oriental carpeting such a delight to gaze upon. The British soldiers gazed covetously.

When the delegation appeared, the soldiers had their first view of Afghans of affluence and importance.

Ali Ahmed carried himself as if he were handsome, and this convinced many people that he was. His jaw was aggressive, and his mustaches framed his nose like parentheses. Like all Afghans of status, Ali Ahmed wore Western clothes, but no one ever knew in what form of Western clothes he would appear. Today he wore a dark green tunic of heavy cloth, thick riding breeches, knee boots and spurs, a Sam Browne belt and sword and pistol. It was a hot day even for July. His headdress was rather like a helmet of ancient times, a brown dome covered with black feathers. The Hindu Niranjan Das, an old man who was very tall and thin, rode a small skinny pony. If these soldiers had been as well read as their political officers, they would have been reminded of Don Quixote on Rosinante. As it was, they marveled at his hat, which had a very shallow crown and a very wide brim, and needed only a cutout to remind the learned of Don Quixote's shaving-basin hat.

The delegates rested for an hour, then departed after some unpleasantness connected with Niranjan Das's hat, which could not be found. Certain of the British soldiers volunteered to help with the packing of the carpets. These were men who had been serving prison sentences in England for such offenses as burglary and shopbreaking, and in 1915–16, in the press of war, had been sent to finish these sentences with the Somerset Light Infantry. It was the hope of all the others, including one of their young officers, that they might put their special skills to use in acquiring one of the Afghan carpets, but their past exploits had not prepared them for the wariness of the Afghan attendants. When the party had gone, taking all its carpets, a light-fingered soldier revealed that he had a trophy after all, the missing hat. Inside it was a label, "Hawkes and Co., Savile Row, London."[5]

At Peshawar the delegates boarded a special train for Rawalpindi, a dusty cantonment in which little was going on. There they saw much that was like their own towns, but the British ruler had set his stamp on the architecture. During this conference the Afghans lived and conferred in wooden buildings surrounded by something totally foreign to their natures, a verandah. Afghan houses all looked inward and presented to the street only a wall, usually of mud. Even the palaces were within walls. When an Afghan wanted to sit on a platform and look out, or be looked at, he went to a teahouse. Many years later, when Moslem names would replace the English names on all these Rawalpindi houses, carpets would be hung on the verandahs to restore Oriental privacy.

The British delegates also came by train to Rawalpindi. An enthusiastic police officer had written on the regulations of the day, "Should there be a tendency on the part of any crowd that may assemble to accord an ovation to Sir Hamilton Grant, this should be encouraged and not checked." No crowd assembled. There was not even any assemblage of the sort that would have been unnoticed anyway, that of spies. A few weeks earlier the North-West Frontier Province Political Officer had sent this advice: "It is understood that steps are being taken by Military Intelligence and Central Intelligence Departments to collect Afghan intelligence from the Afghan party at Rawalpindi. Do you not think this is undignified and possibly harmful? The spy system is very clumsy and we do not want to frighten these shy birds from giving us and our Indian colleagues their confidence." This would be the last time the British would refer to the Afghans as "shy birds."

In a similarly condescending attitude, that of a nanny reproving naughty children, Sir Hamilton Grant had prepared an opening statement: "When there is illness, it is necessary to take the ill-tasting drug first; the sweetmeat that removes the evil taste comes later."

Friday, July 27, was the opening day. On the previous night Ali Ahmed brooded over the fact that his attendants had been deprived of their firearms on entering Rawalpindi, and that his party was openly under police surveillance. He opened with this topic.

"As a friend," said Ali Ahmed, "I will be quite ready to discuss anything in a friendly spirit but Afghanistan is not prepared to accept anything in the nature of a threat."

Grant said, "As regards arms, I trust you have made some arrangement for storing."

"I shall not allow my men to go out without arms," said Ali Ahmed, "but if I myself go out, may I have an armed orderly?"

"Why do you ask for an armed orderly? There is no danger."

"It will satisfy the Afghans."

"The Viceroy has written to the Amir," said Grant, "explaining that he could not allow an escort and that he would be responsible for the safety of the Afghan delegates."

"I asked for the escort only as an honor."

"I cannot permit the Afghan delegates to go about with a lot of armed men."

"This is only a trifle."

"The matter cannot be dismissed as a trifle. We have several things to think of in wartime."

"It is only to safeguard my honor," said Ali Ahmed.

"I will safeguard your honor. In a country where no one is allowed to go armed, we cannot suddenly allow fifty men to go about armed."

"If I go in a motor there will be only four or five persons with me, not more. If we do not have this escort, the people of Afghanistan will say that they have been deprived of everything. That, according to our views, is a slight."

"The custom of my country is that no one goes armed," said Grant.

What they were really discussing was the question of who had won the war, whether the Afghans should be treated like the conquered Indians, and the fact that Grant and Ali Ahmed did belong to countries with different customs. In Afghanistan arms were a normal part of a costume.

The ostensible topic then became the British Agent in Kabul. Ali Ahmed offered to release him if the British would send for the Afghan Postmaster of Peshawar and his imprisoned friends.

"I cannot entertain that idea for a moment. If that is the spirit which is going to be shown, I shall have to do what I have been advised by you not to do, and indulge in definite threats. I shall report to my government what was said, and I shall not be surprised if I am told to suspend negotiations pending the arrival of the British Agent in Rawalpindi."

"When does the British Government want its envoy?"

"At once."

"You cannot give me an order. You can only make a request. Whatever you wish to say will be carried to the Amir. I wish to be treated as a friend."

"I have every desire to treat you as a friend, but I am perfectly astounded," said Grant, "at the lack of comprehension of the position shown by the proposal."

"I think you are very short-tempered and very sensitive," said Ali Ahmed, "and as I myself am very sensitive, I believe it would be better to correspond in writing only."

"I have perfect control over my temper," said Grant, "but when I hear a proposition such as that put forward, I have to state plainly what the views of my government will be on the subject."

He then asked why the British Agent had not accompanied the delegation.

In Kabul the British Agent Saifullah was well enough, but wretched. He was interned under guard in the Agency building, along with members of his mission, one of whom thought that the other members were plotting to murder him and had written to his father and uncle in India naming those to be charged in case of his sudden death.

Next door to the Agency lived Shuja-ud-Dowleh, the young friend of Amanullah who had given him the first firsthand information of his father's death. Amanullah had made Shuja-ud-Dowleh his Chief of Intelligence. For the rest of his life it would be whispered of Shuja-ud-Dowleh that his was the finger that had pulled the trigger on his Amir.

"At 8:30 one evening," Saifullah recorded in his diary, "a woman appearing on the wall between the Agency building and the house of Shuja-ud-Dowleh shouted loudly saying, 'O you men of the Agency! You have enticed our slave girl, who has disappeared, and she has come to you. Hand her over to us instantly, otherwise a complaint will be lodged against you in the Kotwal [police station]!' She was answered gently that the Agency men knew nothing of the girl; she might have gone elsewhere. I called the havildar of the Agency gate guard and told him what had occurred. He said the girl had made a hole in the latrine of Shuja-ud-Dowleh's and coming out therefrom in the narrow lane was passing by the front of the gate of the Agency building when she was challenged by the guard and arrested, taken and handed over to her owner on her telling that she was the slave maid of Shuja-ud-Dowleh and owing to severe persecution exercised upon her she wanted to run away."

But the cruelest hurt to the British Agent was the thought that the British Government had abandoned him because he was only an Indian. "The case must have been different had there been a European British Agent."

Now, in Rawalpindi, when the British asked about their Agent, Ali Ahmed said that the matter had lost importance. They did not press the point. Grant conducted Ali Ahmed to the verandah and a waiting car. Thus ended the first session of peace-making.

That night Ali Ahmed wrote to Amanullah complaining of the restrictions, and Maffey wrote to the Viceroy, "Ali Ahmed is a vain, full-blooded coxcomb."

The next day's meeting began auspiciously because Ali Ahmed found at his place a note he had made at the previous sitting. But soon Grant was saying, "We have ample information that the Afghan Government have already been coquetting with the Bolsheviks."

"They have been coquetting with us," said Ali Ahmed.

"That is probably true. The Bolsheviks have been making promises of support . . ."

"I will tell you the truth," interrupted Ali Ahmed, offended by the word "probably." "It is my object always to be truthful."

"I did not mean to surprise you by all this. I just mentioned it," said Grant. "We cannot help being surprised and amused at the impossibility of such an extraordinary development that two things which are so utterly incongruous as the Afghan constitution and the Afghan social system and the Bolsheviks and Bolshevik doctrine should come together. A violent rabble who hold that kings must be murdered, that monarchies must be abolished, that aristocracies must be swept away, and that all property must be common, even women? Where is the Bolshevik religion? The British Government are not much perturbed by the idea of a Bolshevik flood and they do not keep awake at nights because of it."

"As a friend, I tell the British Government that they should have some anxiety."

"I don't think so. As regards India I am not frightened. I will ask Sir Shams Shah to bear me out."

The Indian delegate to whom he appealed was one of two who were not comfortable in their role of link between East and West. The Afghans regarded them as their own kind, as oppressed persons who should be rescued. They kept embracing them. The Indians knew that the traditional Afghan greeting between men is an embrace and three kisses on alternate cheeks. They knew that the British knew this, but they also knew what Anglo-Saxons think of men who kiss each other. Besides, they did not wish to appear to feel oppressed. After each embrace they assured the British privately that it had been unwelcome.

Now Sir Shams Shah said, "India hates the Bolsheviks, who make no distinction between high and low, good and evil. There are many castes in India. India does not wish to destroy its caste system by adopting Bolshevik principles. The principles of the Bolsheviks interfere with the chastity of women, wealthy people, and trade. The frontier tribes of India are very jealous of the honor of their women and will never let the Bolsheviks enter the country."

Sir Gurbakhsh Singh spoke similarly, "There are a large number of God-worshipping people in India and they look upon the King as an extra God. Those who worship God look down upon the Bolsheviks with great disgust because if they have revolted against the King they have revolted against God."

When Grant spoke of women being common property under Bolshevism and the Indians also spoke of sex, they were making a tiny incident appear to be a universal practice. Early in the Revolution, in a small town on the Volga called Syzran, the officials had issued a proclamation complaining that capitalism had resulted in all the young, pretty women going to the bourgeoisie while peasants and workers had to be content with second-best. In the future women would be communal property like everything else. Lenin, as soon as he heard of this, ordered a halt, and, fearful of the propaganda that could result, imposed the death penalty for taking a copy of the proclamation out of the country. A Russian lady returning to her husband's post in Kashgar, China, smuggled out a copy in her hat, and the British Consul in Kashgar sent it to India.[6]

Ali Ahmed, hearing Bolshevism described by such references, agreed, "It is an evil influence."

"No doubt it is a very evil influence," echoed Grant.

"Bolshevism is worse than plague in India," said Ali Ahmed.

"As regards India, the Government of India have no fears."

"It has spread all over Europe," Ali Ahmed reminded him.

"Only in unfortunate, ruined countries that have been defeated."

"Russia and Austria-Hungary were great kingdoms," said Ali Ahmed.

"The countries that have won—England, France and America—are free from Bolshevism."

Ali Ahmed said politely, "I hope it will not get to victorious countries."

"If we cannot come to an agreement of this sort, and there is danger of Bolshevism coming down to India, then our only course will be completely to close the door into Afghanistan. I am simply telling you what we intend to do if, after peace is established, Afghanistan keeps the door open as it is at present to Bolshevik emissaries and Bolshevik influences. We would do this by completely closing every pass leading from Afghanistan into India. We should not regard the inconvenience caused thereby to trade and the trade of Afghanistan and the Ghilzais would have to find their outlet in some other direction."

For a moment the Afghans were silent. The British were to comment later on their expressions, assuring themselves, "We have a terrible weapon at hand in the closing of the passes."

"Then you will force Afghanistan," began Ali Ahmed, but Grant interrupted him before he could make a threat, and soon the talk turned to Amir Habibullah's contribution to the British by his neutrality and to Britain's failure to pay his subsidy. "Had the late Amir been spared, I do not think there would be occasion for such talk as we are having here today."

Ali Ahmed burst forth, "Amir Habibullah's wise strategy suppressed the feelings of the nation. When he died, and the present King succeeded him, the people had an opportunity of showing their feelings. If he had lived another year and a half, a severe revolution would have taken place in Afghanistan. The present King of Afghanistan is following the ideas of the nation. Diwan Niranjan Das is a civil colonel and in durbar there are four hundred Mohammadzai and Barakzai officers who sit below him. Distinctions have been removed in order to unite nationalities, so that it may be impossible for the Bolsheviks or their class of persons to disunite them. The advantages that the Bolsheviks will have in making friends with Afghanistan will be that they will ask them to help them to induce the Moslem states in Trans-Caspia and Central Asia to accept their rule and they will be willing to hand over tracts of Moslem states to Afghanistan to secure the friendship of Afghanistan.

"Now it is for you to decide whether you will make us friends or drive us over to the Bolsheviks. We are all anxious to be friends. I am very pleased that you have given me the idea."

Seeing that the British secretary was taking notes, Ali Ahmed concluded, "I hope you will give me a summary of these remarks."

Grant changed the subject, expressing regret that Habibullah's tomb had been bombed. He included the phrase, "If this is what actually happened—" and Colonel Ghulam Mohammed broke in, "We are Moslems and we do not tell lies."

"I do not doubt your words," said Grant, "but war is war and accidents will occur."

"You should fight with live people and not with those who are dead," said Ghulam Mohammed.

"It was an accident. When a shell is fired from a gun at a town five miles away, we cannot tell exactly where it will hit. It is the same way with airplanes."

Ali Ahmed said, "It is not customary to send airplanes to countries which do not possess them. It is the same as the Germans sending zeppelins to England."

"In that case the British did not complain but brought the zeppelins down and they did not send any more."

"If we had airplanes," said Ali Ahmed, "we would also bring the British airplanes down."

"I would be glad to see a condition of things in which all nations were equally armed," said Grant, whose government had recently been rejoicing that this was not the case. "A nation with superior armament tries to get the better of the other."

"The British used to complain that the Germans threw bombs on churches and people."

"That was propaganda. We always try to make out that our enemy is doing very bad things. That makes our own people fight better."

"The British published the doings of Germans to the world," said Ali Ahmed.

"Yes. It helped to stir up our own people."

"Look at the forbearance of the Afghans," cried Ali Ahmed. "We do not publish the doings of the British to the whole world but only tell the delegates about it."

"This is very nice of you and will make for friendship."

At the close of that session, Ali Ahmed said that he would hear the terms the British were prepared to offer. "And if we become friends, I will exchange hats with Sir Hamilton Grant and shake hands with him."

"I shall be very pleased."

"If the result is to the contrary, I will pay my compliments to you but I will not shake hands with you."

On July 29 they all met again and Grant, after offering to forego reparations because Afghanistan would not be able to pay, read a proposed treaty in which the Afghans accepted responsibility for the war, expressed contrition, and agreed to a British demarcation of the frontier and the confiscation of money due from Habibullah's time.

No mention was made of British control of Afghanistan's foreign relations. Grant had wired his superiors that this would be impossible to secure.

Ali Ahmed refused to accept the treaty. "Afghanistan has made itself independent and it does not matter whether the British Government recognize that independence or not."

The day was ending in mutual dislike. "We have moved a hundred miles apart," said Ali Ahmed.

But the British served tea in the conference room after the session. Ali Ahmed drank several cups of tea and ate a quantity of rich little cakes. Then he said:

"I would willingly go about with a policeman sitting on my shoulders if you so desire." He explained:

"If you treat me kindly as a friend, you can make me do anything you like."

For three days Ali Ahmed had been talking about his need to be treated like a friend. Now the British, who also are softened by tea, listened to him.

"Afghans are as touchy as Frenchmen," Grant wired the Viceroy, "always on the look-out for offense, vain as peacocks, and yet responsive to kindness and friendship to an amazing degree."

Later Grant was to write, "It is difficult at first to believe, when one is confronted with a number of fine-looking, comparatively fair-skinned gentlemen in frock coats or resplendent uniforms, that they are, beneath a thin veneer of civilization, really very barbarous, very uncontrolled and very childish. Like children, they respond amazingly to the treatment accorded them. But they are high-spirited, willful, rather naughty children who are not to be cowed by hard words or threats. Kindliness, patience and candor alone can win them to see reason. They will accept the refusal of their most cherished desire if it is put to them in temperate, friendly words, and the reason for the refusal honestly explained."

With their new understanding, the British learned that day that an Afghan likes to be host in his own home. So the fourth session was held at the house which, for the duration, was Ali Ahmed's. "The conversation today will assume a very friendly tone because the British delegates have come to visit me."

Then Ali Ahmed took up his copy of the treaty which the British had proposed and suggested that the words "in view of wanton and unprovoked aggression of the Amir" be changed to "owing to war between the two governments"; that "the Amir of Afghanistan" be changed to "the Afghan Government," and that the sentence "The Amir is contrite for the past" be altered, explaining, "The word 'contrite' is rather disagreeable to the Afghan people."

Ali Ahmed put forth also the idea that all the tribes in India known as Afghans be turned over to Afghanistan and that the British Government give Afghanistan one-half the annual sum it spent on those tribes. "For this consideration, Afghanistan would control the tribes in question better than the British Government do."

When Grant reported this to the Viceroy, he felt obliged to explain that Ali Ahmed really meant it.

"The boundary will be demarcated by the Boundary Commission," said Grant. "That is compensation which the British demand for this war. It is no advantage. It is simply to save their faces and to prevent delay."

"I am ready now to settle where the line shall run," said Ali Ahmed, "and an Afghan delegate can go there and demarcate."

Grant told him, "The British public and the British Government are smarting under a sense of very great indignation at the present moment and my own people will make it impossible for me to make peace."

Then Grant said, "I offered you a friendship treaty in six months."

"Why should you postpone it six months?" asked Ali Ahmed.

"Because the British public will not be hit in the face with a fist one day and put its hand into its pocket and hand over rupees the next."

Ali Ahmed said he would like to see the Viceroy. Grant refused. "In this matter I have got full authority and I am going to discharge my functions. There is no possibility of your going to the Viceroy."

Thereupon Grant commenced the strategy of telling Ali Ahmed falsely that he was making all decisions on his own, without reference to his superiors. He did not wish to give the Afghans any ideas about delaying tactics.

"Then peace cannot be concluded," said Ali Ahmed.

"I am very sorry."

"My object is that I should forego something and you will forego something."

"Impossible. One word more. We have decided August 16 is the date on which the treaty is to be accepted. If you are going to reject the treaty, I trust you will let me know as early as possible and I shall have your train ready."

"We can walk," said Ali Ahmed.

The next session on August 6 commenced with Grant's saying, "I shall be glad to hear anything Your Excellency has to say."

"I am waiting for you to say something."

"I merely want to know if you accept the treaty or not."

Ali Ahmed asked for a separate letter or a clause in the treaty specifying the freedom of Afghanistan in its foreign relations.

Two days earlier Grant had asked permission from the Viceroy to write such a letter. The Viceroy wired to London and waited for a reply. None came, so he wired to Grant that he should sign at once if he felt a grave risk inherent in delay, or if there was danger of the treaty's being referred to Kabul, where anything might happen. Later that day London approved. So Grant, who had just heard of new tribal raids, had prepared a letter which he drew forth when Ali Ahmed asked, "What shall I say to my Cabinet and people? They will say, 'You went to India. What have you brought back?' They will laugh at me."

Ali Ahmed looked at the letter and said, "We do not need this letter, as we were free from the date of the war."

"I agree the Afghans do not need this letter, but you have asked for it."

"I only wanted to show it to my people . . . I will go now and inform you tonight or tomorrow morning."

When Grant later had to justify his yielding on the letter, he explained, "Time was an important consideration. We reached a critical point where the Afghans, suspicious of our intentions regarding their independence and the freedom of their foreign relations, were ready to sign if given the assurance they required. Had we shilly-shallied over this matter, the Afghans' suspicions would have been thoroughly aroused, and they would either have refused to sign the treaty and broken off negotiations, or else they would have insisted on referring the matter to Kabul. Referral to Kabul would have involved delay at a time when there was the acutest tension on the frontier and indeed practical hostilities were in progress in the Peiwar and incidents might at any moment have occurred which would have made peace impossible. Moreover, it is uncertain how the treaty would be received in

Kabul. We considered, therefore, that it was all-important to get the treaty signed as quickly as we could."

Now he said to Ali Ahmed, "I do not want to put the matter off three or four days."

"You have telegraphic communication with your headquarters and your people are educated. I have no telegraphs and my people are uneducated. I am even more anxious than you to arrive at a decision."

Then Ali Ahmed protested that Amanullah was not described in the treaty as "His Majesty."

"That is solely in the power of King George," said Grant.

"If the Afghans addressed King George without 'His Majesty,' it would not please the British Government," said Ali Ahmed.

Maffey hastily exclaimed, "It would not!" but Grant said, "It would not seriously trouble us."

"It is only a civilized form of address," said Ali Ahmed.

"It has to be approved."

"The ruler of Afghanistan does not stand in need of being called His Majesty by the British Government."

"Perhaps not," said Grant. "Let him be called His Majesty by the Bolsheviks."

"As we are making friends . . ."

"We are not making friends. We are making peace. Can I ask the King-Emperor to give recognition to a man who is at war with them?"

"The Amir is fighting with the British but he has not been deprived of his kingdom," Ali Ahmed said.

For many years it had been important to the British to make their treaties with the Amirs of Afghanistan, who were mortal, rather than with the Government of Afghanistan, which endured. Faced with the conflict between this principle and a king's social sensibilities, Grant made a hasty decision.

"If at the head of the treaty we insert 'Government of Afghanistan,' instead of the name The Amir, that will remove all idea of indignity."

"I am giving you friendly advice," said Ali Ahmed, "that in the future when the Viceroy writes to the Amir, the words 'His Majesty' should be used. This is not a very difficult matter."

"It is," Grant said. "You do not know King George."

On August 8 both Grant and Ali Ahmed signed "The Treaty of Peace Between the Illustrious British Government and the Independent Government of Afghanistan," which said:

"From the date of the signing of this treaty there shall be peace.

"In view of the circumstances which have brought about the present war . . . the British Government, to mark their displeasure, withdraw the privilege enjoyed by former Amirs of importing arms, ammunition or warlike munitions through India to Afghanistan. The arrears of the late Amir's subsidy are furthermore confiscated and no subsidy is granted to the present Amir. At the same time, the British Government are desirous of the re-establishment of the old friendship . . . provided they have guarantees that the Afghan Government are, on their part, sincerely anxious to regain the friendship of the British Government. The British Government are prepared, therefore, provided the Afghan Government prove this by their acts and conduct, to receive another Afghan Mission after six months for the discussion and settlement of matters of common interest to the two governments and the re-establishment of old friendship on a satisfactory basis." The treaty provided also for an early demarcation of the doubtful portion of the Indo-Afghan frontier by a British Commission whose decision would be binding on Afghanistan.

And there was attached a letter to Ali Ahmed which said, "You asked me for some further assurance that the Peace Treaty which the British Government now offer contain nothing that interferes with the complete liberty of Afghanistan either in internal or external matters. My friend, if you will read the treaty carefully, you will see that there is no such interference with the liberty of Afghanistan. You have told me that the Afghan Government are unwilling to renew the arrangement whereby the late Amir agreed to follow unreservedly the advice of the British Government in regard to his external relations. I have not, therefore, pressed this matter, and no mention of it is made in the treaty. Therefore, the said Treaty and this letter leave Afghanistan officially free and independent in all its internal and external affairs. Moreover, this war has cancelled all previous treaties."

After the signing, Grant asked Ali Ahmed if he had been present in 1905 at the signing of a treaty between Amir Habibullah and a mission headed by Sir Louis Dane. Ali Ahmed said he had. Grant recalled that on that occasion a blot had appeared on the paper, and Sir Louis Dane had quoted the poem, "For a mole on the face of my lady-love, I would give Samarkand and Bokhara."

Ali Ahmed said he remembered this, but there was a condition attached. The interpreter explained that the first sentence of the poem was, "If my beloved win my heart." The offer was conditional on her winning his love.

Grant said, "I would like to offer you this gift of Bokhara and Samarkand but I do not know what the Bolsheviks would have to say." Ali Ahmed would have lingered in India, but Grant hurried him off.

The thunder of nine guns welcomed the news in Kabul. The narrow bazaar streets with their empty stalls had no shoppers on August 13, for all the men of Kabul were crowding toward the thoroughfares to shout their welcome to the messengers who told of a treaty. The military bands played with hope and triumph.

When Ali Ahmed returned to Kabul, his reception in the council chambers was not as enthusiastic as that in the streets. Mahmud Tarzi told him that he had no business giving away Afghan land by letting the British demarcate the frontier, that he had been so overwhelmed by one word, "independence," that everything else had gone out of his head. Nadir was angry because the treaty did not include amnesty for the Wazirs who had defied the British Government to fight for Afghanistan; Nadir had jeopardized his own reputation with assurances to the tribes.

Amanullah himself thought the Afghans had fared very well. Yet policy demanded some show of reprimanding his delegate. He put Ali Ahmed under house arrest.

Then family sentiment, an effective force in Afghanistan, provided a graceful way to rescind that punishment. Ali Ahmed wished to marry one of Amanullah's full sisters, Seraj-ul-Banat, and Ulya Hazrat wanted her nephew for a son-in-law. The wedding was an excuse for the bridegroom's release.

This story was told all over Kabul as one more example of the influence of Ulya Hazrat. In fact, this episode marked a waning of her dominance. The war had been a rite of passage for Amanullah. He had gambled and won. From that day forward, no advice would ever outweigh his own judgment.

On the evening of August 20, in the open spaces of the Idgah Mosque, in the same spot where he had received the turban of Amirship, proclaimed independence, and called his people to a Holy War, Amanullah mounted the steps of the pulpit. Before him stood fifty thousand Afghans surrounded by banners bearing verses from the Koran and the words "Long live our Amir."

"Oh, my proud and gallant nation, I have called you together today to hear good tidings of what you so deeply loved and longed for, the complete political freedom of your country, from protection under an alien nation, the British . . . You and your country are henceforth completely politically free and at liberty to speak to any nation . . .

"Your bloodshed and self-sacrifice alone have brought home to us this happy day of our national liberty, and no nation has granted us this."

Tarzi would say later, "What was achieved now by resorting to arms could never be hoped to be achieved by any other means." Amanullah's father had tried to work with the established order and failed. Amanullah, by fighting, had won. From that time, he was to think of himself as a revolutionary.

Although Bravin was still on his way from Herat, there had arrived in Kabul a Moslem gentleman from Russian Turkestan named Hosein, who according to rumor was the head of a delegation come to mourn Amir Habibullah. He had some sort of official standing, at any rate, and Amanullah used him in this ceremony to represent Russia.

Hosein stood on one side of Amanullah and Saifullah, the British Agent released three days earlier, on the other. "Here is the Russian representative standing along with the British envoy side by side today, a practical proof of our liberty," said Amanullah.

Ali Ahmed formally presented the two men to Amanullah, who shook Saifullah's hand saying, "Your British Government have accomplished and perfected the right of friendship." Then he shook Hosein's hand saying, "It was your government who came first in acknowledging our right of national liberty and political freedom."

Then he appealed to the nation to cooperate with him in spreading knowledge and education. "Hitherto you have been under the despotic rule of one person but now you are free."

Moscow had learned from the press on August 13 of the signing of the treaty, and ordered Tashkent, "Verify without delay."

In London the treaty brought bewilderment. It seemed to many Englishmen that their politicians had given away the thing they had asked men to die for: control of Afghanistan. In Parliament, Lord Sydenham unknowingly echoed a phrase of Curzon: "What has impressed me most unfavorably is the attitude of victors which seems throughout to have been assumed by the Afghans." Montagu drafted a letter to the Prime Minister suggesting that he replace Chelmsford as Viceroy but decided not to send it.[7]

G. of I. was far happier with the outcome than H.M.G.

"Change was bound to come," Grant wrote to Sir Denys Bray, who had succeeded him as Foreign Secretary of India. "It accords with the spirit of the age." On the Afghan-Indian frontier, earlier than in other parts of the British Empire, the postwar era had arrived.

"Our policy in the past was dictated by fear of an aggressive Russian Empire, continually intriguing at the gates of India. That Empire has collapsed and in its place we have Bolshevik chaos. We have, I believe, nothing to fear from Bolshevik influence in Afghanistan unless the whole fabric of the government collapses and Bolshevism finds its opportunity in chaos there as elsewhere."

Grant was still bemused by Ali Ahmed's remark, "If you treat me kindly as a friend, you can make me do anything you like."

"Liberty is a new toy to the Afghan Government," said Grant. "And they are very jealous and excited about it. And we shall be wise to give them free rein in the matter. Later on, if we handle them well, they will come to us to mend their toy when it gets chipped or broken. They want the shadow of external freedom and don't really worry about its substance."

But the military Commander-in-Chief, General Sir C. C. Munro, said, "Our political relations with the Amir must be profoundly changed. We cannot remain with blind-folded eyes on our side of the frontier."

To improve British vision, there was created a special intelligence bureau for the collection and coordination of news from Afghanistan, under the direction of J. H. Adam of the Central Intelligence Division in Peshawar, who became head of the Afghan Intelligence Agency.

One of Adam's first reports, as spymaster for Afghan affairs, came from a traveler who had seen in the Kohat Pass a large standard surmounted by a crescent and star and bearing the name of Amanullah. It appeared there the day after the Treaty was signed.

If Roos-Keppel had been passing that way, it might have reminded him of a sentence he wrote on June 4 to the Viceroy:

"Amanullah has lit a fire that will take us a great deal of trouble to put out."

CHAPTER 7

August 21, 1919, to July 29, 1920

The British Agent Saifullah went driving every evening in one of the official state carriages, an American-made victoria. Amanullah had sent it around on the day of the proclamation of the Anglo-Afghan Treaty, with a message that a daily ride might help repair the damage that captivity had done to his health.

Saifullah did not truly enjoy these drives because, along with the same victoria, the attendants brought always the same pony. It was a small, weak pony, not strong enough for this particular carriage, and inclined to be restive and to prance about, causing discomfort to both driver and passenger.

On August 24, when official peace was just four days old in Kabul, the pony became so nervous that Saifullah got out and told the coachman to walk it back to the stable. He started for the Agency on foot, the empty carriage and the prancing pony following him. The coachman called out that the pony seemed better and the sahib might ride again. Good-naturedly, Saifullah replied that he liked to walk, and the carriage went out of sight.

Then along the road came a second carriage. This was a state phaeton, much finer than Saifullah's victoria, drawn by two full-grown horses who seemed equal to their task, and followed by an Afghan military escort.

In it was riding the new Russian envoy, Paul Alexander Bravin. He had been permitted to enter Kabul on August 21, the day after someone else had represented Russia in the peace ceremony.

Bravin bowed graciously, and Saifullah bowed back, although out-

raged at the humiliation of the British Empire being seen afoot. Around
the bend of the road he met Amanullah, who was also walking, and they
exchanged pleasantries.

"I have since refused with thanks the use of the carriage in the future
so kindly granted me by the trickful Afghan Government," wrote
Saifullah. "They must keep even, if not preferentially, the balance of
respective honors between two competitive elements having come into
existence unfortunately by the new changes in system of the Afghan
Government."

Within a few days Saifullah was offered the use of a phaeton with
rubber tires as good as Bravin's and with two horses just as strong. He
rode through Kabul in it every evening, but informed Mahmud Tarzi
the phaeton was "no favor exclusive to me but it was, on the contrary,
a favor truly speaking on my part to use it, so that the people who have
witnessed the humiliation of the British Agent may also witness the
honor done to him."

This episode marked Amanullah's first experience with the new necessity of playing Britain and Russia against each other in his own
kingdom.

As regards carriages, there was not a balance even now, for he
allotted three phaetons to the Russians. Russia had complimented
Afghanistan in a manner Britain had not done since the 1830s when
she had seemed all too eager to settle down and colonize and thereby
brought disaster on herself, and would not repeat now without much
debate. The Russians had brought their ladies.

Mme. Bravin was enjoying her new adventure. She was a fiery person
who, in Tashkent, had displayed some rifles saying they were being
sent to Turcomans to attack the British in the rear. She was also extremely pretty, with blond hair and fair skin, and the two extra
phaetons had been provided for her and her three lady companions.
They rode out into Kabul's suburbs every day, wearing Western clothes
and without veiling their faces. Mme. Bravin used to toss a veil over
her head and tie it beneath her chin, so that it surrounded her pretty
features. To the men of Kabul, who had seldom seen a young female
face on the street, and certainly not one which used a veil to enhance
rather than conceal, this was a remarkable sight. Admiring boys ran
after her carriage just to look. But older men, in whom the teachings
of mullahs were more deeply ingrained, resented the defiance of their

Moslem customs and muttered about the ways of Christians, not realizing yet that these ladies' politics inclined them to atheism.

Saifullah finally departed for India on September 25, after a splendid reception at the Foreign Office Building to which he and all his staff were conveyed in first-class phaetons with strong horses. During dinner Tarzi said to him, "Afghanistan is infant-like in its walk of life among the nations of the world, and hence it needs most for its advancement on a large scale a helping hand from a strong nation like Britain," to which he replied, "The British have never denied a helping hand to the child but the child is too mischievous and thankless." He was gratified when some of the servants told him they had been with the Afghan delegation at Rawalpindi and had been treated well by the British.

Writing in his diary that Afghans sympathized with the discomfort of his internment, Saifullah asked, "Will not our government feel this as much as has been done by the Kabul public and take it into consideration to secure due amends and reparations when the occasion offers itself properly?" When this diary reached London a penciled note appeared in the margin, "Certainly not."

After Saifullah's baggage had been taken away from the British Agency, including a decoration and a gold sword and a coat embroidered with gold, the gifts of Amanullah, he was preparing to enter a suitable vehicle carrying some of the first gold coins to be struck with Amanullah's name. Suddenly another carriage drove in front of his party. It held a former official of Habibullah's time named Sher Ahmed, who beckoned to a member of the Agent's staff, Hafiz Mutiullah. Taking Mutiullah in his carriage to a secluded spot, Sher Ahmed gave him a message that he said, according to Saifullah's report, came from several prominent Afghans, including Gul Mohammed, who was preparing to accompany the British Agent to India where he would serve Amanullah as first envoy under his new independence.

These people were all displeased with Amanullah, went the message, and with his way of rule, and were awaiting the day when Kabul would be occupied by the British Government and Afghanistan governed by "a rational system of government." Sher Ahmed said that he would be one of the persons to shoot the Amir at the first opportunity, which he was eagerly awaiting.

Then he gave a summary of all the feuds and disagreements in the royal family and those families close to it. The new Envoy to India was a cousin of the lady who had been the last wife Amir Habibullah took from the ruling Mohammadzai clan, and whom he had divorced when he was impotent with her. Gul Mohammed resented the insult to his family.

Gul Mohammed was one of those royal refugees who had lived in India during Abdur Rahman's reign; his son Faiz Mohammed, a friend of Amanullah, was then with his mission in Russia, where observers said he was doing most of the work. This envoy undoubtedly thought well of the British, but he was accompanied by an assistant who disliked everything British and was suspected of being attached to Gul Mohammed's staff to report his doings to Amanullah.

This was Ghulam Siddiq, who belonged to one of Afghanistan's most interesting families. He had three brothers, Ghulam Nabi, Ghulam Jilani, and Abdul Aziz. The four men were more or less contemporaries of Amanullah and his intimate friends. Their father, Ghulam Haidar, had been known as the "Red General" of Amir Abdur Rahman because his hair and beard were flaming red. He was over six feet tall and weighed 280 pounds, and Abdur Rahman had ordered him to ride slowly because he could not afford to lose him. His spirit was as extravagant as his body. Above the door of his house in Charkh, in the tribal area southeast of Kabul, he had written, "He who passes here and does not dine with me is my enemy." His sons inherited all his tribal characteristics, which included not only generosity but a fierce loyalty to each other and to Amanullah. This family called itself Charkhi.

For young Ghulam Siddiq, round of face and figure, it was his first visit to India. The British Agent noted with pleasure that he gasped at sight of the Khyber fortifications.

War was still on the minds of the British inside those fortifications, and in many other minds. According to the treaty arrangement, a party which included Afghan observers had demarcated the disputed boundary whose violation had precipitated the war. The British took the post of Torkham for themselves. On August 29 the Afghans set a table beside the Kabul River near Kam, lighted it brightly with arc lights run by generators, and entertained fifteen British and Indian officers at dinner. The guests were walking back to their own camp, guided by lanterns and escorted by the Afghan General, when all of a sudden shots were fired at them from the high grass of an island in the river eighty yards away. Then a few more shots went over their heads. No one was hit, and the British said the incident was useful in advertising the demarcation.

It was useful also as an early indication to the British that they had made a mistake in imposing a six-month probation period before the final signing of their "treaty in two parts." To many tribesmen this meant that fighting would start again in six months, and why should it stop?

Several weeks passed before the tribesmen knew that peace had been made at all. The Afghan officials dared not tell them, for Nadir had assured their mullahs that the Amir would not make a peace treaty without securing amnesty for the tribes on the British side of the frontier who had aided the Afghans against their own government. In this Nadir made an unsound judgment. The Afghan attitude toward land and people was so humanistic that the British could hardly call it naïve and thought it a bargaining trick, as they would think at the conference where an Afghan delegate would say:

"We cannot understand how you, with your vast possessions, can be so greedy about a few yards of rock, with reference to our country which possesses almost nothing but rocks and prizes every yard of them."

The British delegate would reply, "I understand [Tarzi] to say that the strongest power ought not to seize the strongest place on the frontier. Does he mean this is according to the laws of generosity or according to the rules of international law?"

"Nations are composed of human beings," Tarzi would say, "and international law is the same as the law of humanity. We appeal to equity."

But the British, who would not yield a pebble, saw no reason to give the tribesmen, for whose good will they had always competed, any reason to be grateful to the Amir of Afghanistan.

They had the same problem, themselves, on a smaller scale, and handled it more deviously. There were Afghans who had helped the British. When Lalpura, a village on the Afghan border, was about to be evacuated by British forces and handed back to an Afghan official who was approaching with a hundred armed retainers, an excuse for delay was invented "to give an opportunity of escape to several people who have assisted us."

"There are three states: war, peace and mutual suspicion," the Afghans were to point out when they met the British at their next conference. Among the tribes the division between the first and the third was not clearly defined. These Wazirs and Mahsuds lived difficult lives accountable only to themselves. When they were rich enough, they built their homes like forts, enclosing within a high mud wall spiked with gun towers a small kingdom, where they reigned over family, sons, sons' families, servants and retainers, with space to offer a charpoy—a netting of heavy cord on a wooden frame—as a bed for any passer-by who deserved hospitality.

Once, while the laundry was drying on the roof of one of the mud buildings inside one of these forts, a man from a visiting family stole a trouser string, the cord which is run through the waistband of voluminous Afghan trousers to hold them up. In the following generation the son of the owner of the trouser string avenged the offense by killing the son of the man who had taken it. Such personal and eternal justice was the way of the tribes. It was the style they had evolved for living together, and it was subject only to the Koran. In their enclosed world, where the only direction in which to look was up, the only source of inspiration outside themselves was Allah, their only enlightenment the Koran as read by the mullah, who was often the only person who could read or write at all.

One trifle that concerned them very little was the Durand Line dividing Afghanistan from British India. In "Unadministered Territory" the British Empire wore its powers lightly. In other lands, including India where they had ended the practice of wife-burning, the British gloried that they were bringing, along with their rule, the Anglo-Saxon's justice. Most of the Empire thanked them for it. But these frontier tribesmen they left to their own justice, so strictly that an Afghan from Kabul, where tribal ways were tempered, would accuse them of hoping that all the tribesmen would kill each other off.

To a tribesman, government, whether Afghan or British, offered little that would stir a sense of gratitude and identity. Twice a year the government appeared; once to collect taxes and once to take young men into the Army, and life was so insecure that no family could survive without at least one young man at home. Government always took away. It gave nothing that was wanted.

The British did bring roads, but the tribes did not want them. They could leave home any time they wished to raid or make wars or send delegations to other tribes or to Kabul. And who knew what might enter along the roads in the motor vehicles of the foreigners? When the British wished to make a road, they first secured a written agreement with the tribes. Now in 1919 they decided to build a road among the Wazirs on the basis of an agreement with a previous generation. The tribes rebelled.

"Roads," the British told the Afghans, "are the most civilizing agents in the world."

"We have noticed that roads are always followed by guns," said the Afghans, "and according to our ideas, guns are not a civilizing factor."

"After the guns follows peace and that produces civilization."

"Your civilization may not suit the Mahsuds. Your ideas of civilization may not be the same as ours . . . Our custom after making a quarrel is to forget everything. But the Mahsuds fought for us and yet you are still treating them as enemies and not forgiving them. How can we expect forgiveness from you?"

And then, from the Afghans, the core of the matter: "If you had not fixed the six months' probationary period but had made a permanent treaty of friendship at once, as we wished, the trouble would have settled itself. The probationary period gave an opportunity . . . to work up religious feeling."

In the three months following the peace treaty, the tribes belonging to the British raided their masters' convoys and otherwise conducted themselves with less regard for the Pax Britannica than they had ever shown. The British blamed Afghan intrigue, especially after Amanullah received members of their Mahsud and Wazir tribes in Kabul and rewarded them for their services, telling them that the Waziristan tribes saved his face for him and were the only Pathans of any use. He gave each man a silver medal with a green, yellow and blue worsted ribbon.

"So long as we are suspicious of your intentions, we naturally make what preparations we can," the Afghans would tell the British. "We have seen in the papers that notwithstanding that you and France are friends, yet you are giving money to the Arabs of Mesopotamia and are inciting them against France. This is the way of the world."

Bombing from airplanes had rescued the British in the war with Afghanistan. This seemed the ultimate weapon also with the recalcitrant tribes.

The ethics of bombing disturbed the Viceroy, Lord Chelmsford. He was a mountain man himself, who could picture bombs exploding among lonely ridges on people who had no defense. "I do not like at all the idea of confining our operations to an extensive bombardment by the Air Force of Wazir and Mahsud villages. I am prepared to accept such operations on the part of the Air Force when it forms part of a general move by our forces into their country, but it seems to me rather inhuman and cold-blooded to send our airmen to bomb the villages while the rest of our forces keep the ring.

"I am also not a little concerned as to the possibility of our setting up a feeling of bitterness and rancor among the tribesmen through carrying out such a policy."

On the frontier, having heard from Army headquarters that "our troops are heartily sick of war" and from his own military officers of two incidents in which British troops suffered severely, the Chief Commissioner of the North-West Frontier Province, who was now the same Sir Hamilton Grant who had been at Rawalpindi, disagreed with the Viceroy:

"We did not hesitate to send airplanes to bomb the Maris and more recently to bomb Kabul and Jalalabad without warning, and we must have killed women in the latter place. These bombardments had an excellent effect, hastened the Amir's peace overtures, and have left no real rancor behind.

"The proposal to send airplanes out to drop pamphlets warning the Wazirs and Mahsuds . . . seems to me a most risky performance. The planes will certainly be shot at: we may lose some without having caused any effect; and in a completely illiterate country the pamphlets will be useless. I think it would be a mistake to risk our airplanes—and their subsequent moral effect—in a fruitless endeavor to salve our consciences."

An easy way to victory would have been for Grant the only easy way of anything in his troubled world. He had tried to end profiteering with price control, but gave up. ". . . Our hands are so overflowing with trouble that we cannot well afford to make more over a question of this kind . . . I find that one of my greatest difficulties here is the fact that there is practically no officer whom I can consult about anything . . . though there are many excellent officers serving in this province. They have all lost initiative and I must almost say self-reliance."

The tribes were bombed, but some considerations prevailed; the bombs were preceded by leaflets threatening them, by a certain date, unless fines and rifles had been handed over.

"But [the tribesmen] utilized the period after which we said we would bomb them," complained the British, "to send their women and flocks into places of safety and refused to come in. Then we started bombing them from the air because we thought that was much easier and cheaper than sending troops into their country. But as they have no cities and are scattered over the mountains, our bombs from the air did not frighten them as much as we hoped they would."

Looking back on this period, the British would admit to a further complication: "If a treaty of friendship had been signed immediately, even though the Afghans might have no intention of keeping it longer than might be convenient, its mere publication would have . . . increased suspicion of Bolsheviks against Afghans. Moreover, the conclusion of an immediate treaty would have made it impossible for Afghanistan to play off the Bolshevik against British offers."

The envoy from the Bolshevist Government of Russia, Bravin, was formally received by Amanullah on September 3. "Pompous but frigid" is the way he reported on his reception.

The Russians in Moscow, on the other hand, sent one of the first trains on the newly conquered railroad to take Mohammed Wali and his mission to the capital, where their reception was not only elaborate but warm. The usual ceremony took place at the railway station, and a few days later, on October 14, Lenin himself shook Mohammed Wali's hand saying, "I am very happy to see in the Red Capital of the Workers-Peasants Government the representative of the friendly Afghan people who suffer and are struggling under the imperialist yoke." It was the sort of statement that Bolshevik leaders were making on all occasions, and Mohammed Wali responded in kind: "I extend a friendly hand to you and hope that you will aid the entire East in liberating itself from the oppression of European imperialism."

On information from the Afghan Consulate in Tashkent, the Foreign Minister of Russian Turkestan wired Moscow: "Afghanistan intends to make an alliance with Soviet Russia against England. I consider conclusion of such an alliance main motive for Afghan mission."

Afghans therefore became favored persons in Russia. In Tashkent one family took out Afghan citizenship to save its piano; the government was confiscating all privately owned pianos so that they might have wider use in schools to educate the children of the proletariat, but it would have been impolitic to touch the property of an Afghan while there were hopes of Afghan aid in absorbing India.[1]

Not all individuals in either country were feeling this solidarity, however. When Bravin left Herat for Kabul, the musicians in the military band, disapproving of Bolshevism, refused to play for him. On the frontier the Afghan traders were refusing to accept Bolshevist ruble notes, and one Afghan who protested too loudly on Russian territory was put into prison.

In Tsarist days only caravans had bound Russia and Afghanistan together. It was this trade that put into every Afghan teahouse a shining brass samovar, from which the tea was put into china pots decorated with dainty pink roses, a design originating in a French drawing room and copied by the French-admiring Russians, to be held in strong, rough Afghan hands and poured into equally rose-spattered teacups. Matches and fabrics had gone into Afghanistan. Now the caravans were halted because they could not agree on the currency.

On that northern frontier of Afghanistan there was room for everything, even suspicion, even without the whisper of General Malleson's traveling agents. Here men were limited only by their own minds. No mountains bore down on them. The land reached on and on; the horizon was far away and led to other spaces. These were the steppes of Central Asia. Afghanistan stretched into Russia, and Russia stretched into Afghanistan. The people were Uzbegs and Tajiks, not so quick to rise to trouble as those on the eastern frontier with India, possibly because there was a calming quality to a landscape that placed no limit to a man's motions. Here, also, the boundary was only political and the same families lived on both sides.

But Russia had just endured a change more unsettling than any in its history, and in the part of Asiatic Russia called Turkestan there was even more bewilderment than in the rest of Russia. Almost all the inhabitants were Moslems. The Central Government in Moscow, still loyal to its proclaimed principle of self-determination, was insisting that the Moslems be given representation in proportion to their numbers, while the Bolsheviks on the spot knew that if the principle were followed to the letter these Moslems would choose any form of government in preference to Bolshevism. In January there had been an attempt at counterrevolution by the White Guards. This land was troubled enough, and now Afghans in arms were going back and forth across the border talking of taking Kushk and Panjdeh and of cooperative garrisons.

At a meeting of the Turkestan Soviets the President of the Turkestan Republic, named Kozakov, was accused of not giving the Afghans sufficient help in their war with Britain. His defense, which he made partly in the local press, was that the Russians were afraid to give arms to the Afghans as they could not be sure these arms would not be used against themselves. A protesting letter appeared in the newspaper: "When England was giving hundreds of guns to Kolchak and Denikin to fight against the Soviet, would she not also have given some to Afghanistan for the same purpose? Yes, certainly English arms and gold were offered by British imperialism but were refused and the hand of friendship was offered to the workmen and peasants of Soviet Russia." Kozakov explained unhappily that when Bravin was attacked on the Oxus River carrying arms to Afghanistan, those arms could have been captured by the enemies of the Soviet, since England was employing robber bands to prevent arms from reaching Afghanistan.

"Such a statement is criminal," wired Karakhan from Moscow, where General Malleson's agents did not reach, "as I had instructed the Turkestan Commissary of Foreign Affairs to inform the Afghans that we will supply them with arms immediately the Aktiubinsk obstruction is broken through . . ."

Malleson said, "Both Bolsheviks and Afghans are taking extraordinary precautions against entry of our British propaganda."

Yet a wireless operator in Kushk used government facilities illegally to send a message to an operator in Tashkent asking about possibilities of a transfer "as it is dangerous here as probably those savages, the Afghans, will take over Kushk and all its erection. Under them it would be worse than under White Guards."

With mutual suspicions among the new friends to the north as among the old allies to the east, Amanullah was trying out his new politics.

"Interesting politically" was the most definite description Bravin could send to Russia after his first interview with Amanullah. Amanullah read a letter from Lenin which the new Envoy delivered and replied that he would consider Russia's request for permission to use Afghanistan as a passage for anti-British propaganda into India. The new days had brought a new weapon, words, and Russia hoped to establish a propaganda center in Afghanistan.

Bravin offered to repair the roads through Jalalabad and Kandahar and to establish consulates there; Amanullah refused. It would have meant certain trouble with the British to permit Russians officially so close to India. Bravin spoke of a commercial treaty, but the Afghan

suggestions were all one-sided; duty on Russian goods entering Afghanistan but none in the other direction, and Russia to bear the cost of
insuring Afghan goods against robbery in Russia. When Bravin wished
to offer money, he had to bring forth British promissory notes; Bolshevik currency aroused so little confidence that placards were being
posted all over Turkestan imploring people "not to believe lies circulated by the British mission in Meshed regarding the worthlessness of
ruble notes."

Amanullah received Bravin several times. He was courteous but
evasive. Hearing stories of Bolshevik aggression in the Moslem states of
Bokhara and Khiva, he sent men there without Bolshevik knowledge.
Soon Bravin decided that he had little hope of official permission for
his propaganda center in Afghanistan, so he secretly sent forty men to
the Indian frontier to start propaganda without permission.

Bravin was in a forlorn position. He had lost the essential weapon
of an ambassador, the confidence of his own government. Another
ambassador was coming up behind him. This was Jacob Suritz, who
arrived in Tashkent late in September like a hurricane. With a dynamic
sweep of power, possible because Moscow had entrusted him with wide
authority, he made a tight organization, acceptable to Moscow, out
of the confusion that had been the Turkestan Government. He decided that the policy toward Bokhara and Khiva was arousing too much
suspicion, and he altered its outward aspects. Then he turned his great
energy toward Afghanistan.

"It is said that Bravin's departure for Afghanistan before my arrival
was a mistake," he wired Karakhan in Moscow. And made plans to go
there himself.

Suritz was to supersede Bravin, who would become his subordinate.
But he himself was on a tight string with Moscow. Elaborate special
arrangements were made for him to send information from Kabul, so
that he might receive orders and act only on them.

The British attempted to capture Suritz before he could reach
Afghanistan.

"A Turcoman of note, who was sent by me to organize plan for capture of Suritz party, somewhere south of Yulatan, has returned here,"
General Malleson reported on October 31. "He was unable to effect
anything mainly on account of complete ascendancy of Afghans in
whole region from Merv to Kushk. Afghans are doing everything possible to conciliate Turcomans. Men arrested by Bolsheviks are released,

fines inflicted are remitted and hardships removed by order of Afghans, whom local Bolsheviks implicitly obey. No Turcoman understands situation, or whether Bolsheviks and Afghans are really friends or enemies. But all recognize that Afghans control local situation and position everywhere as protectors of Moslems. In the Sarakhs area, Afghans have composed long-standing Turcoman feud and have warned all to be ready to act when the right time comes."

So Suritz, unaware that he had been the object of a kidnap attempt, rode into Herat on November 11. Almost at once he discovered what the Turcomans knew all along, that the Afghans protect their Moslem religion from even the words of the irreverent. In Afghanistan it was a criminal offense to be heard on the street blaspheming. Suritz was a forceful personality; on his first meeting with the Herat officials he made a remark which offended their religious feelings. That night he wrote a report to Russia warning, "We must be on guard against this."

In the Khyber Pass, a Moslem member of the Political Officer's staff hired a few informers, disguised himself and them as travelers, and circulated at night among the people whose caravans were resting in the serais before the morning's opening of the route into India. If anything in a man's talk convinced these informers he might be something beside a bona fide trader, a messenger carried the news to Peshawar, where the arrival was awaited by police. Suritz had got into Afghanistan despite their watchfulness, but the Government of India wired Peshawar, "Perhaps strengthening of machinery for examination of suspicious person in Khyber, the Kurram, and at Chaman, might make access to India more difficult at all events and frighten some persons from attempting ingress." All along the frontier travelers were being stopped, questioned and detained.

Deep in India, at the Foreign Office, the Foreign Secretary Henry Dobbs summoned the Afghan envoy, Gul Mohammed, as soon as he heard of Suritz's approach, and complained that Bravin was still in Kabul conferring with the Amir.

"That is because the Amir is now independent," interjected Gul Mohammed, "and at liberty to admit envoys from any foreign state."

"This seems a childish argument," said Dobbs, "because, so far as I know, Afghanistan is the only state in the world which at present is receiving a Bolshevik emissary. Do you mean to say that America, France, Italy, and Holland have all lost their independence because they are refusing to admit Bolshevik envoys or to have any relations with the Bolshevik Government? This argument only shows that Aghanistan has not yet learned the first principles of diplomacy. Every state in the world except Afghanistan considers the Bolshevik Government as its enemy. If the Afghans choose, on the contrary, to consider the Bolshevik Government as their friend, well and good; but you will not do this and at the same time claim that you are showing friendship for the British Government."

Soon a British member of Parliament named O'Grady would go to Copenhagen, Denmark, to confer as a representative of his government with the Russian representative, Maxim M. Litvinov, who had been accepted by the British Foreign Office as an unofficial, unacknowledged ambassador, allowed to send messages in cipher, when the Foreign Office sent Bruce Lockhart to Moscow immediately after the Revolution as their own unofficial, unacknowledged ambassador. O'Grady and Litvinov met to discuss the exchange of wounded war prisoners, but they were also making tentative gestures toward the recognition of the Bolshevik Government by Britain and the signing of a trade agreement between Russia and England. There were news stories of this possible agreement.

"We should look foolish if, having made immense efforts to make the Afghans get rid of the Bolshevist emissaries, we had to consent to their admittance," Dobbs would write. "It would therefore be an advantage not to enter upon final discussions with Afghanistan until our future relations with the Bolsheviks are cleared."

Suritz received a similar message from Moscow, telling him to tread lightly while an accommodation with England was pending. It was only a few months since Amanullah had rejoiced in Afghanistan's new freedom to control her own destiny, no longer the subject of decisions by her powerful neighbors. He did not know the new Soviet Russia and the old British Empire were moving toward a rapprochement that might affect Afghanistan, as in the days of his father and grandfather, against her will.

Bravin, after Suritz's arrival, had nothing to do. He should have returned to Russia, but men had returned to their death and the fact of his replacement so soon after his arrival did not indicate approval of his achievements. He had advocated great generosity toward the Afghans in concession of territory; he had urged haste, reminding his superiors in Tashkent, "You can grow tired of mere verbal assurances of friendship." General Malleson would describe his offers to the

Afghans with the words, "Bravin swallowed the bait."[2] His actions, without his knowing it, had been directed by the British and therefore had served British interests and caused the discomfiture of his own country. Once in the past he had been denounced as a British spy, and this was in his record.

Paul Alexander Bravin became one of the Soviet Union's first defectors. He remained in Kabul and Amanullah, who felt strongly the Moslem principle of the sanctity of asylum, made him an Afghan citizen. To a suggestion that he might do Russia the favor of having Bravin killed, Amanullah gave an indignant refusal.

And Bravin developed a great interest in the plants and herbs of Afghanistan. Such an interest is popular among people who work in intelligence. No one may question their excursions into secluded areas if they return with a few specimens, and Bravin, who was a trained diplomat, may even have been able to tell, if asked, the botanical names of the plants which fascinated him.

Throughout Afghanistan are small squares of soil dedicated to Moslems of special holiness who are buried there. At each corner of the Ziarat, or shrine, stands a pole from the tip of which flutters a banner that may have been square or rectangular when fastened there but which the wind has turned into a flutter of ribbons. Along the poles flutter other ribbons which are shreds of fabric tied there by true believers who feel that by doing so they are giving their prayers a stronger chance of being answered. Sometimes there are attached also small hands cut from tin, to signify by the pointing forefinger that there is only one God. At the five daily hours of prayer a popular shrine becomes a mosque; no one approaches it without removing his shoes, and prayer rugs are spread and the ritual of kneeling, bowing, standing, is performed. Since a shrine is often built on a hillside, the flags seen against the sky give the same sense of lifting to heaven that a cathedral spire does, or a minaret.

In Hadda, close to Jalalabad, was one of the most revered shrines in eastern Afghanistan, that of the Mullah Akhunzada, known as the Hadda Mullah, who had once raised the Shinwari tribes against Amanullah's grandfather, inspiring Amir Abdur Rahman to say, "Once the people are aroused and flushed with success, they are beyond the control of any man."[3] The mullah's control, almost supernatural even in life, after death was great enough to inspire his followers' sons to whatever deeds were invoked in his name.

On January 31, 1920, Nadir conducted a great jirga at the shrine of the Hadda Mullah.

To prepare for the day an amphitheater had been cut in the side of a low conical hill, where approximately fifteen thousand tribesmen stood, facing the top of the hill, striped coats or shawls thrown over their shoulders, their best turbans wound around their best caps, a rifle in almost every man's hand. Underfoot there was mud, and the pointed shoes were soiled and damp, for this was Afghanistan's rainy season and the jirga, scheduled for January 27, which was a Friday and a holy day, had been postponed because of heavy rains. Most of the men had come from the Afghan province of Ningrahar, but there were also Afridis and Mohmands from the British territory.

On top of the hill a large canopy stood. A gun boomed twelve times. The tribesmen looked up. They saw Nadir, escorted by three generals and fifty soldiers, take his seat beneath the canopy.

They looked down. A procession was forming at the foot of the hill. A line of twenty-eight men in scarlet tunics carried twenty-eight black standards on which were embroidered white hands, the star and crescent of Islam, and the silhouette of a mosque. The black flag of jehad was being raised. Behind the flags came a horse artillery battery, a battery of mountain guns, cannons, three cavalry and seven infantry regiments.

Nadir arose. He was not tall, but no man bore his stature more rigidly. "The Amir has sent me to speak to you as his representative. These twenty-eight new standards have been brought to you from Mazar-i-Sharif, where they were laid on the shrine of the Saki Sahib and blessed."

He was speaking of one of the most sacred shrines in all Afghanistan, dedicated to Ali, son-in-law of the Prophet Mohammed, raising its many colors of tile arabesques and its blue dome above the wide, wide stretches of the Central Asian steppes.

"The Amir presents three to the Afridis, three to the Mohmands, three to the Shinwaris, and rest will be divided among the tribes of Ningrahar.

"The white hand embroidered upon them is an emblem of unity, and by virtue of this sign you are ordered to lay aside your differences, give up looting one another, and preserve an undivided front." Nadir explained that the hands signified also two other kinds of unity, between the tribes and the Afghan Army and between the sects of Islam, the Shiahs and Sunnis, and that the fortunes of the Afghan tribes were to be linked for the future with those of Afghanistan.

"On the eighteenth of the present lunar month," continued Nadir, "a second conference will be held between Afghan and British delegates . . . If the British Government accede to the Amir's demands, there will be peace for all Islam, but if these demands are refused, there will be war and you must be prepared to take your part in it immediately.

"In the event of war there will be simultaneous attack by Mohmands on Shabkadr, by Afridis on Ali Masjid, and by Ningraharis on Landi Kotal, and Afghan regular troops will reinforce the tribesmen at such points as may appear convenient. In these circumstances I shall give you detailed instructions in full tribal jirga after the conference has broken up. Till then, you are to keep quiet and do nothing rash.

"Do not forget the sacred duty which the Amir has imposed on you and of which these blessed standards are the visible sign."

Solemnly the various tribes sent chosen men forward to receive the standards from Nadir's hands.

"Amen, and God be with your cause."

Then the tribes took their standards to the shrine of the Hadda Mullah, Akhunzada, to be blessed again.

And the story going among them was that Nadir in conversation had said that the Russians had sent four airplanes, and three hundred thousand soldiers to aid Afghanistan against the British.

Nadir rode on his horse back to Jalalabad and motored to Kabul, returning three days later to receive the leading Afridis and Mohmands, British tribesmen, in the garden of his house. The standards were brought from the Hadda Shrine and again presented, and the Afridi standard-bearers marched out of Jalalabad in military fashion accompanied by a band.

When the banner of one of the British subtribes, the Zakka Khel, arrived in its home village, a leading man wrote to the British that it would be impossible now to collect government rifles or bring a representative jirga to Peshawar, saying: "Up to this time there have been raids and dacoities [burglaries] but these have not been so mischievous. Now Islamic standards have been presented to Afridis, Mohmands, and Swatis and these people have come under the shadow of another nation. This is not an ordinary matter but it appears to have lifelong and permanent significance."

All this occurred largely because Amanullah was again awaiting a reply to a letter.

In September he had addressed a letter to King George V of Great Britain, ordering for it a solid leather cover inscribed in gold. On illuminated paper he had written in his own hand, "To His Majesty, the abode of magnificence and grandeur, my dear friend, the most magnificent King George, King of the Great Government of England and Emperor of India." The letter ended, "I am very thankful that the great government of Your Majesty have acknowledged and agreed to the internal and external independence, freedom, and liberty of the Government of Afghanistan."

On the same day Mahmud Tarzi addressed a letter to his counterpart in London, the Secretary of State for Foreign Affairs, "Your Exalted Excellency, the abode of felicity . . . may your glory endure forever . . . I express my great sorrow and say that had an early reply been given to the first and second letters of His Majesty my King, which have been addressed to the Viceroy of India with good intent and sincerity, and had a friendly and sympathetic hand been extended from that side, matters would not have reached this extent, because to obtain the right of independence, which is one of the natural qualities of the human race, and which Afghanistan possessed and was in every way worthy of, there would have been no necessity for controversy or dispute. It would have been secured with great facility and through mutual good offices."

All that London saw was that protocol had been defied. In a society which existed because everyone "knew his place," Afghanistan did not know her place. Not hearing the lesson in Tarzi's closing sentences, His Majesty's Government was offended that Amanullah was trying to conduct his affairs directly with London, as his grandfather had tried, instead of through the Government of India. "The only course seems to be to ignore the letters. Until the period of probation is over, the less we say to them the better, certainly the less we commit ourselves in the direction of recognizing their claims to a new status." Lord Curzon, who had become Foreign Secretary by the time Tarzi's letter arrived, said, "I see . . . that I am stated to have received the letter from Mahmud Tarzi. The sight of it in the file is the only form of receipt of which I am aware." In the curt reply to Amanullah he was not, by direct order of King George, addressed as His Majesty.

Again Amanullah wrote to King George in January 1920, offering to send delegates to advise on the treatment of the Moslem holy places in Arab countries, such as Mecca and Medina, which were in British control. This struck London as so impertinent that King George's ministers could hardly bring themselves to show it to him. "What right has the Amir to lecture His Majesty on the disposal of the Holy Places, i.e., of territory conquered by His Majesty's forces?"

Informers took news of Nadir's jirga to the Government of India, as Amanullah had known they would. The Government of India realized that the date on which Nadir had promised a conference was February 8 by the Western calendar, precisely six months after the signing of the treaty of Rawalpindi. Back in August it had not occurred to the Government of India that the Afghans might assume the six months' probation period meant an automatic conference at the close of it. They feared that on February 8 Nadir would present himself at the frontier and decided they would send him back.

Instead, they received a letter dated February 10 from Amanullah that stated honestly the situation that was disturbing him as he heard nothing from the British but had the Russians at his door and was trying to bargain with them. "No one great civilized power except the Russian Government was our neighbor with whom we could enter into commercial and political relations in a free and independent manner . . . It has nothing to do with their beliefs, religion and behavior . . . The British Government did not show us such warmth of friendship that we should not become the focus of others. There is still time. If useful and speedy remedies are not considered, it is probable that our friendship of today will even turn into coolness."

Amanullah was less frank when he wrote, "I am trying to control the people who are bent on jehad," but it was quite true that "If the war continues and those tribes are subjected to great pressure, it will be impossible to control the Ghilzais." The nomad tribe of Ghilzais, altogether unfriendly to the ruling clan of Kabul, the Duranis, brought an undisciplined spirit every spring as they led their flocks and camels across the mountains into Afghanistan.

To the Viceroy Chelmsford, more sensitive than many officials, it had already occurred that Britain, lacking communication with Afghanistan while Russia was in residence, had better have "frank and personal discussion with the real directors of Afghan policy, Amir and Mahmud Tarzi, who are factors quite unknown to us at present . . ."

From London came, "His Majesty's Government not prepared to take step which would be misconstrued as weakness." The tradition of saving face was strong in the British Empire.

Yet the Government of India did call a conference for April and almost missed getting the Afghans there.

Amanullah and Mahmud Tarzi had been trying to keep Afghanistan balanced in the influence of, not two, but three differing factors. Two of these, Russia and Great Britain, were forced on them by geography. The third Amanullah chose from his heart.

Amanullah always, from his childhood, had a sense of mission of protecting Islam. About his religious duties, the Friday appearance at the mosque and the five daily periods of prayer, he was rather casual, as his grandfather had been. These seemed to him superficialities and he did not understand those in whom these rituals could stir excitement. One of Tarzi's attractions for him was the intellectual attitude they shared toward religion.

But they were both alarmed that the countries whose state religion was Islam, which made them Islam itself, were being threatened from two sides. The Empire of Turkey, home of the Caliph, had lost a war and was about to be the subject of a treaty which would probably dismember her, while the atheist Bolsheviks, in spite of promises, were taking over the small Moslem states of Bokhara, Khiva and Ferghana. On behalf of these nations Amanullah jeopardized his new friendship with the Bolsheviks and British alike.

From a remote camp in Ferghana a Moslem named Mohammed Emin was resisting the Bolshevik conquest and was awaiting the arrival of two hundred Cossacks and machine guns. They never came. He had asked help from England, but, now England was expecting to buy and sell in cooperation with the new Russia, he got a noncommittal refusal.

An Afghan delegation went to Mohammed Emin in the names of the Afghans of Turkish Azer-baijan, presenting a letter which suggested that, after renouncing all sympathies with the British, he should join an Afghan conference to settle the future of his country, which would be assured independence. To this confusing message Mohammed Emin replied that he wished to be rid of the Bolsheviks, but Afghanistan seemed to be cooperating with the Bolsheviks and he sent a letter to Amanullah, requesting that he announce exactly what his policy was. A member of the party carrying the message to Kabul was a secret double agent in the employ of the British Consul in Kashgar, China. Malleson's mission in Meshed, source of the promised Cossacks who never arrived, immediately spread word among the Bolsheviks that Afghans were conspiring behind their backs.

Therefore Malleson was able to continue sending messages to the Government of India, "Bolsheviks suspect Afghans of duplicity in negotiating with Anglophile government of Bokhara . . ." "Under urgent orders from Tashkent a special Bolshevist guard has been placed in Band-i-Sultan, as it is feared Afghans might injure water supply . . ." "In the Panjdeh area, the Afghans are said to be leaving hurriedly for Afghanistan for fear of arrest and confiscation by Bolsheviks." And the Government of India was reporting to His Majesty's Government, "We are keeping [Amanullah] absolutely at arm's length so that we cannot possibly be suspected of complicity in [his] schemes."

During these early months of 1920 the Bolsheviks were becoming stronger and less in need of allies. They were defeating their White Russian adversaries and gaining new lands. They had got back the Orenburg-Tashkent Railway after its capture by the counterrevolutionary workers, but had so little fuel to run it that they were breaking up railway stations and unessential sleeping cars to feed their boilers. The tracks were so badly damaged that a trip of 145 miles took four to five days. And on this railroad an Afghan official party complained of its accommodations, or so the Russians heard.

On January 13 at Kabul the Afghans presented their demands to Suritz. They agreed to renew the war with England, which they feared was inevitable anyway, at the expiration of four months from the delivery in Kabul of eighty thousand to a hundred thousand rifles, fifteen hundred machine guns, and fifty million rubles in gold. They would not, however, put this in writing. They were prepared to make a treaty of friendship on various conditions that included a subsidy of ten millions in gold, machinery for making smokeless powder, telegraph lines and aid in arming the frontier tribes.

These demands had something in common with those Amir Habibullah had made on the German mission during the World War: they were exorbitant. Suritz and the other Russians were astonished. Then they made counterproposals.

The ten million demanded became one million offered. The number of rifles was five thousand and they were offered on condition that Afghanistan not hinder the passage through her territory of ten thousand rifles from Tashkent for tribes on the British frontier. Twelve airplanes, eight antiaircraft guns, a wireless installation, and smokeless powder plant completed the package.

Suritz, who took orders from Moscow, where a commercial treaty with Britain was a hope of the future, kept postponing decisions on a military alliance with Afghanistan. The British, who were already making a list of agreements regarding Afghanistan to take up with the Russians, calculated that they could not afford a war until October.

So in March they invited Amanullah to send delegates to a meeting in April in India, and had no official reply. Suddenly at the start of April Amanullah abandoned hope of the Russians and turned toward Britain.

Captain L. E. Barton, Assistant Political Agent, Khyber, was at his post at Landi Kotal on the morning of April 7, 1920, when he received the information that three motorcars had arrived at the border of Torkham and that the occupants, who seemed important, wished to go at once to Landi Kotal. Captain Barton sought out his Colonel, who was reading at that moment a letter from Afghanistan which should have been delivered the previous night, alerting him to the arrival of delegates for the conference.

Mahmud Tarzi and his mission had come in a motor, followed by a second motor holding attendants and a truck full of luggage. Captain Barton walked to the boundary and, sending his compliments, asked if one of the gentlemen would come to speak with him. The Afghans sent word that he might enter Afghanistan. He went to the car and the Afghans shook hands, not introducing themselves. Captain Barton explained that the letter had just arrived. Surprise and annoyance were apparent in the car.

"We were not aware that our invitation had been accepted," said Captain Barton. The car erupted with excitement.

"There must be more in this than meets the eye!" "It is just like the British to have some ulterior motive." "If you don't want us, we can go back." "We have come for a peace conference and we have written in good time that we were coming and this is an extraordinary kind of reception."

"The Chief Commissioner would like to have you received with the honors and entertainment suitable to a delegation from another country. He cannot receive you today."

"You must be telling a lie, or at any rate a lie is being told somewhere," said Abdul Hadi, a young man who had succeeded Tarzi as editor of *Seraj-ul-Akhbar*, and later joined him in the Foreign Ministry. He was one of the men of humble birth who, under Amanullah, was having his chance to become important, and while this made him completely loyal to Amanullah, he had not learned to temper his thoughts before he spoke them.

A Moslem always is indignant at being called a liar, and the Christian Captain Barton responded with Moslem indignation.

"I do not accuse you of telling lies," mollified Abdul Hadi, "but either you are not speaking the truth or else His Excellency the Viceroy does not see fit to let you know what is going on as he must have received the Amir's letter."

Then a clerk approached from the second car and pointed out that the letter had been signed by the Amir only eight days ago, so it was possible the Viceroy had not received it. Tarzi thought a moment and said this was quite possible. The mood of his delegation softened at once. In a friendly manner they explained that they had been invited for April 5 but snow and rain had delayed them so they hurried through after writing that they would arrive on the eighth.

"This is not the eighth," said Captain Barton. "It is the seventh." Declining the cigarettes and the drinks that had been brought for them, the Afghan party turned back with good nature.

That night Grant wrote a further explanation of the surprise. "Our intelligence in the Khyber of events in the Jalalabad area has of late been rendered very difficult by Nadir's actions in arresting all persons who he thinks are our agents. I understand that there are some ten or twelve of our agents now under arrest in Jalalabad."

On April 12 the same delegation crossed the frontier to be welcomed by a guard of honor. A special train took them on a journey of several days into India. It did not stop in any places where Afghans might meet Indians, but everything that Tarzi saw from the train window interested him. The crops had been good that year, and he was amazed that the workers should look so poor in some places where the land gave forth such abundance. The Afghans' destination was Mussoorie.

This conference had no treaty as its goal, merely talk. "There is a difference between a warm handshake bare hand to bare hand, and the feeling of shaking hands when both persons have thick gloves on," a British official said on the train journey, and Tarzi kept referring to this. During the official proceedings he was to express his aims with a word that the British, in the official report, would reproduce by asterisks. He said, "Peace and war***. I want to remove all the results of the late unfortunate war."

Two of the most significant events of this conference were not part of the proceedings.

Mussoorie had been chosen because it was remote. In the foothills of the Himalayas, between the purple peaks and the plains of India, Mussoorie was a hill station to which the British rulers of India sent their families when the annual burden of heat descended over the rest of India. As high as Kabul but far greener, Mussoorie was a dramatic meeting place with a wide mall running along its ridge beside a sheer drop of cliff. In April the heat had not yet descended, so the English ladies had not come and the Savoy Hotel, center of European comforts, had plenty of space for the conference.

But the Savoy Hotel, even off-season, had some Indian guests. One was the Congress Party leader Jawaharlal Nehru, an advocate of India freedom, who had brought his wife and mother to recover from an illness, along with his four-year-old daughter Indira. "Suddenly one evening," he wrote, "I had a visit from the superintendent of police, who showed me a letter from the local government asking him to get an undertaking from me that I would not have any dealings or contacts with the Afghan delegation. This struck me as extraordinary since I had not seen them during a month's stay and there was little chance of my doing so. The superintendent knew this, as he was closely watching the delegation, and there were literally crowds of secret service men about . . . As I persisted in my refusal to give an undertaking, an order of externment was served on me, calling upon me to leave the district . . . within twenty-four hours."[4]

The departure of Nehru was reported in the newspapers, and since the Afghans felt responsible, Tarzi sent Nehru's mother every day a basket of fruit and flowers. Within a few weeks Nehru was allowed to return. He walked into the courtyard of the Savoy Hotel to see a member of the Afghan delegation holding the baby Indira.

"The Afghans, on closer acquaintance with agitators who did get across," said the official report, "realized the futility of their characters, the hollowness of their declamations, and the hopelessness of depending on them for help."

Nehru would write, "As a result of the externment order from Mussoorie I spent about two weeks in Allahabad, and it was during this period that I got entangled in the peasant movement. That entanglement grew in later years and influenced my mental outlook greatly. I have sometimes wondered what would have happened if I had not been externed and had not been in Allahabad just then with no other engagements."⁵ The Afghans' presence in Mussoorie had sent Nehru one step further in his goal of a free India, and the Afghans had been in the presence of two future Prime Ministers of that India.

At the close of May, the conference was suspended because of activity on the frontier that was more upsetting than usual. Abdul Hadi went to Dakka to report. And during this intermission there occurred an incident involving young Ghulam Siddiq, who had accompanied the Ambassador to India with such wide-eyed eagerness for all new experiences. He was with the group in Mussoorie as Tarzi's assistant.

This is the letter the British were inspired to draft to Tarzi:

"You have already been fully informed privately of the reasons which make [Ghulam Siddiq's] return to India undesirable. I am now, however, obligated by your official letter to inform you of the same officially.

"Ghulam Siddiq, while in Mussoorie, insulted a married European woman by making advances to her, and was under my private advice to you, in order to avoid a scandal, sent away from Mussoorie to Dakka on the excuse that he was required to carry a letter to Abdul Hadi, who was then at Dakka. It was understood that he would not return to India. His conduct has made him no longer a fitting person for the post of Assistant Envoy and if you require this formality, the Viceroy will write officially to the Amir and inform him of this fact."

In the British Colonial world sex never crossed the East-West line by so much as a gesture or a flirtatious glance. The rules of that world were not familiar to Ghulam Siddiq, who in Afghanistan would never even have met another man's wife.

The rule about keeping such matters quiet, which would have prevailed in an Anglo-Saxon gentlemen's club, did not prevail with Mahmud Tarzi. At an official session he complained, "I am at a great disadvantage because Ghulam Siddiq, who was able to write shorthand and who was my right-hand man, has, owing to what I regard as a false accusation, not been allowed to remain in Mussoorie with me. I have done everything in my power to be conciliatory and polite, but I cannot conceal my feelings on the subject."

Ghulam Siddiq tried to cross back into India and the frontier guards would have admitted him but a routine check put the barriers up against him. He was humiliated and angry, and, with the tribal intensity that made him fiercely loyal and fiercely proud, not likely to forgive.

News from Kabul disturbed those at Mussoorie from time to time. Tarzi heard that his influence with Amanullah was in jeopardy and, having had the experience of going from high to low in the favor of Amanullah's father, was eager to finish the business successfully and hurry home. "If he falls, the truculent and ambitious Nadir will be predominant," Dobbs warned his government, saying to Tarzi himself, "A few days before you started for India, Nadir announced that war with the British is inevitable and urged the Bolsheviks to cooperate. But Nadir is a soldier whose thoughts are naturally of war. You and I . . . are diplomatists whose business is to avert war."

Learning that Russia had made offers to Afghanistan, and preferring Tarzi to Nadir, the British sent Tarzi away smiling and victorious. As he crossed the border on July 29, he was carrying a list of things the British would give in the future provided Amanullah was a good boy.

There had been the same proviso after Rawalpindi, and he had been, from the British viewpoint, a bad boy indeed. They could not afford to treat him like a bad boy.

Roos-Keppel had described their problem: "The difficulty of cooing and roaring at the same time."

When Curzon heard the results, he complained, "Afghanistan cannot behave like a prostitute with two lovers." More tolerantly, Sir Arthur Hirtzel wrote, "We could not presumably insist on the Amir breaking off negotiations with the Bolsheviks since he could not reasonably be expected to be off with the new love before he is on again with the old."

According to the metaphors these gentlemen chose, they were thinking of cooing.

CHAPTER 8

Early 1920 to January 10, 1921

It was the anniversary of Afghanistan's winning of independence, and several hundred Afghans were seated in front of a stage watching a theatrical troupe from India perform. A magician doing sleight-of-hand tricks reached into a hat and, with a flourish, pulled out the flag of a foreign country. Everyone clapped.

In the audience a man arose and called for the show to be stopped. It was Amir Amanullah. Few people had known he was there.

"Why are you clapping?" Amanullah asked. "A few clap and the rest of you follow. Think about what you are doing. You have to know what you are doing." He sat down. The performance continued.

The British flag came out of the hat. There was silence. Then the magician pulled out the flag of Afghanistan. The audience erupted in applause. Amanullah had made his point.

Amanullah was a kind of ruler that few Eastern countries had ever seen—or few Western countries, either. No earlier Amir ever went anywhere without such ceremony that all within sight and hearing knew that here was the Amir. Today an Afghan might casually look around and note that the man standing next to him was Amanullah. One might pass him in the road walking and stop for a chat. Early in his reign he disbanded his personal bodyguard. When his family protested, for there had been an attempt to shoot him and a wooden bridge had been cut before he was to drive over it, Amanullah said airily, "The nation is my bodyguard."

"Amanullah is madly in love with the Afghan people," a brother-in-law observed. It did not occur to Amanullah that his great love might not be returned. Those who disliked his ways seemed so few and inconsequential that he assumed the great, loving majority would take care of them.

His optimism and euphoria spread all over Afghanistan. The Amir was the source of all power. He was an absolute monarch. When the government moved with the seasons, it was the movement of one man's household. He ordered and it was law. Other amirs had been a rather frightening sun in the distance. Now this source of power was like a glowing fire at which every man in Afghanistan was asked to warm himself.

"I am very glad that you are listening to my advice," he would tell the people of Kandahar. And he would give them more advice. "It is a kind of flattery that people kiss other people's hands. Don't do that. You want help only from God. Be sure you know a person first and after that admire him."

Amanullah was trying to teach Afghans to think for themselves. This was not common anywhere, and in Afghanistan not many had the strong sense of self that makes one's own opinions seem important. Amanullah had his assurance. Being born into an Amir's family and being the only adored son of an ambitious mother (even though he was afraid of her) and listening to the new ideas that Mahmud Tarzi had brought from the great outside world, all gave Amanullah confidence in himself as a person and the urge to pick out his path for himself. To the men squatting in the teahouses, pushing carts through the bazaars and calling, "Khabardar! Take care!" the tradition that made them part of a small group (family and tribes) before they were part of a large group (the nation) gave them the sense of existing only in the consciousness of the group, of not having any significance in themselves. At any rate, they believed that all things happened through the will of Allah, and so how could they hope to change anything?

Such docility infuriated Amanullah, especially when the Koran was quoted in its defense. Afghanistan was almost totally illiterate; few could read the Persian or Pushto which they spoke, certainly not the Arabic in which the Koran was faithfully presented because it would have been a sin to tamper with the word of Allah by translating it. The Divine Word was filtered to the people through a mullah, and Amanullah often complained that the will of Allah was being confused with the prejudices of some half-educated mullah.

The Promised Land of Western benefits into which Amanullah pledged to lead his people was one which he had never seen himself.

Like Moses, he knew it only from hearsay. He knew of many things
which Afghanistan in her isolation had only glimpsed, but these were
matters on which many in his kingdom were far better informed than
he. The combination of his grandfather's harshness and his father's
clemency had profited the country; Abdur Rahman had forced into exile
many important families, whose sons were therefore educated in Indian
or Syrian schools, where they could learn more than anywhere in
Afghanistan; under Habibullah, these families with their educated sons,
experienced in the ways of other countries, had returned. The Tarzi,
Musahiban and Zakria and the Shahgassi family, to which Ali Ahmed
belonged, all were among these.

Amanullah had never been very far from Kabul; Westerners, when
they learned of his efforts toward modernity, would say, "Of course,
he must have been educated in England." If Amanullah had heard
them, he would have been indignant; he would look toward his traditional adversary, England, for many things, but not for ambition.

Amanullah had been educated by listening, and since he had listened
chiefly to Mahmud Tarzi, and Tarzi had put all his revelations and ideas
into his newspaper, *Seraj-ul-Akhbar*, all the other literate young men
had the same intellectual background as Amanullah. They had read of
trains, of the microscope and the telescope, of stockholders who formed
companies to cooperate in manufacture, of archaeology, of scientific
weather predictions. They knew that once it had been Islam that held
the fountainhead of knowledge, and Islam who sent scholars and learning to the West. The Arabs had invented the zero; one of the earliest
telescopes had been in Ulugh Beg's observatory in Samarkand in
neighboring Turkestan. Over the centuries some Moslems had developed various ways of comforting themselves for their loss of this leadership. Some said that all the inventions of the Western world had
originated in Moslem minds but that the diagrams and outlines had
been carried off by the Crusaders. Many thought that such blessings
should be left alone if they could be received only from the hands of
unbelievers, and Tarzi had consoled these with the words, "A diamond
encrusted with mud is still a diamond." He spoke of applying the
principles of Islam, intelligently.[1]

For most of the twentieth century, the young men of Afghanistan
had been yearning for all the glories that Afghanistan, withdrawn from
the world, had been missing.

Now one of their own was the Amir.

One day early in 1920 the town criers went through the streets of Kabul, beating their drums with curved sticks and calling out that henceforth, by order of the Amir, all slaves were to be free. The Kochis, the nomads, wandering through the bazaars, heard them. Some of the Kochi women were brazen by Afghan standards: they did not veil their faces. They strode along looking where they wished, and knowing that the town people regarded them as outside society, they did exactly as they pleased.

It pleased these women now to burst into private homes, astounding the guardians at the gates, and call out that all slaves within were free. They made a little song of it, to the tune of shaking tambourines. Finding a slave, they would drag her out of the house and into the street.

Few slaves were left in Afghanistan. Amanullah's grandfather had issued a proclamation forbidding future slavery while maintaining current bondage, but even this was not well enforced. Most slaves were Hazaras, of a tribe commonly believed to be descended from the regiments ("Hazar" means "thousands" or "regiment") left behind by Genghis Khan, because their eyes had a slant and their features a Mongolian look. The legend was too picturesque to die even after scientists disputed its accuracy. The Hazaras had revolted against Abdur Rahman, who put them down with great violence and felt great personal distaste for them. Now they grazed their flocks in the Hazarajat in Central Afghanistan, which was even more remote and rugged than other sections, or came into Kabul to do work that no one else wanted to do. Others of the remaining slaves were from Kaffiristan, which means "land of the unbelievers," in an eastern corner so remote that when it came to the attention of Abdur Rahman its tall, handsome inhabitants were still in the wood age of history, not having discovered bronze, and were worshipping spirits in trees and brooks, probably a legacy from the conquest of Alexander the Great. Abdur Rahman made them into Moslems by threat of extermination and named their country, in honor of this enforced enlightenment, "Nuristan" or "Land of Light."

In Amanullah's own household were some Kaffir slaves, inherited from his father. He set them free and, if they wished, paid their expenses back to Nuristan.

There had been many male slaves in the past. One aspect of Abdur Rahman's proclamation had been an end to the practice of emasculating boys so they might serve out their lives in harems. Now the male servants in a harem were boys who had not yet reached a size where a string of certain length would reach around their chests, or men too old to worry about, or young women who wore men's clothing and lost all sense of femininity to such a degree that one of them, sent by Abdur Rahman in the night to fetch the English doctor for his favorite wife, sat on the doctor's bed and watched him dress.[2] There were prominent Afghans who had once been slaves but in whom their masters had reposed such confidence they became sons. Some others were the results of the master's interest in a woman slave; they enjoyed all the titles and dignities of any other son of the house.

In 1920, however, almost all the slaves were women domestic servants. Some of these, dragged outside by the ebullient Kochi women, were terrified by their new freedom: they remained where they were, their status altered only legally.

The younger women slaves saw that a new life was possible. Afghanistan was full of men who had no wives because they could not afford the bridal payment to a prospective bride's family. These freed slave girls were truly free; there was no one to demand a price for them, and they might give themselves where they wished, a luxury available to no other Afghan women. The mullahs performed many marriages in the weeks after Amanullah abolished slavery.

One of Amanullah's first diplomatic appointees, the Consul he sent to Meshed, late in 1919, scandalized the Persians by permitting his wife to go unveiled and to receive visitors. Meshed was easily scandalized. It was very, very conservative, deeply aware of the presence of an especially sacred gold-domed mosque which, fifty years later, might be viewed by women, even Western women, only if they veiled themselves and remained at a distance.

Amanullah himself was not quite ready to unveil women, although he would have liked to. One of his sisters was learning to drive a car. Being closest to the royal warmth, his family were the first to feel its glow. Souraya was already far ahead of the other royal ladies in modernity, and the sisters made haste to catch up. Outside their homes they respected the conventions, but they did not, like many city women, put over their heads the slipcover called a "chaderi" or a "burkah," falling in narrow pleats to the ankles in back and to the knees in front, with a few rows of crocheting to permit vision. The royal ladies wore Western dress and, as nearly as they could manage, they followed the same fashions that Paris and London were wearing. Amanullah looked over each new dress the first time it was worn, and complained if it was not sufficiently simple. Foreign fabrics he forbade; the dresses were Afghan fabrics, usually the heavy silks woven in Herat and Kabul, and two dressmakers from Europe lived at the palace to make them; no more sending off to England.

Across the northern border the Russians were trying to get Moslem women out of the veil. There the veil was far more restrictive; it was a curtain of black horsehair covering the front of the body from head to knees, attached to a quilted cape like a man's coat without sleeves. In this a woman looked as if she had quickly flung over her the thing closest to hand. In a Turkestan village Nur Ali's wife, encouraged by Bolshevik persuasions, dared to appear outdoors without this covering. Nur Ali, while several devout Moslem friends looked on with approval, killed her. When Nur Ali was brought to trial before five thousand other peasants, the question was whether his action had been that of a hero, against a woman who had dishonored his family, or whether he was a criminal. Since this was a "show" trial conducted by the Central Soviet, for the purpose of making Nur Ali into a frightening example for other villages, the verdict was for criminality and the complaisant friends also were punished. Still the murders of women brave enough to unveil continued. Local judges in Russian Turkestan felt as Nur Ali had done toward unveiled women, so they were reluctant to declare this crime a capital offense. It was necessary for the Bolsheviks to introduce politics and describe such a murder as "a terrorist act against an agent of the revolution." Then they could demand a death for a death.[3]

Across the border the men in Afghan Turkestan felt fortunate; their reckless Amir was not going quite so far.

Amanullah on his succession found himself surrounded by stepmothers, the large harem of his father, Habibullah. He told these ladies that they need not spend the rest of their lives in the palace, as they had expected to do, but those without children might rejoin their families and do as they wished. Many married again. Amanullah brought back his half brother Kabir, who had run away several years before. Kabir was a delightful but erratic personality; Amir Habibullah used to assign each of his sons to head a different department of government, but when Kabir came of the proper age, he did not entrust him with his own post but told him to assist Inayatullah. In rebellion, Kabir got into one of the country's few motorcars and drove to India, rushing past the border without stopping for the usual formalities. The British sent him to Burma, where they interned political prisoners, but they found him totally without politics and so affable that the Commissioner's secretary took to playing golf with him. Kabir was lonesome for his family and after the War of Independence the British saw no reason for not sending such an innocuous person home.

Hidayatullah, the nine-year-old son of Amanullah's first marriage, went to school like most other boys, without escort, riding a pony, accompanied only by his uncle Amin Jan, who was about the same age. All over Afghanistan boys were going to school who had never had the opportunity before. They were not many in proportion to the total population, but where there had been almost no schools outside Kabul, now there were forty schools in all the major centers. They were all primary schools, since there was only the beginning class at first, and each year a new class was added, with the students at a variety of age levels because big boys were getting their first lessons alongside six-year-olds.

Amanullah himself walked one evening each week to the Shah-do-Shamshira Mosque, where he conducted one of the classes in reading and writing for adults. Standing at a large blackboard, he pointed out "alef" and the other letters of the Persian alphabet, and answered questions from his fifty students whether they pertained to reading or not. In time Amanullah devised a method whereby, he said, a person might acquire the rudiments of literacy in twenty-three days. Having heard of an English method of teaching languages called Linguaphone, he called his own invention Ghaziphone, after his own title of Ghazi.

Students were now an elite, favored class. They were the men of the future. A special emblem was created for their caps, a combination of saber, inkwell, and pen, to indicate that learning went along with the saber but outweighed it two to one. When a new bridge was built across the Kabul River, this emblem of pen and inkwell was worked into the concrete, and when the students erected a monument to Amanullah close to his birthplace in Paghman, it appeared there also.

Amanullah had twenty-five half sisters, daughters of his father's less important wives. The younger of these began attending a public school, the first school for girls ever to be opened in Afghanistan.

"If you are not educated," Amanullah was to tell a crowd in Kandahar, "try hard to make your children educated. An uneducated person can do nothing. This education is not only for your sons but also for your wives and daughters, because they have to know their way of life and their religious ways. The worst thing in Afghanistan is that people think that women do not have the same rights. Our Prophet has said that all humans have the same rights. So make your wives educated. If your wives are not educated, your children will not be educated. It is a law in our religion that a man can have four wives. Take yourselves as an example. If you have four wives and each wife has five children, how can you support them? So you should have only one wife in order to support them better and give them good training."

Each year a class was added to the girls' school, also, and each class adopted an individual color of dress. For all the Afghan women who were already literate, a newspaper was printed every Thursday on green paper, to distinguish it from the newspapers for men.

The mullahs had monopolized education in the past, giving it such a religious turn that the children learned chiefly how strictly they must obey the mullah. Their method of teaching was rote; gathering the children around them in the mosque, they would have them memorize the Koran in Arabic, without always troubling to ascertain that the students understood what they were saying. The mullahs resented having classes taught by outsiders; yet they themselves had established the pattern by which many of Amanullah's modern schools were conducted: memory and repetition, not logic.

Within a few years some of these mullahs would be meeting with French teachers to discuss a curriculum, and would come to an agreement only after the French made two concessions: they would teach only vocal music, not instrumental, and in teaching about the heavenly bodies they would say nothing to hint at the shape and movement of the earth. This would take place one year before the trial in Dayton, Tennessee, U.S.A., of John Scopes for teaching Darwin's theory of evolution.

All the work that Amanullah was doing took almost all his time. He had to make an appointment with himself to exercise, which he did by walking out or riding at twilight or shooting ducks in the palace compound. Every morning except Friday he was at his desk by eight o'clock. When lunch time came, he invited any visitors who happened to be around to join him at the table. Amanullah ate less rice than most Afghans but remained slightly overweight. In the afternoon tea was brought to his desk, and he sipped it while writing or talking. Otherwise, he took time out only for prayers. A supply of fresh shirts was kept in his office, but he would have worn the same suit for two or three months if no one had suggested a change.[4]

Amanullah was rearranging the entire administration. His country was not a whole, but came in several parts which had not much interest in each other. Official life centered around Kabul, Kandahar, and Jalalabad. To the north, stretching around Mazar-i-Sharif, were the level lands that were literally separated from the Central Government for a few months each winter when snows closed the passes of the Hindu Kush. In the west, adjoining Persia, the lush lands around Herat also led a life of their own. Herat was the cultured aristocrat of Afghan cities. Once it had been the home of so many poets that one of them, seated cross-legged in a group on the floor, sighed, "I cannot stretch out my leg without touching the backside of a poet," to which another responded, "Nor draw it in, either." While most other Afghans were Sunni Moslems, believing that the Prophet had intended the election of his successors, and praying with arms folded across the waist, most Heratis were Shiahs, who believed that the Prophet's rightful successor was his son-in-law Ali. When they needed help from heaven for some extraordinary task like pushing a cart from a ditch, they did not invoke Mohammed himself but cried, "Ya, Ali!" When they prayed, their hands hung at their sides. Yet these strict religionists had been so daring as to paint pictures in which angels were shown as men with wings.

In these fragmented sections of Afghanistan the local governors almost had their own kingdoms. The ruler who appointed a governor was far off in Kabul too remote to interfere. The only telephone lines were those connecting Kabul with Jalalabad and Paghman for the Amir's official use. Now Amanullah decided to exercise a greater control over the provinces, and planned a system of telephone communication. Unknowingly, he copied the pattern of the octopus, which is that of a spy network, in which the various parts can not communicate with each other, only with the head. He admitted that he did this to reduce the opportunities for intrigue, and he applied the same principle to road-building.

A Council of Ministers advised Amanullah. Unlike his father in his brief experiment with a council, Amanullah called it into sessions often and listened to its advice. Not all its members were of high birth. His Minister for Agriculture was the man who had been taking care of the royal gardens. Abdul Quddus, the elder statesman now serving his third generation of Amirs, was Prime Minister, but Mahmud Tarzi as Foreign Minister was the ruling force. Nadir, now reinstated as

Commander-in-Chief, was Minister of War. One of Tarzi's ideas, expressed in early years, was that the government should not be a monopoly of the royal family but should be shared by all classes. Only one close relation of Amanullah sat on the council, Ali Ahmed. Always there was friction between Amanullah and Ali Ahmed, and after one severe personal disagreement, Amanullah dismissed his cousin as Minister of Home Affairs, breaking the only family tie. The replacement was Sher Ahmed, the man who had confided in the British Agent a desire to annihilate Amanullah and his way of government.

The royal family was fascinated by its new head, but uncomfortable. To some it seemed that Amanullah was giving away their birthright. They liked having their hands kissed. And the humble Afghans who bent low to kiss the Amir's hand were often disconcerted to find that they were supposed only to shake it.

One of Tarzi's first letters as Foreign Minister had been addressed to a sardar exiled in India asking him what, since he had been receiving a government pension for years, he was prepared to do to earn his keep. Amanullah's uncle, Mohammed Omar, had maintained one occupation: upholding the distinction of being the offspring of the Great Amir Abdur Rahman and the famous Bobo Jan. He was so fat that a chair had once broken when he sat in it, and so ineffectual that he could talk sedition without getting into trouble because no one paid attention. Now Mohammed Omar, in order to keep his allowance, had to be Director of Personnel in the Ministry of the Interior. This meant going to an office every day and pretending to consider the qualifications of applicants. He hated it and was useless. Amanullah diminished his forefathers' custom of sending cooked food from the royal kitchen to all the members of his family, which meant to a host of retainers as well. Even a royal sardar had to work in order literally to eat.

Even being a Sunni Moslem no longer gave automatic superiority. "I have been always telling you that union is the best thing and persecution the worst thing," Amanullah would say to the Kandahar crowd. "Racial discrimination does not mean Durani and Ghilzai. We are all Moslems. And we are all human. We are all one tribe, our God one, our Prophet one, and no difference between us. My purpose is that you shall have union so that enemies may not attack you, either interior or foreign. For me all Afghan people are the same."

For those whose position was so high that they had no wish to change it, Amanullah's words gave back the echo of the same fear that Curzon would point out in respect to all Asians vis-à-vis all Europeans: "An aggressive spirit of nationalism . . . had led these people to believe that they are not only as good as we, but better." It was the old situation of one man's being more equal than another.

Amanullah cut in half the tax that Hindus in Afghanistan had to pay simply for being Hindus, and he abolished the old ruling that their turbans had to be yellow, whereupon most of them bought red turbans. The only restriction he left on them was a distinctive mark called the "Kashka" or "Tilk" which they still had to paint on their foreheads to protect them from the anger of Moslems who might not understand why they failed to fall to their knees five times a day for prayer or recite the "Kalima," the profession of faith, "There is no God but Allah and Mohammed is his Prophet." One day a Hindu woman was seen to be joining a group in reciting the "Kalima"; she was seized by a crowd that demanded she be converted at once to Islam, and was rescued from forcible conversion only by the intervention of the local Governor.

Amanullah did something that few Afghan Moslems ever had done; he attended Hindu religious services. He also joined Shiah Moslems in their special rites and told his officials not to ignore a man's application for job merely because he was Shiah.

The mullahs of Afghanistan for all these centuries had felt like Islam itself. They had protected Islam so fiercely that no missionary of another religion had ever entered Afghanistan, and only one conversion of a Moslem was on record; this man had become a Christian in India and when he returned to his own country he was killed. Islam they now saw threatened by teachings and inventions from the same infidel West that had sent the Crusaders to kill Moslems in that golden era when Islam held learning in its hands and the West, by contrast, was barbarian. The mullahs knew their own personal power would be diminished when every man could do his own reading and writing and would probably be reading words that would not conform to the Prophet's teachings as interpreted by themselves.

The danger was more immediate than they supposed. Amanullah altered their income as he had done that of the royal family, by making it dependent on work. He also decreed that the money which the faithful paid to the sacred shrines of Afghanistan, for which the shrine custodians had not been accountable to anyone, should go into the public treasury. Even irreligious Abdur Rahman, who had decreed loudly the ignorance of mullahs and once tied two of them together by their beards, never had thus assailed the institution of the clergy. The most lofty mullah in the nation remained Amanullah's friend. Shah Agha was head of the Hazrat family who lived in apartments behind and above the dark shops in the narrow covered streets of Shor Bazaar. He stood at Amanullah's side on all ceremonial occasions, as he had stood in placing the turban of amirship on his head. He had so much learning that he was willing to grant others a little learning of their own, and he endorsed what Amanullah was doing.

Not all the Hazrat family of Shor Bazaar were so generous. Shah Agha had two brothers called Sher Agha and Gul Agha.

Although family names were not generally used in Afghanistan, some individuals had a multiplicity of names. In the privacy of families each child grew up with a private pet name. On occasion the childhood pet name persisted into adult life without being a sign of any emotional immaturity or weakness. This occurred with Shah Agha's two brothers, and the parents who gave the names in that family were prophetic, for the dominant, leading personality, Fazl Umar, was Sher Agha, which means "Mr. Lion," while the follower among the brothers, the quiet and handsome one, Mohammed Saddiq, was Gul Agha or "Mr. Flower." And the name of the head of the family, Shah Agha, means "Mr. King." Shah Agha, who supported Amanullah loyally, would die in 1923; if he had lived, the history of Afghanistan might be different.

Amanullah and his plans for the future, even more upsetting than the present changes, seemed dangerous and heretical to the two younger brothers. The lion-hearted Sher Agha had been decorated by Amanullah and given the title "Light of the Saints" for his services in exhorting the tribes during the War of Independence. That did not prevent his announcing that Afghanistan was becoming a godless place in which he did not wish to stay. Disagreement between an individual and the government was so commonplace that a convention existed for handling it; the individual departed on the pilgrimage for Mecca and did not return. Sher Agha went from Mecca to India, establishing himself at Sirhind and becoming so famous for his piety and learning that disciples pressed food and gifts on him and provided a house. Twice a year the nomad Ghilzais swept across his path to and from Afghanistan; he preached to them and advised them and went into their camps. In India the nomads were called, not Kochis, as in Afghanistan, but Powindahs. A famous mullah known as the Powindah Mullah had recently died; soon, when one said in India "the Powindah Mullah," one meant Sher Agha.

Gul Agha, staying behind in his garden, was more quietly discontented, talking out his fears with such companions as Mohammed Osman, who had been discredited as Governor of Kandahar after introducing at Amanullah's marriage to Souraya a band of entertainers whose leading lady was insufficiently clad by Kabul standards. Like many who say, "Never again!" he went to the other extreme of rigidity. Amanullah gave him the position of Director of the theological school in Kabul; this was not so good as a governorship, but it gave him an opportunity to indoctrinate the new mullahs in Afghanistan.

Shah Agha, however, whose prestige was far greater than theirs, mounted the pulpit of the Friday Mosque in Kabul after prayers on November 19, 1920, and made a speech in which he declared that, as Amanullah was the only independent Moslem ruler left in the world, he was now head of Islam. The Moslem world should salute him as Caliph, and the Khutba should be read in every mosque in the name of Amanullah.

Amanullah was present. He kept silent.

The Ottoman Empire was being torn apart and with it the fabric of Islam. The Sultan of Turkey, the Caliph, had administered the Holy Places, chiefly Mecca and Medina, the shrines of pilgrimage, the two cities between which the Prophet had made his migration in A.D. 622 that began the Moslem era. The Caliph had been defeated by England and her Allies, who in May announced the terms they would embody in the Treaty of Sevres. Turkey was doomed. Nothing would remain to her except Constantinople and a corner of Anatolia; the rest was to be partitioned in various ways among the Allies. Until the last moment the Government of India pleaded for softening on behalf of Turkey, for fear of reprisals from Indian Moslems. Special security precautions were taken in India when the terms were announced, but no great uprising occurred, and Amanullah expressed chagrin that it did not. The Mussoorie Conference was in recess at that time, a matter arranged by the British so they might present a fait accompli to Mahmud Tarzi, whose memory of Turkish hospitality, as well as his feeling for Islam, was causing him to raise this question, which, properly, did not belong on the agenda.

"How will the people of Mecca or Medina, which do not produce anything, support themselves?" asked Tarzi at Mussoorie.

"Do you mean that without a suzerain power such as Turkey it will not be possible to keep the local population from starvation and arrange supplies for pilgrims and that the pilgrimages, therefore, will not be able to take place?" asked the British.

"If you build a mosque in Iraq of pure gold and the name of the Caliphate is not mentioned in it, it will not be called a mosque, it will simply be called a building. You say that you have repaired the mosques and given great help to the people of these places. If you built mosques of gold and Moslems built them of mud, they would prefer the latter.

"As regards the preservation of the Caliphate, it is something spiritual like the Kaabaa [the sacred stone in Mecca] made of stones, earth and wood, which is built by human hands and which only serves as a center on which the attention of all Moslems has to be focused," said Tarzi. "For this reason Afghanistan has a connection with the Caliphate."

As early as 1916 the disappearance of the Caliphate as a power had been foreseen by Colonel T. E. Lawrence, the famous Lawrence of Arabia, the British agent who led the Arab Revolt from which the Arabs had expected their independence. "This war should, if it results in anything, at all, take away definitely and finally the religious supremacy of the Sultan [of Turkey]." Lawrence added: "England cannot make a new Caliph . . . any more than the Japanese could impose a new Pope of the R[oman] C[atholic] church."[5]

Yet England, in 1920, was trying to prevent a Caliph from being made. Three men were being talked about, and the one whose appointment would have disturbed England most was Amanullah. He was already too much of a hero among the Moslems in India. Even as Shah Agha spoke, the Viceroy was wiring to London: "Bitterness of Moslem extremists in India . . . is such that they would accept election of Amir . . . it is unnecessary for us to point out the grave situation for India which Amir's election might bring about, and it seems desirable to take any steps possible to prevent this . . ."

The message included this sentence, "Jemal Pasha is about to reach Kabul under wing of Bolsheviks and it seems possible that he may be bearer of some message on the subject."

Jemal Pasha, the Sultan's War Minister, hated the British with an intensity possible only in one who had hoped for friendship with them once and had been rebuffed. The Turks were still the enemies of the

English, because the Greeks who were fighting them were involved with the Allies, most of whom regretted having ever become involved. Jemal Pasha was going to Kabul to help train the Afghan Army, but the British believed that he had other goals which were linked with the Bolsheviks, who had been the first to recognize Mustapha Kemal's government. In Kabul, when the British representative would meet Jemal Pasha on the road as a result of a flat tire on his automobile, which the British chauffeur helped to change, Jemal Pasha would say, "You English make a great mistake in assuming that the new Anatolian Government is under Bolshevik influence; in face of the hostility of all the world against Turkey, they were driven to seek help somewhere and even to go to an impossible people."

One phrase in particular could raise tremors in the British Empire: Pan-Islamism. If all the Moslems in the world were to unite, they would be a formidable enemy directing their energies against the British, who were the rulers of so many Moslems. The Bolsheviks were urging Pan-Islamism.

An Afghan Ambassador in Turkey would soon be telling a French woman journalist: "Islam is a large body of which Turkey is the head, Azerbaijan the neck, Persia the chest, Afghanistan the heart, India the abdomen, Egypt and Palestine, Iraq and Turkestan are its arms and legs. When you deliver rough blows at the head, how can the rest of the body not feel it?" This Afghan Ambassador was holding receptions every Friday; the turbans, flowing robes and fur-trimmed pelisses in his drawing room indicated a temporary unity of Islam.[6]

Afghanistan was indeed the heart of Islam to many Indian Moslems in 1920. Drawn by affection for her, thousands of Moslems swept through the frontier passes seeking a refuge from the infidel Government of their own country. Amanullah had felt in childhood a strong emotion toward the protection of Islam. Now, like the Jews of the Exodus, Moslems left the land of oppression. Amanullah was truly their King of the West.

Amanullah did not invite these people. Yet a phonograph record was being circulated in India with a song proclaiming that when a land is occupied by infidels, people have the right to move to a better place. "Come to the Light of Islam" went the song. "The Amir of Afghanistan is calling to you."

Committees were formed in India for the Hijrat, the organized movement of the immigrants, who were called muhajirin. At first Amanullah was glad to have them. His idealism responded to their unhappiness, and he saw them bringing capital and talent into Afghanistan.

But most who came had very little of either talent or capital. In the burst of enthusiasm for their exodus and distaste for the British, they sold their possessions in India at ruinously low prices and brought only their hopes. They came through the Khyber Pass with banners flying and drums beating. Soon Amanullah saw that their coming might be a mistake, and sent orders to his trade agent in Peshawar that he was not to issue passes to these muhajirin to enter Afghanistan, for this would lay his government open to the charge of creating unrest in India and also would put him in a difficult position should the British prevent any immigrants from crossing the frontier. The effort was wasted; the British were already blaming Amanullah, and it was part of their policy not to spare him embarrassment by refusing passage to any who wished to enter Afghanistan in this movement; their officials had their orders.

Whole families and groups of families moved together. One family in Peshawar, having sold its property at a sacrifice, became worried about the welfare of a fourteen-year-old daughter on such a long and dangerous journey. Someone told them of a man who was also going to Afghanistan: "a good man" but without any money. They found this man and made him the proposition that if he would marry their daughter to assure her a protector, he might postpone the bridal payment until he had earned some money. With a large party, some riding on donkeys and some in carts, some walking and driving their flocks of sheep before them, they made their way to Kabul.

They camped on a piece of land north of Kabul that Amanullah was giving to the muhajirin. One night, while they slept, the water that flowed through the area for washing and cooking was altered in its course, so that they awoke with the precious water, beyond price when used properly, soaking their quilts on which they were sleeping. Into the next generation they would be telling that the British did it. They would say that the whole movement was instigated by the British to embarrass Amanullah.

And, indeed, Amanullah was embarrassed. These were refugees who had a claim on his hospitality through the Moslem principle of asylum and through the naïve enthusiasm with which they had sought him. For those with some education and skills there was a place in his reorganization of the government as clerks and minor officials. He had need of such persons, although sometimes he would have to restrain their anti-British bias in the interest of foreign relations.

But Kabul was full of persons from India who had no place to stay, no money, nothing to eat but the food that Amanullah provided in hastily thrown-up canteens. Early in August two large caravans of muhajirins passed through the Khyber to seek a new life, and ten thousand more were awaiting at Jamrud their turn to go. Already some earlier muhajirin were passing through in the opposite direction, disillusioned; these included the family with the fourteen-year-old daughter and their son-in-law, the "good man." To their discouraging reports, the ten thousand waiting in Jamrud paid no attention. This was a religious pilgrimage. By August 12 approximately fifty thousand men, women and children had crossed into Afghanistan.

Amanullah gave these people some of the crown lands in Kataghan, and some others settled near Kabul. But most of these people had not done well in India and would probably not do well anywhere. What they were fleeing, though they did not know it, was not the British but their own inadequacy. Even if the gift lands had been more fertile than they were, in their impoverished state the people would not have flourished. Some prominent Afghans were good to them; the Assistant Minister of Finance, Mirza Hashim, gave three hundred of these poor people refuge in his garden. It developed that they had brought cholera with them, and so the garden became a nightmare of death and wretchedness. But the Minister helped as much as he could. Afghans of the muhajirin's class, which was low, did not share this compassion. They saw only more competition in a life already hard enough.

In desperation Amanullah ordered his frontier officers on August 12 to prevent muhajirin from entering Afghanistan. The Afghan Trade Agent in Peshawar distributed notices to this effect to Moslem leaders in India.

On that day, defying Amanullah's order, a party of seven thousand started out from Fort Jamrud. Two days later they arrived in early morning at the barbed-wire fence that marked the Afghan-Indian border. They found the gate blocked and fifty armed Afghan soldiers drawn up to bar their passage. They would not be denied the end of the journey they had made through the cruel heat in a pass where shade and water were scarce. They cried out that if force was used against them, they would use force and fight their way through. One shot from an Afghan rifle would have started a civil war in Islam. The fifty soldiers, opposed by seven thousand muhajirin, many of whom were armed, let them go as far as Jalalabad. This was the end of an emotional pilgrimage that had begun in hope and love.

By October only two thousand were still in Afghanistan, most of them on the gift lands in Kataghan. The government employed about a hundred and sixty. Most of the others returned to India, far worse off than before. Those who had worked for the government in India were told that they could not work again for the regime they had disapproved so dramatically. The others were to be forever suspect; in British correspondence the word "muhajirin" would always be used in a derogatory sense.

About two hundred muhajirin, all adventuresome young men, pressed on, farther west, and reached Russia. There they were welcomed earnestly. In the advancement of Russia's goal of penetrating India with propaganda, these men would have been called a Godsend had the Russians believed in God. They were the ideal agents, natives of India, speaking the language. The Russians offered training in aviation to some; others were enlisted in their army. The most promising were enrolled in the propaganda school at Tashkent, and the cream of those went to Baku for a course in Communist principles. But a Moslem sufficiently religious to make his own individual hegira does not easily turn into a Communist, and the unchanging ones were allowed to leave Russia. Most went home to India, where the British, of course, would never know if they were loyal Moslems or clever agents.

"The present policy," G. of I. would write soon, "is to mark down any returning muhajirin who may be considered potentially dangerous and to send them under police surveillance to their homes. Close watch is maintained over their movements there; we are thus able to secure invaluable information, avoid driving movement entirely underground, and know where to strike in event of trouble arising from this source."

When Mahmud Tarzi was returning home from the Mussoorie Conference, his car stopped in the Khyber to allow the rest of the convoy to catch up. Some Afridis were walking along the road. Tarzi got out and greeted these with the news that he was on his way to make peace. A graybeard told him that all the great numbers of muhajirin who had been passing through had made a deep impression on his tribe; that they, along with eighteen million Moslems in India, were determined to see that the authority of the Sultan of Turkey was saved from destruction. Resuming the journey, Tarzi said to the Political Agent of Khyber, Colonel Humphrys, "The words of this graybeard illustrate the difficulty which is hanging like a black cloud over our negotiations."

In September 1920, Islam had another shattering blow. The Bolsheviks took by force the Moslem Kingdoms of Bokhara and Khiva.

Amanullah had unknowingly prevented this a few months earlier. He protested the Bolshevik treatment of Bokhara, and although the Coup was already in progress, it was postponed, while the Bolsheviks made no further effort to get what they wanted from Afghanistan.

Suritz, the Russian Envoy in Kabul, was trying to find out what happened at Mussoorie. When Tarzi told him that no treaty had been made, which was the truth, Suritz thought he was being evasive. What Suritz wanted especially, and had orders from Moscow not to forego, was permission to establish in Kabul a propaganda center to use against India. The Afghans pointed out that this would mean war with Britain, in which case Russia must go to war also.

Suritz knew that Amanullah was involved in some way with the Amir of Bokhara, but was uncertain exactly how.

"My true, happy, meet-to-be-accompanied, my son, your Imperial Majesty, Lord of Bokhara!" Ulya Hazrat had written to the Amir of Bokhara, "our enemies have made good use of our family disagreements . . . the hearts of such as I, sitting in corners, in prayerful contemplation beyond the veil of the unknown future of Islam, cannot but burn and wither away, feeling the approach of death . . .

"The child of my heart, Amanullah, sets as a first condition of friendship with the Russian Soviet Republic, the independence of Bokhara."

Amanullah sent the Amir of Bokhara a military instructor, two specialists in making cartridges, and six guns, as well as the more romantic gifts of a gun for his personal use, several bales of white shawl work from Kashmir, a prayer mat, English boots, and a horse of an unusual shade of gold. These went with his official Envoy. He had also a spy disguised as a seller of tea. Later this spy would throw off his disguise and become Afghan Ambassador to Bokhara, perhaps the first spy in history to be promoted so immediately to Ambassador, a distinction equaled only by the Russian spy Sorge, whose picture was put on a postage stamp.

Some other Afghans went to Bokhara in disguise; these were soldiers whose assignment was to train the Bokharans, whose city was famous as a center of Islamic learning where mullahs competed in reciting the Koran, but who were so backward in matters of warfare that when the Afghans set up a rifle target at a normal distance, they laughed and asked who could be expected to shoot so ridiculously far.

Finally, in September, Suritz abandoned his hope for a propaganda center in Kabul and told Moscow they had better set up the center in Tashkent, but only temporarily. "I am convinced it will have to be removed to Kabul as soon as the treaty is ratified. In Kabul only can objective be attained."

Russian fortunes were improving; the White Russian and Allied opposition was collapsing. So the treaty was made which provided for a million-ruble subsidy from Russia to Afghanistan and various technical and commercial benefits in return for benevolent neutrality and Russian consulates in five Afghan cities including two close to the Indian frontier, Ghazni and Kandahar. Amanullah succeeded in inserting a clause guaranteeing that Bokhara and Khiva should have a form of government chosen by the people, but the Russians included the loophole, "whatever that form may be."

The treaty was agreed upon, and almost at once Bokhara was attacked by airplanes, armored cars, and armored trains, and a Bolshevik force captured the Bokharans whose soldiers could not shoot very far. They captured also several Afghan soldiers, whom they paraded in triumph through the streets. From the Treasury they removed three wagonloads of gold and precious stones which the Amir, one of the world's richest men, failed to carry off when he fled to the eastern part of his country from where he kept sending the Viceroy of India desperate letters which never arrived.

Amanullah had stated in a Cabinet meeting in May that the Russians were untrustworthy and had not fulfilled such promises as they had made to him and that their real object was to bring ruin on Afghanistan. In September all Afghanistan saw the proof.

"Intense excitement has been caused in Kabul by the overthrow of the Amir of Bokhara," wrote G. of I., "as a result of which Afghan delegates may very shortly be sent to India to try to conclude final agreement with us."

But Amanullah reacted with more poise than the British expected. On October 23, H.M.G., in the person of Roos-Keppel, was writing, "G. of I. prophesied that Afghanistan, terrified by the fate of Bokhara, would press for an immediate alliance with us and for help from us, and in the event of our refusal would reluctantly come to terms with the Bolsheviks. A month has passed and nothing of the sort has happened . . . there is certainly no sign that the Amir is inclined towards us by any fear of the Bolsheviks." Dr. Abdul Ghani, leaving Amanullah's service as Director of Education, passed through Khyber and gave out the information that neither Amanullah nor the Afghans had any sympathy with the Bolsheviks and both desired friendship with Britain, but that the events in Bokhara had so alarmed the Afghan Government that Amanullah was anxious to come to a friendly understanding with the Bolsheviks.

The Viceroy inquired whether Amanullah had given the Russians consulates close to the Indian frontier. "Should any such agreement have been concluded in fact, it would render conclusion of a friendship treaty between Great Britain and Afghanistan impossible." G. of I. had to invent a story about a wireless message of congratulations in order to avoid telling Amanullah they had intercepted Suritz's messages to his government. Suritz had written in Herat, "The English have spies everywhere," and tossed the rough draft of this note into his wastepaper basket, whence it made its way into the British official documents.

Amanullah responded with independence. He was politely evasive and invited the British to Kabul.

But there was one step that he feared to take. His nomination as Caliph of Islam was being endorsed by the Indian revolutionaries who were in touch with Moscow. It would serve the purpose of Russia.

On November 23, four days after Shah Agha had called on him to become Caliph, Amanullah announced in an open durbar that he was forbidding circulation of a pamphlet written on the subject, and wished to hear no more about it. He said he did not intend to join in an intrigue against the British Government which he regarded as likely to lead to the downfall of Afghanistan.

Amanullah now issued a firman to all Afghans saying, "It may not be hidden or concealed from the minds of all Hindus and Moslems that before this, the reputation of the Russian Empire was bad in the Country of Afghanistan owing to rumors given out by the common people. A permanent alliance and unity having been procured between the Russian and the Afghan governments, it has been fully ascertained that the Russians do not bear so much enmity and animosity towards the

Moslems, so that they should cut off their tongues for their prayers and worshipping, nor do the Russian officials tie up their mules and donkeys in the Moslem mosques. And now the Russians have entered into a permanent alliance of friendship and sincerity with the Afghan Kingdom and do not refuse whatever is desired by the Afghan Government, which has no concern with the Russian religion, faith and law.

"Before this the Russians had no such enmity with the English, either, but the latter deceive their subjects in India and have deposited the whole wealth of the subjects in the treasury. The faults of the English had been showing some small symptoms of influence in the Kingdom of Afghanistan, also. The Russian alliance should be reckoned as good fortune."

The British decided they had better get a mission of their own into Kabul, and they convinced themselves that this would not diminish their dignity.

Britain's policy of making agreements with Afghanistan in phases, with a waiting period before each step, had been unwise. The bargaining position of the British Empire was growing progressively worse. In the home islands the economic boom that had followed the war was beginning to fade and soon would be replaced by a recession. The Irish Catholics were rebelling and the Irish Republican Army was a new terror. Mustapha Kemal was succeeding in Anatolia and the Italians were contemplating a separate peace with him. There was trouble still in Mesopotamia. For the Russians, on the other hand, affairs were better. The Tsarist opponents, already deserted by the Allies, were being defeated.

"It seems desirable to take advantage, before it has time to cool, of Afghan resentment against Bolsheviks owing to overthrow of Bokhara," said G. of I., and H.M.G. said, "There is one important fact which is that the Indian Army wants a prolonged period of rest and peace and if this can be gained, it will be a great advantage."

One immediate problem involved in sending a British Mission to Kabul was the manner in which its members should address Amanullah.

Two refusals of the British were completely mystifying to the Afghans. One was the withholding of the money in Amir Habibullah's account which he had requested just before his murder, and the other was the failure to call Amanullah "Your Majesty." These seemed denials of, in the first case, an honest debt, and in the second case, common courtesy.

"Our Mission will be hopelessly handicapped if they are not authorized to address the Amir by the title which he has assumed, and it is more than likely that the whole negotiations may break down upon this petty matter, in which Amir's amour-propre is obviously involved," G. of I. pleaded with H.M.G., who replied regally, "I consider that title should be held in reserve to be bestowed as a reward for a satisfactory treaty, conclusion of which would be a fitting opportunity for His Majesty the King to adopt this means of marking his recognition of Amir's membership in brotherhood of sovereigns."

In reality, only one man was withholding the title: King George, who could not bear the thought of calling Amanullah, "Sir, my brother." The custom was for the British monarch to address directly, using the first person, in such documents as credentials of ambassadors, those whom H.M.G. designated as "civilized sovereigns." These included the Shah of Persia; the King of Siam was promoted to that category one year before the war, but never the Emperor of China, while there was such a person reigning over a people who were creating immortal art when the British were painting nothing but blue marks on their bodies. "Non-civilized sovereigns," whom the British monarch addressed in the third person, included the Emperor of Morocco and the Negus of Abyssinia, the latter receiving a slightly more cordial address than the former since his Christian religion was considered a civilizing influence, though obviously not completely so.

Amanullah's "antecedents" had been described as offending King George, successor to the throne of William the Conqueror, Richard III and Henry VIII. But a different explanation occurred to one sympathetic official: that King George, in a day when "the brotherhood of sovereigns" was being diminished by Hohenzollerns, Habsburgs, and Romanoffs, was reluctant to admit into his exclusive club "a scruffy savage from Central Asia."

Henry Dobbs, Foreign Secretary of the Government of India, was named to lead the British Mission to Kabul. In the few months since he had headed the Conference at Mussoorie he had been rewarded for his services thereto with the title "Sir" in front of his name.

Dobbs was an Irishman. This made him a puzzling personality to the Afghans, who had read of the "troubles" in Ireland and marveled at the presence in the highest ranks of the oppressor of a man who belonged with the oppressed. He had to explain the position of a Protestant land-owning Irishman, which he was, in contrast to the poor Catholic Irishman. His delegates were a Brigadier-General, S. F. Muspratt, two British officials, P. J. G. Pipon, and J. G. Acheson, and the Indian dignitary Nawab Sir Shams Shah. He brought along a medical officer, a military attaché, a fleet of motorcycles with riders to carry dispatches on them, and a signals officer with a complete wireless station. The only wireless in Kabul was operated by a Russian, and he would take no chances in spite of using cipher.

In the mid-morning of January 5, 1921, Dobbs, in formal morning dress, crossed the border and became the first British official to be received in Afghanistan in Amanullah's reign. Amanullah had made elaborate plans for his security. Dobbs drove along a road bare of animals and people, since these were all diverted to a distance of fifty yards and held behind piquets and sentries. He was the fifth such head of a British Mission to enter Afghanistan. Of the previous four, two had returned. His chances were even.

In Jalalabad the strictness ended. Every man in the vicinity was pushing along the road to see the foreigners. Thirteen guns were fired as the leading car drove through the gateway of the Bagh-i-Shahi Palace, a tall-columned blue building with fountains and flowers in its garden. On the steps stood the chief officers, headed by Nadir's brother Hashim, who was both civil and military officer of the district. In the reception hall, while refreshments were being served, Hashim complimented his guest's nationality by discoursing on the state of Ireland and its importance in international politics. Hashim, Dobbs said later, "impressed all who met him as a man of exceptional address and ability. His manner was frank and extremely cordial." The next morning Hashim visited the English party at breakfast and spoke of the recent growth of a general spirit of unrest among the lower classes in Afghanistan, expressing the theory that it originated in Persia. He himself, he said, deplored the spread of Bolshevik ideas.

Dobbs wished to visit Habibullah's tomb. He had already seen evidence of Habibullah's fondness for Jalalabad in the lines of cypress and chanar trees which lined the approaches and the main avenues. Now Hashim led him into the walled garden that once had been Habibullah's golf course. Well-kept roads wound through flower beds and between rows of cypress and Persian pine. The tomb was enclosed in a domed mausoleum open on all four sides and approached by steps. It was, in the usual fashion of the country, a half-cylinder of concrete, but a head-stone and covering of marble cut in a lacy pattern had been added. Habibullah's name appeared nowhere; it was taken for granted that everyone knew who was buried there. As Dobbs approached, an open Koran lay on the tomb and four mullahs were standing by with their hands outstretched, hands upward, in the attitude of prayer. They were accustomed to praying there in this manner. Each of the British party stood for a moment in silence on the top step, the civilians baring their heads and the military at salute.

Resuming the journey, Dobbs heard more conversation about Ireland from two other members of the Afghan welcoming party. Once again the roads had been cleared of other travelers, except at the entrance to the Kabul Gorge where this had been impossible, and the dignitaries had to wait on the passage of a line of Turcoman camels.

The Dilkusha Palace had been built by Habibullah for official receptions; the name, which means Heart's Desire, was more romantic than its function deserved. On January 10 Dobbs and his party, in formal dress, entered the Dilkusha Palace and were face-to-face with an enormous staircase flanked by rows of electric candelabra, and on either side a large bronze urn of impressive intricacy. Mahmud Tarzi, who had accompanied Dobbs, presented him to Nadir. The hall was filled with the important men of Kabul; Dobbs made a mental note that at the durbar for the Dane Mission in 1905, only two personages had met the delegates at the door. These welcoming Afghans all wore uniforms of scarlet and gold; Tarzi was the only civilian note.

Nadir, who had succeeded Tarzi as senior officer of state, led Dobbs up the staircase, over many yards of carpets woven in Panjdeh, one of the spots the Afghans hoped to receive back from Russia. In the long reception hall the delegates were seated at small tables holding sweetmeats and fruits. A table near the entrance held large photographs of King George and Queen Mary.

The Chamberlain entered, carrying a wand surmounted by a gold star, and announced the Amir.

Amanullah, in an inspiration of dramatic effectiveness, in all that mass of scarlet and gold, was wearing simple black and a big hat of sable with a gold star.

When Amanullah first spoke, he was formal and precise, but after he learned that all the party understood Persian, so that no translator was needed, he relaxed and became almost jovial. He said the British delegates would soon learn to pronounce the Persian letter "qaf," since the word "qanaat" or "contentment" would figure largely in the conference. He knew as much about the Mussoorie Conference as if he had been there, including the nickname "malang," or "holy madman," given to one of the British delegates. He also brought up the subject of Ireland and discovered that four of the seven members of the Mission were Irish.

"The Amir's demeanor and presence were commanding and digni- fied," Dobbs reported. "He has a keen sense of humor and an infectious laugh. His manner, when the first attitude of extreme formality had worn off, was cheerful and animated and he has the habit of illustrating his meaning by rapid gesticulation."

Amanullah told Dobbs that he had appointed Tarzi, with certain assistants, to take part in negotiations.

"I am excluding Nadir, as being a man of war," he said, laughing. "Generals never are useful in agreements. The union of Sir Henry Dobbs and Sardar Mahmud Tarzi, both men of the pen, and both Foreign Ministers, is a favorable omen. I hope you will be completely successful."

Nadir replied with a rather rigid humor that seemed half in earnest, "Men of the pen are helpless without men of the sword. I myself am always ready to serve in either capacity."

The durbar ended. The Englishmen who had installed the wireless station returned to India, taking in their empty vehicles five young Af- ghans who were to study telegraphy in Karachi. These were wearing new gray overcoats and gray caps bearing Amanullah's symbol of education, the pen and sword.

Amanullah was host in his own country to the British Empire that he had succeeded in defying.

CHAPTER 9

January 13, 1921, to June 15, 1921

Amanullah met the British Empire face to face in discussion on the morning of January 13. Snow was falling heavily from an overcast sky and Amanullah had a head cold coming as, in his informal costume of short gray tweed coat and black trousers, he greeted Sir Henry Dobbs, wearing formal morning attire. Tarzi and Sir Shams Shah were the only others present.

Dobbs quickly stated his misgivings: "If I were not a friend, I should pretend ignorance of the things which I am now going to reveal. These things are known only to a very few. We keep them out even of our confidential offices. The things that I am going to talk to you about are things discovered by our Secret Service regarding the relations between Afghanistan and other parties, such as the Bolshevik Government, Jemal Pasha, and Mustapha Kemal . . . Our Secret Service is acknowledged to be the best in the world and you would be astonished if I could reveal to you the sources of our information."

"Where do you get your news from?" demanded Amanullah. "If you keep any secrets back from me, I will keep things back from you."

"I must beg to be excused. I could not possibly give away the names of our informers."

"They will be safe with me."

"Suppose, which God forbid, you were to fall ill with high fever and be delirious. You might give away the names and our informers might be killed. You know what happens at Moscow and Tashkent."

Dobbs said that Britain knew that Afghanistan had made treaties with the Bolsheviks and with Mustapha Kemal about which she had told Great Britain nothing. "We cannot enter the conference blind-folded."

Amanullah asked about the League of Nations, under whose rules all treaties had to be public, inquiring what nations had signed it. He was particularly interested in America.

"There are special reasons for America standing aloof at present," said Dobbs, "but whether she signs or not, the one thing against which all Americans are keen is secret diplomacy and secret agreements."

Then Dobbs laid on the table statements from the British Secret Service regarding Afghanistan's agreement with Russia, Suritz's comments on that agreement, and an account of Afghanistan's relations with Turkey and the work of Jemal Pasha.

As each paper was brought forth, Amanullah and Tarzi grew more nervous. Amanullah began to drum on the table with the fingers of both hands as if he were playing a piano.

Tarzi asked, "Where did you get your information about Jemal Pasha? I suppose you have done so since you came here."

"Reflect on all the precautions which you are taking for the safety of our whole party! Do you really think that I have been making inquiries in Kabul? No, I would not dream of doing such a thing. Our Secret Service has got the information elsewhere."

Dobbs read aloud the Persian translation of a telegram which Suritz had sent to Moscow and which the British had intercepted. It said:

"After eight months' negotiations, a Russo-Afghan treaty was concluded on September 16. The treaty guarantees a benevolent neutrality towards us. The treaty will make Afghanistan dependent on us both financially and militarily."

When Dobbs read this last sentence, Amanullah cried out, "I am under no one! I am not under Russia's protection." Dobbs continued to read as if he had not spoken.

"Until ratification of the treaty, the situation is very strained," Suritz had wired, "especially in connection with events in Bokhara. It is essential to avoid any cause which might make it worse, and especially to see that no incident takes place on the frontier. Any frontier incident may spoil the whole situation, as it would be treated by the Afghans as a pretext for breaking with us, and would not be treated as a local affair. It would probably influence the whole policy in the East. Under no circumstances can we afford to irritate the Afghan diplomats until the ratification of the treaty. Any violent act will make the ratification of the treaty impossible."

Dobbs then read of the activities of Jemal Pasha and a secret commission to send propaganda into India. "You are expecting to receive very shortly in Kabul a deputation from Mustapha Kemal and are sending a deputation to him."

"Well, what of it?" asked Amanullah.

"My object is to show that you seem to be trying to run with four different parties: the Bolsheviks, the British, Jemal Pasha and Mustapha Kemal. Now, that won't do."

Amanullah said, "I am going to speak frankly in my turn. I shall tell you what I have told no one else. You are spread all over the world as a result of this war, but that has not added to your real strength. In the meanwhile the Bolsheviks have made themselves strong. They are rapidly recovering from their disorganization and are setting their factories going again and are turning out military material rapidly."

Then Amanullah expanded a bit too much on his personal activities: "My personal standard is hoisted on each public office while I am there."

"May I ask its color?" said Dobbs.

"It is red," said Amanullah. Turning to Tarzi, he complained, "I wish to goodness you and Sir Henry Dobbs would not converse silently with your eyes and eyebrows, like regular old diplomats. I know what both of you are thinking, that red is the color of the Bolsheviks' flag. But let me tell you that the color of the Afghan royal standard was fixed long before the Bolsheviks' was. And I am not going to change it now."

Amanullah looked at Dobbs and spoke so fast he was difficult to understand.

"Well, I remember, when I was small, we were always told that the Russians were the enemies of Islam, raping Moslem women and murdering Moslem men and children and destroying mosques. You were the friends of Islam. You saved Constantinople by your ships from the Russians.

"Now all that is changed. You have alienated the hearts of all Moslems, not only of Turkey but also in Egypt, Mesopotamia, India and Persia. You have no friends. The French are not your friends. I know all about the Italian intrigues against you. Now you have a chance of making Afghanistan your friend. If you help her to become a big power, the hearts of Moslems all over the world will be turned towards you, as they will see that you are helping a Moslem power, and that what you did to Turkey was done from political motives and not from hatred of Islam. That will be a great help to you, and it will lessen your anxiety about India.

"The important thing is to win men's hearts. It is in this that real power consists.

"Think of my position. I was younger than my brothers . . . and my uncle. Inayatullah was in charge of the Army, yet the hearts of men were with me, not only of the people but of the Army; and it was thus that I sat on the throne.

"The position of Afghanistan is pivotal. Consider all these deputations and embassies which are coming to me here from the Bolsheviks, Jemal Pasha, Mustapha Kemal, your deputation and Shaukat Ali [the Indian Moslem leader] wishing to visit Afghanistan. Now, if by generous treatment you make Afghanistan your friend, all the matters that worry you in the arrangements which you say I have made with the Bolsheviks and Jemal Pasha will disappear at once. There is no need, therefore, for me to tell you the details of them, nor whether your information is right or wrong. Let us get quickly to work at drafting a treaty of friendship. It should not take more than five or six days. Then, if the Afghans are content, all grounds of suspicion will vanish."

Dobbs said, "I quite admit much of what you have said about the hearts of Moslems being turned against us. If the Caliphate question had not existed, the extremists would have seized on some other question."

"There would not have been any other questions of this kind or magnitude."

"Things are settling in India. The Germans were absolutely confident that we would not go to war, because all India would rise against us. Instead of that, India helped us."

"Because you made special promises of freedom to them, these new councils, and so forth."

"You must not believe the exaggerations of informers, newspapers, and rumors," Dobbs told him.

Amanullah pressed on. "What about your terms with Turkey? Are you going to modify them? You should do so and turn the hearts of Moslems towards you again."

"I cannot say what are the latest intentions of my government," said

Dobbs. "The British Premier and the Foreign Ministers of France and Italy are still discussing the matter and their discussions have not been made public."

"Aha!" cried Amanullah. "What did you tell me about the League of Nations abolishing secret diplomacy?"

"I said 'secret agreements,' not 'secret discussions prior to agreements.'"

By this time Amanullah was sniffling while the other men were trying not to shiver in the cold room. Before they parted, Amanullah told Dobbs, "Your good name and your credit with your government depend on your returning with a treaty in your pocket. You cannot go back without one."

"On the contrary, the very last message which the Viceroy sent me before I crossed the frontier was a telegram to say that he hoped I would remember that . . . he would not blame me if I returned without one."

"Then the Viceroy has made you free from blame."

The snow had stopped falling, but the temperature had dropped below freezing. It had been a very brief honeymoon.

As Amanullah and Tarzi discussed at Council meetings their first encounter, and news of it spread to others and even to the servants and soldiers and the people in the streets, the cordiality that had warmed the British delegates' entry into Kabul slowly vanished. Some officers and soldiers nodded to them in passing with an informality that they found almost insolent. The passers-by, who had begun by saluting them in the streets, ceased to do so. Wherever they went, an official escort went also; they noted that the Russians went about alone; they did not know that the Russians had achieved this liberty by threatening to apply the same surveillance to the Afghan Envoy in Russia. The guide assigned to the British spoke and understood English, and was observed eavesdropping on their private conversations. Their classical education rescued them and they switched to French. Whenever they attempted to give a tip to a barber or a coolie for some small service, they were restrained, and the escort gave the tip himself. In official eyes it was not desirable for them to become too popular. As the final mark of their disfavor, officers attending the British began to speak often of the good qualities of the Russians.

In official talks Nadir, who took part whenever frontier matters were discussed, was justifying the earlier British description of him as "truculent." He outlined the hostility of almost all the world toward Britain, saying, "Afghanistan would incur such odium from the tribes and from Indian Moslems if she made friendship with Great Britain that she must receive an ample quid pro quo." Tarzi was disturbed by the prospect of the conference's failing to reach agreement, but Nadir declared, "Even if Tarzi signed a treaty on the lines of the Mussoorie Conference, I should refuse to accept it."

H.M.G.'s reaction was, "If any other government in the world (even Germany before the war) used such language towards us, we should . . . close discussions at once."

Bravin, the defeated former Envoy from Russia, who had become an Afghan citizen, left Kabul in mid-January with his pretty wife and went to Ghazni. Everyone thought he was on his way to India, where he would reveal to the British all he had learned as a Russian official, first for the Tsar and then for the Bolsheviks. Some said that he had accepted his post in Afghanistan only as a steppingstone to India and had lingered overlong. Just before the Mussoorie Conference, the British had heard with dismay that Amanullah was considering making Bravin a delegate.

In Ghazni, while Bravin was on one of his flower-gathering expeditions, someone shot him. An Afghan soldier was tried for the murder and executed.

Gradually the people of Kabul began to salute again as the British walked through the bazaar. The officers in attendance encouraged the giving of small gifts for service. Dobbs was gratified to hear foul abuse of the Bolsheviks from an Afghan colonel, and Amanullah, Nadir and Tarzi, the triumvirate of power, sent friendly greetings and queries after his health. Dobbs reported all these nuances to H.M.G., who thought him "mercurial."

This popularity, Dobbs heard, was due partly to Russia's delay in ratifying her treaty with Afghanistan.

In regard to the treaty he himself was negotiating, Dobbs was restrained by H.M.G.'s refusal to make concessions. He was miserable. Finally H.M.G empowered him to offer Amanullah the same subsidy his father had received, 20½ lakhs of rupees. "If Dobbs finds himself pressed up to 20 lakhs, we feel that he should go up to that limit, for the docking of the odd half-lakh would be regarded as a gratuitous pin-prick. If he can secure satisfactory settlement, in these very difficult times . . . he will have done very well . . . 20½ lakhs represent, after all, but a few days' expenditure on a frontier expedition, and is a small premium to pay for a peace-on-the-frontier policy."

On February 27 Amanullah celebrated the second anniversary of his accession. Dinner was not served until midnight because a hurricane had blown down the tent erected for it, smashing furniture and crockery, plates of food, and three hundred electric light bulbs. The tall clock tower on Dilkusha Palace had been hung with bunting; this was blown down, but a red and green electric sign continued to wish the Amir good health in a changing pattern that was fashionable in London street signs.

The Amir wore a scarlet tunic with a collar of small diamond stars of the Order of Almar, which he had created himself, a dome-shaped astrakhan hat with his grandfather's diamond star, and a flowing light-gray coat and gray trousers. Those who held the rank of Sardar-i-Ala, the highest order, wore astrakhan caps with crimson ostrich plumes in front and the military officers had a newly devised black cloth tunic. A few sayeds demonstrated the scorn that a Child of the Prophet should feel for worldly things by wearing their ordinary posteens and turbans.

While waiting for the smashed dinner table to be restored, Amanullah played bridge with some of his relatives while a few mullahs, among them Shah Agha, looked on with interest. Here the Russians contributed to their own belittling, for they had no small talk, while the British had polished theirs in drawingrooms. Dobbs and his companions played bridge and chess and chatted gracefully, while the Russians sat glumly to one side, alone except for an occasional attention from Jemal Pasha.

The entertainment was a recital by the children who had been orphaned in the War of Independence and were now wards of the government. They sang:

"We the orphans were in a sad plight,
Having lost our fathers we were restless.
When our fathers became martyrs,
We were face to face with grief and sorrow.
But on account of the kindness of the Ghazi King
We now possess honor and pride
And think that we
All are the children of the King."

On the following day the Russians ratified their treaty with Afghanistan. But the news did not reach Kabul until March 7. Kabul knew only that the promised cession to Afghanistan of the lands around Panjdeh was slow in taking place.

So Dobbs on March 2 decided on a new move.

That afternoon Dobbs met with Amanullah, Nadir and Tarzi completely alone. The only attendant was a deaf-mute, one of those which every Oriental court maintained for such an occasion. Dobbs even took the precaution of placing the table in the middle of the room.

Then Dobbs told the Afghans the source of all the information he had revealed at their first conference: that for eighteen months the British Secret Service had been reading every single telegram exchanged between Moscow, Tashkent, Kushk, Kabul and other places. They had broken the Russian code. It was safe now to reveal this because the Russians had learned the secret and changed their code.

"This wireless telegraphy is most mischievous!" cried Amanullah. "The various governments make use of this to embitter the relations of other states. I am sure that the Bolsheviks intended those telegrams for your consumption. They tried to play a similar trick on me last year. A long wireless telegram came from Tashkent, giving an account of the treaty alleged to have been signed by my Envoy, Wali Khan, with the Bolsheviks, which would have put Afghanistan completely under the feet of Russia. I was horror-stricken. I had given no authority to Wali Khan to sign any treaty and I could not believe that he had betrayed me. I could not sleep nights, and all my advisers were similarly perturbed. At last a message got through from Wali Khan saying that he had made no agreement of any kind and I telegraphed to Nadir at Jalalabad and Mahmud Tarzi, who was also away, expressing my great relief.

"The Bolsheviks have been trying to play the same trick on you. I will smash up both the wireless installations at Kabul. They only do harm. They both really belong to me."

Dobbs told the Afghans that he knew from the telegrams that Nadir had advocated war with Great Britain the previous year. "I hinted to you at Mussoorie that we knew all about it and Suritz wired later, after you got back, that you warned him that we had found out about it. We learned from these telegrams how the Bolsheviks were planning the overthrow of Bokhara . . . The Bokharan business was deliberately planned by the Bolshevik Government against Suritz's advice. Suritz made out that at first you were very angry about it, and that you declared that you would have your reputation among Moslems ruined by it, but that afterwards you became more reconciled.

"Another thing we learned was that only the day before our mission arrived in Kabul, Amir Sahib told Suritz that he was personally opposed to the treaty of friendship with us, and that he intended to delay negotiations as long as possible in the hope that the Russian treaty would be ratified."

Amanullah said, "That telegram says I promised to protract negotiations with you. Who, pray, is protracting them now?"

"We are perfectly prepared to let bygones be bygones," said Dobbs, "and to forget all these suspicions, if you will only clear the dust from your eyes and realize the honesty of our purpose."

Nations have always been ready to forgive defections in which they themselves might sooner or later be caught.

"All that you have told me," said Amanullah, "only shows the importance of making friendship between us. If real friendship is made, all that is contained in these papers will disappear. Until we sign a treaty, I have a right to do what I like on my side and you cannot object, and you have the same right on your side and I cannot object . . . It is this delay which is spoiling everything between us. You should have made a final treaty at Rawalpindi. Then again there was the Mussoorie Conference at which nothing was settled. If things go on like this, the end will be war between us, and I want peace in all the world and especially with the states bordering on Afghanistan . . . The blame for the delay is on you. I have told you before that these things that you object to may be arranged, though I doubt very much whether I can depart from any of the ideas which I put forward in my draft treaty."

Dobbs said that his treaty would contain the promise that no power other than Great Britain would be allowed in the country bordering on the frontier, and that a reciprocal promise on the part of the British would be made that no consuls of any other powers would be allowed in the Indian frontier area.

"What is the good of that to us?" cried Amanullah. "I am to give you a house and you are to give me a stone. You know quite well that you don't want foreign consuls at Peshawar and other places. You are not giving up anything or giving any reciprocal advantage to us. We must have something real in return for such a concession."

"About Jemal," said Dobbs, "he told me he was greatly attached to you. Later in the conversation, when he had got rather worked up, he said that he would naturally be our bitter enemy and would do everything possible to cause us trouble in India for so long as we did not revise our policy towards Turkey and show ourselves friendly to Turkey."

Amanullah said angrily, "Did he say friendly to Turkey or friendly to Afghanistan?"

"Friendly to Turkey," replied Dobbs. "His whole heart is wrapped up in Turkish interests, I don't blame him for that. Love of country is always good."

"Why don't you love Ireland then?" asked Amanullah.

Tarzi said, "I suppose you have been reading all our ciphers, too. Well, if you have, it doesn't matter. There is no harm in them."

"I should never think of trying to obtain the key of your ciphers from your offices." When Dobbs later sent his report to India, his colleagues noted that he was careful to include the words, "from your offices." Now he added for the benefit of the Afghans, "I came here as a diplomat, not as a spy."

Dobbs was pleased with his day's work; he expected many happy results from the shock he had administered.

A few days later he heard of the signing in Moscow. "This means Afghanistan will be unable to comply with my demands. What shall I do?"

The desperate note in Dobbs's telegram was due not so much to the Afghans as to his own superiors, the unsympathetic H.M.G., even with G. of I. as a buffer. H.M.G. already knew the terms of the Russo-Afghan treaty; British spies were efficient. Yet they demanded to be told by the Afghans. If Russia paid a subsidy, it was unthinkable that H.M.G. should pay one. "Outbreak of war not unanimously accepted as certain," said H.M.G., while G. of I. was calculating how best to postpone war until the weather was cooler.

"We must beg H.M.G. to envisage facts as we see them," wrote Chelmsford, whose term as Viceroy was ending. "Afghanistan is determined to parade her complete independence. From this nothing short of war will drive her . . . Can we, in view of general situation in the Near and Middle East, face an Afghan war? India cannot, and we must venture to remind H.M.G. that it is on India and Indian resources that the brunt would fall . . . It is most important for us to clinch negotiations, if possible, before effect of Dobbs's revelations has had time to wear off."

Chelmsford also wired to "insist again that Britain cannot demand to be the sole purveyor of assistance to Afghans. From the Afghan point of view, it must be remembered that our subsidy represents a rise of about 2.8 rupees in monthly pay of Afghan Army, whereas at least double is apparently required with present high prices to keep it contented at existing strength."

H.M.G., which had complained that Dobbs was beginning to "see through Afghan spectacles," said no.

Dobbs switched his attention to finding a way to maneuver so that the rupture would seem justified in the eyes of the British public.

In his unhappiness he had to send a further unhappy wire: "An enormous and valuable Birjand carpet, worth about 4,000 rupees, has just been sent to me by Amir without any previous intimation with a message that it is not intended as an official present but is a personal gift from him to me. In existing circumstances a gift is most embarrassing but it was impossible to refuse." The next day Dobbs wired in an escalation of misery that he had discovered the carpet was worth 12,000 rupees.

On March 16 the British themselves signed a treaty with Russia, providing for the resumption of trade.

The treaty contained clauses prohibiting hostile propaganda against each other. Roos-Keppel had commented during negotiations, "We only propose that either side shall refrain from propaganda. This will not prevent mutual spying which will presumably go on forever."

All over the world this new development took by surprise many Empire officials who were engaged, by order, in propaganda against Russia. G. of I. hoped that the new communication might enable H.M.G. to ask Russia to relinquish the bothersome consulates. Tarzi tried this direct approach with Suritz, warning him that Britain might acquire similar posts close to Russia. Suritz replied that the British might have ten consulates for all he cared.

Dobbs was packing to go home.

He met with Amanullah and Tarzi for what was intended to be the last time. "I cannot understand, when both countries sincerely desire friendship, how you can break off negotiations over trifling differences," Amanullah said to Dobbs, who privately shared his feeling.

"I have given my word to the Russians about the consulates, and it is very difficult to take it back, even though technically I can still refuse to ratify the treaty. Tell me as a friend how I shall get out of this

. . . If we refuse to ratify the consulates, Russia will probably refuse to make a treaty and withdraw their offer of the subsidy and return of Panjdeh, and either attack Afghanistan or ruin her by propaganda." Dobbs said he thought the return of Panjdeh was largely illusory.

Tarzi asked, "Can you give Afghanistan definite support if she incurs Russian enmity?" Dobbs said there might be a possibility as something of the kind had been considered when Bokhara was overthrown.

The Amir of Bokhara, after wandering over his former kingdom, had come to rest in Kabul. Most of his immense treasure had been lost, the Russians having taken part of it away, along with part of his harem, by uncoupling one of his railroad cars. One gift that he did bring to the country of his asylum was a flock of the finest Karakul sheep in the world, who improved the breed in Afghanistan. He brought also a box of Bokhara soil. This he placed outside the house in Paghman which Amanullah gave him, and into it he thrust two silver poles from which flew two Bokharan standards wondrously embroidered.

Amanullah had sent the outspoken Abdul Hadi as representative to the new Russian Government of Bokhara where, according to the Russians, he was so unsympathetic as to let the diplomatic pouch be used for messages to those still resisting Russian rule.

With still another country Amanullah was making a treaty. An agreement with the Turkish Government of Mustapha Kemal was signed on February 28 in Moscow by Wali.

Amanullah denied the signing when Dobbs asked about it, but said he was contemplating a treaty with the Turkish nationalists. "Until an agreement is reached with the British Government I am free to entertain agreements with other nations and must make provisions in case of a rupture with you." Dobbs was diplomatically unable to call Amanullah a liar. "The doctrine that it is a laudable thing to lie for one's country has been constantly preached by Jemal Pasha and Tarzi and it is unlikely that the Amir will have a higher political morality," wired Dobbs, who had not always been, in the interests of the British Empire, totally accurate.

Dobbs was delaying his threatened departure from Kabul.

On April 16 Tarzi invited him to lunch and spoke of "the extraordinary new methods of the new diplomacy which consists of making demands from your rival and, by simultaneously publishing your demands, making it difficult for him to comply."

The whole world now knew of the Russian consulates on the Indian frontier in the Afghan treaty. Sir Robert Horne, who had negotiated for England the trade agreement with Russia, proclaimed them along with an equally public demand that Russia withdraw. Dobbs abandoned all hope of such a withdrawal, for now "it has become a public trial of strength between us and Russia." This was not the first time Horne had talked too much; it had been he who, by revealing too much knowledge of Russian internal affairs, had cost the British the Russian code.

Through a beautiful spring they negotiated. The yellow crocus bloomed and faded. In April the purple glory of the flowering judas tree covered the terraced hills of Istalif, where potters were turning on their wheels the bowls they would cover with the bright blue glaze that they alone in Central Asia preserved. Peach, pear and apple trees were blooming also. The mountains in the distance, between this brilliant softness and the blue sky, were harsh and brown, enhancing the passing loveliness of the one and the eternity of the other.

Then, as spring grew older, the rains ceased; the snows on the mountaintops, which had made the rivers a torrent, had done their melting. The lakes in Kabul were nearly dry. Nomads, who had driven their flocks a long distance in search of grazing land, now drove them into the empty lake beds to find what damp vegetation they could. The weather was too dry and sultry. Everyone predicted a poor harvest. Food was costing more.

No one was more discontented over high prices than the soldiers. They had expected a large raise in pay; they got a very small one. Their money now brought fewer rations. In the past, under the inefficient, lackadaisical old régime, they had been able to work at other trades and earn extra money, but the Turkish officers whom Amanullah had imported were energetic and made being a soldier a full-time job.

In the Viceregal Lodge in India there was also discontent. The new Viceroy, Rufus Isaacs, Lord Reading, a distinguished jurist, had come to India with the intention of disposing quickly of that petty annoyance on his frontier, the Afghan problem. By May 5 he was writing, "My present more intimate knowledge of Indian affairs makes me desirous to obtain a treaty with Afghanistan, even though it falls short of our requirements . . . There is no counsel of perfection in regard to Afghanistan . . ."

Mahatma Gandhi was writing in *Young India* that "I . . . so far as my creed of non-violence is concerned, can contemplate an Afghan

162   FIRE IN AFGHANISTAN

invasion with perfect equanimity . . . They are a God-fearing people."
Two Moslem leaders in India were imprisoned for having allegedly
sent a letter to Amanullah inviting him to invade India. "I also would
send one," Gandhi said in Allahabad, "to inform the Amir that if he
came no Indian, as long as I can help it, would help the Government
to drive him back."

Dobbs was authorized to offer Amanullah up to forty lakhs of rupees
annually in subsidy.

Still they could not agree. Shah Agha was beseeching Amanullah not
to make a treaty without protecting the tribes that had helped him.
That was one point on which the G. of I. would not yield. It involved
their sovereignty.

A new emissary, Rosenberg, arrived from Russia bringing the treaty
signed there. Amanullah delayed ratifying it.

On June 4 there came one of the occasions which makes good will
possible: the birth of a son to Souraya and Amanullah. Their first boy
had died of cholera; this was their heir, whom they named Rahmatullah. Congratulations were handed all around, not only to Amanullah
but to the grandfather, Mahmud Tarzi.

Again, there was a relaxation at the Moslem Festival of Id-ul-Fitr.
About twenty thousand persons watched as four state elephants capari-
soned in cloth of gold, carrying silver howdahs, unoccupied, paraded
between rows of household cavalry in full uniform that lined the road
between the Arg Palace and Idgah Mosque. It was a gay crowd.
Sweet-sellers sold orange candies bent like pretzels. Children paid a
few small coins to ride on a carousel of wood that flew out and around
when a man turned a crank.

Amanullah rode through on horseback, preceded by a cavalry band.
As he approached the mosque gate he saw that the men of the British
Mission, a few minor Bolshevik officials and three Armenian ladies
were watching from a mound opposite; he decided that he would build
on that mound a permanent grandstand for foreign representatives,
and before the ceremony was over, he had given the order.

Ever since he had become Amir, Amanullah had been working to
create new laws for Afghanistan, which had none except the Shariat,
or religious law as interpreted by the mullahs, which gave almost absolute power to the judge, always a mullah. The Shariat law was severe
and let a man off very little. It was the law of the Old Testament. A
Turkish authority on law who had come with Jemal Pasha, named

Bedri Bey, former Police Chief of Constantinople, was writing a code for Afghanistan similar to that of Turkey, which had been based on the Napoleonic Code of France.

After prayers, Amanullah arose on a platform in the mosque and announced that his new code, called the Nizamnamas, would become law at once.

There was cheering.

He announced that he would meet with his provincial officials and that the people in the provinces must come and heckle the officials to assure that they were doing their duty.

They were still cheering as Amanullah left the mosque and a heliograph sent a signal to the heights to the South so that at the moment of his leaving a salute boomed forth.

Amanullah decided that the way to safeguard this new society that he was building was to link its fortunes entirely with Great Britain's. For five months he had been able to observe both men from Great Britain and men from Soviet Russia.

Suritz sent Amanullah a peremptory note demanding that he ratify the treaty at once. Instead, Amanullah told Tarzi to meet with Dobbs and offer to break off completely with Russia, on various conditions which included a gift by Britain immediately of munitions which had been promised only in event of an attack by a third power. He told Tarzi to list the Russian gifts he would be forfeiting: the return to Afghanistan of Panjdeh, a telegraph line, a smokeless powder factory, five thousand rifles, guns, antiaircraft guns, and twelve airplanes.

"If you will accept our proposal," Tarzi told Dobbs, "we will sign at once and inform Suritz that we will have nothing more to do with Russia. We will make a clean cut. But we feel great uneasiness about the British gift of munitions [contingent on an unprovoked Russian invasion] since they will be required for the distant Northern frontier, and if Russia made a sudden attack, the Afghans could not possibly get them to their Northern troops in time to be of any use. Northern Afghanistan might then be overrun like poor Belgium, and it would be poor comfort to feel that eventually British help might enable us to force the Russians back. We cannot take grave risks of invasion without the immediate gift of munitions. The moral effort of this immediate gift will enable us to give Russia this slap in the face with satisfaction.

"I will force the rupture of relations on Suritz by complaining about the Russian reaction in Bokhara and Khiva without mentioning the consulate question."

Dobbs advised accepting this offer. G. of I. wondered why the Afghans needed so many rifles, since they were demanding almost three times as many as the Russians would have given, but the Viceroy agreed to the terms and in arsenals throughout India soldiers began to gather the gifts for Afghanistan: twenty thousand rifles, two hundred Lewis guns, twelve mountain guns, two batteries of eighteen-pounders, and the telegraph material for a line from Kabul to Kandahar to Herat.

Amanullah, however, was not content merely to have them promised. He wanted them not only delivered but already in the hands of troops at Herat and Mazar-i-Sharif, before he told the Russians he was through with them, with the treaty safely signed in advance.

G. of I. would not trust Afghanistan to this extent. "Nobody can foresee what may happen between signing of treaty and arrival of munitions on Russo-Afghan border. Interval . . . would be considerable; it is estimated by our military authorities in most favorable conditions, at six weeks at least. Afghan procrastination, moreover, is proverbial, and every excuse to put off final rupture with Russia might be made full use of."

The rifles and ammunition were ready to be delivered on the frontier within a week, the batteries within three weeks. Once this gigantic arsenal was on its way, rumors about it would be wild throughout both countries; the treaty would have to be announced at the same time. H.M.G. appreciated the problems and introduced one of its own, a power greater than either H.M.G. or G. of I. That power was British public opinion.

"We shall be precluded from taking openly the line that the Afghan breach with Russia is the consideration for our increased subsidy. Afghan proposal is to engineer break over Bokhara and Khiva questions . . . Publication of treaty itself will not reveal true quid pro quo, and unless and until rupture with Russians takes place, reasons for generous terms of British treaty will not appear."

The British public was already disturbed by the generous terms of the Treaty of Rawalpindi.

"If Afghans carried out promise to break with Russians at end of period, you will appreciate difficulty of defending position in Parliament during interval between publication of treaty and open rupture.

And if after publication of treaty and handing over of munitions, Afghans refused to break with Russians, we should be placed in very awkward position."

No one was willing to trust anyone else, but the British were sufficiently confident to start drafting a letter in which King George would gracefully confer on Amanullah the title "Your Majesty," using the formula for uncivilized states (his officials dared not even bring up the question of the "civilized" formula). The India Office in London wrote to the Colonial Office on June 15 that discussions in Kabul had reached the final stage, and that wording of the treaty should be considered.

While these Englishmen were moving toward a fulfillment, other Englishmen in other parts of the world were doing things that would disillusion Amanullah with these whom he was ready to trust.

CHAPTER 10

March 1921 to February 25, 1922

Since March an Afghan Mission had been going around the world to announce to all governments Afghanistan's independence and desire to be friendly.

Amanullah's dream for his country included an exchange of diplomats with all capitals, the coming and going of businessmen who would invest money in Afghanistan, buy her goods and sell their own, and train Afghans in the technology to which she was coming so late. Since Afghanistan was landlocked, no ships brought and carried news, so the only way to step from her isolation was to go abroad and carry the news herself.

Wali's mission that had gone to Moscow became the international mission, a group of quiet men who would have attracted more attention in the West had they worn native costume, but instead merged with the Western background so well that one journalist who did pay them attention admired in print Wali's powder-blue waistcoat and stickpin. He was accompanied by young Ghulam Siddiq and Faiz Mohammed, and by two commercial attachés and a servant.

The British resented the mission, and their diplomats saw to it that it was not well received by the leaders of other nations. As the British Ambassador in Paris told the French, "We consider Afghanistan, though ostensibly independent, still within our sphere of influence . . . We hope to get into a much closer relationship with Afghanistan in the near future."

No country would chance offending the mighty British Empire for the sake of the wanderers from the tiny kingdom of Afghanistan, which barely seemed real. The exception was Italy, with whom Wali succeeded in making an agreement for commercial relations. July 3 was set as the date when an Italian Mission would start for Kabul. Amanullah was jubilant at this beginning of an international life for Afghanistan.

But the British, hearing of this treaty, brought pressure on Italy and the departure was postponed with the intention of letting it lapse altogether. In the course of this maneuver the British diplomats were so arrogant toward the Italians that it was inevitable the Italians would take revenge. They told the Afghans, who were then in Paris, what had happened.

In Kabul on the morning of June 17 everything pointed to an imminent agreement with Britain. Then the "dak runner," ringing his little bell, brought the mail, and Amanullah learned that he was being pushed back into the old isolation and dependence. He said nothing to Dobbs of this, but all progress toward the treaty ceased.

Meanwhile the Afghan Mission sailed on July 2 for the United States, arriving in New York City.

At the same time, from another direction, another Afghan was arriving in the United States. She was Princess Fatima Sultana, descendant of a close associate of the Amir Shah Shuja whom the British had placed on the throne of Kabul in the 1830s, thereby precipitating, to their sorrow, the First Afghan War. When Shah Shuja entered Kabul as a ruler, no Afghan tossed him either a flower or a smile. When he left, he was fleeing in the darkness, carrying on his person his treasure of jewels. He was killed and abandoned; his noble companion, who knew of the jewels, took them from his body, and henceforth they were the glory of the house of the fortunate companion. And the glory of all the jewels was a forty-five-carat diamond called the Dar-i-Nur, which means "River of Light."

Fatima Sultana and her husband Yakub quarreled with Amir Habibullah; she always told people that she was afraid the Amir would take away her diamond. She took the malcontents' route out of Afghanistan by way of Mecca, and established in Amritsar, in India.

Now a widow, Fatima Sultana arrived in San Francisco traveling on a British passport, and was taken in charge by the British Consul General, who provided hotel accommodations for her and the two teen-age sons who accompanied her, and sent the party on to New York.[1]

In New York the press discovered Princess Fatima Sultana; someone must have tipped off the reporters, for she was too inexperienced to do it herself. And she was what the reporters called "a natural." Having never met the press before, she had not prepared a set of stereotyped reactions, like a movie star, or a politician; she said whatever she thought and felt.

In appearance she was, to the New York reading public, an eccentric. A stout, middle-aged woman, she wore in her nostril, in the Indian fashion, a large sapphire that was one of her ancestor's purloined jewels. The rest of her costume was described by reporters as "Indian above and Western below." One newspaper said, "She wore a coat gown of a striped silk like a man's shirting and with a turnover collar with a four-in-hand tie of old rose. She was enveloped as usual in a veil, this time a pale blue. A pink rosette adorned her glossy tresses as well as her gold hair ornaments. She had pink silver lace on her costume in unexpected directions, and wore a golden chain with its gold Mohammedan sacred writings. She ended up with black stockings and a good pair of Oxford shoes, her patent leather slippers with the gilt buckles being under the table."

One Afghan party was more Afghans than the New York press had ever seen. Two Afghan parties were so rare that anyone with an instinct for the press reaction, in its attack on what it called "the lighter side of the news," could have predicted that in the news stories the Princess Fatima Sultana and the official Mission headed by Wali would be connected, and that the Princess would make Afghanistan seem the unreal storybook land that the British wished it to remain.

Wali was asked if he knew Princess Fatima Sultana. Although everyone in Kabul knew who she was, Wali's first reaction was to cast off this exile who had nothing to do with his purpose. He said that he did not know her.

Princess Fatima Sultana was asked if she knew Wali. She said that their grandfathers were brothers. Informed that he had denied knowing her, she responded with indignation. And he had said that he did not know of her diamond. She and her sons smiled at one another and remarked there was nothing more to be said, adding, "Even the nomads know of this jewel."

The headline in the New York *Times* of July 13, that Wali had hoped would tell of Amanullah's aspirations for Afghanistan, said instead, "Two Royal Afghans Are Not Acquainted."

The press had taken the precaution of asking the British about the Princess. Yes, they said, she was a real princess. In fact, she carried letters from various officials of the Punjab attesting her authenticity. The Mission? Well, the British had no information about this Mission. The Princess was received by the Mayor of New York, John F. Hylan, and she wore her Dar-i-Nur diamond on a chain around her neck, and told reporters that she was hoping to sell it.

The Mission, on the other hand, appeared a bit suspicious. It was not verified by the British who knew everything in that part of the world, and it spoke unchivalrously of a lady. It was not half so interesting as the Princess; its members wore no "picturesque costumes."

An interview with Wali, conducted by the New York *Times* with Faiz Mohammed as interpreter, went:

"Questioned about Afghan home life and whether the Amir had the usual four wives, to which a noble Afghan is entitled, the envoy looked out the window smiling. 'His Excellency says,' interpreted the ready chancellor, 'that the Amir has but one wife and is not in favor of polygamy.'

" 'Were you surprised at the skirts of American women when you arrived in this country?'

" 'We have been in Paris,' said the chancellor, and his answer seemed final enough to end the subject.

"Speaking through his interpreter the Ambassador said, 'I have come to America and to European countries especially to declare the independence of Afghanistan and to inform the President of the accession of the new Amir, and to announce his policies. I am going to Washington for the purpose of establishing relations between the United States and my country.' "

For the tall buildings, the dangerous rush of traffic, the unmannerly haste of people during business hours, all the other liabilities of American life, Europe had been preparing the Afghan Mission. But not for ridicule.

Yet they would not have accomplished their ultimate goal, the presentation of letters to the President and Secretary of State, had it not been for the Princess Fatima Sultana and for a set of circumstances that made the United States Government ridiculous far beyond anyone's imagining.

The Princess Fatima Sultana was doomed by Kismet to be used for other people's purposes. She had an affinity for scoundrels. One minor scoundrel in her life was a man calling himself Zerdecheno, who attached himself to her and was described in some of the news stories surrounding her as "the Crown Prince of Egypt." No one ever knew who he was. He made overtures to various Americans about entering into business arrangements, on the basis of his promising future as the Crown Prince of various Mideastern localities, Kurdistan being sometimes mentioned. A few of these people wrote to the State Department about him and were told to consult the Almanach de Gotha; one got the information that the Crown Prince of Egypt at that time was named Farouk and was one year old.

One of the great scoundrels of the day read the news story about the Princess' reception by the Mayor of New York. This man's legal name was Stephen Jacob Weinberg but he called himself usually Stanley Clifford Weyman,[2] or used other names when he pushed into illustrious circles pretending to be someone else simply for the joy of pretending. A few years earlier he had called himself Lieutenant Royal St. Cyr of the French Navy and attended a dinner in Washington given by the Vice-President of the United States. The previous year he had embarrassed the U.S. Navy by being the dinner guest several times, under another name, of the Commander-in-Chief of the Atlantic Fleet. Five years later, he would pose as the personal physician of the movie star Pola Negri at the funeral of her lover, the screen idol Rudolph Valentino, and would not be prosecuted because Miss Negri would say he was the best doctor she ever had.

In his modest apartment in Brooklyn, New York, Weyman read of the Princess Fatima Sultana and decided to present her to the President of the United States. This ambition may have been enlarged by his reading that the Mission of Wali wished to be presented to the President. Weyman had been trying for years to present someone to some President or the other.

He appointed himself Rodney S. Wyman, State Department Naval Liaison Officer, took the subway train to the Waldorf-Astoria Hotel, and introduced himself to the Princess, who was staying there. He said, to her delight, that he had been delegated to escort her to Washington. Then he called the Third Assistant Secretary of State, Robert Woods Bliss, to announce that he would make arrangements direct with the White House to present the Princess. Bliss, deducing that this caller was operating on orders from higher-up, agreed.

No one was ever to question why a naval attaché should concern himself with a country that had no coastline.

The British were, of course, anxious that Afghanistan should make no alliance with America. They were perturbed that machine guns destined for the Sinn Fein Rebellion in Ireland, bought in America, had been seized by U.S. Customs under regulations prohibiting arms from being exported for use against friendly powers. H.M.G. considered telling the Americans that arms sent to Afghanistan might end up in the hands of frontier tribesmen shooting at the British. But they limited themselves to the letter to the U.S. Ambassador in Paris speaking of Britain's sphere of influence.

So the memo written on July 9 by the Department of Near-Eastern Affairs, U.S. Department of State, to the Secretary of State, Charles Evans Hughes, said, "This Mission [Afghanistan] had already left for the U.S. when we received the first telegram announcing its departure . . . I should, if there had been time, have suggested telegraphing discouraging its departure; however, they are now on their way. It would seem to me in view of the attitude taken by the British Embassy in Paris, which I presume voices the sentiments of the Foreign Office, that we should receive them and act in as perfunctory a manner as possible. You may think it necessary to receive them, as may the President also, but I trust it will not be necessary to take up the President's or your valuable time with this Mission. We have to my knowledge no particular interest in Afghanistan and in view of the British attitude toward the object of this Mission, it would seem to me that we might accede to their desires and pay as little attention to the Mission as we can with propriety do."

Then someone in the State Department read the Treaty of Rawalpindi, with its accompanying letter giving Afghanistan complete independence. "This statement would scarcely coincide with the statement referred to in my former memorandum from the British Ambassador to France."

That was on July 13. On July 14 the same department received a memorandum concerning the Princess Fatima Sultana. "The Department has not been notified by any diplomatic or consular office that the Princess intended to visit the United States. She arrived as a private individual and has not stated in her telegram whether she had letters of recommendation or credentials of any kind. The attached clippings from some of yesterday's New York papers would indicate that her relations are not cordial with the Afghan Mission which arrived here on Tuesday. The New York *Evening Post* states that the Princess left Afghanistan 16 years ago and has since been living under British protection in India. This may explain the absence of cordiality between the parties, as the Afghans are now anxious to assert their full independence. In a memo [the Department of Near-Eastern Affairs] expressed the opinion that there was no need for the President or the Secretary to receive the Mission. If the Mission is not received, there appears to be no necessity for the Princess to be received. Moreover, unpleasant feeling may be created between the Mission and the Princess if the latter is received while the former is not.

"If, on the other hand, it should be deemed advisable to receive the Mission, the importance of its being received might be somewhat diminished should the Princess also be received. Such a course, if it should meet with the Secretary's approval, would probably please the British."

A new angle was presented on the following day by the Office of the Foreign Trade Adviser of the State Department. "It seems rather presumptuous for the British Ambassador at Paris to discourage any proceeding . . . I consider it even more important for American interests to obtain at once such concessions as may be desirable. I, therefore, believe that it would be well to extend to the Mission our proper courtesies."

A compromise was handily available to the State Department with the presence of the Princess, who was not only asking to be received but regally confident that she would be. Weinberg-Weyman-Wyman had a flair for handling such things. Hughes's advice to President Harding was: "In view of British relations I think it would be well to receive her in case the Mission is received, but not until after the Mission is received."

The Princess was offered a choice of dates, and chose the earliest. When the State Department discovered that she had been scheduled ahead of the Mission, it suggested a change, but Secretary Hughes, having had enough of the matter, let it stand.

On July 20, Hughes spoke with Wali and his Mission and received courteously a letter from his counterpart in Kabul, Mahmud Tarzi. He reported to President Harding:

"They are here merely as a special mission to press the request for the establishment of diplomatic relations. Now that Great Britain has relinquished her protectorate, we cannot have any relations with Afghanistan except directly . . . There is still some sensitiveness (with Great Britain) as to the making of any special agreements with Afghanistan, and I understand there was some feeling created by the fact that Italy entered into such an agreement. I think the special ambassador has a letter from the Amir addressed to you which he is desirous to deliver; this letter, I understand, is to the same effect as the one delivered to me and involves no committal on your part if received."

President Harding received the Mission and the letter. He replied to Amanullah, consoling him on the loss of Amir Habibullah, discoursing on the great interest which Americans had always felt in Afghanistan, and stating that an American Legation could be established in Kabul only by a vote of Congress, which was not likely to vote for it in that session.

The Mission's meeting with the President was almost unnoticed by the press, but when Princess Fatima Sultana was received, the Washington *Post* described in detail her outfit of deep pink satin embroidered in gold and black, her nose sapphire, the famous diamond, and the gifts she had brought for the President and Mrs. Harding. Senator Medill McCormick of Illinois showed the party around the Capitol. Princess Sultana was consistently described as Afghan, and as the only woman of her family not to veil her face. In the interviews, the Princess revealed herself as a woman of intelligence and charm, and the officials who met her were impressed. The Washington *Evening Star* printed a photograph of the Princess, her sons, and "Lt. Rodney Wyman."

The Mission sailed away, complaining bitterly of its treatment in America, where now, more than before, Afghanistan was a land from a musical comedy.

But the Mission would never know, and the public would not know for forty-six years, the story that was just beginning with Princess Fatima Sultana. The self-designated "naval attaché" Wyman fell out with her. In September he wired Robert Woods Bliss at the State Department: "Princess Fatima Sultana absolutely penniless . . . unprincipled in her dealings with me and in general is associating with fake crown prince recently exposed by New York *World* . . . Sons immoral and becoming recognized characters . . . She is surrounded by numerous pseudo-advisors . . . Indians studying at Columbia who agitate against British Government." And the Princess wrote that Wyman, "who was sent by the State Department to help me," had "behaved in a very objectionable manner." She wondered what happened to various gifts she had sent by him to Mrs. Harding.

Three days later the Princess wrote that she had given Wyman six hundred dollars to handle for her, which he spent on the trip to Washington, that he had failed to pay the Washington hotel bill, although she had given him the money, that he was evading contact with her.

Then the State Department discovered that it had entertained an impostor and eventually what a famous impostor he was. A special agent, R. C. Bannerman, tracked Wyman down at his home in Brooklyn, under his real name of Weinberg, and retrieved three tablecloths sent by Princess Fatima Sultana to Mrs. Harding. In April 1922 the spurious Wyman was convicted of illegally wearing a naval officer's uniform in his Afghan escapade and sentenced to two years in a Federal Penitentiary.

But in March 1922, Princess Fatima Sultana was writing again to the Secretary of State: "I had upon my arrival in this country, aside from certain funds which I deemed ample for my personal needs, a 45-carat diamond of great historic and intrinsic value. I had been led to believe that I could find a ready sale for my diamond here; the very lowest estimate of its value would be about $100,000 . . . I now find myself without means and with my diamond in the hands of the Sheriff of New York attached in satisfaction of a debt of $2,000."

The Princess had been a victim, but as often happens when victims prove an embarrassment, she was being treated as if she were a culprit. The Americans and the British were both eager to get her out of the country. In January, Bliss had written a memo: "Mr. Chilton, Counselor of the British Embassy, called this morning and informed me that his government was going to undertake to repatriate the Princess Fatima Sultana and her sons to India . . . There is a boat . . . from New York direct to Bombay leaving March 25; his government is desirous, however, of having the Princess leave New York as soon as possible and it may, therefore, send her to India without delay by way of San Francisco, or via Europe with a transfer at some Mediterranean port.

"He said he understood the older son was intriguing to obtain control of his mother's remaining jewelry in order to pawn it, that the Consul-General of Great Britain in New York is now looking after the Princess and her affairs . . . I told Mr. Chilton that the situation regarding Princess Fatima had reached a crisis and that . . . I was contemplating making a recommendation that she be deported to England, inasmuch as I am informed that she is traveling on an English passport. I explained again somewhat fully that her financial situation was difficult in the extreme; that she was now being sued for $2,000 by a man in New York who had loaned her $2,000, with her diamond as security, and that in all probability he would win his case as he had a perfectly clear claim.

"Mr. Chilton said that he had recently received instructions to the effect that the British Government would no longer interest herself in caring for Afghans in China, and that he supposed it was for that reason that no reply had been made to his telegram [to London].

"I pointed out that as far as we knew, this woman, being a bearer of a British passport, was a subject of Great Britain; that we wished to avoid any unpleasant incidents regarding her stay in the U.S., and that it was a most awkward situation as we had no means of caring for her and her family. I further said that she was helpless and the situation pitiable, and that I really thought the British authorities should look after her, especially as she, when entering this country at San Francisco, was taken in charge by the British Consul-General, hotel accommodations being provided; she was then sent on to New York, and since then the British Consul in New York has refused to aid her in any way or give her counsel, other than that she had better sell her diamond and pay her debts with the proceeds."

The Government of India was asked to pay for the return of the Princess or to request Afghanistan to do so. Arrangements were made for her return on a boat sailing in mid-March.

The Princess politely refused to leave. Her diamond was sold at auction for $5,500, but she did not even get all of that, for U.S. Customs claimed duty of $1,400 in addition to the judgments filed against her. The issue in this claim was whether she had brought the diamond to America especially for sale or as part of her personal wardrobe, and the press statements about her wish to sell the diamond worked against her. She engaged a lawyer who claimed that the State Department agent, Bannerman, had advised her to pay the duty, promising reimbursement which never came; the lawyer did not succeed in getting back the $1,400. A year later the Afghan Consul in Calcutta inquired about the sale of the diamond, and was given the name of the buyer, John R. Keim, and the price. And another year later another Afghan Mission was in New York with the less spectacular goal of selling lapis lazuli. It encountered Princess Fatima Sultana, as luckless as any caravan that has been robbed in the desert, still in America. On President Harding's death, she wrote a note of condolence to Mrs. Harding, who wanted to acknowledge this courtesy but could discover no address.

The publicity that had embarrassed the Afghan Mission had also destroyed the Princess Fatima Sultana.*

In June the British had hoped that another month would see the Russians out of Afghanistan entirely. Instead, in July a new Russian Minister arrived, a former naval officer of the Tsar named Raskolnikov, a good-looking man only slightly older than thirty. He brought, along with a forceful personality, a consignment of gold that had been promised under the treaty. He brought also a pretty wife[3] in her early twenties whose bright blue eyes in a round, rosy face, framed by a bonnet frothy with feathers, aroused as much admiration as she drove through the Kabul streets in her Mercedes roadster as Mme. Bravin's veil-wreathed face had caused in that less sophisticated day only a year and a half earlier. Mme. Larissa Raskolnikova had spent very little time in her native Russia, for her father had been such a dedicated revolutionary that for most of his life he had been in exile. Exiled revolutionaries, having not much else to do, develop the art of talking, and Mme. Raskolnikova enchanted the Afghans with her conversation, which was more varied than they were accustomed to hearing from women, especially combined with youth and blue eyes. On the subject of Communism she was far more of a firebrand than her husband; but she had other topics, and at one Foreign Office dinner captivated Mahmud Tarzi with her dissertation on the works of William Shakespeare. In private she fascinated Amanullah and Souraya by performing Russian dances for them.[4]

At the Foreign Office banquet where Suritz was bade farewell and Raskolnikov welcomed, Tarzi made a speech ending, "If the relations of the two states have taken definite shape, it is due to the efforts of Mr. Suritz." As Abdul Hadi, just back from Bokhara, said, "Long live the Russo-Afghan alliance!" the no-longer-favored Dobbs was still asking Tarzi for the facts.

Water, that scarcest of commodities in Afghanistan, was scarcer than ever that year. Almost every afternoon a dust storm blew up, compelling the men to hold the ends of their turbans across their mouths and close their eyes. Although the apricot crop was magnificent, and the nomads who hired out as day laborers every summer were busy gathering in the golden fruit, there was very little wheat, and sheep had died

* In the documents made available to me at the India Office Library there was nothing about the Afghan Mission's visit to the U.S.A., although its activities elsewhere were recorded.

in great numbers on the Eastern frontier. This year Afghanistan would have to eat more of the products from India for which she exchanged her dried fruits.

The prospect of hunger was a situation the British could exploit. "We have a powerful weapon in the closing of the passes," had been said by the British during the Rawalpindi conference. Now Dobbs contemplated closing the passes between the two countries, and not alone against traders.

"The [nomads] ordinarily begin to move down about the end of September or the middle of October; and in a year like the present of severe drought on the Afghan side of the frontier, they are likely to be driven down earlier than usual by want of food grains, fodder, and water. Plans should be put into operation, therefore, by September.

"We should certainly, I think, do all in our power to prevent the immigration by the issue of notices. For once the concentrated torrents of men, women and children, camels and donkeys, begin to pour down through the passes, it will be a dangerous and pitiable task to stop them. The Amir will probably himself be anxious to prevent the immigration, if a breakdown of negotiations takes place; for he will not wish to risk the seizure during the cold weather by the British of all the camels on which he depends for the transport of rations for his troops. But the Afghan authorities have a very loose hold over the [nomad] tribes; and the pressure of famine might be so great that their orders might be disregarded . . .

"We must face the possibility . . . that the issue of notices may not stop the immigration, the impulse to which will be so unusually strong this year. In that case force will be needed. The [nomads] come down in well-armed bands sometimes thousands strong, prepared to fight their way through Wazirs and other enemies. They change their routes at short notice and if they were to hear that the Gumal was blocked, the principal forces might stream through the Zhob and Loralai or even through the Pishin passes. A good intelligence system should be devised to secure early news of the main currents of immigration and small bodies of troops will have to be ready to go to points at which the traffic can be held up.

"Similar steps will have to be considered for the stopping of the usual cold weather immigration of Afghan labor. The distributaries of the Sind Canal (and possibly also of the Punjab canals) are cleared of silt every winter by Afghan laborers, who earn immense sums by this work

. . . They are also employed every winter on road-making all along the frontier. A large part of their earnings passes either legitimately or illegitimately into the pockets of Afghan officials, or is devoted to the payment of land revenue. For the petty Afghan cultivator consumes most of his grain or produce himself, and pays his revenue out of the earnings of those members of his family who can work abroad.

"If it becomes necessary to teach Afghanistan by peaceful blockade how she depends for her life-blood upon India, the lesson should evidently be taught as thoroughly and drastically as possible. And this year of famine is an admirable one for the purpose."

G. of I. thought Dobbs too optimistic and rejected this suggestion: "The forces of nature which prompt this yearly move to the plains of India are so overwhelming that no manifestoes issued against it, whether by Amir or the G. of I., are likely to be effective in checking it materially, in a year of scarcity like this more especially . . . In view of Afghanistan's traditional dread of being entrapped by us into war when [nomads] with their camels are as hostages in our hands, it is open to speculation whether they would be more perturbed at the prospect of the passes being closed before [nomad] migration or after."

All through that hot July they negotiated. Amnesty for the tribes was again an important matter. "Otherwise [Afghanistan] would be accused of selling the independence of the Mahsuds," wrote Dobbs. "This decision would, I believe, be chiefly due to the way in which Nadir's personal credit is involved, although full weight must be given to the Afghan perception that the only fighting force they can ever raise against us is that of our own frontier tribes, and that, if Afghanistan now abandons them to their fate, she can never again count upon their assistance, and they may even turn against her."

On July 31, Dobbs sent a mailbag to India, containing among other letters an account of his protest on the banquet for the Russians. The bag disappeared. The man carrying it said it had been swept away by a flood. The British investigated and found no sign of a flood.

Then the Foreign Office told the story that the bag had been sent, contrary to regulations, by an unarmed mounted soldier who was also carrying a telephone for repair. Along the road he was set upon by five men who robbed him and tied him to a tree. He told them that he was carrying only letters and a telephone box, but the robbers said they knew the bag contained notes and the box contained gold. After a time the soldier wriggled free and went on foot to Jalalabad, where, to save

himself, he told the flood story. It was August 6 before the Foreign
Office heard about the loss. Then a Foreign Office man summoned the
head men of the district and gave them three days in which to bring in
the bag or the guilty parties. They brought both, as a result of the government's promising amnesty if the bag was undamaged.

Dobbs did not believe a word of this story. His theory was that Amanullah had ordered the post stolen in order to see his report on the Russian banquet and its aftermath. He refused to send for the restored
mailbag but insisted on an official bringing it to his house.

One cause of Dobbs's suspicion was a certain passage in an Afghan
note, which bore a strong resemblance to a passage in one of the G. of
I.'s confidential notes to him. However, Denys Bray, Foreign Secretary
of India, reassured him, "Our own description of Afghan policy was
extracted (if I remember right, almost verbatim) from certain Afghan
material that had come into our hands."

So the mailbag theft, by whomever, was accepted with equanimity by
the British, who turned it to their advantage. "Our best plan seems
to be to make the utmost possible capital out of the incident and use
it both for delay and in order to give time for development of the new
world factors, and for display of righteous indignation and exercise of
pressure to get our terms accepted. I suggest it would be useful." G. of
I. told H.M.G., "if you were to send me a telegram couched in a form
suitable to be shown by Dobbs to Afghans, expatiating on the enormity
and barbarity of the incident from the Foreign Office point of view and
taking most serious view of consequences which as a civilized country
may be forced upon us."

The "new world factors" included new fighting between the Turks
and the Greeks, in which the Turks seemed to be losing, to the consternation of the Afghans, and a great famine in Russia which, linked with
rebellion among the newly conquered people in Asia, appeared to be
diminishing Russia's power. Dobbs considered himself justified at an
early August meeting in giving the Afghans "very plain speaking almost
amounting to rudeness."

Wali's mission, in the meantime, had sailed from New York directly
for England, landing at Liverpool on August 8.

This was the first Afghan Mission to step onto English soil since
Amanullah's grandfather Abdur Rahman had sent Nasrullah to ask that
Afghanistan be allowed to deal directly with H.M.G. rather than

through India. The same old issue was at stake now. "Afghans are exceedingly touchy on this point," warned Dobbs, "and think it involves inferior treatment in their case as compared to other states such as Siam."

One day after his arrival Wali was protesting that he did not wish to see the Secretary of State for India; he would see only the Foreign Minister himself.

Haste in making an appointment was necessary, because King George was leaving London for Balmoral in two days, and Lord Curzon was in Paris. Wali refused to deal with the Secretary of State for India, Edwin S. Montagu, although he might have had an appointment that day, and Montagu would have taken him to King George.

"My instructions were precise and absolute," Wali said. "I dare not deviate from them in the slightest, even if I have to leave London as a result." Wali kept talking about the indignity felt by Afghanistan at having to deal with the Government of India while Japan, China, Persia dealt with the British Government. "After the Treaty of Rawalpindi, Afghanistan considered she had severed all connection with India."

"It is for the very purpose of connecting with the British Foreign Office that we have come here," members of the Mission kept saying, and, "If we thought that the invitation to visit England from Washington had emanated from the India Office, we would not have accepted it."

The Mission finally arrived at the Foreign Office on August 17 with an appointment to see Lord Curzon. Before the interview Curzon called their escort, Stewart Pears, to his inner office and pointed out that Wali was in no way entitled to be called "His Exellency."

A few moments later Pears introduced the Mission and its chief was called simply, "General Mohammed Wali Khan."

"I am particularly glad to meet Afghans again as I am one of the very few Englishmen who has ever traveled in Afghanistan," began Lord Curzon. He asked after certain officials of his day, and was interested to learn that Ghulam Siddiq was the son of General Ghulam Haidar who had escorted him to Amir Abdur Rahman.

The personal reminiscence abated, Wali held out the letter he had brought from Tarzi to the Foreign Ministry of Great Britain. Curzon accepted this from his hand and placed it unopened on the table.

Wali presented a second envelope inscribed in Persian "Copy of a letter from H.M. the Amir." He said this held an English translation of Amir Amanullah's letter to King George. Curzon accepted this also and laid it beside the first, unopened.

"I am at a loss to understand the delay that has occurred in the negotiations at Kabul," said Lord Curzon, who went on to mention "the constantly changing attitude of the Afghan officials."

Wali began an explanation of the Afghan viewpoint, finally appealing to Curzon for his good offices in view of Curzon's exceptional knowledge of Afghan affairs.

Curzon interrupted him, "I have no wish to discuss the matters now under negotiation at Kabul which are matters lying within the province of the Secretary of State for India."

"As you asked the reasons for the delay in negotiations," said Wali, "I was attempting to furnish an explanation of these reasons."

"Until the treaty is concluded," said Curzon, "it is possible to receive General Mohammed Wali as a distinguished Afghan visitor only and not as a representative of Afghanistan."

After a few informal remarks, the Afghans took their leave. Curzon handed both letters, unopened, to Pears and told him to deliver them to the India Office.

Wali wired home a report of this meeting.

That letter that Dobbs received on August 28 from Mohammed Tarzi said, "If Dobbs thinks that Afghanistan will ignore her independence for any kind of friendship or enmity, he is making a great mistake. We might show that Dobbs is negotiating at Kabul on behalf of His Majesty the King of England and not on behalf of the Government of India. Therefore my government looks upon these unfriendly actions with the greatest displeasure and strong feeling and wish to make it understood in a loud voice that Afghanistan does not desire relations with any state or tribe which should be wholly or partially against its complete independence and liberty."

The expression by which Tarzi addressed Dobbs in the course of this letter was "Janab-i-Dobb," or "Your Excellency Dobbs." This seemingly inoffensive phrase, Dobbs told his government, was insulting in the way it was used. "According to Asiatic ideas, mention of the addressee's name in body of letter instead of 'that kind friend' is very rude." What Dobbs did not explain is that his name "Dobb" in Arabic means "bear," and the bear ranked along with the pig as the animal to which one Afghan boy would compare another when tempers burst out past the boiling point. It was a prelude to a fist fight. Dobbs knew that Tarzi knew that he knew this.

The Afghan Mission remained in London till September 17, when it left for the European continent to retrace some of its steps with more hope of success. Pears, the only person to say good-bye at Victoria Station, reported, "Wali and his staff have been uniformly courteous throughout their visit although their disappointment has been acute. Wali is a thoroughly well-bred and amiable man of some character and, I should say, some principle."

Ghulam Siddiq already had left for Kabul to carry firsthand news of the Mission's experiences in its travels through the world.

Amanullah ratified in August the Treaty with Russia. He accepted 500,000 rubles from Raskolnikov, the first payment of the annual subsidy of 1,000,000. Two airplanes were delivered, but they came in crates, not flying under their own power, and ironically they were old planes which Russia had once received from Great Britain.

Afghanistan's encounters with Lord Curzon convinced Amanullah that he could no longer flee to the security of close ties with Britain without losing his adult status in the world of nations. To the British, he realized, an exclusive treaty with Afghanistan was the apron-string by which a mother binds a child to herself. He had learned a universal truth, "You can't go home again." Independence compelled him to balance his two powerful neighbors against one another. So he ratified with Russia.

The Russians themselves handed the British in London a copy of the treaty, through the Chairman of their Trade Delegation to Britain, L. B. Krassin. There the British read the same clauses to which they had been objecting all along, which granted Russia consulates in Kandahar and Ghazni.

"For us to linger here longer with the Afghans in the mood displayed by these letters seems useless and will expose British representatives to indignity," complained Dobbs.

Amanullah had expected to climax two years of Afghan independence with a great Jeshyn in Paghman, the suburb which Kabulis often described lovingly as "a green place," for its contrast with the harsh crags of Kabul. At Paghman the summer was cooler, although the hills, so close that one felt almost that an outstretched hand might touch one, sometimes closed out the breezes.

Amanullah had built there a terraced garden of twenty acres, bringing in turf to make grassy steps and keeping it alive with large water hoses. Statues cast from Russian molds were ready to be placed. Always this had been a favorite retreat for the well-to-do. Now it became a point of pride for Amanullah's ministers to have homes there; these were built of wood, unlike the mud and stone of the typical Afghan house. Their architecture was Swiss chalet, with little balconies to overlook the hills and the fruit trees; on the interior walls colored stenciling conformed to the European style of the 1920s while not being at all un-Afghan.

Amanullah put up a five-winged recreation hall that he called "The Star," set atop a hill so that one could look through big windows in all directions. This was for the public in general, who were Amanullah's first concern. For them he was erecting a wooden bandstand in European style and was having a hotel built. In Kabul only a few months earlier the only road lighted by electricity had been that which ran from the main entrance of the Arg past the War Memorial to the main Kabul River bridge. Now the lights ran down the road between the Idgah Mosque and the Chaman Huzuri, the great field where celebrations were usually held. Both roads were bordered with young Persian elms and beds of grass and flowers. At night, when the lights illuminated only the roads and not the mountains behind them covered with mud houses, it was like being on a boulevard in Europe.

Amanullah had expected to bring numbers of people to Kabul from Kandahar, Ghazni, Herat and Turkestan, to have them walk along the lighted Kabul boulevards and beneath the arch in Paghman, celebrating independence, and sitting on his terraces to hear music from his bandstand. It would have been a political demonstration of the first magnitude and Amanullah expected to have his international relations settled by then.

Cholera, one of the dreads of Central Asia, bore down on Kabul and canceled his plans. It was so severe that the sale of fruit in Kabul was forbidden and the fruit-growers, who had been rejoicing in a crop better than expected in this year of drought, were stricken.

On the day when Amanullah would have opened his celebration, he was in Paghman with only a few advisers. Dobbs called on him there, finding him sitting outside an open pavilion in the shade of a walnut tree looking down on a small tank which spouted three fountains. With him were Mahmud Tarzi and Abdul Hadi. Genially Amanullah told humorous stories of the elaborate precautions his Turkish doctors made him take against cholera infection when he visited Kabul. As he chatted, he sniffed aromatic salts, one of the precautions.

This pleasant visit took place the day before the Mission's visit in London with Lord Curzon, and was to be one of the last pleasant episodes with the British for a while.

"The chaotic conditions to which the Amir's impulses have reduced negotiations" was Dobbs's description of the following weeks. Tarzi sent him word that he would make no decision until Ghulam Siddiq arrived from London with his report. "I feel his report is likely to have an unfavorable effect," said Dobbs.

But Tarzi was suddenly not an important man any longer. Amanullah stopped needing his father-in-law, the old mentor, who had been urging him to play both sides for all advantages he could get. "Nadir and his faction have become prominent, and temporarily persuaded Amir that Tarzi has backed the wrong horse," wired Dobbs. "At all costs Nadir party wishes to discredit Tarzi plan of equal advantages from both sides and to put all their money on one side or the other."

Jemal Pasha left for Bokhara to try to negotiate return of Afghan merchandise taken in the overthrow of Bokhara. This deprived Tarzi of an ally. It also enabled Nadir to point to the perfidy of the Russians, for the goods never were returned, and trade across the border was forbidden although in fact there was much smuggling of karakul skins, carpets and silks into Afghanistan and tea, indigo, and dyes into Russia. The presence of the former Amir of Bokhara in Kabul reminded Amanullah constantly of his fate at Russian hands. The former Amir had asked the British to help him regain his kingdom and had been politely declined. Amanullah asked his reinstatement of the Bolsheviks, who declined not quite so politely on the grounds that he had accepted aid from the British.

In Turkey, however, Moslem affairs were progressing. Kemal's troops routed the Greeks in one of the longest pitched battles of history, lasting twenty-three days. Kemal took a title that Amanullah likewise had given himself: Ghazi.

In this confusion Amanullah told Dobbs that he would deal directly with him, asking him to take care that no news of their discussions reached Tarzi's ears. If Dobbs had to write, he should address his letter to the Foreign Minister but see that it reached the Amir.

Ghulam Siddiq, on board the ship headed home, talked with a traveling companion who was a British agent. He said that Wali had instructed him to urge the speedy conclusion of a treaty with Great Britain as it was only in alliance with Britain that Afghanistan could take a strong place in the world of affairs. The men of his Mission were disillusioned over Russia and lucky not to have come to terms with the Soviets as they would have been swallowed up by the Bolsheviks. "Russia is in a dreadful state and the people little better than savages." They had been surprised at the settled conditions in England, although the country that most impressed them was Germany.

Home in Kabul, this young man who hated the British advised Amanullah that his treaty should be made with the British.

All alone, without any adviser or witness, Amanullah met with Dobbs on September 28 and offered to repudiate his treaty with Russia as soon as arms from Britain could be transported to the Turkestan frontier. He would return the money, munitions and airplanes already received from Russia and would take no more. But the British must state clearly the minimum help they would give in case of a war with Russia and among other things he wanted twelve airplanes of which four must be delivered at once in order to give confidence to his people.

"I think that is impossible," said Dobbs.

"I have thought the matter out very carefully and can yield on none of these points," Amanullah replied. "Unfortunately, I cannot show the thoughts of my heart by X rays. You must trust me."

Because of the treatment of his Mission in London, he said, if Russia did not break off negotiations, he would be at liberty to make a fresh treaty with her for exchange of diplomats and commercial products.

Amanullah was offering almost exactly what Britain had wanted three months earlier, but now he had publicly ratified his Russian treaty and accepted money. The game which Amanullah was trying to play was far more intricate than that of his grandfather and father, who had been completely in the hands of one power. In Dobbs, in England, he saw a father figure with whom he would be safe, and he naïvely thought that he could return to the old sheltered days when Afghanistan was England's child. He was learning now once more that you can't go home again. He could not dismount from the tiger.

"Afghan provocation to Russia would be flagrant," Dobbs warned his superiors, and he would not let Amanullah regress from adulthood.

To the east, India was still restless for its independence, and the restless ones were Moslems rather than Hindus. "For this reason," said Dobbs, "at present I regret rupture more than any previous time . . . Rupture with Afghanistan might have serious consequences."

They argued for more than a month. Once Amanullah gave an appointment to the British Indian delegate, Sir Shams Shah, and kept him waiting in the reception room while he argued loudly on the telephone with the Governor of Jalalabad, Nadir's brother Hashim, and finally when he called in Sir Shams Shah, told him he had just defeated Hashim in an argument. He talked about many irrelevant matters, holding forth about the mullahs, accusing them of having perverted religion for their own ends. He spoke a great deal about Islam being for the good of mankind and not for the mullahs. But he kept coming back to the question that troubled him. "Why," he kept asking, "are the British delaying?"

The British were offering many things, but no subsidy in cash. That had been offered only for the expulsion of the Russians, which they no longer sought. Dobbs and his Mission were preparing to leave.

Amanullah summoned Dobbs to his palace for several meetings before his departure. Only Mahmud Sami was with him. Lately, as Amanullah had ceased to rely on Tarzi, he had been bringing into discussions another older man to whom he had once deferred, Mahmud Sami, his teacher in military school. Broken from his mother's dominance, he still craved a strong father.

Neuralgia was troubling the twenty-nine-year-old Amir; he was not sleeping well. At one meeting he sipped tea and nibbled dry toast, saying he had eaten nothing else that day. There were several meetings with only Mahmud Sami, Dobbs and his colleague Pipon. Amanullah kept maintaining that Tarzi knew nothing of what was going on. Dobbs doubted this.

On November 15 at 10:45 P.M., after eleven hours of discussion in a single day, Amanullah said he was satisfied with the treaty. He started clapping. Mahmud Sami, Dobbs and Pipon clapped too.

The following day Mahmud Sami was to take a new bride. Amanullah gave a dinner at the Arg which proclaimed the ascendancy of Mahmud Sami, for Amanullah put on the uniform of a cadet which he had worn while studying under the General. Amanullah had selected the bride, whom Mahmud Sami had never seen. He kept telling the General that his bride was lame in one leg and quite bald. Each time the bridegroom received the news with mock despair, pressing his hand to his forehead, moaning loudly, raising his eyes to the heavens.

Many considered Mahmud Sami a very vulgar man. For Tarzi, who concurred in this opinion, it was painful to watch the man who had usurped his position; he looked glum throughout the party and seemed embarrassed whenever he spoke to the British delegates. Unfortunately his dinner partner was Mahmud Sami. Nadir disliked the bridegroom also, but he and his brothers were present and chatted with Dobbs. Two of their family had been very ill, and the physician of the British Mission had cured them. Nadir was effusively grateful.

Finally Amanullah took before his Council the draft treaty which provided for the exchange of legations and consulates, the right for Afganistan to import arms and munitions through India so long as her intentions were friendly, exchange of information on the tribes, and, in a separate letter from Tarzi, the denial to Russia of consulates in Kandahar and Ghazni in return for customs concessions. There was no subsidy.

The Council asked about Arnawai, which the British had wanted. Amanullah said that he had been forced to agree to the return of Arnawai, a frontier area taken from Chitral by Amir Abdur Rahman, in return for the cession of Torkham in the Khyber Pass.

The Council exploded in fury. Some of its members told Amanullah that he had given way on every point.

On November 22 Dobbs and Tarzi signed the treaty, with Tarzi making a speech in which he demonstrated his old skill at satire by congratulating the Amir on being able to carry through the treaty without the help of the Foreign Office. Dobbs, in his speech, said that evacuation of Arnawai and Torkham would be carried out simultaneously. The Afghan delegates said they knew nothing about this. They began an argument, but Dobbs said that the Amir had personally waived his claim to Arnawai, and everyone went outside to be photographed.

Tarzi insisted that he and Dobbs should talk with Amanullah. Amanullah denied that he had made the agreement to which Dobbs referred. "I informed my Council that no objection would be raised to Afghanistan's keeping Arnawai. On that understanding I obtained their consent to the whole treaty."

Amanullah was forgoing one advantage he might have used: his absolute rule. His father and grandfather would not have troubled to obtain anyone's consent.

Amanullah took Dobbs aside and described his difficulties with the Council. "I simply must declare our treaty null and void, although I have already published it to my people, unless you can give me a letter assuring that the question of Arnawai will not be pressed."

Later Mahmud Sami spoke on Amanullah's behalf to Dobbs, who told him, "If the Amir goes back now on an understanding clearly arrived at . . . all hope of the British Government helping him in his large policy, which he has set his heart on, will vanish . . . Moreover, Afghanistan will be publicly disgraced on the occasion of its first entry into world politics."

A farewell dinner was held for the Mission. Tarzi began to praise the treaty, and the Minister of Commerce, the outspoken Ghulam Mohammed, interrupted to say he would prefer war to such a treaty. Dobbs pretended that he thought this was a joke. He suspected Tarzi's remarks, anyway; he thought it likely that Tarzi would enjoy wrecking the treaty in order to show Amanullah that he could not get along without him.

"On the other hand, the whole Nadir band of brothers is going out of the way to show pleasure in the treaty and is sending of late frequent private communications," wrote Dobbs. "It is impossible for me to stay more than a few days longer, as there are already signs of a desire to speed the parting guest, and we shall expose ourself to humiliation by obviously outstaying our welcome. The hitch that has occurred is so far known only to a narrow circle and those outside it are unable to understand delayed departure." The British Mission had been in Kabul for nearly eleven months.

Amanullah's trouble with his throat, diagnosed as severe quinsy, had become so bad that the doctors decided to operate.

While he was having this operation, the whole question of Arnawai was taken from his hands by some of the tribesmen about whose welfare he had been so solicitous. These were Wazirs who had taken refuge from the British and asked for land in Afghanistan; only a month earlier he had settled them in a colony at Shahjui. At this moment two hundred and fifty of those men chose to raid across the frontier into British territory at Barshor, killing two British officers and forty soldiers, burning a fort and some villages, and then going home satisfied with themselves.

Against the advice of his doctor Amanullah received Dobbs, sitting in an armchair, in a dressing gown with his throat bandaged. In a feeble voice he said that he had been working night and day to show the world that Afghanistan was an honorable and civilized state, and this incident had almost made him despair of his people and officials who could not recognize where their interests lay. He yielded Arnawai on condition that no fortifications be erected there. "I will keep my kingly word and remain steadfast in pursuit of my policy of friendship with Great Britain."

During an interval when Dobbs left the room while Amanullah made a telephone call, Mahmud Sami begged him to promise a gift of a first-class airplane on which Amanullah's heart was set. He said that he and Nadir suspected the Russian gift planes were ancient duds furbished up for presentation but quite useless. Dobbs said this had never been considered. The atmosphere remained, as he described it, "indescribably friendly."

The Mission said farewell at a durbar to which Amanullah wore a robe adorned with the stars of two Afghan orders. He gave Dobbs a gold cup and saucer and a gold watch and chain. There was an hour of pleasant conversation. Then Amanullah suddenly arose and, speaking from notes, said, "There is no doubt that these relations are not friendly but of mere acquaintance and neighborhood . . . You should never think that Afghanistan will be your friend when the rest of the Islamic world is vexed with you, or that the inhabitants or the Government of Afghanistan will sit carelessly by when you take measures against our sacred Islamic observances. In India also you should closely observe your actions."

H.M.G. was outraged: "The Amir will have to learn that independent sovereigns do not criticize the domestic policy of other independent sovereigns." And: "It is a humiliating experience, due, I think, largely to recent handling of Afghan affairs, that we should have to listen to a lecture from the Amir of Afghanistan on how our Government should behave in India."

The treaty was ratified in Kabul on February 6, 1922.

The Afghans wanted Dobbs for their first British Minister, but Dobbs declined with a diplomatic statement that was also true: he needed a long vacation. Stewart Pears was nominated but Amanullah said, "Conversations and reports of Ghulam Siddiq have caused Pears's name to be so inextricably connected in my mind and in my people's minds with the diplomatic rebuff that Wali sustained in London, although I much regret it, I must ask for suggestion of another name."

"Pears was only carrying out orders," explained Dobbs.

"And on no account will I accept a representative of Indian nationality. That would look as if I were still under India," Amanullah said vehemently.

Several British officials were considered. The one who wanted the job most seemed the least qualified, being only a Colonel, but finally Francis Humphrys, former Political Agent of the Khyber, became Great Britain's first Minister to Afghanistan. He crossed the frontier on February 25, 1922; he and his staff were to hold a party on the occasion of being in Kabul for six weeks without being murdered.[5]

Abdul Hadi was Amanullah's appointment as Afghan Minister to London. The British recalled him as blunt and antagonistic. Curzon was tempted to reject him in revenge for the rejection of Pears. But the warning of Lord Reading prevailed, "In regard to Afghanistan there is no counsel of perfection." The two independent states exchanged ministers.

CHAPTER 11

1923

Amanullah needed to remind the frontier tribes of his authority and to tell them what he had in mind for Afghanistan. Wearing the turban, short cloak and pointed shoes of the Afridi, he gathered four thousand Afridis and Mohmands in the garden surrounding his father's tomb in Jalalabad on February 26, 1923. "Solemn promises should be made in solemn places."

He spoke in Pushtu, the language of the tribes of the eastern frontier, which he had been studying for several months and used now with grace. Pushtu, he said, should be the tongue of all Afghanistan, as a call to tribal unity replacing the courtly Persian. Pushtu was a complicated language that had accumulated, like Afghanistan itself, from fragments of all the many languages that had been spoken in those mountains.

Amanullah solemnly pledged himself to oppose with every means in his power any enemy of their religion and independence. A memorial had been newly erected to those who fell fighting at Dakka in the War of Independence. He tossed a few flowers on this, and some of the tribesmen did also.

"Allah-o-Akbar! Allah-o-Akbar!" cried Amanullah. It was the Afghan war cry. "My brothers, although I wish to shake hands with you all individually, time does not permit, and it will inconvenience you as well. Hence instead I look upon your tribal banners and kiss them. I leave you all unto God now."

In the palace the next day he gathered a selected jirga of about eight hundred delegates from the Shinwari, Afridi, Mohmand, Khugiani, Ghilzai and Ningrahar Wazir tribes. It included four spies that the

British had specially summoned from India to supplement the work of their regular spies; they paid this extra attention because they feared this meeting, since it was attended by tribesmen from British territory, might have repercussions on their own affairs; they were particularly curious what attention Amanullah might pay to one tribesman, who was a fugitive from the charge of murdering a British officer and his wife.

Amanullah announced that he was going to read the Nizamnamas, the code of laws that he had promulgated for Afghanistan more than a year earlier, setting out the first formal secular constitution. His purpose, he said, was to enable them to know in the future whether or not his officials were carrying out his instructions.

For three hours Amanullah read and explained.

A British tribesman with a history of rebellion interrupted to ask for aid to his fellow tribesmen.

"That has nothing to do with the Nizamnamas," Amanullah said, and continued reading.

One of the Hazrats interrupted him next, the brother of the distinguished Hazrat Sahib of Chaharbagh.

"The Nizamnamas appear to be injurious to the progress of Islamic teaching," said the Hazrat. Amanullah went on reading.

When he had finished, he asked for criticism of himself or his officials.

The first to speak was Badshah Gul, one of the three sons, all with the same name, of the famous Haji of Turangzai, who had been stirring up tribes against the British for eight years, burning the houses of men who cooperated too happily with the conquerors. Badshah Gul suggested that tribal jirgas should be interviewed as often as possible. Amanullah agreed this would be good.

Someone proposed that, as Afghanistan was now an independent country, its ruler should take the title of Sultan. Amanullah replied that he preferred the title of Amir Ghazi, but if his people wished him to be a sultan, he would be.

An Afridi asked that arrangements be made for the education of Afridi children. Amanullah promised to see to it.

At the end of this meeting, even some of the tribesmen who had been bitter toward Amanullah, for his failure to secure amnesty from the British, were feeling fondness for this new kind of ruler. He had made himself one of them in appearance, although his careful mustache and the glow in his eyes were far too worldly to make him seem a true Afridi. He had spoken cordially and with sympathy, giving them all the dignity of their manhood.

Nadir distributed allowances the following day, and some of the warmness disappeared, since the allowances were lower than in the past. One band showed its displeasure by kidnapping an Afghan official, whom they later released. Amanullah attended some of the small conferences of tribesmen that day, wearing his Afridi clothes; only one mullah recognized him.

Next Amanullah went on a tour of the frontier. The British were building a railroad through the Khyber, a masterful engineering feat since the track kept disappearing into the mountain and then reappearing and then darting into a mountainside again. This was the railroad they would have preferred to take into Afghanistan, before the War of Independence; it had been begun only after Amanullah showed he would not "walk in the shoes of his father."

Most of the work on the railroad was being done by coolies, men who ranked low on both sides of the frontier, because their function was to pick up things and carry them for more fortunate people. Amanullah crossed the dividing line into British territory, wearing again his Afridi dress. He went up to these coolies and introduced himself; he shook their hands and embraced them. Never had they been treated so graciously by any person of distinction. Some wept.

It disturbed the British authorities that the Amir of Afghanistan ignored protocol to such a degree as to walk unannounced and unauthorized onto their soil, but they had learned that Amanullah liked to upset them.

A few mornings later he got into his car at 3:30 A.M., and with Queen Souraya, Inayatullah, and his secretary drove through to Kabul without stopping, to the consternation of his officials who did not expect him. He liked to throw them off balance, too.

It was significant that the Nizamnamas were interrupted at Jalalabad by two attitudes, indifference and hostility. Through them the average Afghan was presented with many rights, some similar to those for which men in the Western world had defied kings and fought. Legally, an Afghan had no rights at all up to that moment.

Some of the provisions were:

"Torturing with racks, etc., is absolutely forbidden and only such punishments as are mentioned in the Civil and Military Penal Codes can be inflicted."

"Houses and residential quarters of all Afghan subjects are immune from aggression, and no one on behalf of government, or of the public, can make a forcible entry into a house without permission, except under orders issued according to the law."

"Personal freedom of the subjects is immune from all sorts of interference and aggression, and no one can be put in confinement or inflicted with punishment except under Islamic and administrative laws. Slavery is absolutely forbidden in Afghanistan and no one may employ any man or woman as a slave."

"Afghan subjects can jointly or individually submit a complaint to a government department against a mamur or other officer, if they find him behaving contrary to Islamic Law and government regulations. But if the Government pay no attention to their complaints they should approach their superior officers and on failing to obtain justice from them, a petition can be submitted directly to the King."

Such laws and their enforcement led the Afghan Minister in Rome, Sardar Azimullah, in a conversation at the British Embassy to recall regretfully "the days of Abdur Rahman, when twenty and thirty men were executed each morning and then criminals were loaded with chains on their necks, arms, bodies and legs, whereas now only a single chain on the leg is employed, which is manifestly inadequate."

In the bazaars also there were whispers that lamented the days of Abdur Rahman. Crime was more prevalent. Some saw in this the effect of Amanullah's reducing the size of the Army—"These are the days of the Pen, not of the Sword," he said in public and in private—so that many men were set loose unemployed. But to most, and to all those working for law enforcement, this was the fruit of the new regulations, which imposed less cruel penalties and therefore made a criminal less fearful.

Raids and burglaries increased. The old enmity between Hazaras and Ghilzais over grazing lands in the Hazarajat flared up. The most daring bazaar robbery of all time took place in Kabul; on the road to Paghman one of the Amir's own guard was murdered.

And in Kandahar there was more than simple robbery when a young woman organized her robber band into an entire government in competition with the government of her province. She called herself "Dakhtar-i-Ishakzai" or "Daughter of Ishakzai" and sent word to the Governor that her jurisdiction began, and his ended, at a point four miles north of Kandahar. She established departments of war, revenue, justice, and public safety, and raided with such success that soon she was the chieftain of fifty young men and, following the instinct of the Queens of Egypt who used to put on beards to signify the masculine nature of power, changed her name to Sardar Badshah, or Prince King. The Kandahar authorities eventually decided to arrest her, but there was a conflict between the police and the military as to who should perform this act. The military officer of that district declared flatly, "It is no part of a soldier's duty to send an expedition after a woman."

Finally a policeman was persuaded to disguise himself, pretend to join her band, and then kill the lady known as Prince King. Her brother, captured, was tied to a gun and the gun fired, sending him into bits. This was a form of punishment that the British originated during the Indian Mutiny of 1857, and which was so popular with Amanullah's predecessors that whenever the gun was heard in Kabul at any time other than noon, it was known that some offender had ended his career. The gun could not have sounded a deterrent to others, however, for this lady had begun her own career only after her husband had been executed in precisely the same manner.

The Governor in Kandahar, facing a police strike, pleaded the limitations imposed on him by Amanullah's Nizamnamas, that he could not punish for a crime unless there were eyewitnesses, whereas in the old days he had wide scope for his judgment. This did not satisfy the traders who had complained. If the situation did not improve, they told the Governor, they would appeal to the Amir.

And people did appeal to Amanullah, and he did suspend his own leniency at least once. In the diary of the British Military Attaché the episode was described:

"About three months ago a treasure chest containing something over a lakh of rupees on its way to the commissariat department in Khost disappeared at a stage on the Logar Road.

"Fifteen suspects arrived in chains in Kabul. The detective in charge soon afterwards reported that the necessity of observing the Nizamnamas made all progress with the case impossible. The Amir then gave a reluctant assent to the employment of older methods. The one selected by the detectives, the Bazaar says, included a free application of boiling mustard oil, with the result that the whole treasure was at once discovered in a garden belonging to the nephew of the commandant of police."

The mullahs detested the Nizamnamas. No man had any business

making laws, they thought; that belonged to God. The laws set down
by the Prophet had been assembled in a form known as Shariat, and the
mullahs interpreted this. The new code abridged their powers.

In the palace at Jalalabad, on the evening of the same day that Amanullah announced to the tribes that he would oppose any enemy of their
religion, he watched a dramatic entertainment attended by many officials and the diplomatic corps, who were charged one hundred rupees
for their seats for the benefit of charity and education.

Written by the Turkish legal authority Bedri Bey, who had also com-
piled the Nizamnamas, the plot concerned the moral downfall of a
Moslem Prince who divorced his Moslem wives to marry a European
actress. The role of the actress was taken by the wife of a German government employee; the Moslem wives kept purdah.

In one scene a mullah was depicted as a monster of corruption, obviously as prototype of the depravity of all mullahs. Amanullah enjoyed
it thoroughly and showed his pleasure. So did most of the audience.
The Persian Minister privately expressed his surprise that such a presentation, which would have created an uproar in Tehran, should have
been shown in Afghanistan, which was supposed to be a hotbed of
fanaticism.

The mullahs preached from their pulpits the next Friday against plays
which showed religion in disrespect. Finally Amanullah found some
mullahs so openly hostile to all his policies that he put several under
arrest. These had two chief complaints: the education of the young by
Europeans who might fatally flaw their religious natures, and the tendency to give undue freedom to women. While visiting the power station
at Jabal-ul-Seraj, Amanullah met with the leading mullahs of Kohistan,
the area north of Kabul, and tried to reassure them about his policy,
saying that he was not trying to destroy Islam.

From his point of view, Amanullah was keeping his pledge to the
tribes to do nothing against their religion. To him, these mullahs were
not religion.

One June day in 1923 anonymous notices, exactly alike, appeared
on the walls of a Kabul mosque and of a popular teahouse. They accused
Amanullah of a breach of faith with his people, recounted the promises
that he had made at the time of his accession and his declaration of
war against Britain, and pointed out that these were still unfulfilled.
There were vague but ominous threats against him.

"The common people can only think of their temporary and apparent advantages," Mahmud Tarzi had written. "They do not understand their permanent and real advantages."

Amanullah's son by his first marriage, Hidayatullah, age twelve, was the youngest of thirty-five Afghan boys who were studying at the Lycée Michelet in Paris. When the official photograph was taken, he leaned back and stretched out his legs in the characteristic pose of a bored man of the world.

The President of France, Aristide Briand, assured the British Embassy in Paris that he had given instructions for no special notice to be taken by the press. Yet a Paris newspaper described their special porkless meals, their ablutions and their prayers.

"What surprised them most? The swiftness. They could not understand that people should hurry. The secretary who accompanied them, Zulficar Khan, explained that at home the more noble one is, the more suitable it is to be slow. Vivacity denotes a plebeian origin . . . What impressed them most was the Tomb of Napoleon."[1]

By mid-1922 there were forty-eight Afghan students in Germany, thirty-six in France, six in Italy. Tarzi's son Abdul Wahab was studying at Oxford University at a cost to his father of £600 yearly, an enormous sum by the standard even of a rich Afghan. This helped explain why only one Afghan student was in England. In Germany £400 would serve for four years, and besides, the Germans had none of the snobbishness toward Orientals to which the British admitted. The Afghans, many of whom looked no different from the British, might have avoided this snobbery, but they had heard stories from Indians, whose brown skins gave them away.

The look of Kabul was changing. Always there had been many sorts of faces in the crowds that passed through with the seasons or the flow of trade, but they had been Asiatic faces. Now there was a leavening of Anglo-Saxon noses and chins, of blond hair and blue eyes, of open Teutonic stares as well as the withdrawn Asian glance, of the skin that gets red under the sun, of vivid Gallic and Mediterranean features. Afghanistan was still secluded to the extent that no foreigner might enter without official permission, and the British had not yet removed their famous sign from the Khyber forbidding entry into Afghanistan. But Amanullah was granting admittance to diplomats with whom he was exchanging courtesies, and to Europeans whose skills he hoped to use.

Wali's Mission, after its disappointment in London, had returned to the Continent and, now that the British were resigned to a future of sharing Afghanistan with other nations, succeeded in making treaties with France, Italy and Germany. On Wali's return in June 1922 to replace Tarzi as Foreign Minister, he was accompanied by the Italian Minister and his postponed commercial mission. Soon there came a French Mission whose object was to uncover archaeological treasures which it would share with Afghanistan, half and half. Germany established a mission. Then there were also legations from Persia and Turkey; to these two Moslem neighbors Amanullah gave buildings that had been his own residences as a prince.

All the jealousies and intrigues of Europe came with these people. The British Minister, Humphrys, described the foreign colonies in Kabul as "divided into two camps, one the Russian and Turkish, the other British and French, with the Italian and German ministers anxious to keep on good terms with both and the Persian Minister too timid to express himself at all." Every Sunday the Italian Legation held an "at home"; alternate Sundays were for the British and French, while those in-between were known as "Red Sundays."

The French were alarmed by the influx of the Germans, whom they had been fighting so recently, and suspected them of plotting a new "Move to the East." The British also suspected the Germans, who were coming in particularly large numbers because, in the defeated state of their country, they were willing to work cheaply. One party of German craftsmen, passing through India en route to Kabul, was kept under surveillance lest it make contact with Bolshevik intriguers. The British suspected also their friends, the French, having heard that the French teachers and archaeologists were paid a salary by their own government to augment what they received from the Afghans, and wondering if these were part of the Alliance Israélite, which had the aim of advancing French interests in the Middle East.

Amanullah insisted that he wished no nationality to have preeminence in Afghanistan; like his forefathers, he remembered that India had become a vassal when it let foreigners purchase land and manage things. Any preference he showed was to countries so remote from his own borders that any designs they might have would not be territorial. The Italians, Germans and French all remarked at one time or other that the Afghans might do better being educated by the British and Russians, on whom their futures depended, but Amanullah never heard them.

Francis Humphrys, the new Minister of Britain, had a face that added to the ethnic interest of Kabul, typically British and ruggedly handsome. But it was seldom seen in the bazaars, although he did not obey the order of Lord Curzon, that he must never appear in public without six Bengal lancers riding before him and six riding after.

There were no Englishmen in Afghanistan except the staff of the Legation, and even when the American journalist and lecturer Lowell Thomas[2] went to Kabul in the summer of 1922, to make the first movie travelogue of that country, Amanullah refused entry to an English assistant so Thomas had to replace him with an American. The British kept to themselves more than other nationalities; even when their wives joined them, the wives might almost have been in purdah for all the impact they made on Kabul's social life. The British did not need to mingle to know what was going on. They had underlings who could blend with the milieu far better than they and serve their purposes well, for they controlled all India.

The noisy group in Kabul, as it turned out, were the German colony. One problem which foreigners brought into Afghanistan was the alcoholic beverage. In obedience to the teachings of the Prophet, wine and beer and whiskey were forbidden in the country, but special arrangements were made for the foreign legations to import their own. In one year the British listed their requirements as ten thousand bottles. The Germans' first importation was thirty thousand bottles of beer, which had to be strictly accounted for, lest they sell any to Afghans. The French and British marveled at this quantity and wondered if some of the bottles might contain explosives. From a psychological standpoint, they did. The day after the first bottles were opened, the Indian butler at the German Legation remarked to the butler at the British Legation: "I have seen sahibs drunk in India but sahibs who get drunk and fight with bottles in the street at two in the morning are a new thing which I have not seen until now."

The day came when the British in Kabul received a query from their colleagues in the North-West Frontier Province: "It would be interesting to know from official sources whether the report is true that some of the Russian women who have arrived are young, well educated in languages, and desirous of giving lessons to the wives and daughters of Kabul sardars." The reply from the British Military Attaché was:

"Some months ago, certain Russian personnel in Kabul were getting into trouble with Afghan women.

"About twelve unattached women were, therefore, imported for them. These . . . live in the house which bulk of the Russians occupy near the Legation . . . As certain of them have started going to Afghan houses, the purpose of their importation—that is, to prevent trouble between Russians and Afghans—is unlikely to be fulfilled.

"The above is with reference to the request . . . asking whether certain of the Russian new arrivals are young and have been brought for the purpose of educating Afghans."

In the clash of two societies professions also suffered. So successfully had the Prophet Mohammed convinced his followers of the evil of worshipping idols that they could not be changed quickly. The French archaeologists were ecstatic to uncover near Jalalabad a stupa from Buddhist days containing many statues of Buddha, large and small. Putting a guard on the excavation, they sent for the French Minister to come and behold their treasure, but before he could arrive, followers of the late fanatic Mullah of Hadda, at whose shrine Nadir had put flags during his 1920 jirga, had come and, with a sense of doing their Moslem duty, destroyed all the Buddhas. Amanullah was furious and ordered an investigation, but the disheartened French did no more excavating in that spot for a while. An Italian expert in the raising of silkworms was baffled by the death rate among his worms. He found the cause in Ramzan, the Moslem month in which no food or drink must pass the lips between sunrise and sunset; the silkworms were being treated as Moslems.

Yet matters progressed. By the middle of 1923 the French School in Kabul, called the Amaniah, had 320 pupils, and the headmaster reported that the parents' attitude was surprisingly free from obstructiveness. The students learned both Persian and French, and tiny Afghans sang in class, "Il pleut, il pleut, bergère."

"These children will stop their professors in the school corridor to ask the meaning of a word they have just heard. Their curiosity is insatiable," said the French professor. "When they go back to their homes, these students have not a book, not a table to write at, not a single sheet of paper. A notebook is all they have. All Moslem schools, where respect for the teacher has an almost religious nature, have a rather military aspect, which suits the Afghan character."[3]

To counteract the influence of the French, another school was opened with German instructors, and soon small Afghans were singing, "Rös-lein, Röslein, Röslein rot, Röslein in dem Heiden."

Queen Souraya presided often over the awarding of prizes at the girls' school in Kabul. She invited wives of foreign diplomats, who were generally less interested in the students than in the chic Western outfits which Souraya and the princesses wore.

Souraya, who had suffered from a lisp, was becoming a poised public speaker, although she spoke only to women's groups. She had difficulty pronouncing the letter "r." Her father Mahmud Tarzi wrote her speeches. Amanullah, hearing her rehearse, sent one speech back to Tarzi with the offer of a gold coin for every "r" that he could change into an "l." He paid off promptly.

Kandaharis were dismayed at education for women; they saw in it the threat to remove their own womenfolk forcibly and send them to Kabul for education.

Doctors came from Europe, including some women doctors: Russian, Italian, French and German. A German woman doctor, Fraulein Lehn, joined with the wife of an Italian doctor, Signora Tanzi, in establishing a hospital for women.

German engineers were trying to make a good road between Kabul and Jalalabad, cutting through a gorge that was one of the most pre-cipitous and rocky in the world. They privately estimated the job would take fifty years at the present pace. Amanullah had the dream of a good road all the way from Mazar-i-Sharif to the Indian border, putting Kabul within eleven or twelve days of Moscow by connecting with the Russian railroad. He departed from his anti-British policy to ask the British to find the skilled labor for him in India; negotiations failed be-cause, as Humphrys reported, "a Royal Engineers' subaltern deputed to Afghanistan expects more than the official pay of an Afghan Commander-in-Chief." Telephones spread out; the wireless was built, and the Afghan students who had been studying wireless in Karachi returned to operate it. Amanullah refused to let any foreign legation have its own wireless operator or set, so that all messages had to go through the Afghans. Diplomatic messages were in code, anyway. The British objected to Amanullah's using telegraph wire, which had been given to him under the Kabul treaty, to establish wireless com-munication with Russia. "I cannot make you a promise," said Amanul-lah, "as this would savor of dictation in a matter in which I am a free agent, but, speaking as man to man, I will tell you that the material will be used between Torkham and Kabul and Kabul and Kandahar." One piece of wire was much like another, anyway.

Amanullah would have liked recognition and help from that colossus of Western technology who was too far away to be a threat: the United States. In 1922 he entertained for three months a representative of the U.S. State Department, Cornelius Van H. Engert, who had been assigned to look Afghanistan over. Engert's secret report pointed out the faults of the country, such as the lack of protection for foreigners under law, but in his summation he advised recognition by the United States and not only for her own commercial interest. "Conditions through this vast area have become little short of alarming," wrote Engert. "Great Britain alone has during the past five years been near enough to exercise any influence in favor of law and order, but possibly owing to an extra couple of blunders and possibly owing to her sudden determination to retrench, she has lost a great deal of her former prestige aside from the fact that her geographical proximity had always caused her motives to be regarded with more or less suspicion by the natives. If, therefore, we were to enter the field, we would not only be able to reap the material benefits that our position as the only politically absolutely disinterested power would give us, but we could lend our moral support to all those elements which are trying to prevent chaos in a part of the world that is otherwise certain to prove very troublesome in the near future."

Engert's report sat in the files of the U.S. State Department. Nothing was done.[4]

The matches made in Afghanistan were far superior to those made in India and Russia, according to the prejudiced opinion of the British.

The cloth woven in Afghanistan was also admirable; the British credited this to the fine British looms.

As with most developing countries, it was cheaper for Afghanistan to import many things rather than to make her own, but to remain forever a supplier of raw materials and a purchaser of manufactured articles would not have been an entry into the world of nations. And in the case of the cloth, Amanullah had a dramatic resource for assuring that the domestic product would have preference.

In the bazaar he saw a Hindu shopkeeper sitting cross-legged on the platform that was his store, surrounded by folded lengths of silk that would be wound into turbans. Amanullah stopped and examined the turbans. They had come from India.

While the bewildered merchant protested, Amanullah piled the cloths all into the center of the passageway. Then he struck one of the Kabuli matches and made a bonfire.

Turning to the merchant, he gave him a sum of money which would replace twice the number of turbans he had burnt, but he warned the merchant to sell only Afghan merchandise.

The men of Amanullah's family and court tended to disdain the local fabrics, when made up by Afghan tailors. The ladies' dressmakers in Kabul produced dresses that compared favorably with the Paris couture, but between the work of men's tailors in Kabul and those of Savile Row, London, the difference was greater.

Amanullah began to carry around a small pair of manicure scissors. When he observed that a relative or courtier was wearing cloth made outside Afghanistan, he moved in close, and surreptitiously brought out his little scissors, and before the man knew, the offending suit was unwearable.

The Persian Minister was once the victim of this maneuver. It was only one more source of annoyance for him; Amanullah had decreed in his Nizamnamas a limit to the amount of money that might be paid for a bride. Fathers had been in the habit of valuing their daughters too highly; even fifty years later the Kabul newspapers would be complaining of young couples being beggared by a father's demands. The daughter of the Persian Minister became engaged to a young Persian employed by the Afghan Government, and a price of nine thousand rupees agreed on; then the Minister was told he could receive only thirty rupees. The wedding was postponed until both parties could get back to Persia and out of Amanullah's reach.

Amanullah ordered the bootmakers of Kabul to cease making the sort of shoes known as "loop-the-loop," the typically Persian boat-shaped shoes whose pointed toes culminated in long strips of leather curving up and round. Henceforth, he said, only European styles should be made. This was logical in a country where the climate was closer to the European than to that of India, where the Punjabi shoes originated, but Amanullah's aim was psychological. He also increased the import duty on used clothing. The Afghans, who had been going about for years in the castoffs of other nations, were to be pushed into making clothes for themselves.

Dar-ul-Aman, a city, was to be the physical monument of Amanullah.

Other Amirs had thought of building a new city, for it was apparent even in Abdur Rahman's time that Kabul was outgrowing its boundaries.

To the east of Kabul, just beyond the crowded clusters of mud houses, Amanullah started to give reality to a new city. Its center was to be a Parliament building in the European style, reached by a long, wide boulevard framed in trees. When this boulevard was being made, Amanullah went out among the workmen, seized a shovel, and did some of the work himself. After that, the road progressed faster, and when finished it led dramatically between rows of shade trees to a spot where an impressive building would raise itself.

On the exterior of the Parliament were to be several stone plaques. Amanullah's coat of arms was on some of these; he had adopted an "Amani hat" in emulation of the "Pahlevi cap" which the new Shah of Persia, Riza Shah Pahlevi, the Army sergeant who had made himself ruler, was putting on Persian heads. The Amani hat was a straight-visored helmet like that worn by many Central European armies, with a stiff brush arising from the front. On the official arms it was underscored by crossed swords.

That represented Amanullah's present, but he planned also to put on two other plaques two designs which depicted the future of Afghanistan: an airplane and a locomotive engine.

Beyond the Parliament building Amanullah cut off the top of a hill, as a site for a palace that would stand surrounded by mountains. Both German and French architects worked on the plans, with curved porches at each end. The design in stone for the entrance porch had a motif of lions, but the lions that emerged were typical of Amanullah's personality rather than symbols of ferocity. They had a whimsical, friendly air; an Afghan prince would later compare them to the comedian Danny Kaye, and they would remind some of the lion in The Wizard of Oz. Certainly no one would look at these lions and think of war.

On the lower level, beside the terrace where the royal family expected to relax, were designs of gentler animals, a cat and a monkey.

Amanullah expected his ministers and courtiers to build themselves houses nearby, and several did. In his dedication speech Amanullah said that had he been a despot, he would have built a city fifty miles from Kabul instead of five miles, and forced them to establish there, whereas he was allowing them to pleasure themselves in regard to doing so. In order to carry materials from Kabul to the building sites, a railroad was built, the only railroad ever to exist in Afghanistan. It was not much more than a toy, like the train on the plaque on the building. On a very narrow gauge track ran several small open cars.

The unfinished buildings, throughout the years, advancing slowly toward completion, reminded Amanullah of his dream, reminded some other Afghans of all the money his dream was costing. When he made a speech comparing Dar-ul-Aman with Rome, the British maliciously said that it had something in common already in that it was not built in a day.

"The theory that regarded Afghanistan as a kind of appanage to India is no longer tenable," said H.M.G., "and there seems to be nothing left but to make the best of the new conditions."

The first Afghan Minister to Rome was Sher Ahmed, whose doubts about Amanullah had started with his accession.

"I returned from my three-year stay in Europe," he told a member of the British Legation in 1923, "very disheartened and pessimistic as to the possibilities of any real progress being made in the near future by Afghanistan.

"When I left Afghanistan, I had a sense of my own power and my own fitness to hold my own with the politicians and diplomats of Europe. After a short stay in Europe, I realized that I was nothing, that I lacked the education, the savoir-faire, and every other qualification necessary to compete on the same level with Europeans.

"So great is my sense of disappointment that I have refused to accept any government appointment in Afghanistan. I have no spirit left to tackle affairs which I feel to be futile. The Amir, who has not been abroad and is therefore quite incapable of realizing the backwardness of his country, is attempting to emulate the hare, when the pace of the tortoise is really more suitable. The Amir expects his country to advance a hundred miles a day, and thinks that progress can be attained by the mere giving of orders, instead of by the slow process of educating people and gradually opening up the country. I told the Amir that the project of erecting a city at Dar-ul-Aman must take years to materialize, if it ever materializes at all, and that it is wrong to sink money into unproductive bricks and mortar, which could be used to much better advantage in more productive ways."

From one country Afghanistan withdrew its representation. Bokhara, the Moslem Amirate toward which Afghanistan had such a brotherly feeling, was absorbed so completely into the Soviet Union that any pretense of its independence became a farce, and its deposed Amir removed his silver standard from the box of Bokhara soil in Kabul.

The moment of truth arrived on August 5, 1922. Its victim was Enver Pasha, the sophisticated nephew by marriage of Sultan Abdul Hamid of Turkey, who had entertained the Kaiser in Constantinople and had studied warfare in Germany. The Soviets thought he was their man; instead, he was as ardent a Moslem as any Afridi or Wazir fighting on the frontier in the hope of becoming a ghazi. The Soviets sent him to Bokhara to do their work. He turned against them and put himself at the head of those called the "Basmachis," a term originally meaning "bandit" but in that case meaning "die-hard," for these men refused to give up their ambition for a free Bokhara.

Secretly the Afghans again sent men and munitions to help against the Russians; Nadir directed their operations from a spot close to the Afghan-Russian frontier. Amanullah, much troubled, met privately with Francis Humphrys and asked Britain's aid for Bokhara. Britain, who had refused the Amir of Bokhara, refused the Amir of Afghanistan.

In the Bokhara village of Deh-i-nau, where he thought himself safe, Enver Pasha and his troops were surrounded on the morning of August 5 by Soviet cavalrymen, led to his hiding-place by the Soviet intelligence agent Georgei Agabekov, who would soon be in charge of Soviet intelligence in Afghanistan. Trying to escape from his headquarters, Enver called to thirty of his officers to fight a rear-guard action, holding high above his head a Koran to remind them of the Paradise that awaited ghazis. A Russian saber lobbed off his head and made him a shaheed; the Koran was taken to Russian intelligence headquarters.[5]

Enver's dream had been also one of the dreams of Amanullah: a union of the Moslem peoples of Central Asia. That saber stroke was fatal for Amanullah's plan as well as Enver's life. The Afghan Foreign Office found it expedient to publish a denial of any desire to interfere in the internal affairs of Bokhara.

This episode completed Amanullah's disillusionment with the Bolsheviks, whose revolution he had heralded, as many had done, as a new dawn of liberation. Now the Russians had two excuses for not ceding Panjdeh and for not giving all the material they had promised under the treaty: this Bokharan interference and their failure to get consulates in Kandahar and Ghazni, although they themselves had agreed with the British, in the interest of trade, not to press for the consulates.

"In public," wrote the British Minister in Kabul, "[Amanullah's] attitude toward Raskolnikov's pose of honied subservience has been unusually cold and sometimes brusque to the point of rudeness. On more than one occasion, the marked courtesy shown by His Majesty to this Legation seems to have been dictated mainly by a desire to annoy the Russian Minister. The refusal of permission to the latter to accompany his wife to Kandahar was also significant."

The British were not convinced that this hostility would continue, and protested to Russia about its activities in Afghanistan, in a note specifying Russian infiltration of the tribes with money, in an effort to get propaganda and arms into India. They would have liked to assure that the old affinity was not renewed.

When the Russians wanted to bring in a team of archaeologists, Amanullah said no; he did not want the British digging in remote places, either; he hesitated such a long time before admitting one of the world's great archaeologists, Sir Aurel Stein, that Sir Aurel, whose only offense was being British, had little more life left when he finally arrived. Any foreigner who wished to visit Bamiyan to see the giant Buddhas was admitted, but not the British.

Having brought the world to him, Amanullah was trying to keep it from overwhelming him.

Amanullah was having problems also with his own people. He had achieved an ironic position; at the same time that he was reducing the size of his army, he was being reviled for putting people into it.

"These are the days of the pen, not of the sword," Amanullah repeated in July at a religious observance in Kabul. "Therefore, send your sons to school. Our martial qualities are sufficient. It is education that we lack."

Every tribesman in Afghanistan would have agreed with him about the sufficiency of his martial qualities. Tribesmen were the first line of defense of his nation, and they knew it; in every conflict the victory had been won by the tribes.

"There are indications that the Afghan military authorities are now convinced that their true policy is to reduce the regular army far below the figure aimed at by Abdur Rahman, while borrowing from him the idea of a well-armed national levy to be embodied only when necessity arises," reported Humphrys. "To this end conscripts are to be passed in as large numbers and as short a time as possible."

"Hasht nafari" was the phrase for the policy of conscription. "One in eight" was its meaning, for a number equal to one eighth of the eligible young men was to be drafted. Amanullah did not invent this system; it had existed in Abdur Rahman's day. But under Amanullah it was being enforced with an energy never concentrated on it before. Those two words, "hasht nafari," were being spat out with hatred from one end of Afghanistan to the other.

No one was in the bazaar of Kandahar on November 27, 1923. On all the shops the shutters remained in place. Few men were in the streets, either. Most of Kandahar had crowded into the city's most sacred mosque declaring they would stay there until assured their young men would not be conscripted.

The Shinwaris and Khugianis, two of the most unruly of the Afghan frontier tribes, were cooperating for once and swore to uphold each other in resisting attempts to impose conscription on them. They told the authorities that, while ready to support the Amir with their own strength in time of war, they would not submit to compulsory service in time of peace.

They were offended by the suggestion that they, fine warriors, should need instruction in the thing at which they excelled, fighting.

"The application of the laws appears to be subject to gross abuses and a source of no small profit to those responsible," the British Minister noted. "The names of those to be summoned are supplied . . . and if reports are to be believed, these are in order of ability to pay the exemption fee. Postponement of calling up can be secured by bribery of officials . . . The payment of the exemption fee is supposed to secure exemption for a year . . . It is understood that the principle of compulsory military service has been expanded to one of universal national service in any capacity which may suit the state. The justification for impressing laborers for the construction of the new capital is that they are being trained in a service useful to the state. Physical unfitness is no protection—the conscription of a man blind in his right eye, and of another over forty-five years old can be vouched for—nor is the fact that a man is the sole support of his family always accepted as a reason for exemption in spite of provisions of the conscription law."

Amanullah kept urging honesty and fair play on his officials. Having never been tempted, himself, to be other than honest and fair, he thought that exhortation would suffice. But every change in the social order seemed to stir afresh the avarice of those far down along the administrative ladder. This was a beginning of an era of exceptional corruption in a country which took for granted a certain amount of corruption. Abdur Rahman had taken such steps as making his clerks sign an agreement that if they made an erasure in the accounts, their right hands would be cut off. Amanullah, having never been a poor exile like his grandfather, marveled at such steps. The pen, in his experience, was always honest.

The trouble in Kandahar began when the Governor tried to enforce a demand for twelve hundred men. By spontaneous agreement almost all Kandahar went into the mosque. The Governor sent messengers to them. The messengers were manhandled. The Governor made offers of postponement; these were ignored. The bakers inside the mosque were not baking bread. Soon the men outside, unable to buy their staple of diet, were rioting also. Life resumed in Kandahar only after an influential mullah, the Hazrat Sahib of Deh Khwaja, stood in the doorway of the mosque and promised exemption, taking a religious oath that, if the hasht nafari scheme were again proposed, he would join them in the mosque.

Later this Hazrat refused to receive an emissary from Amanullah, saying that he feared he intended to oppress God's creatures in Kandahar as he had done elsewhere.

Amanullah was expected to take a certain sum from the treasury each year as his salary for being Amir. The officials discovered that he had let several years pass without drawing anything. They asked him to take his pay. He sent word that he was too busy.

CHAPTER 12

February 26, 1923, to April 30, 1923

With the passing years the British Empire was deeper and deeper in trouble. Some historians would date from the year 1921 the beginning of its end.[1] In India there were problems both financial and political; neither Moslem nor Hindu would give any surcease from strident demands for independence.

Few men of the Empire were so wise as to realize that these were terminal problems. The public in England, confident that it still sat triumphantly on the seat of power, could not understand, for instance, why the great British Empire was not more assertive toward the insignificant country of Afghanistan. The public did not suspect the dread with which India contemplated even the chance of a war with Afghanistan, or of Afghans coming into India to aid its own malcontents.

One man who saw was the ignored Mr. Engert of the U.S. State Department, who would have speeded America's stepping into a vacuum in Central Asia being left by the British Empire. Another was the Prince of Wales, later King Edward VIII and the Duke of Windsor, whose visit to India in 1921 was boycotted by the Congress Party; he wrote to his hosts that by filling empty seats at his appearances with Boy Scouts, high school students, and other substitutes, they had made him look a "b.f." (bloody fool).[2]

In their weakness the British on the frontier used the easiest method of chastising the tribes for various offenses: bombing. Bombing became routine. After thus punishing from the air a party of Wazirs who seemed to threaten their outposts, they received this letter from a Wazir, Mullah Mustaqin:

"To God the Victorious, Omnipotent and Merciful we pray . . .

"In its great strength the British Government caused its airplanes to bomb the whole of the Wazir lashkar at its place of meeting, and also the district of Birmal. Men, women and children and the cattle of the poor Moslems fled. The women were disgraced on account of their coming out of purdah.

"It was not fitting that Government should have belittled its dignity and degraded its grandeur in the eyes of its helpless subjects. It has transpired that strength and tolerance are no longer qualities of Government, for when a drum is beaten for the gathering of a few men in Khorasan, Englishmen in India tremble.

"Government should have ignored this lashkar until it had fired on the posts of Government. Even then, the officials of Government could have heard the firing and wondered whether it was rain or only the crackling of a fire beneath a cooking pot."

Mullah Mustaqin's sentiments were endorsed by fifteen men of his tribe, all mullahs and maliks, who affixed their thumbprints.

"Strength and tolerance are no longer qualities of Government" was an observation far more discerning than many more literate men would make for many years. Weakness continued to impel the British to discipline recalcitrant tribes by bombing from the air. The Viceroy Lord Chelmsford had recorded his misgivings on the grounds both of sportsmanship and of the ill feeling that might be engendered.

At the jirga in Jalalabad where Amanullah dressed as an Afridi, in February of 1923, much of the conversation dealt with the bombs that had fallen on the tribes. Men compared notes. They discovered that many pregnant women, forced from the homes and fields, were impelled by haste to reveal themselves more freely than propriety required and had miscarried. There was a lament over an old man, a hafiz, who had committed the entire Koran to heart; one bomb burned him to death, robbing the old man of his life and the tribe of its Koran all at once.

What appeared to the British as just one additional weapon, a peculiarly convenient one, was to the tribes an innovation totally unforgivable, war against a civilian population.

With such new insecurity in their lives, with the sky no longer dependable for shelter, the tribes stirred toward their British masters. They still raided. But instead of the picturesque attacks on each other, they attacked more frequently the British, and as if in revenge for the action against their own families, they began more often to take their vengeance on British women.

"Towards the end of 1920 came the horrible affair when Colonel and Mrs. Foulkes were murdered in the dead of night in the center of Kohat cantonment. Colonel Foulkes was an officer of the Indian Medical Service noted both for the skill in his profession and his kindly nature and disposition." So wrote A. M. S. Elsmie in the London *Times* in 1923; he had commanded the Army forces in Kohat.

"The cold-blooded outrage, involving, as it did, the murder of an English lady, was of a nature quite different from anything which had occurred before in the long history of the frontier. A short time previously a lady had been carried off from Peshawar into tribal territory and subjected to treatment which cannot be described, but at all events murder had not been attempted."

"The new type of frontier villain that has arisen" and "a worse state of affairs than has ever been known before" were some of Elsmie's phrases.

How much did Amanullah have to do with this? The question aroused conflict between two intelligence agencies. His jirga at Jalalabad on February 26 was covered by the British Minister in Kabul, who sent the principal Indian employee of his Legation, and also by the Chief Commissioner of the North-West Frontier Province, whose own spies were always going back and forth.

The man whom the British, and most of his fellow tribesmen, considered guilty of the murder of Colonel Foulkes and his wife, had gone into Afghanistan, where the British law could not touch him. India had no treaty of extradition with Afghanistan, and as such treaties work both ways, did not want one. The social standards of the Afghan tribes were such that once an animal, running from a huntsman of noble birth, darted into the mud hut of a poor woman, and the woman, when the huntsman rode up with his retinue, proclaimed that it would violate the principle of asylum were she to surrender this pursued animal. Mirzali, the suspected murderer, was still in Afghanistan with his friends and relatives and the British suspected he would be bold enough to attend Amanullah's jirga. He was.

The spies differed in their accounts of how much honor Amanullah had paid Mirzali in the way of allowances and such rewards as royalty can bestow just by being in the vicinity. The North-West Frontier Province got the report that Mirzali was especially favored, which meant encouragement to his crime, they said, and an inspiration to others who might do likewise.

Not at all, said the British Minister Humphrys. At Amanullah's jirga Mirzali had been merely one among thousands, and Amanullah could not have rejected him completely without doing violence to his traditions. Later, when the crimes would increase, Humphrys would attribute them to other causes. One was the spate of road-building, on which the British and the Afghans had disagreed at Mussoorie as to whether it was civilizing; and one was the stepped-up pace of bombardment from the air.

Besides, continued Humphrys, Afghan wooing of British tribesmen was nothing new; British and Afghans had always competed for the loyalty of Afghan tribesmen, and there were many shrewd ones who accepted allowances from both sides. For a generation Amanullah's uncle Nasrullah, the fanatic who saw the British as infidels intending incalculable harm, had been the instrument of inciting hatred against them. Now they considered their chief enemy to be Nadir, aided by his brothers in the various provinces, and Humphrys remembered this whenever confronted socially or officially with Nadir and "his usual sermon on the mutual advantages of Anglo-Indian friendship." Humphrys knew that Nadir had actually asked two of their tribes to send twenty-five boys each to military school in Kabul, and said that his brother Hashim kept a constant stream of agents going between Jalalabad, where he was Governor, and Tirah in British territory, opposing the building of the railway in the Khyber Pass. Nasrullah had been a forthright adversary.

The competition and incitement were old, said Humphrys. The virulence of the crimes was new.

The British went on with plans for bombing the Tazi Khel, a subtribe so close to the border at Tochi that in the same families there were both Afghan and British subjects. "Tazi Khel will not be induced to come in for a settlement by a single visit of airplanes," wired the Political Agent at Tochi, "but will probably move to Khost [inside Afghanistan]. I think this will have an excellent effect since it will cause them considerable inconvenience and make it difficult for them to raid in Tochi. We might bomb them once again when they collect about the beginning of April to migrate, if they continue to give trouble."

By mistake the planes dropped bombs several miles inside Afghan territory and killed three Afghans who belonged to the Tazi Khel but who had moved in exactly the opposite direction from that forecast by the Political Agent; they had gone not toward Khost but, because of a disagreement with the authorities there, away from it.

"Mistake was due to occupants of encampment turning out and firing on airplanes," said G. of I. "There seems to be nothing for it but to tell Afghan Government the facts, frankly emphasizing such facts as tell in our favor."

The Government of India had a regular scale for reparations in such cases:

Man killed . . . 3,500 rupees (Kabuli)
Man permanently disabled, two limbs . . . 3,500
Man, loss of one limb . . . 1,750
Tribal sepoys at same rate.
Women at half rates throughout.
Man severely wounded . . . 500
One man and two women slightly wounded, for all three . . . 500
One man seriously wounded and treated in hospital till recovery . . . 150.
Camel . . . 300
Cow or bullock . . . 35
Sheep or goat . . . 18
Horse . . . 200
Donkey . . . 100
Cash equivalent of British machine gun or service rifle . . . 800

A joint commission of Afghans and British agreed on compensation to the Tazi Khel. G. of I. reported:

"For one man and one woman killed, one man permanently disabled, one man and one woman seriously wounded but not disabled, one man and one woman very slightly wounded, total 7 persons, and for 160 livestock killed . . . [we] work this out at 9,125 rupees (Kabuli) or 485 pounds. In addition, you may pay blood money for Sheikh Pir, which was excluded from findings as he was found to have been killed on British side of line. Resident suggests that this should not be paid unless heirs satisfy the Political Agent that he did not fire on airplanes. Livestock damaged: 2,454 rupees. Express to Afghan Government appreciation of ready spirit of cooperation displayed by Hakim of Khost. "Hope this will enable you to turn evil to good." And H.M.G. in its turn noted: "If a further display of generosity is made, it may well be that the incident will turn out something of a blessing in disguise."

For by the time the settlement was made in late May to the Tazi Khel, blood had been shed that the British found worth far more than £485.

On April 8, 1923, two majors of the Seaforth Highlanders, stationed at Landi Kotal in the Khyber, decided to take a walk before dinner along the Mullagori Road. Such a stroll would have been forbidden to them a few years earlier, but a long familiarity with tension breeds nonchalance, and Majors N. C. Orr and F. Anderson were doing only what others of their group had often done. The road, at any rate, had been decreed to be "civilized." Although there was one set of rules in the independent tribal area that began a few feet from the road, the road itself, according to British dictum, was in civilization, and any acts upon it were to be treated by the same laws as in England itself. Majors Orr and Anderson were insufficiently aware how close the two worlds were coming.

From the hills back of the road, past what the British called civilization, shots were fired. Both men were killed instantly, each with three bullet wounds. One of the murderers ran up and snatched a white pith helmet which had fallen onto the road. The spot where they died was three and a half miles past Landi Kotal Fort and not far from the Afghan border. Some Afghan Shinwaris heard firing and went in the direction of the sound. Twenty minutes later they found the bodies.

Earlier that day a man had passed on the road two Sangu Khel Shinwaris from Afghanistan, and the reputation of that particular clan in respect to its neighbors was such that he warned those whom he encountered later to be careful of their flocks.

"There are a good many Sangu Khel [Shinwaris] working on the Khyber Railway. They are in Peshawar," wired the Commissioner of the North-West Frontier Province. "I am taking steps to arrest a number of these before they slip through our fingers." And later, "Four Sangu Khel Shinwaris have been arrested in Peshawar and 26 in Khyber where they were employed as coolies . . . A number belong to Nazian, where suspected murderers live, and one is said to be a relative of Nur Rahman." Nur Rahman was a Sangu Khel Shinwari who had been hanged in 1909 in Peshawar, and the long memory of a vengeful Afghan was notorious. No one suspected that these coolies on the railway had anything to do with the murders. The British were following a custom known as "barampta" and in other parts of the world as "taking hostages," whereby members of a tribe or group were kept imprisoned until the tribe had surrendered another member or otherwise met a demand. It was considered humane to rotate the hostages.

Ardali and Daud Shah, two Sangu Khel Shinwaris, were the men whom the British soon singled out as the murderers. People arriving by caravan told stories of the display of the pith helmet in a teahouse in Dakka in Afghanistan; the men had boasted of avenging Nur Rahman's execution fourteen years earlier; and then, evidently having been warned of the dangers of talk, they had disappeared from the teahouse.

The British were remembering that in the previous December a lieutenant of the Royal Engineers had been murdered and that in March an attempt had been made to kidnap two British officers.

These violent events overshadowed temporarily the matter of Ajab and the rifles.

During the disturbances in 1920, which the officials attributed to "a small minority of evil-doers," the cavalry magazine in Kohat was raided and 120 rifles carried away. This was a major theft. British rifles were obviously valuable in the tribal areas. One reason for the British hesitance to send the Afghan Government a supply of their rifles was that "the temptation for Afghan Government in time of financial stringency . . . to sell such rifles supplied to them by H.M.G. would be strong." In the Kohat Pass the tribal armory was always turning out imitations of these rifles, but the copies were good for only a few firings and even the spare parts of the originals were valued.

Guilt for this theft was fixed by the British on an Afridi from the Bosti Khel named Ajab, who already had a reputation as a skilled burglar. It would not have harmed Ajab's standing among his fellows had he admitted to this crime, but he declared his innocence so vehemently that he soon made apparent a full-blown persecution feeling against the British officers of Kohat.

"I gave full authority that the British Government should produce some eye witness who might have seen me on the spot and recognized me as the man who carried away ten rifles," Ajab was to write. "I had permitted the Government if it could produce even two witnesses from any one of the five tribes inhabiting our Independent Darra [valley], and these witnesses could prove me guilty, I would undoubtedly pay indemnity to the British, otherwise the British Government could settle the matter with me according to the Moslem's Shariat . . . The

British, however, did not hear me, and without any proof showed me as the man responsible . . . [They] prohibited my entry in their dominion . . . For two years I cried that my guilt should be proved, and when the Viceroy of India came on a tour of the frontier and passed through Akhor Pass in our Independent Territory, I gave him my written protest . . . his attention had been invited to the fact that his tyrannical officers of the frontier were holding me guilty for the 120 rifles of the cavalry without any proof . . . but even then the British frontier officers did not cease their wickedness and when Amal Khan was bringing our goats to our Independent Darra the political officer, Kohat, caught him and sold our livestock by auction."

After the auction of his goats, Ajab took a step that settled for good the question of whether he was a rifle thief or not. He raided the Kohat Police Magazine on February 14, 1923, and stole forty-four rifles.

The mullah who wrote for him his letter of protest put at its head a quotation from the Koran, "Practice violence upon those who oppress you." "Peace be upon him who acts up to advice." He said, "It is the national habit of the English nation that men of other religions, especially Moslems, are their servants by nature and are their inherent property inasmuch as the English nation has suppressed the liberty of every simple-minded Moslem throughout the world."

For the latter theft the British had witnesses; they had, in fact, too many, and the wrong kind, for one of these witnesses told them that Ajab, or one of his gang, had disguised himself as a woman and was concealing a rifle in his garments. Later, when the case became famous, it would be said that one man had actually been captured wearing the burkah, or all-enveloping chaderi, in which a rifle was hidden. This was not likely. Although a chaderi would have been a useful hiding-place for a rifle, the appearance of one in Afridi territory would have made the wearer an object of immense curiosity. Since they worked in the fields, Afridi women did not veil themselves in that manner; they flung scarves over their heads to complement a costume of full-skirted dress and trousers. This custom was to confuse some of the less experienced British officers, who did not recognize it as a matter of economics rather than morality. They thought that the Afridis were less jealous of their women than the men in Kabul and Peshawar. They were even more so.

To recover the stolen rifles, the village of the Bosti Khel was raided on March 4. A raid into Independent Territory was a difficult business, so the soldiers went at night, and at a time when they knew that Ajab would not be at home. The poor village, surrounded by its mud walls, was quiet, and people within the enclosures were sleeping on rope beds or curled upon the ground on the posteens they wore during the day. Suddenly there were noises and threats, and the raid was upon them. The soldiers, who were Indian Moslems, led by British officers, entered the huts and found the rifles and took them. But the sum did not add up to forty-four. The officers remembered the story of men disguised as women.

Thereupon they insisted that the women of Bosti Khel, who had been awakened from sleep, should come out and file slowly past them, while they looked into each face to assure that this was really a woman. Under threat of arms, the women did it. The officers would explain that they did not touch any woman. If the searchers, either soldiers or officers, had touched one of these women, it would have been adultery. What they did was, by Afridi standards, bad enough.

In this night Ajab lost more than the rifles. He lost his reputation as a raider and burglar, since his own premises were successfully attacked, and, more importantly, he lost the respect of his women. The Bosti Khel matrons teased him, and his own mother reproached him daily for the shame he had brought on the women of his family and the fact that he had not avenged their honor. Finally, desperately, Ajab brought a Koran to his mother, and placing his hand on it, swore that he would commit such a crime as had never been committed before.

The date of his revenge was forced upon him, for the British demanded recompense for the still-missing rifles from the Bosti Khel Afridis, to whom Ajab and his brother Shahzada belonged, and from the Tirah Jowakis, the tribe of Sultan Mir and his brother, also named Shahzada, whom the British considered equally guilty for the theft. April 16 was the date set for payment of twelve thousand rupees in Peshawar, and once the tribes had surrendered this large sum of money, there would be no more honor or prestige for Ajab.

Major Archibald Jenner Ellis lived in a bungalow in Kohat cantonment next door to the Commanding General's, where there was a military guard. His wife, having heard of the murders a week earlier of the two British officers at Landi Kotal, was nervous about her safety and that of her eighteen-year-old daughter Molly. She began to keep a whistle by her bed.

At 2 A.M. on the morning of April 14, Ajab and his friends crept into

the Ellis bungalow, according to the charges later made. They were so
adept that they did not awaken the guard at the General's house, nor
the British officer sleeping in the bungalow, nor the servant sleeping on
the porch.

Mrs. Ellis was the principal target. Later it was deduced that Ajab
and his friends needed her for a hostage to improve their bargaining
position. One of them tried to carry her away. But this was not the
fanciful romance in which the Western woman is swept away by the
glamorous man of the East. This was reality; Mrs. Ellis was a middle-
aged woman and she was heavy. The man could not lift her.

Mrs. Ellis managed to reach her whistle and blow it. At that sound of
alarm, the man took out his knife and cut her throat.

The servant sleeping on the porch was awake now, and he awakened
the rest of the household before he ran away. When help came, Molly
Ellis was gone.

The British were then faced with their own reality, with a nightmare that was their ultimate in dread: a young Englishwoman alone in
the power of men of a different race.

"The gang are practically without friends," went the word from
Kohat the next day. "Action against Bosti Khel is not advised at present
moment as all Bosti Khel are out in pursuit cooperating with us. Anxious as I am to strike a blow, I feel we must give tribal jirga a chance,
and also wait for definite information which should not be long delayed.
The gang are acting with extreme caution and secrecy."

Before the sight of an eighteen-year-old girl in hostile hands the
British Empire was powerless. To send in armed men might mean
Molly's death.

The only recourse was the tribes' own custom of negotiation. And
a tribal feud often came to an end when revenge had been spent on
all the men and the chain of vengeance reached only to a woman. The
tribesmen had their chivalry toward women. Therefore, as their emissary seeking the freedom of Molly Ellis the British chose, not one of
their men, but one of their women.

Lilian A. Wade Starr was a nurse at the Church Missionary Society
Medical Mission in Peshawar, where her father had been a missionary
and her husband a physician. The husband, Dr. Vernon Starr, had
treated a young Pathan boy who, after being cured, had made inquiries
about becoming a Christian. So enraged was his father at this treachery
to Islam that he killed his son. Then he had gone with a friend to Dr.

Starr's door and, when he answered the knock, stabbed him to death. Now Mrs. Starr was again at the Peshawar Hospital tending fellow tribesmen of the man who had made her a widow. Even if she had not heard of the Ellis crime, she would have known that the frontier was troubled because many of her patients were leaving the hospital before they were cured and discharged; they were Afridis fleeing possible vengeance.

Sir John Maffey, who was now Commissioner of the North-West Frontier Province, asked Mrs. Starr to go into Independent Territory, into places where few Englishmen had gone and no Englishwoman, and to release Molly Ellis. She agreed to do so and volunteered, if necessary, to replace Molly as a hostage.

A slight, blond woman with a slim, aristocratic face, Mrs. Starr set out on horseback wearing riding clothes and a pith helmet. At the last minute one of her Indian escorts wrapped a turban around this helmet, fearing that a fugitive looking down might think he was seeing an English officer and fire. In her bags Mrs. Starr was carrying, along with medical supplies, two Afridi women's outfits for herself and Molly; these had trousers tight from knee to ankle, unlike the full trousers of other tribes, full black skirts and black shawls edged with red. Later in the journey Mrs. Starr would simply throw a shawl over her pith helmet and would be assured that any passing tribesman would recognize her instantly as a woman; this was the costume which, according to the report that started all the trouble, had concealed a rifle.

All Mrs. Starr's companions were Indian Moslems. One was Mullah Abdul Haq, son of the influential Mullah of Karborgha who three times, publicly in the mosque, had placed a curse on Ajab's gang for their crime, crying out that an attack on a woman was against all Moslem law. Abdul Haq never spoke to Mrs. Starr on their journey, but his presence protected her life. Also with her was an Afridi, the Indian personal attendant of Sir John Maffey, an officer named Moghal Baz.

When this party set out into the dangerous area where the British Empire did not tread too heavily, it was accompanied by forty men who comprised the jirga of the first khel, or clan, through whose lands they were to pass. Whenever they reached the limits of one khel, the escorting jirga handed them over to the men of the tribal area they were entering. Without this official sanction they could not have gone with any safety. Mrs. Starr was handed in turn to five khels. One debated for an hour before accepting her, and she overheard them saying, "Now we know why the feringhi rule Hindustan [India]. Their women are as their men."

The British had no certain idea, when Mrs. Starr began her journey, where Molly might be. But they knew that Ajab had as associates a father and son, Sultan Mir and Gul Akbar, who were of the Jowaki tribe of Tirah, the wildest area of those mountains. Sultan Mir's house near a village called Khanki Bazaar seemed as likely a place to look as any.

On the second day out Mrs. Starr received a letter from Sir John Maffey formally addressed, "Mrs. Starr, Independent Territory." In the most remote hills, in parts where a traveler had to have the correct credentials to survive, where the amenities of the twentieth century were only a dream, communications could be very good. A man, running or going by horseback, could make his way almost anywhere, and could catch up with a party that had gone ahead. Maffey's letter said, "I have just sent a telegram to the Government of India telling them of your enterprise, now that it is too late to stop you. Do not be disappointed too bitterly if success does not come. It is not going to be easy."

Molly had been wearing only her nightgown when the men dragged her out of bed and up into the hills overlooking the Kohat Road. For a whole day they lay high on the hillside looking down with field glasses at the frantic search in the caves for them. In the night they went westward to the higher mountains. Walking by night, resting and hiding by day, they soon were far out of the part of the world known as "civilized."

One of the gang gave Molly his coat. They procured an Afridi woman's shawl for her head and a pair of native woolen socks with leather soles so that her feet would not be cut on the rocks. For five days they walked, and were finally high in the mountain peaks that are always covered with snow. Molly was cold; there was no bedding; the food was hard bread.

After eighty miles they reached the place to which Maffey had reasoned they would go: Sultan Mir's house about seven miles from Khanki Bazaar. This was a mud fortress with a two-story watch-tower at each corner. Molly was put into one of these towers. They brought her paper and pencil and she wrote five letters to her father, glad of the chance to communicate at last. Ajab dictated exorbitant terms for her release.

Ajab was not the leader of the gang; it was his brother Shahzada who gave the orders. But Ajab was the writer of a notorious series of letters, so that his would be the name always associated with the crime.

And he would exult in this moment of power, even in retrospect: "Almighty God who is our Master and creator granted me such courage that I kidnapped Miss Ellis, which raised a horror in the whole British Empire . . ."

Ajab's religious leader was a mullah of the family known as Akhunzada, a kinsman of the famous mullah buried at Hadda in Afghanistan on whose grave Nadir had laid the banners of jehad. He ruled over all those hills and had hundreds of followers who gave him money, craved his prayers and feared his curses. "His mosque has shady friends," Maffey had said, but nevertheless he had written to Kohat to denounce the crime.

This night the mullah was giving dinner to all who had come, according to the custom of mullahs of his stature, and there were more than usual because about two hundred tribesmen had made a pilgrimage to this holy place to talk over the dreadful problem of the British woman in their midst.

One who came to listen rather than to talk was Kuli Khan, Assistant Political Agent of the Kurram Valley, who managed to confer privately with the mullah and persuaded him to send for Ajab and his followers, only a few miles away, for a conference.

But on hearing that Mrs. Starr was coming toward his home with an official of the British Government, the mullah was perturbed. Mullah Mahmud Akhunzada was leader and inspiration to many Afghans; he had his own political consequences to worry about, just as the British and Afghan Governments had theirs, and this official intrusion threatened his position. He hastily sent a note to Mrs. Starr's party: "It is very necessary that you should not come with the Englishman; if so, then there is no pardon. Absolutely lady-doctor and her company are prohibited. This is very urgent order. In default of this there will occur very long fighting." Moghal Baz accepted this note and kept coming.

Talking with the mullah and Kuli, Ajab and Shahzada were coy about confessing their role in the upheaval. Finally they admitted what the British had feared: that they were planning to take Molly farther west into Afghanistan, where they could keep her indefinitely while bargaining. Rescue would have been almost impossible in that case; the Afghan Government's political situation would have been a disaster.

Mrs. Starr reached Khanki Bazaar expecting the hospitality of the mullah. He would not admit her. It was now evening and she had no

place to stay. But there was in the village a sympathetic man who had
served before retiring in the 46th Punjabi Regiment, and fortunately
his house was on the highest level in Khanki Bazaar. He told the mullah:
"I fear till the day of resurrection between your house and my house
there will be a feud over this matter. My house tops yours and we are
ready if need be to fight. You cannot fire on a woman. What can you
do?"

The mullah in desperation told him to take Mrs. Starr to his own
house. Then, relenting slightly, the mullah permitted Kuli to send Molly
a letter, food and a riding habit. And at midnight Molly, asleep on a
charpoy in Sultan Mir's tower, was awakened and was brought down to
Khanki Bazaar, carried the whole seven miles on the back of Gul Akh-
bar, the youngest and least important of the gang. Mrs. Starr was asleep
when she arrived and, even after waking, was not permitted to see her
for several hours. Then Mrs. Starr was finally admitted to the mullah's
house and there saw the object of her search lying on a bed, tired but
not injured. "I treated Miss Ellis . . . as a respectable guest," Ajab was
to write. "Following to our utmost power our true religion of Islam,
we regarded Miss Ellis as a trust and a deposit."

A report was sent by the dependable system of communication to
Sir John Maffey, who, however, had not relied entirely on one delegation. While the gang were bargaining with the two Indian officials,
their own messengers brought word that a lashkar of Afridis from the
Khyber was descending on Sultan Mir's house with intent to burn it.

Shahzada, who had lost control at the Ellis house at the sound of a
whistle and killed Mrs. Ellis, again gave way to violence. He raised his
hands and in a loud voice called on Heaven to witness that it was under
the instigation of the mullah himself that this treachery had been
worked upon him and his friends.

This was blasphemy toward the spiritual leader of the place. The
mullah, like Jehovah driven past endurance, turned upon the gang and,
with shrieking passion, hurled verbal thunderbolts. He cursed them.

While the mullah's sheikhs, his permanent attendants, were trying
to drag the gang from his presence, suddenly all bravado went out of
them. They removed their turbans and laid them at the mullah's feet.
They begged forgiveness. They implored that he remove the curses.
With bad grace, he did.

Now it was fairly easy to bargain. Moghal Baz, acting for the British,
agreed to the release of two of Ajab's gang who were only thieves, not

being known to have murdered anyone. Messengers left at once, and the released prisoners were on their way to Khanki Bazaar in time to be given into tribal keeping as Mrs. Starr's party was leaving. Molly put over her head a shawl that Mrs. Starr had brought, and they started home.

Just before they left, the mullah, who had not yet spoken to either woman, handed Moghal Baz a gift for Molly, a Pathan necklace of gold coins.

They made the return trip of thirty miles in eleven hours, with Molly carried on a stretcher during the hottest part of the day. It was dark when they entered Administered Territory, and Mrs. Starr had to use a small flashlight. Seeing the pinpoints of light coming down the slope, the men waiting at the bottom knew that Molly was almost home.[8]

The British paid fifteen thousand rupees to Mullah Mahmud Akhundzada. Reluctant to admit that they had paid a ransom, the Government of India attempted to conceal the expenditure in a manner common in sophisticated societies. They said the sum was paid "not as a purchase for Miss Ellis' release but to defray the mullah's heavy expenses." Parliament was so informed. This did not deceive persons along the frontier who knew that the mullah's only entertainment expense had been a few sheep slaughtered. No more did it take in the gentlemen at Whitehall to whom entertainment expenses meant picking up the check at Claridge's in London. "It is not at all certain that the mullah would distinguish between ransom and entertainment allowance in the circumstances," said H.M.G. privately, "and the rumors that have grown up show that the tribes and others have failed to draw this distinction."

When the expenditure was reported to the Legislative Assembly of India, a Hindu member asked, "Did the Government of India take any effective steps or any action before this in cases in which Indian girls or Indian women were kidnapped or abducted?" The reply was noncommittal.

The Afghan woman of Tazi Khel on whom the British bomb fell by mistake was valued, for her life, at 1,750 rupees.

Not until April 30 did Humphrys talk with Amanullah about these murders. Meanwhile he was arguing with his own government about the extent of Afghan responsibility, which he thought very dubious and unprovable.

"I fail to see how the Afghan Government can fairly be held in any way responsible for the commission of this crime," Humphrys said. He was instructed to hold Afghanistan responsible.

Humphrys managed to see Amanullah alone, as G. of I. had suggested, "for the coupling of his name in tribal gossip with outbreak of fanatical outrage (dangerous potential implications of which are obvious) is clearly matter for his ear only." He was annoyed to find Amanullah ebullient, saying he could not attend a conference in Turkey, as reported, because the many reforms which he had initiated in the country could not be brought to completion without his guidance.

"Neither I nor my ministers," said Amanullah, "even remotely suggested the encouragement of a hostility toward Great Britain. On the contrary, we exhorted the tribesmen to drop their feud, cultivate a spirit of unity, and abstain from raids and all forms of violence."

Then Humphrys reached the subject that he had come to discuss. The two murders at Landi Kotal and Kohat had been received with horror and indignation in Great Britain and India.

"I have conclusive evidence that the Landi Kotal murders were committed by two Sangu Khel Afghan subjects, who have since publicly boasted of their crime. As there is no extradition treaty between our two countries, I cannot demand that the murderers should be handed over for trial by a British court, but it is the plain duty of a neighboring and friendly state to arrest and punish the murderers in the promptest possible manner.

"Should there be any failure of justice in this respect—which I could hardly conceive possible—the British Government and public will draw their own conclusions."

Then he solemnly warned Amanullah, "The treatment of this case will be regarded as the test of the good will of the Afghan Government and of their claim to be reckoned a civilized state."

This was not the first time a British official had lectured the Afghans on the behavior of a civilized state. At Mussoorie three years earlier, Sir Henry Dobbs had told them that civilized countries, and he named the United States as one, permitted friendly countries like Britain to send police into their territory against persons who threatened the British political régime; this was what the British wanted to do in Afghanistan against various Indians. Again, the Afghans were told that civilized countries did not fortify all the way to a frontier line; in fact, there is no convention to this effect, but so many other factors influence defense that the matter of using the last inch of territory is seldom mentioned among military men. Now Humphrys told Amanullah that he should capture men and punish them for a crime committed in British territory and he pronounced that this was the test of a civilized state. In this he was demanding something that Great Britain would not have done for any other nation. In 1879 Britain had passed an extradition act which imposed several conditions before she would surrender fugitive criminals to another state, and forbade the turning over of any person to another country for a political offense.

But the British were saying that Afghanistan would not be civilized unless she punished Britain's fugitives for her, and Amanullah wanted above all for his country to be civilized. He wrote down the names which Humphrys gave him as being guilty of the Ellis crime. "I will personally supervise the investigation of this senseless and abominable crime," he said, "and the result will be the test of my authority."

It had been Humphrys' idea that pressure should be applied to Amanullah by refusing temporarily the passage through India of some armaments which Humphrys knew he had ordered. Humphrys now made that threat, bringing forth a copy of the treaty of 1921 and pointing to the clause whereby permission to import was given "as long as Afghanistan should show itself friendly to Great Britain." As a sign of friendliness, he insisted on the prompt arrest and punishment of Ardali and Daud Shah, the two Afghans from the Sangu Khel of the Shinwaris suspected of killing Majors Orr and Anderson.

"The program and welfare of Afghanistan," Amanullah told him earnestly, "depend primarily on the friendship of Great Britain. My policy, and that of my Ministers, will be directed in all sincerity toward strengthening that friendship."

"The time has come to translate such assurances into action," Humphrys said coldly before he withdrew, taking his first steps backward as is proper in the presence of a monarch.

CHAPTER 13

April 1923 to March 20, 1924

"The arrest and trial of Afghan subjects for a crime committed in British India would have been a departure from all precedent in Afghanistan. Amir Habibullah, even when in receipt of a subsidy, had never gone so far."

Even while the British thus admitted the extraordinary nature of their request, they marveled at the confusion and resistance that it created in Afghanistan.

"The reasons for the constant shufflings, evasions . . . must be largely a matter of conjecture," went the official reports, "but one of them may be found in the existence of two rival parties in the State. Wali . . . fresh from his tour of Europe . . . seems genuinely to have aimed at conducting the foreign relations of his country on a civilized basis . . . He was, however . . . abysmally ignorant of frontier matters.

"There is considerable evidence to show that his chief opponent was Nadir. Between the diplomat and the soldier, the man of international affairs and the frontier expert, there seems to have been a lack of sympathy . . . and Nadir saw in compliance with the British demands the thin end of the wedge which would in time shatter Afghan influence with the frontier tribes.

"With a view to his own appointment as Foreign Minister, he is therefore employing his undoubted abilities for intrigue to obstruct the fulfillment of the promises made by the Amir and Wali for the satisfaction of British demands. His motive would be, by discrediting Wali's conduct of foreign affairs as having led to a crisis in Anglo-Afghan relations, to pave the way for his own appointment as Foreign Minister and then, by a speedy fulfillment of British demands, to appear as the man who had twice saved his country, in war by his generalship and in peace by his genius for diplomacy.

"A more dangerous possibility is suggested by information recently received from Europe, which goes to show that Nadir is aiming at supplanting not Wali but the Amir himself, and is working to bring about not merely a political crisis but a revolution.

"In whatever form the theory appears, it shows Nadir as the villain of the piece, plotting to ruin either the Amir or the Foreign Minister for his own advancement. It serves to explain many contradictory features in the present situation; as, for instance, the repeated discrepancies between Wali's assurances and the actual conduct of Afghan officials on the Indian frontier . . . The antecedents both of Wali, whom so impartial an observer as Mr. Pears regarded as sincere, and of Nadir, lend color to this theory. So long as it is regarded as such, and facts are not unconsciously distorted to support it, it may usefully be borne in mind as a possible explanation of much that is obscure in the present situation."

Local officials on the eastern frontier were unhappy at having to comply with certain British demands, particularly in dismissing from Afghan service the tribesmen who, in order to join the Afghan forces, had deserted from the British.

"The lot of an Afghan provincial officer is not a happy one," wrote the British. "The Afghan regular garrisons . . . are inefficient and unreliable, and he has to maintain his position largely by diplomatic conciliation of public opinion . . . Present Governor . . . was certainly afraid of possible outbreak of dismissed Wazirs.

"Local opinion in the Afghan provinces must certainly have been in favor of Nadir's policy, while the general inefficiency of Afghan administration facilitated the evasion of orders from the capital . . . When to these factors is added Russian and Turkish influence, with the probability that Russian money was being employed for payments to our tribes, it is not surprising the fulfillment of the Foreign Minister's assurances was slow and halting."

Nadir was now the Second Gentleman of the Land. According to the Nizamnamas, whenever the Amir left Kabul he had to delegate a regent to wield his power. Nadir was that regent. But his pre-eminence was threatened.

His family was close to the First Family of Afghanistan. Three of his brothers were betrothed to three sisters of Amanullah, full sisters who were the daughters of Ulya Hazrat. One was a daughter by adoption; she was the child of a wife who died bearing her, and Ulya Hazrat at her husband's request had made no distinction between this girl and her own daughters. This was the bride of Shah Mahmud, the stocky, square-faced brother who had been Governor of Khanabad. Another sister was married to Shah Wali, the tall, slim brother with a jaunty air whom the British described as a "beau sabreur" type, meaning he would have looked quite at home as the "dashing officer" hero of one of their own imperial romances; if they thought him a trifle superficial, that also conformed to the romantic picture.

The pampered baby of Amanullah's family, Princess Nur-us-Seraj, was betrothed to Hashim, the brother with an Oriental fullness to his eyes and an almond face. He was not a full brother of Nadir, but resembled him enough to be extremely congenial, having the force of personality which Shah Wali seemed to lack. He had been Military Governor of Herat at the time of Amir Habibullah's murder, when the "Bastard" battalion had led Nadir and Shah Wali in chains to Kabul; recalled from that post in the aftermath of the murder, he had become Governor of Jalalabad, where he had been energetic in the interest of Afghan influence among the tribes, both British and Afghan, the same sort of energy for which men of less secure social standing were now to be dismissed.

Nur-us-Seraj was Amanullah's favorite sister. Growing up surrounded by love and admiration, she gave off love in return. She had been well educated. The old inhibiting conditions prevailed still in many ways in the royal household; when menservants carried platters of food from the central kitchens to the dining tables of the princesses, a large cloth was thrown over all the heads, platter and all, and a little boy led the servants into the harem. On each excursion out of the palace, they wore some sort of veil to conceal their faces, even though their dresses and shoes might be of the same type that ladies were wearing in Paris. But within their own social circle they met men and talked with them freely; they were not limited, like the Afridi women for instance, to brothers, fathers and first cousins. Nur-us-Seraj met foreign diplomats; Humphrys described her as "charming." And for Hashim this was not an arranged match, sought solely for the prestige of being the husband of the King's sister. He would not be seeing his bride for the first time in a mirror beneath a cover at the wedding ceremony. He was truly in love with

Nur-us-Seraj; years later someone would say, "The name of Nur-us-Seraj could always excite Hashim."

Amanullah had agreed to these three betrothals, and the marriages to Shah Wali and Shah Mahmud did take place. But he could not bring himself to give the favorite little sister to Hashim. He said that Hashim was too old for her; there was talk that Amanullah became perturbed at the sight of so much power going to this single family, and decided to limit it. There was gossip about the family's involvement in the murder of Amir Habibullah.

The man to whom Amanullah finally gave Nur-us-Seraj was Hassan Jan, the son of his first cousin Mohammed Omar. Hassan was close to Nur-us-Seraj in age. He was also the right age to be a little brother to Amanullah. Ulya Hazrat's only other son had been born when Amanullah was twenty-three.

The wedding did not take place until 1926, but eventually he married his baby sister to his surrogate baby brother, and by making Hassan Jan his companion of honor insured that Nur-us-Seraj would remain in his family.

To break a betrothal announced publicly was an affront. When Hashim failed to get Nur-us-Seraj, it was heartbreaking—he never married anyone else—but pride was as strong an emotion as love with Hashim, and to Nadir, who lacked the understanding that love might have given, it was even more of an indignity. Hashim, in April of 1923, went to Europe with his father, who was seeking medical treatment, and instead of returning, visited one European capital after another.

Nadir remained. Again the family's pride was affronted through a young relative who was a student of the Harbiyeh Military School. He died, and his death was attributed to a beating he had received as a punishment from the Commandant of the school, General Mahmud Sami. Nadir's wrath for vengeance was legendary; the story went around that the General was to be dismissed. Amanullah ordered an investigation, which showed that the boy had attended classes for several days after the beating and even had taken part in physical exercise. Mahmud Sami was acquitted, but only partially so, for he had to pay damages to the boy's family. During Habibullah's reign Nadir's enmity had forced Mahmud Sami into exile for several years; now it had new food.

With all these personal blows to his esteem, Nadir was worried about the esteem which the tribes felt for him and his country. Ardali and

Daud Shah were caught by a violation of safe-conduct which one Moslem should not visit upon another. Nadir, whose prestige with the tribes was one of the pillars of his position, did not wish to be associated with a policy which offended them; he tried to draw good, at least, from this evil.

He dined at the British Legation on June 16 and told Humphrys, "We are making unprecedented efforts to carry out your demands. The arrest of Daud Shah and Ardali was no ordinary achievement . . . [and is] considered by the people of the Eastern Province as a sign that the Afghan Government is under the domination of the British . . .

"But be patient," implored Nadir. "Realize the danger that may result if we give in too hastily to the demands of the British Government." Humphrys was not moved.

"In order to justify the Amir's present attitude in the eyes of his people," persisted Nadir, "may not some generous gesture be made toward Afghanistan by Great Britain? For instance, if a single airplane can be flown from India and presented to the Amir, it will make a wonderful effect on the Afghan people." This had no effect on Humphrys.

The men of the Bosti Khel and the neighboring country signed an agreement with the British: "We the maliks of the Gallai agree to destroy on May 22, 1923, the houses of Ajab and Shahzada who have committed murder in British territory and to destroy the mela of Kawan Khan Sheraki for his guilt in the Foulkes murder case and others." The men agreed to accept a road through their land and the posting of military guards. "Should any of our tribes commit murder in British territory we shall at once expel him from our limits and his house shall be burnt and destroyed and we shall assist Government in any action against him which may be deemed necessary." There was an agreement to expel outlaws hiding in their district at the request of the Government. The British considered this a landmark in their relations with the tribes.

"As regards outlaws," reported Sir John Maffey, who personally supervised the burning of Ajab's house, "I made some concessions regarding outlaw residents of old standing, since in many cases there are marriage and other ties. As one old elder remarked, 'You have taken off our shirts. Leave us our trousers.' "

British bombs, the primal cause of all this trouble, had been dropped again, without warning, on the territory of these Orakzai and Afridi clans shortly before they came together for this jirga. "This swift and unexpected rending of their curtain carried a warning to Orakzais, whose attitude had not been fully satisfactory. Its effect on their morale is demonstrated by the fact that no protest against visitation was made. The subject was discreetly avoided."

Ajab and Shahzada were being harbored in the home of Malik Mansur, a Sangu Khel Shinwari. The Governor of Jalalabad, hearing this, sent messengers to Mansur to bring pressure to make him desist from giving shelter to his friends. Mansur could not believe he was hearing aright; surely he was not being asked to abandon a fellow Moslem fleeing from those unbelievers, the British. He was summoned to Paghman, where Amanullah had gone with his court for the warm months, to hear an amplification. He still found it hard to believe.

Amanullah knew that Afghans and their relatives across the frontier were not without a code of behavior, and a strict one, but the Western world did not know this. When the *Daily Mail* of London published the charge that Amanullah's policy of exciting the tribes had contributed to the murder of Mrs. Ellis, his official newspaper *Aman-i-Afghan* described these charges as "an unprincipled attempt to lower the prestige of Afghanistan in the eyes of the world. The spirit that caused these murders was not created by any speeches of the Amir or his officers but by the tyranny and oppression under which the people of the frontier are groaning. While condemning with the utmost abhorrence all murderers of women and children, we ask who are the most guilty, those who murder one woman or those who murder hundreds."

Englishmen close enough to recognize a difference in attitudes admitted: "What we regard as murderous outrage may sometimes appear to others as killing in an open fight . . ." And Humphrys told his superiors, "There are strong grounds for believing that the Amir and all educated Afghans are anxious to show that the old tradition of fanaticism and barbarism in this country has been officially abandoned, and that Afghanistan is engaged in proving its title to be regarded as a civilized state."

"Civilized" was the word that the British kept using when they talked with the Afghans. Amanullah, wanting so much to be regarded as civilized, looked past the good opinion of the tribes, which meant so much to Nadir, and further, to the good opinion of the Western world. So did his Foreign Minister, Wali, who had been in that world. They were not conversant with Western jurisprudence, so they did not know that Britain was demanding of them, in the name of civilization, something that civilized nations would have thought uncivilized, punishment for a crime committed outside its borders.

So Amanullah put Ardali and Daud Shah on trial for the murder of two officers on British territory.

The British were so determined that Ardali and Daud Shah should be punished that they speculated on the chance of their being convicted in an Afghan court, and suggested that "our man," if Afghan conviction seemed doubtful, should "move the prosecution to press for surrender of accused to us for trial in India." The solicitor of the Government of India considered, "The case as it stands would have fair chance of success in British Indian Court, and if confession by accused be proved to have been voluntarily made by them, I think that conviction would be assured . . . but capital punishment [in Afghanistan] cannot be awarded by law in present case in which non-Moslems have been murdered by Moslems."

"Our man" to the British was Lieutenant C. R. Wombwell of the Seaforth Highlanders, the regiment to which the murdered majors had belonged. Under Moslem law any trial for murder had to consider both "the rights of God" and "the rights of man." The former, represented by the justice of the state, punished for offenses; the latter, in the person of the next-of-kin of the victim, had a right to demand retribution in the form of hand-to-hand reprisals (there had been a next-of-kin who cut off a convicted prisoner's head) or blood money. The British set out to conform to Moslem justice.

Lieutenant Wombwell's role was disturbing to both British and Afghans. He was to attend court every day and be seen as a living symbol of British influence. "We think Minister should endeavor to maneuver the Afghans into accepting our man to assist them in their own Government prosecution. For us definitely to assume the role of prosecutors in this murder case would create hostile atmosphere from the outset which might prejudice trial, and would incidentally be great breach of Afghan sovereignty if Afghan Government knew it."

On the night of August 17–18 Ardali and Daud Shah escaped from the lockup in the Arg.

Six days passed before Wali told Humphrys about the escape, which made unnecessary all the plans for the trial. The British would always write the word "escape" with quotation marks around it, although they admitted that people sometimes did effect authentic escapes from Afghan jails.

But they heard that Ardali himself attributed his "escape" to the efforts of Nadir, and they spoke of "the possibility that either Bolshevik money or Nadir's sinister influence had been at work."

Amanullah himself came under their suspicion. "The arrangement . . . whereby British counsel would attend the Kabul courts each day from the British Legation would very likely have been regarded as an attempt to dictate the verdict in the case by diplomatic pressure. A conviction . . . might have inflamed public opinion. The result, in fact, might well have been a popular uprising against the Amir, particularly in the Eastern Province, which is notoriously fanatical in sentiment, and where the executive at this time was notoriously weak. There were already signs of internal disorder, and the Amir may have thought that even the risk of rupture with Great Britain involved in an 'escape' would be preferable to the repercussions of such a trial. At the very least it might have been feared that the presence of British counsel in the court would expose the crudities of Afghan judicial proceedings to the ridicule of the Anglo-Indian press, and to ridicule the Afghan is always hypersensitive."

One step which the British took, not typical of British judicial proceedings toward men who had not yet been tried, was to get a promise from the Afridis living in Tirah that if Ardali and Daud Shah went into their area, they would kill them.

The Afghan officials whose "negligence," if such, had been responsible for the "escape," if such, were given sentences of four years to six months. Still Humphrys wrote to Wali:

"If . . . the prisoners should remain untraced or escape to a place where the Afghan Government will be unable to recapture them, I must warn Your Excellency in the plainest possible language that this deplorable occurrence will be regarded by my Government with the gravest concern and cannot fail to have a lamentable effect on the relations between our two countries."

The other pursued group, Ajab and his followers, had gone into Afghanistan and their women had followed by a different route. The British knew this; several years later, writing of a different offender, Humphrys warned against expelling him into Afghan territory. "Expulsion was deliberately engineered in the case of . . . Ajab and Shahzada, and when we insisted that the Afghans should deal with them, they replied, not without reason, . . . that as we were unable to punish our criminals, we called on them to pull our chestnuts out of the fire."

The Government of India did not really expect Amanullah to surrender Ajab and his friends. "It is even doubtful whether he could flout public opinion by embarking on action so unprecedented and contrary to Afghan doctrine of asylum . . . Nevertheless, of such wide-reaching importance would this solution be for us, not only in satisfying public opinion [in England] but in impressing the whole frontier, that we think that Minister should again press for it in his conversations. He will, of course, enlarge on the profound disappointment of His Majesty's Government, should Afghan Government contrary to their confident expectations, fail to mark Afghans' professed entry into the comity of civilized nations by abandoning barbaric attitude of giving asylum to heinous criminals."

Meanwhile, they decided to use the weapon that was temporarily in their hands.

Afghanistan had bought arms abroad, and was expecting to bring them through India. Britain had agreed to such import in the treaty, with a loophole "so long as relations continue friendly." Dobbs had given Tarzi a letter promising not to use trivialities as an excuse for preventing an import.

Nadir, in his June 13 conversation with Humphrys, had said that his country's boast of "independence" was a sham if Great Britain were coldly disposed toward her:

"Take for instance the question of transit of arms through India," Nadir had said. "There might come a time when the immediate acquisition of arms might be a question of life or death to Afghanistan, but if the British Government were apathetic, what could be easier than for them to say, 'The ship was delayed' or 'The heat in India is very great.' "

The idea was not new to Humphrys.

A shipment of arms from France arrived at the port of Bombay on September 11. Wali asked Humphrys to make arrangements for their passage. Humphrys replied that the arms would not be permitted to pass until Afghanistan had again arrested Ardali and Daud Shah and given them a real trial, had done something spectacular about arresting Ajab and Shahzada, and had made reparations for earlier raids, among other concessions.

Nadir met Humphrys and asked him to have patience for one month more. He was dining again at the British Legation. "If it were to become generally known that the British Government has refused the passage of arms for Afghanistan at a time when Russia is just beginning to deliver the arms promised under the treaty, the anti-British party will get the upper hand and the country will head toward destruction."

"I cannot avoid the impression that Your Excellency is inviting me to extricate the Afghan Government from a mess of their own making."

"Wait one month more," begged Nadir. "If your demands are not met by that time, a twenty-four-hour ultimatum will be justified."

"I am not dealing with ultimatums. In spite of many disappointments, I have not lost faith in the sanity of the Afghan people."

H.M.G. noted, "Nadir is the most important personage in Afghanistan after the Amir. Colonel Humphrys is not to be deceived by his glozing tongue."

Three days later Humphrys made his position formal in a letter to Wali, ending, "As soon as Afghan Government has given proof that its policy is no longer unfriendly and provocative, [G. of I.] are prepared to permit the passage of the arms in question."

A second shipment of arms was ready to leave Italy. The Afghan Ambassador to Rome, Sardar Azimullah, called on the British Embassy and asked that a personal request lifting the embargo be sent to Lord Curzon, who knew Afghanistan well.

"This consignment is very small," he said, "while practically the whole of Afghanistan is already armed, so these additional munitions cannot reasonably be held to affect the situation."

Then he declared in confidence that the real reason for the Afghan Government's anxiety to secure the delivery of arms was to enable them to show the Soviet Government that Bolshevik Russia was not their only source of supply. For this purpose, he gave the Embassy official to understand, the actual number of the consignment would be greatly exaggerated in public announcements.

At this time seventeen hundred pack animals were on their way to Kabul from Herat, bringing the war material that Russia had promised under its treaty and was now delivering.

"The stoppage of arms is worse than death to Afghanistan," Amanullah told Humphrys on November 7 with much emotion. "Each country understands its own interests and Afghanistan is prepared to sacrifice herself."

"Don't play with fire," advised Humphrys. Until then only a few persons knew that the arms shipments had been held up: chiefly Amanullah, Nadir and Wali. The Council had not been informed; there was enough trouble with hostile demonstrations of tribesmen in Kabul, and Wali hoped that the steps he had already taken would suffice.

The two sets of murderers had now joined forces; that is what Nadir told Humphrys early in November. Nadir knew many of the secrets of the tribes, for he had been in charge of frontier affairs for many years. Now, his pride was again offended. In this crisis, he was relieved of his post on the frontier and Wali, as Foreign Minister, supplanted him.

"Nadir is said to resent keenly the loss of power which this transfer involves," reported the British.

Paid spies ran a regular route for the British between Nazian in Shinwari country and the fort at Landi Kotal. This was an accepted fact of tribal life. Now the Shinwaris of the Sangu Khel began to worry about their fugitives whom they were sheltering; they attacked any man whom they suspected of carrying information about Ardali and Daud Shah; one former inhabitant who returned for a visit was besieged by other Shinwaris, who accused him of betraying Ardali, and pushed out of the area. The spy system in the Khyber foundered.

Wali was persuaded by Humphrys to agree that, since Ajab was hiding close to the frontier line, the British Afridis "need not be squeamish about crossing the undemarcated frontier if they come on the trail of the gang."

On November 12 Wali said the Governor of Jalalabad would be ordered to dispose of Ardali and Daud Shah within a fortnight. Was this not sufficient to release the arms shipment? It was not.

For two months the secret had been kept from the Council; Wali had asked Humphrys to withhold his official note announcing the embargo of arms shipments. Now he asked for the note to be sent.

Finally, all Afghanistan knew what a drastic step Britain was taking to force her to break her rule of asylum, and was outraged.

Humphrys applied more pressure. He withdrew all British women from Kabul.

Mrs. Humphrys was already planning to return to England for a wedding. This fact was not announced. Neither was anything else, "Afghans being left to draw their own conclusions."

Since Mrs. Ellis' tragedy, writers of letters to the *Times* had been demanding the removal of British women from the frontier, or at least better protection for them. Protection was being provided. At Kohat and Bannu a barbed-wire fence, lighted electrically, was put around the cantonments; the gardens at Kohat near the Foulkes and Ellis bungalows were cut down, not as an act of vengeance but to prevent their giving shelter; all high-growing crops surrounding the other cantonments were cut. There was a whole summer to prepare when ladies always left the hot frontier. When they returned home that fall, they found guards doubled.

The barbed-wire had not yet been placed around Paracinar, in Kurram very close to the frontier, not far from the protected cantonment of Bannu. On the night of November 7, Captain Watts of the Kurram Militia and his wife went to bed in the bungalow of their Commandant, Major Campbell. Early in the morning Major Campbell awakened briefly but lightly, thought he heard a sound somewhere in the house like a sweeper moving a piece of furniture, and fell asleep again.

What had happened was that some persons had tried, about dawn on November 8, to peep through the bedroom window by cutting an inch-long slit in the screen and lighting matches outside it. The bedroom curtain was drawn; they could see nothing. Then they went to the dressing room window, which had no screen, and first tried by the light of matches to force the framework open with a piece of iron. They managed to break the pane nearest the lower bolt, and it was easy to reach in a hand and unfasten the window. One man climbed in this way and admitted his companions by the easier passage of the door.

One went into the bedroom and picked up Mrs. Watts, bedclothes and all, and carried her into the dressing room. Captain Watts awoke at once and started up. A man standing just inside the bedroom door fired at him with a musket; the light was dim; he missed. Mrs. Watts, awake and struggling, seized a curtain over the dressing room door as she was carried past and tore it down. Captain Watts's revolver was in an unlocked suitcase just inside the dressing room door. He went there after it. The man with the musket was too quick. Both men were strong, but they fought at close range, and the intruder had a knife as well as a gun. The Wattses had two spaniel dogs. One tried to protect its master by biting the intruder, who smashed its head with the rifle butt. Mrs. Watts was stabbed. The men took some of Captain Watts's clothing and jewelry, ignoring Mrs. Watts's rings and watch, and fled.

Major Campbell, awakened at 6:30 A.M. by a servant who said something dreadful had happened, went into the bedroom and heard only two sounds: the ticking of Mrs. Watts's wristwatch and the whimpering of the other spaniel, sitting on a quilt which had been pulled off the bed.

The tracks of three men, one in nailed sandals, led toward Afghanistan.

At tea parties in British drawing rooms in Peshawar, where the British ladies went, the great topic of conversation was which lady would be the next to be carried off and murdered.[1] It was significant of the intensity of the times that two other murders of Britons had taken place in July and September without creating so much excitement. Female blood had been tasted. The July and September victims were men, officers, shot while wide awake and in one case evidently by accident. Then, on November 30, Major H. C. Finnis, Political Agent of Zhob, while driving toward a jirga, was fired on and killed. It was also significant of change that the local tribesmen almost at once captured one of the suspects and handed him over to the British.

When the ladies left Kabul, one departure cut into Amanullah's own household, to the satisfaction of the British. He had hired a young Englishwoman, a Miss Borland, to attend Souraya in childbirth, with the idea that she would remain to teach midwifery. Miss Borland was not a member of the official British colony, but Humphrys, reminding her that she would be the only British woman left in Afghanistan, persuaded her to go in the last motor of the evacuation.

The Italian chargé d'affaires called on Humphrys to comment on the alarming suddenness of the ladies' departure, and asked Humphrys to give him some days' warning if it were decided to withdraw the British Legation. "I have reason to believe," Humphrys reported with satisfaction, "that my French and Italian colleagues are genuinely alarmed at the prospect of rupture of Anglo-Afghan diplomatic relations and, it appears, advise the Afghan Government to meet the British demands quickly."

The British demands were for a set of men loose in the mountains and valleys where traditionally people had looked hard without finding. Ajab kept sending letters to the tribes in British territory which indicated that he understood the principle of the "civilizing influence" of roads: "As long as we do not commit any offense on the road, you should not confront us in any other place. If except on roads you come forward anywhere else to help the English by stopping us, then you should rest assured that you will find yourself in Hell . . . Remember henceforth, that it is the English who had disgraced our nation and it is I alone who have been compelled to go into exile. I am pleased with

my lot and may God accept this . . . If you did not read this letter out
to all Moslems, may your wives be divorced from you."

Ajab and the other hunted men were living by now in their own kingdom. Their wives and children had joined them so that they had a
colony of considerable size in a spot in Afghanistan known as Mandatai.
Nothing is secret among the tribes, and the British Afridis were so well
informed that they protested being assigned to search the Morgha
mountain range, saying that in view of the gang's universally known
residence in Mandatai, this mission was farcical and unjust to them.
These Afridis suggested a joint conference on the problem to the Sangu
Khel Shinwaris, who turned them down.

A guard of unprecedented vigilance protected the fugitives. The villages where they lived might not be approached by any stranger, nor
by anyone at all whose purpose and good faith were not well established.
Malik Mansur, the chief protector of the group, the man who had been
summoned to Amanullah to be told why he should surrender them, led
a fierce attack on a village in the Nazian Valley, because it was the home
of some men he suspected of having informed to the British, and burned
the houses to the ground. Some of Ardali's relatives were killed in the
process.

But an extraordinarily clever British agent, a tribesman, penetrated
the hideout at Mandatai and talked with the mullah who had actually
written Ajab's voluminous correspondence for him. He said that Ajab
had sent letters before the Watts murder in order to comply with the
Moslem requirement that a warning must be given before any attack.
Ajab wrote a letter to the Chaknawar Mullah which might be interpreted as admitting the Watts crime in order, again, to acquire a hostage; it was his bad fortune that he gave the letter for delivery to this
British agent.

Knowing so much about the fugitives, the British reasoned that the
Afghans must know this also. Besides, two of their Afridis had reported
separately that Nadir had offered their jirga fifty thousand rupees if
those in their tribe who had received allowances from Afghanistan
would show their gratitude by accepting the gang into British territory
for shelter.

"Eyewash" was a word that Humphrys used in reply to Wali's prot-
estations, which included the reminder that Ajab's successful flight
was being financed by British money paid to ransom Molly.

Then Ajab sent still another warning. Someone, not a British agent this time, put it into the mailbox at Thal on British territory. He said that unless Government came to terms with him, he would be forced to the commission of an offense which he would not otherwise contemplate. Knowing what he had contemplated in the past, Amanullah moved quickly.

Troops were sent out from Kabul toward his hideaway. They did not go marching openly; there had been enough talk and unrest already, and some tribesmen had made a hostile demonstration in Kabul itself. These soldiers went in small groups, as if on leave, walking or riding on horseback or reclining in tongas. Three miles out on the Jalalabad road, they assembled and became military units again. Their goal was Mandatai; their mission, to coerce the Sangu Khel into giving up Ajab and the rest.

They failed. At least, so their Commanding Officer reported to the Governor of Jalalabad and to the British Military Attaché, who had gone to Jalalabad to hear the results. They had searched every hill and valley, he said, without success. The criminals and those who harbored them had fled.

The Commanding Officer assured the British Military Attaché that he would not relax his efforts to find them and, if he could not arrest them, to kill them.

"Time, which is regarded by your Ministers as a mere figure of speech," Humphrys told Amanullah on December 27, "is a most essential factor . . ."

Humphrys suggesed a joint Anglo-Afghan attack on the Sangu Khel, reinforced by British airplanes.

"If those measures were carried out, they would probably result in a general Sangu Khel insurrection," said Amanullah, "since the identity of the British officers and their party cannot be hidden. Likewise, it would be extremely dangerous to use airplanes." Then he added, "These demands in the English press, that the murderers should be handed over to the British authorities for trial, would, if complied with, result in my own murder."

Talking among themselves, the British had accepted the fact that they could expect no more from Amanullah than deportation of the fugitives to some place like Turkestan in the north, where they could not harm British people anymore. Amanullah suggested this on his own initiative, and gave Humphrys a promise, which he asked him to keep secret, that he would have the men treated with special severity in Turkestan.

"I will never rest until these murderers are disposed of, but if this takes longer than expected, please do not break off relations. That would undo all the work of the past two years."

On the evening of January 8, 1924, Ajab was sitting in the office of the Governor of Jalalabad. He went away without being arrested; this was the preliminary step in a negotiation which the British were trying to observe as closely as they could despite the fact that it was being conducted behind their backs and the Governor of Jalalabad seemed as concerned about their informers as he was about Ajab.

Ajab already had another asylum arranged and a jirga to take him there. But he was tired of being a fugitive. In his letter to the Chaknawar Mullah, he had complained that he was crushed "between the upper and lower kingdoms." To have two countries pursuing him, despite all his tribal connections, was taxing. So, as soon as Ajab stepped within Afridi limits, putting himself out of reach of the Afghans, he sent the Governor of Jalalabad a message that he would talk surrender. The Governor telephoned Wali, who, without hanging up the telephone, summoned Humphrys.

Would the British Government be satisfied with Ajab's deportation to Turkestan? The decision had to be made at once. Humphrys accepted the bird in the hand.

On January 28, three lorries left Jalalabad carrying most of Ajab's group, including their women and children; Ajab was transported separately and picked up after the caravan had passed through Kabul, to avoid trouble. They all went into exile in Turkestan, where they knew no one and where even the language was strange to them. Ajab was interned at the Mazar-i-Sharif cantonment, but the severe treatment which Amanullah had promised did not materialize.

Two years later a traveler from Peshawar was in Mazar-i-Sharif and recognized the famous Ajab of the Ellis case, who was surrounded by thirty-five followers. They exchanged greetings, and Ajab told, not without pride, exactly who he was. He said the Afghan Government had given him sufficient land for his maintenance and thirty rupees a month to each of his men. He asked the Peshawari to remain there with him, being one of his countrymen and therefore congenial.

The Peshawari, declining to stay, said that he would like very much to be photographed with the famous Ajab Khan Ghazi and his followers, and, bringing forth his camera, asked if someone would take a picture. Ajab became enraged: "As you appear to be in British pay, I will not have my picture taken." The traveler begged his pardon and left him hastily.

Ajab's land was valuable, adjoining that of the Governor of Mazar. Water in all of Afghanistan was so treasured that constantly there were disputes and feuds about the streams that ran through pieces of property; diverting the course of water might draw blood. One day the Governor's servants dammed the water which ran through his garden into Ajab's land. Ajab seized one of the Governor's men, beat him, ducked him in a pool of water, and let him go. The Governor, hearing this, summoned Ajab, who brought fifteen armed men to the interview. The Governor berated him: instead of being grateful to the Afghan Government for giving him land, he had shown his ingratitude by almost drowning one of his servants. Ajab should realize his proper position. Ajab threatened to shoot the Governor if he had any more trouble.

But the other men were still at liberty. The arms were not yet released.

Aman-i-Afghan published an accusation that the real motive of the British was to keep the arms in the damp climate of India until they became useless from rust; that then they would hand over a useless heap of iron and claim that they had fulfilled their treaty obligations.

The consignment from France was sitting on the dock at Bombay, but those bought in Italy still had to be shipped, and Amanullah was making plans to bring them through Russia. He had done this before, until Russia, during the Bokhara upheaval, showed her displeasure in the same way that the British were now showing theirs. The positions were reversed. Grigori V. Chicherin, the Foreign Minister of Russia, had informed the Afghan Minister in his country that the Soviet Government was prepared to order mobilization in Russian Turkestan if British forces entered Afghanistan. The bazaars in Tehran, Persia, had closed for a day in sympathy against "the British ultimatum."

Ardali and Daud Shah, who unlike Ajab were Afghan subjects, had found a refuge among the Mohmands of the British side. The Governor of Jalalabad sent word to them, also, asking them to come in on safe conduct and giving surety that they would be treated well. They accepted.

Four Mohmands came with Ardali and Daud Shah, to surrender them at the appointed place, a fork in the Kabul River not far from Dakka, where two Afghan colonels and some soldiers were waiting. As they

came in front of this party, the story was later told, one of the Mohmands' revolvers dropped and went off.

Hearing the shot, the Afghan soldiers believed that they faced a fight.
They lifted their rifles and fired at the men who were walking toward
them. Ardali was killed at once. Daud Shah, wounded, escaped after
killing one of the soldiers. The Afghans kept firing, but the place was
full of high weeds, and their targets had escaped.

Daud Shah was lost, and when Wali told Humphrys that he was in
British territory, this time Humphrys believed him. "Daud Shah has
twice put faith in the Afghan safe conduct, and twice it has been shamelessly violated. On the first occasion he was brought to Kabul and imprisoned, and on the second he was fired at and his companion was
killed at his side in the presence of Mohmand escort. In addition, he is
charged with killing an Afghan soldier. It therefore seems most unlikely
that he will seek refuge in Afghan territory for the present, or that he
will trust again any messenger sent by the Governor to bring him in."

From then on the Governor of Jalalabad had a bodyguard wherever
he went, and was secretly offering large rewards from his personal fortune for Daud Shah's arrest; his life was in danger while this man whom
he had betrayed was at large.

The British decided that Amanullah had learned his lesson, and that
the world at large had been shown what British power could do. On
March 20, 1924, they agreed that arms and other instruments of war
might now be shipped through India to Afghanistan. The crates of
ammunition waiting at Bombay continued their delayed journey, and
the English ladies returned to Kabul.

But Amanullah had ruined his reputation with his people. The tribes
were indignant at the betrayal of two sacred principles: that of asylum
and that of a promised safe-conduct. The British Consul at Jalalabad,
watching the faces of the people watching Ajab's family being loaded
into lorries for deportation, and listening to discussions of the "murder"
of Ardali, said:

"If the element of apprehension from the Amir as a ruler were eliminated, there is no doubt that fatwa of kufr [a denunciation of him as an
infidel] would be passed against him."

People said that Amanullah was so abject toward the British that he
had killed one of his own subjects to please them. It did not help their
sense of justice that no Afghan court, had Ardali's guilt been proved

black as sin, would have given him for this crime the punishment which the Amir, in their opinion, had given without a trial.

The news of the arms release was greeted, said Wali, "with affection." But Amanullah complained, "My performance was not properly appreciated in England. All this was without precedent and carried through in the teeth of public opinion. No Amir has previously made reparations of any kind to the British Government. My submission has enormously weakened my position on the frontier."

A month later Humphrys was writing, "The case of Mirza Painda Mahomet Khan will, I think, convince you that the question [of an extradition treaty with Afghanistan] is no 'sleeping dog.' Here a man who was known to our frontier officials to have been convicted of murder and sentenced to death by an Afghan Court took refuge in Administered British territory, whence his son was allowed to start for a raid in Afghanistan. One can imagine what capital Abdul Hadi would make out of this if he were in Kabul."

Abdul Hadi had made the comment during the Mussoorie Conference: "Perhaps Afghanistan does not consider the civilization of so-called civilized countries real civilization."

CHAPTER 14

1924

Almost at once the rebellion was upon Amanullah.

It broke out in Khost, an area of the Southern Province which protruded like a peninsula into Waziristan, where the tribes that the British found so difficult were always imparting some of their wildness to their neighbors. The Mangal tribe who lived there had rebelled in 1912 against Amanullah's father, charging repression and greed to his officials. Kabul soldiers came back from that expedition saying that they had never seen such rags and tatters as the poverty-stricken Mangals wore, and even in Kabul a tear in a garment was never any reason for not wearing it in public. The panic that besets most poor people was theirs; a deflection of an irrigation stream or a foot placed accidentally on a seedling could inflame them to kill one another.

The gossip that went through the hills and valleys, almost as fast as if telephone wires carried it, had kept them aware of all the searching for Ajab, Ardali, Daud Shah, and the rest; they sympathized with the tribesmen, and resented the betrayals. The capitulation to Britain shamed them. Their neighbors the Wazirs related their disappointment with the Amir of Afghanistan for failing to provide amnesty for them after they had fought their own government for him; they did not know how desperately he had tried on their behalf. Some Wazirs who had deserted from the British militia had been enlisted in the Afghan militia in Khost. Now, under the policy of trying to fulfill "neighborly" relations with the British, the Governor of the Southern Province discharged these Wazirs, who again felt abandoned and complained to the Mangals.

It was the mullahs of Khost, however, who precipitated the rebellion. They feared the Nizamnamas, the new Administrative Code of Laws that Amanullah had set forth to displace the religious Shariat that gave them so much power. They feared the day when an ordinary man would no longer be dependent on his mullah to read or write a letter, being able to do so himself. In a land rimmed by mountains, where theirs was the only effective law, they found it easy to arouse these always desperate men to attack the garrisons of their faithless Amir.

Troops left Kabul for Khost at night, in an attempt to forestall alarm. Few of the soldiers had been in the Army for very long, but Shah Wali, Nadir's brother who was the Army Commander, made a speech saying that mullahs from Kabul were on their way to negotiate and the matter would probably be settled before they arrived. He sounded more optimistic than Amanullah felt. There were six thousand Mangals in a bad mood facing four thousand reserves from other tribes. The Governor ordered them to hand over the rebellious mullahs for punishment for sedition; they refused. The Governor again put into his militia the deserters from Waziristan whom he had dismissed; having been trained in the British Army, they were as good fighters as he had, and if he did not take them, they would certainly join the rebels.

Two mullahs from Kabul, one of them Sher Agha, the Hazrat Sahib of Shor Bazaar, reached Matun, the principal town of Khost, ahead of the soldiers, and found themselves in enemy territory. Matun was entirely occupied by the Mangal rebels. The mullahs spoke with them and showed the letters from Amanullah authorizing a discussion about the Nizamnamas with their own mullahs, and promising to abolish his new laws if they were found contrary to Shariat. Reason prevailed. All the mullahs agreed to go to Kabul for a discussion.

Peace seemed very likely.

Nadir had led the government forces that had subdued the Mangals in 1912; then he won his first fame and made his first friendships with the tribes. Now Amanullah asked Nadir, in this same situation, to take command again.

Nadir refused.

He told Amanullah that he could not face those tribesmen to whom promises had been broken. He could not command an army toward which Amanullah was showing so much indifference.

Nadir had recently recovered from typhoid, convalescing at his home in the suburbs. Now he went back there. It was the first time in his adult life that he had not been in the center of public affairs, and Kabul gossiped. The gossip reached Khost, where it turned into rumors that Nadir was suspected of complicity in their rebellion. For five years his had been the hand that distributed the allowances from Kabul; just a few months earlier he had drawn up, keeping the fact a secret from Wali, whose responsibility it was, a list of allowances for the British Mahsuds. Nadir was the tribesmen's champion and benefactor.

Nadir dined at the British Embassy on April 4. He appeared not only sick but dejected. To inquiries about his health he replied that he had recovered from the typhoid, but that his heart was very sore.

After dinner, settling himself in one of Humphrys' most commodious and comfortable British chairs, Nadir gave the sigh which often precedes the gathering of strength for a difficult task. He began what Humphrys later described as "the most fulsome praise of British institutions, methods, characters, and stability which I am accustomed to hear from his lips," and Nadir's propensity for praising the British to their faces already was a joke among them.

He congratulated Humphrys on the fact that a peaceful solution had been found to the recent troubles on the frontier.

Up to this moment Nadir's attitude had been one that Humphrys described later as "almost cringing civility."

Then, as Humphrys wrote, "the mask appeared to drop from his face for an instant."

Bitterly Nadir said, "You have achieved success, it is true, but at what cost to myself and to Afghan influence with the frontier tribes."

Then emotion fell again into the background. Diplomacy was ascendant. The mask was in place again and Nadir's disciplined face was gracious and polite. He commented on the serious unrest that had broken out in Khost. Humphrys said that he understood the risings had subsided. Nadir said they had not.

"This unrest is not of a transitory nature," said Nadir, "but is due to the policy of the Amir, who has obstinately refused to listen to my advice."

Nadir then proceeded to catalogue Amanullah's errors.

"First, Amanullah tried to push through his reforms far too precipitately. Afghans as a race are fanatical, bigoted, conservative. It is not safe to run roughshod over their cherished customs and attempt to dragoon them into civilization on the European standard.

"It is commonly believed by the people that the new administrative code violates the canons of Islamic law. Therefore it is extremely unpopular with the mullahs and the orthodox party. Yet this code was introduced suddenly without any attempt being made to explain away doubts as to its validity."

Nadir became more personal.

"The men chiefly responsible for this indecent haste are Mahmud Tarzi, the author of all those political squibs which used to be published in *Seraj-ul-Akhbar*, and Jemal Pasha, the Turkish adventurer who captivated the imagination of the Amir with his ultra-modern ideas."

Nadir and Humphrys both knew that the Afghans disliked all Turks at that time, because they had abolished the power of the Caliph.

"Hatred and contempt for the Turks . . . is now general throughout Afghanistan, and the reforms connected with Jemal Pasha's name for this reason are still more suspect than they were before . . ."

Nadir said that any day there might be seen in the streets of Kabul dozens of foreign doctors and engineers, strolling idly about without employment.

"I do not blame the foreigners. I understand that most of them are genuinely anxious to work. A never-ending stream of these expensive experts is pouring into Kabul, but no one has ever taken the trouble to think out beforehand what they are to do or where they are to go. What is the use of fifty foreign doctors when there is only one disgracefully equipped hospital for them to work in? In the present conditions two doctors could have amply sufficed to initiate medical reforms in Kabul. Careful preparation is necessary, but everything was rushed through without regard for the morrow. There is no program for the engineer, no plans to work with, no tools to work with."

Nadir became more and more excited.

"Education is being run on the most haphazard lines, and money is being poured out like water. Is it surprising that this reckless and purposeless extravagance is resented by the people? Unrest is spreading. I hope that a halt will be cried before it is too late."

The Army was Nadir's chief concern; he was still Minister of War.

"Meanwhile the Army has been ruthlessly cut down, and the power of the state is scarcely able to cope successfully with the disorders which have arisen in the provinces. All these blunders have been committed in the teeth of my warnings, and since my advice has consistently been disregarded, my heart is no longer in my work. I am determined to abandon my military career, and I decline all responsibility for the consequences of a policy which I deplore."

Nadir said that he intended to live in retirement until he was given a diplomatic assignment outside Afghanistan. His brother, Shah Wali, had resigned his post as General in command of the Kabul troops and was now merely one of the Amir's aide-de-camps.

Nadir poured out his complaints so fast and so intensely that Humphrys could not speak until he had finished. Then Humphrys said the Amir was doing his best according to his lights to further the prosperity and civilization of Afghanistan.

"This is no easy task," Humphrys assured Nadir.

Nadir would not be calmed. "No real improvement in the progress of my country," he said, "is possible without the friendship and assistance of the British Empire." He was back at his favorite theme.

The conversation shocked Humphrys. He wrote to his superiors: "It is remarkable that Nadir would so freely criticize the policy of the sovereign, of whom he had invariably hitherto spoken to me in terms of servile adulation. The whole tenor of his conversation certainly seemed to show that he was extremely dispirited, and lent color to the popular report that he has had a violent quarrel with the Amir and had resigned the post of War Minister in consequence. The bitter remark concerning the loss of his own and Afghanistan's influence in general with the frontier tribes seems to indicate that his policy of anti-British intrigue . . . has been temporarily, at any rate, rejected by the Amir.

"But whatever the immediate cause of differences between the Amir and himself, it seems very clear that he is for the moment discredited and feeling very acutely the loss of his former paramount influence with the Amir. The family of which he is the chief representative is so powerful that the Amir cannot afford to leave him unemployed and disgruntled for long."

Within a few days it was announced that Nadir would be replaced as War Minister by Wali, and that he would go to Paris as Afghanistan's Minister to France. He wanted Shah Wali appointed as his assistant, but Amanullah refused. His brother Shah Mahmud was transferred from command in Northern Afghanistan to be head of the military school in Kabul, which was a petty post for a man of his position. Hashim was appointed Minister to Russia; he was still traveling in Europe, and instead of returning to Kabul, the disappointed suitor of Nur-us-Seraj went directly to Moscow.

All this indicated, thought Humphrys, "that the Amir's present policy in regard to [this family] is either to remove them from Afghanistan or else to keep them under close observation in Kabul."

It was July before Nadir left for Paris, and meanwhile the rebellion in Khost was so intense that Amanullah put into active service the men of the "Bastard" regiment who had arrested Nadir and his family after Habibullah's murder. One of Nadir's first acts on being reinstated as Commander-in-Chief had been to dismiss these men. Their reinstatement was considered a deliberate insult to him. But Amanullah needed trained fighters.

The nomad tribe of Ghilzais was returning to Afghanistan with the spring, and whenever trouble came in the spring, there was always the fear that the Ghilzais would add to it. One Ahmedzai Ghilzai, Ghaus-ud-din, whose father had led the Mangal uprising of 1912, and who in 1917 had lured two exiled sardars into an attempt on the Afghan throne, was arrested. History was repeating itself. Two more exiled sardars were trying to get into Afghanistan disguised as Ghilzais; the British caught them at Parachinar and turned them back.

The mullahs from Khost had not gone to Kabul for discussions after all. They were still in their homes, protesting, and the story was that they were getting support in their defiance of Amanullah from one of the mullahs whom he had chosen to talk with them, Sher Agha.

Wali took charge of the government forces, and led them successfully through the Altimur Pass into Khost, whose Governor had already prepared for defeat by sending his favorite pony and thirty thousand rupees in gold to Peshawar. The Ahmedzai Ghilzais were persuaded to support Amanullah by Ghaus-ud-din, whom Amanullah released from prison to argue with them. By early May two out of three of the rebellious Khost tribes had submitted and Wali expected to be home in a fortnight.

Then the Ahmadzai Ghilzais went over to the rebels. The report went out that Ghaus-ud-din had merely pretended to cooperate with the government in order to get the rifles.

Amanullah issued a proclamation: "To all my sincere subjects: As required by the strict order, 'Consult the people in affairs and when you have decided, trust in God,' I always cherish the desire that in the transaction of important affairs of state and those affecting the prosperity and happiness of the nation, the representatives of the people should, as far as possible, also take part, and both in thought and words, help and assist me in bearing this heavy burden."

He called for a Loe Jirga, a Great Assembly, to be held in Kabul at the end of July. It was time to communicate with his people.

An Afghan Air Force was one of Amanullah's dreams for his country, but he had not yet succeeded in having one Afghan plane in the air. There were five airplanes in the country, and three German mechanics, Linthe, Weiss and Brustmann, were trying to get them into flying condition, but all they had done so far was to paint them horizon blue with two-foot black bands on the wings. The two presented by Russia had a type of rotary engine which no one in Kabul understood, and were underpowered for Kabul's mountains and were in bad condition anyway. Two bought in Italy for the suspiciously low price of £200 also were useless; the rumor in the bazaars was that the British had deliberately flung them off the ships when unloading them in India. The truth was that the trip to Kabul, over rugged roads and passes, whether on camel back or in a lorry, was damaging to a sensitive instrument like an airplane part. The only airplane which seemed likely to fly, in the German's opinion, was a British one which had been described as "sent by God." It had crashed in Afghanistan just before the Kabul conference and had been kept there. None of the mechanics understood its Rolls-Royce engine or was able to tune up the fuselage or get the wings at the right angle of incidence. What they needed, although they never asked for it, was a book of the maker's instructions.

"The only machine the Amir has ever seen in flight," surmised Humphrys, "was British." This had been the plane that bombed Kabul in 1919. "And at the moment, therefore, it is only British aircraft in which he has any faith." In discussing the prospect of a gift of aircraft to Afghanistan, which he thought less potentially dangerous than one of heavy artillery, he suggested these "to be flown to Kabul by British airmen and formally presented to the Amir. Discredit of their subsequent fate would be bequeathed to foreign personnel, whose failure would form the subject of unfavorable comparisons with the skill of their first pilots."

The acting Foreign Minister, while Mahmud Tarzi was en route from Paris and Wali was in Khost fighting the rebels, was Sardar Sher Ahmed, who had been Minister to Rome and was now President of the Shora, the Council. He asked the British for six airplanes, and he wanted them at once, within ten to fifteen days. He specified six planes, four of them bombers, and two equipped with machine guns.

"Where do you want delivery?" asked Richard Maconachie, who was chargé d'affaires during Humphrys' holiday in India.

"If the Government of India objects to the German pilots crossing the frontier and taking the machines over at an airdrome in India, these might be brought up in British lorries to Kabul. If the machines can be supplied, I shall be glad to know the price and whether this should be paid in cash or in carpets, hides, and so forth."

"It is fantastic," said Maconachie, "to suppose that six machines can be delivered at Torkham, complete with spare parts and accessories as you desire, within fifteen days of such a proposal being submitted to His Majesty's Government."

"Time is a very necessary factor," said Sher Ahmed, "but if six machines cannot be supplied in that period, a small number, say four, would be better than nothing."

"I doubt whether there are six machines available for this purpose in India."

This remark of Maconachie amused Sher Ahmed very much. "I know on excellent authority that the British have vast numbers of airplanes in India. What are six? Absolutely nothing. The British Government will not even notice their loss."

"My information on the subject is extremely scanty, but it seems to me reasonable to suppose that this vast number of machines of which you have told me are kept by the government for its own use, and not for sale, like toys in a shop."

He explained, "Airplanes are brittle things and, if brought up by road from Torkham to Kabul in lorries, would very likely be damaged. Should this happen, the Afghans will say we did it on purpose."

Maconachie suggested that the airplanes might be purchased on the Peshawar airdrome and then flown by the British pilots, with one Afghan officer as passenger in each to show the sightseers at Kabul landing ground that they really were Afghan property.

"This idea is absolutely impossible!" cried Sher Ahmed. "There would be panic in Dakka, Jalalabad, and every village within sight of the planes while they were in flight, and in spite of any previous proclamations and propaganda to the contrary, everyone in the Eastern Province would believe that the British were on their way to bomb Kabul. The Afghan Government simply cannot face the prospect of this."

Sher Ahmed had proposed that Afghan boys be sent to India for training as aviators. Maconachie next discussed this.

"Casualties might be heavy. However inconceivable it may be to you or me that my government wished to kill Afghan boys, or that, if they did, they would choose so expensive a method of doing it as sending them up in airplanes, there is apparently nothing too improbable for Afghans to believe, provided it suggests a dishonest motive for whatever the British Government does."

"You must not mind what ignorant bazaar people say about the British. The Amir has decided to trust your government completely."

"I had not been thinking of teashop gossip, but of newspaper articles of a kind still published in the Afghan press."

"It does not matter what the people think," Sher Ahmed assured him. "The Amir, I am sure, would not resent any number of casualties. His Majesty, in fact, expects them. Boys die at all times and in all places when it is their fate. Sardar Nadir's son, for instance, has just died in Paris; not in an airplane, it is true, but the principle is the same. No one accused the French Government of killing him. Two Afghan boys are learning to fly in Italy. They have not yet completed their course, but each has crashed twice so far. They have not been killed, but that is no credit to the Italians. They ought to have been, and in that case no one would have held the Italian Government responsible. Casualties are of no consequence whatever."

In London, Foreign Secretary Ramsay MacDonald told the India Office that "in the case of the Amir resisting the strong temptation to indulge in anti-British intrigue during the coming Great Assembly, H.M.G. might later on very appropriately offer him a present of perhaps two Avro training machines. In this connection it is understood that the Russian Government are despatching a consignment of airplanes in sections on camel or mule back to Kabul . . . In the not unlikely event of these machines being found on reassembly to be unfit for flying, Russian prestige would, in a country such as Afghanistan, receive a serious setback . . . such an eventuality provides an additional argument against H.M.G.'s supplying airplanes with undue haste and without careful preparation."

The rebels in Khost had a leader now; he was called the Lame Mullah, or Mullah Lang, although his true name was Abdullah, because he walked with a slight limp. He wore a cloak of green, the color of the Prophet. The Lame Mullah would become a figure in the folklore of

Afghanistan. In later years people would relate his exploits in telling Mangals, as if inspired divinely, "Go look under such a tree, and you will find money." And they would go and look, and the money would be there. And then the story would end, "Of course, the British had put it there, because they wanted people to follow the Lame Mullah."

"The Lame Satan" is what the Ittihad-i-Mashriqi called him in an article so obscure as to be hardly intelligible, which contained the sentence, "I was in the _____ Legation when two gentlemen, etc." The official Kabul newspaper *Aman-i-Afghan* suspended publication for a period in June because it was reluctant to give out news of so little success in Khost.

The Lame Mullah argued with the negotiators that Amanullah had sent and they reached agreement on all points except education and hasht nafari. Regarding education he demanded that only the limited number of boys who were likely to have to deal with foreigners should receive a modern education. As for girls, he said that the less they had to do with foreigners the better, but he would agree to their being educated provided they were taught only the Koran and they were not kept in school after reaching a marriageable age, and their male teachers were not younger than eighty years of age.

Hasht nafari was unnecessary, the Lame Mullah said. If war broke out with a foreign power, the Mangal tribes would provide the Amir with a hundred thousand men who would serve voluntarily without any pay. But for training in peacetime they would supply not one.

"Why do the frontier tribes need training?" he asked, and he challenged to take on, in a marksmanship contest, any twenty of the Afghan regular troops. The Lame Mullah was a noted marksman, and no one accepted the challenge.

In Kabul, which was feeling the loss of grain normally brought through the rebellious area, Amanullah had issued orders forbidding the employment within twenty miles of the capital of the nomad Ghilzais, several subtribes of whom used to make their livelihood in midsummer by hiring out to gather the harvest. The farmers around Kabul depended on them, but Amanullah said that he wished to keep the Kabulis occupied with their own business, such as cutting crops, as a means of preventing gossip with outsiders about the uneasy state of affairs. What his proclamation said was:

"The harvesters are in the habit of receiving one out of every twenty sheaves as payment for their work. This is against the Koran, which forbids payment in kind. Owners of crops lose heavily as the harvesters make the sheaves they are to get much bigger than the rest. Also, as their womenfolk do the gleaning, a further opening is given to them to rob the owners.

"The harvesters, through continually being on the move, avoid the census for purpose of enlistment in the army, education of children, and payment of animal taxes. The government has undertaken extensive irrigation work and is prepared to supply land at cheap rates to the nomad tribes if they will only settle down and cultivate it."

The crops were in danger of rotting in the fields, while two bands of nomads camped on either side the steep cliffs of the gorge on the road to Kabul from Jalalabad. They were waiting to see what would happen; everyone said that if they did not get their usual harvesting work, they would take to robbery. The officials, concurring in this opinion, issued rifles to the villagers living along this road.

The Qita Namuna, the crack regiment that Jemal Pasha had trained, was on its way to fight in Khost. Amanullah personally thanked the men for their services, and the two principal ladies in his family, Souraya and Ulya Hazrat, appeared in a military ceremony in which no lady had appeared before, and handed each man a nosegay and a handkerchief which infolded some gold coins. Their faces were veiled beneath smart brimmed hats, but the soldiers had their first opportunity to see what women's Western attire looked like, and what a royal lady's legs looked like.

One man who accepted Souraya's gold-laden handkerchief had been a ne'er-do-well from Kala Khan in Kohistan, north of Kabul. He was a brave and skillful soldier, but he had more affinity for the profession which he embarked upon as a boy when he destroyed the vineyard of a rich Kohistani farmer; he was not the first boy of his village to steal grapes; many varieties were grown on those hillsides, and the little black grapes which appeared first of all had a special lure for youngsters. But this man would later describe his act as an altruistic feat of revenge, inspired by a rude remark the vineyard owner had made to his father, who occupied one of the lowest rungs in the social ladder because his function was to fill a goatskin with water every morning and walk over the roads with it, sprinkling the dust away. This man's future would display the two propensities he had shown in the vineyard incident; for taking other people's property and for justifying the seizure with a show of nobility. He would desert from the Qita Namuna to devote his time to banditry, adopting a professional name that recalled constantly his father's occupation. He was the Son of the Water-Carrier, or Bacha Sacao.

At a religious ceremony on July 13, Amanullah was not the dramatic figure, sword in hand, that he had been at other such observances. His manner was nervous. His speech was hesitant and uncertain. When he looked into the crowd standing before him in Idgah Mosque, he saw mostly mullahs, for he had been careful to honor these by filling the first rows from their ranks. Inayatullah was not present; he had become more popular lately, as those discontented with Amanullah had noted the contrast between the two brothers, and the bazaar said that this, coupled with his distaste for politics, kept him away.

"A Moslem people can progress only if the people themselves are of one accord," Amanullah said in a short speech he made after leading the prayers himself. Mullahs usually led prayers and delivered the sermons. At the same time his Chief of General Staff was saying to a British official, "A lot of ignorant tribesmen have put the Afghan clock back by at least a year."

Nadir prepared finally to leave for Paris. "His departure may ease situation somewhat," the British Military Attaché said in his diary, "as, though there is no evidence to show that he is concerned in present movement against Amanullah, his continued presence in the capital may well have gone a long way towards encouraging the rebels in the South."

Nadir admitted frankly that he did not want to go to Paris but had come to the conclusion that the Amir's order must be obeyed.

"I think the Afghan Government knows very little about the progress of operations," he said. "Wali is at Gardez and the Afghan Government must surely know what is going on in the immediate neighborhood of that place, but they are, perhaps, ashamed to say."

It would have pleased the British had Nadir elected to travel through Russia rather than through their own domains of India. They did not trust him. Just before his departure, Maconachie asked him why individuals in Afghanistan were so fond of expressing their friendship for Great Britain in private but not in public. Nadir replied that it was because the present Afghan Government was really anti-British in sentiment; that they feared British policy would destroy Afghan influence with the tribes, and they feared the British wished to keep Afghanistan weak and hinder her progress.

So Nadir crossed the frontier on July 12 and was out of Afghanistan during the Assembly, at which many had feared his influence.

The men who came to Kabul to the Great Assembly were important men in their own places; when they spoke, others heeded; that is why they had been chosen as representatives. Summoned by the monarch to the capital, they found their opinions more eagerly sought than ever. Some of them had come a little timidly, in spite of their outward assurance, wondering about the acceptability of their turbans, their shirts, their cummerbunds. Here they were given food and shelter, and, to their gratification, two sets of eminent people were seeking to influence their minds. The Amir's close advisers, Sardar Faiz Mohammed, who had been all over the world with Wali's mission, and the Judge Abdul Wasi, who was the Amir's chief counselor on religious matters, talked to them in favor of the new code, the Nizamnamas, pointing out its advantages and dismissing as nonsense any notion that the code offended Islam. Then there were mullahs whose association with the mighty implied a great amount of learning, who kept urging on them the abolition of the Nizamnamas.

At the beginning, almost every delegate spoke vigorously against hasht nafari, the most violent speakers being from Kandahar where, eight months earlier, the entire male population had shut itself up in the mosque as a protest. Amanullah spoke just as vigorously. He told the men that their opposition displayed a complete lack of responsibility in that they refused to agree to fresh taxation which was needed if the voluntary system they proposed as an alternative were to be of any use.

Amanullah's logic won; the Assembly voted to maintain hasht nafari, but the exemption fee was reduced to half, and a conscript was allowed to offer a substitute in the form of another man willing and able to serve.

About the education of women, Amanullah had to capitulate. He had not realized how bitterly men felt in the outlying provinces of his country. He agreed that female education should end at the age of twelve, and he showed so much concern over the opposition that many were speculating that the girls' school in Kabul would not open when vacation ended.

These were some of the measures passed by the Great Assembly which virtually annihilated portions of the Nizamnamas:

"Marriage of a girl below age of puberty is admissible."

"Females should receive their education from their near relatives who are their 'mahrans' [those who have admission into the harem]."

"The execution of a thief after repetition of an offense is legal."

"Sentences of imprisonment for life should be remitted in part if the prisoner shows signs of repentance."

"The study of languages of non-Moslem people to meet ordinary requirements is allowed provided it does not create a bad effect on a man's belief and provided a man has completed his religious education."

"Marriage of a second, third or fourth wife should not be made subject to approval of previous wives, or other conditions. In the case of a man not treating his wives equally, the husband can be brought into court at once."

"Freedom in the fundamental articles of faith and religion have never been, should not and will not be permitted, but the word 'freedom' used in the Nizamnamas meant 'freedom in personal rights,' not as regards faith, religion, and politics. As the said word was comprehensive, an explanation of the same has been given in the Nizamnamas and a correction has accordingly been made."

In these matters, and others, the mullahs of Afghanistan, many of whom could barely read and write, revised a code of laws which had been inaugurated by Napoleon Bonaparte in France and adapted to Turks and then adapted again to Afghans. What resulted was in many cases so obscure that, when the time came to apply the criminal laws, no one could understand what was meant.

Some delegates wished to pass a vote of censure on the Foreign Office for not making Russia live up to her treaty obligations. Men from the North, whose lands in Afghan Turkestan adjoined those in Russian Turkestan, were particularly bitter toward Russia for her absorption of Bokhara. A few mullahs would have declared all Turks infidels because they had abolished the clause in the treaty with Turkey that acknowledged her religious dominion.

The Chaknawar Mullah, one who had been angry with Amanullah over the surrender of Ajab, Ardali, et al., made a closing speech in which he praised Amanullah for having agreed to all suggestions made by religious leaders, thereby bringing his Nizamnamas completely in line with Shariat. When a rumor went around that the delegates from

Kandahar, where men had been nearly as rebellious as those in Khost, had been looted by rebels from Khost of all their possessions, including their commemorative medals, it looked as if civil strife might be over.

Always a threat to the ruler in Kabul were the descendants of former rulers who had lost the throne and been exiled to India where the British Government, feeling that British interference made them somewhat responsible for these people's dispossession, gave them allowances.

Abdul Karim was the youngest and least important son of the late ex-Amir Yakub, the man who would always be held in scorn by Afghans because he had granted Britain in the Treaty of Gandamak control over Afghan foreign relations. Abdul Karim, whom the British considered unstable, had run away four times. In 1917, after his father discontinued his allowance and after an incident in which he called a policeman a pig, he went into Afghanistan, whence he was lured by the British promise of an allowance. They made this promise in the expectation that his father would share his own money. Amir Yakub would not, dismissing Abdul Karim as the son of a concubine, and the British had to pay his allowance themselves. That was when he bragged to the British that his father loved him best of all his children. In 1920 he started to walk away from Dehra Dun but was caught and put under house arrest for two weeks. "I lived in [Benares] city . . . and worked as a goldsmith in my leisure hours to earn my livelihood, as the allowances paid to me by the Government were barely sufficient for a man of my position," he said of that period. When the Moslem movement of protest against Britain spread to his city, he went with a group to the police station seeking to be arrested, and was successful in winning more than three months' imprisonment, although he did not really care about self-government for India; he was feuding with the officials.

Abdul Karim's fifth flight took place while the Great Assembly was convening. Its goal was the seizure of a birthright from his hostile father, something to which he was entitled only by being the son of the father who openly called him a bastard. He would become Amir of Afghanistan. History was finally with him. There were Afghans who, as everyone in India knew by this time, would welcome a new Amir.

Besides, he was having disputes with the local police and was finding his allowance inadequate.

Abdul Karim rode his horse from Benares to a station eight miles away, took a train to another station, and alighted to escape detection. Then he walked to Rawalpindi; it was a journey of several days, and he spent the nights free of charge in various mosques. By a combination of train and steamer he reached Bannu in Baluchistan, and hired a man to take him to Miranshah, where the British had a fort. There he met an Afghan tribesman to whom he confided who he was.

"There is a rebellion now in Khost," said the tribesman, "and it is an opportune time for you to regain the country which your father lost."

The two walked for two days, and reached a village in Afghanistan called Nawakot, where they stayed with one of the tribesman's relations, Burland Khan, who was a leader of the Jadrans.

Soon all the countryside knew that a son of the former Amir had come among them. They went to Nawakot in crowds to see Abdul Karim. They paid him homage. A proclamation in Persian was prepared proclaiming him Amir of Afghanistan in place of Amir Amanullah, and many men from various tribes put their thumbprints to it.

Abdul Karim, who had never had even respect before, spent several weeks there enjoying himself. And the rebellion, which had nearly died down, suddenly was intensified.

The British were embarrassed. It was routine for them to keep under surveillance all former Afghan royalty in India, especially in time of discord, and this notorious malcontent who had eluded them was a man whose intelligence they had often disparaged. They felt some reparation was required of them.

Abdul Karim, therefore, was responsible for Amanullah's getting what he had been wanting all along: two airplanes in good working order.

Sher Ahmed and Maconachie discussed the delivery of planes, and the German pilot Brustmann was summoned to be asked if he were prepared to fly a British plane delivered by air at Dakka from Dakka to Kabul.

He said yes, but then went on: "The government owes me over five hundred rupees and I can get no one to listen to my claim. The government has treated me badly. I was promised rises in pay if I did good work, and since I was furnished only with airplanes that are useless, I have not, through no fault of my own, been able to earn any increase in pay."

Sher Ahmed decided that the planes should be delivered by air at

Kabul by British pilots. "I hope, however, that your government will allow Afghan officers to travel in the machines from Peshawar," he told Maconachie, "and that the Afghan Government will be given a free hand to camouflage this transaction by representing the purchase as being completed in Peshawar and Afghan officers as being in command. It is important that the British pilots who deliver the planes should have as little as possible to do with the British Legation, and therefore, I do not think that they should be your guests."

H.M.G. had this opinion: "The escape of Abdul Karim, coinciding as it does with a recrudescence of the Khost Rebellion, may not improbably be regarded as an act of British bad faith and strengthen the existing suspicion that we have incited or at least connived at this movement. Refusal to supply such a paltry number of airplanes at this juncture must inevitably confirm such a suspicion." And H.M.G. was correct. Fifty years later the Afghans would be blaming the British still for sending Abdul Karim into the Khost Rebellion with the intent of replacing Amanullah with a more amenable Amir, and Abdul Karim would still be described as a bastard.

There was a question whether sending planes to the Afghans would conform to the Versailles Treaty, since Germans would fly the planes after delivery. But G. of I. was so eager to end the rebellion that it promised the planes before getting official permission. "This is a case," H.M.G. explained to itself, "in which urgent local political considerations for supporting the Amir have outweighed the necessity for adhering to the spirit of the Treaty of Versailles, and the Government of India have, not unnaturally, succumbed to the former."

Boys of sixteen and seventeen made up much of the Afghan Regiment known as the Sar Nigahban (Self-Sacrifice). When Kabulis heard that this regiment had been given equipment and one blanket per man, they reasoned that matters must be desperate for the Afghan Government forces.

The youthful regiment went off to battle and was encamped in Logar when, before dawn on August 4, it was suddenly overwhelmed by rebel tribesmen. The commander was killed; the rebels covered his body with gunpowder and set fire to it. They had done this earlier with the body of the former Governor of Logar; their emotions had reached a violence to which not even the dead were sacred.

Many rebels had no weapons except axes. They swung these axes with ferocity, and as they swung out at boy soldiers, who were barely in their teens, they shrieked abuse of the "Kaffir Amir," the "Infidel Amir." To those who survived that massacre, the memory that made them shudder was of the insane gleam in the eyes, the cries of pure hate writhing from bearded lips. All the fury of jehad had been turned against their own.

Ghulam Nabi, the former Minister to Russia, went to Charkh, where his father had offered hospitality to all who went by, and asked for allies. Ali Ahmed was appointed Governor of Jalalabad and his post was raised to the importance of Kandahar and Turkestan; he had influence with the Khugiani tribes, from which much was hoped.

Old Abdul Quddus, the Prime Minister, in his flowing robes, and stylish Shah Wali, in tailored military uniform, departed for Logar carrying sealed Korans to assure the Mangals they came to talk. The Mangals sent word that they welcomed Shah Wali as a member of a family to whom they were deeply grateful. Some time earlier a rebel force had lost the Altimur Pass because its various groups neglected warfare to argue about who should be the Amir, with one group supporting Nadir.

What these officials had to tell the tribes was that they themselves might become the object of the jehad, the Holy War, with which they were constantly threatening others, if they did not make peace.

Two officials drove into the Southern Province to recruit soldiers for the Army from the small villages. Having little success, they went for the night to Ghazni, where they found the people sick with apprehension of an attack at any moment by the Suleiman Khels, their Ghilzai neighbors to the south who kept them in frequent states of fear. On the morning of August 14 the driver who had taken the officials to Ghazni set out to return to Kabul with his empty lorry.

The first valley through which he drove was quiet, but when he reached Sheikhabad, halfway to Kabul, he found the Suleiman Khel aggressors that Ghazni had been dreading. There were thousands of them, and a band of other nomads had joined them.

The Wardak River ran just south of Sheikhabad. The wooden bridge that crossed it was in flames. The heat of the fire and the heat of the sun reflected from the pale road made the air go in shimmers, through which the driver saw hostile faces and chests hung with three bandoleers of bullets apiece. The rebels crowded around his lorry and shouted at him. But they listened more than most mobs. They gathered that he was from Peshawar and so had no part of their quarrel, and they permitted him his neutrality.

Was he carrying any letters? He said no. They did not believe him, so he showed them the only piece of paper he had on him, a ten-rupee note. They had seen money before, but not much paper money; these were Indian rupees. So bitter were these men against anything with writing on it that they tore up the driver's ten-rupee note, lest it contaminate them.

Had he been to Ghazni? How was it fortified? They asked so many questions about Ghazni that the lorry driver deduced they were planning an attack. Then he noticed that all the flames he was seeing did not come from the bridge, but the rebels had pulled down the telephone wire from Kabul to Ghazni and were burning the telephone poles and cooking their food over them.

In midsummer the Wardak River had not much water in it; the driver decided to take his lorry across the river bed. When the rebels saw what he wanted, they crowded behind him and with a push here and a shove there, in the generous manner of Afghanistan where a traveler can always find assistance, they got his lorry across the river.

Then they told him that he should take as many as possible in his lorry to Kala Durani, in the direction of Kabul, where there was a detachment of Afghan Government troops that they wished to mop up. They did not wait for permission, but scrambled into the lorry. Any Afghan conveyance, even in normal times, was likely to be packed tightly with passengers, and these rebels, hungry for fighting, pushed so greedily into the lorry, in such numbers, that in a moment one side began to sag ominously. They had made a tire burst.

This calamity of the lorry driver dissolved, all at once, their threats and demands. He was no longer to be used, but to be pitied. They would trouble him no more, the rebels said, as they scrambled again, this time out of the lorry.

Reaching Kala Durani on his patched tire, the driver reported his experience to the military detachment whom that blowout had saved from annihilation, and the commander sent a message to the War Office in Kabul.

Amanullah had received an earlier report, that of the fighting at Logar with the regiment of young boys. He tried to extract some propaganda from the event. That morning town criers went through the streets sounding their drums and proclaiming that the Government had won a victory in Logar and that the triumphant men would return that afternoon. The Jeshyn of Independence had been scheduled to open the next day in Paghman and everything was ready for it. Amanullah suddenly postponed it, giving as excuse the sudden snap of cool weather; the truth was that he and his ministers had too much on their minds to try to control a rebellion from any place except the capital. As a result many people who had put themselves in tune for a celebration had nowhere to go, and that afternoon about five thousand gathered near the War Office.

The men came, riding in tongas, and they heard the officiating Minister of War make a speech of congratulations. But there were only fifty of them.

Many more, about 250, were carried in lorries to the hospitals at Bagrami and Sherpur on the outskirts of Kabul. Those who worked with them saw their deplorable state; they saw that many of the wounds could have been made only with axes. Amanullah knew that there was really no victory. Souraya, when she heard what had happened to these boys, sent gifts to each of the wounded, 210 rupees, silk garments, and a wristwatch.

That same day Amanullah insisted on a proclamation of jehad against the Mangal rebels who had defied their ruler. And the mullahs of Kabul complied.

Abdul Karim was now signing letters Amir Abdul Karim Khan Khadim Islam. His Kismet was fulfilled, at least partially. He was now an ally of the man who knew how to use him, the Lame Mullah.

He had gone to Utman, a village sixteen miles southwest of Matun, the largest town of Khost, and four miles from the frontier, accompanied by what he later described as "a large group of my followers," who were actually his leaders because they were taking him to the home village of the Lame Mullah. And when the Lame Mullah limped to the place where Abdul Karim was staying, and went through the motions of doing obeisance to him, he had found the element that had been missing from his war against Amanullah. In a son of former Amir Yakub, a grandson of the Amir Sher Ali, at last the Lame Mullah had someone with whom to replace Amanullah.

He knew how to use his prize. Abdul Karim's reaction to any sort of responsibility, to any problem, had always been to run away. By comparison with the men surrounding him now, who had been tempered by their mountains and by the seasons, he was a handsome, conceited weakling. His only personal superiority over the tribesmen lay in his education, and as Amanullah in Kabul was discovering, these were the days of the sword and not of the pen. The Lame Mullah did not press any responsibility upon his treasure. He arranged for three leading mullahs of the Jadran, Mangal and Ahmedzai tribes to approach Abdul Karim and beg the honor of giving a daughter in marriage. Three brides kept Abdul Karim occupied, and in the intervals there was always some tribesman coming to pay homage.

Meanwhile, the very fact of Abdul Karim's presence was giving a new impetus to the rebellion.

On August 22 Amanullah received the means of ending his troubles. Two British airplanes arrived. No one shot at them as they flew from Peshawar, the first planes to enter Afghanistan by wing since 1919, possibly because their British Army emblem had been painted out and the words "Allah-o-Akbar," "God is Great," painted on. When the pilots alighted at the airfield in Kabul, they found flowers flying toward them; their arrival had been advertised, and there would have been more flowers if some Kabulis had not stayed away remembering a previous disappointment with Russian planes. One plane broke its tail post on landing, but the English plane that had crashed in 1921 had truly been sent by God; being a Bristol fighter like these, it supplied the spare part.

During the next two days the British pilots demonstrated for the education of the Germans who were to take over the planes and for the fascination of the onlookers. Amanullah was the first Afghan to fly in one. Sher Ahmed obtained a promise from the airmen that he would be the second, and he was waiting by the plane, dressed in goggles and helmet, when Abdul Aziz, a nephew of Ulya Hazrat, who was acting head of the War Office in Wali's absence at the battlefront, reached over, removed Sher Ahmed's goggles and helmet and, putting them on himself, took his seat in the plane. He had a twenty-minute ride, which he pronounced perfect, and he gave the British a receipt, saying that the Afghan Government had decided to purchase. Later Sher Ahmed had his flight, during which he waved a bright handkerchief at his friends below.

The airmen and the mechanics departed, carrying medals given to them by Amanullah at a grateful interview. Afghans were as glad to see them go as they had been at their arrival, for they had feared these foreigners might drop bombs on the rebels, who after all were their own.

Amanullah prepared leaflets to be dropped in Khost before any more serious steps. They were addressed, "Oh, my ignorant, simple and unfortunate sons of [Khost], whom mischief-mongers have misled." They announced that a fatwa [proclamation] of jehad had been proclaimed, but did not mention any tribe by name, saying merely "evildoers."

"You still belong to us, however high you may jump into the air," said the leaflets. "On this account Government has no intention of destroying and exterminating you . . . Oh, my foolish sons, these airplanes which are flying over your heads and which are dropping papers full of my love and regard for you, these can also drop missiles of fire upon you."

Rebels had been assembling; when they saw the planes, they dispersed. A German pilot was approached in Kabul a few days later by two old men, graybeards from the Logar Valley, who had come to beg him not to drop bombs on their village.

Within a month there were signs of success. Sher Ahmed told Maconachie as much when he visited him on September 17.

"The outlook is more hopeful since there are signs of dissension among the rebels who are running short of ammunition. Ghaus-ud-din seems to be repenting of having deserted the King so hastily."

"There scarcely seems to be any need of repentance on the part of Ghaus-ud-din," said Maconachie. "Presumably his defection was a ruse carefully arranged by the Afghan Government to break up the rebels' councils."

"Well," said Sher Ahmed, "if you know as much as that, there is no harm in telling you more. The fact is that Ghaus-ud-din now is in Kabul, at this moment. He is being interviewed by the Amir. He brought in some of his Ahmedzai maliks with him, and this very evening he will return to the Logar front."

"What about the rumors that Abdul Karim is receiving British support?"

"Up to the present the Afghan Government are satisfied that Abdul Karim has not received a single rupee or cartridge from the Indian frontier, which is continuously and carefully watched by Afghan agents."

In Paris, Mahmud Tarzi, now Afghan Minister there, had given a newspaper interview blaming the British for initiating and financing the rebellion.

Maconachie mentioned the report that Abdul Karim was in possession of a large amount of British sovereigns. Sher Ahmed replied that he believed this to be entirely untrue, that Abdul Karim had no money and was issuing promissory notes which could be cashed when he ascended the throne of Afghanistan.

"If this is official information that you have from the Afghan Government," said Maconachie, "a very heavy responsibility lies on those who are deliberately misleading the Afghan people in the matter and spreading propaganda to the effect that the rebellion is receiving British support."

"At the present moment," said Sher Ahmed, "the necessity of discrediting Abdul Karim outweighs everything else, and the best chance of success in this direction lies in making it known that he was acting as the tool of the unbeliever. Otherwise, as you may have guessed, Kabul would refuse to accept the declaration of a Holy War as justifiable in any way."

"You are playing with fire," said Maconachie. "Fanatical excitement and international misunderstandings are more easily produced than cured."

"It is a case of unpleasant necessity. As soon as Abdul Karim is out of the country, the Afghan Government will announce that further investigations have made it clear that he has received no British support." Sher Ahmed produced a leaflet in Pushtu offering a British reward for Abdul Karim's arrest, and said he had shown it to the Amir, who was greatly impressed by this fresh evidence of British good faith.

Suddenly Sher Ahmed sprang to his feet. He was a talkative man who made expansive gestures with his conversation; now the gestures were heroic.

"My career is finished. I have just heard that Mahmud Tarzi has landed at Karachi!

"As long as I have been at the Foreign Office, I have worked for friendship between Great Britain and Afghanistan . . . I am an Afghan and a Moslem. Both Russians and British in my eyes are foreigners and unbelievers. Neither one has any claim on me. But I have no enmity with either.

"As a matter of common sense I can see that the policy of Russia is essentially aggressive and that what she wants is to get India, which

FIRE IN AFGHANISTAN

she cannot do until Afghanistan has ceased to exist as an independent power. Great Britain on the other hand has no particular love for Afghanistan, but she is not aggressive and entirely in her own interests desires that Afghanistan should remain strong and prosperous as a buffer against the Bolsheviks. So much for the official and patriotic standpoint."

Sher Ahmed's usually smiling face was contorted. Maconachie had never seen anything but affability in this man. Now he saw hatred.

"My private interests are entirely the same. It is all very well for upstarts of low birth like Mohammed Hashim Khan, Minister of Finance, or Abdul Hadi to look for their advancement to a Bolshevik domination of their country, since it is always the Bolshevik way to choose their leaders from the gutter. The only favor that I as a member of the royal family could expect from the Russian conquerors would be an efficient firing party.

"The British know how to treat a sardar. I have, since in the existing conditions anything may happen, been looking up the histories and I have found that Lord Roberts when in Kabul always treated the Afghan nobles with the greatest courtesy and even consulted them regarding the administration of-the country."

Maconachie tried to change the subject by saying: "It must be a severe blow to Tarzi to find that the progressive policy of which he is generally regarded as the author has led his country into civil war."

"Mahmud Tarzi made this mess," Sher Ahmed replied. "It is for him to put it right, but God knows what he will do. He may even be fool enough to turn to the Russians for assistance. For my own part I will continue as President of the Council to urge the necessity of a friendship between Afghanistan and Great Britain."

Sher Ahmed then told Maconachie why he had asked him to come for a visit.

"On September 14 Weisz [the German pilot] flew to Gardez with peremptory orders from the Amir to land there at all costs. Wali had been ordered to prepare a landing ground eight hundred by eight hundred yards. He prepared one five hundred yards by three hundred. Five and three, you see, make eight. The result was that Weisz on landing taxied into a ditch. The machine pitched on its nose and broke the propeller. Weisz and the Afghan passenger were not hurt, but the question now is how to get another propeller to Gardez and then how to fit it."

They agreed that a spare propeller would be sent to Kabul as quickly as possible by road.

Then Maconachie asked Sher Ahmed if he could account for the impression which all the legations in Kabul seemed to have that the British machines had been supplied free of charge.

"I started this story myself," said Sher Ahmed. "It was a very good idea. It has enhanced my reputation as a diplomat."

"I have contradicted the story already," said Maconachie. "I intend to contradict it whenever I am asked about it."

"This is very ill-advised on your part. It is as much to your interest as it is to mine to say that the airplanes were presented free to the Amir by the British Government. A general belief to this effect would make your government and you very popular in Kabul."

"Even if this were so, there are perhaps other considerations to be taken into account."

The German pilot Weisz did manage to examine the machine and, by disguising himself as an Afghan, to get back to Kabul to report that it could be repaired.

Then the German Minister in Kabul almost destroyed the new Afghan Air Force when he asked the British chargé about the Versailles Treaty, which, after all, had been imposed on Germany by Britain and her Allies. His concern for technicalities was most unwelcome to the British, who had known all along what the Versailles Treaty said. They had just agreed to supply bombs to Amanullah, and were not willing to take upon themselves, immediately thereafter, the burden of depriving him of the only means of dropping them by preventing his only pilots from flying. "Great Britain is constantly accused in India of making promises to the ear and breaking them to the heart (I think that is the formula)" read the minute paper in London. "Could there be a clearer example of procedure than this would be? We sell airplanes to the Amir knowing the purpose for which they are required and the fact that there are only Germans to fly them, and then at the last moment we refuse to let them fly. If the principle must be asserted, which seems proper, I suggest that no difficulties be made at Kabul."

A Moslem scholar once said, "Necessity makes lawful that which is forbidden."

"Government planes from the north" would be arriving immediately, the town criers proclaimed in the bazaars on September 30, and the next day four service planes and a passenger plane arrived from Russia, flying. Crowds watched them in flight over Kabul, dropping confetti and flowers. These planes were offered as a gift, but another gift went along with them, the continued presence of Russian personnel to fly and maintain them. Amanullah offered to pay for the airplanes on condition the Russian personnel return at once to Russia. "His supposedly pro-Russian sentiments are one of the reasons for the Amir's unpopularity," reported the British, "and some go as far as to assert that the arrival of the Russian planes would be the last straw . . . Mullahs and a large section of upper classes reported not to like signs of increasing friendship with Russia and are freely expressing opinions."

While the two nations argued about the string attached to the gift, the Russian pilots, whom the Afghans were paying by the day, continued to fly. They dropped some bombs in the vicinity of the rebels, not close enough to hurt, only to threaten.

With the new weapon of the twentieth century, and with their old weapons, including the approach of cold weather which took the nomads down to the plains of India, the rebellion reached a stage which enabled Amanullah to decide that Victory, although not complete, was visible and present.

CHAPTER 15

January 21, 1925, to August 31, 1925

The Lame Mullah was captured and taken to Kabul, a tragic figure in his cloak and turban of the Prophet's color, green. He looked as if no harm could possibly have come from him.

"These so-called mullahs from whom even Satan himself would seek protection" was the way Amanullah described him and his chief lieutenant on January 21, 1925, when they were publicly condemned in a ceremony the final details of which were not reported in the newspaper because the man who took the shorthand notes was overcome with weeping amid the shouts of "Long live the King!"

Abdul Karim was accompanied now by only a few men of what he called "my personal bodyguard," and some of these would have sold him to the British. He left them behind and went out of Afghanistan, where he would have been executed if found, exactly as he had entered it, on foot: all he carried was a blanket.

Winding a turban around his head, so that he might pretend to be a mullah, he went to Tirah and on to Thal. On the way he met some travelers who discussed the rebellion and expressed sympathy with Amanullah, so Abdul Karim did not tell them who he was. At Thal he took a train, buying a third-class ticket. Later he would say that he chose third class to conceal his identity, not for economy, since he was carrying one hundred English sovereigns and eight hundred Kabuli rupees. When, after a change of trains, he reached Peshawar, he went to the bazaar and exchanged his Kabuli coins for English money; in this center of commerce between India and Afghanistan, this aroused no attention.

Another train ride and a walk on foot took Abdul Karim to an important khan whom he knew in Bajaur, in Independent Territory. To this
man Abdul Karim revealed his identity, asking him to negotiate with
the British for airplanes and machine guns. The khan was too busy; he
was preparing to invade the land of another khan, who was an enemy,
and Abdul Karim's project of invading Afghanistan from another corner, although more ambitious, was far less immediate and personal.
With typical Pathan hospitality, he asked the young man to remain a
few days.

Before leaving, Abdul Karim entrusted to this man for safekeeping
the document with many signatures which proclaimed his election as
Amir of Afghanistan.

Abdul Karim's mother and small son, the child of a wife who had
died, lived with his wife's brother, Sardar Abdus Samad, an extra-
assistant commissioner who had been transferred to Gujranwala about
the time of Abdul Karim's departure for the frontier. Abdul Karim took
a train, again in the crowded discomfort of third class, where he managed to sleep a little, to Gujranwala, and not having visited his family
there went to the district court to find out the address. He was told
that Abdus Samad had been transferred to Gurdaspur.

Taking a tonga back to the railway station, Abdul Karim paid the
driver, using some coins that he had tied in a handkerchief. Then he
noticed a large cut in his shirt. He felt for his purse, which had been
fastened at his waist under the shirt. It was gone. While he had dozed
in the train, someone had cut it off.

In the turban which he had put on as a disguise, which he never would
have worn in India under his own identity, Abdul Karim had tied up
six rupees and a few annas. With these he bought a ticket to Gurdaspur.
That night he reached his destination and was once more with his
mother and sister and small son.

He told them that he would return to Afghanistan to become Amir,
that he had stopped by only for help. His mother began to cry and
begged him to give up this foolish plan. She pointed out that his brother-
in-law would be approached by the government, for which he worked,
to reveal his whereabouts. Abdul Karim saw the logic of that.

"Considering that my arrival had become known, and I would be arrested," he related later, "I took leave of my mother at about 10 P.M. and
returned to the railway station and lay down in a mosque close by, as I
did not like the idea of being removed by the police in the presence of

my mother and other relatives. I had hardly been in the mosque for a few minutes when a head constable and a constable came up and conveyed me to the city police station."

Amanullah asked the British to give him Abdul Karim in reciprocity for what he had done for them in regard to Ajab and the others. They refused, saying he was a political offender, but they sent him away from the frontier to internment in Burma.

"Sinister influences are at work in Kabul to precipitate outburst of savagery which could only lead to recrudescence of rebellion in still fiercer form," wrote Humphrys in May 1925.

Later Humphrys described the punishment of the rebels as "extremely moderate in view of the grave peril which threatened the government, the indiscriminate murder of Afghan soldier prisoners by the rebels, and the necessity in a country like Afghanistan for strong deterrents."

The number executed was seventy-five out of about five thousand prisoners. All Mangal, Zadran and Ghilzai women and children prisoners were released except for the Ahmedzai Ghilzais of Altimur, the worst offenders, who were deported with their male relatives to Turkestan, where they were given land.

Souraya held a harem durbar for the rebel women and told them that their men richly deserved any punishment that might come to them, and that they themselves, since they had encouraged the men, had been treated extraordinarily well.

One execution, that of the Lame Mullah, kept Kabul in upheaval because it was delayed until late May, and meanwhile the Lame Mullah had the power of speech and there was speculation as to whom he might implicate. It would have surprised no one to hear of his sudden death shortly after his arrest. There was even talk that Wali had some involvement with him which accounted for the delay in defeating his forces. Prominent persons were said to have sent the rebels, at a time when they seemed likely to win, encouraging messages which they now regretted.

Amazingly, no important persons were arrested.

Two victory parades were held, one for Wali and his forces, which Amanullah attended, and a second for Ali Ahmed, which Amanullah did not attend. In both processions the women prisoners were displayed on camels and donkeys.

This arrest and display of their women offended the Ghilzais, who sent a deputation of elders to Kabul under safe-conduct to protest; the elders were put into jail. This was the sort of official behavior that might have caused the rebellion, not completely subdued, to ignite again. Amanullah, after a warning by Humphrys, released the elders. It was on Amanullah that all the discredit fell; after the Lame Mullah was shot in a public ceremony, some Afghan soldiers trampled his body underfoot. Although Amanullah had nothing to do with this, bitter people complained, not of the soldiers, but of their Amir.

Amanullah did agree to the punishment that perturbed his friends; that of the Qadianis.

The Qadianis were a very small and unimportant Moslem sect in India. Qadiani beliefs differed from those of orthodox Moslems in their concession to man of more right to use his free will; not all things were ordained by Allah, they said, but instead Allah had given man an initiative so that he might employ it. They believed also that a new Prophet had followed Mohammed.

Two members of this sect entered Afghanistan in the summer of 1924, preaching their doctrines, and were arrested by the ecclesiastical courts and charged with heresy. One recanted and was set free. But the other, Maulvi Niamatullah, questioned the legality of his arrest. According to the Nizamnamas and the announcements of Amir Amanullah, he said, complete religious freedom existed in Afghanistan.

Maulvi Niamatullah had entered an alien country to collide headlong with its history. He displayed his courage at the most virulent stage of the Khost Rebellion, when the Great Assembly was being convened and Amanullah's outstanding need was to placate the orthodox religious faction. Besides, Amanullah himself had been accused on the frontier of being a Qadiani. His exhortations to his countrymen to use their own judgment, in such things as whom to applaud and whose hand to kiss as well as more practical matters, indicated that he set great store on free will.

On order of the ecclesiastical court Maulvi Niamatullah was executed for his beliefs on August 31. And the form of his execution was this: he was led onto an open place at Sherpur, just outside Kabul, and those who attended took up big stones and threw them at him until he was dead.

Forty years later an American novel would describe the stoning of a woman for adultery at Ghazni,[1] supposedly taking place after the

Second World War. The Afghans, having forgotten about Maulvi Niamatullah, would be indignant. They would deny that any execution
had been carried out in this form since very early days. It was shocking
also in 1924.

A week after this stoning Amanullah spoke in the mosque following
midday prayers and asked for the denunciation of all Qadianis, who he
said would be executed according to law. In February 1925 two more
Qadianis were stoned to death.

Stoning was sufficiently medieval to alarm even Moslems who were
not particularly liberal. In India, whence the Qadianis had come, news
of the stoning was a source of distress. The leaders of the Moslem
League in India wrote Amanullah a strong letter of protest; Indian
newspapers carried such condemnatory articles on the subject that the
official Afghan newspaper, the *Aman-i-Afghan*, felt it necessary to defend both the conviction of Niamatullah and the manner of his execution. In three articles on April 1925 it said about the first:

"Islam confers complete freedom of faith upon its non-Moslem subjects. But a Moslem is not permitted to change his faith and become
irreligious like Europeans and their followers . . . Every Moslem has
responsibility toward his religion. This is not possessed by Europeans
who have become worse than wild beasts in their strayings from human
qualities."

A few months earlier *Aman-i-Afghan* had quoted a Turkish newspaper's account of the lynching of a Negro by white men in the Southern
part of the United States, giving all the gruesome details. It reached
the conclusion that "Western nations, which pretend to regard Oriental
punishments as barbarity, are themselves capable of committing atrocities when it suits their book to do so."

Now, in defense of stoning, the newspaper described methods of
execution in other parts of the world. The story of the lynching, passing through Turkish and possibly other languages, was misunderstood and led to the erroneous statement that the American Congress
had recently passed a law permitting the emasculation of criminals and
lunatics. The article closed, "Executions are according to the disposition
of the people and should be such as to prevent crime."

In spite of his public optimism and vigor, Amanullah privately was
worried about the future. He issued an order forbidding any more arrests of Qadianis, but there lingered the history of having betrayed
his principles. As for those who already thought him heretic, they were

so hostile that he who once had gloried in saying, "The nation is my bodyguard," now did not dare to move publicly without having the most undesirable characters in each locality sequestered beforehand. Again placards were posted threatening his assassination.

The Hazrat of Shor Bazaar who had supported him, Shah Agha, died in 1925. Sher Agha, who found him dangerous, now was head of that powerful family and in 1925, after service in the Khost Rebellion which had led to conflicting opinions as to which side he was on, he and Amanullah agreed that he would be better off in India. It was then that he left Afghanistan for an exile that would make him the spiritual adviser of many nomads.

It had always been part of Amanullah's independence that he refused the "capitulations" by which some other Oriental countries agreed that Westerners accused of crime would be tried by their own courts.

An Italian engineer named Dario Piparno shot and killed, in a panic, an Afghan policeman who had come to arrest him, and was secretly executed. Italy was enraged, demanding an apology and indemnity, which Amanullah gave only a short time before the Italian Legation would have broken relations with Afghanistan and departed.

Later a German, Dr. Stratil-Sauer, riding a motorcycle across Asia as a publicity stunt, killed an Afghan in what he said was an accident. Unlike Piparno, who had collided with Afghan pride at a moment when Amanullah, beset by the Khost Rebellion, was obliged to display his independence of foreigners, Stratil-Sauer had a public trial. Although condemned to several years' imprisonment, he was immediately pardoned and set free.

Both these men had killed Afghan Moslems. When one German killed another German, Afghan law interfered only to assure that the relatives of the dead man would bring no reprisals.

After these episodes, members of the British Legation were ordered to put their revolvers away at the bottom of their trunks and keep them there.

Abdul Karim was sent to Shwebo cantonment in Burma, where he was given a bungalow and an outbuilding for two servants. The Government that provided these accommodations did not provide anything for him to do. One day a new district magistrate arrived in Shwebo and, recognizing in an "unstable, excitable and virile youth of about twenty-five [he was three years older but looked young] with nothing to do or to occupy his mind" a source of potential trouble, arranged for him to obtain a riding pony from the Military Police Lines. In his letters to India he managed to convey his restlessness to his mother, who offered to send him a wife.

The friends that Abdul Karim drew around him were mostly young Burmese boys still in their teens, who were impressed by him. This man who had tried to be a king was still trying to be "king of his company."

He was friendly also with two Englishmen named Watt and Macnamara. He talked with these about the Christian religion, and finally bought a Bible and began to attend evensong services at the only Anglican church in Shwebo.

Early in 1927 Abdul Karim told the rector of that church, the Reverend Stockings, that he wished to become a Christian.

The Reverend Stockings was in no hurry to collect the soul of Abdul Karim. He had been sent there to minister to the Anglo-Saxon population, not to convert the natives. British policy was to leave native religion strictly alone, except for removing such excesses as human sacrifice and widow-burning. During Lord Curzon's Viceroyalty a bishop who had been his close friend lost his post in India because he forgot where his ministry ended. Besides, it was not difficult to deduce that this urge toward Christianity, on the part of so unstable a young man, might arise from some motive other than deep religious conviction.

Conversion to any religion other than Islam would end, for all times, any possibility of his ever ruling Afghanistan. But it also was the greatest insult to Afghanistan that Abdul Karim had in his power to impose. He wrote of his plan to his mother, and this unhappy woman, reared in a society where the only known convert to Christianity had been killed for it, replied with lamentations. She wrote back to Abdul Karim that if he did such a thing, she would give him none of the money that his dead father had left with her in trust for him. Since money was always lacking in Abdul Karim's life, he wired that she had been mistaken.

The Moslem community in Shwebo knew what Abdul Karim had in mind, and although the Reverend Stockings personally did not think there was enough interest in this young man to cause any concern, Sergeant Watt told him that they were annoyed. So when Abdul Karim went to the Reverend Stockings and asked to be baptized in the Christian faith, he was prudently told to take his time and think the matter over.

About the beginning of February, Abdul Karim began to talk in a disturbing manner. First he said that his life was in danger, that the Amir of Afghanistan was his deadly enemy, who had sent men to Burma to kill him, and he asked a friend in the police force to watch out for possible assassins.

Then he began to talk about suicide, not for the first time. In Benares jail he had tried to hang himself. He had made the threat once to officials in Burma.

One night, while Watt and Macnamara were visiting him, he showed exactly how he would go about shooting himself.

"Do it through the mouth. That is the simplest way," advised Watt, who considered the conversation a joke.

"That would spoil the features," objected Abdul Karim.

Two looking-glasses were in his house, placed parallel and opposite each other. Abdul Karim was very proud of, first, his good looks, and second, the flexibility of his body. He used to study his appearance in one mirror and then, without turning his body, look over his shoulder at the reflection of his back in the other. It was a trick with which he often amused visitors.

Now he showed how, being so flexible, with a small pistol he could perform a feat not possible to everyone: shoot himself in the back of the head.

Such talk aroused alarm finally even in Sergeant Watt, and the district magistrate who had provided the pony became concerned enough to send a policeman to Abdul Karim's house on February 17 to see if he had any firearms. He had none. But the query was unfortunate in its suggestion. The next day he acquired a German Mauser pistol four inches long.

That night he made an appointment with a sixteen-year-old Burmese friend, Maung Po Tun, to meet him early the next morning to go shopping for socks and ties. He was always seeking company.

But after his friend had gone, Abdul Karim closed all his doors and windows, placed a table and chair between the two mirrors, wrote his will and some farewell letters, and killed himself exactly as he had told the two Englishmen he would.

Po Tun, finding his friend's house locked and no answer to his calls, summoned the servants and reached his slim hand between the shutters of the window, opened it, and looked into the room. He called the police. Abdul Karim had done his work so well that the police had to finger through his thick hair for some seconds before they found the bullet hole. The official report said, "The deceased was a good-looking man."

In one of his farewell letters Abdul Karim had asked, although he died before his baptism, to be buried as a Christian. Instead, when the news of his death reached his half brothers in Dehra Dun in India, he was mourned with the Moslem "fatiha," prayers for the dead, attended by all the men of the Afghan colony in Dehra Dun and about thirty-five Afghans who were in town on business, some of whom had fought in Abdul Karim's name during the rebellion of 1924. No political speeches were made, but privately there was speculation that, instead of committing suicide, he had been murdered on orders from Kabul.

On the table before Abdul Karim when he died was a letter addressed to his son, which he asked to be published in the newspaper. It was not. In it he told the son, if he became the Amir of Afghanistan, to be good to the Afghans.

CHAPTER 16

October 1925 to August 1927

Kandahar, in its long history of conquering and being conquered, of the passage of people from the Far East to the West and back again, had never known anything like Amanullah's visit of October 1925.

He prepared them with a general notice in advance saying that the Amir would accept petitions concerning:

1. Complaints against any of the local officers.
2. Applications for restoration of confiscated property.
3. Pardons for outlaws.
4. Pardons for prisoners condemned to long terms of imprisonment.

"Considerable nervousness is being displayed by the local officials who, in anticipation of the Amir's visit, have refused to take any bribes for the last few weeks," wrote the British Military Attaché. "Prices have risen abnormally owing to the large collection of supplies for the Amir and his entourage. In spite of official desire to display a satisfactory state of affairs, the number of thefts and robberies in the vicinity of Kandahar shows no sign of decreasing, and regular gangs, who are believed to be in the pay of local gentlemen of importance, continue to commit offenses unchecked."

Ulya Hazrat preceded her son to Kandahar with a retinue of forty ladies and a great deal of jewelry as gifts for the Kandahar ladies, who were her own tribe. Amanullah left the following day, October 11, with many government motorcars and lorries carrying his baggage, and forty other lorries and motors hired for the trip at a price far above the market prices.

Outside Kandahar, Amanullah alighted from his car and greeted the crowd awaiting him, then rode through their cheers to the mosque of the Khirqa Sharif, where another crowd was waiting, this one including many mullahs. He shook hands all around.

One day a few weeks later all the bazaars in Kandahar were closed, as they had been during the hasht nafari protest, but this closing was by official order. Several thousand persons collected in the Arg of Kandahar for a Durbar-i-Makafar, or Durbar of Recompense, where Amanullah made an opening speech, then discussed each department of the administration. He dismissed the Director of the Hospital Department and made him leave the durbar in disgrace. The doctor was fined a week's pay and compelled to stand for an hour to be gazed upon by persons who contemplated his offense, which was, like that of the Director, making false accounts of the numbers of patients treated.

The Chief of Police was deprived of his medals and reduced in rank; his chief clerk was dismissed. Amanullah found them guilty of negligence.

The Director of the Agriculture Department, whose brother was Governor of Kandahar, was dismissed because Amanullah, after discussing his duties with him, found him ignorant.

The Magistrate was found guilty of treachery, and arrested and ordered taken to a Kabul prison and his property confiscated.

Officials of the treasury, post office and education departments were commended and decorated. As for the Customs Director, the British Military Attaché said that he, "a notorious rascal, who, however, knows whom to bribe, was decorated with a medal and proclaimed an honest man." This was the Postmaster in Peshawar who had given so much trouble in 1919.

The district officers had an especially difficult time, for Amanullah examined each of these on the contents of his code of laws, the Nizamnamas. Only one man knew enough about the laws to answer Amanullah's questions with any degree of competence. Amanullah promoted him immediately and appointed him to a post in Badakhshan. One other officer had a smattering of knowledge; Amanullah said he would undergo a further inspection. As for the others, Amanullah said in the durbar, in front of all the population of Kandahar, that they had failed miserably and would shortly be replaced by more efficient officers sent from Kabul.

As for the Governor of Kandahar, Amanullah referred to him as "honest and respectable but slow and negligent."

During Amanullah's visit he was told that a prisoner had recently been executed for taking part in a jail break, when actually he had been admitted to prison only the day after the break. Amanullah put the responsible official in chains.

Later in Kabul he reported on what he had found in Kandahar: "I have this complaint against the Governor, that he did not put up to me any proposals concerning the government, progress and prosperity of Kandahar, and other important affairs. His only request was that permission should be given to kill people accused of mischief and that rewards be given for Hindu converts to Islam. If a man embraces Islam, it should be for the sake of doctrine and deeds and no reward is required in this case."

Regarding education, Amanullah said, "Petty, unrecognized schools are still in vogue. I have ordered that they should be closed down and that the number of regular schools should be increased. People who had withdrawn their sons from the school, or had not sent them to school, were fined five rupees each. My speeches on education had the effect that they sent their children to school. In consequence about six hundred to eight hundred new students joined the schools in a few days.

"Schools for traders, Persian-speaking people and Hindus were separate. This separation causes division in a nation. Everyone who lives in the lands of Afghanistan is an Afghan, irrespective of the religion he professes or the sect or class to which he belongs and there is no distinction among Afghans. The Persian-speaking people and the Afghans are Moslems and there is no difference between them. The Hindus, of course, have different religious beliefs. All Hindu and Moslem students should study in one school. For the period of theology the Hindus should go to their special room and teacher, and the Moslems to their special room and teacher. Separate schools should not be maintained for people of various religions, classes or sects."

Traders had been accustomed to paying a tax for education of ten pice each; Amanullah made them agree to raise this 900 percent to one rupee. "In this respect they have exceeded the traders of Kabul," he pointed out to the Kabulis. "In Kandahar trade is mostly carried on by individuals. I have advised them to form companies. I have ordered canals to be dug to make use of cultivable land now lying untilled." Amanullah suggested that machines be obtained for works which would add to the people's prosperity.

"Justice and police affairs in Kandahar were in a state of confusion,"

Amanullah said. "The Commandant's office, especially, was in a very poor state. Thefts were so common that no one could sleep in peace. There was little difference between killing a man and hunting an animal. The old Commandant had, owing to negligence and carelessness, executed a man who did not deserve death. The Commandant and the Superintendent of Police have, therefore, been imprisoned for five years. The head clerk of the Police Office has been dismissed. The new Commandant has been reduced one grade as he has not displayed any activity in restoring law and order. Theft was so rife that every khan and notable maintained thieves and vied with one another in the skill of their thieves. Some of the people always disobeyed the laws and inclined others to do the same. Others had made it their profession to smuggle goods. With regard to such people I ordered that they should be brought to Kabul and detained here until they re-establish their reputation and the public change their opinion about them. Some other people . . . who were professional theives and highway robbers, and who, according to the Shariat, deserved to be killed, were sentenced to death. I also ordered that the khans should be held responsible for thefts committed by their servants."

Amanullah mentioned 1,800,000 rupees as the deficit in Kandahar's treasury due to tax arrears. "The people requested that the revenue should be slightly increased to cover arrears outstanding and that arrears should be remitted. But I did not agree to this and tore the petition to pieces."

Kandahar was to have its own Dar-ul-Aman. Amanullah said he had chosen a site for new Government buildings. He was not aware of the displeasure of the Kandaharis over the site he had chosen, which would take away some of their best orchards. "People desirous of building private houses there can do so provided they follow the government's plan."

He had also ordered rules to restrict the hands of guardians so that they might not be able to dissipate the fortunes of minors in their charge.

Kandahar was not the same for a while. Six months later the British intelligence officers were reporting, "There has been an improvement in the work of the officials since Amir's visit to Kandahar and rumors of a future visit will keep them on their toes."

It was shortly after this that an airplane flew over Kandahar and dropped leaflets bearing the message from Amanullah to "his children of Kandahar," in which he said that "the extraordinary love infused into his heart" by the Kandaharis during his last visit made another early visit essential. Wrote the British Military Attaché: "This has considerably frightened the local officials who now expect a sudden, unannounced visit and in consequence all officers are showing great devotion to their duties."

Amanullah was resilient. The Khost Rebellion was over and he was going ahead with all his plans as if it had never happened.

"The Pillar of Knowledge and Ignorance" was what he called the monument to that struggle. That was the way he regarded it: as a conflict between two abstract qualities, knowledge on one hand and ignorance on the other. That it was also between two groups of people did not enter into his calculations. Always he looked upon issues as abstractions, without considering that they all involved living people who had emotions which might be illogical or foolish or totally opposed to their interests, but nevertheless existed.

"This lack of discernment in Amanullah may have come," as a French writer later theorized, from "an excess of his good qualities; his beautiful boldness and the quickness with which, without casting a look around him, he put into execution the plans which, in his opinion, conformed to the interests of the nation. Perhaps, also, while possessing certain gifts, he lacked virtues that are more humble but indispensable: circumspection and the discernment which enables people to penetrate the souls and the ambitions of men, to foresee the consequences of events."[1]

Between two human beings there are many nuances; a choice, always difficult, often disappears into compromise. Between knowledge and ignorance, there is only one choice.

Amanullah launched the subscription for the monument soon after the Rebellion ended. He dedicated it on June 22, 1927, a pillar in granite and marble on a rock above the Kabul River, with the jagged ruins of the old Bala Hissar, which the British had destroyed, seeming to point down the hillside to it. A description of the rebellion was carved in the marble of the front face and the words inlaid in gold. On the other three faces were carved the names of more than three hundred officers who had died in the campaign.

Toward sunset all the diplomats, ministers and their assistants, troops, and ten thousand spectators were waiting at the base of the pillar and along the road. At six o'clock a bugle sounded and the military band struck up the "Salaami," the melody which saluted the Amir. Amanullah drove up in a silver Rolls-Royce. Queen Souraya was with him. This was the first time that an Afghan Queen had ever attended a public function.

Souraya wore a dress and hat that were Western and stylish, but the hat had a thick black veil which made it impossible to distinguish her features. In the second car came two of her young daughters, who also wore European-style dresses and, over their faces, no veils at all. These princesses were getting into their teens, an age when, according to old Afghan tradition, a girl became a woman and should cease to show her face. Amanullah was thereby dramatizing his desire to abolish the custom of purdah.

"To gain independence Afghanistan successfully dealt with its external enemies and in order to introduce knowledge, modern science, education and civilization within the country Afghanistan had to combat ignorance," Amanullah said in his speech. "Some selfish people, for furtherance of their own motives, did not like to see knowledge spreading in the country, and this was the cause of the revolt in [Khost]. Thanks to God the Afghan Army succeeded in putting out this fire!"

Amanullah said that it gave him no pleasure to say that he crushed his own brothers in Khost, because no one could be happy in cutting or injuring his own arm or any other organ of his body. But "I want to let it be known that whoever may be an enemy of knowledge will be considered as the King's enemy." And he referred particularly to the mullahs.

A few nights later Ulya Hazrat entertained the royal family at a dinner to discuss whether or not Amanullah should make an official visit to Khost. She herself was violently opposed, as she feared assassination there. A year earlier there had been reports of rebellions and excursions in the Southern Province. "These are common," wrote the British Intelligence Service, "but for the past weeks have been so persistent they seem to be put out by interested parties. Whether they originate with the people, or Amir is starting to induce malcontents to show their hands, since he feels strong enough to cope, is not known. Name of Inayatullah mentioned."

Amanullah felt "strong enough to cope," if not on the 1925 visit to Kandahar, then on the 1926 return when he was in a far better humor because he found far less to criticize.

"My dear ones!" he said in his farewell speech, "the greatest sacrifice that can be offered to God is life, because everything else can be easily replaced. And life is the dearest thing; therefore this should be offered as a sacrifice to God. But how should this be done? Not by committing suicide, by shooting oneself with a revolver, but by defending one's religion and country against its enemies . . . There are several advantages in the preparation for war. It prevents differences appearing among you . . . If there is nothing to divert your attention, dissensions are bound to appear in your minds."

Amanullah exhorted the Kandaharis to send their children to schools, girls as well as boys. He deplored the Afghan custom of treating women badly and exhorted his audience to follow his example by limiting themselves to one wife.

He inspected the schools, where one girl asked him to release her imprisoned father, which he did. He went to the military cantonment in disguise; only a sentry recognized him, and he promised this soldier a rise in pay if he did not disclose the fact.

"I am very pleased with the Kandahar officials. There is no comparison between this year's work and last year's. I regret the execution of certain robbers and criminals during the previous year, but justice demanded it and the criminals had only themselves to blame."

He announced a sanction of a hundred thousand rupees as a loan to ten traders with insufficient capital to carry on their work, another sum of thirty thousand rupees on a loan to cultivators for agriculture development, and an appropriation of thirty-five thousand rupees for repairing the road between Kabul and Kandahar.

"Last year when I came here I could not see a single piece of country-made cloth. But now as I find that the people of Kandahar are inclined toward locally manufacturing cloth, I have advanced the sum of ten thousand rupees to Baqidad Khan, who is desirous of developing local cloth manufacture but prevented by lack of funds."

Amanullah had one criticism: "The students of the Kandahar Schools are slow in their movements and did not know how to salute properly. They require to be trained in these things."

Souraya, like Ulya Hazrat, reared chiefly daughters. Her first son died of cholera. There was another son, born in mid 1923, who died of bronchial pneumonia at the age of eighteen months; German doctors tended him; at the last moment Amanullah called in the surgeon of the British Legation, who said that all possible had been done. The following year

Rahmatullah, the son whose birth in 1921 had softened the tension of the Kabul conference, was desperately ill, and Amanullah called in virtually all the doctors in Kabul, ten in all, of various nationalities. Nine agreed on a diagnosis; one Italian physician had a different opinion and was given a few days' leave; Rahmatullah recovered, and Amanullah expressed his and Souraya's gratitude to the various legations and individuals who had helped. The following year Souraya gave birth to another boy, who died young. Many babies in Afghanistan did not grow to be more than babies.

Rahmatullah had four sisters; Amenah, born 1915; Sultan, born 1917; Abedah, born 1919; and Hamidah, born 1923. It seemed likely that, if Amanullah's plans for his country went well, none of his daughters would ever have to be veiled.

The harem serai in the Arg at Kabul was lively, for this family was augmented by another family, the children of Amir Habibullah, some of whom were almost as young as Amanullah's own children. Souraya and Amanullah were warm and affectionate with them all. No one in Afghanistan would have found this surprising.

Afghan families seldom consisted of only a couple and offspring; relatives, even cousins several times removed, expected to be sheltered and people whose principles would not let them refuse asylum to a stranger, even a criminal, were not aware that there were homes in the world where a relative might not be welcome. The higher a man's position, the greater the throng he enfolded into his hospitality.

Driving along a Kabul street one day, Amanullah saw a woman whose story he knew. A blond European, who did not veil, she was conspicuous, and in Kabul, as the British sometimes complained, "everything is known." This was one of the German wives whom an Afridi had brought back to the frontier hills after the Great War; a British officer, talking about such marriages, had expressed incomprehension because the Afridis were in Germany only, he felt, by the grace of the British Empire, since they had been sent there to fight in the Great War; it did not occur to him that it was the British Empire which owed gratitude to the Afridis for fighting. These men, so redoubtable at home, were so little impressed by the cause of the Allies that, after they got to Europe, they deserted.

Between a German fraulein and an Afridi tribesman it was natural that a flame should ignite. When a man of the Middle East is in a fantasizing mood, he always says that he would like "a beautiful girl with golden hair." He never omits the "golden hair," and this the German women had in abundance. To the women, weary with war, seeing their own men return disheartened and weak, these dark, intense men with their look of not giving a damn were like phoenixes rising from the ashes of war. The marriages which surprised the British officer were demonstrations of the adage that opposites attract.

Some of the Afridis enlarged upon their status in Afghanistan, made themselves princes when talking to the girls; even when they did not, the glamour that envelopes a far-off unknown place gave the girls much to hope for; more than they found in reality. Many a fraulein went to the mountains to discover she was not the only wife, but number three or four; some would tell stories of having to sleep on one side of a mutual husband while the other incumbent slept on the other side. But they made the most of it, and this lady had two children before she found herself in Kabul with her children, having left her husband, trying to make a new life in a strange land.

This day on the street she was amazed to see a motorcar stop and a person of importance get out. Any person who had a motorcar was important. The man told her who he was. It was the Amir himself, Amanullah. There on the street he offered her a home. She went to live in the house of Ulya Hazrat, who gave her two rooms and asked nothing in return. She left only when, feeling that she and her children could not live forever as guests, she married an Afghan man.

Amanullah's daughters and half sisters attended a school for girls of noble family, which was a device to circumvent the promise he had given the Great Assembly during the Khost Rebellion to limit the education of women. At first a selected group of girls attended classes in the Arg. Then, in April 1925, even before accounts had been settled to the extent of the Lame Mullah's execution, again girls were being educated publicly.

"The milk of ignorance which the Afghans imbibe from their mothers" was Mahmud Tarzi's explanation of the Khost Rebellion. "Progress is impossible until the women of the country are educated." That explained the deep bitterness which made the subject of female education the most emotional of all the conflicts. That explained also why the mullahs tried to stir to opposition all those whom they could influence; they knew Amanullah and his advisers were making remarks like Tarzi's: "Those whose duty it is to interpret religion are, as in most other countries, generally the most ignorant of all."

Alarmed as he had been by the raging hostility which female education could evoke, which he had never suspected until the Great Assembly, Amanullah persevered. He even suggested opening a girls' school in Khost, the center of the rebellion where it was most needed but most opposed. He would have sent the girls of Kandahar to school except for reports of even greater opposition he would face; it caused alarm in Kandahar when a shipment of books arrived along with a lady rumored to be "an educationist."

When Amanullah visited the Kabul girls' school in June 1926, he advised the girls to learn riding and other modern arts. A Kabul newspaper published a short article saying that American women were even taking part in swordplay. So now the Afghan girls of the school played volley ball, in contrast to the activity of other aristocratic women.

"You should even take the opportunity, if offered, of taking a trip in an airplane, as European women do," Amanullah told the girls. "I consider that the purdah system has been enforced to an absurd degree in Afghanistan . . . the real purdah is that of the soul and the purdah should not be allowed to interfere with the progress of the nation."

Several months later a firman was posted in the streets: "His Majesty, desiring to improve the education of his people, orders all inhabitants of Kabul to send their sons of the age of seven years and over to school. Those failing to comply with the order will be sentenced to imprisonment for a period of one to ten weeks or a fine of from thirty to forty rupees.

"All Government servants are ordered to send their daughters to the girls' school, failing which they will be dismissed from Government service."

A little later still he would say in Kandahar, where 1,658 students were going to school, all boys: "I have obtained my main purpose . . . Now we have high schools and after that we will establish universities. I am grateful to God we are succeeding."

The world was coming into the royal palace every evening. A wireless set had been installed, and now Amanullah and Souraya and their relations and guests could hear what people were saying as far away as London and Paris.

The French and British were competing as to who should provide Afghan wireless and therefore control it; the French openly, through a firm, Sauvage Brothers, who gave an installation to replace the worn-out Russian wireless and thereby demonstrate their skill; the British secretly, as they dickered with Marconi as a form of insurance in case the French deal collapsed. What the British really wanted was to keep Russian hands off that wireless.

It was already possible to go to the movies in Kabul, and later, also in Mazar-i-Sharif. The first cinema in Afghanistan was an education in the ways of the Western world, for the films all came from America or Europe; they were those which had passed the first flush of interest in their own countries, and since they were silent films, without Persian or Pushtu subtitles, which most of the audience would not have been able to read anyway, all the knowledge of plot or social background came from the pantomime.

During the first months, as each film came to an end, a man would arise and discourse on the depravity of Western civilization as the audience had seen it. Soon everyone had heard the warning, for the cinema theater was crowded from the very beginning, and it ceased. But the editor of *Aman-i-Afghan* was concerned enough to suggest a board of film censors and a ban on the following classes of films: those picturing Western morality and love stories, Biblical films, and those produced for anti-Asiatic propaganda. This, as the British noted, would have eliminated most available films, and Amanullah himself did some censoring for political reasons when a film on the Russo-Japanese war began to show the Russians in a particularly bad light. He arose in the audience and ordered the showing stopped.

Souraya and her sister-in-law entertained with a new dimension that had been missing from Ulya Hazrat's purdah parties. While the men were celebrating the anniversary of independence in 1925, Souraya gave her own social function in the Arg for the ladies of what later newspaper accounts would describe as "the gentry of Kabul," as well as the ladies of the diplomatic corps and some other foreign ladies. As she entered the room, instead of simply greeting her guests and having her hands kissed, as Ulya Hazrat had done, she made a speech, to which one of the Afghan ladies responded with another speech. At intervals she joined her guests in doing the "attan," the Afghan national dance performed in a circle, with the dancers leaning into the circle and then out. She suggested to the Europeans that they should dance in their own style. But none of them knew any dances that did not require a man as a partner and music quite different from that which the Afghan musicians behind a screen were playing on the rubabs, underarms, and tambours.

Dinner was served in two rooms; the wives of diplomats dined with Souraya, the other foreign ladies in the second room. Something went wrong with the arrangements; the second room, unknown to Souraya, did not get the proper service. And the Russian and German ladies went home saying they were disgusted. The British were immune to this particular diplomatic dilemma, since the only British in Afghanistan were diplomats and their wives had priority on dining privileges. But the Russian Ambassador, Léonide Stark, made an official protest to the Afghan Government.

Madame Stark was in room number 1, and therefore had her dinner in style. But Stark had other interests among the Russian women in Kabul. He had virtually adopted, though unofficially, the traditional Moslem number of wives. There was the official Madame Stark, his Armenian wife. There was the secretary with whom he was having an affair; there was the wife of a newly arrived member of his Legation, who also shared his affections. It was announced one day that Mme. Stark had died suddenly.[2] Her body was put on an airplane for transport to Russia with much ceremony, and members of the British Legation paid their respects at the airport, believing as they did so that Stark had murdered her.[3] In fact, she had killed herself, leaving Stark with two women in Kabul, one pregnant.[4]

The British concern with Stark's love life had nothing to do with its variety, but rather with the delicate constitutions of his wives which necessitated them to pass the winter in a warm climate; namely, in Jalalabad, from which official Russians were banned by the Anglo-Afghan Treaty. Stark was a well-born son of a Navy family, who had deserted from the Tsarist Navy at the age of fourteen to become an ardent revolutionary. When time would make him dean of the Kabul diplomatic corps, the British would consider him unsatisfactory "as he would almost certainly betray the interests of the corps as a whole if he could thereby gain any credit for himself with the Afghan Government."

A succession of Mme. Starks was the subject of protests by the British; when Stark accompanied a wife to Jalalabad, he was in an area where they were positive he would intrigue against them more forcefully even than he did in Kabul, where he was financing an efficient spy system and even had Amanullah's Chief of Police on his payroll with an agreement to imprison as an English spy any person whom the Russians might designate as such.[5] The British did not object to the lady's presence near their frontier, only her husband's. "A woman alone cannot do much harm," commented the Government of India, whose allies a few years earlier had executed Mata Hari for doing harm alone; yet they thought it suspicious that Stark should have such a weakness for women with weak lungs. In 1930 the British Minister in Kabul would be writing about Stark: "His new wife, Comrade Olga, arrived recently by air from Russia. She is a lady of some physical attractions and does not believe in masking her batteries."

During the second reception for women, a few months later, all the guests were European ladies; the Germans and Russians forgot their previous disappointment and attended in numbers. Amanullah himself was present; his purpose was to invest Souraya formally with the insignia of a high Afghan order, which never before had been conferred upon a woman.

The wife of the Turkish Minister was embarrassed at the prospect of confronting a man outside her family. Although Mustapha Kemal was preparing then to compel the unveiling of Turkish women, her old-fashioned instincts prevailed, and she was permitted to withdraw before the entry of Amanullah.

Souraya qualified for a decoration in one important direction: she had courage. When Amanullah paid in 1927 a visit to Khost against which Ulya Hazrat and Souraya warned him desperately, both of them accompanied him. The sight of women on a royal visit was new to the men of Khost, and one important landowner, who had a flock of sheep ready to present to Amanullah, designated some of the sheep for the two Queens.

Amanullah already had rescinded most of the punishments exacted on Khost for the rebellion. Now he promised a general amnesty and the abolition of forced labor except for construction of roads. He said that primary schools would be opened and that all who wished might send their sons to Kabul for education at public expense.

Asked what were their grievances, the men of Khost described the tyranny of the military governorship and the unjust rules of their mullahs, and asked to be governed by the same laws as the rest of Afghanistan.

Amanullah told them that the Nizamnamas against which they had rebelled were those very laws he had established to bring peace and justice.

The men of Amanullah's family were not all as happy with the new order as the women were.

His cousin, Mohammed Omar, son of Amir Abdul Rahman, peevishly refused to continue to pretend to be a director of personnel as payment for what he regarded as the luxury owed to him. He went to India with his wife, three children and two nurses; the surgeon of the British Legation gave him a certificate saying that his wife needed medical treatment obtainable only in India; the wife, on the other hand, told the British Legation that Amanullah made unwelcome advances to her. The opinion of the British was that Mohammed Omar wanted to lead a life of ease. He refused to return to Afghanistan even when invited by Amanullah.

Kabir, Amanullah's half brother who had once run away to India, was earning his keep as Minister of Health. Kabir performed his job by announcing to the German doctor in charge of the civil hospital that an X-ray machine would be installed. The doctor pointed out that the initial cost of such a machine was small but its running expenses very large, and that money was needed more urgently in other directions.

"There will be no running expenses," said Kabir. "It will not be used. But we must be able to say that we have an X-ray apparatus in Kabul." This X-ray machine was Kabir's disgrace, for he resigned after Amanullah's Persian secretary purchased one for one-tenth the sum that he was preparing to spend.

Amanullah was working ten hours a day, even when he moved to Jalalabad where it was hot and unhealthy in May. "His father at this time of year," the British commented approvingly, "was in the habit of disappearing into and not emerging from his harem for weeks at a time." Along with supervising the administration of Jalalabad, assisted by Ulya Hazrat who inquired vigorously into the characters of all the officials, he had workmen busy preparing a secondary palace at Jalalabad for the royal family's use, so that he might give the major palace to the people for a hotel. Already there was a hotel in Paghman whose employees had been sent for training to the famous Taj Mahal Hotel in Bombay.

One day Amanullah arrived unexpectedly at Istalif and found that the sentry was absent; he ordered the man to go out and arrest a notorious outlaw, whereupon he would be pardoned, otherwise he would be shot.

On another day General Mahmud Sami, who had recently been promoted to the rank of Corps Commander, appeared at Amanullah's office wearing several rows of medal ribbons. The General, like everyone around Amanullah, was very careful to wear only garments made of Afghan-woven cloth. Looking at the ribbons, Amanullah inquired if those had been made in the State factory. They had not been. With his scissors, he cut the offending ribbons from the General's chest.

Always there had been an air of suspense about the court of an Afghan ruler. Under Amanullah's grandfather a man had never been sure whether he would be alive the next day; now he was never sure what Amanullah would do the next day, though it would probably not mean his death. Once a week Amanullah took over spiritual affairs, preaching the sermon at Friday services in the mosque; this was not customary but Amanullah told his listeners that otherwise God would not heed their prayers. In one speech, while advising them to abide in all things by Islamic law, he made a great point of theory that widows should be allowed to remarry freely.

Although the sacred day of prayer was still Friday, the day of rest, when offices and shops were closed, was now Thursday. When Amanullah made this change, he had in mind the custom of India, where the British, whose day of rest was Sunday, had imposed their own cycle for so long that it was accepted now without question. On Friday a two-hour break in business gave time for worship. Amanullah hoped eventually to make Sunday the day of rest, conforming with worldwide practice in anticipation of the day when Afghanistan would be part of the commerce of the world.

On the first Friday of the new order he made a personal tour of every office in Kabul to be sure people were at work. He also checked attendance at the mosques.

A few months later the Customs officials confiscated a box of leaflets which Amanullah ordered to be burned. Signed by certain religious men in India, they criticized on religious grounds the change in holiday.

Inayatullah, always a gentle, unambitious person, was not a political threat anymore. When Amanullah moved to Jalalabad, he now permitted his elder brother to stay behind in Kabul, not under his supervision.

What it took to arouse the ire of placid Inayatullah was Sher Ahmed, the man who had been Acting Foreign Minister during the rebellion. At a pigeon shooting outing in Paghman, Inayatullah claimed to have wounded a bird. Sher Ahmed called him a liar. They abused each other and would have fought if friends had not separated them. Later the case came before the local magistrate, but was not settled so far as family emotions went because a few months later the youngest daughter of Mahmud Tarzi, while a spectator at an official conference, suddenly broke up the conference by crying in a loud voice that she and her family were determined to die rather than pass over the insult offered to Inayatullah by Sher Ahmed.

What it took to handle Sher Ahmed was Ali Ahmed. This flamboyant cousin of Amanullah, with the big mustaches, expressed his opinion at another conference openly to Sher Ahmed's face. He said that Sher Ahmed deserved to be shot and that he expected him shortly to be shot.

Ali Ahmed was popular at both the British and the Russian Legations. Everyone had the same explanation for his frequent visits to both: the imported whiskey served there for which his fondness was legendary. Each of these Legations, operating on personal knowledge, had its theory as to why the other invited him: to elicit information from an official in his cups.

One person with whom Ali Ahmed was not popular was Amanullah. Their rivalry, going back to childhood, never reached the pinnacle which popular rumor credited to it, of Amanullah's wishing to kill Ali Ahmed. But the older cousin did not hide his reluctance to accept the younger as Amir. At a social function, for instance, Amanullah would make it known that everyone should wear evening clothes; Ali Ahmed would appear in riding breeches and a tweed jacket. This was a trifle, but Amanullah's kingship did not shrink from trifles.

Both men attended the Id-ul-Fitr feast in Idgh Mosque in 1927, which the British Military Attaché described thus:

"It was expected that [the Amir] would arrive on foot from the Arg, and the route of about a mile and a half was lined with police at irregular intervals, unarmed except for occasional batons and wearing cherry red.

"In the ancient grandstand certain diplomats gathered for the royal arrival, which proved dramatic. Whir of powerful engines, a flash as of silver, and the Ghazi King, driving his own Rolls-Royce, had come and gone. Mme. Vorobchievieci, the Queen's dressmaker, explained 'il

1. King Amanullah and Queen Souraya with their children (left to right) Amenah, Adelah, Maleha, Ihsanullah, Crown Prince Rahmatullah, Abedah.

2. The wedding of Nur-us-Seraj, favorite sister of King Amanullah, and Hassan Jan. Seated on the left is Inayatullah; on the right wearing glasses is Mahmud Tarzi.

3. The Jeshyn of 1928. The members of Loe Jirga in Western clothes; Nur-us-Seraj and Queen Souraya unveiled.

4. Ulya Hazrat surrounded by the ladies of the harem. Amanullah is the young boy standing at her right. The photograph was probably taken by Amir Habibullah.

5. Bacha Sacao after his capture in 1929.

6. Queen Souraya in 1928.

7. Sher Agha is shown after Amanullah's expulsion still wearing the symbolic headgear and decoration given him by Amanullah.

8. Amir Habibullah with the most modern of his wives, Ulya Janab, sister of Nadir.

9. Amanullah in tribal (Afridi) dress attending jirgah in 1923.

10. Bacha Sacao addressing the Jeshyn of 1929. Amanullah's symbols still remain on the dais.

11. Official photograph of King Nadir Shah.

12. Amanullah and Souraya arriving in Egypt in 1927. This photograph was used to arouse the tribes, who were shocked by the public visibility of the royal women's faces.

13. Amanullah as a young prince.

14. Tomb of Amanullah at Jalalabad.

15. Khyber Pass.

16. Durand Line.

17. Buddha carved in a cliff at
Bamiyan.

18. Hamidullah, bandit brother of
Bacha Sacao.

avait peur,' which, whatever the truth thereof, can hardly, in view of her position, be regarded as the essence of discretion.

"Although King is at moment by no means a popular idol, it is more probable that he was unwell or pressed for time. The Oriental's inability to appreciate the princely virtues of punctuality was certainly ludicrously in evidence for Sardar Inayatullah, whose title of Muin-us-Sultanat might pardonably lead one to suppose that he is the heir to the throne, arrived driving a two-seater in the middle of the service, while Habibullah Tarzi, an official in the Foreign Office, appeared in a tonga a few minutes after it was over.

"The service though brief was not unimpressive, as, in response to the kingly voice, five thousand backs proclaimed in bending unison the infallibility of the Prophet. One gained the impression that, if that voice were not prematurely stilled, there might after all be a future for Afghanistan.

"That the King was really nervous is doubtful, for on the return journey he was still at the wheel driving very slowly down a fairly crowded highway. If he anticipated danger, he would have been altogether more wise to allow someone else to act as chauffeur, as a car driven by a preoccupied monarch would be liable to depart from its legitimate course. Everybody seemed very glad to see him and his free hand was continually employed in acknowledging the greetings of his subjects.

"This quite successful exit was, however, completely eclipsed by the Governor of Kabul, Shahgassi Ali Ahmed Jan, who departed astride a well-looking black charger whose glossy coat and prancing mien vied with its master's imperial moustachios and statuesque form to complete a picture the entirely medieval dignity of which the noble equestrian appeared to be by no means unconscious.

"Thus was a curtain provided for the play, and thereafter a heterogeneous procession of functionaries passed and were quickly lost in the crowd whose gay apparel and cheerful faces announced the tedious passing and rapid climax of yet another fast of Ramzan."

On yet another occasion Ali Ahmed eclipsed Amanullah: on the extinguishing of the fire at the British Legation. Amanullah chose to go there in disguise to watch unobserved. Ali Ahmed brought along his riding crop. It had been the custom in Kabul that, whenever a building caught fire, a mob rushed in to carry off anything that could be lifted. A few Afghans attempted this, while flames were licking at the Legation building that had once been Abdur Rahman's reception hall and where the Durand Treaty had been signed. Ali Ahmed struck out with his riding crop and felled the looters to the ground. He was the most conspicuous person there.

The report of the fire by the Military Attaché, W. K. Fraser-Tytler, said, "Baron von Kaltenborn, employed in the Afghan War Office, who is a stalwart monarchist and refuses to live under a republic in his own country, lived up to his principles and his three Iron Crosses by assisting at great personal risk in saving intact the full-length portraits of the King and Queen.

"Saved one Christmas pudding, 12 bottles champagne, and 36 bottles of whiskey."

Ali Ahmed was Governor of Kabul, the post from which Amanullah had leapt to the Kingship. He was behaving with the same concern for his constituency that enabled Amanullah to build a reservoir of good will on which to call in a crisis. He often visited the city on patrol duty and gave out that anyone having proof of corruption by officials should report to him and he would personally inquire into the complaints. Twice a week he summoned the flour merchants, butchers, etc., and fixed the price of food to the delight of the consumers. He became noted for his courtesy.

Ali Ahmed was acting exactly like Amanullah, so naturally it was not long until an intelligence report said, "Ali Ahmed has aroused the suspicions of the Amir."

Nur-us-Seraj was betrothed to Hassan Jan in October 1926. The betrothal service for Amanullah's nineteen-year-old sister was unique in Afghanistan in that it was strictly a civil ceremony. No mullah was present.

The marriage ceremony marked the diminution in importance of still another of the matrimonial cast of characters: the bridegroom. An Afghan wedding was, despite all the attentions of the women who had few other outlets for their social instincts, a man's affair. The bridegroom gave the wedding feast, which derived its social importance from his social status.

To celebrate this particular joyous occasion all the couples in Afghanistan who married on the same day received gifts. And this had nothing to do with the bridegroom, whose royal birth did not make him distinguished, but everything to do with the bride's being the ruler's favorite little sister. The ceremony itself was in the tradition of the West, wherein the bridegroom is an essential nonentity. Nur-us-Seraj wore a veil of illusion and a white bridal gown made by the Romanian dressmaker Mme. Vorobchievieci, whom the ladies of the court called "Mme. Zizi." It was definitely Nur-us-Seraj's wedding, not Hassan Jan's.

At this wedding feast was one invisible presence on which everyone commented, although not in the hearing of the royal family. There was a ghost at the table—a whole family of ghosts, the Musahiban family headed by Nadir, whose brother, Hashim, had expected to marry Nur-us-Seraj.

Nadir resigned as Minister to Paris in the fall of 1926; the reason he gave was ill health; he went to Switzerland for treatment for tuberculosis and said nothing about returning to his own country.

Hashim had been Minister to Russia but at about the same time he was transferred to Tehran. He wished to return to Kabul before taking his new post. Amanullah refused permission but gave him leave of absence to visit Nadir in Switzerland.

Some of the family remained in Afghanistan, but none was present when Nur-us-Seraj, who had once been proclaimed officially as the intended of Hashim, became the bride of Hassan Jan.

Meanwhile the activities of the family known to the British as "Nadir and Company" were causing interest in London.

On January 10, 1926, Nadir had a conversation with Sir Richard Hodgson, British Minister to Russia, who was in Paris on leave. He asked for an opportunity of expressing his views to "some person having the confidence of the India Office." And his views were in favor of stronger alliance with Britain and opposition to Russia. He said he and his brother Hashim, the Minister in Russia, who shared these views, expected to be recalled shortly to Kabul.

"Our presence in Kabul is, I think, necessary. I intend to use every effort to bring about the understanding with Great Britain in which I see the only guarantee of my country's independence."

Then Nadir said, "A friendly arrangement in the matter of frontier delimitations would assist powerfully, for a natural frontier does away with many causes of dispute." He suggested that Kunar River as boundary, which would have added to Britain's lands at the expense of Afghanistan.

This was not the first time Nadir had attempted to talk with some representative of the British Foreign Office. On May 13, 1925, Colonel A. D. Enriquez, a retired Indian Army officer who had met Nadir both in Kapurthala, where the Colonel had been in charge of the Maharajah's sons, and in Paris, called on the Foreign Office. Acting as Nadir's emissary, Enriquez asked for a meeting between Nadir and the Foreign Office. This would have violated all protocol. The proper procedure for discussing Anglo-Afghan matters was between the respective ministers in Kabul and London and the governments themselves. A month later Nadir had initiated with Lord Crewe, British Ambassador in Paris, a discussion of aid to Afghanistan centering on a railway built by British capital; he seemed unaware of talks that Amanullah was having with Humphrys about roads. "The Afghan Government is too weak really to assert itself," he said discussing a policy of friendship with Britain.

Combined with these incidents, the report of Nadir's talk with Hodgson led to the following letter to the India Office from Sir Denys Bray, Foreign Secretary to the Government of India:

"Thus I myself find it difficult not to link up this particular conversation of Nadir Khan's in Paris with a more interesting conversation of which we have some knowledge, that took place in Moscow between Tsukerman and a mysterious and obviously highly placed Afghan some time before December 13, 1925. In both conversations much is said of the unrest and disquieting situation in Kabul. Hashim Khan (for who else could the mysterious personage be?) said a great deal about the Amir; his brother not a word. Hashim talked almost open treason and put out feelers for Russian neutrality in event of a rising. Nadir I admit said nothing overt on this score; but then he said he wanted to air his views to somebody in the confidence of the India Office! Yet he made a very definite bid for our support, and what Afghan in his wildest dreams could suggest giving us great blocks of God-granted Afghan soil except for our support in some coup d'état?"

In August 1926, Hashim received a year's leave of absence in order to join the ailing Nadir.

He himself told the British Ambassador Hodgson that the Commissar for Foreign Affairs "looks upon me as a hostile personality with whose presence he can well dispense."

Hashim said much more to Hodgson.

He predicted a revolution in Afghanistan in the near future.

"The feeling is gaining ground," he said, "that the Amir, who is relapsing into indolence, is incapable of taking a decision and, without a policy, has come under Russian influence and is on the way to betray his country . . . I myself would welcome an upheaval, for I am convinced that the popular conception is correct; that, failing radical changes in the present régime, the process of Russian penetration cannot be met."

He advised Hodgson against discussing confidential matters with his successor.

The destiny of nations was the theme of this conversation. But it took place very close in time to an event in Kabul that was purely personal: a nineteen-year-old girl in a white wedding dress and a bridegroom who was not Hashim.

In 1927 Paghman, the scene of Jeshyn, looked now like a European town with a scattering of mud houses, rather than like an Afghan town infused with the flavor of Europe. Looking down from one of its hills, one could pick out instantly the buildings that owed their existence to Amanullah. They were big, often wooden, square, full of little verandahs and stenciled designs. A park offered the municipal look of geometric flower beds, of statuary reincarnations of ancient Romans and Greeks, of a bandstand. The new hotel, the Bahar, was a success before it opened, with every room reserved a week before the start of Jeshyn. Amanullah, so pleased that he gave fifty thousand rupees to buy dishes, had lunch there every day.

Souraya attended and, while watching the clay pigeon shooting competition between Afghans and the British Legation, was inspired to take a rifle and participate. She did very well.

While making his speech, Amanullah did something that had never been done in Afghanistan. He turned to the women, segregated in a special area, and addressed them directly. His words were of their duty to the nation and posterity and their responsibility in the education of their children.

Later he opened an arts and crafts exhibit: "A few years ago this exhibition of Afghan produce was accommodated on one table; this year it fills a fair-sized house and its adjacent grounds; shortly it will require several houses and fields to show off all the exhibits . . . Foreign countries are now producing imitation Afghan goods, which in itself is proof of the excellence of, and demand for, Afghan products."

Satisfying though it was, this Jeshyn was not on the scale of other years. Amanullah had too much on his mind.

He was preparing to go out into the world of the West. Soon the Promised Land would be more than hearsay.

CHAPTER 17

1927

The country that first invited Amanullah to pay a state visit was Italy, with whom he had been on such bad terms two years earlier that relations had come close to being severed.

No other Afghan monarch had ever stepped on European soil; the refusals of his two predecessors were attributed to a fear of leaving the throne unprotected.

"Amanullah's unprecedented decision speaks for his confidence in the stability of his internal situation," said the Government of India, "and also of his personal position. We trust that his confidence in the latter is not misplaced . . ."

On September 22, 1927, the Afghan Minister in London, who was now Amanullah's old friend and director of intelligence, Shuja-ud-Dowleh, announced to the Foreign Office in London that Amanullah would leave his country in the middle of December and would like to visit England. In various capitals, including Moscow, other Afghan ministers were making the same announcement.

"On the whole, we stand to gain," wrote G. of I., "for it would be a case of King meeting King."

Amanullah was really a King now, not an Amir. In June 1926 he had adopted the title as more meaningful in the modern world, and the British, who had disputed at the beginning of his reign his right to the title "Your Majesty" now noted this as a matter of routine.

Neither London nor Moscow had inaugurated Amanullah's visit, and Russia did not approve. But each was curious what would happen in the country of the other. This curiosity was more intense because of an incident which had taken place in May of that year. Scotland Yard agents had broken into an office at 49 Moorgate in London and found evidence that Russians ostensibly engaged in trade had actually been spying. Immediately Great Britain broke off her diplomatic relations with Russia.

This severance followed three years in which Great Britain, led by a Labor Government, had given the current Bolshevik Government the gift of recognition as the rightful government of Russia. G. of I. had speculated that this new amity might cost Afghanistan her "artificial importance."

"It is to the conflicting interests of her powerful neighbors that Afghanistan owes her international importance," Humphrys had written to the Secretary for Foreign Affairs, Sir Austen Chamberlain. "If Afghanistan were bounded on the northwest by an Arctic Ocean, she would be merely a petty border state which could give no concern to H.M.G."

But Afghanistan was bounded on the northwest by Russia, which between 1925 and 1927 gave Great Britain not less, but more cause for alarm. Some of the messages passing between England and India in 1925 and 1926 were:

"It is a matter of first importance to keep Amir on his throne. Unsatisfactory as he is, there is no one better in prospect; and revolution is what the Bolsheviks are playing for."

"There is every reason to believe that the Russian menace will increase."

"A late member of the Russian Legation recently remarked to my Italian colleague [in Kabul] that Soviet policy in Afghanistan could be summed up in a single word, 'revolution.' "

"A danger does exist in my opinion," wrote Humphrys in June 1925, "that the Afghans will allow the pendulum to swing too far towards Russia if our treatment of them appears cold . . ."

On August 31, 1926, Amanullah had signed a new treaty with Russia. The following week he met with Humphrys in a private room, completely alone, and assured him that this treaty was not directed against British interests. He mentioned an episode which had sent the pendulum of Afghan opinion swinging away from Russia, the occupation by Soviet troops of an island in the Oxus River called Urta Tagai which was part of Afghanistan. Eventually the Russians evacuated it but only after much bitterness.

"My eyes have been opened by the Urta Tagai incident to the imminent danger of Russian penetration," said Amanullah. "This instrument is intended solely to protect Afghan territory against further Russian aggression, insofar as it is possible to do so by a paper agreement." He asked Humphrys' opinion of the treaty.

"I assume that the very fact that a fresh agreement has been concluded with the Soviet Union indicates that Your Majesty is satisfied with the manner in which the Soviets have observed the terms of the previous treaty."

Amanullah leaped from his chair and paced up and down the room, talking with an agitated sputter about Russia's failure to observe the treaty of 1921. "I am aware that Soviet agents are trying to spread revolutionary doctrines among my people and I am not so blind as to suppose that a Communist Government could be anything but hostile to myself and my throne."

"Why do you continue to tempt providence," asked Humphrys, "by entrusting one of your fighting arms to Russian personnel?" The Afghan airplanes were still being operated by Russian pilots. Additional Russian planes had arrived, in which these pilots had treated the citizens of Kabul to flights in a ceremony which Humphrys, on horseback, had watched unseen.

"Airplanes are a necessity to Afghanistan," said Amanullah, "and I failed to get either the material or the personnel from any other quarter. If only you will tell me how to secure their services, I will gladly make over control of my air force, until young Afghans are sufficiently trained, to British or other foreign personnel and get rid of the Russians tomorrow . . ."

"It is constantly impressed on me that the Afghan Air Force is a military force. If it is manned by British pilots and civil war breaks out again in Afghanistan, Your Majesty will certainly feel that you have been betrayed if the pilots refuse to bomb the rebel Afghan tribesmen, and yet it is certain that the British Government cannot allow them to take part in such warfare. If your air force were intended merely for civil aviation, the matter would be different."

Belgian or Swiss pilots would not be under the same handicap, suggested Humphrys.

Amanullah said the expense would be prohibitive. "Although Russian pilots are paid by the Afghan Government, they are content with a far lower salary than would be the case with other foreigners."

"Let me warn you against the folly of being a catspaw in the interests of others," said Humphrys. "Are you aware that a portion of the Russian pilots' pay is regularly set aside for revolutionary propaganda?" Amanullah had heard this and again said the Russian pilots would be eliminated as soon as possible.

"Is there any truth," asked Humphrys, "in the rumors current in Kabul that a Russian bank is shortly to be established with a network of Soviet Government agents throughout the country?" This rumor was so disturbing to Humphrys' Government that it was persuading the Chartered Bank of Delhi to make overtures to Afghanistan as a countermeasure.

Amanullah ridiculed the idea that he might make over control of Afghan trade to the Russians.

"A horde of Russians seem to have been let loose lately for road and telegraph construction," persisted Humphrys. "Their activities will have to be carefully watched."

Amanullah offered to turn the road and telegraph building over to the British.

Before the two parted, Amanullah said, "Whatever may appear superficially to be my object, my settled policy is to draw closer and closer towards England if she will allow me to do so, and merely to keep on terms of good neighborliness with Russia." In that sentence was an echo of the pledge his father had given and kept during the Great War, to maintain his friendship despite appearances.

"I am considerably disappointed," he added, "that the response of the British Government to my advances for friendship is much colder than I anticipated . . ."

"I cannot escape from the conviction that you are playing a dangerous game with the Soviets."

In fact, the British had decided to bid against Russia for Afghanistan's favor, but as subtly as possible. They would not give cash, which might be spent in ways not acceptable to the donor. One gift which seemed to be without flaw was the construction of a road from Kabul to Khyber by way of Jalalabad. Amanullah had asked for it a year earlier, saying:

"Every traveler entering Afghanistan is struck by the extraordinary deterioration of the road as soon as he crosses the Indian frontier into Afghanistan. For the honor of my country and for the development of trade, it is essential that the road from the Khyber to Kabul be realigned and improved without further delay. In the present circum-

stances new lorries are converted into scrap iron in six months and
motorcars which ought to run twenty miles to the gallon are able with
difficulty to do five."

The British, after many letters, telegrams, and conferences, agreed
to do exactly as Amanullah wished. In effect, they were giving a subsidy, just as they had given his father and grandfather, and just as Russia
had promised but had given only sporadically.

But they were keeping the subsidy a secret from him. They earmarked
an annual expenditure of seven hundred thousand rupees for Afghanistan, but instead of giving it in cash regularly, they would make a gift
that had to be requested each year as a single entity. Amanullah must
not come to take it for granted.

The project of the new road proceeded as far as a preliminary survey
by British engineers. But Amanullah's Council rejected the gift in the
form in which it was offered. They requested the cash outright, to spend
themselves. The British declined. They attributed this situation to the
desire of Amanullah's ministers for graft and the support of Wali and
Mahmud Tarzi to the fact that their positions gave them less opportunity.

When word came that Amanullah was planning a visit to Europe, it
seemed that the most fruitful application of that idle 700,000 rupees
would be to demonstrate to him at first hand the glories of the British
Empire.

Amanullah had bade farewell in February to Sir Francis Humphrys,
who was on his way to England for consultation. He said that he himself would be leaving Kabul soon to go to Mazar-i-Sharif to suppress
the Bolshevik propaganda in his northern province.

One intelligence report from Mazar-i-Sharif that had perturbed the
British was a remark made in Peshawar by a "yokel" from Mazar: "In
Mazar the Russians move about without any restrictions. When passing
the shrine of Sakhi Sahib they all take off their hats. One of them gave
the imam of the shrine a considerable sum of money." This led to the
comment: "In Mazar less than a year ago the Russians were adopting an
arrogant and intolerant attitude. In the last eight months there has
been a very marked change in their behavior towards Moslems in general and Moslem religious leaders in particular. It seems clear that orders
have been given to ingratiate themselves with Moslem countries."
Taken in conjunction with a statement of the President of Uzbegistan,

which was the name Russia had given to the lands adjoining Afghanistan, anticipating the day when North Afghanistan would be included in the Soviet Uzbeg Republic, it was ominous.

Camels and pack ponies filled the streets of Kabul in the days when Amanullah was preparing for his Mazar visit. He was taking a very strong contingent of all arms, consisting of the best troops in Kabul and practically all the mobile artillery in the Kabul corps, a force out of all proportion to a royal escort. He feared to cross the Hindu Kush without such a strong force. He might need it there. He might need it to return. It was not wise to leave it behind in Kabul for anyone else.

Ali Ahmed, still Governor of Kabul, invited a guest to dinner on May 14, during the absence in Mazar of his cousin and brother-in-law, Amanullah. This guest was Basil J. Gould, chargé d'affaires at the British Legation during Humphrys' absence.

"What attitude would the British Government adopt if Russia were to invade Afghanistan or interfere openly in its affairs?" Ali Ahmed asked Gould. Then he showed that he was not talking academically.

"I anticipate that this question may need to be answered practically within a few weeks or months in the following circumstances.

"Afghanistan is heartily disgusted with the persons and methods of King Amanullah and of his advisers, all of whom are subservient to Russian interests, and most of whom belong to an objectionable 'new' school. This disaffection extends to a large part of the Army, to most of the population of Kabul and Jalalabad and Kandahar districts, and to all the frontier tribes . . . I, myself, on the other hand, am most popular with the frontier tribes.

"The time is approaching when the responsible patriots and British-loving party must assert itself. Plans are already far advanced but not actually complete. If there is no interference from outside, there can be no doubt that a coup d'état will succeed, almost without bloodshed.

"In the event of a coup d'état, will the British Government keep Russia out of the field? A coup is inevitable, but it may be necessary to make terms with Russia, unless the influence of that country can be neutralized."

Gould's description of that conversation began, "I have never met so candid a conspirator." He gave Ali Ahmed a lecture on loyalty.

In London, Humphrys heard of the incident and said that Ali Ahmed

had tried to sound him out on the same subject. "His chief characteristic is vanity."

A few days later Amanullah returned to Kabul saying his visit to
Mazar had been as successful as it was opportune, that he had brought
northern Afghanistan into the focus of the capital.

At about the same time Amanullah's Minister to London, Shuja-ud-
Dowleh, who loved him dearly, was causing him trouble.

The British had considered rejecting this young man of about thirty-
six when he was named to succeed Abdul Hadi, for their files contained
the rumor that Shuja-ud-Dowleh, who had been Chief of the Royal
Servants at Amir Habibullah's court, was the person who fired the bullet into the Amir's brain in 1919. Humphrys reported that, although he
had heard other names mentioned in connection with the deed, he
had not heard that, and the Foreign Office official Sir Victor Wellesley
noted, "If it had been definitely established that he did murder the
Amir, I think we ought to object, but mere rumor is hardly sufficient
to go on."

Murder is not the only offense, however, and in London this young
man showed himself guilty of two qualities that the British found repre-
hensible: presumption and bad manners. He wrote them a note:

"Request you to be so good as to provide me with facilities for the
erection of a private tennis court in Kensington Gardens at a spot near
these premises so that I may be able to play tennis there without any
loss of time. At the moment, I cannot play any other game but tennis,
which is necessary for health reasons . . . In case I have the assistance
of the desired facilities, I shall accept some of the minor expenses which
might be involved in erecting a private tennis court."

Early in 1927 a trivial misunderstanding over passports evoked from
Shuja-ud-Dowleh a rude note critical of Sir Francis Humphrys, and
Sir Victor Wellesley, who had given him the benefit of doubt as regards
murder, called him for an interview. An interpreter was present, but
there was some gap between Wellesley's English and the Afghan Minister's Persian. All that Shuja-ud-Dowleh communicated was "truc-
ulence."

The British Secretary of State for Foreign Affairs, Sir Austen Chamberlain, conferring a few days later on another routine matter, was
amazed to hear from Shuja-ud-Dowleh a tirade antagonistic to

Humphrys which closed with a demand for his withdrawal from his post in Kabul.

At least, Chamberlain thought that was what Shuja-ud-Dowleh said. Again, since the words were filtered through an interpreter, he considered the strong possibility that he had misunderstood. But suppose the Afghan had really said that? Was he acting on his own, or had Amanullah really attempted to remove Humphrys from the British Legation in Kabul?

Ghulam Siddiq was acting as Foreign Minister, since Mahmud Tarzi had gone to Switzerland with Amanullah's daughter Sultan Jan, who needed treatment for tuberculosis. The Foreign Office talked about Ghulam Siddiq's expulsion from Mussoorie in "the woman case"; the possible intrigue of the Turkish Minister who was temporarily dean of the Kabul diplomatic corps and would lose his prestige on Humphrys' return from his leave of absence; the possible desire of Amanullah to have a more tractable Minister in Kabul, since the time was approaching to negotiate a new treaty. But no one was absolutely certain that Amanullah had anything to do with this demand, even if it had really been made, so the vague and unpleasant matter was dropped.

Except, of course, from British memories, especially Sir Francis Humphrys' memory.

Humphrys received Amanullah's travel schedule on October 29 from Ghulam Siddiq. The program in India was unsuitable, Humphrys complained, because of "the shabbiness of the route." What he meant was that the route bypassed Delhi, the capital, the only place where the Viceroy felt his dignity would permit a welcome.

"The program is irrevocably fixed," said Ghulam Siddiq.

"I will explain matters fully to King Amanullah."

Both men knew well Amanullah's attitude toward the Government of India. In view of the long period when the British had entrusted their relations with Afghanistan not to London, but to India, thereby relegating Afghanistan to the rank of a second-rate power in the world's eyes, Amanullah wanted nothing to do with Delhi.

Now the Afghans were planning to go over India's head to discuss directly with London, as Ghulam Siddiq indicated almost at once by saying, "I am confident of convincing the British Foreign Secretary in London that the Government of India's frontier policy is dishonest and harmful to Afghanistan. I will also disabuse the British Cabinet of its groundless apprehension of a Russian attack in India."

"Such language is highly improper," said Humphrys.

To Amanullah, Humphrys said later, "My government is entitled to be fully consulted about the intermediate program in India."

"I had not originally intended to visit India officially," Amanullah told him. "My own wish is to pass through India as quickly as possible in a private capacity."

Amanullah said he had already chosen a name to use on this incognito passage through India. He would be called Azizurrahman.

"The fact that you will be skulking through India unknown by a merchant route instead of by royal highway will create a deplorable impression."

"I do not care a button what people think."

"What reply shall I give my government?"

"Tell them that I have spoken."

"This is not an appropriate reply."

Humphrys reported, "Before I took my leave, the King resumed his old affectionate manner towards me and said he was sorry to thwart me, adding that his mind was made up before my arrival."

"Tranquillity" was not a word often used in connection with Afghanistan, but reports of the period when Amanullah made his plans for Europe spoke of "the present tranquillity," and predicted that all would be well if he returned before the snows were off the mountain passes. One of the best harvests ever known was being reaped. There was no more unrest than would always be expected. Amanullah had a regent to leave behind who had already deputed for him on other absences and whom he trusted.

The regent was Wali, who was one of the young men who owed his rise in the world completely to Amanullah, who had no powerful family to support him in controversy, only Amanullah; for this cynical reason, as well as for his past record of sincerity, the choice was admired.

"A rapid and sound worker with a constructive mind," was Humphrys' appraisal of Wali. "He appears to be well equipped to balance conflicting interests . . . Wali's task during the coming months will be to hold together Afghanistan until the King returns from his travels. If any man in Afghanistan is capable of a masterly inactivity, he surely is that man. I feel, however, that he may judge that, in order to rule, he must act."

There was speculation as to whether the King would be wise enough to keep Nadir and his brothers out of Afghanistan during his absence. After the departure of Nadir and Hashim for assignments abroad, another brother, Shah Wali, and a cousin, Ahmed Shah, had asked for similar assignments and been told that two of the family in foreign posts were enough. However, Shah Wali had been sent to Paris to escort a party of students, so now there were three of the brothers together in Switzerland.

Of a brother who remained, the British Military Attaché was writing in his diary in April 1926: "Shah Mahmud, brother of Nadir, continues to display great reluctance to take over the appointment of Governor of Jalalabad district as he correctly thinks that the Amir does not trust any member of his family. He asks to be allowed to consult Nadir before he accepts the appointment." Once in Jalalabad, Shah Mahmud almost seemed to be governing in the name of Nadir, and well, for the diaries said: "The Governor is keeping up his family tradition of friendliness to our frontier tribes. On the other hand, the party of Afridis who came to Kabul some months ago are still waiting for someone to take notice of them." Later there would be the rumor that Shah Mahmud while in Jalalabad as Governor had tried to spread propaganda for transferring Afghanistan into a republic with Nadir as the first President.

Amanullah wrote to Nadir while he was arranging his trip, asking him to return to Afghanistan. As everyone had heard that Nadir's health was at its lowest point, no one believed that Amanullah was so reckless as to want him back. It seemed evident that Amanullah was trying to assure good relations with this influential family before departing for Europe especially after he sent Nadir one thousand pounds for medical expenses.

Meanwhile Shah Mahmud, quarreling with the Minister of Court, resigned as Governor of Jalalabad but Amanullah asked him to stay on until replaced, and failed to appoint anyone else.

The first member of Amanullah's party to leave for Europe was the dressmaker Mme. Vorobchievieci. She was going to select and buy the clothes for his ladies, who had no intention of wearing native costumes. They would meet the women of Europe on Europe's own terms.

Another departure took place at nearly the same time. Gul Agha,

Hazrat of Shor Bazaar, and his nephew Masum traveled through the
Khyber Pass to Sirhind where his brother Sher Agha was living.

In London the Foreign Office busied itself with memos as to what
would entertain an Afghan monarch:
"It is understood that Humphrys does not wish to stress education,
other than at Eton and Oxford, as it is not at present very popular in
Afghanistan."
"The evenings seem remarkably free of engagements but it will no
doubt be possible to arrange theatre parties and perhaps some private
dinners. It is to be hoped that the King will not wish to take up political
conversations at that hour."
"I should think that the less His Majesty is left with nowhere to go
in the evenings except music halls and theatres, the better for his project of receiving some respect for our civilization. As he cannot understand what is said on the stage, and probably would find no attraction
in Western music, the only kind of theatrical entertainment likely to
interest him would be the spectacular kind afforded by lightly draped
danseuses."

Ever since the days when Amir Habibullah had assigned Mahmud
Tarzi to translate Jules Verne's *Voyage to the Moon*, Afghans had been
interested in the farthest reaches to which people could go. For the nine
years of Amanullah's reign, his newspaper *Aman-i-Afghan* had been
publishing little paragraphs about inventions in travel: a device to enable an airplane to fly by night, a prediction that a rocket would carry
men to the moon and that it would weigh four hundred tons and speed
along at four hundred miles per hour.
Now *Aman-i-Afghan* was writing of Amanullah's travels, and so much
of wonder these travels held that the moon would have seemed no more
incredible a place for an Afghan King to go than Europe.
Amanullah was punctual for his farewell reception to the diplomatic
corps; this was taken by the Europeans as a good omen. The next day,
before a large gathering outside the palace, he made the people raise
their hands to promise solemnly that they would behave well while he
was away. He and traveling companions raised their own hands in a
pledge that on all occasions they would observe most rigorously the
injunctions of Islam.
Then, because there was not time to embrace everyone, Amanullah

chose four men representing four classes of his subjects, and he embraced with tears in his eyes a soldier, a student, a clerk and a dweller in the bazaar.

He went to India by way of Kandahar, which he entered on December 1 to a salute of twenty-one guns. There he said to officials and students:

"In the beginning I thank God and the Prophet Mohammed, then with tears in my eyes and a warm heart I want to tell you good-bye. All these things you mention, I have not done. First, God has done them, and second, you have done them. I thank God and I thank you and I want more help from God to work for you. My purpose in traveling outside Afghanistan is for your benefit. I want to pick up new things which we have not had. Anyone who wishes may travel outside the country. The religious men are saying that if we go outside, we do not know if we shall return or not. I should like very much to come back to see you, but if I am not able to come, there is advice which you should keep in mind."

He told the people to be patriotic and to defend their land, and to remember they were all one nation.

"The King has no vote and no right to give commands. Who abolished this right? Myself, and by my own counsel. Because God has said that we should consult the people. So listen to my advice and never live under a dictatorial king. Don't be superstitious. For instance, some unwise mullahs have put religion in chains for you, and have told you falsely about religion, and you have been deceived. The only things you should do are what God ordered and the Prophet ordered; don't believe what mullahs say.

"Also, I tell you that you must not think of any difference between men, civilians, educators. You are all one country and you are brothers.

"For this advice I want a vote of approval from you." The people raised their hands.

"I also suggest that you act properly toward your wives. Don't treat them badly, because they have hopes in God and they are also human beings and they have rights. Don't have more than one wife, because you won't be able to bear the expenses. You should send your children to school and to foreign countries. You should spend all your wealth for your children's education.

"All I have told you is from orders of God and the Prophet."

On December 10 Amanullah's party drove from Kandahar to the frontier preceded by one hundred and fifty pieces of luggage. Souraya would be the first Afghan queen ever to step outside her country. Their only surviving son Rahmatullah, aged six, Nur-us-Seraj and her husband Hassan Jan, and Souraya's sister Bibi Khurd and a Turkish lady-in-waiting accompanied them. Amanullah was taking along Ali Ahmed because it was not safe to leave him behind. He was taking Sher Ahmed, who would not have got along with the regent Wali. Ghulam Siddiq was already planning how he would handle foreign affairs in Europe. The royal party, including the dressmaker, doctor and servants, numbered thirty-one.

They drove between low hills and orchards into a dry torrent bed that seldom was lighted by sun because on each side rocky hills arose as steeply as fortresses. Then across a wide plain and down a low pass till they were driving past Dubrai serai, a windowless building of twenty-eight rooms which Amanullah's father had built to shelter men and animals whose caravans were carrying the supplies of life between Afghanistan and India; the loopholes for riflemen in the parapet running around its top showed that the passage could not be assured always to be peaceful.

Farther on was another reminder of conflict, a square fort with walls zigzagging up the hill to towers, and a small bazaar where no one was trading because the men had been stirred from villages invisible in the distant hills, not to buy but to partake in the general excitement that everyone could sense.

From here the road across a plain was sandy, and wheels tended to sink and be stuck. To speed the King's way a special road had been built, which no one had used before.

Amanullah's car drove over the new road between two of the white pillars standing like sentries to mark the frontier. And beyond that row of pillars, the world was waiting to welcome him.

CHAPTER 18

December 10, 1927, to March 8, 1928

The British were there in uniforms and braid, a guard of honor standing ramrod stiff with no prospect of stirring a muscle until Amanullah should inspect it and proclaim it perfect. A military band was playing the Afghan national anthem, which it had just learned. Planes of the Royal Air Force, once so alarming in the skies of Afghanistan, dipped their wings in the skies of India. Amanullah was handed a telegram in which King George V made him welcome to his empire.

About a thousand Afghan tribesmen had come down from the hills to the border, and some who had seen the King's car passing by had leaped on their horses and ridden along with him. Now they pressed forward in an onsurge that threatened to engulf the ceremony; they forgot that the frontier was there, and this was as symbolic of Anglo-Afghan relations as anything else taking place.

A gun boomed thirty-one times. The customary salute was twenty-one guns. But someone in the Foreign Office had discovered a book of memoirs by a retired General who told of thirty-one guns being accorded on one occasion to the ruler of Siam. Although one particularly levelheaded official pointed out the unlikelihood that Amanullah, who did not read English anyway, was familiar with this obscure book, it was important not to take any chances on offending him.

Amanullah's refusal to travel via Delhi had made him, officially, unofficial; the Government of India's first reaction had been to withdraw the offer of trains, ships, residences, etc., which had been made on the assumption that he would be a state guest while in India. But remembering that Britain would need Afghanistan on her side in case of a war with Russia, the Government of India remembered also that the hospitality had been offered unconditionally.

Amanullah beheld his first train, and if he thought that this was what all trains looked like, he would be disappointed forever after. Its two carriages were white and gold, painted with the royal crest of Afghanistan. The Union Jack and the green banner of the British court fluttered from their roofs. The carriages were lined with Burma teak; in the white tile bathroom the fittings were silver; blue and antique gold decorated the bedrooms. These carriages had been made especially at a cost of £15,000, and Amanullah had even been consulted as to whether he and the Queen would like separate bedrooms; at first he had asked for separate, but at the last minute had changed his mind.[1]

The party with luggage and escort boarded the train, which looked as if it had strayed onto the wrong track, its baroque elegance an anachronism beside the railway station of this last outpost of Empire in Baluchistan being stared at by bearded men who fingered rifles. The train began to move, toward the sea and away from Afghanistan. Amanullah's grand tour had begun.

At Karachi he saw the sea for the first time and boarded the ship *Manela* for Bombay. "What impresses everybody is the King's amazing keenness," reported the London *Times* correspondent on board. "One feels that here is a monarch and a man, a rare personality in which the dominating thing is vitality."

When the *Manela* docked at Bombay, only then was Amanullah truly in India; Karachi had been a way station. Here was the great arch known as "The Gateway of India" which had welcomed thousands of Englishmen to the subcontinent that was the glory of their Empire.

Before he landed, he was told that the Viceroy was ill and could not receive him.

Everyone always would suspect the Viceroy's illness, as the convenient "diplomatic headache" that was probably incurred when he heard that Amanullah would not travel as the Government of India wished. Indeed, the Viceroy, who was Lord Irwin, later to be Lord Halifax, had written his father, "I am afraid Bombay will be a tiresome week, very full of engagements and with this dreadful Afghan visit stuffed in on top of everything else. I would like, when it is over, to go to bed for a week."[2]

Lord Irwin was in bed earlier than he expected. He came down with malaria. And he was soon writing again to his father: "The Afghan

visit went off quite well. One or two were inclined to be tiresome at
first and Sir Francis Humphrys had to speak very plainly to them. I
believe that when they heard that I was ill and not going to meet them
at Bombay, they decided it was not necessary for them to land in full
dress and accordingly packed all their full dress up in their heavy luggage which they were sending on shore, when Humphrys went on
board to pay his respects to the King. He protested and said they must
at once get it all out again, and when they demurred, said to them, 'If
King George heard of this, he would say you were a lot of barbarians
who ought never to have come down from the trees in Kabul.' "³

Of course, the Afghans did not believe in the Viceroy's illness, and
Humphrys, though not as plain-spoken as he described himself to the
Viceroy, spoke swiftly to get them out of the "flannels" in which they
were dressed and into attire more appropriate to the procession awaiting them. In the confusion Amanullah, who was always courteous although unfamiliar with Western etiquette, forgot to thank the captain
of the ship.

"Ghulam Siddiq had the impertinence to urge that the Vicereine and
the Governor of Bombay should sit with their backs to the horses," reported Humphrys. "It was always to be expected that Ghulam Siddiq
would devise some method of creating embarrassment." The Government of India had not forgotten the circumstances in which this young
man had been expelled from India more than seven years earlier, and
knew that he remembered. The State dinner in Bombay was delayed
while he argued about the seating arrangements after everyone was
ready to walk in. In the process he kept Lady Irwin waiting; it had been
another English lady who had caused his humiliation. Often the British
had complained of Tarzi as Foreign Minister. Now they wished for him
back.

The people of India, on the other hand, were ecstatic.

Messages to London from Bombay said:

"Roads were packed by unprecedented crowds whose enthusiasm,
which was not confined to the Moslem element, accorded him very
evident pleasure, especially when his carriage was surrounded by surging crowds, chiefly Pathan and Afghan who broke through the barriers."

India had been fascinated by Amanullah ever since he took from
England what so many Indians would have liked for themselves; control of his own affairs. The British had marked this attraction as a matter for caution. But they were unprepared for seeing it flower in the

cries of welcome, the outstretched hands, the light of admiration in the dark eyes of Moslem and Hindu alike. The heir to the British throne had been received with a riot that killed 450; here was a welcome spontaneously given.

Amanullah once stood up in his carriage and cheered like a schoolboy.

In the bazaars they were calling him "The Lightning of God."

Amanullah welcomed Mahatma Gandhi's wife on the platform with him at a Moslem meeting and declared the Hindus his neighbors and brethren and asked for religious tolerance. In London they said, "Whether it was 'good form' for him to undertake the mission of peacemaker while on a brief visit on foreign soil probably this much of Pan-Islamic propaganda had to be expected from one in the position of King Amanullah and had better be swallowed with good grace by the Government of India. Let us hope at least that King Amanullah will keep off the prayerbook when he arrives here."

The *Rajputana* was escorted to sea on December 17 by airplanes and royal salutes from several batteries, and the R.I.M.S. *Clive* kept her company for the first ten miles, then boomed a salute of thirty-one guns and departed. The Afghan party settled into shipboard life with an ease that impressed everyone on board, especially as the ladies were discarding their veils in public for the first time. Christmas, of which they had scarcely heard, came while the *Rajputana* was at sea. Souraya, who had made friends with many of the children on board, gave them a Christmas tree and presents. Amanullah inspected everything and asked intelligent questions.

Humphrys sent a wire to London from the *Rajputana:* "I have been discussing with King and his ministers inconvenience of return journey via Russia and think there is a good chance of their accepting return passage by P&O steamship from Port Said and travel thence via Bombay and Peshawar to Kabul . . . Special train might be kept in readiness for journey through India some time next summer."

Going through the Suez Canal, the Afghans saw something with which they were familiar: camels. But instead of ambling lazily, their oversized feet flapping along dusty roads beneath burdens of cargo, these camels were disciplined like horses as they carried in a military manner the soldiers of the Camel Corps turned out as an escort for Amanullah, who could not spare them much attention as he was too busy watching the ship float through the different locks.

On December 26 the *Rajputana* docked at Port Said and the entire ship's company cheered as the Afghan party landed, to be met by the brother of King Fuad. This time there was no complaint about costume: the men wore their most brilliant uniforms.

And when Souraya and Nur-us-Seraj walked ashore, they were wearing veils again, but the veils had changed since they had left Asia behind. Only a sheer film of black tulle covered each face, no more concealing than a silk stocking would have been. If the Moslem men who escorted them ashore in Egypt were surprised, they did not show it. Newspaper photographers were at the dock; they snapped photographs which were printed all over the world, and in these the whole world could distinguish perfectly the beautiful features of Amanullah's womenfolk.

Afghanistan was hearing all about Amanullah's success. The British Foreign Office had seen to that, and assured that all news reports carried the signature of Reuters, the famous news agency, "whether Reuters' own, the British official wireless, or concocted in the Foreign and Political Department in Delhi . . . This point is very important. Reuters messages, to which the Afghans are accustomed and which in this case they will believe to be the same as messages on the subject sent all over the world, will be of far greater value than British official bulletins, labelled as such, which would be regarded as propaganda."

These "Reuters" dispatches, however, were only words. The photographs of the royal visit appeared in publications in Europe which were seldom seen in Afghanistan. But now copies were being sent there and circulated, especially those with photographs of Souraya disembarking in Egypt with only gossamer between her face and the infidel world. Even the tribesmen in the hills, where few could read, saw this photograph.

As the kings Fuad and Amanullah rode through Cairo's streets in an open carriage, crowds and parading students shouted, "Egypt and Afghanistan!" When Amanullah addressed the Deputies, there were cries in that august assembly of "Long live the Afghan nation! Long live the democratic King!" These were aroused by his reference to the Egyptian Parliament as "the only sacred place where the nation manifests its will."

"His pleasant, natural manner and the eagerness with which he interrogates all and sundry on local affairs have combined with a certain ingenuousness of speech to win him the sympathies of many who blame King Fuad for a contrasting attitude of proud and stiff seclusion," reported the British High Commissioner, Lord Lloyd. "King Amanullah's manifest zeal for the welfare of the Orient and his apparent success in its championship against the West naturally confirm these sympathies . . .

"In one quarter only is King Amanullah's visit unlikely to have enhanced his reputation. When not in uniform he has worn a gray frock coat and top hat, which have been hailed by modernists as the authentic insignia of progress. In these garments he descended upon a somewhat scandalized Azhar [Mosque]. The performance in a top hat of the ritual genuflections of Moslem prayer is no easy feat, but the ulema appear to have withheld every expression of appreciation. Indeed, it is credibly reported that a reception in His Majesty's honor, which was to have been organized by the ulema [the body of religious leaders], was prevented by their disapproval of the royal headdress."

What shocked the orthodox Moslems was that Amanullah had prayed with a brim shading his face. Even a soldier, whose military cap has a visor, takes care to turn his hat around before praying, so that nothing comes between his face and heaven. The brim of that hat had cost Amanullah a gesture of religious support.

He sailed on January 5 for Europe, and there in Naples on the threshold of new enlightenment, he found part of the old order in Afghanistan.

Nadir and two brothers, Hashim and Shah Wali, came to see him. Much had changed since he and Nadir had parted two and a half years earlier. Amanullah had gone much higher. Here he was not the ruler who, despite his power, was tied to Nadir by the threads of custom and interlocking family which even he could not ignore. Here Amanullah was the man of the hour; Nadir could not pick up a newspaper without seeing his picture. Amanullah apparently had won his gamble with progress. Nadir, on the other hand, had no official status anywhere. He and his brothers were private citizens. Yet when Amanullah suggested that Nadir return to Afghanistan, Nadir made conditions.

They were not simply political conditions regarding the pace of development and the concessions to tribal prejudice. Nadir went into personalities. He insisted that before he would return, Amanullah must discharge from official positions a number of persons whom he named: Wali the regent, Ghulam Nabi, Mahmud Sami, Ghulam Siddiq, Mahmud Tarzi.[4] Some were persons who had replaced him in positions; with some he had standing disagreements.

For Amanullah to agree would have meant throwing aside all those who had helped him to this pinnacle; it would have meant Nadir and Nadir alone directing the state. He said no.

The brothers talked with him again when he visited the French Riviera. Hashim did not meet Nur-us-Seraj. There were to be rumors as to the heated nature of those meetings, and Nadir would describe his reaction as "disgusted."

In the large expanse of India where people came and went across the frontier of Afghanistan, something was happening. Compared to the upheaval of a few years earlier that had led to the Khost Rebellion, it was no more than a suspicious rustling of leaves.

The frontier itself, where unrest was so normal that tranquillity was a relative state, was quieter than usual. The British, observing this quiet, deduced that Amanullah had paid especially larger allowances to the tribes to keep them peaceful during his absence; they knew that some of the most energetic mullahs had been given lectures about behaving themselves.

No, the trouble was taking place farther into India.

"Even a man who knows nothing about intelligence work can realize that something is being hatched," said one of the least informed agents of the Baluchistan Intelligence Bureau. "Undoubtedly something is afoot," he said, in Dera Ismail Khan, a town separated from the Afghan frontier by a distance that would be only a hundred miles for a bird, but for a man would lead around and up and down the hills where the Wazirs were jealous of their own sovereignty, and then one would be in the Afghan country of the Suleiman Khel Ghilzais, that clan who were part nomad, part settler, and who had frightened the people of Ghazni and penetrated close to Kabul during the Khost Rebellion.

"The Hazrat Sahib is mixed up in it," the agent added.

Sher Agha was the Hazrat Sahib he referred to. After departing Afghanistan by mutual agreement with Amanullah, whose reforms he detested, he had settled in the Indian city of Sirhind, but on December 18 Sher Agha had arrived in Dera Ismail Khan to meet thousands of nomads, who revered him as the Afridis revered their Mullah Mahmud

Akhunzada, to join them in the annual celebration at the Zakheri Ziarat.

The rustle reached the ears of the editor of a Lahore newspaper, *Tarjuman-i-Sarhad*, who put it not only into print but into what many Indians and Afghans, suspicious of British intentions, were to consider its proper context.

"The Snare of a Pir [Religious Leader] Who Has Been Expelled from Afghanistan.

"A Pir who has been expelled from Afghanistan is living in Dera Ismail Khan since some time. He is called Pir Fazl [Sher Agha's real name was Fazl-i-Umar] and the [nomads] visit him. People look upon him with great suspicion. It is said that he is the son of a well-known deceased pir of Afghanistan in whom Amir Habibullah had great faith. He took a leading part in the backward movement against the Nizam-namas in spite of Amir Amanullah Khan's advice and the movement resulted in a rebellion. His Majesty simply expelled him from his dominions and gave him no further punishment out of respect for his father. After coming away from Afghanistan, this Pir went to different places in India and settled at Dera Ismail Khan . . . It is thought that Dera Ismail Khan has been selected to carry on propaganda against the Government of Afghanistan and its reforms as the [nomads] pass this way and it is somewhat obscure as compared with the independence-loving Peshawar. His having no ostensible standard of livelihood, his high standard of life, the visit of the [nomads] to him, Dera Ismail Khan's situation in the way of [nomads] and his getting two houses are not facts that can be regarded as accidental."

The editor stated that the two houses had been given to him by the Political Agent, which would have meant the British Government, and for this he was severely chastised.

The British, on the contrary, had been suspicious of Sher Agha since the previous August, when the Baluchistan Intelligence Bureau reported that he was in regular correspondence with the following important men in Afghanistan: Sher Ahmed, President of the Shora; Mohammed Osman, the former Governor of Kandahar who had lost his position after introducing an inadequately clad dancer into the wedding festivities of Amanullah and Souraya, and was now head of the theological school in Kabul; Abdul Aziz, acting War Minister, who had been competing with Wali for supremacy; Zalmai, a Mangal malik who after helping direct the rebellion in Khost had fled to India, but recently had been allowed by Amanullah to return to Khost; and a hakim of Ghazni, and one of the obstreperous Suleiman Khel Ghilzais.

These men, according to British information, were all murids, or disciples, of Sher Agha.

"It was hinted to me," said the intelligence agent of Baluchistan, "that Sher Agha was perhaps trying to engineer a plot against the Afghan Government."

Even earlier, in March of 1927, a memorandum had gone out to the governments of two Indian provinces and of Burma, the internment site of potential troublemakers: "A report has been received of the existence of an invitation to the eldest son of the late Sardar Mohammed Ayub Khan [one of the exiled members of the previous dynasty] signed by some leading men of Kandahar asking him to come to Kandahar where affairs are ripe for a rising against the King of Afghanistan. At present the Government of India are not inclined to attach too much importance to the report but there undoubtedly exists some disaffection in Kandahar and it would be advisable to keep a watch on the more important Afghan refugees." And a week later, "Enquiries in progress in Quetta point to there being some foundation for the report." And two names mentioned were those of Akram and Azam, the two sons of former Amir Ayub who, twelve years earlier, had been encouraged by the Ghilzai horse trader Ghaus-ud-din to make an abortive attempt to enter Afghanistan with a view to taking over the throne, and had been stopped when their Ford had a collision with a cow.

Now, in January of 1928, other reports started coming in to the intelligence bureau.

In Kandahar there was a scandal that ended with the dismissal of the Hakim of Baldak, who mentioned that he expected to see Sher Agha either at Lahore or in Dera Ismail Khan. "In order to watch his movements, I was able to get a man of mine to accompany him as a servant.

"[He] realized that he had made a slip in mentioning his intended visit to [Sher Agha] as he subsequently tried to eradicate the impression that he had given."

At the same time another mullah who lived in Ghazni passed through Quetta; he was one of the instigators of the Khost Rebellion who would have been arrested on Amanullah's visit to Gardez in the previous year had not Ali Ahmed warned him in time to escape. He also was headed for Dera Ismail Khan in company with another mullah who gave the

British secret information on still others who were coming; one was a Zadran malik who had escaped arrest in Khost; another was the son of a man imprisoned in Kabul. Sher Agha seemed to be the point towards which they were all moving, and he had arrived in company with several mullahs, some of whom were from Kabul.

A meeting was to be held, and this is what the British heard:

"My informant states that the reason for the calling of the meeting is to formulate plans whereby the Jadid, or New Party, in Afghanistan [the party of reform] can be overthrown. He stated that the ulema and the common people of Afghanistan were entirely opposed to the New Party in the plans of which they see only disaster to Afghanistan and to Islam. They are not actively against the King but they desire to bring off a coup during his absence by obliterating the New Party and with this as a fait accompli to force the King to break away from his present attitude as regards the tenets of Islam. If, however, he refuses to do so, they are prepared to set up a republic."

Paniala, a small village north of Dera Ismail Khan, was the scene of the meeting sometime between January 28, when Sher Agha went there at the invitation of a follower, and February 1, when he returned to Dera Ismail Khan after visiting several nomad camps.

Paniala is so small that it does not appear on many maps, a quiet place where the people raise enough food for themselves and not much more. But it became an important place in the history of Afghanistan from the meeting of which the informer, an Afghan mullah who was present, gave the British an account.

Sher Agha, said the informer, came amply prepared to incite in Khost a rising similar to that which had almost toppled Amanullah in 1924. He had already received at a secret meeting pledges of support from the maliks of the Ghilzai clans that spent the winters near Dera Ismail Khan. They resented Amanullah's efforts to conscript them into his army; they found Afghan soldiers insolent when they drove their flocks westward for the summers.

In spite of Sher Agha's careful plans, there were some who wished to amend those plans to their own ideas. Two of the royal Afghan exiles in India, two sons of the late Sardar Ayub, had made an abortive attempt to enter Afghanistan several years earlier, enticed by the Ghilzai chief Ghaus-ud-din, whom the British credited with the nefarious intent of taking their money and then betraying them to the Amir for more money. Now some men suggested that these men be introduced into Afghanistan as part of the plot against Amanullah, to serve as a rallying point as Abdul Karim had done in the 1924 rebellion. Two Ahmedzais, from Ghaus-ud-din's own clan, were on hand in Paniala saying they had come with the express purpose of helping these men escape into Afghanistan, one into Jalalabad and the other into Khost, on the night of February 7 during a religious observance.

Sher Agha did not like the introduction of royal pretenders into his scheme. There would come a day when many Afghans would believe that he wished the throne for himself and therefore would back no other candidate. What he said to the mullahs gathered around him at Paniala was that these royal exiles would confuse the issue. Khost, he said, was ready to rise for the sake of Islam to cast out an infidel king. The cause was now purely religious; the men of Khost would never fight so hard simply for a change of dynasty, and all their expected support would be jeopardized. He finally agreed that one of the young men might enter the area around Jalalabad, but Khost was his alone.

Having disposed of this complication, Sher Agha now laid his foundations by discussing Amanullah's defects in the light of religious law, assuring all present that by rebelling they would be serving the cause of Allah and the Prophet. Then he unfolded a careful scheme.

Already, said Sher Agha, two of his kinsmen were busy for the cause in Kabul: his brother Gul Agha and his nephew Masum, son of Shah Agha. He expected the active cooperation of Zamindawar, a region near Kandahar that was considered a stronghold of Amanullah's own clan, the Durranis. A judge from Kandahar was expected at Paniala. Sher Agha had sent a telegram to him in Lahore, where he was visiting, but he did not arrive.

Roles in the rebellion were assigned to various mullahs. Haji Dost Mohammed was told that he should await Sher Agha's signal to travel through Duki, Loralai and Thal, to stir up the Ghilzais who would be returning to Afghanistan from India with the approach of spring. Two mullahs, Mohammed Hassan alias Abdul Rahim, and Mohammed Jan, were told to leave immediately for Khost to arouse rebellion among the Mangal and Zadran tribes. Malik Biland also was assigned to Zadran, while Malik Ghulam Khan was ordered to Gurbaz, a district that had seen a slight insurrection in the previous year.

"The mullahs . . . are very anti-Russian," said the informer, Haji Dost Mohammed, "and hope that Russian help will be forthcoming to the Government, as they then consider that all Afghanistan will be cemented to their cause."

He quoted Sher Agha as naming among important men in the plot Shah Mahmud, Nadir's brother, who had just been recalled as Governor of Jalalabad; Abdul Aziz, officiating War Minister, and Mohammed Osman, a former Governor of Kandahar now in charge of Kabul's theological school.

With this news the British ordered special surveillance for the sardars in India, Akram and Azam, in case they were about to be spirited across the frontier. They were attending the races at Lucknow. February 7, the date for their supposed escape, came and they were still at the races. March 8 came and there was no uprising.

Sher Agha went to Bannu to see the nomads but returned to Dera Ismail Khan a week later. "A man who has previously worked for me has arrived from Dera Ismail Khan and has informed me that Sher Agha is 'courting' the Hazrat Sahib of Paniala. The latter is paramount among the Ghilzais. Sher Agha himself has been frequently visiting the Ghilzais."

In London, wondering if Shah Mahmud's dismissal indicated that Wali had wind of the plot, an official wrote, "The situation in and around Khost is highly inflammable and a move on the part of Nadir and his brothers might put a match to it." They checked also on the whereabouts of Nadir, who was living in the south of France, in Grasse, and getting medical treatment in Switzerland.

Basil Gould, who was directing the British Legation in Humphrys' absence, showed Wali the newspaper story on Sher Agha as an excuse to ask his opinion. Wali thanked the Government of India for wishing him to be consulted, said that he had some knowledge of this man, whom he did not think a probable source of danger, but that he would speak again about him in due course.

The British then took action on their own. Most of what they knew about Sher Agha was in the cloudy area of secret reports, but he was quite open about one thing: his violent disapproval of Queen Souraya's showing herself unveiled in Europe and the education of Afghan children as "infidels." He talked so publicly on these topics that he laid himself open to arrest under a law forbidding abuse of monarchs friendly to India.

The Deputy Commissioner of Dera Ismail Khan ordered Sher Agha to appear before him. This man who was accustomed to giving orders, not taking them, refused and was arrested. On his appearance he admitted having received the order but said the object with which he was summoned was not explained, that if the Deputy Commissioner wished to see him, he should explain the purpose. "The demeanor of [Sher Agha] was somewhat truculent during the interview . . . I have arranged that [he] shall leave by Darya Khan tonight. His destination is Lahore." Thus Sher Agha was moved away from the Afghan frontier, where his preaching was most dangerous.

"I explained to him the reason for his having been summoned," said the Deputy Commissioner, "but he denied that he had taken part in any such activities."

In Lahore, Sher Agha, after meeting with one of the sardars whose introduction into Afghanistan had been suggested, was joined by his mother. He told his disciples that he would go either to Sirhind or to Bombay. But he made a final attempt to return to the frontier in a letter in May to the Chief Commissioner of the North-West Frontier Province, in which this proud man humbled himself before "The Benign Government" with a plea that "the petitioner may be set free to visit the frontier province occasionally when he is required by his disciples to do so . . . It is an admitted fact that Your Honor's petitioner has no other source of income. He is supported by his disciples; as well, his family and dependents are supplied board and lodging by the said disciples. If he is restricted in this way, he will not be able to earn his and his dependents' and family's livelihood. His resources will suffer and he will be put to starvation with all his family and dependents. He does not see if the Benign Government is willing so. In addition he mentioned that he has to go back to his country [Afghanistan]. If he is restricted in this way he will not be able to earn to pay for his return expenses. This is the prime cause he requests the cancellation of the order. Or, if it is possible, he requests that Government may kindly manage for his livelihood as well as for the maintenance of his family and dependents."

"He was expelled solely in order to prevent him from using this province as a basis for intrigue in Afghanistan," said a memo from the Commissioner, Sir Norman Bolton. "I suggest asking at Kabul if they still want him out." Sultan Ahmed, Deputy Foreign Minister, cousin of Faiz Mohammed, said that Sher Agha had asked permission to return to Afghanistan, that a display of excessive apprehension might tend to enhance his importance in the eyes both of himself and of the world.

But he deferred a decision and the British continued to keep Sher Agha, at the request of the Afghan Government, away from the frontier.

The Afghan Trade Agent at Quetta was buying the illustrated newspapers and sending them to Kabul so that the officials there might see the same photographs of Queen Souraya in Western clothes that were passing from hand to hand among the tribes. He made a remark to an Indian officer which was being whispered by both the well-wishers and the enemies of Amanullah: that it was possible Amanullah might be a state guest in other countries for the rest of his life.

CHAPTER 19

January 8, 1928, to March 13, 1928

"The royal customers approach," wrote one newspaper.

To the optimist—and most Westerners of the 1920s were optimists —it was apparent that a country which had bought nothing for centuries must need everything. Many of those people, when they heard of the approach of the King of Afghanistan, had to run to an atlas to learn where Afghanistan was. They would later assure Amanullah of a life-long interest in his country. Some clever woman had uttered a memorable phrase, "Oh, to be naked with a checkbook!" which symbolized the ideal customer. In the aspirations of much of Europe, Amanullah was naked with a checkbook.

The resources of that checkbook were unknown to them, as they were unknown to most Afghans. Four years earlier an Italian expert assisting Afghanistan with its finances had said that there was plenty of money for Amanullah's projects.[1] The Khost Rebellion had devoured a large part of those reserves. As much had gone for bribery as for fighting; Ghaus-ud-din had got 150,000 rupees for his intricate double-play with the Ahmedzai Ghilzais. But Amanullah's journey, which seemed to many Afghans such an expensive luxury, was not costing as much as they thought. Amanullah was a professional guest. He went only to those countries that entertained him completely. The journey through India and on the *Rajputana* to Egypt, despite the talk about the "shabbiness of the route," had cost the Government of India nearly ten years of the secret, uncollected subsidy, or 6,300,491 rupees. It irritated G. of I. that Amanullah never seemed to realize who had been his host, but insisted on paying his thanks to H.M.G.

In Rome, Amanullah, through his Minister to Italy, made overtures to the United States. But he was told that he would have to bear all the expenses of an American visit himself, that he would not be a state guest although he would be met at Quarantine by an Assistant Secretary of State. The instructions from Washington had been to discourage a visit, and this response did.[2]

Most of Amanullah's expenses for the trip were paid from his personal treasury in the Arg. As to the official purchases, he hoped that some of the men who were so eager to sell would come to Afghanistan along with their products, thereby bringing capital. The giants among nations had not yet devised the policy which, twenty years later, would make smaller nations burgeon, by not only selling them articles but giving or lending the money with which to buy them. In this interplay of interests Amanullah was a hopeful novice in a field where the larger nations were no more experienced than he.

The King of Italy, wearing a gray-green uniform, was quite overshadowed by Amanullah in a blue uniform and a black hat with aigrette plumes. When they met at the Rome railway station, there was present also the real ruler of Italy, Premier Benito Mussolini, with whom people were comparing Amanullah with such enthusiasm that some could even detect a resemblance in the two faces, one square and one round. Amanullah was being called "the Mussolini of the East." The cliché with which the Mussolini of the West was described was "He made the trains run on time."

After the greeting Mussolini slipped out a side door and drove down the back streets in a bulletproof limousine; that was a difference between the two men. Amanullah stepped into an open carriage beside King Vittorio Emanuele for a ride through cheering crowds. Souraya, carrying a bunch of red roses that had been presented to her, rode with them. It was her first experience at taking part in a public ceremony unveiled, of acting as a Western consort acts.

King Vittorio Emanuele liked Amanullah far beyond the conventional amenities paid to another head of state. His Queen, who came from Montenegro, a place as wild as Afghanistan, also liked Amanullah and Souraya. They were two royal couples who, if Kismet or Fate had not put them on thrones, would have been going on picnics together and showing pictures of their children to each other. The prize of the Italian visit was this friendship.

After three days at the Quirinal Palace, Amanullah had to move to the Grand Hotel in order to pay a visit to Pope Pius XI, who was "the Prisoner of the Vatican" and could receive no one who came from the King's official residence. Amanullah was the first ruler received by any Pope whose country held not only no Catholic missionaries but also no Catholics. It may have been the only such country in the world. The Pope considered his courtesy a beginning step that might lead to Catholic missionaries some day in Afghanistan, but with the long patience of the Church he did not openly mention this wish.

Amanullah had not been briefed in advance about the man and the church that were receiving him. When asked if there were any Catholics in his country, he replied that they were there in abundance, showing, first, that he wanted to please his generous host, and second, that he had no real idea what a Catholic was.

Arriving at the Vatican, he asked Prince Massimo, the Papal Master of Ceremonies, not to fail as they entered the Throne Room to point out the consort of His Holiness. The Prince said that the Pope had no wife; Amanullah was amazed. After the audience he visited the Papal Secretary of State, Pietro Cardinal Gasparri, with whom he discussed this surprising lack. He asked about the Sacred College and learned that its members also did not marry. Amanullah then assured Cardinal Gasparri that he thought that he, at least, might be exempted from celibacy. In Islam there was no thought of this abstention; it was incredible that anyone should hope to please Allah in such a fashion.

Also surprising to Amanullah was the Pope's status as "Prisoner of the Vatican." He told Pope Pius, "I hear there is a conflict between you and the King. I cannot understand that; why, the King is such a good man! You will see, Your Holiness, that in three or four years you will come out of the Vatican. I am sure of that."

Vittorio Emanuele, in his turn, was so impressed by Amanullah that the decoration he chose to confer on him was the highest in Italy, the Collar of the Annunziata, which was limited to twelve holders, who included the Kings of Spain and England. This conferring made the two kings "cousins," and Vittorio Emanuele was to show himself, later, a cousin indeed.

Frenchmen lost no time in discovering that Souraya's name was almost the same as "sourire," the French word for "smile," and making the most of it. Souraya's secluded past had left her with just enough shyness to make her poise and charm extremely piquant in a setting of Frenchwomen who had studied from birth to handle themselves in the company of men. The dressmaker had done well; she wore elegant clothes with enough originality to attract comment.

Souraya was unfortunate that her entry into the Western world came at a time when skirts were worn very short, "flapper style." Her legs were not her best feature, although only one journalist was so ungallant as to call attention to that. Her figure reflected the children that she had borne. The dressmaker was wise enough not to make Souraya a flapper, but to clothe her on classic lines with skirts falling a few inches below her knees. It was a style which the Queen of England, ten years later, would be wearing while other women's skirts were still short.

Amanullah and Souraya left Rome for Nice on January 19 and for five days they enjoyed themselves, with only the unpleasant interview with Nadir to mar the sunny days of the French Riviera. "I want to see everything in Europe, both good and bad," Amanullah told reporters, thereby proving himself more realistic than most state visitors who pretended that everything was good. He visited the gambling resorts and watched Hassan Jan play. Amanullah, who did not gamble himself, was amused that Hassan Jan lost.

The special Presidential car reserved for foreign dignitaries was attached to the "Blue Train" to take the royal party to Paris. Newspapers had been calling Amanullah "Asia's most independent and astute monarch; this is the visit of the whole government of his country, for, more than Mussolini, more than Stalin, Amanullah is the whole government of his country." One Paris dispatch listed his goals thus: "He wants France to help his banking business, Germany to encourage the exploitation of natural resources, England to sell him ammunition, and Russia to worry the others."

Along a two-mile stretch of boulevard the French regimental bands played the Afghan national anthem, which they also had just learned. Hidayatullah, the son of Amanullah's first marriage, was waiting at the Afghan Legation for a reunion in private with his father, whom he had seen for only one brief holiday since his departure for France more than six years earlier. The sun was shining, and the entire French Cabinet was waiting with the President, Gaston Doumergue, at the Bois de Boulogne station when the Blue Train came to a stop so deftly that the door of Amanullah's special car was even with the red carpet on the platform.

Amanullah and Souraya stepped out. Souraya, who had been studying French, said, "Bonjour": She held out her hand. The President of the French Republic took her hand and bowed over it.

At that moment the photographers snapped their picture.

The sight of a Queen of Afghanistan actually touching a foreign man sent shock waves all along the mountains of the Suleiman Range which was home to the most formidable tribes of both India and Afghanistan. The shock waves reached as far away as Bombay, where a newspaper published a cartoon showing a mullah being horrified by the spectacle of an unveiled Queen. A Lahore newspaper, *Milap*, stated that it had received a letter over the signature of Mohammed Ayub Khan, a Pathan, asking the editor to refrain from publishing such items of news as that which appeared in a recent issue to the effect that the Queen of Afghanistan had attended a banquet unveiled. "For this slander," wrote Mohammed Ayub Khan, completely erroneously, "the Afghan Government has sentenced one Mahasha Mhursand to death and his head will be struck off with the dagger of Islam in the presence of the King. The editor should either ask pardon or drown himself in the Rabi, thereby reaching Paradise, where nymphs will bathe him." The editor noted that to be sentenced to death for publishing the truth is not an unenviable fate, and that he was indifferent to nymphs.

Some in Kandahar, sharing the incredulity of this letter writer, were saying that these photographs of the unveiled Queen could not possibly be genuine but must be circulated by the British as propaganda.

In Herat the Russian Consul, Poliak, was happy to give out the news that the Queen of Afghanistan was unveiling on her tour. In London, where cinema records of the journey were being made, the comment was, "We have to bowdlerize the film sent home." Someone wondered about the reaction to a shot of Souraya scratching her nose.

Wali discovered sometime in January that he was suffering from a kidney stone; he decided that after Amanullah's return, when his regency would be ended, he would go to Europe for treatment. Meanwhile, he was concerned over possible danger in the spring, when the Ghilzais and other nomad tribes would sweep back into Afghanistan; he ordered extra ammunition moved into the area around Khost. It was ominous that the Mullah of Tagao, an influential religious leader from the area north of Kabul, requested permission to sell his property and move from Afghanistan to Mecca; this was reminiscent of Sher Agha; Wali postponed a decision till the King's return.

He was trying to keep in tranquillity a group of tribes of whom an official had said, in exasperation, that if all the mountains were made of solid gold, and all that given to these tribes, still it would not be enough. He tried to implement Amanullah's ambitions for education by opening a school in Ghazni and requiring boys to attend; the citizens of Ghazni were indignant. In Kandahar a convicted murderer was handed over to the family of his victim and publicly slaughtered according to the old principle of "qisas" which Amanullah had vowed to abolish. A malik living near Kandahar was arrested for failure to pay his arrears of revenue and told, after hostages had been taken from him, to go to Kabul, but instead he went in a direction that would have alarmed Wali had he known all that the British knew: he went to Dera Ismail Khan while Sher Agha was there.

Wali, like everyone else, heard the ominous rustle. The diary of the British Military Attaché said: "Unease in Eastern Provinces reported from Jalalabad as a result of rumors of intrigues against the King. It seems pro-Republican propaganda in Eastern Provinces must have emanated from Shah Mahmud, former Governor, not Kabul. Several of Shah Mahmud's adherents who held responsible positions in Eastern Provinces now transferred." The comment in London was "[The rumor] is formidable insofar as it is supported by the tribes who are still no doubt much influenced by the views of this family [of Nadir]."

Then at the end of April the rumors about designs on the throne by the exiled sardars in India, Akram and Azam, burst into reality with the appearance of a mysterious twenty-four-year-old stranger on the frontier, accompanied by a nine-year-old girl who he said was his sister. All up and down the frontier and in Kabul went the story that Akram had appeared among the tribes. Arrested and brought to Kabul, the stranger said he was Karam, grandson of ex-Amir Yakub, and told a romantic tale of a beggar who guided him to his destiny at the home of a sayed in Bannu, one of the Indian towns where, whether by coincidence or not, Sher Agha had been visiting, and of the equally mysterious sayed's sending him into Khost. There was no record of a grandson of Yakub by that name. Some rumors said he was Abdul Karim, who had been in Khost during the rebellion; not everyone knew that Abdul Karim had killed himself in Burma, and some who had heard this did not believe it.

A mystic might have called him the materialization of all the rumors and imaginings. There had been so much talk about Akram and Azam that Wali had already expressed his willingness to have them in Afghanistan where he could keep them in custody. The stranger, whoever he was, was never anything but mysterious. He was never heard of again.

But Wali had other troubles, principally a gang of bandits who were arrested in the Koh-i-Daman area with incomplete success. Some of the offenders escaped and fled toward India, and eventually were arrested in Peshawar. One bandit, who was the brother-in-law of Wali's gardener at his Koh-i-Daman estate, before fleeing sent a message to Wali asking for amnesty. Wali replied, through his gardener, that he could make no such promise in the absence of King Amanullah.

"The Afghan Government makes an oral but insistent request," reported the British chargé d'affaires in Kabul, "that they should either be imprisoned or removed from the frontier. It is clear that Afghan Government would be seriously perturbed if these men were set at liberty."

Two of the captured men, named Azam and Usman, were told to furnish security from someone who could satisfy the Peshawar magistrate of their future good behavior. They had friends in the Kurram, the area around Parachinar, who were willing to provide bond of three thousand rupees each. But the magistrate would not accept bond from persons outside Peshawar district, so they were sentenced to three years' imprisonment.

Some of their party from Koh-i-Daman were luckier. There was, for instance, Sayed Hussein, who had abandoned a respectable family for the pursuit of banditry. The Peshawar police could not catch him. There was also a man who briefly earned, for the second time in his life, an honest living. He served tea from a samovar in a teahouse in the section of Peshawar known as Nimak-Mandi. But tea-serving did not fulfill him. He and his brother were implicated in a burglary and arrested; they gave their residence as Koh-i-Daman, Kabul. The evidence did not suffice to convict them; they were set free and soon disappeared from Peshawar.

The first instance of this man's earning an honest living had taken place before and during the Khost Rebellion, when he had served in the crack Qita Namuna Regiment before deserting. It was he who had publicized his father's honest profession by taking the name Son of the

Water-Carrier or Bacha Sacao. It was also he who had asked Wali for the chance to become respectable.

When Amanullah went shopping in Berlin, he used to withdraw his attention from the merchandise long enough to peep from behind a blind to see if the crowds in the street, gathered to watch him, had diminished or increased. Most of the time they had increased, for this gesture became generally known and anticipated, and while Amanullah was peeping at the Berlin public, the public was peeping at him. They loved him for this.

His approach on Berlin had presented the Republic of Germany with two problems, one minor and one major. The minor problem was how to feed him. Most of the German cuisine was built around pork, the animal forbidden to Moslems, so sausages, wursts, Westphalian ham, many German specialties were dismissed at once, and, of course, what remained could not be washed down with beer. "The careful supervision of meals by the Afghan Embassy has meant simpler menus and more drinking of plain water than has ever been recorded on any public occasion in Germany," said the London *Observer*.

Back in Afghanistan, Amanullah's enemies were accusing him of eating pork and drinking wine. He did neither. Even in France he responded to a toast "in the limpid and pure water of France."

Germany had been a Republic only since her defeat in the Great War had sent the Kaiser into exile. Amanullah was the first monarch to visit in Republican days, so there was no established protocol to take care of him. Some Germans would have gone to the extreme of republicanism as they had gone to the extreme of Prussianism, and made his reception austere. But the craving to defer to rank cannot be legislated away.

As it was, nothing was austere except the black coat and tall black hat which President Paul von Hindenburg wore as he saluted Amanullah and handed Souraya a bunch of orchids. Amanullah's outfit, a red and blue uniform and a military hat to which a white plume was clasped by a jewel, was more in keeping with the tone of the visit.

Some newspapers of the left complained that "a grander reception would hardly be possible and what will be done if, instead of a minor Oriental despot, a King or President of a real power visits?"

What mattered was that dressmakers of Berlin were kept busy producing gowns suitable for meeting royalty, and Government officials were complaining of social climbers who wished to entertain the guests. Since there was no official residence suitably elegant, the Republic of Germany paid a large sum to the Crown Prince whom it had deposed in order to rent one of the palaces it had permitted him to retain, the elaborate Prince Albrecht Palace on the Wilhelmstrasse. Amanullah and most of his suite stayed here. The overflow was accommodated at a hotel.

Germany showed him her military might. But because of the Treaty of Versailles, it was makeshift in everything but intention. No planes flew overhead to impress the Afghan ruler whose first aviators had been German; they were forbidden by the treaty which would have prevented his using Germans to put down the Khost Rebellion if Britain had not chosen deliberately to ignore it. Nor were there any tanks; when Amanullah watched the maneuvers from a grandstand, men wheeled bicycles on which were attached cloth-and-wood replicas of tanks.

"It was evident that the soldiers had been trained to the highest point of efficiency," reported the New York *Times*. "It was also a big day for President von Hindenburg. Though the scene was familiar to him, his face showed that he enjoyed seeing it again." A nationalist newspaper wrote, "What a heartfelt joy once again to see such well-disciplined, soldierly fellows marching in closed ranks! The glory of Prussia! The old iron troops!"

The political significance of this episode was lost on Amanullah, as was another incident, when a group of left-wing Germans gathered in the street and shouted at him, "Down with this loafer! He should learn to work!" Not knowing what they were saying, Amanullah smiled and doffed his hat. Then the men began to shake their fists. He could understand that, so the police dispersed the critics.

Among the German women who had married Afridi men and gone with them to Afghanistan was Charlotte Boettcher of Berlin. She was unhappy with her husband Abdullah and tried to leave him, but even more unhappy when he died. Abdullah's body was being carried out of the poor mud house where they lived, to be buried, when his brother grabbed Charlotte's wrist and said, "You are my wife now."

The custom of a widow's being passed to another member of the family was an old one. Abdur Rahman had done his best to abolish it, saying that it was possible for a woman who got into the clutches of an evil family to remain a prisoner all her life. Amanullah would have forbidden this had he known. But Charlotte was not concerned about the marriage, for she knew that her brother-in-law had no interest in her. He wanted the small amount of gold that Abdullah had left. She gave it to him.

But there were four children, whom she feared he might take. One of the friends who had come to her home that day was another German wife, the woman to whom Amanullah had given a refuge in his mother's house. She had thought it prudent to wear a chaderi. And now the chaderi proved of some value, for she took up under it the youngest of Charlotte's children and, without the brother-in-law's knowing, carried him off.

She took the baby to the German Hospital and to one of its doctors, Fraulein Lehn, who on hearing the story offered to shelter Charlotte and the older children in the hospital. She said that she would give a certificate saying that they all needed medical treatment; many law-abiding persons, confronted with a situation they considered inhumane, discovered within themselves great resources for manipulating the rules.

The German Legation intervened on Charlotte's behalf and was told that she was free and could leave Afghanistan any time she wished. But the children were given into the custody of the local authorities and Charlotte would not leave without them. She remained, while the Afghan Government gave her an allowance of thirty dollars a month; this sum was more than an Afghan white collar worker would be earning forty years later, when prices and incomes had advanced.

In Berlin Charlotte's mother, an old lady named Emma Boettcher, prepared a petition asking Amanullah to allow her grandchildren to come to Germany with their mother. The German Foreign Office permitted her to approach Amanullah and present it. He granted the plea, asking her, although he did not make this a condition, to rear the children as Moslems.

Amanullah was visiting the General Electric Company works in Berlin when he suddenly dashed at one of the onlookers, seized him by the hands, kissed him on both cheeks, and drew him aside for a few minutes' conversation. This was von Hentig, who had led a mission to Afghanistan during the Great War in an attempt to persuade Amir Habibullah to forsake his neutrality and join the Germans and Turks. Amanullah called von Hentig "my oldest and best acquaintance in Berlin."

Amanullah was busy also acquiring things. The German Government presented him with a three-engine Junkers passenger airplane which it called "a symbol of friendship between states separated from one another by great distances, for it is the means by which they can always remain in communication with each other." Amanullah had already been observed to clap his hands when a speech of welcome expressed the hope that the aerial lines connecting Berlin with Moscow would soon be extended to Kabul. He began negotiations for a line linking Kabul, Herat and Tehran.

Germany gave Amanullah a credit of five million gold marks without interest for eight years and presented, in addition to the plane, a motor lorry in which Amanullah planned to transport children to school.

With his credit, Amanullah bought a printing press, two small Junkers airplanes, and mill and factory machinery including machinery for the making of soap. He made an agreement with a German company to sell lapis lazuli, the bright blue stone which was found nowhere in the world of better quality than in Afghanistan, for three years at 830,000 rupees a year. Amanullah was carrying around Europe specimens of the various minerals of his country; a number of European firms looked at these, but mining in Afghanistan was such an unknown enterprise that no one could make any definite promises, although he did come to an arrangement with Krupp regarding iron ore.

Amanullah saw in the German fields some horses of a kind unknown in his country: stocky horses called percherons that were useful in farming and for pulling heavy loads. He made a note to import some and distribute them throughout the farm areas of Afghanistan.

Italy had given him an armored car and the promise of aviation training for twenty-five Afghans, and he had bought there thirty-two guns. France gave him arms and permitted him to buy five armored cars, two field batteries, one mountain battery and two lorries. Belgium agreed to admit certified graduates of Afghan schools to its own schools.

Considering all the rewards of his trip, which had not even reached the halfway point, a British official suggested that the complaints of Afghans at home might diminish if they were told that their King's journey did not mean merely expense for themselves, but that it might pay its way or show a profit.

Amanullah did send word back to Kabul. When the mullahs heard of the soap-making machine, some of them said that Amanullah intended to melt down the corpses of Moslems to make his soap.

CHAPTER 20

March 13, 1928, to April 5, 1928

King George V, who had once expressed the hope that he would never have to call Amanullah "Your Majesty," did so.

The time was March 13, 1928, and the place was Victoria Station, London. Many years earlier Amanullah's grandfather had drawn in his mind a fantasy of being received by Queen Victoria in London with the House of Lords on one side and the House of Commons on the other. Abdur Rahman's grandson was fulfilling this fantasy, and if Abdur Rahman could have heard of this in Paradise, it would have given him more pleasure than all the nymphs and houris, considering the respective value he had put on those things in life.

Amanullah and Souraya rode to Buckingham Palace beside the British monarchs in open carriages escorted by uniforms, plumes, bands. Almost all of London watched. The London *Times* recorded every event of the royal visit so thoroughly, both before and after, that any Londoner knew exactly where to go in the hope of seeing Amanullah, and a cursory reading of the *Times* gave the illusion that nothing else was happening in the world.

That evening at a state dinner Amanullah became the first Afghan ruler since approximately 1737 to behold the great diamond known as the Koh-i-Noor, or Mountain of Light. This diamond had been the property of the Crown of Delhi when Nadir Shah swept down from Persia and conquered the Moguls of India. The Mogul Emperor, meeting his conqueror to make peace terms, hid in his turban his one remaining treasure, this diamond. But he was as unlucky with his diamond as Princess Fatima Sultana with hers. Nadir Shah heard of the concealment, and suggested that they mark peace in a traditional manner, by exchanging turbans. The Mogul could not refuse. Nadir met his death with the violence with which he had lived, and his Queen gave the diamond as a reward for service to the chief of his bodyguard, who was the Ahmed Shah Durrani who founded the dynasty that had culminated in Amanullah. But between the two rulers had come the unpopular Shah Shuja; one of his diamonds had gone to Princess Fatima Sultana's ancestor; the Koh-i-Noor was taken from him as a compulsory gift by Ranjit Singh, who took Peshawar from the Afghans, and who in his turn, overcome by Great Britain, found it expedient to offer it to Queen Victoria. Most of the time the Koh-i-Noor reposed in the Tower of London to be admired by tourists among the other Crown Jewels.

On this night, however, Amanullah beheld it on the breast of Queen Mary. It sparkled on her silver tissue gown next to the star and ribbon of an Afghan order, Almar-i-Ala, which Amanullah had just bestowed on her.

"It is difficult at this stage to predict what the ultimate effect of the visit may be," Humphrys was to write a month later. "First there is the danger that the impressions which Amanullah has formed of Great Britain may be blurred or even completely effaced by the glamour of his subsequent experiences in Russia."

In the cause of making Amanullah's visit indelible, the British mobilized every plume, every horse, every flower. No ceremony was omitted.

"Britain holds the highest cards, the King, the Queen, and the Prince of Wales," wrote the New York *Times.* "Britain is chuckling at the story that Berlin played her highest cards of cheap goods and industrial efficiency and failed to impress. Russia is expected to play her 'you and I' card. Russia and Afghanistan are both Oriental and against Imperialism.

"London feels it had a better 'you and I' card than that. It is the pomp and pageantry of a royal reception offered by the Emperor of India, the largest Mohammedan Empire on earth, to a fellow ruler over Moslem subjects. 'We are both members of the same club' is what, silently, the presence of the British monarchs will tell the Afghan monarchs."

It was the same strategy that had kept Amir Habibullah happy in his wartime neutrality by sending him a handwritten letter from the same King George who was now expending far more money and energy on the son. Again the royal strategy succeeded.

Amanullah confided in Humphrys his impression of the other countries he had visited:

"The French and Italians are excitable and rarely know their own minds. Germany is crushed by poverty, and half the people want a King and the other half a republic. There is no stability. In England everything is carried out with precision and strict regard for punctuality—there is no confusion. I was taken in great comfort from place to place without apparent effort and without hesitation. On the continent my program was so haphazard and my hosts appeared so bewildered that I rarely consented to go through with it. At a State function in Paris more than half an hour was wasted before it was discovered that Queen Souraya had arrived. They were much more efficient in Germany, but the people sometimes embarrassed the President by shouting, 'Long live the monarchy and down with the Republic!' "

About England he said, "From the moment when I landed at Dover and shook hands with the Prince of Wales, I felt that I was in a royal and friendly atmosphere, quite different from the cold republican atmosphere of France and Germany."

And one of his suite said, "No Englishman has a right to go to Heaven when he is dead, as he has already enjoyed it on earth."

A reception was given at Hatfield, where the famous garden included a maze. Amanullah insisted that one of his staff enter the maze without a guide, and found his unfortunate official quite incapable of finding his way out. Amanullah was delighted. He said that this was a thing which he must institute at Kabul, since it would provide a more merciful means than was sometimes used in that country of getting rid of an inconvenient rival.

At a civic reception in Liverpool, Amanullah performed sleight-of-hand tricks and produced the ace of spades from behind the Lord Mayor's ear.

He spoke his first English phrase in England, "How do you do?" to the Secretary of State for Air just before he became the first royal personage to fly over London in a plane. This took place on March 21, the Afghan New Year's Day.

His second English sentence was spoken while he was seated with Souraya in a Rolls-Royce sports car in the showroom where he had intended to stay an hour and stayed two and a half hours. He started the engine of his car, raised his hat, and said in perfect English, "Well, good-bye now. I go to Kabul." He drove the car a few yards, then rested in the seat as if reluctant to leave.

Souraya learned enough English to pick up and kiss a four-year-old girl who presented her a bouquet, saying, "You darling, I love little English girls but I have always been too shy to kiss one of them." At the Queen Charlotte Hospital she deplored the high rate of infant mortality in her own country. Looking at the babies, she suddenly turned to the matron and said, "I would like very much to see an absolutely new baby." No new baby was found but she saw the delivery room and a group of expectant mothers. In India the Englishwomen who spoke with Souraya at purdah parties had reported her "barren of conversational topics and difficult to entertain." After about three and a half months of emancipation from Afghan restraints, she was universally described in England as "charming."

Amanullah did understand English well enough to know at Oxford University, where he became an honorary Doctor of Civil Laws, that when his diploma was read, the language he was hearing was not English. He was informed that it was Latin.

Souraya, who had surprised the British Legation at Kabul by joining its men in a pigeon shoot, visited a Sheffield factory with Amanullah and was invited to shoot at a figure of an infantryman wearing a bulletproof vest. She surprised her hosts, first by accepting, and second, by being only half an inch off the target. In Sheffield, the platform where the royal train arrived was banked with nearly three thousand plants and the Manchester *Guardian* commented, "It recalled the idea of a royal reception in the old days, before our own reigning family had come to that agreeable habit of dispensing largely with formality."

At the Greenwich Observatory, Amanullah stood astride the meridian on the silver clock, with his right leg in the Western Hemisphere and his left leg in the Eastern Hemisphere and said, "See, I am now myself a Westerner."

What most endeared England to Amanullah and Souraya was, as the New York *Times* predicted, England's high cards, the King and the Queen, the personal attention of the royal family. The member of that family whom they found most appealing was the Duchess of York, wife of King George's second son who would eventually be King George VI. At one formal, flower-decked lunch a distinguished Persian scholar was on hand to interpret for Amanullah and the Duchess, but they waved him away and enjoyed themselves communicating by gestures and laughing at their own confusion.

"There are no Communists in England. They are all King-Worshippers," Amanullah remarked in Liverpool after driving through one of the poorest quarters and finding that the residents had festooned the street with garlands.

"Of the visit to Windsor Castle," he said, "I cannot speak without emotion." King George and Queen Mary had invited him into their private lives with a warmth seldom shown even to a fellow sovereign. "It is the perfect abode of mighty kings who have reigned through the centuries, and its charm and grandeur cannot be compared with any other palace in the world." Driving away from Windsor Castle, he and Souraya told each other that they could hardly bear to leave the "castle of their dreams."

Politics, and with it reality, entered the picture briefly when Sir Austen Chamberlain, the British Secretary of State for Foreign Affairs, called on Amanullah on March 20. Chamberlain had expected the invitation sooner, since Amanullah had parried all questions of journalists with "I shall know about that after I talk with Sir Austen Chamberlain."

The topic that Amanullah brought up, and not very pleasantly, was the perpetual one of the frontier. Their talk had an unsatisfactory ending when Chamberlain said, "I cannot myself make proposals for remedying a grievance which appears to me purely imaginary."

"Imaginary" was a word used also by Ghulam Siddiq when Chamberlain, at Amanullah's request, spoke with him a few days later. "It will be apparent from a glance at the map," said Ghulam Siddiq, "that Russia cannot make a threat on India except at incalculable cost and with the utmost difficulty in the transport of men. If [the newspaper] reports of British fear of Russia are inaccurate, then it must be an imaginary danger which underlies the action of the Government of India, probably a suspicion that Russia, in cooperation with Afghanistan, will attack India. Such an idea has never entered the head of King Amanullah, and Great Britain should furnish proof of her suspicions."

Ghulam Siddiq was now completely in charge of Afghanistan's foreign affairs. Mahmud Tarzi had left for Kabul before the party reached England, which, considering the role he had played in putting Afghanistan in her present high bargaining position, was like Moses' being deprived of the Promised Land. The rumors said that he was returning to Afghanistan to deal with threatened unrest; he was also disheartened at being passed over in the councils of his son-in-law, whom he had started on the path that led to Buckingham Palace.

In Berlin, a journalist had quoted Ghulam Siddiq, "We are going to England to see our worst enemies at home." They were not surprised at his antagonism. But they did find it puzzling that the Afghans should have waited so late to ask for something and then have made the request secondary to complaints on frontier policy.

"What shall we give Afghanistan?" had been a question for debate in London and India since the royal visit first was mentioned. The problem was not merely to benefit Afghanistan but to benefit the British Empire in the process, and not solely through making her the object of gratitude.

Russia seemed so menacing in these days that in 1927 a subcommittee of the Committee of Imperial Defense had examined and reported on the defense of India with special reference to Russian aggression in Afghanistan. It had considered the possibility of war with Afghanistan and the frontier tribes and "the greater contingency of war with Russia." Its findings affected the decisions on Amanullah's gifts.

Road-building was one gift the British were willing to continue to offer, provided the roads went to the right places. The same applied to railways, provided the rails went from Chaman in India and not from Kushk in Russia.

Also in Britain's own interests, there were gifts which she would not think of giving Amanullah. One was machinery for Afghan factories, "in view of the undesirability of devoting Indian money to the purpose of British machinery to turn out goods which would oust Indian goods from the Afghan market," and "gifts of airplanes, spares, etc. . . . , for their Air Forces as long as it is in Russian hands."

The Government of India wished to exclude from the list of possible gifts any machine guns, saying "our military advisers do not wish to facilitate the acquistion of such weapons by Afghanistan as we cannot altogether ignore all possibility of Afghanistan being ranged against us, and we are reluctant to expose our troops to possible risk of coming under fire of automatic weapons similar to those with which they are themselves armed and supplied by us. Explanations appear hardly necessary, but if any have to be given, we suggest that the Afghans be told that we have none to spare."

"I have read some strange things," an India Office official, Sir Claude Jacob, wrote on this memorandum, "but the sentence in the Government of India telegram . . . 'We suggest the Afghans be told that we have none to spare,' is about as lame an excuse that could be offered. Fancy the British Empire having no machine guns to spare! I do not see how we can refuse the King of Afghanistan anything now that we have gone so far. After all, it is the man behind the gun that counts and not the gun itself, and I think our Indian army well led by British officers would defeat any Afghan Army no matter how well armed it may be."

Amanullah needed lorries; the unimproved roads were wearing out those that he had. Before leaving Kabul he gave orders for many to be junked, assuming he would acquire new ones. The British planned a gift of lorries, but the Germans were shrewd enough to sell him some of their own and persuade him to cancel his request for the six-wheelers the British would have presented.

What the British finally gave Amanullah was armament costing more than one million rupees. The gift included three Rolls-Royce armored cars, six Vickers machine guns with pack equipment, one battery 3.75 howitzers with pack equipment, one battery 2.75 guns with pack equipment, one battery eighteen-pounders with harness, and five hundred shells for each of the above batteries, and one thousand .303 rifles and one hundred thousand cartridges.

At least, they gave the promise; it was August before the list was complete, and since all the articles were not available at once, the delivery would have to be spread over several months. "This will afford time to judge of the value of the experimental policy of a 'subsidy in kind,'" said the prudent H.M.G., which was spending the money of G. of I.

Amanullah got a personal gift of a Rolls-Royce; not the sports model which he had admired in the shop, but the limousine with his coat of arms painted on the side which he had used during his English visit. It cost £2637 in addition to the cost of shipping it to Bombay and taking it to Peshawar on a closed truck.

He bought the Rolls-Royce sports model for himself, however, paying cash for it, and then he ordered two other Rolls-Royces made up to special requirements, paying a deposit.

Souraya, who came from a country where carpets were knotted painstakingly by hand and sent around the world to be the pride of families who could afford them, bought a carpet woven on a power loom in Axminster. She bought two suites of bedroom furniture, one in gray and one in light brown, in a style that was known then as "English art furniture." She bought library furniture in the Adams style, including two bookcases, several bed-settees in embossed velvet, bronze bowls for goldfish, marble statuary and Royal Doulton china. Amanullah accompanied her on some of these shopping expeditions, with such interest that he often asked the salesman to place an article in position so that they might judge the effect.

They were furnishing the new palace in Dar-ul-Aman. Work on this palace had ceased during the Khost Rebellion but Amanullah had decided that on March 21, 1929, New Year's Day, exactly one year after the New Year's on which he had become the first monarch to fly over London, he would move into his new palace.

Salesmen were surprised when Amanullah and Souraya ordered electrical appliances; they had not suspected that Afghanistan had any electricity, even for royalty. Amanullah was fascinated by the automatic electric phonograph; he bought three of these for his palace, and then decided to buy another as a gift for Queen Mary.

Gifts for Amanullah and Souraya arrived every day, at palace or hotel, in every country. Commercial firms who hoped to sell to them presented specimens of their wares. In Afghanistan there was no prejudice against tradesmen bearing gifts. For centuries a caravan or a trader had insured a welcome with judicious offerings to tribal chief or ruler. So Amanullah and Souraya saw no reason to decline, for instance, the gold and silver electric coffee percolator that was sent to them after the existence of electricity in their palace became known. There were also ceremonial gifts, like the ship's model from the Corporation of Liverpool, and guns and saddlery.

When the Afghans left London, ten lorries were required to carry their luggage. They dropped some on the way in the form of gifts, including four of the silky-haired, slender hunting dogs known in Afghanistan as "tazis" and in England as Afghan hounds. A memorandum went to the port authorities at Karachi asking them to look out for shipments that would be arriving soon marked "H. M. King Amanullah, Kabul, Afghanistan."

Amanullah had been writing his mother letters extolling the hospitality he was receiving. He had sent Wali letters of instructions. One had been orders to halt government construction until his return, since his visit to Europe had given him many ideas for buildings. Another was the announcement that Afghanistan had joined the International Postal Union.

Now he had decided to stay away longer than he had planned, and like most travelers who extend their journeys, he wrote home for money.

CHAPTER 21

April 6, 1928, to June 20, 1928

The Russians had the same problem that had faced the Germans: to entertain Amanullah in a manner likely to satisfy both him and their own interests while still maintaining their public posture as people who despised his rank. They were aware of the advantage that the British possessed in "a matter of King meeting King."

Fortunately for the Soviets, their hero-leader Lenin, on writing the first letter ever addressed by a Russian ruler to an Afghan ruler, had called Amanullah "Padishah" or "King." This gave sanction for recognizing his royalty. Having done this, they prepared a palace for him to stay in.

While Amanullah was still in England, the London newspapers kept denying the rumors that England was trying to prevent his visiting Russia. The explanation of these rumors is that they were true. A British Colonel advised several Afghans, in confidence, that it would be better not to visit Russia. When some of Amanullah's suite expressed a disinclination for Russia, the fact was passed on to the press.

"A risk," Humphrys said of Amanullah's visit to Russia. But he added, "This is a risk which I feel should be faced with equanimity. For, however clever the camouflage, the King is too shrewd an observer to fail to notice some of the uglier aspects of the political and economic life of the Soviet Union. His Majesty told me privately that he did not intend to adhere to any fixed program in Russia but would go where he pleased and try to see things as they really existed. On the other hand, the Soviet Government will doubtless do their utmost to furnish him with proof of their power and stability, and subtle advances will be made to induce him to link his fortunes with Moscow."

Yet Amanullah had given a message to Humphrys to take to Kabul, where he would arrive before the royal party. "Tell them that I have been able in three weeks to accomplish more towards the increase of Anglo-Afghan friendship than my Foreign Office has been able to do in two years."

"I believe that in his heart," said Humphrys, "he will feel a bias, prompted alike by self-interest and personal inclination, towards England. This is all that we can reasonably expect of an Afghan ruler."

The Russian visit had to wait while Amanullah had his tonsils removed.

A year earlier the surgeon of the British Legation in Kabul had wished to operate but Amanullah was too busy visiting Mazar-i-Sharif and his other provinces. His throat had troubled him constantly; although he was a dynamic speaker with a powerful voice, always he had to keep a glass of water nearby when speaking in public and take frequent sips. A throat ailment had weakened him at the close of the Kabul conference in 1921. Now he went back to Germany as a private citizen staying at the Afghan Legation, while doctors removed the infected tonsils that had marred his visit to Belgium. Eight-year-old Sultan Jan came from Switzerland, and the father and daughter both had their tonsils out, an operation generally considered a child's, at the same time in Unger's Clinic, Berlin. Amanullah gave tips of one hundred dollars and more to the nurses and other employees, and promised to pay for ten years the expenses of any patient chosen by the hospital and the Afghan Legation to occupy his bed. In all the cities that he had visited, he had made contributions for the poor. It was the way of Afghan royalty.

The Secret Service guarded him in Berlin, despite his private status, and was in turmoil one day when he eluded them and walked alone to the radio tower which was a sightseeing attraction and stood in line with the Easter Monday holiday crowd to buy his ticket.

But Germany had been in a greater turmoil than that ever since Amanullah's first visit. He had arranged in advance for a Berlin jeweler to make a large number of Afghan decorations, which he intended to present there; and before the war the medal-loving Germans would have accepted them with glee, but now they had a new constitution. He departed, and the London *Times* now recorded: "Good Republicans were shocked to learn that Amanullah presented decorations and despite the clause in the Constitution forbidding decorations from foreign governments, they were not refused. The Almar-i-Ala, the highest order and also the Red Ducal Cloak, were accepted by President von Hindenburg, and [other officials]. Others said they accepted the decorations in their private capacity as pretty gifts . . . The conservative press says that other prominent Socialists accepted. Some denied this, but not all."

Far away in Oberlin, Ohio, U.S.A., a man was inspired to write to the New York *Times* pointing out that in ancient Afghan tradition robes of honor were distributed only to one's subjects and that acceptance meant accepting overlordship. "It would be well for the German Republic to consider carefully the desirability of accepting His Majesty's gift, and before doing so to ascertain the precise implications of acceptance, for if the historical significance of the institution still holds, Germany will become one of the outlying provinces (wilayat) of the Kingdom of Afghanistan ruled over by the Amir Hindenburg."

"In the past century," said the New York *Times* dispatch from Berlin, "probably no monarch big or little has received so much free entertainment from European governments or set so many European chancelleries by the ears." The German press had just calculated the cost of entertaining Amanullah: 185,000 marks for the gift airplane, in which he had just requested that a desk replace two seats so that he might work in flight; 400,000 marks for other gifts, which included two completely automatic telephone plants; 80,000 marks for rental of his palace and 67,000 marks for the street decorations, reception, etc., a total of a million marks or about $250,000.

Amanullah and Souraya spent May Day in Poland. It displeased the Russians to see their prospective guests spend their own special holiday in the country which had stopped the Bolshevik advance through Europe and with which they were on bad terms. The visit to England they had accepted as natural, but so far as anyone knew, only four Poles had ever stepped inside Afghanistan: Count Potocki, who had stayed at the British Legation and received from the British the highest compliment in their power; namely, that he was mistaken for an Englishman; and three unfortunate refugees from Russian justice who had been arrested in Herat and sent, penniless, to jail in Kabul and had been released after British intervention, whereupon one became a Moslem and the others disappeared.

But Amanullah made a treaty with Poland, and the Poles welcomed him with a fanfare of trumpets and spread costly carpets to shield his feet from the pavement, and displayed their prowess in fire-fighting so deftly that he asked them to send fire-fighting experts to Afghanistan.

The May Day decorations were still brightening the streets of Moscow when Amanullah arrived, on May 3. They had been left especially for him. He was the first monarch to enter the Soviet Union since Nicholas II, and the Soviets, who had renounced kings and murdered Nicholas, treated him like a king. The title they always used for him was the Persian "padishah," which may have served to confuse the Russian people, already confused by the style of his reception, as to exactly what he was. The railway platform was covered for his arrival with Oriental carpets; Mme. Alexandra Koliontal, the Soviet Ambassador to Norway, who had been recalled to Moscow especially to be hostess to Souraya, handed her guest the traditional capitalistic bunch of roses. Mikhail Kalinin, President of the Soviet Union, wearing a plain dark overcoat and soft hat, greeted Amanullah, who was dressed in a suitably proletarian fashion in contrast to the sable trimming on Souraya's blue coat.

Only two hundred privileged spectators were admitted to the station in addition to the troops and officials, but about fifty thousand people were lining the streets to applaud as he passed. Western newspapermen observing the parade wondered if all those people had come out to see Amanullah or to see their own leaders, who remained usually out of sight. But there was no doubt about the enthusiasm at the Moscow Hippodrome when Amanullah sat in the former Imperial box decorated with flowers and flags. Many thousands had waited for hours to see his car pass. They surged onto the race track cheering Amanullah, and only when mounted police spread out across the track did they finally go and let the races begin. A special prize called "Independent Afghanistan" of one thousand rubles was offered in Amanullah's honor for the best trotter; the red chestnut who won it was named Bonaparte, and the newspaper *Izvestia*, which had published a special edition in Amanullah's honor, pointed out that Napoleon Bonaparte was the first modern statesman to realize Afghanistan's importance as the key to Indian trade routes and thus attracted the attention of his enemy, England, to the country that after a vivid past had practically dropped out of history.

Amanullah and Souraya stayed in a palace built by a capitalist sugar king just across the Moscow River from the Kremlin, and in Leningrad they occupied the suite that Alexander II had used at the Winter

Palace. The Soviets put on full evening dress and danced beneath sparkling chandeliers at a ball where Amanullah played the proletariat in simple khaki uniform.

During the latter part of the nineteenth century, Tsar Nicholas II, who was then only a crown prince, had been entertained by the French Ambassador, Maurice Paléologue, at a reception which he later described in his memoirs. The memoirs had been read by the Afghan trade representative in Moscow, Abdul Madjid Zabuli, of the Hakimof company, who decided to reproduce this royal reception for King Amanullah on behalf of the Afghan colony in Moscow. For eight days he pre-empted the section of the Grand Hotel which led to the dining room on the second floor. This made it possible to plant a certain kind of lichen on the carpet of the corridor and staircase, and with controlled electric heat, humidity and light, it was arranged that the lichen covered the whole area by the time Amanullah arrived for the festivities. He walked over lichen, just as Nicholas had done. Flowers also bloomed indoors, so that the cost of decorations alone was four thousand dollars. Ninety-two guests sat down to dinner at a cost of fifty dollars a head, and during six hours were entertained by orchestras from various Republics of the Soviet Union, especially Ukraine and Caucasus, whose round trip travel expenses were paid in addition to their fees. The entertainment cost six thousand dollars. Of this $14,600 party the New York *Times* wrote, "It may open a new vista to the Soviet Treasury Department in the treatment of private businessmen."

With Grigori V. Chicherin, People's Commissar of Foreign Affairs, Amanullah had a serious discussion on May 7, which he opened with "I love Soviet Russia. I have seen in her a friend from the very beginning and I shall hold onto her, be assured of this and do not worry."

"I have to make more precise our relations with England," Chicherin told him. "We know that persons in England have tried to suggest to you the thought that the Soviet Government is an aggressive force both against England and in general against everyone. We feel sympathy for all peoples who are struggling for full independence and in one way or another we support them insofar as this is possible. But this does not mean that we want to fall upon England and to throw ourselves into a war with England, as our enemies are saying. Most of our population have feelings toward England which absolutely are not tender, for from the very beginning of our existence, on all fronts everywhere, England has created difficulties for us, has played a principal role in the intervention, and is now trying to press us to the wall. But this does not in any way mean that we are striving to throw ourselves onto England, for by virtue of the character of our power we cannot favor an aggressive military policy.

"It is not England who has reasons to fear an attack from us, but it is we who have reasons to fear an attack from England. Whether England herself prepares war against us, we shall see later. England has always striven to push others in place of herself into military activities. She may push Poland against us; I personally regard rather calmly the treaty between Afghanistan and Poland, but in the minds of our public this treaty arouses apprehension."

Amanullah asked Chicherin to calm public opinion concerning Poland. "This is the simplest treaty about establishing normal relations without any kind of obligations." Chicherin told him that he had heard the Poles wished to take over the cotton production of Afghanistan. "I would never agree," said Amanullah, "to any decision which would mean control by any sort of foreigners over any part of my country, so you have nothing to fear from the Polish plans."

The conversation came to a climax, from Amanullah's viewpoint, when he said, "It is necessary to take advantage of this trip in order that something concrete shall result. In other countries I have always done something for my people; either I bought machines or weapons, or came to an agreement on sending Afghan students or on an invitation to Afghanistan of engineers. I shall be very disappointed if during my stay in a most friendly country nothing is accomplished for Afghanistan. I brought with me the Deputy Minister of Foreign Affairs, Ghulam Siddiq, and I have summoned the Minister of Trade, Abdul Hadi, so that conversations about actual questions may take place now. I have especially chosen two most current questions: the construction of a highway and a trade treaty."[1]

Amanullah mentioned several times his desire for a trade treaty and for the privilege of transit through Russia. "I cannot leave Afghanistan locked in from all sides as at the present time."

The Russians never granted him either. They did not explain, but observers guessed that they feared reprisals from the British Empire. They had the same nervousness of the British designs on them that the British had of their designs, except that what the British feared was not Russian arms but their propaganda.

About another request of Amanullah, for a fourfold alliance comprising Russia, Turkey, Persia and Afghanistan, the Russians were quite frank. Leo M. Karakhan, the dapper Commissar for Foreign Affairs in the East, who was closest to Amanullah of all his Russian hosts and even played tennis with him, reported, "We pointed out the impossibility of a military alliance or of a mutual guarantee among these four governments, explaining that the formation of relations among the four countries would be understood as an aggressive combination against third countries and would be misunderstood. Ghulam Siddiq agreed that now was not the time to speak about a military alliance or of any sort of combination of mutual guarantees."

Amanullah asked also for a modern road from Kabul up through Mazar-i-Sharif, replacing the caravan trail, to which the Soviets agreed "in principle." The reality of that road was further off than the British Army guessed.

Chicherin and Amanullah spoke of arrests of Afghan merchants for disobeying the Russian currency regulations (Amanullah asked that they not be arrested without good cause) and of an Afghan who had approached Amanullah in the streets of Moscow and complained of six hundred sheep being stolen from him.

Before they parted, Chicherin mentioned a report in a German newspaper that Amanullah had concluded in London an agreement about the subordination of the Afghan Army to British officers. Amanullah laughed loudly. "I earnestly ask you not to believe all this gossip. I have concluded no such agreement in London and never thought about enlisting the services of English officers. These reports of the newspapers are useful because they show what the enemies of Afghanistan indeed want and in the same way show what Afghanistan must avoid. I am therefore grateful to these newspapers, for I learn from them what I must not do."

The immediate fruits of Amanullah's visit to Russia were a gift of four agricultural tractors, two tanks, two airplanes, and numerous albums with photographs of Soviet projects. As personal gifts Amanullah received a sword and saber and Souraya a rifle (being treated on the sexless terms of a Soviet woman) as well as a set of dolls in Russian costumes and a complete table service for seventy-five persons which had once belonged to the aristocratic Yusupoff family.

Karakhan reported, "I believe the most important result of the padishah's stay with us was perhaps the personal contact with statesmen which probably was closer for him with us than in any other place

in Europe. When he was bidding us good-bye, the padishah more than
once personally called by name Kalinin, Chicherin, Voroshilov and
Rykov . . . The Moscow maneuvers made a big impression on the
padishah, and he, so chary of statements, said to Comrade Voroshilov
that he was delighted with everything he had seen and that he considered our friendship so firm that any other power which might replace us would be his enemy. For a statesman especially in the position
of Amanullah a pronouncement of this kind has to be acknowledged as
very responsible and important."[2]

"Chary of statements" was not an observation that officials of other
countries had made about Amanullah. The Russians had more sources
of information on his feelings than Karakhan's pleasure in being called
by his name. An agent of the Russian secret police, the O.G.P.U., an
important Persian of Duzdap, had been offered an education in Russia
for his son; actually, the son was a hostage for the father's performance
of his assignment to obtain the secret orders of the Persian Army. In
Moscow Amanullah wished to engage a valet. The Soviet Agency which
provides domestics for all foreign legations sent around this young man,
with instructions to listen and not to reveal that he understood Persian.

Once as he was serving tea, Souraya said in Persian to Amanullah,
"This tea seems cold to me." He was on the point of blurting out, "Excuse me, it is boiling," when he saw that Amanullah was looking at him,
and he stopped just in time.[3]

So he survived in his position to report to the Russian officials the
true sentiments that Amanullah and Souraya expressed in their private
conversations, which were not favorable. They were finding many, many
flaws in Soviet civilization.

Amanullah was asked to participate in the presentation of forty-nine
combat planes to the Red Air Force, but refused when he discovered
that they had been purchased by a "Reply to Chamberlain" Fund established after Joseph Stalin in an emotional outburst had attributed
aggressive designs on Russia to Sir Austen Chamberlain. At the Lenin
Institute Amanullah listened with a smile while the director informed
him in Russian that he was "an enlightened monarch who will never
tolerate the dominance of Great Britain over Afghanistan." When
Amanullah heard the translation, his expression changed. He frowned.
In his formal reply he said, "I was tremendously impressed by much of
what I saw in England. I am convinced of the good will of the British
Empire toward Afghanistan."

As a result of this, added to their natural suspicions, the Russians wondered if Amanullah might not have a secret treaty with the British. Their agents checked through all the luggage of the Afghan royal party, surreptitiously hunting such documents. They found none. But there were two bags to which they could not gain access, of which they became inordinately suspicious. Amanullah's party was well into the Ukraine toward the end of the journey when the agents managed to steal these well-guarded bags. All they found was Souraya's lingerie.[4]

The Russians turned Amanullah over to the Turks in the middle of the Black Sea. A Turkish delegation arrived on a liner to receive him and since Amanullah reverted to his former habit of being late, they had the opportunity to talk with Russians on the escorting liners, giving rise to speculation as to what alliances might result.

At the railroad station in Ankara Amanullah kissed on both cheeks the leader who was awaiting him, Mustapha Kemal Pasha, called Kemal Ataturk or "Father of Turks," who had already accomplished much of what Amanullah wished to accomplish. In the same month of 1919 the two men had set forth to their destinies: Kemal to Anatolia and a fight for freedom from the past, Amanullah to independence and the same social liberation. Turkey had progressed much further than Afghanistan.

But the people whose lives Kemal was changing were more sophisticated than the Afghans, for they had known Christians and Moors, had been the seat of the Byzantine Empire, had watched ships sail up to their shores and sent ships out in turn, and their country was partially in Europe. Yet Kemal had gone into the most remote sections of Turkey, where these influences were not known, and ordered the women to unveil and the children to learn to read.

In doing this Kemal had been ruthless. He had slashed at lives as coolly as any Caliph ordering heads to fall into baskets. One of his biographers wrote of Kemal that there was not one tender anecdote about him. About Amanullah there were hundreds of lovable stories.

After paying his respects at the new inland capital Ankara, formerly Angora, Amanullah went to the old capital, Constantinople. There he visited the Chamber of the Sacred Mantle, which held the most sacred objects in the Moslem world: a mantle which the Prophet Mohammed had worn, a flag he had carried, his staff, sword and bow. In the days of the Caliphs and old Turkey, no lay Moslem ever beheld these relics.

Once a year specially privileged guests were permitted to kiss, through its cover, the casket holding the mantle, that was all.

Amanullah asked to see this casket. Kemal Ataturk had abolished all the trappings of religion, just as he had abolished the temporal power of the Caliphate, and the Chamber of the Holy Mantle had never been entered since that time. The custodian at its door was disturbed by such a request of the distinguished visitor from Afghanistan, which would have given these sacred objects an importance that Kemal wished to prevent. Then he rose to a diplomatic level that an ambassador could not improve upon, he said that his key would not open the door. Disappointed, Amanullah told him that Afghanistan had a Prophet's mantle also, then left for a display of sculpture in the round, one of the works of man that was absolutely forbidden to the orthodox Moslem.

Amanullah, unlike Kemal, was not singlemindedly striding toward his goal. He might hate the mullahs but his heart was with Islam. Sentiment was part of him. He could not go all the way as Kemal had done.

"Let us hope," wrote the New York *Times* correspondent, "that the custodian of the chamber will receive the praise he deserved for keeping the door closed and reminding Turkey's newest Moslem pupil that the tempo of progress is jazz and not a hesitation waltz."

The Turks gave Amanullah, besides a jeweled sword, rugs from the fur of Angora goats and a jeweled album of photographs showing the development of Ankara. For Souraya they had gone to great trouble to find a pair of fluffy white Angora kittens.

The visit to Persia began officially June 6 on the shores of the Caspian, when the Minister of Court Teymourtache welcomed the party in the town that had been Enzeli and now was called Pahlevi after the army sergeant who had made himself ruler of Persia, Reza Shah Pahlevi.

Souraya was going back into the Moslem atmosphere of seclusion that she had left behind. For the first time in five months she put on a veil, as did Nur-us-Seraj, her sister Hurya, and her mother, who had come to meet her. Although the Shah of Persia was trying like Kemal to alter the customs of his country, it would be nine years before he would tell his wife and daughters to go out unveiled.

The veils which Souraya and the other Afghan ladies wore in Persia were not the chador, the big sheet of fabric in which a Persian lady wound herself, holding it to her face so that not much more than two eyes could be seen. In Afghanistan the Queen and Princesses had progressed to European hats with veils falling from the brim. This is what they put on now, and the veils were transparent. They knew that they had re-entered a different world from that of England and Russia when, instead of joining the men for ceremonies as they had become accustomed to do, they were escorted to a separate party with the Queen of Persia.

The British Legation in Tehran described the Persian visit:

"The man in the Tehran street has vociferously acclaimed the King and Queen on every available occasion. Both of the Afghan sovereigns have endeared themselves by their sympathy, their affability and their complete lack of arrogance or pride to the populace of Tehran. Their stay has been one long crescendo of applause and friendliness. They have gone about alone in the streets of Tehran and the country places around, the King often driving the car himself, and everywhere they have been greeted with a warmth of feeling quite extraordinary in a Persian crowd.

"It must be said that the sovereigns have almost gone out of their way to be kind and gracious to the most humble, and the public have not been slow to draw comparisons between the apparently innate graciousness and kindliness of the Afghan monarch and the usual sullen bearing and scowling features of their own Shah . . .

"The Shah has been in a vile temper on more than one occasion during the stay of the Afghan sovereign, more especially at the dinner given by the Prime Minister in the Farmanieh Palace when His Majesty's chauffeur was unfortunate enough to take a wrong turn in a narrow country road and the Shah not only arrived late but was compelled to walk part of the way. He vented his fury on his ministers for the bad arrangements and left immediately after dinner.

"His attitude must also be ascribed in part to jealousy at the more evident popular success of his guest, and he is even said to have given instructions for the police to dampen the enthusiasm.

"The Queen has come in for her fair share of welcome from the public and the fact that Her Majesty has on occasions gone about unveiled in the streets has not excited the slightest comment. Her simplicity and graciousness have quite captured the hearts of all Tehranis.

"The heads of all missions with their wives have been invited to all dinners given for the royal guests but the Queen appeared at none of them, not even at the final banquet given by the King himself.

"The royal guests leave Tehran today [June 16] for Meshed and the Afghan frontier by motorcar. Amanullah has bestowed on Reza Shah the Order of the Almar-i-Ala and has received in exchange a high Persian order. Amanullah has received also from the Government a tea service in gold."

The ulema of Persia had sent Amanullah a letter asking that in Persia he veil his wife's face. He had ignored that, and continued to ignore it in Meshed, where Souraya and the other women of her family went without veils to prayers at the great mosque with a huge dome of pure gold, where no unbeliever was ever permitted to walk in the neighboring streets; where a distinguished scholar who entered it many years later, with official permission, was mobbed because he was not a Moslem; and where the Shah's wife, nine years later, would be refused admittance because she came unveiled.

Souraya was not refused admittance, but her unveiled presence was considered sacrilege. The Mosque of Meshed was a mosque of the Shiah branch of Islam, while Amanullah and most of Afghanistan belonged to the Sunni branch; this increased the insult to Meshed.

"It is difficult to believe that the King is actuated by a deliberate and well-thought-out policy in this behavior," wrote the British of the Meshed visit. "It certainly does not pave the way for a welcome from all sections of his countrymen which should be the crowning feature of his remarkable tour . . . Anything may be expected of Amanullah after his return, from the disestablishment of the Sunni faith to the declaration of his title to the Caliphate . . . and the repercussions of any ill-considered step he takes will inevitably be felt not only on the frontier but throughout the Moslem community in India, judging from the amount of interest which the Indian press appears to take in Souraya's departure from the traditional costume and etiquette of a Moslem lady."

On June 20 Amanullah drove his own car across the frontier and six months and ten days after he had left Afghanistan, was once more home.

CHAPTER 22

June 20, 1928, to August 1, 1928

Amanullah said in his first speech in Kandahar:

"I visited Europe not for pleasure, recreation or the purpose of machinery, but in order that I might explore the real road to progress . . . Even at feasts and garden parties given in my honor I devoted myself to discussing means of progress with the great statesmen of the West.

"Whatever I learned will shortly be laid before the nation. It will then rest with the nation to judge which was my object—the betterment of my country and nation or the personal interests of Amanullah and Queen Souraya. If my objects are selfish, the nation is at liberty to reject my suggestions, but if such is not the case, I hope that Kandahar will be the first to carry them out. Kandahar is dearest to me of all places in my kingdom. A father loves best the son who obeys the most."

Amanullah then accused the officials of slackness. He said, "There is no satisfactory arrangement for posts and telegraphs nor is any trouble taken to improve the roads. Is it not shameful that the posts of Afghanistan are still carried on men's backs?" He told of meeting a man riding a donkey, and learning that this was a postal carrier who had not had a donkey to carry his heavy bag of mail, had acquired the donkey only for the return trip.

"Now take the telegraph. The line to Farah has been left incomplete and the work postponed. Why? Because it is too hot and the men cannot work! It is a pity that the King of Afghanistan should sit in Kandahar and be ignorant of what is happening in Herat. Why? Simply because of the slackness on the part of the officials.

"Compare this state of affairs with other parts of the world. Take

London. There every morning and every evening you obtain news of
what is happening all over the surface of the earth.

"Now take the state of the roads of the country. How bad they are!
Why? Because the people are very delicate! They cannot bear the heat
and cold! They leave the most urgent works simply because 'it is too
hot,' 'it is too cold,' 'it is raining' and for such other excuses!

"Are you more delicate than the women of Europe, who boldly work
in front of furnaces in workshops and factories never complaining of
excessive heat or cold or hard labor? Is it not shameful that the women
of Europe are more laborious and more active than the men of Afghanistan? I have personally witnessed in Europe that the women there work
on equal terms with men and take an active part in every branch of life
and in all matters, whether political, social, commercial, or any other,
you will find there women in offices, women in workshops and factories
operating the machines and working in front of fires, women in political circles, and in short women everywhere you go. On the other hand
the women of Afghanistan only know how to sit idly in the houses, and
they do nothing more. Why should not then such a country be backward, while countries where women share equally with men are prosperous?

"Afghanistan is situated between two very strong powers, England
and Russia, neither of which wishes to see her prosper. And this is only
natural; for you too would not like to help a neighboring country and
to see it grow stronger than your own. Why then should England or
Russia help you and why should you expect help of them? You may say
that you have no money. But neither England nor Russia is going to
supply you with it.

"What then can you do? Try hard to earn money yourselves. You
possess in this country mines of every kind. Work them and make use
of them. Form companies and start factories and workshops. Expend
a little labor and courage. You will then find money in plenty. Unless
you help yourselves, it is absolutely impossible for you to move with the
world and to safeguard your interests. Therefore be active and bold.

"You cannot reach your goal merely by sitting idle. Amanullah cannot do everything for you. He advises you, implores you and presses
you, but beyond that he can do nothing. You may rest assured that
Amanullah will carry with him to the grave all his ambitions of seeing
Afghanistan advanced and prosperous, unless you rouse yourselves from
your deep sleep."

Amanullah came home to Afghanistan in a bad humor. He remained indoors for his first two days in Herat. Then he met the principal Heratis at tea and made a speech in which the most memorable statements were that he was quite aware of what the officials had been doing in his absence, that some of the petitions of the people had reached him, that urgent work in Kabul made it impossible to stay but he would return later in the year to investigate the people's complaints and to scrutinize his officials' conduct.

In the next city, Farah, he spoke to the Governor only twice, once concerning the climate of Farah and once to say, "Thanks," when wished a pleasant journey.

It was nothing new for Amanullah to be critical of his officials but now he was suffering from what a later generation would term "culture shock." He looked upon his people with eyes that had seen London and Paris.

The decorations, archways and lights which his subjects had erected for him could not compensate for the burden of administration that settled upon him the instant he crossed the frontier. He spoke of corruption and of official misbehavior, two worries of which he had been free in the past six months. In his absence a Kabul newspaper had run a contest offering a prize for the outstanding account of official corruption. No one would have dared such a thing under his father or grandfather, but no such quantity of examples flourished then. A combination of new things and new people produced an excess of corruption under Amanullah, who was so lacking in greed personally that he did not even draw his own salary every year; the new things gave opportunity for bribery and deceit, the men newly come to influence were not inhibited by social custom from making the most of it. A classic story arose concerning a man who could not get a document signed because the official kept telling him there was no ink in his inkwell; the man finally understood and, taking the inkwell to fill it, brought it back stuffed with money.

By the time Amanullah reached Kandahar, at the wheel of the car with Souraya and Nur-us-Seraj as passengers, he was not quite so cross. Kandahar was the home of his mother's family, and he had a special affection for it. Yet after an effusive speech of welcome his reply was the discourse in which he told the Kandaharis, not how glad he was to see them again, but what was wrong with them.

When a newly married couple returns from the honeymoon to life among old acquaintances, the complaint often is heard that everyone encountering them looks first at the bride's stomach to see if she is pregnant. Likewise, when Amanullah and Souraya came home from Europe, glances usually went first of all to Souraya's face, to see if it were covered or not. When she entered Kandahar, her hat had a heavy veil which satisfied everyone. But later in her visit she wore a veil so thin that members of the British Legation, who were playing the game as earnestly as anyone, reported to London, awaiting the news, that her features were easily discernible.

"The King is a kaffir and will make us all kaffirs," said some of the mullahs who had been conversing pleasantly with Amanullah before they saw his wife.

The royal party camped in the Wardak Valley southwest of Kabul on the night of June 30 so that Amanullah might make a triumphal entry on the morning of July 1. While planes circled above dropping flowers, the crowds in the streets and roads almost pushed each other down in the struggle for a glimpse.

What they glimpsed was, in addition to their King riding in an open Rolls-Royce, the Queen of Afghanistan wearing a type of veil that had seldom been seen there. It was fastened around her head at the bridge of her nose, just below her eyes, and covered only the lower part of her face.

Women in Syria and some other Middle East countries wore such veils, and so did actresses in Western musical comedies dealing with the Mysterious East. One evening in London, while Amanullah was attending a type of social function that fulfills Moslem male supremacy but is an English convention, a stag dinner, Queen Mary had taken Souraya to the theater. The attraction was the operetta *The Desert Song.* This delighted the same people who had rejoiced that in London Amanullah and Souraya would be living as in their own palace, not considering the illogic of traveling halfway around the world in order to be as at home. So Souraya had been treated to an unrealistic, romanticized view of a culture supposed to bear some resemblance to her own, which she was qualified to judge.

The actresses in *The Desert Song* had been veiled in a fashion that concealed as little as possible the expensive faces for which they had been hired. They wore veils below the eyes, so gossamer sheer that a true realist would have wondered why the hero gasped when the heroine removed hers.

Souraya and her ladies wore such veils, not so sheer as in an operetta, but the first such veils seen on Kabul streets since Ali Ahmed's wife, Amanullah's sister Seraj-ul-Banat, had worn one in the victory parade after the Khost Rebellion.

The King and Queen went to Dilkusha Palace, where both shook hands with all members of the diplomatic corps (Souraya now found it natural to shake hands with a foreign man) and withdrew. Later Amanullah came and finally expressed delight at meeting again his dear people.

"I do not believe that there are in the world any enemies of Afghanistan. Nonetheless, I thank God that during my absence my brave and devoted nation has done nothing to provoke any kind of complications."

And saying that he and his companions had been true to Islam, as they had promised, he embraced, as he had done on parting, a soldier, an official, a countryman, and a student.

A three-day holiday celebrated his return. Each shopkeeper had been ordered to illuminate with no fewer than a dozen electric light bulbs, and to paint his shop green. The bazaars were so full of people that walking was difficult and driving homicidal. Lights shown on the palaces and legations, a fair was held in Abdur Rahman's old palace of Bagh-i-Bala, and there were dinners and garden parties. Souraya twice entertained, but only for ladies; she had regressed to her old social life.

Just before Amanullah's return the rumors began again to rustle along the northwest frontier of India.

These new rumors said that Afghanistan was preparing for war against India.

"This excitement may be nothing but 'midsummer madness,'" reported in secret from Parachinar the Political Agent of Kurram, "but the conviction that something sensational will happen very shortly in Afghanistan is remarkably widespread and firmly held here."

The Political Agent heard on June 9 from a Mangal tribesman who had just spent a week in Afghanistan: "Whenever I stayed in Afghan Territory I heard the news that the Afghan Government was going to start 'badi' with the British Government. Moreover small numbers of soldiers were constantly coming to Gardez from Kabul and they were said to be Turks, Arabs and Bolsheviks.

"I did not see any Afghan official as I have enmity there. There is a charge against me in connection with certain Afghan rifles there."

Another man said, "A declaration has come from the Amir Sahib that he is highly pleased with every nation except one, of which the name is not mentioned."

This latter information came from an informer who lived at Kharlachi on the border adjoining the area of Afghanistan known as Hariob, just north of Khost. The following day, June 11, another man of Kharlachi told the Political Agent, "A proclamation affixed on the gate of the office of the Governor of the Southern Province runs: 'I am pleased with all the nations but against one only have I grievances.'"

The British did not doubt that they were the nation referred to. They wondered if Amanullah had really said this. Their agents talked with tribesmen who had gone to Kabul for Amanullah's return; no one from Waziristan, Khyber or Tirah reported any such statement from Amanullah; the rumors all were heard in one section of Kurram and farther north in Bajaur. Someone was deliberately spreading that report, the British concluded. They were correct; Amanullah was speaking instead of his friendship with them so ardently that his Persian secretary remarked it was nothing short of hypnotism that had changed the entire outlook of the King and his ministers in one month in England, from deep-founded suspicion of British policy to their present friendly and trusting attitude.

The British therefore were puzzled by the rumors they kept hearing from some areas and not from others, and generally not from Afghanistan itself.

"Pir Mohammed Qasim of Makhezai, who is, according to my information an Afghan intelligence agent and generally has a pretty good knowledge of what is going on across the border," the Political Agent of Kurram reported on June 12, "also called on me today and said that one of his informants who had just returned from Khost reported all quiet there, and that he himself could not account for the general belief along the Kurram border that the Afghan Government were preparing for war.

"The statements are poor stuff and do not reproduce the emphasis with which the authors declared to me their conviction that trouble was brewing."

Searching for an explanation of these wild rumors, the Political Agent suggested:

"The King's tour in Europe and especially the abandonment of purdah by the Queen have given rise to comment that the King has been corrupted by the British and is now subservient to them. To counteract the effect of such talk the Afghan Government are putting out anti-British propaganda to show the King's independence and orthodoxy.

"It has also been hinted to me that it is a precaution taken by conspirators against the King to ensure a refuge in case of failure."

By August the rumors had almost died down. The Political Agent decided that perhaps the Russians had started them "with object of disturbing present peaceful conditions and counteracting effect of London visit and closer relations they think may follow between us and Afghanistan."

Souraya wrote an article on Moslem women which was published in *Aman-i-Afghan* on July 25, in which she said that before the coming of Islam, women were subject to their husbands, parents and sons, but that Islam had given them equal status with men.

About purdah Souraya said, "It is generally seen that common customs and practices have in course of time become one of the religious obligations, or regarded as a principle of faith. This is to be found among all nations and religions. The same case happened with the purdah system. It was simply a national practice first, but has gradually developed into a strict regulation of our religion, according to the belief of the common folk. The reference which is made in our Holy Koran, in this connection, is only on the basis of civilization and morals. It is never a command which could be followed by punishment if disobeyed.

"What is really ordained in the Koran with regard to purdah is equally for the males and females both. The females, according to religious regulations, are required to conceal from human eyes their whole body except their face, their palms and their feet, which concealment and exposure are necessary during daily prayers and pilgrimages to the Holy Ka'aba—and so also there are regulations for the male sex in Islam. This sort of purdah is not an invention by Islam; rather, it has also been referred to in all the other holy scriptures of the universal religions . . .

"If the prevailing views regarding purdah remain unchanged, then there is no possibility of any progress in the life of the Eastern people, particularly among Moslems. For as a matter of fact, the women have proved themselves a great factor in the civilization of mankind, and I daresay that unless and until the woman-population of the East get proper training, in accordance with the modern methods, it is impossible for them to become useful.

"And they who, on account of their narrow-mindedness, say that the woman could get proper education even inside purdah, have really misunderstood the meaning of education. It does not mean simply reading or writing. It has got quite a wider sense; education means the training of man through some practical course, lesson, experience and experiment, which a university alone, or any common center of education provides, and which apparently seems impossible inside purdah. However, for the benefit of my Eastern people, I advise them to reject the common belief regarding purdah and adopt what Islam actually prescribes for women, regulating thereby their own special costume. Otherwise the practice of copying Western fashion, which prevails so widely in the East, is sure to snare the people sooner or later, and to the utter dismay of those who favor strict purdah, purdah will be effaced altogether and will never remain even to the extent that religion has laid down."

Even before the publication of her views, Souraya had been talking to women. First she addressed the girls' school at Kabul, saying that it was out-of-date to wear veils and urging them to work for the abolition of the purdah system, which would have to be without compulsion. No one took this very seriously.

Then she called a group of women to a meeting in Dilkusha Palace and told them they must take an equal part with the men in the general work of the country, which of course was impossible while they remained like prisoners in their homes. The human being is the highest form of creation, Souraya said, and beauty a thing of joy which should not be hidden.

"The women of Europe are predominant in industry but the women of Afghanistan, who are physically stronger, do not take any part in the progress of the country," said she. "This is solely due to the universally condemned practice of purdah."

Then she called another meeting and organized the women; Kabul was divided into districts and a representative chosen to be responsible for the education of girls and for the welfare of women generally in each district.

Kabul began to take the prospect of unveiling more seriously.

Amanullah himself called the women of Kabul to Dilkusha Palace; only a few came, and those were veiled because the King was no close relation of theirs. They heard that they had lived a life of subjection to the unnecessary tyranny of their husbands and were virtually prisoners in their own homes. He told them that he had proof that many women, simply because the veil cut them off from air, were dying of tuberculosis.

"I have had the advantage of having traveled and have come to the conclusion that in no Moslem country other than Afghanistan, not even Turkey or Persia, are women 'buried alive.' Veiling has retarded your progress in education and has deprived you of the opportunity to take up professions, in contrast to your Western sisters. In fact, it forces you to be completely dependent on your husbands. I wish to see you disregard the wishes of your husbands in regard to veiling and attending places of amusement."

Amanullah went on to advocate the shooting of interfering husbands and said that he would himself supply the weapons and that no inquiries would be instituted against the women. Irony is dangerous unless it has a sophisticated recipient able to recognize what it is; these women, whose extremely sheltered lives were the cause of Amanullah's complaints, took him seriously. So did their husbands when they heard about it.

Amanullah delighted in giving the people of Afghanistan beautiful surroundings. Their own setting of mountains and sky was beautiful, but closer, in their lives and homes, the poor people had little to look upon except walls made of mud. A few years earlier he had given them beauty at the expense of his own family and friends, for he had ordered the reduction to eye level of the garden walls surrounding the homes of the nobility, including that of his mother, and now the poor people, to whom an aristocratic residence had been nothing but another expanse of mud wall, saw trees and paths and flowers. This made a walk through Kabul a stroll through a gorgeous private estate.

In Paghman, the resort sixteen miles north, Amanullah already had made a park of paths and statues and flower beds, with iron benches and a bandstand. Now he had parks built at his new city of Dar-ul-Aman, encircling like a giant wheel of flower beds the Parliament building that was standing, mammoth and rather Germanic-looking, at the end of a long boulevard. This building and the more remote, delicate palace were still not completed, but work had been resumed.

And in these gardens Amanullah ordered that no woman should walk wearing the old-fashioned head-to-foot veil, the burkah. He had expressed himself as favoring, if one had to veil at all, the Syrian veil which covered only the lower part of the face. This, too, seemed a nuisance to him, but less ridiculous than covering oneself completely.

Once Amanullah himself, in the garden, saw a woman wearing a burkah. "What are you doing with that piece of cloth?" He reached out and uncovered the lady, who stood terrified and humiliated in what, to her, was nakedness. Amanullah struck a match and burned the offending burkah there in the path. The lady had to go home in her shame.

Amanullah saw a man wearing his hair long at the sides. Beneath a turban it did not matter what a man's hair was like, or if he had any. The Sikhs from India never in a lifetime cut their hair but wound it around their heads. But Amanullah intended to abolish the turban, and he had ordered that no man's hair should be long at the sides. He had this offender arrested. As the man was being led to jail, he passed a hairdresser's shop; Amanullah let him stop and go inside to have his sideburns sheared. Then he was pardoned.

No one was allowed to wear in Paghman or in the public gardens at Dar-ul-Aman either a turban or the classic peaked hat of karakul lamb, only Western hats with brims. Even the drivers of motor lorries delivering goods had to remove their headgear before entering the forbidden precincts. The loose, full pantaloons that Afghans had been wearing for years also were forbidden; Amir Abdur Rahman had enforced a reduction of the yardage of cloth used in these, but they were still baggy. Their advantage was that the men already had them. Amanullah ordered the wearing of Western jackets and trousers. Most men already had a jacket of some sort, no matter how old-fashioned or tattered by Western standards, and Amanullah could not regulate the degree of excellence. But Western trousers they did not own, nor the shoes, socks, tie and other appurtenances that went with a complete outfit. The outlay for a required wardrobe came to about one hundred Afghanis, or fifty India rupees, a major expenditure which some men could not manage.

At first the requirement was only for Paghman and Dar-ul-Aman, where most people had the privilege of staying away. Then it was extended to all of Kabul, and a fine of two puls, or one fiftieth of an Afghani, was imposed on those who violated it, but the ominous news was that on the next New Year's Day, March 21, 1929, no form of dress but the Western style would be legal.

Aman-i-Afghan explained that people who dressed in this manner "feel a sort of revolution and modernization in them." It pointed out that, while some think the shape of the hat is bad, they should realize after consideration that hats are more useful than round-winding turbans.

This was not merely whimsy on Amanullah's part. He had been to Turkey, where one reason for his warm welcome had been his understanding of the problems of Mustapha Kemal. Early in Kemal's career as a young army officer he had been sent on a mission to France, and after contributing some very intelligent advice, he had been told that no one would take him seriously, "As long as you wear that thing on your head." From that moment Kemal had hated the traditional Turkish headgear, the red fez with the tassel atop.[1]

To the European and American reading about Mustapha Kemal's throwing fezes into the Bosporus, the situation was funny. There was something comical about people making such a fuss over any kind of hat.

Amanullah went to Turkey and he did not think any of this was funny. He understood the implications. Kemal had reasoned that people became what they looked like, and while he could not alter immediately their pattern of thought, it was comparatively easy to alter the outward appearance. Amanullah did not see why the same methods would not work in Afghanistan.

As in Turkey, there were things that were comical to the European Legations looking on. An Afghan man got hold of a woman's straw hat and put it on; the policeman who was ordered to arrest people for violations was nonplused. This was not a turban; it was a Western hat, perhaps, but something about it was odd. Some clever Afghans cut melons in two, ate the meat, then inverted the melon shells on their heads and went to Amanullah sighing that this was all the hat they could wear, having no money to buy anything else. Amanullah, tender-hearted, gave them money.

"From the aesthetic point of view," the Kabul military attaché wrote in his diary, "the streets of Kabul are losing much of their former picturesqueness." That was a viewpoint which, forty years later, Westerners would still be expressing and the Kabul newspaper would ask why Westerners did not continue to wear the costume of a previous century.

The homecoming gifts that Amanullah brought to his young half sisters were radios. In his absence, more progress had come to Afghanistan. A broadcasting station had been opened in June in the house that Nasrullah had built after a London model. Every evening from seven-thirty to nine-thirty a program was sent out, chiefly music. Only Amanullah and a few of his relatives had sets to receive this program, but there was erected close to the royal workshop, not so very far from the broadcasting station, a large receiving set to which the public might come to hear the programs. By the time Amanullah returned home, a man had already left for Kandahar to supervise a similar broadcasting station there and to install a few sets.

New schools had opened, including a reformatory for boys who continually stayed away from the other schools. Evening classes in foreign languages had been started and the enrollment reflected the international interest in Kabul. There were eighty students for English, twenty for Russian, thirty for French and ten for German. Some boys from the Mohmand subtribe of Usman Khel, who had come to Kabul for school rather reluctantly, went back to their homes. Amanullah's sister Banat gave each of them some money and a gold bracelet, telling them to spend the money on a holiday and to give the bracelets to their mothers; as a result Kabul heard that many more Usman Khel Mohmands would be coming to school. Even some of the Ghilzais had accepted teachers to accompany them in their wanderings.

A new hotel opened in Kabul across the street from the cinema, with sixteen rooms, electric lights, bells and, as a special mark of progress, flush toilets. The British praised this hotel greatly until the toilets ceased to flush.

A French firm was making a survey for a railroad, and a German company was doing the same. The British kept a close watch on the activities of the French team, which was headed by a young man in his twenties named Michel Clemenceau, grandson of a former Premier of France. Young Clemenceau described his experiences in Afghanistan in letters to his father beginning "Cher Papa." His father sent his letters to Sir Basil Zaharoff, the munitions magnate, who had an interest in the matter, and Sir Basil sent them to the British Foreign Office, which had thereby an inner knowledge of the project even beyond what Clemenceau was giving them himself. The British lent him a map of Afghanistan, then thought better of the action and asked for it back.

At the time of Amanullah's departure for Europe, when European and American newspapers were speculating on effects of his trip, there had been visions of the possibility for a man, sometime in the future, to board a train in Paris and travel straight through to Shanghai. Any such route would have to pass through Afghanistan. The British would have liked a railroad on their own terms, and kept close watch on all developments so as to see that they did not veer toward Russia; already at Chaman in a warehouse were stored the materials for extending into Afghanistan the railway that stopped in the Khyber Pass; this was a war emergency supply, for the British had figured that they could build the railroad faster from their end than the Russians could from theirs, and thereby gain a priceless commodity of wartime, a few weeks.

The prospect of being a link of commercial air service was also part of Amanullah's plan. He had discussed it in Germany, thinking to link with Tehran through Junkers Aircraft, which had already flown to Kabul the planes he had purchased and been given. Fearful of a German monopoly, the British were contemplating air services of their own between Kabul and Rawalpindi, but there they faced another fear stronger than fear of Germans. The question was whether establishment of air service over the frontier "would not entail opening of that portion to private aircraft of all states who are contracting parties to the convention relating to Regulation of Aerial Navigation? Answer is obviously one of great moment, seeing that Russia (to take the extreme example) would apparently have little difficulty in becoming a contracting party to the convention, and would certainly have no scruple in subsidizing her nationals to fly in 'private aircraft' over this critical portion of India's frontiers, if she were given opportunity. Of such moment, indeed, is it, that if no satisfactory solution can be found, it will be necessary to examine possibility of India's withdrawing from convention."

The secrets of the frontier were already revealed, the British Legation in Kabul had discovered, in some photographs available in a Kabul shop, which showed all the fortifications in the Khyber Pass in detail that would be extremely useful for aerial bombing. The Legation sent a man around to buy the pictures; the shopkeeper happily told him that the Russian Legation had them now, but as soon as they were returned, he could order all he wished.

Amanullah was suffering from that restlessness which increases when the fulfillment of a long-sought goal finally comes within sight. He was still annoyed with his officials, saying they had not only taken bribes in his absence but had been drinking alcohol. He threatened to order doctors to rip open their stomachs and examine their livers to see if they had been drinking or not. To find out about their bribes, he would have an expert examine their expenses and compare these with their incomes and private means.

There was so much to hope for that the troubles seemed easily overcome. But there was one worrisome matter: crime. Shortly after his return a convoy from the north bringing money to Kabul had been attacked near dawn at Charikar and about sixty thousand Afghani rupees had been stolen. Charikar was in the section north of Kabul called Kohistan or Koh-i-Daman, meaning Land of Hills or Foot of the Hill. The men there, while not having the wild reputation of the Pathans in the east, were wild enough to cause trouble and in 1926 Amanullah had sent Ali Ahmed there to put down an uprising, which he had done so effectively as to inaugurate a brief reign of terror. This was the home land of the bad characters who had escaped to India the previous year, including the notorious Bacha Sacao, who, in all opinions, probably had stolen the rupees.

The movement of money was important because there were no banks in Afghanistan. "One serious cause of anxiety at present," the British Military Attaché had written in June, "is that the local treasury in Kabul is quite empty and has exhausted its resources. There are no banking facilities, so the Treasury is freely used by local merchants and officials as the only place of security in Kabul. Amounts of deposit to an account in the treasury can be remitted to any of the provincial headquarters by a paper transaction at a charge of 1%. On account of the insecurity of the roads, this means of transfer of money is freely used. Now trade is almost at a standstill, and there is some discontent in the local bazaars. This situation has never before occurred in Afghanistan." In July, after Amanullah's return, he was writing, "From ordinary people, it is said, 10% is deducted on all checks presented and for the most influential checks are paid only in installments on excuse of lack of cash available. Treasury officials give out that there is a large reserve sum belonging to the King, who does not want it expended. This story is thought propaganda to give sense of safety to depositors."

The story of the large sum in Amanullah's private treasury was not propaganda; it was there, and Amanullah intended to print paper currency, a new thing in Afghanistan, which would be secured by his own treasury. The problem was one of moving money back and forth, so when Bacha Sacao robbed the convoy, he upset the balance.

Every year since 1919 Afghanistan had celebrated the anniversary of its independence with a Jeshyn in August. This year was the Tenth Anniversary; it was the year of Amanullah's greatest effort, for he had proved himself in the world to which independence had taken him.

He sent out a proclamation of a greater Jeshyn than usual, to be followed by a Loe Jirga, or Great Assembly, to which the people throughout the nation would be asked to send delegates to discuss the issues of the day. The British Legation was warned to expect no Afghan officials at any social functions, for they would all be busy making plans for Jeshyn.

Women were to be represented at the Loe Jirga, and Amanullah's sister Kubra Jan would address them on behalf of the women of the country. Souraya expected to entertain several of the "older and more intelligent women of Kandahar" who would go back to disseminate information about the new life in store for Afghan women. This was not the first women's conference ever proposed to Kandahar. During the reign of Amanullah's father the suggestion had caused an eruption of protest against the Governor, who was then Mohammed Osman, the man who, having lost his position over other protest connected with liberality of outlook, was now the extremely orthodox head of the theological seminary. Some Kandaharis made threats against the delegates whom they were sending to the Loe Jirga, saying that if they returned after agreeing to the unveiling of women and female education, they would be killed.

Afghanistan approached this Loe Jirga with apprehension. One subject for discussion was already announced: Amanullah had ordered his officials to have only one wife; for those who already had more, this posed a problem which the Loe Jirga would be asked to settle. Amanullah had announced also that only 29½ Kabuli rupees might be taken for a woman to be given in marriage and that anyone who disobeyed these orders would be severely punished. There would be proposals for more such alterations in a man's normal way of life. Whoever went as a delegate would be going to a revolution.

According to an intelligence report, one woman in Kabul talked a great deal in favor of the proposal to unveil women. Her husband killed her and cut up her body.

CHAPTER 23

August 1928

The Jeshyn of August 1928 would be remembered for many things. One of these was the introduction of a new business in Kabul, the renting of Western clothes. No one was permitted within the Jeshyn grounds at Paghman, not even a coolie delivering a burden, in any other costume.

The delegates who came for Jeshyn and the Loe Jirga that would follow did not have the expense of renting, for Amanullah gave each one black trousers, rather long black coats, and black hats which had been made in advance. If any delegate was willing to add a clean-shaven face to the picture he presented, the barber was waiting.

As they feared, Amanullah in his opening speech brought up the subject of women. He had added a new astonishment: he said that he would send a party of Afghan girls out of their country, to Turkey, to study midwifery.

Up to now, said Amanullah, the government had been content to establish peace, and friendly relations with foreign powers, but all the time he had been studying what would best serve Afghanistan's future. Now he was ready to implement his ideas.

He continued to talk about women. He quoted from the Koran to the effect that polygamy is permissible only when wives are treated with absolute equality; this is almost an impossible ideal and therefore, he said, no man should marry more than one wife. The future prosperity of the country, said Amanullah, depended on the mothers and the fostering of the new generation.

The delegates, listening to their King, were seated in an open amphitheater. The backdrop of mountains close at hand was beautiful.

To one side, in a special enclosure as usual, sat the women, most of whom were wearing half veils. Amanullah admonished them to be pure and chaste, but to be free and not in bondage to their husbands.

Later Amanullah visited among the delegates in their seats, and with him came Souraya and Nur-us-Seraj. They wore no veils, but the fashionable cloche hats. They chatted with such delegates as were not too embarrassed to talk with an unveiled woman.

Every evening a full band played in the public gardens of Paghman, while men formed a circle and danced the attan. The first ball in Afghanistan was given, a fancy-dress affair where Afghans dressed as courtiers of Louis XVI and other personages who seemed as exotic to them as the average Afghan would have seemed to a courtier of Louis XVI. Most of the ladies who attended were wives of foreign diplomats, but many Afghans said, after the ball was over, that next time they would bring their wives.

In the seven-hundred-seat theater Amanullah had built at Paghman, every evening a variety show was staged by a troupe recruited from India. The artists came from a variety of nations and showed varying talents. A lady contortionist twisted; a dancer from India named Idan Bai undulated. Humphrys was shocked, not at the sight but because the program was conducted in English, and he feared the shocked orthodox might blame his country.

By the time Jeshyn was over, the Afghan officer who had threatened to start a fistfight, if necessary, to keep an Afghan woman from talking to a European, would have found his ideas of etiquette quite changed if he had not been in jail.

The party that was Jeshyn ended, and the Loe Jirga settled to work.

More than a thousand delegates were on hand. Amanullah, wanting to sound out the general sentiment, had a private meeting with a few specially selected delegates. He suggested some of the reforms he had in mind:

The abolition of purdah and emancipation of women generally, the outlawing of polygamy, compulsory education of both sexes, divorce of church from state by introduction of civil laws not necessarily founded on Islamic code, licensing of all firearms in Afghanistan, increase of taxation on landed property, the introduction of a national bank and the issue of currency notes.

No one approved of any of it. The reaction was utter horror, especially among the delegates from Khost and other frontier areas. The good will generated by the lavish entertainment all at once vanished into rancor. Amanullah was angry; he would have persevered but Wali and Ghulam Siddiq and some others begged him to modify the proposals. He agreed on the excuse that the Loe Jirga consisted of uneducated and uncivilized persons who were unable to give a sound opinion on matters requiring special knowledge.

Amanullah rose before black-coated delegates in the theater at Paghman on August 28. The female delegates were seated in the gallery along with some other ladies, opposite members of the diplomatic corps.

No proposals would come before the Loe Jirga which would violate in any way the principles of Islam, Amanullah assured his audience, and he talked about those principles. In doing so he described the Koran as an instructional and historic book and the Prophet Mohammed as a servant of the community and a soldier. The men sat and looked at him without expression, but their emotions were as black as their clothes. Amanullah had made an error that had already caused much trouble in many other religions, in many other countries. He had discussed in a cerebral and intellectual context a subject which, for his listeners, shimmered with the untouchable halo of emotion. He was making the Prophet sound like a public official and the Koran like a textbook one might find anywhere, instead of being the supernatural emanations of Allah that every delegate knew them for.

Then he outlined a proposal for a constitution similar to that of Turkey, under which the present Council of State, consisting of about fifty members appointed by the Government, would be replaced with a National Assembly of 150 representatives, who would be elected (in theory) by the people for a term of three years. These should be between twenty-five and seventy years of age and literate, but in the less civilized areas there would be a grace period of six years during which literacy would not be required. These representatives would live at Kabul but be allowed to return home for four months each year at harvest time. This Assembly would not replace the Loe Jirga, which would meet every five years.

In five sessions the Assembly agreed with most of the things that Amanullah asked of them. They rejected only one proposal, which had to do with the topic on which he had expected to demand most and then reconsidered: women.

Amanullah would have made it unlawful for women to marry before the age of eighteen and men before the age of twenty-two. Passions were stirred and the men shouted with indignation when this was proposed. They said no. But they confirmed his pronouncement that no official should have more than one wife. By definition, the Loe Jirga contained no public official.

The second most heated discussion was provoked by bribery and corruption of officials. Amanullah said this practice was leading the country to destruction, that the people were to blame as much as the officials since it was as harmful to give as to receive. For once the delegates really agreed with him. One of them arose and told of an official whose servant was living on a scale that was ten times the salary of his employer. Many said that some posts carried such small salaries that the incumbents could not live without illegitimate additions to their pay. A committee was appointed to inquire into the living standards of officials, and it was decided that a service book should be kept for each one, in which would be shown his pay, his monthly expenditure, the number of servants he kept, and so forth. In the past it had not been permitted to inquire into a complaint of official bribery after the passage of a week; the Assembly extended that period to two months.

A new national flag was suggested to replace the old one which Amanullah described as looking like the flag of a ship. Its colors were: black, signifying the blot on the country before it gained independence; red, denoting the sacrifices made in gaining independence; and green, showing the progress made since becoming independent. The words "Allah" and "Mohammed" were inscribed above a sun rising over hills covered with growing corn to signify the rising sun of a hilly but agricultural and prosperous country. Except for the two words this did not contain any religious symbol, as the old flag had, but the delegates sullenly approved.

They agreed at his request that mullahs who acted as teachers or preachers would have to present themselves for examination and obtain a certificate attesting sufficient knowledge for these duties. Amanullah said that he would expel from the country all Indians and other foreigners who had been taught at Deoband Theological Center in India, calling them "mischievous, traitor and foreign propagandists." Deoband was a center of Congress Party activity aimed toward Indian freedom, and its mullahs were also fanatic against Amanullah.

Amanullah announced that he now had eight times as many modern rifles and sixteen times as many modern guns as he had last year; there had been no elephant races at Jeshyn because the elephants had gone to Russia to bring back the munitions given there. This was a result of purchases for which he was levying five rupees on each man and asking each Government servant to give a month's pay. No one objected. Whatever the pretense of consultation, Amanullah was really an absolute monarch, and they knew it.

Then came an announcement of which the Loe Jirga approved with every indication of sincerity. Souraya, veiled, led out eight-year-old Prince Rahmatullah wearing a military uniform and knee-high boots. Amanullah told the delegates that since his elder son, Hidayatullah, was born before he ascended the throne, he was considered an unofficial son. This was in keeping with Persian tradition, which had it that the only sons who might inherit were those "born to the purple." Rahmatullah, eldest son of the Queen, he proclaimed the true Crown Prince. The men cheered. In honor of this proclamation seventy male and four female prisoners were released from jail.

When Amanullah bade the delegates farewell, he said, "I leave the question of purdah; that is to say, if any person sees any advantage in being unveiled, she may remove her veil; if anyone is in favor of being veiled, she may remain veiled. Should I order all females to be veiled, a large number of my subjects, nomads and villagers, will find it very difficult to observe the order. Should I, on the other hand, order purdah to be abolished, I will have to face a great opposition against an ancient custom in the cities like Kabul and Kandahar. I will therefore follow the injunctions of the Islamic code and will punish those who expose the parts of the body which it is ordained therein should be kept covered."

Thereby he sounded like a severe Puritan while remaining as liberal as he ever was.

A traveler from Badakhshan in northeast Afghanistan met the delegates returning from the Loe Jirga. They told him that the King had abandoned his religion and that Afghanistan was no longer a fit place for a Moslem to live in. Some Badakhshan people were threatening to move to Russia, where they would be let alone.

The conspiracy against Amanullah began to move.
Sher Agha's men in Kabul, his brother Gul Agha and his nephew

Masum, set out upon the first step of the plan that Sher Agha had organized in January at his meeting of mullahs in Paniala, India.

On September 5 the sessions of the Loe Jirga ended and the delegates began to return by various ways to the mountains and valleys which they had left to confer with the government of Afghanistan. But Gul Agha did not wait for the final outcome of these meetings. He could prophesy that when the delegates began to report to their neighbors on the events in Kabul, they would speak with a disapproval that might be aroused to anger and action, and it was part of the grand plan to be ready to turn the sparks of discontent into flame.

Gul Agha and Masum left on horseback on the last day of August, accompanied by other mullahs, an important Kabul judge, and a servant, nine mounted men, all bearded like the Prophet, all wearing the turbans that no king on earth could make them relinquish.

Their destination was Khost, the area southeast of Kabul that four years earlier had almost destroyed Amanullah, and still felt bitterness about its punishment. It would be the easiest place in Afghanistan to stir to another rebellion.

Gul Agha was carrying a manifesto signed by four hundred mullahs proclaiming that the King was a kaffir who would turn Afghanistan away from the principles of Islam and the people should rise up against him.

Forty Mangal tribesmen had joined him by September 2 when he arrived at the home of a sympathetic Mangal in the small village of Sara Khel, having gathered his escort in another village called Machalghu. The presence of such distinguished men, on so mysterious an errand, in these obscure villages caused the local official to investigate. "You should inform me after ascertaining the actual nature of the matter," the hakim wrote to his assistant, "and having taken necessary steps for the arrest of those who appear to be open to suspicion, you should detain them."

When the official heard "the actual nature of the matter," he arrested Gul Agha's party in a raid in which one servant was killed. Gul Agha and Masum and their companions were taken in custody to Kabul.

They were still defiant when they reached the capital. They denied the attempt to overthrow Amanullah, but they maintained that they were headed toward India as an alternative to living in the wicked place that Amanullah would make of Afghanistan.

But the manifesto they were carrying told the story. In those four hundred signatures Amanullah saw how much they hated him and how far they were prepared to go. He saw also that his attempt to mollify the Loe Jirga by limiting his demands had done no good, that they had not waited for his compromise.

The Hazrats of Shor Bazaar were the most influential mullahs in Kabul, perhaps in Afghanistan. No hierarchy of clergy exists in Islam, only a loose brotherhood of men who take upon themselves to learn the Koran and teach it to others. No central control and no standards existed. When Amanullah had proposed that no mullah should appoint himself to teaching or preaching without some test to see if he were capable, he had struck at the livelihood of many men who were mullahs only because they said they were.

The Hazrats were not among these unlettered men who preached in mosques on holy days for whatever donation they could get. The Hazrats had all the Islamic learning that anyone could acquire. And if there had been among the Moslems of Kabul any position comparable to that of Archbishop of Canterbury, it would certainly have gone to one of the Hazrats of Shor Bazaar.

The aristocrats and well-to-do people of Kabul knew this, and wishing to give their children the best instruction and the most authoritative learning in religion, they sent them to the Hazrats of Shor Bazaar. The men who took their religion from Sher Agha or Gul Agha were known as their murids, or disciples. In Kabul therefore almost every man of any importance was a murid of the Hazrats.

And when their religious leader was brought into Kabul in the custody of soldiers, his hands bound, and put into prison, there was no other subject for Kabul to talk about.

Amanullah summoned his Council of State and all agreed that Gul Agha was a rebel who should be punished. There was one exception, the eminent Judge Abdur Rahman Begtuti, who had lost none of his prestige as a result of once being arrested on a charge of accepting bribes, and who had accompanied Gul Agha. Amanullah asked this judge to issue a fatwa, a religious proclamation, against Gul Agha. The judge refused. Faced with rebellion even in his own Council, Amanullah ordered the dissident arrested, and the furor grew.

The Kabul newspapers attempted to calm the uproar. The official paper *Aman-i-Afghan* wrote that the opposition of the Hazrats and the judge were directed against a decision taken by the Loe Jirga to fix penalties for certain crimes in advance before waiting for the crime to be committed.

This was commonplace in Western law, and the newspaper said there were precedents for it in ancient Islamic law. But in Afghanistan for centuries the judge had imposed whatever penalty pleased him upon the culprit standing before him, whatever the crime. The Nizamnamas of Amanullah contained a clause fixing penalties; the Great Assembly of 1924 abolished it, but now it was revived, and the judge whom Amanullah arrested would have lost thereby an enormous power, the power of life or death over a whole population.

In a plea for an educated, trained police force to replace the present short-term conscript force, the newspaper *Anis* cited an incident connected with the arrest of Gul Agha, the report that a policeman cursed himself at being obliged to carry out such a duty. Had this policeman been an educated man, said the newspaper which was unofficial but controlled, he would have known that Gul Agha was really an offender, that Gul Agha chose for his propaganda a part of the country where nearly all the inhabitants were uneducated, that if his cause had been just, he would have resorted to some enlightened and well-informed part of the country.

This article was intended to help Amanullah. What it did was to point out the opposition of the simple, humble people of Afghanistan, and if anyone in that troubled time had been calm enough to think through the significance of its comment, he would have opened a whole new set of moral dilemmas which would not confront the West for two more decades: the responsibility of an individual for the commands he obeyed, which would emerge to perplex the world at the Nuremberg Trials following the Second World War. In his home-coming address to the people of Kabul, Amanullah had told them to obey the laws, but only lawful laws. There was the dilemma already; the mullahs were disobeying the laws of the government, but in their own minds they were doing exactly as Amanullah had told them, choosing to obey a different set of laws.

A date was set almost at once, September 8, for the trial of Gul Agha and his companions for treason. But there were more to be arrested; the manifesto gave their names.

Soldiers went out arresting and bringing to the prison at Kabul more of the influential religious leaders. One was Mohammed Osman, seventy-one-year-old head of the theological school, and his son

Ghulam Farouq, who had just returned from India. Another was a mullah in Khost who had been sentenced to death after the rebellion there but pardoned by Amanullah. One was Mullah Dad Mohammed of Logar who had been carrying out propaganda in the suburbs of Kabul. About ten mullahs were arrested in Kabul, about ten in Khost and about fifteen in Kohistan.

"It is surprising," wrote the weekly *Sarhad*, a newspaper in Peshawar, where the news had reached, "that no one raised a finger against the arrest of such an influential man, who is a pir of the royal family. Through fear of the King no one dare speak. It is heard that many respectable people have been interned in Afghanistan. It is said that Mohammed Osman and [Judge] Abdur Rahman are arrested because during Jeshyn they endeavored to raise the Mangals against the Government."

The nomad Ghilzais, those who had passed with the seasons through the places where they were likely to talk with Sher Agha, were restless. The season had come around when they were about to seek warmer climates and better grazing lands.

"There is no truth whatever in the rumor that the Ghilzais have been ordered by the King not to undertake their annual migration to India this autumn," wrote Humphrys, "nor if such an order had actually been issued is there the remotest likelihood that it would be obeyed. Annual migration of Ghilzais, like annual migration of duck, is due to natural causes with which Kings are powerless to interfere."

The grazing had not been good in Afghanistan that summer, so there would be more nomads than usual crossing into India. Some of the tribes altered their accustomed route to pass west of the territory of their fellow Ghilzais of the Suleiman Khel. These had been robbing caravans with an energy exceeding even that of the unruly past which had made them notorious . . . They also had heard rumors about forcible removal of beards and other threats. One rumor said that Amanullah had bought in Germany a machine to burn corpses; this was a variant on the earlier rumor about the soap-making machine, but now were added the embellishments of a price list: thirty rupees to burn a rich man, the poor man to be burned free, and all mullahs burned to avoid spreading of disease.

The village of Machalghu, where Gul Agha had found help and shelter in Khost, was attacked by soldiers and many Ghilzais of the Ahmedzai subtribe were arrested. The border posts in Khost received orders that no Ahmedzai Ghilzais and especially the Bazu Khel sub-section, which had aided the mullahs, should be allowed to cross the border without examination to see if they were plotting treason, and that anyone aiding them should be punished. A census of certain groups of the Ahmedzai Ghilzais was commenced, to include lists of their herds and flocks.

In Kandahar soldiers, acting on telegraphed orders from Kabul, went on September 10 into the shop of Haji Azizullah, watchmaker, and arrested him and two companions, whom they sent to Kabul under strong escort. "[Azizullah's] shop was a rendezvous of many influential men in Kandahar," reported the Baluchistan Intelligence Bureau. "Perhaps object of his arrest is to obtain disclosures under pressure against individuals in Kandahar . . . There are indications that well-to-do individuals of the trader class are considering the advisability of transferring themselves and their money to India owing to insecurity in Kandahar. Lawlessness is increasing . . . The story in Kandahar is that several leading men have been arrested in Kabul and their whereabouts unknown."

The commander of an Army post at Pir Serai discovered that twenty-five of his soldiers were planning to desert with their rifles; they said it was because they disapproved of the arrest of the Hazrat of Shor Bazaar.

In Kohistan, north of Kabul, the spirit of unrest stirred more vehemently than elsewhere. One of the mullahs arrested had been Abdul Ahad of Kohistan, who was one of the Hazrats and the brother-in-law of Gul Agha. This mullah had a large following in Kohistan, which was loyal to its own, and which had troubled Amanullah immediately after his accession in 1919 because he executed the Mustaufi-ul-Mamalik of that region and gave his property to Wali. The Mustaufi had been harsh on the Kohistanis and taken their money, but they were attached to him in a way an American statesman would later put into words: "But he is *our* son of a bitch."

Bacha Sacao, after his period in Peshawar serving tea and sitting in the jail, had returned to his birthplace, Kalakhan in Kohistan. According to a story told later about his sojourn in Peshawar, a large safe was stolen there and the authorities knew that Bacha Sacao was guilty because no one else could have lifted it. Perhaps that was the instance in which he was arrested for burglary and set free for what would appear to a British court as lack of evidence. His physical strength was famous even when he was a poor water-carrier's son in Kalakhan; one could sense it looking at his stocky, square body so much like a bull's. Now Bacha Sacao had economic strength also, and, as an inevitable result, political strength. He was eminently successful in the profession at which he truly excelled, banditry.

When Bacha Sacao had robbed the government convoy of money, in Kohistan only the officials had really minded. The Kohistanis regarded government property as being in the public domain. Bacha Sacao gave them some of the money, and if he kept most of it for himself and his gang, no one objected because they themselves were better off than before.

Bacha Sacao's gang robbed some caravans that were taking goods to merchants, and sent a receipt to Customs authorities for the merchandise they had stolen. That was a good joke in Kohistan. They sent other insulting letters to other officials; Bacha Sacao himself could not write and read, but there was always someone to do this for him, and the word of his humor enlivened the hard life in the hills not many miles from the city of Kabul where so many people were leading lives that were so much easier. A joke on those easy-living Kabulis was always welcome.

Then Bacha Sacao kidnapped two Hindu merchants and made their families pay six thousand rupees in ransom.

Next he almost kidnapped Herr Freye, the German manager of the Deutsches-Afghanisches Company; he stopped Freye on the road near Charikar but released him later without making any demands.

Whatever money he collected from rich merchants, or would have collected from a foreigner had he thought it politic to do so, Bacha Sacao shared with the villagers. Since his victims were unlike themselves, and therefore not to be worried about, the Kohistanis had a new hero. Even Malik Mohsin of Kalakhan, who had once employed Bacha Sacao as a domestic servant, forgot that he had discharged him for pilfering and was proud of the association.

Soon no one would travel on the Kabul–Charikar road except by necessity. Three times during September a military force went out from Kabul to capture the bandits, and three times they made contact with the gang but three times they were beaten. Eight soldiers were killed and several wounded.

The influential mullah of Kohistan was released, Bacha Sacao's forays subsided and there was a report that his gang had dispersed and that he himself had gone to Afghan Mohmand country near Jalalabad. On October 1 Amanullah was able to visit Kohistan without incident. He had already made two trips to Khost, where military reinforcements had been sent, so the danger seemed to be past.

Although many other mullahs were released, Gul Agha and Masum were kept in prison, and the judge, Abdul Rahman Begtuti, was sentenced, along with some others, to death.

No one, however, had any doubt as to which mullah was really behind the conspiracy: the one in India.

"Sher Agha, brother of Hazrat of Shor Bazaar, should be watched very carefully. He may try to get to Khost via Kurram or Tochi," the frontier officials in India were ordered. Wali had asked Humphrys to send such a message.

The Government of India, having expelled Sher Agha from the North-West Frontier Province in March, had lost sight of him. They found him in Gondal City in Kathiawar on the coast between Karachi and Bombay. "He is said to be passing his time in prayer and in company of his followers," wired the Political Agent there. "I will report his movements."

Here is how Sher Agha looked to an American, Ben James, who saw him two years later and knew nothing of his role in the conspiracy:[1]

"He was a man of enormous frame who looked stubby despite his great height and seemed to be built of blocks of meat. His head, a huge cube; his black beard, cut square, dropped down over the white cape he wore; . . . Yet his eyes, large and smoldering beneath the thicket of his brows, dominated the whole countenance with their cruel, tragic luster.

"The prophets of old, who scourged the wicked and warred for righteousness, would have envied such demeanor. King and Cabinet faded into the background before his epic-like hero of Islamic faith. I had watched him, spell-bound, and speculated on what words of doom had been formed by his thick, hard lips."

To the people of Kathiawar he was the surrogate of Allah. He was a protective presence at all their ceremonies, insuring the benignity of all the forces that he seemed to gather into his large, unsmiling person, or at least the absence of malignity. He attended marriages and funerals, and in gratitude for his condescension the devout Moslems pressed money and clothing upon him, usually, since the price of protection is always stabilized, nine hundred rupees. "The custom of presenting purses is not unusual in Kathiawar," wrote the agent who was delegated to watch him. "Indeed, it may be regarded as a practice where a man of real or supposed religious eminence is concerned."

Some of Sher Agha's followers were so impressed by him that they started a subscription to buy him a house, but he stopped that. He was already living in a disciple's house, anyway.

If he did not regard his residence in Kathiawar sufficiently permanent to justify owning a house there, the fact did not appear in the intelligence reports.

CHAPTER 24

September 1, 1928, to October 10, 1928

Those who loved Amanullah most were desperately concerned about him.

Disaster was ahead. Superficially it seemed that swift arrest had prevented the immediate disaster invoked by Gul Agha's conspiracy. Those closest to Amanullah, like Wali, Mahmud Tarzi, Sultan Ahmed, Abdul Hadi, the Finance Minister Mir Hashim, his Consul in Bombay Mohammed Akbar, Ghulam Siddiq and his brothers, all knew better.

Mahmud Tarzi had advised him to surround himself with a strong army, as Mustapha Kemal had done, before he tried to force so many reforms on the Afghans. Amanullah spoke disparagingly to other people of this proposal, saying that Mahmud Tarzi, the teacher and adviser of his youth, who was sixty-three, was senile. Souraya was no more likely to listen to Tarzi in spite of his being her father. The Afghan Trade Agent at Quetta, while mailing to Kabul the European publications which showed Souraya unveiled, had been bitter about her recklessness. Yet it was easy to forgive Souraya for her unwillingness to return to the old veiled ways. With Amanullah and Souraya alike, their critics were handicapped by one inescapable fact: they meant so well.

Amanullah's friends forgave him many slights, and kept forgiving. The Amanullah who returned from Europe was not as attractive and lovable as the Amanullah who had gone. Eventually it would become an established legend of Afghan folklore that the British, by making what one Briton called "an unconscionable fuss" over Amanullah, had deliberately puffed up his ego in order to speed him to his downfall.

One of Amanullah's charms had been his awareness of other people. Such a quality, appealing even in the powerless, was irresistible in one who had absolute power and refrained from using it. Now he used his power. By the fall of 1928 Amanullah was in fact the absolute ruler that he said he was not. At the opening of the Loe Jirga he had stated that his forebears had been autocrats but that he was ruling by the counsel of the people. He was mistaken. Amir Abdur Rahman, who had seemed the ultimate in tyranny, had left people's customs alone. The reins of Central Government had been very loose; now the Central Government was coming into a man's home.

There were some who would have liked a republican form of government. Any Afghan who was progressive enough to want a republic would have elected Amanullah as President. The Loe Jirga had voted for a national assembly but postponed the election.

Instead, a Prime Minister and a Cabinet, persons of experience who could make decisions, were sought as an immediate solution. And Amanullah promised to name this body.

As Prime Minister he named Sher Ahmed.

Many of those whom he selected for the Cabinet refused to serve under Sher Ahmed.

And Amanullah himself was going to the individual Cabinet members in secret, advising them to refuse service.

This deceptive gambit distressed the well-wishers against whom it was aimed; it showed that Amanullah would go to any lengths to pretend to satisfy them, but in fact intended to rule as he pleased. All this took place in the month of September, against the background of the Hazrats' arrest and all its ominous connotations which showed how greatly restraint was needed.

There was much about Sher Ahmed that was not known to Amanullah or his advisers. They did not know that in 1919 he had approached the British Agent with suggestions of deposing Amanullah, and even of killing him. They did not know the extent of his pride of position which led him to tell the British that they knew how to treat a sardar. In the British dossier on him, he was described as "a man of some ability but indolent and corrupt." The British, on the other hand, were unaware of the intrigue swirling around his appointment; they told each other that the ministers refused to serve because Sher Ahmed was "a ridiculous puppet."

On September 22 Amanullah finally said that it was impossible to form a Cabinet with a Prime Minister, so he himself would continue to be the Chief of State and Government.

But he would not concern himself immediately with the day-to-day affairs of government. He had plans for reorganizing the life of Afghanistan which required him to withdraw for a while to think them out. Wali, who had postponed his trip to Europe for treatment of the kidney stone, was appointed permanent regent, and Amanullah announced that for the period of his contemplation Wali would govern from the King's own office in the palace. Amanullah moved into a small office in the Foreign Ministry.

Amanullah could still make a gesture like giving up his office; that was one of the reasons why they could not abandon him but continued by his side to what they suspected was destruction.

The Council did achieve one success on September 29. Amanullah was persuaded to send an emissary to Sher Agha in India, asking him to return to Afghanistan and come to an agreement with the government. He had shown himself too powerful for any other treatment.

The emissary, a magistrate from Kabul, set out toward Kathiawar to find the sinister Hazrat. Ghulam Siddiq asked the British to permit Sher Agha to cross the frontier into Afghanistan only if the emissary made such a request; otherwise, to continue to keep him away.

"The mullahs are fighting for their lives," the British had been saying for some time. An Indian visitor to Kabul had seen a soldier forcibly ejecting a venerable mullah from a public place and had been reminded of the treatment in his own country of untouchables.

"The mullahs now realize," Humphrys reported on September 21, "that if they wish to maintain any of their former prestige they cannot delay much longer in asserting themselves. It is also noticed that the King himself appears to have renounced, to a great extent, his former religious observances and it is now a rare event for him to attend a mosque . . .

"It is an evident fact that King Amanullah has never taken sufficient interest in his troops, and has done nothing to establish that feeling of personal loyalty which would be of particular value in his case.

"The pay of the soldier, fourteen rupees per month, is absurdly inadequate at the present day. In the time of the Amirs, a soldier, receiving this pay, employed other means of adding to his income; while on guard duty he would practice his trade as a cobbler, stone mason, private servant or even unskilled labor. Under the present régime, this is not allowed. Parades and other duties, while not adding to general efficiency, have become more arduous and nothing is done for the comfort of the troops. Barracks have been freely demolished but no new ones built, and many of the troops, at least in the central divisions, are housed under canvas which is almost inhuman during the severe winter months; particularly as firewood is difficult to obtain, and only at a price quite beyond their means.

"Lack of funds does not permit the men being even decently clothed, and although it is boasted that the electrical system supplies eighteen thousand units to Kabul, yet no lighting has been installed in any barracks.

"It is true that artillery, cavalry and infantry schools have been established; a good attempt is being made to improve the training of the officer, and up-to-date war material has been imported, but none of these affect the routine of the private soldier whose treatment at the hands of his officer is at times almost brutal, officers entirely lacking all sense of duty towards their men.

"At one time the great advantage of the soldier's life was the power he exercised over the civil population, but the Government is now issuing statements and generally making it known that the people should not obey any but lawful orders given by authorized officials . . .

"Under the above circumstances, it is certainly possible, if not probable, that the Army would welcome and support any popular movement which would carry a personal appeal and hold out hopes of an increase of pay and amenities."

Outside Kabul, in the provinces, people were freely expressing the opinion that the King must be mad. That left him for support only the official class of Kabul. These were the people who had held out both hands for all the progress that he could bring; it was said that they were sycophants who told Amanullah what he wanted to hear, and some were, but usually what he wanted to hear was what they really thought.

Even they were suffering from Amanullah's zeal. He was planning to check on their income and expenses as a means of ending bribery through which some had paid for their motorcars and European dress.

"A good king but a bad politician," a friend called Amanullah. He had not drawn allies around him or shored up his position. He was almost all alone.

"The situation in Afghanistan has undergone considerable changes since the return of King Amanullah to Kabul on July 1," Humphrys wrote. "Since his arrival he has played into the hands of his enemies and has now produced a situation in which all the cards would be on the side of a revolutionary leader should the opportunity produce the man."

On the last day of September Amanullah commenced a series of lectures which lasted for five days, talking three hours each day. A large tent was erected in the compound of the Foreign Office, and here about six hundred persons sat to hear him, including Queen Souraya and a number of ladies, all wearing the sheer veil that had become fashionable since her return.

The first evening's talk was preceded by a farewell ceremony for a hundred and five young men and fifteen young women who were going to Turkey to study. The girls evoked more attention than the men, for they were the first Afghan women ever to be sent out of the country. Their faces were covered in sheer black cloth as they heard Amanullah and Souraya wish them well in their study of midwifery, and then they marched past the audience and entered motorcars which drove off at once, taking them through the Khyber Pass to Peshawar on their first step toward an education outside Afghanistan. By the time they reached Peshawar, they had removed their veils. Their eyes were tinged with blue makeup, which was not uncommon among Afghan women, even those who worked in the field, and they were wearing lipstick.[1]

Amanullah said that his tour had cost £70,000 and resulted in useful gifts of arms and machinery to the value of £460,000, a profit to the nation of £390,000. Everyone had been waiting for this accounting. There was much talk that the trip had been ruinously expensive. Even now some wondered if these figures included the cost of transportation of these articles, which were arriving at the Customs Houses on the frontier every day.

He reformed the Army. His changes ranged from a year's military duty for all high school graduates, who would become reserve officers, to the issuance of cooked rations to his royal guard, service in batches of four as his aide-de-camps "in order that they may have opportunities of associating with the King," establishment of a club for officers to be financed by a month's pay from each officer, and the preparation of a map.

Amanullah said that no soldier was to be a follower of any religious leader or take part in politics. "Your spiritual leader must be your rifle."

The police got two changes: they were removed from control of the Ministry of Justice and the color of their uniforms was altered.

Fat men, said Amanullah, are usually fat because of idleness, and since fat men are unfit for military service, any man who exceeded a standard weight in relation to his height would be discharged from the Army. He said that no Afghan married to a foreign woman might be employed in the Foreign Ministry unless he divorced his wife.

Coeducation was part of his proposals: girls from six to ten years of age, he said, should study in the same schools as boys, to save the expense of separate primary schools for girls. He asked his listeners to agree with this; they did.

An old-age pension, a social innovation that would not reach the United States of America for nine more years, he proposed for Government workers and soldiers, who would support it with contributions during their working years.

Amanullah promised to take control of Afghanistan's trade himself if the traders did not show more enterprise by going farther afield than Peshawar or Lahore.

All this, and more, took Amanullah five days to present. The climax came on the third day.

"Religion does not require women to veil their hands, feet or faces, or to wear any special kind of veil."

Queen Souraya arose in the audience and tore off the light transparent veil she had been wearing. The audience applauded. Other women present arose and tore off their veils. The men looked upon their faces. It was October 2, 1928, an important date in Afghan history when unveiled women for the first time were socially accepted.

"Women should now discard the old burkah and either go unveiled or wear modest garments and a light veil," said Amanullah. "Outside Kabul the decision of the whole matter must rest with the individual. But tribal custom must not impose itself on the free will of the individual."

As regards the number of wives, Amanullah pointed out that he, his brother Inayatullah, and the regent Wali, had only one wife apiece, but had between them twenty-eight fine children. "This shows that one wife can suffice to keep the Afghan nation from extinction."

It had been a magnificent, formidable performance, not merely in the physical energy of the five days but in the range of Amanullah's mentality that had covered the whole of Afghan life, from the trivial to the momentous, and set his mark upon it. In those days of contem-

plation he had organized it all. Those who had thought him a genius
had more reason now than ever.

Those who worried about consequences also had more reason.

Each of the exciting five days had seen the projection of a different
movie film showing Amanullah's trip. People had anticipated an interesting reaction to the sight of Souraya's unveiled face in the films,
but after Souraya unveiled herself in person, this was an anticlimax.

What was observed was the inspiration to imitate the things that
Afghans had seen as, cinematically, they had taken Amanullah's journey
along with him. Within a few days seven airplanes were in the sky attempting formations, as the planes of other countries had done, and
the cavalry school was carrying pennons of the new Afghan colors on
its lances, just like British cavalry.

Equipment for playing cricket arrived at the Kabul schools, and the
Afghan Sports Club, which had been a joke before Amanullah's return,
was besieged with applications for membership now that he had told
Afghans they should exercise. "On the playing fields of Kabul," read
the British Military Attaché's diary, "members of this Legation have
come in contact with young Afghans and, while learning themselves
to sympathize more fully, may perhaps by example lay some long cherished bogey of suspicion. The King has asked for the measurements of
a squash court, and the day is not far off when every kind of sport will
be going full swing. This must have a civilizing influence on a people
whose physical activities in the past have been employed in sterner
pursuits. The King paid a delicate compliment in a public speech by
saying that the British were the finest race physically he had met in
his travels. But if the Empire's reputation in these contests is to be left
in the hands of the British Legation, it will soon be necessary, with
the increasing standard of Afghanistan, to hang a notice outside its
walls, 'Internationals only need apply.' "

Kabul, however, was not all of Afghanistan. There a vision of library
and hotels and an introduction to cricket had meaning. In the houses
behind the mud forts on the mountainsides and along the rivers, where
rice and wheat were grown with hope, where the fertility of a flock meant
the difference between hunger and plenty, different things made people
happy and different things distressed them.

The Mohmands of the Usman Khel had been made happy briefly
when some of their boys, whom Amanullah had taken to school in Ka-

bul, returned for vacation carrying gold bracelets as gifts from Amanullah's sisters to their mothers. They had even decided to submit others
of their boys to education. But dissatisfaction was their natural state.
In 1925 they had rebelled against the Central Government, and the
result was that Amanullah had taken away their land, which lay near
Jalalabad on the opposite side of the Kunar River, and given it to a
Khugiani named Abdul Wadud. He gave them other lands nearby,
but they regretted their own.

Then Abdul Wadud behaved like King David, who, although having
everything tangible in sight, still coveted another man's woman. The
lady in question was a widow, but she was a Mohmand of the Usman
Khel and under the control of relatives to whom Abdul Wadud was an
enemy. Abdul Wadud raided the village where she lived and took her,
and incidentally killed a Mohmand.

The Mohmands determined to take back not only the woman but
the lands which they had lost. Their men were summoned to form a
lashkar, under threat of a fine of two bullocks and one load of wheat
for anyone who refused to join. Soon two thousand armed Mohmands
were entrenched by the riverside opposite Jalalabad. They sent a letter
to Shah Mahmud, the Army Commander of the area, stating that they
were willing to join battle with the Afghan Army at Kama, where their
lost lands were. At Kama was a garrison of four hundred soldiers.

Government officials went from Kabul to talk with the Mohmands
and invite them to Jalalabad. They refused to cross the Kunar River,
the officials had to go into their encampment and listen to their
threats to sever relations with the Afghan Government if their demands were not met. Finally their elders looked at the crops of maize,
now ripe and yellow, and decided that its harvest was more important
than revenge, and agreed to postpone discussion a month.

The Mohmand demand was that Abdul Wadud and the woman
should be handed over to them to be stoned to death. Their real complaint, however, was that the King had abolished the purdah system in
Kabul and wished to extend that order to Mohmand territory and that
the abduction of the Mohmand woman and the murder of the
Mohmand had been carried out at the instigation of King Amanullah.

On October 10 Afghan ladies attended a reception at the British
Legation for the first time. Several Afghan male guests suggested that
their wives might be included in future invitations.

CHAPTER 25

October 2, 1928, to November 29, 1928

"The stir created by the King's reforms suggests the advisability of our feeling our way cautiously and avoiding association in public eyes with the proposed reforms until we know which way the wind is blowing," G. of I. wired to H.M.G. Already G. of I. was refusing permission to Englishmen who wanted to enter Afghanistan,[1] and one who did get through, during Jeshyn, was advised by Humphrys to leave quickly in case there was trouble.[2]

This wire was sent October 2, before Amanullah had even completed his exposition of those reforms. October 1928 was a month of transition for Amanullah; he intended it to be a transition between the presenting of his blueprint for a new Afghanistan and, following a short rest, a start toward fulfillment.

The railroad through Afghanistan was one project that was moving toward fulfillment, and now Amanullah was talking of linking Chaman in India with Kushk in Russia, and of carrying freight and passengers from Western Europe to Kabul in fourteen days. The Turkish Ambassador told Humphrys that this rail link was a question of worldwide significance which would, if carried out, vitally affect the strategic and economic problems of the Middle East.

The British knew all about the strategic problems involved. Such a rail link would remove from India the protection of Afghanistan's status as a buffer state. India would be linked with her menace.

Amanullah was dealing with a French group and a German group, neither of which was associated with its government. He had told Michel Clemenceau's French party that work should begin simultaneously on the line between Kabul and Kandahar, which would benefit the British, and a line between New Chaman and Kushk, which the British would have done much to prevent. He told Lenz and Co., the Germans, that he wanted the British connection at Thal, where the track was only two and a half feet wide.

Of the two governments that really were interested in Afghan railroads, the Russians had been talking with the Germans and the British had been conferring at every step with the French. The British interest was not as benevolent as young, baby-faced Clemenceau thought it was, but a channel to early information which they would put to use in thwarting his goal. All this time Humphrys was writing: "We should at this stage neither obstruct nor encourage any of the foreign prospectors, but if necessary exercise diplomatic pressure to defer as long as possible the construction of a railway likely to threaten Indian security." He knew that the instant such a railway appeared in Afghanistan, India would feel impelled to move many more troops to the frontier.

Then, during the second week in October, young Clemenceau put some pressure of his own on the British. Having completed the survey, he had a conversation which Humphrys reported, "[He is] persistent in pointing out that Amanullah is determined to have the railway and that the economic and material progress of Afghanistan is such as to make the early construction of this railway inevitable. Under these circumstances, [he considers] that the British Government should now support [his] project which has been framed to suit British interests as far as it was possible to do so."

In Clemenceau's plan, the track gauge would be four feet, eight and a half inches wide, the gauge used in Europe, which would connect with British tracks in the Khyber but was narrower than either the Russian gauge of five feet or the Indian gauge of five feet six inches. Nationalism had made it impossible for anyone to go from Europe to the East by rail by any route without changing trains. Amanullah insisted the line should continue to Herat and to Kushk, which Clemenceau thought the British should accept. What the British military men had dreamed of was a line connecting Kabul with the Khyber and Kandahar with Chaman, which would have linked Afghanistan only with India and given her no interior connections to speak of.

The support for which Clemenceau was asking was financial. And Humphrys had put the matter to H.M.G. in logical steps which disposed of Clemenceau and his railway: "There is no money in the country to finance construction nor security to offer. A foreign-built railway connection with India would be more expensive than one built by the Indian Railway Board and be heavily over-capitalized. No extensive foreign-built railway operated with the help of foreigners would pay interest on capital, and increased taxation would render railway unpopular. For these two last reasons, and because of the alignment, British backing should be withheld from the present project. Without our political and financial backing, it is unlikely that any foreigners would sink much capital in the country. Failing foreign capital being available . . . the King will turn to us."

And on the happy day when Clemenceau's ambitious plan should fail, and when Amanullah would reject the Germans' more modest but less appealing plan, Humphrys expected that Amanullah would appeal to the British and, in return for a railway from India, forgo a railway from Russia.

"The King is genuinely desirous for railways to be introduced into Afghanistan," the naïve Clemenceau kept telling the British. He told also of bribes demanded by Amanullah's ministers. "King Amanullah has impressed [him]," wrote British intelligence. "The King appears to have confided . . . that he is alone and cannot trust his ministers to do anything honestly."

In the air the British faced the same situation. With the German firm of Junkers planning air service from Tehran to Kabul, and the Russians having a contract for air mail service twice monthly from Termez (although the planes did not keep their schedule), the only route not served by at least the promise of an airline was that from Kabul to India. For this also the British had plans: "Afghans to be excluded from all real control while admitted to full share in credit attaching to service . . . At start, machine to reach and return from Kabul same day. Otherwise our personnel would have to live alone, some way out of Kabul, and it would be difficult to prevent Afghan Government treating them as if they were its own employees. Afghan Government would be more likely to agree if planes simply called at Kabul . . . Fare to be low at start . . . to encourage air habit."

Here, also, the plan called for Amanullah to be "maneuvered" into asking for an air service.

There were twenty airplanes in Afghanistan, but half were temporarily or permanently out of service. One was a plane which the Afghans had bought against British advice during the Khost Rebellion, when any plane seemed infinitely desirable. A former R.A.F. officer named

Murphy had sold it, and three others, to which the British referred thereafter as "Mr. Murphy's planes."

"The history of the airplanes which Mr. Murphy has sold to the Afghan Government is as follows," Humphrys wrote in 1925. "They
are part of a consignment presented as a gift to the Government of
India by His Majesty's Government in 1920, and subsequently handed
over, free of charge, to the M.C. Aviation Syndicate. The machines
were not new when they came to India and, if my information is correct, have since been in open storage at Karachi for four years, during
which period there can be no doubt that they have greatly deteriorated
. . . It is stated that these machines are out of date and unlikely to be
of any lasting value to Afghanistan . . . My opinion, therefore, in which
I feel sure that I shall have the support of all who have any knowledge
of flying conditions in Afghanistan, is that the machines will either
never reach Kabul from Peshawar, or that, if they do arrive there, they
will be found entirely useless."

The planes were bought and one reached Kabul. The other three
remained in Peshawar, where a storm did even more damage to them.
A complaint of Amanullah's father, that Westerners tried to take advantage of Afghans, still applied. There was the matter also of rifles
bought in Poland which an expert described as "fit only for a South
American brigand." Those had not arrived either.

The British, however, felt that the advantage-taking was attempted
in the other direction, and after Ghulam Siddiq, still Acting Foreign
Minister, proposed that Britain and Afghanistan sign a new treaty,
Humphrys wrote:

"Ghulam Siddiq and his friends are opposed to [generous assistance
in kind] because it gives them few, if any, opportunities for enriching
themselves at the expense of the State, and the King himself would prefer to handle cash and recruit his employees at his own discretion; but
there is no getting away from the admission, which Mahmud Tarzi once
made to me in a moment of irritation at the behavior of his colleagues,
that if the British Government were to fill the Kabul Valley with gold,
the country's communications would be no how improved thereby.

"The Afghan, both by temperament and habit, possesses a capacity
for the unprofitable absorption of gold to an unlimited extent. What
he entirely lacks is the aptitude for organization or the honest application of funds. I will quote two examples to illustrate these failings. Three

years ago about a mile of useless road embankment was constructed near Dakka at a cost to the Afghan Government of £50,000, and last year the King paid twice this sum out of his own pocket for the building of a cement factory in Kabul which has never turned out a single ounce of cement."

October 1928 nevertheless was a month of hope. Amanullah hoped to import £750,000 worth of agricultural equipment from England; which he would buy with three quarters of £1,000,000 loan in which English bankers were already interested to the point of asking for what he had most difficulty offering: security. He was arranging to improve the breed of Kabul's karakul sheep, whose fur was his country's chief product for export, by sending there some of the better rams from Mazar-i-Sharif. The match factory had begun to employ women.

Ghulam Siddiq had told Humphrys that Afghanistan was more in need of war material for consolidation and defense than of anything else.

Amanullah was negotiating to buy fifty thousand rifles and fifty million rounds of ammunition from a British firm, and was expecting five tanks, two field batteries, one mountain battery and two ammunition wagons that he had ordered in France, in addition to the munitions being given by England. His major military problem was a temporary shortage of trucks in which to transport all this, for the replacements had not yet arrived for the trucks which in his optimism he had scrapped.

The success of his restriction on traditional dress was visible in the streets of Kabul, where his orders were implemented so earnestly that even the former Amir of Bokhara, once one of the world's most powerful men, was stopped by a policeman and fined for wearing his turban. More women were going unveiled. Souraya had organized courts to hear complaints based on the newly emerging rights of women: against husbands who did not give their wives enough to eat, who beat them, who wanted divorces. A feminine secret service was also being formed to watch out for any reactionary movements among the men of Kabul, or even among the women themselves. Elderly women were to be authorized to go into homes to see if women were being treated properly; never had any law officer been given such a right to burst into an Afghan home uninvited by the man.

All this was part of Amanullah's master plan, which he was still devel-

oping in his small office at the Foreign Ministry. He had not yet returned to the day-by-day administration. He was sequestered with the
future.

The Shinwaris, one of the Pathan tribes that gloried in the legend
of being a Lost Tribe of Israel, lived in the area called Ningrahar southeast of Jalalabad. The southern boundary of their lands was the frontier
between Afghanistan and India, the range of mountains that extended
from the hills around Kabul eastward for two hundred miles to the Indus River in India. This range was called Safed Koh, or White Mountain, because its highest peak was 15,620 feet above the sea, and the
lesser peaks were from 12,000 to 14,000 feet high, so there were only
a few summer months when one could not look up toward the Safed
Koh, from a great distance, and see shining there a white covering of
snow. From this eminence the Safed Koh sent fingers down into Afghanistan and India, long spurs of gradually diminishing mountains,
and on the northern ridges of these, in the eastern area closest to India,
lived the Shinwaris.

They lived between two worlds: the Afghan peaks of the Safed Koh,
which faced northward and did not begin to lose their snows until midsummer, long after the peaks toward India were showing brown; and
the rich alluvial valley around Jalalabad, where the apricot and walnut
trees gave their fruit, and the rice paddies were green. Looking down
from their jagged hills, they could see the tempting caravans plodding
toward India and back laden with good things. They lived between
hardship and plenty, always an unsettling situation.

Below the peaks of almost perpetual snow the grazing grounds
could nourish a multitude of sheep in the appropriate season, and the
edible pine grew there alongside the wild olive and the acacia. The Shinwaris therefore had their own resources. But they were a suspicious
tribe so notorious as troublemakers that the British on the southern
side of the Safed Koh had made up a little verse warning the listener
not to trust:

". . . these three:
A snake, a whore, and a Shinwari."

Each Shinwari family appropriated for itself a knoll in one of the
crevasses between the spurs of the mountains, and built there a cluster
of houses surrounded by the usual Pathan fort with a tower in each
corner. From these they often raided the caravans passing in the low-

lands; then they took refuge in the highlands, knowing that country so inhospitable to human life would be hostile also to their pursuers.

Now in October there were rumors about the Shinwaris; one rumor said that they planned to swoop down on the Afghan girls who had to pass that way to Turkey. This did not happen, but it was what people expected from Shinwaris. The Sangu Khel Shinwaris, who had memories as long as any Afghan, still resented the treatment of Ardali and Daud Shah, which they considered a betrayal of the principle of asylum to Moslems (they did not know that the principles of non-Moslem countries had been betrayed as well).

Now they were perturbed over the ways of Government with a passion that went far deeper than shock at seeing the girls' faces headed for Turkey. Their own women did not cover their faces, although they did use circumspection in talking with men to whom they were not married, and of course, they stayed at home. But as an issue, the bare faces on the roadway served. They served a Sangu Khel malik named Afzal who had fought on Amanullah's side during the Khost Rebellion, but now was saying, among other things, that the girls should not have been sent out of the country but that midwives should have been imported to train them. They served another malik, Alam, who had a lifetime history of arousing Shinwaris to war. He had tried it in the reign of Amanullah's father, when his target was the British, and he had been deprived of his army rank as a result; his holy war had been inspired by Amanullah's uncle Nasrullah, whom he forcefully supported as Amir of Afghanistan. Alam was a friend of the family whose head was Nadir.

The mullah from whom the Shinwaris drew most of their spiritual sustenance announced that he was going to India to live; the local officials detained him; they had orders to keep mullahs from leaving, in view of the trouble being caused by one who had left.

In Kabul, Amanullah showed the mullahs and the rest of Afghanistan that he had accepted the challenge they had given him for the rule of his country: he carried out the sentence of execution of the judge Abdur Rahman Begtuti, two members of his family and another mullah involved in the plot against him.

Kabulis said very little openly about this, but in whispers and private conferences they were wondering how they could secure the release of the Hazrat Sahib of Shor Bazaar, Gul Agha, who more than any of the others represented the power of the clergy and the force of religion. This concern of comfortable, prestigious people in Kabul was shared by the nomads, following their laden camels through the enclosed mountain passes into India, pitching their low black tents at night while their dogs kept alert to snap at anything unfamiliar. These nomads kept asking for news of the arrested Hazrat Sahib, Gul Agha.

Amanullah was trying more desperately than ever to get Sher Agha back into Afghanistan for a confrontation and compromise; the Afghan Consul in Bombay sent emissaries; an Afghan secret agent went to Lahore to his agent there. But at the same time the mullahs in Afghanistan secretly were sending Sher Agha messages warning him to stay away. They feared Amanullah would lure him to destruction.

Other mullahs were being arrested. Rumors kept distorting the already twisted sensibilities of the country. On October 15 Kabul even heard that a strange red airplane had been sighted over Kandahar, but nothing was known of any British planes in that area, of any red planes or any world fliers.

In the Kurram Valley in India, nine murders were committed during three weeks of October. "No particular cause for this increase can be discovered," said the North-West Frontier Province intelligence diary, "but it is noticeable that in no less than six of these cases the persons concerned were immigrants from Afghan or tribal territory."

Some nomads moving toward India unwisely strayed into the domain of the Suleiman Khel Ghilzais, and had their caravans plundered. They protested to the authorities at Gardez and were told that they could take their own revenge. The mullahs of the Suleiman Khel Ghilzais were also going to India, and no official could stop them; they were telling the tribes across the border that Amanullah was interfering with the divine law of the Shariat, and that they who had fought for him in 1919, in spite of not being his subjects, should repeat their indifference to frontiers by rising against him now. Farther south on the road between Chaman and Kandahar, three trucks were robbed and the drivers killed, and the Governor, a new man who was proclaiming the virtues of Amanullah in the mosques of Kandahar, arrested three suspects and had them blown from the gun.

To the west of the restless Shinwaris the fort of Abdul Wadud, the Khugiani who had abducted the Mohmand widow, was being besieged and about a hundred families were shut up there like mice in a hole guarded by a cat. And across the valley from the Shinwaris the Mohmands, who were keeping the guard on Abdul Wadud's fort so that he might not escape before they were ready to deal with him, pondered what they would do when all the maize was finally harvested.

In June, just before Amanullah's return, the British had commented on the unexpected tranquillity along the frontier; whatever troubles were rumored were less than they had expected. Now they looked back and said that June's quiet had been unnatural, like that which preceded a cataclysm. They were more discerning in October.

When November came, rumors were flying along the frontier that Queen Souraya had been assassinated and that the Afghans had rebelled against King Amanullah because of his policy against the mullahs.

At the beginning of November, Amanullah sent a summons to the Tagao Mullah to come to Kabul. This mullah was old enough to have been influential during the reigns of Amanullah's grandfather and father. He had worked for Amanullah in 1919 by preaching jehad against the British, and he was one of three mullahs (the other two were the Hazrats of Shor Bazaar) whom Amanullah had endowed with a special title: his title, Fakhr-ul-Mashaskh, meant "Pride of the Saints." Now he was turning all that energy for Holy War against Amanullah.

Tagao, where "Pride of the Saints" represented the word of Allah, was the beautiful valley of a tributary of the Panjshir River, which flowed southeasterly to join the Kabul River at Sarobi between Kabul and Jalalabad. Long ago this valley had been the principal route for caravans; now the main road went elsewhere, but it was a link between the Jalalabad area at one end and Koh-i-Daman at the northwestern end. Its mullah was a man of importance also in Ningrahar, the land of the Shinwaris.

Tagao had been the home of Inayatullah's mother. To the people of Tagao, who had expected this son of theirs to become Amir, Amanullah's accession caused more disappointment than it did to Inayatullah, who seemed content to be known in Kabul as "Lala," or "Elder Brother," and to live without responsibility. In 1920 a regiment in Tagao which Inayatullah had formed in his days as heir apparent had attempted an unsuccessful coup in his behalf.

The Tagao Mullah was named on a list of mullahs conspiring against Amanullah which the British received from an informer in the circle at Khanki Bazaar in Tirah around Mullah Mahmud Akhundzada. The Afghan Government, sharing the British suspicions of activities in

Khanki Bazaar, had its own agents there to keep eyes and ears open. Mullah Mahmud Akhundzada himself seemed preoccupied with his running feud with his neighbors of the Shiah sect of Islam and with two personal matters; first, mourning the death of his favorite wife, and two months later, making a politically advantageous marriage to her replacement. But to both governments he seemed a likely focal point of intrigue.

When the Tagao Mullah was summoned by the King to appear at Kabul, he refused. Amanullah sent a detachment of soldiers into the Panjshir Valley to bring him by force. As the soldiers approached his home, they were attacked from ambush, and several were wounded before the armed men protecting the mullah succeeded in driving them back toward Kabul.

The ambush was directed by Bacha Sacao.

The only authority which Bacha Sacao respected, besides that of a rifle, was the mystic authority in the symbols of religion. Around his neck on a string he wore a small leather pouch enclosing a piece of paper on which a mullah had written a verse from the Koran. To him this was assurance that, no matter how audaciously he defied the conventions of law-ruled men, heaven would look out for him. Many Afghans wore such amulets. A story went around that Bacha Sacao had received this amulet from a mullah of the Khyber Pass whom he met in the Suleiman Serai in Peshawar while he was serving tea there, and that he expected to live only two months after the death of this mullah. Whoever had given him the amulet, and wherever he had been since his last burst of banditry in Koh-i-Daman, he was still uninjured and successful in Tagao as he defended the mullah of that place against the Government.

A few weeks later the intelligence report of India's North-West Frontier Province would read, "Report serious dacoities [thefts] have been committed in Tagao . . . The Tagao Mullah is said to be not unconnected with these affairs, and to divert suspicions from himself, he has moved to Koh-i-Daman."

And the British Military Attaché would write in his diary, "Hear Bacha Sacao has collected 400 men and joined forces with the Tagao Mullah."

In Koh-i-Daman on the night of November 13/14 Bacha Sacao was confronting another detachment of Afghan soldiers. He had been raiding near Charikar so disastrously that Amanullah was desperate to stop him. The troops found the house where he was staying; they surrounded it.

Suddenly flames began to flicker within the house, and then to lick out of the windows, and smoke billowed and covered it. While the soldiers coughed and blinked through the smoke, Bacha Sacao and his companions wriggled through a hole in the back wall and ran off into the mountains. It was he who had set fire to the house.

That night the Sangu Khel Shinwaris were also busy. By the next afternoon they had succeeded in halting all traffic on the road between Dakka on the frontier and Batikot in the valley. Then with their rifles they made a foray into the civil headquarters at Achin. The official in charge attempted to flee; they captured him and imprisoned him.

The news reached Jalalabad, and its hakim informed Amanullah by telephone.

Amanullah said that he had airplanes, troops and also arms, and since his kingdom rested on an international basis, he did not care much for these rebellions.

"As the rebels are Afghans, and Afghans have a great regard for jirgas," suggested the official, "a jirga should be sent to them."

Amanullah replied that the jirga should include no mullah, hazrat, or sayed [descendant of the Prophet]. Since most jirgas were composed of these very people, the official was perplexed as to whom he should send. He finally chose three men: the editor of the newspaper, a Jalalabad man who had been official of the Shinwaris in the days of Amanullah's father, and a man who had come from India in the religious movement of the 1920s. They went on horseback, accompanied by tongas carrying baggage, to Ghani Khel just below Batikot, one of the besieged places, and sent word to the Shinwaris to meet them. The Shinwaris came. There were seventy or eighty. They were armed. And instead of talking, they set fire to the tongas and carried off the horses and baggage. The three men managed to get back to Jalalabad.

Now the Sangu Khels had been joined by the other clans of Shinwaris and on the second day of their rebellion they went to the army post at Pesh Bolak, where the soldiers, having heard of their King's designs on their religious lives, were so sympathetic that they made only a superficial resistance. The Shinwaris ended with a large sum of money from the treasury and with a larger armory of rifles than they had started out with. On November 16 they fired into the frontier town of Dakka, which was crowded with the caravans and trucks that would have proceeded toward Jalalabad had it not been for the shots from Shinwari rifles which threatened anyone who moved onto the road. The Sarhaddar of Dakka was expecting to be attacked at any instant by the Sangu Khel Shinwaris and he had only sixty men to defend his post. He could not send quickly for reinforcements because the Shinwaris had cut the telephone and telegraph wires which linked him with Jalalabad.

On this day a band of nomads, later than most in their passage toward India, encountered the belligerent Sangu Khels and a fight was inevitable. The nomads lost some animals, but three men of the Sangu Khel were killed, and they ceased defying the law long enough to appeal to the law for revenge. The nomads, however, were allowed to depart in peace. This appeared as proof of bribery and the corruption of the King's officials.

In Kabul on November 16 nine corpses were being brought from the north. They were men who had been killed in a ferocious raid in Koh-i-Daman by Bacha Sacao. One body was that of the Governor of Charikar.

Along the eastern frontier there was talk that revolt had arisen also to the west. But the location named for that revolt was Tagao.

The Mohmands had not joined in the fight. Their attention was centered on the more personal matter of Abdul Wadud and the kidnapped widow. They had issued an ultimatum to the government: if this couple were not handed over to them to be stoned to death, they would attack the Army posts. The last of the maize was being harvested. Soon they would carry out their threat, and to Amanullah, who had already ordered to Jalalabad what troops he could spare from Kabul, it was imperative that their fierce tribe should not add to his troubles.

The religious leader of the Mohmands was an old man known as the Chaknawar Mullah, who over the years had blown hot and cold toward Amanullah. Like many mullahs of the frontier, he would have delighted to have Nasrullah for Amir; in 1919 Amanullah had ordered his arrest, which he had evaded. A few years later he had reconciled himself to Amanullah sufficiently to make a propaganda tour of the tribes in his behalf, and he had helped settle a territory dispute, for which the Afghan Government had sent him a large sum of money. Then he provoked Amanullah's displeasure by acting like an independent monarch, surrounding himself with armed men, summoning tribes to raid on his enemies, with such arrogance that the Government rebuked him. He had been warned not to cause trouble in the King's absence; for his peace he had expected a large reward on Amanullah's return, and gossip said he was dissatisfied with what he got.

The Chaknawar Mullah was named as a conspirator by the informer at Khanki Bazaar. But now he agreed to work for Amanullah. The Mohmands asked him if the King was an infidel; if he were, they were free of the Koran's injunction to obey civil authority. The Chaknawar Mullah defended Amanullah. He not only kept the Mohmands from fighting, but he made them responsible for the safety of the road.

But he had a price. He demanded that Amanullah revoke all laws concerning the education of women and extend an amnesty to all who had rebelled. He also wanted Abdul Wadud and the widow.

Then the Mohmands got Abdul Wadud by their own efforts. On a subterfuge he was persuaded to leave his fort, and he was killed, not by ritual stoning as they would have preferred, but by a bullet. This revenge satisfied the Mohmands for a while.

North of Kabul, however, Bacha Sacao was a menace greater than ever. Now he was not merely an outlaw; he was a hero and champion to the people of Koh-i-Daman with whom he shared his spoils. He had no doubt that Amanullah was an infidel who would ruin them all; the mullahs had told him so. To his greed was added self-righteousness. When Amanullah sent an official into Koh-i-Daman to recruit men to fight the Shinwaris, not only were there no recruits, but the official's escort was attacked and he barely escaped alive.

In 1919 the British, confounded by the war on the ground, had found a solution in the airplane. Now the Afghans had planes, and six of these, manned by Russians as well as Afghans, bombed the Shinwari concentrations on November 20 and 21.

Amanullah prepared also a war of words. They were the same words that he had used after the Khost Rebellion: "The conflict between learning and ignorance." He still saw the conflict as one of abstract qualities, not of human beings fighting for their identities. His recruiting notice said: "The conflict between learning and ignorance has been the cause of many accidents since the creation of the world. The young Afghanistan under the guidance of the progressive rule of His Majesty Amanullah Khan is striving hard day by day for the consolidation of the faith, the driving away of the enemies of the country and religion . . . Ignorance has always been the enemy of peace and the progress of mankind . . . Now some of the wicked Shinwaris . . . have rebelled and have joined the ranks of those who are lost in this as well as in the next world. The Ministry of War wishes to suppress these wicked people and teach them a lesson. It is therefore promulgated for the information of the devoted sons of Afghanistan that on reading this notice they should at once present themselves at the Ministry of War."

Those who volunteered most eagerly were students, those who had really allied themselves with learning as against ignorance. In Khost, which had fought for ignorance, the reserves whom the Army attempted to call were unwilling to fight for learning; they announced that they would not go among the Shinwaris but would serve only in their own province. And several clans voted to ask the British Government to take over the administration of their country; they intended to offer hostages as a pledge of good faith.

On November 24, Sir Francis Humphrys met Amanullah for their first conversation since Jeshyn; Amanullah, having yielded temporarily the administration of government, was not accessible to ambassadors and ministers.

The folly of alienating the sympathies of all classes of his subjects simultaneously was the subject of Humphrys' discourse to Amanullah. He told him that priests, farmers, merchants and soldiers were seething with discontent at the new reforms which were being supported by increased taxation and forced contributions.

"The Shinwaris have been inflamed by my enemies the mullahs who are spreading false rumors about the nature of my reforms," said Amanullah.

"The mullahs are fighting for their existence," said Humphrys.

Humphrys then told Amanullah that his bombing from airplanes was not likely to make him popular with his subjects, especially since the persons dropping the bombs were Russians. "You are being accused by the tribesmen of offenses against Islam and the fact that you are employing professed atheists to bomb your people into submission will lend color to these accusations."

A few days later two Russian pilots dropped their bombs by mistake on Afghan Government troops, killing thirty soldiers and wounding many. The pilots were dismissed, but Amanullah's own soldiers were saying exactly what Humphrys predicted they would say.

In Jalalabad the officials nearly made the same mistake when a band of armed men approached. They almost fired on friendly Khugianis who were offering their services. But these were mistrusted by the military officer whom Amanullah sent to Jalalabad, Mohammed Gul. Convinced that these Khugianis were only looking for loot, Mohammed Gul sent them home and also halted the distribution of arms to various other tribesmen who had arrived as volunteers. He remembered that, a few days earlier, a hundred men sent to stop the rebels had secretly joined them instead.

In Kabul, Ghulam Siddiq asked Humphrys to remove Sher Agha from Gondal City in India to some point even farther from the Afghan frontier, since he was said to be collecting money for propaganda against Amanullah. There was no longer any prospect of compromise with Sher Agha. Humphrys unsympathetically reminded Ghulam Siddiq that he admitted in Afghanistan some persons doing propaganda against the British in India.

Ghulam Siddiq was, despite his travels and his sophistication, a man of the tribes. He shared their capacity for intense loyalties and animosities; he understood them in his bones. His father had been a hero to them. So Amanullah sent him into Shinwari country as his personal mediator.

Ghulam Siddiq fared better than the three men who had gone out from Jalalabad. He was admitted to the fort and allowed to speak. But he convinced no one. The British in the Khyber heard from an informer that the Shinwaris had told Ghulam Siddiq that he was fit only to deal with eunuchs and women. This report reached London, where urbane men at desks, who had heard of Ghulam Siddiq's ambitions toward the British lady in Mussoorie in 1920, wrote in their small, precise handwriting marginal memos which took pleasure in this verbal castrating.

In Jalalabad martial law was proclaimed by Gul Mohammed, who ordered the inhabitants of the city to prepare their own defenses by digging trenches around the cantonment. Every rustle from a distance sent the Jalalabadis into an alarm, for they had heard that the Shinwaris were planning to attack almost at once, and one story was that the Chaknawar Mullah, while holding the Mohmands in check as he promised, was encouraging the Shinwaris to attack Jalalabad in order to force the Afghan Government to accept his terms. It was chilly and a heavy rain was falling.

Gul Mohammed telephoned to Amanullah and demanded additional troops at once. Unless they came, he said, Jalalabad would be lost in three days.

But Kabul itself was in danger of being lost. Bacha Sacao had expanded his threat even further beyond that of a bandit. He was now a power; in the ferocity with which he attacked every outsider who entered Koh-i-Daman and fought off the government troops who tried to subdue him, Bacha Sacao was like an invading force. He no longer headed a band of outlaws. Men who considered themselves respectable had heard the rallying cry against the King who threatened their religion, and Bacha Sacao was so confident of success that he sent a message to Amanullah, not threatening to kill him, but announcing that he would.

Amanullah sent fifteen trucks of war material and eight mountain guns to Jalalabad. But he had to consider also the defense of Kabul. In the hope that peace would come before a pitched battle, he told Gul Mohammed to refrain from battle until December 1. On that day, if Jalalabad was still in jeopardy, he would unleash all the force he had.

Meanwhile he sent a tribal chief who had always been loyal to him, Mir Zaman of Kunar, to Jalalabad with his tribesmen in the hope that their influence would be as effective as their rifles. On arriving Mir Zaman took three regiments and a hundred men of the King's Guard to a place three miles from the Hadda gate to repulse the rebels there. Rain had been falling steadily for thirty-two hours.

On November 29 the Shinwaris swarmed toward Jalalabad and entered through the Kabul gate. By the time they reached the gate the government schools outside the city were in flames, smoldering and smelling because the rain had soaked the wood.

Fifty Shinwaris went into the British Consulate and closed the doors. The Consul, a Moslem from India, was there with six servants. He had also a guard of six Afghan soldiers, but when these soldiers saw the rebels pushing their way into the building, they hid their rifles and fled.

The Consul had been putting a message into code and still held the code book in his hand. The rebels informed him that they intended to loot the Consulate.

"My staff and I are the guests of King Amanullah and of the Afghan state." The Consul recognized some tribesmen whom he knew and appealed to them personally. He mentioned the sanctity of consulates, of which they knew nothing.

"Amanullah is an infidel," said the tribesmen, "and his guests are entitled to no consideration." They opened the safe and found three hundred rupees but no papers. They took chairs, tables, everything they could move, and went into the outbuildings to see what else was worth stealing. The Consul and his servants had to remove most of their clothes and see them carried off by the Shinwaris, who permitted each man to retain a shirt, a pair of trousers and a cap. Gasoline for motors was scarce and valuable but these tribesmen had a can which they had found in the garage. They poured this over the floors and when the Consul and his men saw them preparing to set fire, they fled into the garden. The Consul was still holding the code book. While his house burned a few feet away and no one was observing the actions of one already looted man, the Consul dug a hole and buried the British secret code.

He spent that night in the garden compound listening to the sounds of looting and burning. Amanullah's beautiful palace, with the graceful columns reflected in a pool, was in flames. So was the hotel. Every minute some new tribesmen came into the city to take what they wanted and burn the rest. A garage holding twenty lorries was burned; so was the airplane hangar and several planes were damaged. None of these things burned as brightly or as disastrously as they would have if the rains had not soaked everything.

In the Khyber Pass ammunition was being sold very cheaply. The tribesmen to whom the defenders of Jalalabad had issued it, in the expectation of help, had put it on the market.

At the first attack Mir Zaman had led his troops into the cantonment and shut the gate. The rebels left Jalalabad with their booty but they were still in the countryside, still a menace. They were not only on the side toward Shinwari country but had encircled the city to put themselves on the road to Kabul. And they had cut the telephone and telegraph lines leading to Kabul.

Amanullah would soon offer the throne of Afghanistan to Inayatullah, who would not want it.

CHAPTER 26

November 30, 1928, to December 16, 1928

Amanullah saw only one means of buying time to gather his forces against the Shinwaris: to buy off the other menace, Bacha Sacao.

In the east Ghulam Siddiq had been spending money freely and was managing, despite the attack on Jalalabad, to keep a fair amount of control for the Government. Bacha Sacao seemed fully as purchasable as the mullahs and the other leaders of the Eastern Province. His whole life had been an attempt to get money, never mind whose.

Bacha Sacao made the deal. He agreed to refrain from raiding for six months, and not to put any obstacles in the way of recruiting in Koh-i-Daman, which he had paralyzed. His reward was 400,000 rupees and in addition the rank of General in the Afghan Army and a number of rifles with which to arm his men.

It would have been a master stroke to put the two enemies, one from the north and one from the east, to fighting each other. Bacha Sacao as a high Army officer was quite believable. During the Khost Rebellion he had been brave and efficient before he deserted; there were men who recalled him for his legitimate exploits in the crack Qita Namuna Regiment as well as for his subsequent illegal ones. No one could dispute his gift for leadership; he had that combination of qualities which would later be known as "charisma."

Wali, who had been negotiating Afghanistan's "contract" with the bandit, even sent to Bacha Sacao one of the standard marks of courtesy. Just as it was customary for an Afghan visiting a home for the first time to carry a package of sweets, or for an American in certain circumstances to approach with a bottle of whiskey, Wali presented Bacha Sacao with an especially fine rifle, the currency of etiquette.

For a while the problem of Bacha Sacao seemed to vanish. One person in Amanullah's family already had defied successfully the challenge of Bacha Sacao. In the previous year, after his outburst of depredations in Koh-i-Daman, when he had fled to Peshawar, Ulya Hazrat had made a highly publicized visit to Koh-i-Daman to show that there was nothing to be afraid of.

Ulya Hazrat's strength, which her son Amanullah had not needed for such a long time, was still available, and her son needed it.

Amanullah was stunned. He was like a man who, through keeping his eye on a distant goal, has failed to see the ditch at his feet and has stumbled into it and broken his leg so that his great goal becomes, in an instant, unattainable. Only a few months ago he had been sitting with other kings and learning from them; he had come home, and suddenly he had to face what the kings of the Western world had never taught him about, but which a Western philosopher had defined: "Ignorance with spurs."

All the self-assurance of the past ten years, accumulated by steps that had led, in spite of detours, inexorably forward, vanished. Where, now, was the substance to justify it? From being an independent man Amanullah went to the support of his childhood. He was once again Ulya Hazrat's bright boy. And Ulya Hazrat, who had been living in the shadow of the modernity and initiative of Souraya, whose ways she hated, now had a use for all her powers.

Much of her power she drew from natural sources. "Superstition" had been Amanullah's word for them. Now she cast around to see if those sources could help her boy.

Faqirs, or holy madmen, were often seen in Kabul. Some of them carried oval begging bowls into which the devout put food or money. Some carried the curved ax that was a symbol of holiness, or, lacking an ax, a straw whisk for fanning flames that had the same shape as an ax blade. Rags were the common attire of a faqir, but they were stylized rags. Some women sewed together, very carefully, small bits of cloth of different colors, so that a faqir shimmered iridescently as he passed through the streets in what he would have sworn was the abasement of poverty.

Supernatural powers were credited to some of these faqirs, and because Ulya Hazrat was known to believe in such powers, all the news of faqirs was carried to her.

Now, while her world was shaking, she was told of an extraordinary faqir to be found in a mosque of Kabul meditating silently. It was his custom to remain silent for twenty-one days at a time. Then he would emerge for a day of speech before going back into another twenty-one days of silence. And on that one day his speech was said to be full of prophecy.

Ulya Hazrat sent for this faqir. He was just emerging from his silence, and would soon be inaccessible for another twenty-one days, so her servants were impatient to bring him hastily to her palace. He resisted. He did not know who this woman was who wished to see him. When brought at last before her, he showed remarkable innocence of all things political. He did not even know that the King of the country was named Amanullah.

Politely the faqir lowered his head and silently communed with the forces that Ulya Hazrat so respected. Then he lifted his head and told her that her son Amanullah would be put off the throne by Habibullah.

Habibullah was a common name in Afghanistan. What Habibullah? asked Ulya Hazrat. The faqir simply repeated "Habibullah," and she finally let him go.

That evening when Amanullah came to visit her, haggard from worry and lack of sleep, she demanded that he consider what man named Habibullah could be a threat to him. They could think of only one Habibullah with sufficient prestige, personality, intelligence, and another requisite against which Abdur Rahman had always guarded: distance from the control of the capital. He was Governor of Mazar-i-Sharif.

The proposal that Ulya Hazrat now made was something Amanullah had denounced in the mullahs. But he was too weary and spiritually weakened to resist anything as forceful as his mother. He recalled Habibullah from Mazar-i-Sharif and replaced him with Ghulam Siddiq's brother Abdul Aziz Charkhi. This new Governor was so fat that he would not have qualified for the Army under Amanullah's new rules, but efficiency was not what he was seeking.

Snow was falling in Kabul almost every day, and it was colder than usual for early December.

On one of the clear days, December 4, an airplane flew above the Shinwaris and dropped, instead of bombs as some planes were doing, the message:

"The King has sent my daughter also to Europe carrying on good work. This machine will do you no harm."

Hearing of this message, the British in Delhi wired, "Please let us know if it is regarded as emanating from any wide body of sympathy in Kabul or is individual message."

Another wire to the North-West Frontier Province said, "Estimate of effect of rebellion on our tribes may please be reported by telegram. We should like to know whether it is likely to produce serious unrest on our side and how far we are associated in eyes of tribes with injudicious reforms? Apart from perturbation at Amanullah's recent antics, please let us know how far you consider sympathies of tribes permanently alienated from present regime and how far developments on Afghan side of frontier are likely to be influenced by their attitude."

Mahmud Tarzi had once remarked to Humphrys, "The ways of the British are inscrutable, but they always seem to attain their own ends without compromising their dignity or their honor."

One reason for this success of the inscrutable West was the British Government's constant preoccupation with the opinion of the world. It did not wait for others to see the virtues of its actions and approve, but considered what actions would produce approval and direct its course, when not prevented by other aims, toward that. And a swing in the mood of these tribes of the North-West Frontier Province could commit British troops or could free them for other duty.

"It is difficult to prophesy," went the reply, "but so far reactions of rebellion on our tribes have been favorable to us. There are no indications of serious unrest and tribes do not associate us with His Majesty's reforms. They are inclined to regard Amanullah as an infidel but a definite pronouncement by mullahs is awaited by them. This does not mean their permanent alienation from Durani dynasty. Amanullah still has a *locus penitentiae*, but they would probably prefer to see him deposed in favor of a reactionary . . . Tradition of mutual help between Afridis and Shinwaris against either Kabul or India makes Afridis side with Shinwaris and many arms captured by Shinwaris have been deposited in Tirah for safekeeping . . . On December 5 the Mohmands put in a petition for permission to capture Dakka for the British. This was not due so much to hostility to Kabul as to belief that Dakka was lost to Kabul and Shinwaris, their traditional enemies, would get it first. Little interest at present being shown by the tribes further afield both north and south. It is significant that at a dinner given last night by my personal Indian assistant at which Wali of Swat and Afridi Nawab were present there was no mention at all of Kabul affairs. Present attitude of aloofness and disposition to regard rebellion as personal quarrel between King and Shinwaris should tend to localize rebellion and be favorable to Government of Afghanistan."

On the day this wire was sent, December 5, the Russian Ambassador in Kabul, Léonide Stark, was telling the Italian Minister that he had positive proof that the Government of India had instigated and was encouraging the Shinwari rebellion. A few days later *Aman-i-Afghan* hinted at the same, which would soon be echoed, in less veiled language, all over the world. Amanullah, addressing a group of tribal levies, said that the British Government were his friends and no one should believe the absurd stories that the rebellion was backed by the British.

This rumor against them was rather reassuring to the British when secret sources told them that on December 9 the Politburo of Russia "decided to instruct the Soviet Government to place troops in Central Asiatic Military District on a war footing, also to reinforce the Afghan frontier. [General] Dibenko was told to do a personal reconnaissance of Afghan border. As it is Soviet belief that we instigated the Afghan rebellion prior to a possible advance through that country, the above steps appear to be defensive measures rather than offensive ones."

Suspicions of a "possible advance" were limited to the Politburo. Other people were saying that the British wanted to keep Afghanistan a backward buffer state and therefore had taken steps to halt Amanullah's reforms.

In the South of France Nadir's brother Hashim called on the British Consul at Nice, J. W. Keogh, on December 7, and, handing in his card, told him that he and his brother were well known at the British Foreign Office.

Hashim asked the Consul to pass on to London this message: that he and Nadir had important information to communicate concerning the present conditions in Afghanistan, and that they might be returning to that country very shortly.

He requested that the Foreign Office send someone to Nice to talk matters over with Nadir and receive his information before their return to Afghanistan. The greatest secrecy was necessary, he said, and for that reason he and Nadir could not travel to Paris or to London.

The visitor from the Foreign Office should be one who spoke Persian or Urdu, Hashim added, for he did not speak French and could not explain himself properly in English.

When Humphrys heard this, he was harried by the rebellion and its rumors and trying to decide at what point he should evacuate the Legation. Curtly he wired back to London: "Nadir Khan: If he has anything to say, he can write it in English. I do not recommend any one official or otherwise should be sent to interview him without concurrence [of Kabul] which would probably be conveyed through me. Neither he nor his brothers should be given transit visas through India."

Nadir was told politely that no one was available to visit him. In a confidential inter-office memorandum the Foreign Office had written: "There is every reason to suppose that the brothers intend to return to Afghanistan to cooperate with the rebellious sections of the population."

No wheeled traffic had passed between the Khyber and Jalalabad since the Shinwaris first attacked. A camel caravan that had been caught in Jalalabad made gifts of food to the rebels and thereby bought a safe conduct to Landi Kotal. Some nomads got through by judiciously distributing a large quantity of raisins.

Between Kandahar and Chaman the road was open but truck drivers had gone to Chaman and stayed there. The Governor of Kandahar was trying to get trucks from India into Afghanistan by offering to pay for the empty running to Kandahar and twelve hundred Afghan rupees for the journey from Kandahar to Kabul. Warm new clothing had been issued to a regiment in Kandahar as a prelude to going to Kabul but there was no transport for them.

Amanullah asked to be allowed to purchase trucks in India. "This request has its comic side," said the India Office, remembering that Britain had been planning a gift of trucks to Amanullah until the Germans talked him into buying their trucks, and that he had prematurely scrapped his old ones.

Technically the Shinwaris had made a truce concerning Jalalabad, but in fact they were trying to get in, either overhead with scaling ladders or underground by tunneling. Mir Zaman fought them off but many of his men were killed, including his son.

Yawar Mahmud Khan, the officer in charge of frontier affairs, was sent with troops toward Jalalabad. He was halted by Shinwaris at Nimla, site of the famous garden of Shah Jehan, defeated and captured. Among the casualties were some of the magnificent cypresses which had stood for three hundred years against the background of the Safed Koh.

Then the two leaders of the Shinwaris, Alam and Afzal, issued to the world a manifesto signed by Alam but written by Afzal, who knew how to write:

> In the Name of God the Merciful and Beneficent.
>
> This proclamation is made to all Muslim brethren whether they belong to Afghanistan or elsewhere in the world.
>
> You might have heard that towards the east of Afghanistan there is a tribe known as Shinwaris, who have risen in revolt and have spread dissension and disorder and that the Government of Kabul have taken measures to suppress this revolt and have sent troops to enforce peace and order.
>
> For the information of my Muslim brethren and to remove any misapprehension, I acting on the proverb that "Hearing is not like seeing," have taken this opportunity to lay before them the following facts:
>
> (1) The tribe which has come forward, at the sacrifice of life and property, to fight the cause of righteousness . . . is the Shinwaris, its fighting strength is more than 20,000 . . . They have with the advice of their brethren, living in Safed Koh and in eastern Afghanistan, united themselves for this cause.
>
> (2) The first step taken by them was to reform their rulers, who were addicted to bribery and corruption and to the issuing of orders contrary to "Shara," e.g., to discontinue prayer, to shave off their beards and mustaches, to abandon purdah of their women and not to have any regard for Shariat. After this the Shinwari Lashkar invested a fort which contained troops and other ammunition of war and after slight resistance the fort fell into their hands with all that was therein.
>
> (3) As the shrine of Hazrat Akhunzada Sahib of Hadda is a sacred place and the meeting place of all the Ulemas and Sheikhs . . . they all collected there . . . conferred with the eastern tribes and came to an agreement to cancel the reforms . . . repugnant to Shariat and to murder Amir Amanullah who is lost. Accordingly in pursuance of this pact the Khugianis, who have a fighting strength of 20,000, attacked the Kabuli troops of 9,000 strong who had been sent as reinforcements and who had reached the limits of Nimla and defeated them and their officers are still prisoners. Their leader is Mahmud, a trusted General of Amir Amanullah.

(4). . . all connection of the Kabul Government has been severed, the eastern territories are now governed according to laws and rules of Shariat . . .

(5) The City of Jalalabad is still invested. Some supporters of the Afghan Government, who are enemies of Islam, are living in it. As the residents of the City cannot get out of it, the tribal troops cannot assault the City for fear of innocent men being killed . . .

(6) The cause of all this disturbance is not any personal motives of the tyranny of the rulers, but it is simply to remove these reforms which are heathenish . . . Accordingly, I would mention here the following instances of Amir Amanullah's irregularities:

(a) The framing of his own codes and disregarding Shariat.

(b) That no suit is to be entertained without documentary proof.

(c) The marrying of four wives, which is allowed by the Koran, has been limited to one wife.

(d) The forcible divorce of the wives of his officials.

(e) The cutting of the hair of the women, the discarding of the chaderi of the women and keeping naked their arms and breasts.

(f) The removal of purdah of women.

(g) The sending of grown-up girls to Europe.

(h) The changing of Friday and the day of Haj.

(i) The encouragement of bribery and corruption.

(j) The opening of theaters and cinemas and other places of amusements.

(k) On the day of the great jirga, Amir Amanullah uttered words disrespectful to Mohammed, the prophet of God, on whom be peace, in the presence of all the elders of Afghanistan. He has thus become a kaffir and deserves to be put to death.

(7) Before his return from Europe . . . he was introducing these reforms, which are against Shariat, secretly and politically . . . But after his return from Europe, he introduced his evil reforms publicly and as the population of Afghanistan generally belong to Hanfi sect they have made up their minds to dethrone him and murder him.

(8) . . . Islam contains all the elements required for civilization and religion . . . hence today the whole Afghanistan desires to unite and to free itself.

(9) . . . I assure my Muslim brethren that on the day Amanullah is deposed and some honest and faithful to Shariat King is selected by the whole of the people of Afghanistan in accordance

with the Shariat, then I shall be the first person to tender my allegiance to him. At present, I, Muhammad Alam Shinwari, with the consent of the well-known "Ulemas," without any personal motives, have undertaken to do all this for the glory of the religion.

(10) . . . our casualties do not reach to one hundred, because our fighting men know that this struggle of the people is for the "ghairat" of the religion. They do not wish to use their ammunition, which is intended for their enemies, against their own kith and kin.

(11) The Southern and Northern tribes know that the gathering of the Eastern tribes is for righteousness and therefore no one assists the Government and they are solidly with us.

(12) In order that nothing may remain secret and the real facts may be known to friends and foes alike, I propose to start a paper which will be called *Al Iman* to contradict the news which are published in *Aman* so that the Islamic brethren may know the future of the Afghan nations.*

Amanullah told Humphrys that he now agreed with him about the way to save Afghanistan.

"In order that I shall not be misunderstood again," he said, "I have determined not to permit, even if people ask for it, female education for twenty years. I shall allow mullahs to take over control again of the primary education. To stop this senseless civil war that is ruining my country I promise to do everything I can. It is useless to run the risk of force except in defense."

He knew in detail what the Eastern tribes were demanding as the price of ceasing their fight. Ghulam Siddiq had returned to Kabul with the ultimatum and the tribes had agreed, although no one trusted the agreement very much, to cease firing until they could get a reply.

The tribes insisted that Amanullah:

1. Divorce Queen Souraya.
2. Banish the Tarzi family from Afghanistan, with the exception of Mahmud Tarzi whom they wished to imprison.
3. Close all schools for girls.
4. Recall the Afghan girls who had been sent to Turkey.
5. Abolish all foreign legations except the British.
6. Abolish the new code of laws, the Nizamnamas.

* Many Afghans consider this manifesto a composition far beyond the literary skill of Afzal, who claimed to have written it.

7. Reduce taxes.
8. Abolish the laws pertaining to European dress.
9. Restore purdah in its previous form.
10. Make Islamic law the law of the land.
11. Give the mullahs a place in the Government.

About the fifth demand, the British heard that its exception in their favor was "due to the fact that the British during the past seven years have not attempted to exploit Afghanistan to their own advantage as the Germans have done, and also that the British Legation has taken no part in wine-drinking or dancing parties, nor has given any encouragement whatsoever to social revolutions introduced by the Afghan Government." Afghans more liberal than the tribesmen had been impressed by the dignity which the British always maintained in public, even when it expanded into aloofness. Another point in favor of the British: they were there. The Eastern tribesmen had looked to them for help and would look again.

The hatred inspired by Queen Souraya's emancipation was a shock to Amanullah. In later years the story would go around that a composite photograph had been circulated in the mountains which showed Souraya's head superimposed on the body of a nearly naked dancing girl; this would be cited as proof of British involvement, since a composite photograph takes a certain amount of technical craft. Yet the Queen's face was not well known to the tribesmen, and a photograph of a brunette dancing girl could have been passed off as Souraya without alteration. There was another explanation for the story being told among the Shinwaris, how Amanullah had taken his Queen around Europe naked. This was the wide disparity between European evening dress and Afghan tribal costume. Fashions in Europe had not achieved the scarcity of the strapless evening gown which, when its wearer was seated behind a table and a bowl of flowers, was nowhere in sight. Souraya was photographed in décolleté evening dress with no sleeves; in the mountains of Afghanistan, this was the same as being naked.

To anyone who knew Amanullah, there never was any idea that he would divorce Souraya. But some British officials, considering the reports in Delhi, formed a theory purely from their imagination. They knew that Ulya Hazrat disliked Souraya (Lady Humphrys, who referred to Ulya Hazrat as Kuku, called it hatred), and they wondered if Amanullah's mother might solve that problem by killing his wife.

If Mahmud Tarzi had had any influence, he would have used it in a direction approved by the tribesmen by modifying Amanullah's pace toward reform. This was the end of the road which Mahmud Tarzi had set upon when, after so much trouble and humiliation, he had left Turkey for Afghanistan.

Even while Amanullah studied this list of demands, the Chaknawar Mullah was sending word to mullahs in Kabul that nothing would really satisfy the tribes except the departure of Amanullah.

Bacha Sacao was impressively tall; his eyes were penetrating and flashing; his beard was luxuriant and always carefully trimmed. There would be times when his photograph, taken when he was wearing the accouterments of affluence, would be mistaken for that of Nadir. He had great intelligence, sharpened by many complexities of life and a keen perception in seeing the relations between things and in expressing those relations with a quick wit.

He deserved more from life than the expected fate of a son of a poor water-carrier in Kohistan.

In 1928 Bacha Sacao was nearly forty years old, or approximately Amanullah's age; no record of births was kept in Afghanistan, and certainly no illiterate family ever noted the date when a new child arrived. When Amanullah had come to power, Bacha Sacao had been almost thirty, and although Amanullah had begun at once his move toward universal education and opportunity for all, the new order came too slowly and spottily to do anything for Bacha Sacao.

To a man in his position who felt surging in himself powers and abilities that his present life could not fulfill, there was only one way in which to become an effective man, and that was the way which Bacha Sacao took.

Everything in his career indicated, however, a yearning to be a respectable part of the establishment. He performed well in the crack regiment during the Khost Rebellion, deserting only when he was convinced that Amanullah was indeed an infidel. Later he captured a bandit less efficient than himself and brought him to the authorities, naïvely expecting to be a hero, only to find that to the authorities he was a deserter with a stolen rifle.

Even in his banditry he had, by distributing his loot judiciously, made himself more than a thief. Robin Hood had enjoyed a certain status in medieval England; so did Bacha Sacao in Kohistan. Yet he would have relinquished this status in order to enter again the society he had known for only part of his life, that of respectable men. Then he had somehow become attached to that venerable symbol of authority, the Tagao Mullah, who created his own society and had assured Bacha Sacao that in defending him against Amanullah he became one of the elect.

What Bacha Sacao had always wanted was now in his possession. The rank of General may have meant far more to him than the money Amanullah gave him, for he never had trouble getting money, but the title and the King's assurance meant a place for him among men who mattered. Bacha Sacao at last was truly somebody.

The telephone service between Kohistan and Kabul, equipped to handle only official messages, was of a party-line type. There were several extensions, but they were all linked up so that only one conversation was possible at a time. A lift of the receiver of any telephone along the line would permit a listener to hear what was being said between Kohistan and Kabul by anyone else. This was the line on which Amanullah communicated with the man who was handling the negotiations which made Bacha Sacao a General.

Some time around December 12 Amanullah and this man talked, congratulating each other on the removal of Bacha Sacao as a menace. And Amanullah said, with a laugh, something that indicated that he regarded the truce with the bandit only as a temporary measure until the Shinwari problem could be settled. To the King of Afghanistan a real alliance with a bandit was preposterous; perhaps he thought that Bacha Sacao had entered upon this agreement as cynically as he himself did. Anyone listening to that conversation would know that Amanullah had no respect for Bacha Sacao, who had not won any position with his armistice, and that Bacha Sacao had no future within the law.

Bacha Sacao was listening on one of the extensions.

Among the lower classes of many societies, and even among classes not so low, a romantic illusion often hovers about the pinnacles of power and prestige. Being so far removed from the people of these pinnacles, a poor man tends to feel that the superiority of the possessions of the high and mighty must be accompanied by the same superiority in feeling and character. A poor water-carrier's son who had reached up to those pinnacles would be dashed down by the sudden knowledge that it had all been a pretense. There was a practical aspect to the information that Bacha Sacao had got on the telephone extension, but equally shocking was the disillusionment with his King and the loss of his own dream.

On December 14 Bacha Sacao attacked Kabul.

He came down from Koh-i-Daman with his old friend and lieutenant, Sayed Hussein, and a man from Tagao and between two thousand and three thousand tribesmen, all brandishing rifles, some of which had been given to them by the government against which they now planned to fire.

Traveling from Koh-i-Daman to Kabul is a matter of unfolding scenery. First the hills enclose the traveler into one view, then, as he journeys through each pass, he is enclosed by different mountains and he looks at a different view. Bacha Sacao and his men moved southward, crying out, "Allah-o-Akbar!" ("God is Great!") while many mullahs rode among them on horseback, cheering them ahead with their own well-informed shouts to Allah, and while banners fluttered from poles they carried. They passed from view to view and finally were looking at the hill known as Bagh-i-Bala where Abdur Rahman had built a small palace of domes and columns, which had been a military hospital and now was neighbor to a fort. The men in the fort were outnumbered by the rebels, who took Bagh-i-Bala with ease.

At the British Legation east of Bagh-i-Bala, a handsome house whose heavy doors shut out all ideas that one was in Afghanistan and created another England, the news was known before it reached Kabul. Humphrys was saying good-bye to the French Minister Feit, who had come to discuss the prospect of revolution in Kabul itself and its effect on the Europeans in the city. Every foreigner was frantic with the fear that the rebels, blaming their troubles on outsiders, might rise and kill every person in sight who was not an Afghan.

B. J. Gould, Humphrys' second-in-command, entered the paneled library where Lady Humphrys was reading. He asked where the Minister was, saying with the legendary British understatement that an interesting situation had arisen on Bagh-i-Bala which he might like to see.

"It's begun," Humphrys said when he heard. Feit jumped into his car and drove rapidly back to his own Legation.

Lady Humphrys in her diary for December 14 wrote: "We all stand outside and watch the taking of the fort, which is a leisurely proceeding. Bacha Sacao's men begin marching along the main road to Kabul but gradually a large crowd collects at the corner shops and I see it sweep across to our further gate. I dash down to find Minister and hear his voice from the front porch, 'Shut the gate.' The scene then becomes one of racing orderlies, while an attendant locks the big gates.

"Our Afghan guards press their rifles into the unwilling hands of the orderlies who, however, are forced by Minister to return them and the guards vanish under the nearest cover and are seen no more. Next news of them is that they are sitting under the back wall with their rifles buried.

"The mob is now at our gates and the Minister goes out to face them."

Bacha Sacao himself was at the gate of the British Legation. He spoke with passion to Humphrys, telling him that King Amanullah was an infidel and that he intended to kill him and set up an administration of his own.

"This is the British Legation and we are the guests of your country," Humphrys spoke to Bacha Sacao exactly as the British Consul in Jalalabad had spoken to the Shinwaris there. But Bacha Sacao's reply was different from the Shinwaris'.

"I have no quarrel with you," he said.

Humphrys warned Bacha Sacao that he must respect all Legations, and Bacha Sacao repeated this order to his men. He forbade them to loot.

Leaving a guard at the Legation gate, Bacha Sacao moved on with his cheering men toward Kabul. Soon the guard moved on with them. Later in the day a member of the British Legation was trying to fight his way against the tide of advancing bodies back to the Legation from Kabul; Bacha Sacao saw him and sent an escort to take him home.

Amanullah was astounded when, in early afternoon, he got the news of the attack and when, by four o'clock, he could hear from the palace the firing to the north. Assured that Bacha Sacao would no longer be a menace, he had felt secure enough to send more troops to Jalalabad. Planes had flown above Koh-i-Daman dropping leaflets proclaiming that the bandit and the government were at peace. *Aman-i-Afghan* had published a sentimental article sighing that even a bandit's heart could be touched by the plight of his country.

Now, in the afternoon of December 14, Bacha Sacao led his men and mullahs from Bagh-i-Bala, close to the magazine where the military ammunition was stored, farther toward the city.

Amanullah had no more than fifteen hundred regular troops in Kabul and could not summon back quickly those who had gone to Jalalabad because the telephone and telegraph lines were cut. A regiment had come from Mazar-i-Sharif, bringing eight machine guns and 2,100,000 rupees. About five hundred irregulars from Hazarajat and about two hundred or three hundred from the Southern Province had come as auxiliaries, and a detachment was expected from Kandahar.

Eighteen students at the military schools saved Kabul from capture that day. As the unruly tribesmen walked past the school, the cadets opened fire and, in the narrow road, performed the same service that in ancient Roman days Horatio had performed at his famous bridge. The time that these young men, fighting for knowledge as opposed to ignorance, gained for Amanullah was half an hour, but it sufficed until eighty members of the Royal Guard could take over the defense. The Royal Guard fought for two hours after which Bacha Sacao and his men were sufficiently bloodied to retire to the village of Kolala Pushta and to Habibia College. By that time Amanullah's men had brought up one weapon which the rebels did not have: a big cannon. A few shots from this, well-aimed, sent Bacha Sacao back toward Bagh-i-Bala. It was getting dark, anyway.

At the first sound of rifle fire, all the shopkeepers in the bazaar had put up their shutters and gone home. The schools were closed. The gates of Amanullah's palace, the Arg, were shut. People began to dig holes to bury their valuables, but the ground was frozen, for this distress had come upon Kabul in a month of unreasonable early and bitter cold.

During the next day the rebels were boasting that they had captured two more forts and that reinforcements would arrive soon from Tagao, whereupon they would occupy the city proper. This did not happen. Instead, they felt the effects of another weapon available only to the Government. Three airplanes dropped bombs on them, killing two men. The tribesmen reacted just as the people in Kabul had done toward the British planes in 1919; they fired their rifles skyward.

The wireless in Kabul had stopped operating in the middle of a sentence in a message from the British Legation to Peshawar. The break was ominous to the Government of India. Forewarned of trouble, they knew that, in Humphrys' words, it had begun.

Although the wireless functioned again, the British Legation was still incommunicado, for the telegraph office was in the heart of Kabul, separated from the British Legation by a mass of fighting men. No one could get through with the messages.

Bacha Sacao again rescued the British Legation from a predicament.

He sent one of his own men to escort its orderly to the wireless office with messages, and such were the intricacies and confusions of the situation that this escort from the rebel leader got the orderly into an office operated by Amanullah's government. He gave in his messages, but they were laid aside and not sent for some time. The Legation would complain later that telegraph signals kept going toward Russia while their own messages were ignored.

When the telegrams did get through, Humphrys arranged to receive news at certain hours from Peshawar on his own receiving set. He cautioned Peshawar to remember that others might be listening, that a message like "Jalalabad has not yet fallen" might be interpreted as the expectation of Jalalabad's fall and encourage the theory that the British were responsible for the uprising.

This theory was making the British Legation unsafe; Amanullah's men were causing far more damage there than the rebels.

"I do not think hits [from guns] on Legation were deliberate," Humphrys said later, "and most could not have been observed from soldiers in gun emplacements owing to intervention of trees. On other hand, many rifle shots fired into Legation were deliberate. These came chiefly from a building held by undisciplined Mangals. It was observed that these men shot down many royal cavalry who were on their own side. I have no reason to suspect that any of the shooting into the Legation was done under orders from Afghan officers . . . Another reason for King's troops firing into the Legation with rifles was probably due to an entirely unfounded suspicion that some of the rebels were inside our grounds. The fact that loyalist troops did in fact enter our grounds on several occasions would strengthen this suspicion. One of the King's soldiers was killed and at least three wounded severely before they could be expelled from inside Legation grounds."

It was soon apparent that the only soldiers who had any enthusiasm for protecting their King were his own bodyguard. Some soldiers had actually gone over to Bacha Sacao. Men came into Kabul from the surrounding territory and were asked to take part in the city's defense. Rifles were handed out to these, with two hundred rounds of ammunition for each rifle.

Amanullah had stockpiled, a few years earlier, a large number of rifles. They were part of a shipment from Russia which had come into Kabul by several caravans of mules, all at night, and the British Legation had posted men in the shadows to count the mules to estimate how many rifles were coming. Now these were brought out. They were unwrapped, and people saw that the paper in which they were packed had Russian writing on it. The story would spread, because of this, that Russia was backing Amanullah with arms.

On the third day of fighting Lady Humphrys wrote in her diary: "Region around our gates is very hot. Secretary dashes in to say that two men waving German flags are trying to get in. Beitz and Kutz arrive with messages from German Legation where the German colony is collected. Report that all quiet there. That danger was only in crossing road from the vineyards. Battle continues too fiercely for them to return. Power House Mistri comes in to report trouble at gate where rebels, who are now attacking Nau Burja [a fortified village] from which they had been fired upon, are demanding entrance. They say they require oil, obviously because they want to burn down the Burja. The Power House Mistri offers them oil in a saucer but they beg for lamp oil. Minister and secretary go out to gate. Minister, as usual pipe in hand, explains that we cannot let them in nor supply oil. They ask how we light our houses and when we say by electricity are disconcerted. They then disperse and the battle rages anew and continues all night. Minister walks around house all night and the east wing does not sleep much.

"Before retiring for night, Minister, who has revised plans owing to change in situation, 3,000 tribesmen in retreat being now around the British Legation, explains that he will not fight if an entry is forced. Baits in the way of loot are left downstairs and the arsenal is removed from our bathroom. We do not undress."

Meanwhile the precious ammunition that Amanullah had issued to the newcomers was being wasted. The men, having in their hands fine rifles and bullets which did not cost them anything, did not wait for the appearance of an enemy but kept firing into the air. Ordinary citizens stayed indoors, wondering at each shot if Bacha Sacao had come closer. Occasionally a man would go out to beg the other men to stop shooting, to point out that a stray bullet might strike a child. Town criers with drums went around calling out the same plea. No one minded. To many of these tribesmen, fighting that did not involve their own emotions was a festival.

A rumor went around to disturb Kabul even more: that a member of the royal family had deserted to Bacha Sacao. The deserter was not royal. He was Ghulam Mohammed, the blunt soldier, who had been a member of the delegation at Rawalpindi in 1919. He came from Tagao; his sister had been Inayatullah's mother, and now he was abandoning Amanullah to return to Tagao to try to put his nephew Inayatullah on the throne with Bacha Sacao's help.

Ghaus-ud-din, the Ahmedzai Ghilzai, who traveled and traded and looked like a bundle of rags with a beard and sharp black eyes, came to Kabul. He had helped Amanullah in devious ways during the Khost Rebellion, and now Amanullah gave a rifle to each of the two hundred men Ghaus-ud-din brought with him, and they left, but, as in the earlier rebellion, no one was sure what side he was on. A man observing him said later:

"[Ghaus-ud-din] left for his own country abusing the Amir Sahib and took no part in the action against Bacha Sacao. People's opinions regarding him were divided. Some said that, as in the Mangal Rebellion he had rendered great services to the Amir and had been inadequately rewarded, he was displeased with and opposed to the Amir, and it was for this reason that he had deserted after taking the rifles, with the intention of raising a rebellion in his own country against the Amir. Others thought that he was a very cunning man and that he went to his country in order to raise [troops] for the Amir Sahib under the latter's orders. On the way we heard that in order to allay the suspicion with which his tribe regarded him he had taken an oath on the Koran at the shrine of the Hazrat Umar Benais that he was one with his tribe."

This same man reported also:

"In the course of the fighting when the Bacha Sacao's lashkar retired from the Shahri-i-Ara Burja [Fort], I saw about eighty corpses scattered about, which were said to be those of Kohistanis. The Amir's troops cut the heads off three or four of these in my presence and tying the headless trunk of one on a motorcycle took it through the city. I heard that one of the Bacha Sacao's men in the uniform of the [King's guard] had made an entrance into the Arg but was immediately seized and killed. It was said that he had entered the Arg with the intention of assassinating the Amir Sahib and was the brother of the man whose corpse had been taken around the city tied to the motorcycle."

Amanullah had Gul Agha and Masum brought from prison and told them they were free on condition that they talk with the Tagao Mullah and try to detach him from the cause of Bacha Sacao. He also sent another emissary to India to tell Sher Agha that his brother had been released.

At almost the same time Sher Agha sent a friend toward the frontier on the secret mission of getting news of Gul Agha.

And also at this time British intelligence on the frontier decided that the Shinwari Rebellion was not an isolated incident but part of a wide conspiracy.

CHAPTER 27

December 18, 1928, to January 14, 1929

The man who loves power for its own sake has a great advantage over the man who regards power only as a means of achieving something else. There are many ways in which to exercise power. When life, with a sudden jolt to the fortunes, makes its exercise impossible in one direction, often there is another way to power and another object on which to use it, if power is all one wants.

Amanullah did not have this consolation.

Even now he had the possibility of remaining the first Afghan among the Afghans; he could have salvaged power within the limits set by the mullahs and still have wielded far more power than most men. But it had never been his ambition merely to reign in Afghanistan, not even to rule it. What he had wanted was to lead Afghanistan toward what he thought was good for her.

The classic style for a monarch in his situation would be to send forth a challenge, to hurl defiance at those who had defied him and press on to victory. But Amanullah knew, like everyone else, that victory would not restore the climate in which his desire could be fulfilled. That climate was forever destroyed.

Two months after Amanullah had cried out, "Advance, Afghanistan!" he had nowhere to go.

On the fourth day of the siege of Kabul by Bacha Sacao, Amanullah finally did what everyone had expected him to do the first day: he addressed his subjects. His mother prodded him to it. Dispirited, the King who had delighted in talking to his subjects, either in ceremonial gatherings or as individuals, was embarrassed to face them. He had nothing to say.

Ulya Hazrat, however, was one who liked power itself and would fight for it. She had spoken to Afghans whenever her speech was needed, even though custom demanded that she veil her face while doing so. It was unthinkable to her that her son could depart from the accepted behavior of sovereigns. Her whole life was cast in the old heroic mold.

She told Amanullah that he could not continue to hang around the palace like a woman, that he was a man and a king, and he could no longer delay showing himself to his people and acting like their leader.

Amanullah went out of the palace on foot. Only a small guard accompanied him. He walked into the public gardens nearby, where a great many men had been waiting in the hope of some word from their King. It would have been easy to overlook him if the whisper had not gone around that the King was in the crowd. In his days of hope, Amanullah had made good use of drama. Now, when a flourish to stir the imagination was most needed, he seemed to be deliberately avoiding drama. He had many costumes, with which he had dazzled Europe. But on this day he wore the most drab of them all, a dull gray military uniform. The day also was dull gray.

Amanullah looked around him for a place to stand. He saw a pedestal which held a flowerpot. Removing the pot, he stepped on the pedestal and spoke.

He told his people that it was up to them whether they wished to be captured or not, that these bandits would loot their homes and rape their women, and that salvation was in their own hands. He had ordered arms and ammunition to be distributed. Only those who stood close could hear him. His voice had no resonance; his words sagged like the lines of his face. No one would have recognized the man of that five-day speech in October.

An elderly man spoke up. He said that a long time ago he had tried to warn Amanullah what would happen if he did not slow the pace of his reform, but that an official—and he indicated a man standing nearby as the person he meant—had prevented him from seeing the King. A second man spoke up and said the same.

These remarks irritated Amanullah. He would not listen to more, but stepped down from the pedestal and walked back into the palace. That was his sole public appearance in Kabul during the crisis of his life.

On December 21 he sent the women of his family and seven children to Kandahar by plane. Souraya and Nur-us-Seraj were both pregnant and they went for safety. Ulya Hazrat went as a warrior. Already the walls of Kandahar were posted with messages from Amanullah begging for aid from his "Mama Khel" or his maternal uncles. This was the home of Ulya Hazrat's family, and she went to exert to the utmost all the influence of her birthright and her nature.

As the plane lifted into the air, it dropped a flare to inform Amanullah that Queen Souraya on this occasion had overcome her fear of flying and had not backed down the ladder.

Ghulam Siddiq was on the plane also, carrying a large sum of money. He was going as the advance wave of a move that seemed dreadful but with every day more probable: the transfer of the government from Kabul to Kandahar. Even now the various legations in Kabul were debating whether they should move with the government, and looking up the precedents of similar situations in other countries.

Two legations, those with most stake in Amanullah's fate, were looking even further into the future. On December 18 in Moscow the Politburo decided to offer him sanctuary if he needed it. Five days later a message from the British in Baluchistan to Delhi treated the same possibility in more detail: "In view of . . . remote possibility of Amanullah's seeking asylum in British territory, presume he shall not be debarred entry. In that event it would be as well to be prepared beforehand, and I would suggest that he should be immediately removed from the frontier and sent by special train to Karachi or any other place which Government of India may decide upon."

Although Amanullah had discarded, before the conflict, most of the psychological weapons that should have been available to him, still he had one valuable resource. Most of the slaves in Afghanistan at the time of his accession had been Hazaras; when in 1920 he proclaimed an end to slavery, it was they who entered a new life. In the previous century the Hazaras had rebelled against Amir Abdur Rahman, who put them down with a severity that was extreme even for him, and who always had an unreasoning dislike of Hazaras. Their slanting eyes and Mongolian cheekbones gave them the high visibility which is an inducement to being disliked as a class.

The Hazarajat, where they lived in Central Afghanistan, was painfully rugged, yet it had tufts of grass where sheep might graze in the summer, and these tufts aroused the acquisitiveness of the Ghilzais, who had yet another grievance against the Hazaras in that they worshipped Allah in a slightly different manner. They were Shiahs, in contrast to most Afghans who were Sunnis. A religious and economic feud was constantly causing trouble between the Hazaras and various groups of Ghilzais, usually those of the Suleiman Khel. The Afghan Government settled these disputes, and since the Hazaras were the party with most to gain by an equitable settlement, they had cause for gratitude. For this, and for his tolerance of their Shiah faith, and for their freedom, the Hazaras were loyal to Amanullah.

In his season of need, the Hazaras offered him men, and he sent a general into the Hazarajat to work with them. They did not like the general and sent Amanullah a message that they would take no leader less than one of his own brothers. The half brother whom he sent them was Amin Jan, who had just returned from the school in Germany. With no military experience Amin Jan became the leader of several thousands of Hazaras. He loved and respected them, and they returned him affection with equal respect, although he was only seventeen years old. Amin Jan was clever and resourceful and his devotion to Amanullah, to whom he also owed a new world, was unquestioned.

Ali Ahmed's loyalty, on the other hand, always had been doubtful and his opinion of Amanullah's reforms was not a great deal higher than the mullahs'. But he understood the men of the Pathan tribes, and so Amanullah sent him toward Jalalabad, where some optimism was being stirred by stories of the rebel tribes' falling out among themselves. Snow kept falling around Kabul and reached the depth of two feet, so Ali Ahmed kept postponing the difficult journey through the gorge. On the road to Ghazni men were being offered six hundred rupees per stage to clear the snow.

On the day of Amanullah's appearance in the garden, December 18, a bullet struck Bacha Sacao. He fell from his horse in the sight of his comrades in arms and many of his enemies. In almost no time the news of his fall was being told all over Kabul. On the whole, more prayers were said for his recovery than for his demise, for Afghans admire physical courage and forty years later he would be described by men whom he had injured as "a brave warrior."

Bacha Sacao was hit in the backbone by a fragment of shell, suffering a deep cut. His men took him to Paghman and put him in Amanullah's own summer home.

A day would come when Bacha Sacao would tell an anecdote about the arrival of a surgeon from the British Legation to treat his wound. This story would enter the legends of Afghanistan and would be taken

as evidence that the British had deliberately put Bacha Sacao in Amanullah's path.

If the British paid this tribute to the rebel leader in return for his
favor, they would have been acting to protect the British Legation not
only for their personal survival but as a defense against a catastrophe
to the British Empire. They would have thought they were even serving
to prevent another World War.

Looking into the possibilities of the future, Humphrys saw a chain
of events which, if the first event was allowed to take place, would go
on inexorably to disaster.

"We should inevitably demand reparation if any members of the Legation were killed," Humphrys described this series of events, "and
under present conditions Amanullah would be unable to give it and it
appears to me that war would then be inevitable. Our Legation in
Kabul is thus a hostage to fortune."

In those telegrams that finally reached India, it had been arranged
for a plane to fly from Peshawar at a certain time on December 18
and circle over the Legation. In preparation for its arrival, symbols in
white cloth were arranged on the ground meaning, "All well. Do not
land. Fly very high."

"Heavy shelling," read Lady Humphrys' diary for one day, "and three
shells hit the house between 9 and 10:30. Very disturbing to Minister's
ablutions and the shell is afterwards found to have come within nine
inches of the bath . . . Corridor windows becoming unhealthy . . .
Mangals try to take shelter in councilor's house and doctor's house,
where one mortal casualty is left. A wounded man is found in councilor's kitchen. Our orderlies patrol to keep the combatants off British
territory."

A group of Mangals, who were fighting for Amanullah, kept firing
behind a wall near the Legation gate. Lady Humphrys recorded, "The
Mangals fire at every one and in reply to a message from the Minister
say that they will fire at any one they see. Bacha Sacao's men, however,
cease fire when our airplane comes over on receiving notice that it is
ours and do not fire on our people."

The next day she wrote, "Glorious weather and fortunately warmer,
although heavy snowfall might dampen enthusiasm. Our garden man
has continued to drive his two donkeys about our garden, each day with
complete unconcern, but the day has come when there is only one

donkey left. No messages through to Kabul wireless for three days now as our men have not been able to get through the cordon."

On December 21 Bacha Sacao sent a message to the British Legation, which he seemed to be taking under his protection, to the effect that no one should leave the grounds that day. He was recovered sufficiently to take part in the fighting again. Emissaries from Amanullah were going to Bagh-i-Bala with a Koran, which was the symbol of armistice as a white flag was in the West. But Bacha Sacao did not intend to make peace. He said he would force his way into Kabul that day.

He did not. He retreated to Bagh-i-Bala and the troops around the British Legation were government men.

"I see King's men trying to break down the gates," wrote Lady Humphrys, "and rush to warn [the Legation staff]. In another second they are in and, led by an officer, are charging for the big house. Minister goes out. A soldier levels his rifle but the officer dashes it down. Minister commands them to leave British territory and the officer calls off his men. But it takes an hour to clear them all out, and Minister has to go out so often that relays of tobacco are necessary. Nothing calms our servants so much as the Minister's pipe or so disarms the invaders . . .

"We women and children are sent to our rooms when the gates are broken in and our only consolation at the critical moment is the arrival of our airplane which is a great moral support. A Russian plane [an Afghan plane piloted by a Russian] comes over and complicates the situation as we fear it may drop bombs and cause Bacha Sacao to suspect us of double dealing. From now on a Russian airplane always goes up to watch ours when it comes over."

This British plane did drop something on the people of Kabul: leaflets reminding them of the sanctity of Legations with the warning, "Should, however, staffs or premises of English Legation or consulates be subjected to any acts of aggression at your hands, British Government will exact the fullest retribution for any damage done to them or their property."

Although Amanullah did not openly condemn the British as the instrument of his undoing, still he was not in a friendly mood toward them. The Russians, whose Embassy was in the city and therefore not cut off, were showing far more sympathy and an additional military attaché had arrived, while planes were still carrying mails between Kabul and Termez. Moreover, the Russians had been sending him bombs and airplane gasoline, and signed on December 24 an agreement to send him sixteen airplanes with spare parts by the end of the following April, as well as a great deal of artillery. The British were still trying to make up their minds about letting him buy trucks in India.

The people on whom these British leaflets fell reacted with quite as much bitterness as Amanullah; he and they thought it a violation of Afghan sovereignty to threaten reprisals independently. Moreover, the Russian Ambassador once picked up a wounded soldier of Amanullah and carried him in his car to the hospital for treatment. The people contrasted this with the closed gates at the British Legation and the indifference toward the wounded or dead soldiers found there.

"It may be necessary with help of tribal escort to evacuate ladies and children to Peshawar if, as seems probable, Amanullah is deposed and weather conditions make flying impossible," Humphrys told the Government of India. "Might have to travel under protection of tribes whom I could trust via Panjshir, Tagao, Laghman and Mohmand plains if ordinary route is unsafe."

In their desperation to save their Legation from "an incident in the history of the British Empire which in its developments might easily prove catastrophic," some of the British considered accepting the aid of a Shinwari tribesman whom Humphrys described, without irony, as "a man of the world."

Sometime in the 1880s an actor from Australia visited the Middle East and was impressed by the resemblance between the deserts there and the vast stretch of barren space which Australians called "the Outback." It occurred to him that there, also, camels might serve as transportation. The result was the importation of many camels, along with their drivers, many of whom were Afghan.

One of the most successful of all was a Sangu Khel Shinwari named Abdul Wahid who was called "the Camel King of Australia." Abdul Wahid learned to speak English fluently, although his accent was always pure Australian. He gave himself the English name of Mr. Wade, and returned to his native country with his son by an Australian wife and a large sum of money. Like Bacha Sacao, he intended to make himself a member of the establishment in the place where he had always been a nobody. Unlike the bandit, he had an entrée to that establishment in a plan to develop the minerals of Afghanistan, of which there were many legends although lapis lazuli was the only mineral really found abundantly, and that was so plentiful that one bathroom in the royal palace was covered in tiles cut from the pale blue, less desirable veins.

In 1925 the British Military Attaché's Diary had said, "Abdul Wahid visited the Legation during the week in order to obtain a visa for India . . . He is still uncertain about the result of his mining venture at Kandahar, the decision regarding which will be made by those in England who are financially interested. He intends to accept the position of Khan of Kunar and to exploit the timber and other wealth which he believes is there in abundance."

Then Abdul Wahid had repeated a theme familiar to the British: "It is his avowed intention to use his whole influence in support of the British connection and in this he is convinced that he will be assisted by Nadir, with whom he had spent some days in Paris last year."

But Abdul Wahid achieved none of his grandiose ambitions. The mining project fell through, and he lost £10,000 he had given the Afghan Government. The opportunity to accept the position of Khan of Kunar was never his, for Amanullah gave it to Mir Zaman, the man who was now defending Jalalabad for him. Again like Bacha Sacao, Abdul Wahid was disappointed and ready for revenge.

He was in Peshawar when Bacha Sacao attacked Kabul, and there he made a proposition to the Commissioner of the North-West Frontier Province who on December 18 wired to the Government of India: "Safety of Legation has been guaranteed by Abdul Wahid Shinwari, alias Mr. Wade Australian, in his offer to go to rescue of airmen [of British plane that had crashed near Jalalabad] provided he is permitted to go to Kabul. His great influence with the Chaknawar Mullah and also with rebel leaders is well-known, as well as his bitter hostility to the present Amir. He pressed for assurance the British Government will refrain from interfering on behalf of Amanullah provided Legations are not harmed. Circumstances would appear to justify my permitting him to go. He should start this evening."

But the Government of India had no intention of giving such flattering terms to Abdul Wahid Shinwari alias Mr. Wade Australian. "We leave it to your discretion to employ Abdul Wahid as also any other tribal agent . . . You doubtless realize supreme importance of avoiding any action capable of being construed as political engagement or encouragement. All inducements should be confined strictly to cash basis. This means that Abdul Wahid cannot be given assurances he asked for."

Government of India did not think it needed this man, anyway. A later wire from Peshawar said, "That it is unlikely that insurgents will harm British Legation is the general opinion in Peshawar and among frontier tribes. Provided no foreign power intervenes they are confident of being able to dethrone Amanullah and will do their best to avoid giving cause for interference to British Government." In Peshawar also the safety of the British Legation was worth cooperation with the rebels.

Amanullah also saw the danger that lay in possible injury to the Legation—he did not know how close he had come to fresh disaster when that soldier had aimed his rifle at Humphrys—and so consented for British planes to fly from India to remove the foreign women and children. At five-thirty on the cold morning of December 23 Lady Humphrys and the other women of the British Legation set out by foot toward the Italian Legation, which was close to the field where the plane would land. Afghan soldiers sent by Amanullah escorted them. From the French and German Legations other women were setting forth, and from Amanullah's own palace his wife's Romanian dressmaker and his children's German nurse were departing. They went by back roads and winding ways, for the main road was not safe. This was a period of comparative interlude in the fighting, but still there were snipers.

The pilot left behind a wireless transmitting set for the British Legation. Amanullah knew about this; it violated the terms of his treaty with Great Britain, but he was too harassed to object.

The following day another British plane arrived. It had come to take away the Legation luggage, but Humphrys decided that humanity should prevail over property and used it to evacuate some additional foreign ladies. The ladies, however, did not share his unconcern for property. A German woman could not resist checking in the baggage compartment to see if her possessions were stowed properly; she had been warned not to; the propeller, which never stopped whirring, struck her on the head. This possessiveness cost her the chance to get away, for she was injured although not fatally, and almost cost the whole party their chance, since her head broke the propeller.

On December 25, which was Christmas for the Europeans but only another day for the Moslem Afghans, Amanullah's fortunes improved slightly. Bacha Sacao's forces left Bagh-i-Bala altogether and retired to Paghman and Jabal-us-Siraj. "Legation out of firing zone for the first time since December 14," wrote the British. "Considerable numbers of King's troops and levies streamed back into Kabul from direction of Paghman during the day in high fettle. They boasted of having dispersed the remainder of Bacha Sacao's band at the point of the bayonet, but after eight days' close observation of their tactics, their stories were difficult to believe."

In Jalalabad, Ali Ahmed was spending money freely to bribe the Mohmands and Khugianis into promises of peace. The Shinwaris were still antagonistic, and now more dangerous than ever because they had captured some big cannons which they were bringing up to use against Jalalabad. They also were engaging in their old habit of looting caravans; they offended the Chaknawar Mullah by raiding a large caravan which was heading toward India under his protection; when the news reached India, passage west was forbidden to all caravans. In Peshawar a rumor began to circulate that Amanullah had left for Russia; Afghan officials and traders became so disturbed that they removed two hundred thousand rupees' worth of karakul skins from the Afghan warehouse. The Hindu Sikhs on the border removed their sacred book, the Granth Sahib, with much ceremony to Landi Kotal.

In Kandahar money was being spent also by Ulya Hazrat. On December 24 she made a speech with far more fire than her son had displayed. She belittled the difficulty with the Shinwaris, which at that moment was actually far less threatening than the trouble with Bacha Sacao. She demanded that all soldiers who had been discharged after serving their time should now re-enlist, and kept insisting on the renewal of the policy which had caused a riot a few years earlier in Kandahar, hasht nafari, or the drafting of one man in eight. That occupied her days. In the evenings she was going to the private homes of people who owed favors to her family.

Now the posters in Kandahar had lost their sentimental appeal to the "maternal uncles" and were proclaiming the death penalty for all who did not comply with the call to arms. Kandaharis, like the Kabulis, were burying their money and jewels. There was a rumor that the bridge of boats over the Helmand River, built for Amanullah's return, had been deliberately broken.

In Kabul the Turkish Ambassador took tea with Humphrys and told him that neither Amanullah nor his ministers knew how to deal with the present difficulties. He himself was perturbed by the imminent arrival of Kiazim Pasha, a famous Turkish general being sent by Ataturk to reorganize the Afghan Army even further. Turks were already unpopular enough without one more influx of Turks to take precedence over Afghans.

Later that day Humphrys had tea again, this time with the Italian

Minister, and heard that Léonide Stark, the Russian Ambassador, who had previously been optimistic about Amanullah's chances, now was pessimistic. Having reached pessimism later than the British, Stark was later in the evacuation of his dependents, but on December 30, three large planes came from Termez to carry them off.

During that day of tea-taking Humphrys heard another piece of news which provoked him to exclaim that anyone who believed it must be out of his mind. He was slow in hearing it, for it was known all over the world and believed by many. The rumor that the British had engineered the Shinwari rebellion was already old, but now it included the name of a man supposed to have managed it all: Lawrence of Arabia.

Since May 26 Lawrence had been living ten miles from the Afghan-Indian frontier at the R.A.F. post of Miranshah.

Thomas E. Lawrence was not one of the bright, eager young officers of the North-West Frontier Province whom some journalists suspected of enterprise on their own "which would have caused the hair of their superiors to stand on end." Lawrence was forty years old and tired. At Miranshah he was Aircraftman T. E. Shaw, although the other twenty-four Britons there knew his true identity. Shaw was his name legally, but he had entered the Royal Air Force in August 1922 under a third name which was assumed, and his admission had been imposed by the R.A.F. directors, who had to try several doctors before finding one who would approve him on physical grounds. This was managed not for any good that he could do the service but for his own benefit, to give him "an asylum in the R.A.F."[1]

Lawrence had told friends he wanted a "brain sleep." His brain and body had worked strenuously during the Great War, when he was ostensibly a Colonel but actually a member of the British Foreign Service, an agent who stirred the Arab Revolt with promises of independence after the war. He did not do this in good faith, as would be believed for many years. In the first draft of his story of that period, *The Seven Pillars of Wisdom*, he wrote, "Better win and break our word than lose" but deleted this at the suggestion of his good friend George Bernard Shaw, after whom he had named himself.[2] What distressed Lawrence was the way the world was arranged after the war; he resented the position of the French;[3] this helped account for the fascination of the French Legation in Kabul at all stories of his activity and for the articles that kept appearing in French newspapers about Lawrence, Afghanistan and "les cavaliers de St. Georges," referring to the symbol on British gold sovereigns, which were credited with buying almost anything.

The R.A.F. was uncongenial for Lawrence-Shaw, who was such a misfit in it; but he remained an aircraftman and in December 1926, four years after he had begun his "brain sleep," he was transferred to Karachi in India.

But his brain was not totally asleep; in June 1927 he wrote a friend from Karachi, "Do you know, if I'ld known as much about the British Government in 1917 as I do now, I could have got enough of them behind me to have radically changed the face of Asia?" And in the same letter:[4]

"We can only get at Russia here through Turkey or Persia or Afghanistan or China, and I fancy the Red Army is probably good enough to turn any of those into a bit of herself, as the Germans did Romania . . .

"The most dangerous point is Afghanistan. Do you know I nearly went there last week? The British Attaché at Kabul is entitled to an airman clerk and the depot would have put my name forward if I'd been a lot nippier on a typewriter. I'll have to mug up typing; for from '14 to '18 I served a decent apprenticeship in semi-secret service work, and Russia interests me greatly. The clash is bound to come, I think. It's quite in the cards Russia may have her go in our time."

Russia as a threat was greatly on the mind of the British Empire in regard to Afghanistan at the time of Lawrence's transfer to India. Amanullah was on his way to Russia, the possibility of closer relations between Russia and Afghanistan was strong, and many see a connection between British unease and this transfer of an apparently useless enlisted man.

On May 2, 1928, the day before Amanullah left Poland for Moscow, Lawrence wrote to his brother, "I am leaving Karachi for some squadron upcountry." He told his brother what solicitors had his will, how he wished his estate divided, and that he had an unpublished manuscript, "The Mint." "I'm not conscious of dying, but while I'm informing you of the existence of 'The Mint,' I'ld better put you informed of the other arrangements. Handy-like, to have it in a nut-shell."[5] He told Sir Hugh Trenchard, who headed the Royal Air Force, that he asked for the transfer to get away from an officer who threatened to beat him up.[6]

"Here they employ me mainly in the office," he wrote a friend on

June 30 from Miranshah. "I am the only airman who can work a type-writer."[7]

The skill on a typewriter of this Oxford graduate who had shaken nations, and written a famous book, and was a trained intelligence operative, was often an issue in his letters. He described himself to George Bernard Shaw as "typist and in charge of the file and duty rolls," but added, "I'm not much good as a clerk though I type better than this during the daylight . . . It's awfully hard to make up a sensible letter on a typewriter."[8] And to E. M. Forster, the novelist, he wrote another indictment of the Air Force's training for typists: "Do not swoon with the eccentricity of this typing. I am doing it in the dark and there is not a bell to ring at the end of lines . . . and I cannot feel with my fingertips exactly where I am striking the keys."[9] Touch-typing had evidently not been in his curriculum.

One subject on which he was silent was the landscape surrounding him. "We live behind barbed wire," he wrote, but he who had described the Arabian Desert so vividly had nothing to say about the jagged peaks of Waziristan.

"What is your game, really?" George Bernard Shaw wrote to him once at Miranshah, and his reply was, "Do you never do something because you know you must?"[10]

One of Humphrys' last messages from Kabul before Bacha Sacao's attack was: "I should like to be informed by telegram of Lawrence's whereabouts and to be authorized to give absolute denial to statement that he is in neighborhood of frontier or that he has visited Afghanistan." At the same time the North-West Frontier Province was reporting: "Photo of European has been sent to Sarhaddar of Dakka from Kabul with orders to arrest him if found. Photo is said to have been supplied from India and is supposed to be of Lawrence."

Humphrys was told that Lawrence had been transferred recently to Peshawar, but he had not been; he was still at Miranshah.

One of the legends of Afghanistan would tell of a pir who appeared in its eastern hills during the rebellion and then disappeared, and had never been known there before or after. His name was given sometimes as Pir Karam Shah and sometimes as Pir Munshi Shah, and the belief was that he was Lawrence. Blue eyes would not have disqualified Lawrence for the role since many Pathans have bright blue eyes. Ineptitude in Pushtu would have, and Lawrence with all his Arab experience had never spoken Arabic so perfectly as to pass for an Arab when he had to talk. Four mysterious pirs actually were walking through the Afghan hills, agents sent to contact the Kabul Legation, and they were Indian Moslems who could have passed.

In Lahore an authentic pir was set upon by angry Indians who thought he was Lawrence and almost killed him. A man in Afghanistan was identified by the British to their own satisfaction as the object of some rumors: "I hear that the European who was recently arrested at Matun wearing a false beard," Humphrys wired, "may be a German called Sparling. Spare built, sand complexion, above medium height, age about 27, wild-looking. He disappeared from Kabul some weeks ago. Sparling has embraced Islam and has been mixed up in some exceedingly shady financial transactions with the Afghan Government . . . Suggest that if individual referred to turns out to be Sparling endeavors should be made to apprehend him. This is the European whom Afghans suspected to be Lawrence." In London a sigh went up in a Foreign Office Minute Paper: "It looks as though the production of Sparling . . . might do much to scratch the Lawrence myth. But his capture at Matun would perhaps be difficult to arrange with our tribes without involving ourselves in somewhat unneutral proceedings."

Later, however, when public speculation on Lawrence as a kingmaker was forcing some kind of explanation, there was a suggestion in London for "the issue of a chronological statement regarding Shaw's [Lawrence's] service in India and—if possible—a categorical exposition of the way in which he spent his leave period, if any. The assertion—if true—that he is still ignorant of Pushtu might be useful."

The reply displayed misgivings about "free-lance" provocation during leave periods. "It is proposed to say (on information supplied us by Air Ministry) that we understand that Aircraftman Shaw had not been granted any leave in India up to January 1 last. It is possible, however, that he may have had a few odd periods of local leave which would not be reported to us by Air Ministry; and even if we obtained the full dossier suggested, we should almost certainly not be able to say exactly how he had spent any such periods. Unless we know in advance that we can make out a water-tight case, I think it would be inadvisable to attempt to prove by records that Aircraftman Shaw could never at any time have had any opportunity of crossing the frontier and creating trouble."

And the Under-Secretary of State for India, Sir Arthur Hirtzel, in the middle of negotiations with the Air Ministry, would wire to the

Government of India: "It might be well that Government of India should have [Lawrence-Shaw] watched closely lest when confronted with departure from India he would bolt."

Hirtzel added: "If both he and Omar disappeared, it would be very awkward."

Thus Omar and his disappearance from India provoked Ghulam Siddiq, who had returned from Kandahar, to tell Humphrys: "The Mangal rebellion in 1924 was practically suppressed when the escape of Abdul Karim from India caused it to break out again at enormous cost in blood and treasure to the Afghan Government. It would be calamitous if Omar came to Afghanistan at this present crisis. I shrink from contemplating the cost to Afghanistan if Omar, a far more dangerous individual than Abdul Karim, succeeds in reviving a revolt which at last seems to be subsiding."

At every crisis in Afghanistan the British doubled their surveillance on the royal persons in India whom they continued to call "refugees" although some had been born in India and never known any other home. Sardar Ayub had gone to India in 1888 with three thousand relatives and partisans whom the Government of India supported. By 1928 support was being given only to nineteen of his descendants, but all were presumed to be eager for the Afghan throne, and during this particular crisis most of these were moved to Burma. Local officials protested several removals. One Political Agent asked indulgence for two men aged sixty-five and seventy-four respectively who had never shown any inclination to rule in Afghanistan.

Before these precautions were taken, the next-to-youngest son of the late Ayub, by name Omar, escaped into Afghanistan.

Omar was about thirty-two years old, with large eyes in an oval face, short clipped mustaches, and a way of smiling slightly when he spoke which gave him a rather effeminate appearance. He lived in Allahabad, which he managed to leave sometime on December 22 with an ease which precipitated an investigation in the Allahabad Police Department. He was accompanied by an older friend whose police description included the phrase "is always taking snuff without sneezing."

Omar walked slowly and talked slowly, and the slowness combined with the perpetual smile could never have survived the difficult life of the frontier, so the British felt confident in saying, "Men of his type even when disguised could scarcely escape detection for a day in tribal territory."

"I have received a secret warning, from a man in touch with the Russians," Humphrys wired, "that the King is being advised to have an outrage committed on this Legation. The idea is that British and Russian forces would then enter the country and the King would divert attention from domestic strife by calling on the Afghan nation to resist the invaders who had plotted his country's downfall.

"If Omar proclaims himself Amir, Afghanistan will regard this as definite proof of British intrigue."

In London, Shuja-ud-Dowleh wrote another rude note in his role as Afghan Minister blaming the British for Omar's excursion. "We have independent evidence," said a Foreign Office minute, "at the moment that Shuja-ud-Dowleh is egging on his government into animosity against us over Omar and over the excursions of our aircraft over Afghanistan . . . In the circumstances, while no doubt if Shuja-ud-Dowleh were an ordinary person and the Afghan Government an ordinary government, it would be proper to refuse to receive the note . . . It may be remarked that Shuja-ud-Dowleh is used to being kept waiting for a reply to his communications and there is perhaps no need to act with undue precipitancy in answering him."

Shuja-ud-Dowleh was answered with an oral statement, which left no trace. The British were taking no chances in their primary objective of the moment, to safeguard their Legation in Kabul and along with it the peace of their Empire.

Meanwhile British Intelligence linked Omar's escape with two persons: the Tagao Mullah, who had been the link also between Bacha Sacao and the Shinwari rebels, and Abdul Wahid Shinwari alias Mr. Wade Australian, the man-of-the-world who had made a fortune in Australia and visited Nadir in Paris.

The Afghan Government, having its own intelligence service, had forbidden Abdul Wahid's entry into Afghanistan, but he was still trying to get in. In Peshawar he again asked the British to send him, and this time he offered to find Omar for them.

In Jalalabad things seemed quiet, but this quiet was ominous because it had been achieved by Ali Ahmed, armed with a great amount of government money, and there was the story that when Ali Ahmed met with the Shinwari and Khugiani tribes at Charbagh, he offered to open the gates of Jalalabad to them and divide ammunition and arms if they would accept him as their King, and that the religious leader of those tribes had wound a turban around Ali Ahmed's head, the gesture which was a coronation. The messages that Ali Ahmed sent back assured Amanullah that he was working for him, having to play a devious game to do so. To Amanullah, who had felt the sting of Ali Ahmed's rivalry before, this was not reassuring.

The Shinwaris and Khugianis, before his arrival, had decided to forget their quarrel, and join forces again in the fresh hope of success that they found in the news of Amanullah's trouble in Kabul. Now they were peaceful toward Jalalabad as well as toward each other. Some Ghilzais who had been threatening were also peaceful, but they were said to have decided that Jalalabad might be left to other tribes because there would be so much for them in Kabul.

"Air of optimism prevails among Afghan community here," went the report from Peshawar on December 27. "Trade agent has 10 truck loads of petrol ready which he says will start from Jalalabad tomorrow. Deutsche-Afghanische Company says that they will resume business within a week. Yesterday trade agent sent 10,000 rupees to Dakka. This gives appearance of truth to rumors current that some sort of peace has been made with Khugianis and Chaknawar Mullah is again able to protect road."

South of Kabul, however, there was a fresh burst of trouble. An official was attacked and a mail truck plundered between Kabul and Ghazni, and five poles of the telegraph line were maliciously uprooted.

Some maliks from Hariob in Khost asked the British Political Agent of Kurram for an interview saying that the Jaji Mangals and Zadrans had decided to hand over their country to the British Government. The Political Agent refused to see them. Amanullah, of course, did not know this.

Also he did not know that important maliks of the Suleiman Khel Ghilzais were writing a letter to the Political Agent in South Waziristan: "It is quite probable that shortly after this a very pious man who will be obedient to God, the Prophet and the laws with the consent of the ulemas, government officers and Afghan people will be placed on the throne of the Kingdom." They were also saying, "Apart from this one [Bacha Sacao] who is against the King, together with the Mangals and Zadrans, all are trying to cause heavy bloodshed . . . The King is left alone . . . God knows what will happen in the future, may God help Islam. If you may want anything, please order us."

"You should be entirely at ease and none of you should pay any attention to absurd talk and silly rumors," Amanullah had told his people in leaflets that he dropped over their heads from airplanes. He had quoted the Koran: "He who obeys his King obeys me and he who rebels against his King rebels against me." But he himself did not share this optimism.

He needed arms and ammunition, and he had been so close to so much of these. He managed to fly in some machine guns being delivered from Europe, and the Russians had flown in more bombs for him, but one of the planes crashed near the palace, killing the Russian pilot outright and injuring his Russian observer so badly that he died a few days later. The Russian colony was getting panicky.

Amanullah knew now that he would have to make a public announcement rescinding his reforms. Some had suggested that he make in his own life a gesture that could be displayed to the tribes as a turning from the new ways back to the old traditions. He made such a gesture. He forsook monogamy.

Yet Amanullah did not proclaim this change as he might have done for political capital. It remained personal.

His uncle Nasrullah, from whom he had taken the throne, had a beautiful daughter named Aliah who was then nineteen years old. Being a cousin, Aliah had visited the palace freely and was a friend of Amanullah.

Now, with Souraya in Kandahar and events pressing on him so that he needed all the comfort he could find, Amanullah called Aliah to the palace and, although tradition would have demanded that an intermediary handle this matter, he asked Aliah directly if she would marry him. He did not say anything about politics or the need to impress the tribes with polygamy. He told Aliah that he loved her.

She said that she would marry him. One of the mullahs who had remained friendly was called, and the marriage was registered with only Amanullah's private secretary as witness.

So Aliah became Amanullah's third wife.

The girls' school had been closed when Bacha Sacao made his first attack on December 14, like all the other schools, but Amanullah issued a formal proclamation that there would be no more education for girls and to prove the finality of this decision he had the furniture in the school auctioned off and turned the building over to another function.

He announced that the girls who had been sent to Turkey would be recalled, that the wearing of a veil would be compulsory for all Afghan women including the Queen and Princesses, that all regulations on the wearing of European dress were canceled, that any mullah might teach without a certificate to guarantee his skill, that foreign mullahs including those from Deoband in India were permitted, that any soldier might be the disciple of a pir, that there would be no hasht nafari conscription, that Friday instead of Thursday would again be the holiday.

Amanullah abolished also his entire Nizamnamas, his code of laws, and announced that mullahs would "look after the religious law of the State and bring it into accord with the requirements of the time and see that there is no extreme action in the policy of the State." As a final concession to religious scruples, Amanullah said he would appoint an official to see that no one drank wine.

Almost a decade of loving work vanished in this announcement. It was such a loss to Amanullah that in the streets of Kabul and Kandahar people were advising each other not to take him seriously because in better times he would return to the same old progressive ways.

Amnesty for the rebels was included in the announcement, with two exceptions. He would not pardon Bacha Sacao or his chief lieutenant, Sayed Hussein, or their hundred closest followers. He offered a reward of forty thousand rupees for the heads of the first two and four thousand rupees each for the other hundred heads.

The terms that the Shinwaris had named had been harsher than these, involving the divorce of Souraya and expulsion of her family. He awaited more news from them in Jalalabad.

"It would be hard to conceive a more inconvenient season in which to be asked by the Amir to make good our promise to present him with arms," G. of I. wired to H.M.G. on January 3.

". . . refusal to do so would deepen the suspicions of our bad faith . . . On the other hand, compliance could hardly fail to associate us definitely in tribal mind with his repressive measures. Apart from all other considerations, safety of Legation is so dependent on good will, not merely of Afghan Government but of rebels, that we cannot afford to let our help to King take a form definitely provocative to the tribesmen . . . We . . . do not believe possession of more arms would help . . . Well-advertised reports that we were presenting them might do so. But its immediate effect at dangerous point, viz., around our Legation, might be to provoke the rebels to attack it.

"Practical conclusion thus seems that we should help the Amir by presentation of lorries he has asked us to sell him and be dilatory as far as we decently can over delivery of arms promised him.

"But difficulties and dangers inherent in implementing promise of arms at present juncture are forcing us to examine the advisability of our seeking to liquidate the promise by a corresponding gift of cash. On this point in particular we should be glad of Minister's view while we are clarifying our own.

"Line of approach with Amir might be desirability of avoiding inevitable delay over collection of arms promised, and fresh discussions of this nature might incidentally enable us to mark time without giving the impression of unhelpfulness."

H.M.G., contemplating this wire, made the realistic reply:

"The problem seems to be, not how much we ought or can afford to help the King at this crisis, as how little we can safely pay as an insurance premium against his possible reaction if ultimately victorious. And in this calculation it must not be forgotten that Afghans are apparently destitute of permanent gratitude for past favors and that, if winter in fact stabilizes the situation, the struggle may be prolonged for some time yet."

H.M.G. commented also:

"However strongly we may desire to see a central government emerge successful from its conflict with internal disorder in Afghanistan, we cannot afford to risk antagonizing the tribal belt as a whole for the 'beaux yeux' of King Amanullah, especially if he goes under after all. Nor would it be well lightly to lose our present good reputation with the mullahs thanks to not being identified with anti-Islamic reforms."

Kabul was expecting a decisive battle very soon.

Bacha Sacao had been besieging the fort at Jabal-us-Siraj and finally captured it. The fort, however, was less important than the power station there. His men diverted the stream that supplied electric power to Kabul. Suddenly everything modern stopped. In the homes of the Afghans outside royal circles, this did not mean much as they had no electricity anyway, but in the arsenal no more ammunition could be made.

Only fifteen miles from Kabul at Kila Murad Beg, Bacha Sacao was driven back by Amanullah's men commanded by Wali.

Then on January 8 Humphrys reported:

"As a result of heavy fighting in Koh-i-Daman Valley about seven miles northwest of Legation, Bacha Sacao reoccupied Kila Murad Beg and advanced to foot of Khairkhana Pass which separates Kabul from Koh-i-Daman Valley. Day has gone very badly for King's troops. Logaris, Mangals, Jajis and Wazirs fighting on side of King suffered heavy casualties. Wazirs were dissatisfied with tactics employed which involved being shot in back by comrades and so they withdrew.

"Gul Agha failed in his mission to detach Tagao tribesmen. They have joined Bacha Sacao . . . On account of this reverse people are again burying their valuables and consternation in city. Palace is defended by Hazaras under command of notorious robber and large quantities of supplies are being stored there. Underground retreats also being dug in palace.

"Mahmud Tarzi who has long dispensed with religious observances was seen today reciting Koran and telling his beads in company of seven mullahs. Ghulam Siddiq whom I saw yesterday is growing a beard and all Foreign Staff discarded European hats."

The following day Bacha Sacao began to use a new tactic, that of dividing his force into small parties which made unexpected raids in different directions. The British Military Attaché was writing: "Five French guns were this day on southwest corner of airdrome. They looked clean but it appears that no one knows how to handle them. The artillery ponies have the most crude type of harness, which appears to be held together with pieces of string."

The Turkish Mission, which could have taught the Afghans to use those guns, were headed toward Kabul from Kandahar, having left their wives behind in India, where they had tarried in indecision whether to come at all.

Posters began to appear in unexpected places, placed there by Bacha Sacao's men and offering sixty thousand rupees for Amanullah's head. Amanullah, who was expected to attend prayers at the mosque, sent word that he was indisposed.

For the first time flour was scarce in the bazaars of Kabul.

On January 13 Humphrys wired at eight o'clock in the evening:

"Bacha Sacao has today expelled King's troops from Koh-i-Daman Valley . . . rebels are attacking the villages of Deh Kipak about two miles north-northwest of Legation, having advanced under cover of darkness mist. Headquarters of General Mohammed Omar, commanding the King's army, are in Deh Kipak, and an Indian doctor who was in charge of hospital there has come to Legation. He says that General is surrounded and it is expected that unless he is relieved from Kabul his force will capitulate during night. The doctor declared that earlier in the day Bacha Sacao captured Hazara Kila, the fort in Koh-i-Daman nearest to Kabul with its garrison of three hundred men.

"There is a mist over hills and snow is falling. Tomorrow bids fair to be an exciting day."

That mist and falling snow were Amanullah's worst enemies that night. Out of the mist a voice called out to his General that he was surrounded by eleven thousand men and should pile up his arms and surrender. Unable to see what was around him, and expecting anyway to be overwhelmed, the General told his troops to pile up their arms at the command of the voice, which belonged to Bacha Sacao's younger brother, who had only one hundred and fifty men with him but many more waiting to come up.

The rebels occupied the fort and with its big guns began to shell Bagh-i-Bala and the high hills. At noon on January 14 Humphrys wired:

"King's artillery are not replying. King's troops are seen to be retreating in disorder. Likely Bacha Sacao will enter city tonight."

While his own guns had been shelling his own fortification, Amanullah had been asking Inayatullah, as he had asked him many times before, to take the throne. What had put Afghanistan into this tragedy was his own personality. Inayatullah, who had always said no, looked about him at disaster and said yes. Easygoing and unambitious, he had never wanted a throne; but now he bravely took it when there was no power to being a king, only pain.

Amanullah made plans to announce his abdication and leave Kabul.

Physical courage had never been lacking in Amanullah. The Kings of Afghanistan had faced many terrible fates throughout that country's turbulent history: blinding, long imprisonment, torture. But these things had been done to them by men who were also royal. None had ever fallen into the hands of a bandit. During the negotiations with Bacha Sacao, there had been a time when, under the prodding of the mullahs of Kohistan, Bacha Sacao had demanded that Amanullah sign his amnesty on a Koran, and Amanullah's Council had refused to let him do this, being ashamed to pay so much homage to a bandit. Now Amanullah refused the homage of personal challenge. Bacha Sacao was even further from respectability than he had known.

"It may seem surprising," Humphrys was to write, "that a man of

Amanullah's proved courage did not place himself at the head of his troops and risk everything in a final counter-attack. He would probably have taken this desperate course if his antagonist had been a person of royal blood. What he could not face was the enduring disgrace to his house of being tied to a tree and shot by a bandit."

CHAPTER 28

January 14, 1929, to January 19, 1929

For several days an airplane had been kept at the airport filled with fuel, the pilot standing by, prepared to take Amanullah off to Kandahar, but even the brief journey from the palace to the airport would have been dangerous for him. It was safest to travel south, but there had been reports of rebel bands even on the road toward Kandahar. Abdul Ahad, the officiating Minister of Interior, went ahead in a car to Sheikhabad with orders to await Amanullah there if the road was safe. Abdul Ahad saw no rebels and waited.

At eight o'clock on the morning of January 14 a group of cars drove from the palace carrying Amanullah, Mahmud Tarzi, Ghulam Siddiq and Yakub, the Minister of Court, who had accompanied Amanullah to Europe, and twelve members of the royal bodyguard from Kandahar.

Amanullah had always been happy at the wheel of a motorcar, and his endurance was legendary. At the close of a 1927 visit to Khost, he had galloped forty-three miles on horseback to Gardez, dismounted, and without waiting for food or rest stepped into this same Rolls-Royce and driven at high speed eighty-five miles to Kabul, arriving there in better spirits than the Army officers whom he had left behind in Gardez exhausted from the horseback ride alone.

But this journey toward Kandahar was sheer hell. Despite the rewards that had been offered for clearing the road between Kabul and Ghazni, the snows that had been falling at close intervals for the past two months had been blown here and there into drifts which the intense cold had frozen as hard as stone. It should have taken only a few hours to drive to Sheikhabad. It took eight hours through the ice and snow. There Abdul Ahad was waiting and Amanullah made a telephone call ahead to Ghazni to order the hakim to bring food to the roadside, but to tell no one he was coming. He also gave orders for the road toward Mukur to be repaired hastily wherever it might be impassable.

At eight o'clock that evening, twelve hours after his departure, Amanullah was driving into Ghazni, having traveled ninety-eight miles. He and his companions did not get out of their cars to eat the food brought to them but dined sitting where they had sat for the past twelve hours. Amanullah told the hakim of his abdication and Inayatullah's succession, and said that he was going to Kandahar to get pledges of allegiance to his brother.

Then he drove toward the next stage, Mukur, and as he went south, the snow ceased to be a menace, but nature had another menace, rain. Rain had been falling long enough to swell the streams and wash out the bridge over one of the tributaries of the Ghazni River eight miles north of Mukur. There was nothing to do but to try to drive through the muddy bed of the stream. The cars stuck. Amanullah sent one of his men ahead to get ponies, but the man was slow in returning and Amanullah could not bear to sit in the car any longer, so when a curious villager came up to inspect the strange cars stuck in the mud, Amanullah took him as a guide and on foot, through the pouring rain, set out for Mukur. Abdul Ahad and Ghulam Siddiq trudged along with him. After about four miles of walking they met the man with the ponies, mounted, and rode into Mukur at midnight.

On the Mukur telephone Amanullah tried to talk with Inayatullah in Kabul, but he could not get any connection beyond Sheikhabad. Nothing answered in his palace. Then he put a call through to Kandahar and spoke with members of his family, with Souraya, Ulya Hazrat, Hassan Jan, telling them that he was safe. He spoke also with the Governor of Kandahar, to reassure him with the false news that affairs in Kabul were going well and that a settlement would soon be reached in Jalalabad. He insisted to all these people on secrecy about his arrival. He also asked for cars.

At two o'clock in the morning Hassan Jan drove from Kandahar in a Rolls-Royce belonging to Ulya Hazrat with eight other cars following. Amanullah was having breakfast when they arrived at seven o'clock at Mukur. It was four o'clock when Amanullah drove into Kandahar, having required 32 hours to travel 313 miles.

His royal red flag was flying from a turret. No one there knew that he had abdicated.

In Kabul toward noon on January 14 the town criers went around beating their drums and calling out that all should gather at two-thirty outside Dilkusha Palace to hear a message of importance. Being starved for a word from above, the men of Kabul gathered. A chamberlain appeared on the balcony and read Amanullah's announcement that he was giving up the throne to avoid further bloodshed and had sworn allegiance to Inayatullah, as should all Afghans. Inayatullah then appeared and Gul Agha placed the turban of kingship on his head, saying he might rule only as long as he obeyed religious laws. It was an insulting coronation.

While Amanullah was fighting the snow and rain, in Kabul the sun had come out. The sky was clear. All afternoon Kabulis were going into the palace to offer their signatures as a pledge of allegiance to King Inayatullah. Many of them felt they had been relieved from the war as they had been relieved from snow and rain. Bacha Sacao had always maintained that his fight was only with King Amanullah, not with the people, so they assumed that peace would come with the new King. Inayatullah was a comforting figure. For Amanullah the turban with which he was crowned was virtually the only turban he ever wore; Inayatullah, who had appeared in traditional dress before, now took care that he was seen only in robes and turban; he had never parted with a short beard.

Inayatullah's first act was to call together the leading mullahs, Gul Agha among them, and asked them to take the news to his own advance troops and to the rebels. These mullahs went in a wagon toward Bagh-i-Bala, each man carrying a white flag, which was the symbol of truce according to the Western style which they had just defeated, but here was a symbol of Islam. White flags were more noticeable than Korans. When they returned to Kabul, four thousand rebels came back with them. The sound of the rebels' rifles still made a staccato in the cold air, but these were shots of pure joy.

Shortly after midnight heavy firing began from the direction of the city. "All night firing was kept up with great ferocity with guns, machine guns and rifles," wired Humphrys on January 15. His wireless was the only link with the world outside Afghanistan, for the Kabul wireless had stopped sending. "[Firing] still continues though volume is less. It seems that at present neither side trusts the other."

Now Gul Agha made the final thrust of the grand plan begun by his brother Sher Agha.

"A pious man" would be proclaimed King, so had gone the message on the eastern frontier ten days earlier. Both the brothers were pious. Sher Agha was the leader and he was still so active in India that the British were on the track of new discoveries about him, keeping a surveillance on his mail that did not cease even after a postal carrier dropped and lost the message about that surveillance, thereby jeopardizing it. But Sher Agha was far away and Gul Agha was not only pious but present.

Gul Agha told Bacha Sacao that Inayatullah was not to remain as King. He himself, Gul Agha, would take the throne. Bacha Sacao was to see to it.[1]

By this time Bacha Sacao had had enough of the establishment. Power and prestige no longer impressed him. He would later remark that his own past record as a courteous highwayman appeared to be almost blameless in comparison with Amanullah's perfidy and cowardice and the sordidness and disloyalty of his ministers. He knew that only the force of arms which he controlled would command respect for him, and he knew that his force was the only power in Kabul.

Bacha Sacao told Gul Agha that he was mistaken. He himself, Bacha Sacao, would occupy the throne of Afghanistan.

So the bandit from the hills took over the establishment that had repulsed him. After a lifetime of being known as Bacha Sacao or "Son of the Water-Carrier" he called himself by his true name, which few people had taken the trouble to learn.

He became Amir Habibullah.[2]

The General who had commanded Amanullah's forces now was atop the major gateway of the city aiming a large cannon directly at the palace. He had gone over to Bacha Sacao. So had Amanullah's old friend and teacher, Mahmud Sami. Two of Amanullah's brothers had gone to Bagh-i-Bala to accept the bandit as their King: Hayatullah, who had been overlooked in the scramble for the throne in 1919 and whose position as the second oldest son of an Amir was difficult to remember; and Kabir, who had once fled to India.

About fifteen thousand tribesmen, mostly from Koh-i-Daman, were milling about the city. Their greatest violence flared up when a large airplane sent by the Russians flew over Kabul; so many bullets went hurtling skyward that the pilot turned around and went back to Russia without landing. The Russians who had been keeping Amanullah's air force alive, and who had dropped bombs on these very tribesmen, were dismissed peremptorily and told to go home.

Enormous crowds were trying to get to Bagh-i-Bala to pay homage to their new self-proclaimed Amir. This kept them so busy that the universal looting that everyone had feared did not take place. Bacha Sacao maintained discipline over his men; a few were caught looting and were shot. Yet, "it is becoming increasingly difficult to control this mob," Humphrys wired.

Most of the irregulars who had come to Kabul to serve Amanullah had gone home, each man taking at least one rifle. The palace was the only part of Kabul not in Bacha Sacao's control; that still had its defenses, and from its pierced ramparts shots were fired at anything that seemed to move menacingly.

"Strenuous efforts are being made to secure the peaceful surrender of the Arg [Palace]," Humphrys wired. "If it is captured by assault it will be almost impossible to stop a massacre and looting of the Treasury."

This was the situation that day as Humphrys saw it:

"King Inayatullah was closely besieged in the Arg with a garrison of 5,000 men and provisions for at least a year, while the State Treasury, reduced to three-quarters of a million sterling, and enormous stores of munitions were in his hands.

"Habibullah [Bacha Sacao] with a force of 16,000 men, occupied all the strategic positions commanding the Arg and was in possession of the aerodrome and most of the guns, but was very short of shells.

"A large tribal force which owed allegiance to neither party was hovering in the rear with the intention of looting the city and picking up all the arms they could in the general melee.

"[Bacha Sacao] prepared 1,000 scaling ladders and drew up his guns under cover to within 50 yards of the Arg gates. He then delivered a 24-hour ultimatum to Inayatullah to surrender peacefully, and promised in that event to spare the lives of the garrison. The alternative was an assault with scaling ladders, the blowing in of the gates, and no quarter. To accomplish this he was prepared to lose 7,000 men, and the inevitable result would have been the looting of the State Treasury, the massacre of the garrison, the explosion of the immense arsenal and the destruction of the city and foreign legations located inside it; that is, all except the British Legation. He could not afford to wait."

Inayatullah had already seen that resistance would mean catastrophe to many besides himself. He was willing to surrender. Someone was required to mediate between the King and the bandit.

Gul Agha, still maintaining his position near the source of power, took that upon himself. He went back and forth between Bacha Sacao in Bagh-i-Bala and Inayatullah in the Arg Palace, always running the risk of being shot, and arranged an agreement.

On the afternoon of January 17 Gul Agha went to the British Legation and asked to see Sir Francis Humphrys, and for the first time in his life he spoke face to face with a man who was not a Moslem. He carried a letter written by an official from Koh-i-Daman named Sher Jan who already held the title of Minister of Court for the new ruler:

"Prince Inayatullah having abdicated and having made voluntary obeisance to His Majesty Ghazi Habibullah, he has requested that he and his family of 20 persons (many of whom are children) should be sent to Kandahar by airplane. We have no suitable airplane so we request you to provide one to land at Sherpur Airdrome between 8 and 10 tomorrow morning."

This was the only way to prevent the destruction of Kabul, said Gul Agha. Humphrys replied that no British airplane could go to Kandahar as there was no guarantee of its safety there. But he agreed to ask his government to send two large planes to carry the royal family to Peshawar, whence they would be taken by train to Chaman and sent into Afghanistan again.

On the previous evening the Afghan Trade Agent in Peshawar had arranged a celebration in honor of Inayatullah's succession. The Afghan Legations in Europe had received the news of Amanullah's abdication in a message which the Afghan Foreign Office sent over the British wireless of which it was officially unaware. In London, the Foreign Office had decided there was no problem in recognizing Inayatullah, that the situation was the same as in a succession by death.

Now, only a day later, Humphrys was wiring to Peshawar: "Should an arrangement be reached I assume that two Victorias [airplanes] will be sent as our help in time of urgency may be only way of saving Kabul from destruction. Delay may spoil everything. I shall telegraph to Peshawar again and in that case [an airman] will lay out T on Sherpur Airdrome tomorrow. If T is not out on airdrome, Victorias should return without landing to Peshawar."

The weather in Kabul, fortunately, continued fine.

At eight o'clock on the morning of January 18, Humphrys wired Peshawar to send the two large planes immediately.

Meanwhile Inayatullah signed a paper:

"With the Name of God the Benevolent, the Beneficent, My brother, Habibullah Khan!

"Every one knows that I have no intention or desire for becoming a King . . . Now for the welfare of the Moslems I forego this and abdicate the Amirate of Afghanistan and, as all other Moslems have tendered their allegiance to you, I also tender you my allegiance."

He then listed the men of importance who were with him in the palace and said that they also tendered allegiance to Bacha Sacao.

Amanullah still could not get a telephone message through to Kabul; he could get only as far as Ghazni, from which he heard that Inayatullah was a prisoner. He knew nothing of what was happening.

Two days after his arrival in Kandahar, Amanullah called a meeting of a thousand prominent men of the city and, still disdaining drama, refused to let them pay him the usual homage of standing to hear him speak. He himself sat as he described the risings, blaming that of the Shinwaris on a conspiracy, and finally told the Kandaharis that he had abdicated and they should give allegiance to Inayatullah.

This last news inspired an uproar and protests of unhappiness. One judge refused to accept Inayatullah, crying out that Amanullah was still his King, and most of those present called out that Amanullah was King. This loyalty, far from pleasing Amanullah, left him in a bad temper and he rose to break up the meeting.

He had already ordered the royal flag to be taken down as there was no King in Kandahar.

But he had sent a man to Quetta to take by hand a message that he did not wish to send through the telegraph from Kandahar. The wire went from Quetta to London and to his old friend, Shuja-ud-Dowleh, the Afghan Minister there, who transmitted it to the British Foreign Office.

Amanullah's abdication, he said, was a device to secure his escape from Kabul, and Amanullah had hopes of restoring himself and his family; he begged the British Government to help him, by supply of munitions, to recover the throne; for such aid he promised undying gratitude and undertook to give a guarantee binding on himself and his successors to pay the cost of those munitions.

Shuja-ud-Dowleh added that he was confident no similar request had been made to Moscow.

"I always suspected that Amanullah's abdication . . . was a 'box and cox' arrangement," was Humphrys' reaction. "I have often been told by Amanullah that in time of trouble he would first appeal for help from Great Britain and if that failed, he might be compelled to appeal to Russia . . . In present circumstances it appears evident that we cannot give Amanullah help of any kind and I would suggest if feasible that H.M.G. should communicate a warning to Russia of 'hands off' as regards supplying troops or war materials to Amanullah.

"I suggest that reply to Afghan Minister should take following form: 'Abdication of King Amanullah has been communicated officially to H.M.G. and nominated successor to Afghan throne has surrendered the capital and is at present traveling through India on his way to join his brother ex-King Amanullah in Kandahar. H.M.G. are therefore unable to recognize authority of Afghan Minister in London to hold official communication with the British Foreign Office until present obscure situation has been regularized.'

"I feel that a direct negation if possible should be avoided as it would give Amanullah the opportunity for which perhaps he is looking to make overtures to Russia."

This was the procrastinating game that the Foreign Office set out to play with Shuja-ud-Dowleh, regarding his request as "unofficial and personal." The Foreign Office later said: "We were thinking of ignoring [this request] but the Legation rang up to ask when a reply might be expected."

The reply was a very polite one from the Secretary of State for Foreign Affairs, Sir Austen Chamberlain, who had called upon Amanullah nine months earlier in the royal suite at Claridge's and had promised him a world of armaments which would have meant more than a world to him now:

"His Majesty's Government has given this request their most sympathetic consideration but they much regret that international considerations prevent their interfering in the internal affairs of Afghanistan by giving assistance in the form of arms to one or another party when there is no generally recognized ruler or government in the country. I need not add that if H.M.G. can show their friendship for His Majesty in any way which does not involve such interference, they will be most pleased to do so."

Amanullah's abdication, followed by Inayatullah's, had solved a problem for the British Empire.

The cynicism in London was balanced by a heroic act of *noblesse oblige* in Kabul. Men of the British Legation, without arms, went into the Arg Palace at one o'clock and escorted Inayatullah and members of his family to the airplanes, which waited with their propellers spinning. Bacha Sacao's discipline held. Unmolested, the two planes were flying in a few minutes back to Peshawar with the last hope of Amanullah's dynasty.

"Khilafat Committee advertise a meeting tomorrow in Shah-i-Bagh where Afghan affairs are to be discussed," reported Peshawar. "A large number of trans-frontier tribesmen, mostly Afridis and Mohmands, held a meeting in Peshawar today and agreed by acclamation to take arms in support of Afghan royal family but not necessarily Amanullah.

"All this points to necessity of transferring Inayatullah and his party as quickly as possible from Peshawar."

One plane from Kabul had a stowaway: Amanullah's uncle Mohammed Omar had accepted the bandit as King, but his chauffeur darted into a plane, unnoticed in the excitement, and hid under a seat.

Inayatullah and his party were put onto a train that would take them to a point inside India from which they could go to Kandahar. Inayatullah had not heard from Amanullah since he drove off from the palace; he did not know if he had reached Kandahar or not. When the train halted at Chaman, Inayatullah suddenly asked if he might not wait to ascertain what would confront him in Kandahar.

"I consider it essential that Inayatullah and his party should be sent across the border for Kandahar as soon as possible," Humphrys wired. "Before Inayatullah left Kabul this was solemnly agreed to by both parties and was the only condition on which a British airplane was supplied to convey him to Peshawar. If he stays in India, we shall be accused of a breach of faith and he should be deported from Chaman by force if necessary."

In the early afternoon of January 22 a second deposed King of Afghanistan was driving toward Kandahar.

In the south of France the British Consul at Nice received on January 19 another visit from Nadir's brother Hashim who asked for a visa for himself and his brother, Shah Wali, to transit India on their way to Afghanistan.

The Consul consulted a list of persons to whom he was not to issue visas without special approval and saw there the names of the brothers from Afghanistan, who had been put on the list in late December at Humphrys' request. He told Hashim that he would not be able to grant the visas without referring to Paris.

Greatly annoyed, Hashim asked that the Consul telegraph to Paris. He said that two others of his brothers already had left for Afghanistan. The next morning the Consul received a wire from Paris requesting information as to the whereabouts of Nadir. He had none.

Within a few days Hashim had gone to Paris to repeat at the British Embassy his plea for visas for himself and Shah Wali. There he heard that the matter had to be referred to London. Thinking he might wish to pursue the matter in person as he had in Paris, the British Embassy gave him a visa for England only, but instead he went back to Nice. "We were informed by a secretary of the Afghan Legation that Shah Wali was staying at Nice with Nadir," reported the Paris Embassy, "so we presume the latter was there until recently."

The ban on visas for Nadir and his brothers had been imposed "in order to avoid embarrassment to Amanullah at a time when he was fighting for his throne." In the altered circumstances, Humphrys no longer recommended that visas be withheld.

"It would be difficult now to justify refusal, even if [Bacha Sacao] took our action ill, and it is quite possible that the arrival of any or all of these sardars who possess some of the best and most honest brains in Afghanistan might have a steadying and unifying effect on the country."

Hurriedly, in order to forestall a visit to London by Hashim, who might ask for an interview, the Foreign Office sent instructions to Paris "to grant diplomatic visas to Nadir and his brothers if required and to avoid giving the impression that delay in granting these visas was due to any idea of refusing visas to them personally."

The plane carrying off Inayatullah and his family was still visible from Kabul when Bacha Sacao's men entered the palace of the Arg.

This was not as peaceful as the departure a few minutes earlier. The first man to enter was a malik from Koh-i-Daman who had not wished to take part in the rebellion, but all the men of his village had been aroused and were eager to go. He saw that he could not stop them, and he was their malik, their leader, and he would be a leader no longer if they went to Kabul without him. So he made the sweep southward, and at each stage of the journey he found a group of mullahs waiting with whatever was needed: lanterns, ammunition, food, information as to what was ahead.

Such a highly organized operation was new in this man's experience. Life in his Koh-i-Daman village was far more haphazard. Awestruck, he perceived that there could be only one explanation: God was doing all this.

All reluctance fell from him and he marched on with as much vigor as any others of the shouting tribesmen, to do God's work. When he was carried by the throng toward the palace and realized that he would be the first inside, it came to him, who knew nothing of what Bacha Sacao had planned, that God must intend for him to be Amir.

He crossed the threshold. A bullet—he never knew if it came from his own side or from the King's men—sped between his temples. For the rest of his life he would be blind. He would always think that this too was done by God.

In the harem serai of the palace there was almost panic. The unmarried daughters of Amanullah's father, the woman-loving Amir Habibullah, were all in their teens. Some had left the palace but returned at Amanullah's invitation to be educated. Many young women were living there and they saw themselves the spoils of war.

Instead of the swarm of unruly rebels that they dreaded, they were approached by an elderly man sent by Bacha Sacao, who said that arrangements had been made to take them to Inayatullah's house. The next day their relatives came. All had maternal kinfolk, who, because of Habibullah's penchant for women of various tribes, came from all parts of Afghanistan. These relatives had come to Kabul or had delegates there. They carried off the women of the palace to a variety of homes which were humble but safe.

On that first afternoon Bacha Sacao made himself at home in the palace. He had already given his men a list of the ministers and officials who had served Amanullah with orders to bring them at once in whatever condition they were found. Some of these men were at home wearing the traditional loose pajamas and shirt; others had gone into the bazaars hoping to mingle with the crowd and hear what was happening. The Governor of Kohistan had spent the night dangling from a tree by one leg, having been tied up by some of Bacha Sacao's neigh-

bors whom he had punished in his day of power. The rebel tribesmen
dragged these officials to their leader without giving them time to put
on coats; the way led through muddy streets, and some of the dragging
was done literally. The Kohistan Governor was cut down and taken off
at once.

Eighty of these men were taken into the courtyard of the palace,
where they had to stand in the cold and look through a window at Bacha
Sacao eating. The window that separated him from them was almost
the first glass window he had known; some of his followers would toss
chicken bones in the direction of the outdoors and be surprised when
the bones bounced back, for they had never been inside any house of
luxury except to rob it. Some would find clothes in the palace closet and
try to put them on, marveling at the small size and strange cut, not
knowing they were wearing garments left by Queen Souraya. In the
bathroom tiled with lapis lazuli they would have to be shown, not what
lapis lazuli was, but what the various appointments were for.

Bacha Sacao finished his meal and had this glass window opened.
He stood there in his tribal dress and turban, with two bandoleers full
of bullets across his chest and a belt of bullets at his waist, so that he
seemed to be clothed in bullets. Sher Jan, his new Minister of Court,
said, "His Majesty wishes to address you," and then brought each of
the shivering men to the window for presentation. Sher Jan knew most
of these officials personally, for he had been a humble official when
they were important ones.

He observed protocol. First Amanullah's uncle Mohammed Omar
came, then the brothers Hayatullah and Kabir, who had already placed
themselves on the winning side.

On meeting the Governor of Kohistan, who once had held virtually
power of life over him, and who had been hanging in the tree, Bacha
Sacao observed, "You are the dirtiest man I have ever seen!"

The Minister of Finance, Mir Hashim, was presented. Bacha Sacao
leaned out the window and called, "The big kaffir!"

"I am not a kaffir," said the Finance Minister. "I am a true Moslem
and a sayed."

"Have you not introduced the budget?" asked Bacha Sacao.

"What is a budget? It is the old system of having accounts. In the
house, in the shops, we all have budgets. It is a new name."

"Was this not the same as being an infidel?" asked Bacha Sacao. The
Finance Minister said it was not.

"I asked you to have lunch with me, gentlemen," said Bacha Sacao.

"The Minister of Court will present a paper, and you have to sign."

The former officials were taken to a room downstairs usually used by servants and given the most austere of meals, rice and raisins.

Then Sher Jan entered with a scroll attached to a copy of the Koran and, unrolling it partway, indicated a spot where the officials were to sign. He did not permit them to read what they were signing, but since they were in no position to protest anything, they all signed anyway.

Only Abdul Hadi, when his turn came, had the courage to open the scroll and read it. Abdul Hadi had been a poor boy to whom Mahmud Tarzi had given a position on the newspaper *Seraj-ul-Akhbar*, and then taken into the Foreign Office, thereby starting him on a career in which his way to success was to drive straight through all opposition; although clever enough to observe that other people said flattering things and compromised, Abdul Hadi always behaved in a fashion which was "straightforward and forthright" to his friends, "blunt and rude" to his enemies, who included the British toward whom he was always on the defensive. Even the British, however, said that he was "unbribable." He was just as independent now to the man who held Kabul.

Abdul Hadi saw that he was about to sign a paper not only accepting Bacha Sacao as King, but denouncing Amanullah as a kaffir. He signed, as he had to, but wrote beside his name, "The details of religion belong to students of theology."

Mullahs had prepared this document in which they told the world at their moment of triumph exactly which acts of Amanullah had stung them most deeply and provoked them to drive him from his kingship.

"All his acts were contrary to the orders of the Koran and to the example set by the Holy Prophet. The following are clear examples of his violation of the Shariat of the Prophet and of introducing his own inventions instead.

"1. He abandoned the forms of salutations and introduced instead a sign after the fashion of the unbelievers and against the example of the Prophet, and forcibly persuaded the Moslems to adopt this method.

"2. He introduced hats after the fashion of the unbelievers and abandoned the turban which was worn by the Prophet, with which headdress only can prayers be performed completely. A man who violated Amanullah's rule regarding hats was subject to punishment.

"3. He changed the Islamic dress which was used by Moslems of the past, and gave orders that all should resemble the unbelievers in manner of dress. The new dress is still in use.

"4. The Koran says that men and women who are strangers should not show their eyes to one another. Amanullah, however, cast aside this grand order of God and gave orders for the unveiling of women.

"5. The religious lawyers consider it unlawful that a grown-up woman should go out of her house without the permission of her husband. Amanullah, however, gave orders that all women and girls should go to schools. He has thus disgraced the Moslems.

"6. The growing of the beard and clipping of the middle portion of the mustache was the practice and order of the Prophet, but Amanullah's orders are against the same.

"7. He ordered that boys should go to schools. Boys have the same legal position as grown-up girls. In these schools religion, Shariat and the Koranic laws were not taught, but subjects were taught which interfered with the faith of the students. The boys became shameless . . . By education only knowledge regarding the orders of the Koran is intended and not the knowledge of writing European languages and figures, or knowledge about countries or about the kings of the past, or the languages of unbelievers.

"8. It is not, and has never been, the practice that grown-up Moslem girls should be sent away from an Islamic country for the sake of learning European writing and arts. On account of this undesirable action, we Moslems were ridiculed by all Islamic and non-Islamic countries. Never did and never will any king practice worse tyranny on the people than this."

The document spoke of Amanullah's adopting the solar year, like European countries, in place of the lunar year; of his making Thursday a holiday in place of Friday; of his opposition to the Lame Mullah in the Khost Rebellion and his imprisonment of Gul Agha.

Coming close to the true, deep reason for the rebellion, the mullahs had written, "He abolished allowances of the mullahs, of the callers to prayer, of the servants of the mosques, which these people received from the previous kings . . . He liked to curse the ulemas and their teachings."

Included among these charges was the clarion call which had summoned men to wars before, which that first man over the threshold of the Arg Palace had heard in his heart as he praised God and felt the bullet:

"The actions of Amanullah . . . are centered on the short life of a few days in this temporary world and are based on selfish motives. He did not care for the progress of religion which leads to everlasting life."

CHAPTER 29

January 19, 1929, to February 13, 1929

On January 19 a telegram from Peshawar arrived in Kandahar. It was addressed to Amanullah as "His Majesty" and did not mention political affairs, only hoped that Amanullah was in good health. It came from Inayatullah, who signed himself "Moin-us-Sultanah," the title he had held as a prince, and in this guarded message Amanullah learned that his brother had also abdicated.

But Amanullah was puzzled that the telegram came from Peshawar and wondered if it had been relayed through that city from Kabul or if Inayatullah was actually there. He sent an urgent-reply prepaid telegram to the Afghan Trade Agent in Peshawar asking these questions, but soon he knew the answer from travelers from Ghazni.

The royal standard again was hoisted above the turrets in Kandahar to flutter in a nest of machine guns. Amanullah was making himself King once more, taking over the throne for the second time after Inayatullah had renounced it.

Only his mother's family, however, were showing much enthusiasm for him. Others in Kandahar were preoccupied with the scarcity of grain and food.

Many of the rich Kandahar traders were Hindus fearful they might suffer for their religion. Under Amanullah they had been the equals of any Moslems and were grateful to him and now were kindly when he needed kindness. Now, as a sign of the weakening authority of the King who condemned religious bias, there were again flashes of religious hostility.

Amanullah decided that he should go to Herat. This was the advice of his neglected friend and father-in-law, Mahmud Tarzi, who did not believe that the British would help Amanullah and figured that he would be no worse off, and possibly more likely to find allies, in the vicinity of Russia.[1]

Tarzi himself, weary and weak in health, wanted to leave Afghanistan. Like Amanullah, he was not one who cherished power for its own sake. With the wit that he had put to use early in the century in awakening Afghan youth, he had favored Amanullah's decision to leave the throne of Kabul with a pun on two Persian words. "Takht" means "throne" and "takhte" means the slab on which the dead are laid out; Tarzi said that in Amanullah's present situation, one was as good as the other.

Through the Consul in Bombay, Tarzi was asking the British for a visa to transit India but they remembered how he had stood up against them and Humphrys was told, "Government of India feel the only kind of visa which could at this juncture be given to a man like Tarzi would be visa conditional on his going direct from Chaman to board ship." And he wired back: "Mahmud Tarzi may possibly try to cross Chaman border without a visa with intention of carrying out propaganda in India. I would suggest that careful watch be kept." And later: "The trouble is that Tarzi even if he accepts these conditions will probably try to evade them." They did not know how tired and discouraged he was.

The Kandaharis, faced with the prospect of Amanullah's imminent departure, suddenly saw that he was their only hope against the bandit in Kabul. Their leading mullahs, who had been refusing to put the power of their religion behind him, decided that he might be repentant enough to qualify for their support. They considered proclaiming Bacha Sacao a kaffir, not for anything he did to Islam but for taking the throne.

To them, and to those companions who also wished him to stay, Amanullah replied that he had two reasons for going. The first was that the Afghan nation had destroyed his labors of ten years during which he had worked for the good of his nation. "In consequence I have lost all ambition to rule over such ignorant people." He considered that he should depart voluntarily for Herat according to his own schedule rather than wait until he was forced to go, as he had been forced from Kabul, with "my cup of bitterness overflowing." Secondly, he said, during the past months it had become obvious that the Kandaharis were merely prevaricating and that they were making no response to his call for men, that even those men who had enlisted were not pre-pared to fight.

They agreed to help him and that he should reign from Herat to Ghazni; he finally agreed to remain in Kandahar. He gave a large sum of money to a contractor for purchasing trucks in India. Five buses ordered in happier days arrived in Kandahar. The first use of these buses, which could seat 210, was to rush reinforcements toward Kalat to rescue troops which he had ordered toward Kabul but withdrawn after Inayatullah's flight; they had been attacked by Ghilzais on their way home. Weather again was hostile to Amanullah; heavy snow was falling between Kandahar and Kalat and some of his soldiers were suf-fering from frostbite and unable to march.

As Foreign Minister in the new capital he again named his old friend Ghulam Siddiq, whom the British described as "our most impla-cable enemy in Afghanistan," and it was Ghulam Siddiq's first duty to announce to various nations that Amanullah had withdrawn his abdica-tion and taken the throne of Afghanistan again.

"I advise that no notice be taken," said Humphrys.

Inayatullah reached Kandahar on the evening of January 23. The fol-lowing day Amanullah called a public gathering.

If the public of Kandahar was truly loyal to him, he said, they should pledge their loyalty on the Koran. He asked which King they wished, himself or Inayatullah. If they did not favor him, they must tell the truth and he would go to Herat, Mazar-i-Sharif, Maimana for help. If he could find no help in any of those other places either, he would go to Mecca and spend the rest of his days in the guise of a dervish and would undergo religious mortification by observing a forty-night vigil.

Drama, which had been lacking in his speech in the Kabul garden, was here in abundance. It vibrated in the spirits of the men of Kanda-har. Again they wept. Inayatullah disclaimed the throne for himself. The people cried out that they wanted no one for their King but Aman-ullah. The day of Inayatullah's flight from Kabul had been a Friday, and even while he was an exile in Peshawar the Khutba was being read in his name in the mosque of Kandahar. He never heard himself thus designated a King. When Friday came again, the Khutba was read in the name of Amanullah.

Along the eastern frontier the tribesmen who had started this chain of events by rebelling in November were amazed to hear what they had wrought. Bacha Sacao's accession was reported to them first by returning soldiers who had gone toward Kabul to fight for Amanullah at the time when he thought it safe to remove some troops from Jalalabad. The triumphant men of Bacha Sacao took away these soldiers' arms and sent them back east. Then some of the planes which Bacha Sacao had acquired along with the rest of Kabul flew above Jalalabad and dropped a proclamation, "To my dear brethren of the Eastern Province," praising them for deposing Amanullah ("He was proud and was careless of God") and announcing "Laws framed by him have been canceled and the Shariat of Mohammed (Peace be upon him) has been reinstated."

"You must not believe in what mischief-mongers may tell you," Bacha Sacao told the tribes of the East, "but you should think it over and use your brain. The statement of a plaintiff is generally untrue. You should not disturb peace of mind by false statements of enemies. Most of your notables have come to see me, the road is open and you can also come when you like to do so. I will very soon send pious and good-natured commanding officers."

These assurances did not diminish the shocked distress of the Shinwaris, Mohmands, Khugianis, and other tribes who had been creating chaos in the eastern part of Afghanistan. The more knowledgeable among them knew that there was a connection between Bacha Sacao's attack and their own revolt; the letter earlier that month promising "a pious man" as Amir had even referred to Bacha Sacao by his true name of Habibullah, which was not then generally known.

But in looking forward to the new order which would arise from the one they were destroying, they had imagined it in the framework of tradition, with an Amir whose family and background qualified him: one of the Hazrats of Shor Bazaar or Nadir. It never occurred to these singleminded tribesmen that the forces they had unleashed might get out of their control.

"General conclusion," reported the British in Peshawar, "is that while Amanullah was regarded as dangerous to Islam, accession of Bacha Sacao is insult to Pathan race." Quickly the news had got around that Bacha Sacao was a Tajik, of a tribe to the north of Kabul to which tradition never granted any right of importance in Afghanistan. Although most of the tribesmen could not read or write and some were not above raiding a caravan, still they desired an Amir who was better in these respects than themselves.

So all along the disturbed frontier, on both sides, a wave of sympathy for Amanullah swelled up. Part was human compassion, part was the feeling that he had been better than what they had got.

"Thus though [Bacha Sacao] has obtained possession of Kabul," summarized the British, "he has only the support of the Kohistani tribes and the Tagao and Kabul mullahs. The tribes of our own frontier and the Jalalabad and Khost provinces of Ghazni and of Kandahar are all against him . . . Lower classes are disgusted at accession of Bacha Sacao and they would like to see restoration of royal family in person of some orthodox member." A few days earlier the report had been: "It is increasingly evident that the Ghilzais are taking an interest in present turn of affairs. It is also reported that Ghilzais and Shinwaris have agreed to support Nadir as a candidate for the crown of Afghanistan."

Ajab, the Afridi who had murdered Mrs. Ellis and kidnapped Molly Ellis, had become a folk hero along the frontier. Men forgot that he had acted against helpless women and remembered only that he had defied the kaffirs of the great British Empire and that Amanullah had served the kaffirs' cause by exiling him. Now rumors about Ajab began to fly. One said that he had murdered Bacha Sacao; another said that Bacha Sacao was Ajab in disguise. The British, knowing that Ajab had been kept away from them in Turkestan all these years solely through Amanullah's good will, were worried that Ajab in the flesh might really appear to give them trouble.

In the Indian towns of Lahore and Peshawar the Moslems sympathetic to Amanullah's cause were passing resolutions offering support of his family.

Amanullah's loyal supporter Musa Khan was gathering men to march on Kabul, and some who joined him were Mahsuds from the British side of the frontier; they met with misfortune, and never reached Kabul.

Meanwhile a caravan of eight thousand camels escorted by armed Shinwaris was approaching the British frontier. Another caravan of twenty-five hundred camels got through to Landi Kotal escorted by one thousand Shinwaris to whom the nomads paid a fee of nine rupees per camel. Rebellion was profitable. Travel in the other direction was not so easily bought. A convoy of seven Afghan trucks headed from Peshawar for Jalalabad that same day was attacked and two trucks went up in a wild blaze from the gasoline they had been carrying to government forces. The other five got through. One was carrying one hundred thousand rupees to Jalalabad; it would be the last shipment of money on that road, for Inayatullah during his brief stop there had instructed

the Afghan Trade Agent to send no more Government money to Jalalabad, but to send it all to Kandahar.

Ali Ahmed was still in Jalalabad, where government money as well
as his empathy with the tribesmen had been helping him keep his control. He had just repulsed an attack by Ghilzais on nearby Jagdalak.

For the tribal distress at events in Kabul, Ali Ahmed had a solution.
He had always wanted to be Amir.

Despite all the demands that rebellion had made on it, there was still
a fair sum in the Treasury. Later it would be charged that Amanullah
had run out of money, thereby contributing to his downfall. Although
there had been financial crisis, the British, who studied the matter,
would decide that he had been adequately protected financially. Inayatullah on his departure had been permitted to take three hundred
thousand rupees and still there was a great deal left.

Yet Bacha Sacao, looking at more money than even he himself had
stolen, was offended not only by Amanullah's name and insignia on
the coins but by the dates, which were those of the solar calendar, which
the mullahs thought irreligious. He ordered his own coins struck with
the dates according to the lunar calendar, 1347, Year of the Hegira
(of the Prophet Mohammed) instead of 1307. He discovered stacks of
paper currency which would have been the first such currency in Afghanistan if Amanullah had reigned long enough to issue it. Bacha Sacao
was shocked at the sight; this was obviously not money, and he berated
Amanullah for wanting to cheat the people of Afghanistan.

Bacha Sacao took the financial step which seemed to go with every
accession: he announced an increase in the pay of the Army. He also
forgave the arrears of certain land revenues and abolished Amanullah's
new taxes.

"Educational schools, which were of no use except that a lot of government money was wasted on them, have been closed," he proclaimed.

To emphasize this last, he decreed an auction of all the books that
Amanullah had been amassing for his schools. Most of those who
bought the books were the students who had been studying them.

Even such rudimentary acts of state were, to a degree, beyond the
power of Bacha Sacao's background. He was being advised by a set of
ministers who were a strange mixture of his old bandit companions
and educated men. His Minister of War was his closest friend, who had
shared his life for years and whom he named in his proclamation of

accession almost as his equal. Sayed Hussein, a few years younger, was the son of a well-to-do landowner in Charikar. On his father's death he had quickly squandered the legacy in pleasure and assumed the only profession he ever had, that of banditry. Cruel and ruthless, he had none of the good qualities that were being discovered in Bacha Sacao.

"Sayed Hussein, unable to forget his old profession, has twice abstracted daily receipts from Customs Houses and sent the money to his home at Charikar," reported Humphrys.

Another old robber companion became Bacha Sacao's aide-de-camp and his younger brother, Hamidullah, acquired a prestigious title previously awarded only to such notables as Mahmud Tarzi and Nadir, that of Sardar-i-Ala. The Governor of Kabul was Bacha Sacao's former employer in Kohistan, Malik Mohsin, a respectable man who was to reveal by his cruelty that at heart he too had always been a bandit.

Associated with these were educated men who knew something of affairs of state, men like Sher Jan and his brother Ata-ul-Haq, the Foreign Minister. His Treasury officer was Gul Agha, who knew nothing at all of finances.

"Outsiders, thousands of whom had come to Kabul to do homage to Bacha Sacao, were ordered to return to their homes after depositing their arms in Arg. This is necessary if it is hoped to restore any kind of order," wrote Humphrys on January 20.

"At present bazaars are crowded and small parties are taking this opportunity to hunt down old enemies and loot houses of persons against whom they have a grudge. It is said that two ex-Cabinet ministers are hiding in a sewer."

A few days later he was wiring: "Houses of two Germans employed under late government which are situated a few miles outside Kabul have been completely looted. Also many houses of Mohammedzais [the ruling family].

"Ghulam Yahya, former Assistant Secretary, Foreign Office, was last night left with only the lower half of his pajamas."

Yet the rampant lawlessness which people had feared did not develop. "I have made inquiries from prominent Indians in Kabul city," reported Humphrys. "They state emphatically that Bacha Sacao's men have scrupulously respected the rights of British Indian subjects . . . Trifling thefts were due to Indians being mistaken for Afghans and full compensation had been paid . . . The order kept by Bacha Sacao's men in the city so far has been remarkable."

Internal security had swiftly been established so that Bacha Sacao could begin to worry about outside threats: Ali Ahmed in Jalalabad and the Shinwaris who were threatening to attack him on their own. He sent a group of mullahs east to negotiate with the Shinwaris and began to fortify the approaches to Kabul. His best protector was the intense cold which, combined with snowfall, made it unlikely that any attacker would get through the Kabul gorge.

"The wildest stories are circulating here referring to an imminent attack on Kabul by Ali Ahmed in person from the direction of Jagdalak," wired Humphrys. "Some of my colleagues believe these stories but they seem to me to be only propaganda designed to terrify any wavering supporter of Bacha Sacao.

"Today Sayed Hussein's small son shot at some fish in the Kabul River near the public gardens. This resulted in a *sauve qui peut*, people shouting, 'The Shinwaris are on us!' and trampling each other under foot."

Sir Austen Chamberlain made a formal statement of British policy toward Afghanistan in Parliament on January 29 replying to a question which he had arranged to be asked. Great care was taken in the wording of this statement; the Secretary of State for India, Viscount Peel, did not desire any specific reference to Amanullah or "anything in the nature of a promise to the future central government of Afghanistan, the nature and tendency of which we can form no idea at the present."

When Chamberlain arose to speak, by mistake he held in his hand a discarded early draft of this statement. What he said, and what was reported all over the world, was:

"His Majesty's Government have no intention of interfering in internal affairs of Afghanistan by supporting or assisting any of the parties at present contending for power in that country. They earnestly desire the establishment of a strong central government and they will be prepared when this government is established to show their friendship for the Afghan people by giving it such assistance as they can in reconstruction and development of the country. King Amanullah has formally announced his abdication to His Majesty's Government and consequently until it is clear that in spite of this abdication he is regarded as their king by the people of Afghanistan generally, His Majesty's Government are unable to regard his government as the rightful Afghan Government."

The approved statement had said merely that "It is for the Afghan people alone to determine who is to sit on the Afghan throne and His Majesty's Government await their decision." Chamberlain apologized to Peel and asked him to apologize to the Viceroy, and then they all tried to make the best of what had happened.

Russia, they hoped, would read this statement. Such inspired articles in newspapers were the only form of communication available to the British Empire since it had severed its diplomatic relations with Russia in 1927. "No direct warning to Russia not to interfere is diplomatically feasible," said a minute paper in London. "Britain's own position is ambiguous." So Britain proclaimed publicly its own neutrality.

"It is reassuring," the Viceroy Lord Irwin wrote to Peel, "to see that, if we can believe the Russian telegrams that we intercept, the authorities in Moscow are inclined, as we are, to play the waiting game and avoid embroilment. Indeed, if the chances of Amanullah's restoration are, as Humphrys seems to think, of the slenderest, it is not easy to see what Russia stands to gain at the present time by intervening on his behalf unless she decides to go for something much bigger."

Lawrence of Arabia was still being discussed in newspapers in every language and in many imaginations he was roaming the hills of Afghanistan in attire as picturesque as that in which he had been photographed so often among the Arabs, making and unmaking kings.

On January 8 Lawrence had finally been removed from Miranshah so hastily that he had to leave behind a phonograph that was a gift from George Bernard Shaw. Humphrys, wiring frantically on January 9 to ask where Lawrence was, learned that he had left the frontier only the previous day. Lawrence was taken to Lahore and then to Bombay for transfer to England, his own choice since he was offered alternatives.

Naturally the papers asked, "If Lawrence was not up to anything in India, why all this secrecy about his return?"

The resulting rumor was that this man who finally arrived by ship at Plymouth was not Lawrence at all but a double, that the real Lawrence was still at work in Afghanistan.

In London Lawrence stayed in seclusion in his apartment by official order, then broke that order and went to the House of Commons where, in the lobby, he introduced himself to Ernest Thurtle, a member who had been asking embarrassing questions. The question that embarrassed Lawrence, however, had to do with his fictitious name of Shaw, later legalized; he was sensitive about his birth, which was illegitimate.

Lawrence showed Thurtle the manuscript of "The Mint," written before his transfer to Miranshah, as evidence that he had been too busily occupied otherwise to spy. Thurtle accepted this; he became a friend of Lawrence and the recipient of many of his famous letters. But some other Englishmen were so unconvinced as to burn Lawrence in effigy.[2]

Humphrys now had only a cursory interest in denying rumors about Lawrence. He was concerned with getting the foreigners out of Kabul. Although his own staff had been cut to a minimum of key people who would be the last evacuated, he had a responsibility toward the Indians in Kabul who were British subjects, and a moral obligation toward members of other legations and the foreigners from other countries. In the precarious state of Bacha Sacao's power a sudden collapse was possible any day, and it might be followed by a season of mob rule in which non-Afghans, held responsible for all the ills that Amanullah had visited upon the pious, might be massacred.

Ata-ul-Haq was sufficiently familiar with government to know that it was important to Bacha Sacao's prestige to keep foreigners in Kabul, that their mass departure would advertise to the world their low opinion of the ruler he represented. Besides, in all this ferment of illiterates trained only in banditry, Ata-ul-Haq needed people with other skills. Many of these, including some Indians, had signed contracts by which he tried to hold them.

A powerful weapon was in Ata-ul-Haq's hands. The British were sending a plane into Afghanistan several times a week, bringing mail back and forth for everyone in Kabul and carrying evacués to India. They flew only by Ata-ul-Haq's permission. When he protested to Humphrys about the newspapers in India, which were bringing out all their most vilifying adjectives toward the bandit now ruling to the west, he used in a more or less subtle fashion the threat of stopping these flights.

He did not threaten again, but the possibility of a threat existed when a question arose about the mails that passed through India.

On January 10 the Afghan Legation in London had sent a mail bag to what was then the only government in Afghanistan, to Kabul. By the time the bag reached Peshawar, there were two governments, so Shuja-ud-Dowleh, the Minister in London, asked the Foreign Office to direct this bag to the man for whom it was intended, to Amanullah in Kandahar.

In Kabul, Ata-ul-Haq told Humphrys that all official posts should be sent by British air mail to Kabul.

The bag remained in the Peshawar Post Office for several days while in the high places of London and Delhi a decision was being pondered what to do about it. Meanwhile that bag was joined by another in a similar situation from the Afghan Minister in Paris.

"It is an awkward problem," Humphrys wired. "Amanullah having abdicated and left his Cabinet in the lurch, it does not seem fair that he should have any official mails diverted for him from Kabul to Kandahar . . . The fairest solution seems to send both private and official post to the postmaster of the place where it was originally addressed."

"But it does not seem possible for us as neutrals to deliver one headquarters mail which are known to be intended for another," objected the India Office in London. "It is impossible for us in this way to interfere with choice of loyalties of Afghan officials abroad. From neutrality standpoint we seem to have no option but to comply with Shuja's request."

Meanwhile someone in Peshawar examined the bag more closely and saw that, although addressed in English merely to the Foreign Office, Kabul, it bore in Persian the name of Ghulam Siddiq.

"I trust Government of India will not lose sight of fact that if we refuse Ata-ul-Haq's twice repeated request, he will lose interest in post and there will be danger that we may lose privileges of postal and other airplane landing in Kabul," wired Humphrys. "These and other matters affecting Legations in Kabul are dealt with by *de facto* head of Kabul Foreign Office, and whilst we remain here we are to some extent obliged to humor him. Ghulam Siddiq's connection with Foreign Office at Kabul has clearly ceased forever. I request no diplomatic bag for this or other legations should be sent up from Peshawar pending decision on this important point. If nobody in Kabul received an official post, it may help diminish chagrin of Kabul Government."

In London the situation was puzzling. "There is no evidence that Ata-ul-Haq would know that a bag which had arrived in Peshawar addressed to the Kabul Foreign Office had subsequently been diverted to Kandahar. But it is to be assumed that he has spies in the Peshawar Post Office or wherever such bags are kept."

In Delhi the Viceroy, perturbed, sent a private and personal wire: "We feel that to refuse to divert these bags would be an act of intervention which we could not reconcile with policy we have so far endeavored to adopt, and it is, moreover, repugnant to our ideas of fair play. If, as seems to be fairly certain now, Nadir Khan intends to link up in some way with Kandahar, it would seem even more desirable not to let these bags fall into Bacha Sacao's hands."

But Humphrys kept insisting from Kabul: "If we divert Kabul's bags to Kandahar on grounds which are entirely beyond Ata-ul-Haq's comprehension, however reasonable and correct they may be, we shall offend him and run the risk of having number of our planes cut down. Present Kabul government is far more generous in matter of airplanes than Amanullah's government would probably have been. All Afghans have a distorted idea that passage of airplanes in large numbers represent some sort of foreign invasion of their country."

All Englishmen concerned expressed distaste at what they finally decided to do. "Safety of Legation must emphatically override objection which normally might be conclusive," wired the India Office with the approval of the Foreign Office.

The mail which had been intended for Amanullah was sent to the Government of Bacha Sacao.

The benefit of evacuation, so dearly bought, was not cherished by all who might have had it. On the day Inayatullah left Kabul, London had wired to its ambassadors in the nations represented in Kabul, offering evacuation in British planes to all Legations there. "My Italian colleague," Humphrys reported on January 24, "tells me that Hikmet Bey [the Turkish Ambassador] told him yesterday that he was convinced that chaos in Afghanistan was first stage of war between Russia and England for domination of Asia. It would therefore be obligatory for the Turkish Government to retain their representative in Kabul in order to receive firsthand reports of this homeric struggle. He definitely did not believe that British Legation would ever leave Kabul." By February 8 Humphrys was writing, "My German, French and Italian colleagues wish to leave if I do but are tied by their nationals. The Persian has received no orders from his Government and is terrified at the prospect of remaining. Turk with Kiazim Pasha's mission is waiting for Armageddon."

"My three European colleagues," he was wiring four days later, "have been clinging to hope of evacuating most of their nationals with their baggage by road and at first affected to misunderstand notes to their Government . . . as implying I would arrange a lorry convoy to Peshawar. I have explained to them that this idea is illusory.

"I have also pointed out to them that while it would be possible for

a German merchant, a French professor or an Italian engineer to remain
in hiding in a cave in the Hindu Kush for months until expected storm
blows over, it would be hardly a dignified solution for a first class power."

Ata-ul-Haq did not yet know that the British had decided to close
completely their Legation in Kabul. Humphrys, knowing he would protest, planned to tell him at the last moment. The European countries
who had legations in Kabul were privy to the secret, but the British
decided it would be too great a risk to tell the two Moslem governments,
Persia and Turkey, who at any rate had announced their intention of
staying.

All this time Humphrys was establishing British policy toward Afghanistan by his evaluations, which were read in London and Delhi
with great respect as coming from "the man on the spot." One sentence
in one wire was a summary of this significant opinion:

"Amanullah's cause is dead."

Ali Ahmed was now an Amir. On January 20 he was turbaned in
Charbagh as ruler of the Eastern Province by two mullahs as important
among the tribes of the East as the Hazrats of Shor Bazaar in Kabul.

One was the Hazrat of Charbagh. The other was the very elderly
Naqib of Baghdad, a mullah who outranked even those of Shor Bazaar
in prestige, but who had renounced politics and was content with religious matters.

Now the Naqib of Baghdad showed his nonpartisan spiritual nature
by admonishing Ali Ahmed that he must consider himself not the real
Amir but a caretaker for an Amir to be chosen.

Even a man of Ali Ahmed's self-esteem had to observe that he was
not universally acclaimed. All through the tribal area and even in British Government offices people were saying that for a figurehead he
would suffice. Some tribes, however, were holding jirgas and deciding
he would not suffice even for that. The reason was always the same:
his character. And the outstanding element of that character was his
disobedience to the Prophet's prohibition against intoxicating liquids.

This characteristic was so well known that before he could be an
Amir, he was compelled to take an oath on the Koran, in front of all
those present, that he would no longer drink whiskey.

Then Ali Ahmed returned to Jagdalak with twenty-one trucks and
cars full of Khugianis, the tribe most enthusiastic about him, and began

to act like an Amir. He held a jirga the following day for his Khugianis, the government troops and some Ghilzais. All these accepted him as Amir, the royal salute was played by the band, the royal red flag called the Amiri was run up over his headquarters in an old rest house.

A week later Ali Ahmed began to publish his own newspaper, extolling himself as "courageous and religious . . . His enlightened thought had always been engaged in reforming the nation and country." He made the announcements that were required for a new Amir: abolishment of Amanullah's laws, obedience to the Shariat and the Koran, twenty rupees per month for soldiers, who would not be conscripted. Ali Ahmed performed a ceremony at the tomb in Hadda of the famous mullah whose spirit was guiding the rebellion now, and on Friday he heard the Khutba read in the Jalalabad mosque in the name of Amir Ali Ahmed. He was making his own obeisance to the forces of reaction.

Nowhere in Ali Ahmed's newspaper was he mentioned as a surrogate of Amanullah. This was a delicate matter. The Shinwaris were fearful that he might turn over the throne to Amanullah and therefore declined to support him; others would have supported an ally of Amanullah but not Ali Ahmed himself.

Ali Ahmed had collected all the money which Indian traders owed to the Afghan Government and spent it. Now he asked his friends around Jalalabad to subsidize his reign by paying land revenues in advance. Friendship did not extend so far.

He was ruling in a land where a traveler said: "The people are under no control with no fear of authority."

On the Khyber Pass the Chaknawar Mullah thought he had established some sort of order with a schedule of fees, for escorting caravans: Girdi and its neighbor villages would get two rupees per camel to Landi Kotal and the village of Lalpura two rupees for the remainder of the trip to Dakka. A caravan of 1,361 camels arrived at Torkham under this arrangement and safety henceforth was predicted for that portion of the road. It did not last. One large caravan which had left Kabul several weeks earlier paid forty-two rupees per camel and needed ten days to travel from Jalalabad to Peshawar, finding the greatest danger between Jagdalak and Jalalabad because Ali Ahmed's allies, the Khugianis, were fighting among themselves.

In Khost, which had rebelled in 1924, Ali Ahmed attempted to find help. The men of Khost did not respond. No one was ruling there either.

Having been dissatisfied like most frontier tribes with all forms of government, they now had a government they could be comfortable with: anarchy.

But one man had ambitions in Khost, the horse-trader Ghaus-ud-din whose armament included many rifles he had taken from Amanullah. When Ghaus-ud-din held a jirga of his tribe and the Zadrans at Gardez in Khost, the British commented: "Ghaus-ud-din may be expected to show his hand very soon." He sent Ali Ahmed a pledge of allegiance, but at exactly the same time he was showing his hand to the British. His messenger delivered a letter for the Commissioner of the North-West Province, saying that "former irreligious and worthless King has gone toward Russia," and that when Russia moves, Afghanistan will be helped by British. He asked that if the British Government have any intentions with regard to Afghanistan "then someone might be deputed to discuss the matter with him as he could speak for the whole of the Southern Province and in order that his friendship with the British Government may be established."

This did not strike the British as impertinence. Ghaus-ud-din himself could have observed that, if Bacha Sacao could be an Amir, anyone could be. With approval in Delhi and London, the British Empire sent the disheveled nomad trader of known rascality a courteous version of the statement in Parliament: "It is for Afghans to choose their own King and our policy is not to interfere in Afghan affairs. British Government, however, entertain sincere friendship for the Afghan people and British Government will show proof of their friendship when Afghans have settled their own affairs, provided the people of Afghanistan remain friendly."

In his ecstasy at being addressed like a sovereign state, Ghaus-ud-din sent back a reply which imposed a condition. He asked that future correspondence be conducted in the Hindustani language. He himself could not read or write any language, but this was a way of using his newly discovered power.

Ali Ahmed on February 3 sent a letter to Peshawar to be carried by plane to Humphrys in Kabul. It said that all Ali Ahmed required of the British Government was: one million pounds sterling, 100 motor trucks with driver and two mechanics each, 2,000 tents, serge uniforms and overcoats for 2,000 men, 20,000 rifles and 20,000,000 rounds of ammunition, 30 mountain guns each with 1,000 shells, 1,000 horses complete with saddlery, 12 wireless telephones with operators, a certain number

of military airplanes fitted with machine guns and large passenger planes
with British pilots, plus 80,000 gallons of aviation spirit and petrol.

"As prophesied by me," wrote Ali Ahmed, "Amanullah has proved
himself utterly unworthy of the throne. Bacha Sacao is a mere brigand.
Kabul is shortly going to be attacked from all sides. Bolsheviks are
scheming for a republic which would ruin Afghanistan. They are like a
rotten apple which spoils the whole basket." Calling himself an old
friend of the British Government, he said that Britain had a unique
opportunity to establish a friend on the throne which would never recur
"if British diplomacy was too proud to grasp it."

"Bacha Sacao and Ali Ahmed have lately been exchanging abusive
and threatening messages." Humphrys wired, "About 2,000 troops with
guns have been sent by Bacha Sacao to mouth of Kabul gorge defile,
15 miles east of Kabul, and he is also covering approaches to Kabul from
Logar and Tagao. Ali Ahmed's tactics appear to be to hold Bacha
Sacao's troops on Jalalabad road and to make an encircling movement
with his main force . . . through Tagao and Panjshir which would
eventually threaten Bacha Sacao's rear and cut off his men from their
homes.

"Ali Ahmed has sent warning to Kabul that he will destroy every
house in Kohistan and Koh-i-Daman Valley unless Arg is peacefully
surrendered to him. Kohistanis in Kabul City are very uneasy and some
of them have already begun to retreat northwards."

But snow was falling. Every night the temperature dropped below
freezing leaving a legacy of ice. In such a season in 1840 the British
refugees, going in the opposite direction, had been cut down till only
one man arrived in Jalalabad. "It is hard to believe that tribes from
Eastern Province will risk making advance at this season," Humphrys
wrote. "They would have to traverse ten miles of windswept barren
country."

Ali Ahmed advanced.

What defeated him was not the weather but another force of nature:
treachery. Two Khugiani leaders were in Ali Ahmed's confidence. One
crept off to Kabul and made a deal with Bacha Sacao about which Ata-
ul-Haq would brag to Humphrys. Ali Ahmed was betrayed. Khugianis
and Shinwaris entered his headquarters on pretext of pledging allegiance. Instead they attacked him, and in a few moments he had nothing left, not even his uniform.

He himself later told how, searching for loot, they went to his bedroom and tore at the bedclothes. Under his mattress they found a bottle of whiskey.

It was the first bottle of whiskey these tribesmen had ever seen. The English label meant nothing to them. They demanded of Ali Ahmed what it was.

Ali Ahmed said that it was medicine to cure the sores on camels' backs.

These men were shrewd and suspicious of any unfamiliar fluid; on the rare occasions when they encountered a carbonated soft drink, they did not take a chance with the bubbles, lest this was what the Prophet meant. They sniffed and did not believe that Ali Ahmed's bottle held medicine for camels' backs. They told him he was not fit to be an Amir anyway.[8]

Commenting on this episode, the British would note that Ali Ahmed had committed the irretrievable error for a Pathan: he had made himself ridiculous.

A ridiculous figure, he escaped from the custody of these men whom he had hoped to rule, disguised as a mullah, and, without even a rifle, without money, he found refuge in the home of an agreeable Ghilzai. He was hiding there when Humphrys received his letter with the extravagant demands.

The Shinwaris and Khugianis followed up their success at Jagdalak by entering Jalalabad, ousting the garrison, and beginning to loot everything in sight.

But Ali Ahmed's tragedy had given the Jalalabad garrison some time for preparations. They arranged a time-fuse bomb to blow up the arsenal after their flight. The dynamite exploding in a storehouse of ammunition sent a column of black smoke four thousand feet into the air; observers from afar commented that it was shaped like a mushroom. About eight hundred of the men looting Jalalabad were killed and the city itself was set on fire; all over the Eastern Province on the night of February 10 the sky was red.

Three Shinwaris who had carried five machine guns a sufficient distance from the arsenal to escape destruction continued to bury these guns to prevent them from being seen and looted by other Shinwaris. But many had to stop their looting to search the burning ruins for the bodies of their friends and kinsmen, and to tend to the wounded, many of whom were finally taken by difficult means to the Mission Hospital at Peshawar.

This is what would have happened in Kabul if Inayatullah had not surrendered.

Before the elimination of Ali Ahmed, Bacha Sacao was persuaded to send for Nadir.

Nadir's brother Shah Mahmud had been appointed Bacha Sacao's private secretary. This was the brother who had been Governor of Jalalabad and had spoken disparagingly of Amanullah even while holding an appointment from him. About Bacha Sacao he said that, although illiterate, he had great strength of character and was just.

In a long conversation with Humphrys on February 5, Shah Mahmud compared Bacha Sacao's coup to that of Reza Shah Pahlevi, the army sergeant who had made himself ruler of Persia, but expressed the opinion that Bacha Sacao could not last. He himself was being sent to tour the Eastern and Southern Provinces to persuade the tribes to stop fighting and agree to an early conference to elect a king acceptable to the Afghan nation.

Bacha Sacao would certainly, in Shah Mahmud's opinion, be prepared to abdicate in favor of an Afghan nobleman who was generally approved by the tribes provided he was not a member of Amanullah's family. Everything, he said, depended on the early arrival of Nadir and his other brothers; he was sure that Nadir would not fight and he did not think he would accept the throne, but his influence in settlement by conference would be immense.

All along the roads in Afghanistan people were saying that if Nadir were only present, he could calm the upheaval. Enough important people were saying the same to Bacha Sacao, and enough remnants of his respect for the establishment persisted in his spirit, and he could see enough chaos around him that he was statesman enough to deplore. By the time Shah Mahmud spoke to Humphrys, Bacha Sacao's emissaries were on their way to the south of France to bring Nadir home.

The two men who were to bring Nadir back were his cousin Ahmed Shah, who was married to a sister of Ali Ahmed, and Abdul Aziz, Hashim's maternal uncle, the former Minister to Persia and Rome, elderly and extremely deaf. They traveled to Peshawar as couriers on the British postal plane of February 6; the Government of India was reluctant to establish a precedent of passage on their planes for Afghans, but again yielded to the theory that "obviously this is necessary for the British Legation to keep on terms with the *de facto* government in order to carry out its evacuation."

"Rail and steamer tickets must not be purchased by us for Ahmed Shah, who must himself wire to the P. and O. [steamship] Company," went the instructions to Peshawar. "If it is necessary to advance money, it is essential that utmost precautions be taken to keep our participation in the contract from becoming known."

There was another problem: to assure that these Afghans, whose idea of time was flexible and who had never been compelled to make a train schedule, arrived in Bombay in time for their sailing.

"Please reserve for two Afghans in Peshawar," Bombay was ordered, "the two-berth cabin engaged by the Foreign Office. Afghans will telegraph for passage direct."

And the following day from Peshawar: "Ahmed Shah has not succeeded in getting money from the Trade Agent and is now trying to raise it in the city."

The Trade Agent, Amanullah's man, had been ordered by three different persons, Amanullah, Bacha Sacao, and Ali Ahmed, to hand government funds only to them. As a result he was handing funds to no one. But he called a conference of Afghan traders, many of whom were going bankrupt, and they decided it would be wise to give the money.

"I will see that Ahmed Shah and Abdul Aziz leave tomorrow by Bombay Mail and will get station master to give them ticket whether they pay or not. Cannot do anything about payment of P. and O. tickets but hope to get Ahmed Shah to wire for them."

And later: "Sent them to Dean's Hotel. They left without paying hotel bill or taking tickets. Their tickets paid with batch of refugees who arrived yesterday and left also on Frontier Mail.

"Trade Agent paid Ahmed Shah £480. Heard he had £600 brought unknown to Abdul Aziz."

But on the day these men were to board their ship in Bombay, February 9, the three brothers, Nadir, Hashim and Shah Wali sailed from Marseille.

On February 13 the Viceroy wrote a private and personal letter to Viscount Peel:

"Altogether I think, in spite of the malicious propaganda that has been set on foot, things are shaping themselves so far pretty favorably for us. I hope we may succeed in getting Nadir Khan in without giving rise to too-intensive an anti-British agitation, and indeed it seems as if in this respect too things were working out not unfavorably for us in that he appears to be generally regarded by all parties in Afghanistan as the *deus ex machina.*"

One of the mullahs who had attended Sher Agha's planning session in Paniala, India, more than a year earlier, set forth toward Gondal City to tell Sher Agha it was time for him, too, to come home.

CHAPTER 30

February 7, 1929, to February 25, 1929

Amanullah also had wired to Nadir through the Afghan Legation in Paris, asking him to come to Kandahar and become his Prime Minister.

Of the sort of times through which Afghanistan was passing, a Western poet would write:

"Things fall apart; the center cannot hold."

For a decade Amanullah had been the center of his country. Now he was only a fragment. He was the falconer of Yeats's poem whose falcon could not hear him. He himself could no longer hear the rest of the country. He did not know that Bacha Sacao also had sent for Nadir.

The rest of the world was equally remote and unhearing. To the British Empire the honored guest of Windsor Castle in April was by February a greedy outsider asking for things to which he had no right. One of his requests was for the gift of armaments offered with such careful attention to his specific wants. When he asked for it, he discovered that the gift was not for him, the Amanullah who had dined with King George and received the Victorian Chain, but for the Afghan Government, with which he was presumed to have no more connection than any nomad following his camels across the hills.

He did not know that the British had intended from the first to send the gift bit by bit, in order to extend his gratitude, that this careful parceling out had postponed the first delivery until things fell apart.

Also he did not know that when Sir Austen Chamberlain, his former host, called him by name in Parliament in denying his kingship, that was what the Viceroy described as "a curious little accident."

Ghulam Siddiq was handed a copy of Chamberlain's statement by the Indian Moslem who was British Consul at Kandahar. He replied angrily, "Amanullah has already been recognized as King of Afghanistan by the British Government and a treaty exists to that effect. An internal rebellion does not cancel Amanullah's right to recognition. If British Government refuse to recognize Amanullah, it is a violation of treaty and tantamount to interference in internal affairs of Afghanistan which will have evil results. The reply is obscure. A clear answer should be given early.

"Amanullah's abdication was only a ruse," continued Ghulam Siddiq. "The attitude of Russia is the real danger. Amanullah does not intend to ask for either British or Russian troops, but the fact that the British Government has published it does not recognize Amanullah will be seized upon as an excuse by the Russians to occupy Turkestan and Herat on pleas of self-protection. The Afghan Consul-General at Tashkent reports that 150,000 Russians are already concentrating on the Herat and other borders. We do not understand why the British should not recognize Amanullah when he is recognized by Russia, Germany, Italy, Persia and Turkey. I solemnly warn Sir Francis Humphrys that war will be inevitable if Amanullah's government is overthrown."

Humphrys reported the conversation commenting, "Above is typical of Ghulam Siddiq's confused, ill-balanced and bombastic utterances." Humphrys knew that the backing he described was largely imaginary. The British had been told in confidence by the German Minister of Foreign Affairs that they "had no intention of mixing . . . up with the internal affairs of Afghanistan by recognizing Amanullah."

The reply that Humphrys proposed to give Amanullah after Ghulam Siddiq's outburst repeated Chamberlain's statement in an abrupt form that was less courteous to the grandson of Abdur Rahman than the reply given to the nomad horse-trader Ghaus-ud-din. London thought it "cynical" and softened it.

"It is a sad fact," said Humphrys, "that neither Amanullah nor Ghulam Siddiq have hardly a friend between them in the country." That was the only sentence written by an English official in all the correspondence dealing with Afghanistan to contain an error in grammar. To this extreme Humphrys was driven by his emotions in regard to Amanullah. The sentence was also an exaggeration; the "fact" was that Amanullah did have friends.

"We are fully alive to the dangers of pro-Amanullah propaganda emanating from Kandahar," the Government of India acknowledged.

Amanullah had at Kandahar ten mountain guns, about three thousand rifles, about fifteen machine guns. The cash at his disposal was approximately £70,200 in Afghan rupees, £15,000 worth in silver bricks, and £40,000 pounds in gold. He had tried to get a coin-making machine from India to turn the silver bricks into currency. Already coins minted in Bacha Sacao's name were being circulated in Ghazni.

At the Indian port of Karachi were sixty machine guns that Amanullah had bought in Europe; he had expected to pay for them from the Afghan State Treasury. The machine guns remained in Karachi.

He sent 1,100,000 rupees to Chaman to pay for rifles also lying in Karachi. He could not get them. He had ordered rifles and ammunition from the Birmingham Small Arms Guns Ltd., in England, which was now informed privately and confidentially that there was no prospect of a license being issued for the export of arms to Afghanistan and asked by the Foreign Office to allow the matter to drop. Shuja-ud-Dowleh asked to buy for cash from the Woolwich Arsenal (in other words, from the British Government) two thousand rifles and one million rounds of ammunition which he would carry with him through Germany and Russia. "Consult India Office," wrote the Foreign Office, "but 2,000 rifles and a million cartridges are fantastic—the bottom would fall out of the train." And Sir Austen Chamberlain decreed: "The request is absurd."

Yet a few miles from the Afghan border, in the Kohat Pass, the only industry of any kind in that whole large area was turning out rifles which it sold to anyone. More than twenty years earlier an enterprising Afridi had imported steel from Bombay and begun to produce rifles which were not as good as European makes they imitated but much cheaper. Tribesmen using primitive tools made these rifles by hand, and the Kohat Pass rifle was as famous as the Lee-Enfield and Martini-Henry whose names it often carried.

"With reference to report that Afghan rebels are being supplied with rifles by us," the North-West Frontier Province wired on February 7, "I incline to view that some action is necessary to check manufacture of and export of rifles at Kohat Pass. Trade in rifles now surpasses all previous records. One consignment consisting of 200 rifles en route Khost is known to be held up in Zaimusht territory. A very large number of persons of our own tribes and of Afghanistan are visiting pass to purchase rifles and there is little doubt that all purchases are taken to

Afghanistan. Also it is believed that machine guns and rifles stolen from Afghan Government are for sale in the pass."

The G. of I. saw no reason to keep these particular rifles out of Afghanistan, but it did consider the matter. "Supply of munitions to belligerents by subjects of neutral states (in contradiction to supply by the governments themselves) is technically lawful and we are therefore not obliged by duty of neutrality to prevent it. However, question of neutrality is one thing, question of political expedience another."

Neutrality and political expedience coincided sufficiently for the Government of India to decide that the Kohat Pass rifles did not have to transit British India and theoretically were open to sale to all parties. The fact was that any rifle carried from the Kohat Pass into Afghanistan had to transit a few miles through Independent Territory. The fiery nature of its residents made Independent Territory too troublesome for the British to administer, yet every inch of it, as they often pointed out to the Afghans in the course of negotiations, was part of India. "We could close factory down, of course, but result would be to drive it completely out of our control elsewhere. Afghan tribes are now so glutted with arms that inferior arms from this source will make no appreciable difference and at present we are inclined to leave things as they are."

Amanullah tried to get his rifles and machine guns from Karachi by saying they were consigned to him personally since his name appeared on the documents. The British said it did not matter.

So Amanullah could look only to Russia.

Russia was perplexed all during the rebellion in Afghanistan. Her Chief of Intelligence in Afghanistan would report later, when he defected to the West, that she had no definite idea of what was going on.[1] To the new reactionary government that had taken over Kabul the atheist Bolshevik government was anathema. After first shooting at Russian planes the rebels under Bacha Sacao's orders had permitted them to land.

"Internal situation in Russia is bad," went a British intelligence report which comforted the Viceroy of India, "and appears to be growing steadily worse from every point of view, financial, industrial and political. Shortage of food in towns is serious. There is much discontent among peasants. The state of railways is bad. Industries are still below pre-war level of production. There is open opposition to the present dictator, Stalin, who is endeavoring to purge part of his opponents;

nevertheless, inertia of populace and lack of leaders render a revolution improbable and government will no doubt survive crisis.

"It is not likely that government will or can attempt any large-scale operation in Afghanistan in view of internal situation. They will doubtless seize any opportunity for anti-British intrigue and propaganda but we understand that they are puzzled by present confusing situation and are beginning to wonder whether they have not backed the wrong horse . . ."

For several days and nights early in February smoke candles were kept burning on the Kandahar airport to guide Russian planes that might be unaware of its location; under Amanullah's treaty with Britain, Russians had not been allowed to visit Kandahar. On February 8 the planes arrived bringing eight Russians, one a member of the Foreign Office of Moscow named Solovieff. They brought with them a form of communication that Amanullah had been lacking: a wireless set.

Three times a day the British official wireless transmitted a program of news from Rugby. On February 7 after the noon broadcast a message went out over the Rugby wave-length: "A persistent rumor is in circulation in Peshawar that Russia has delivered an ultimatum to Habibullah [Bacha Sacao]. It is declared that unless [he] ceases robbing the Treasury and pays to Russia £3,000,000 within eight days for equipment and ammunition supplied to Amanullah the Russians will bomb Kabul." Everyone who intercepted this message, including all the military installations in the Empire, thought it part of the official British broadcast; it was not, and no one knew where it came from.

The editors of the *Daily Express* of London, through "their own sources," as they explained to the Foreign Office, heard a different version of the rumor which they published on February 8 giving the time limit of the ultimatum as forty-eight hours. Even Parliament had to take notice; in reply to a question, the Foreign Office denied all knowledge: "The situation in Afghanistan is obscure."

Rumors about Russian help were more likely to be started by Amanullah's enemies than by his friends. Any foreigner who arrived among the tribes unexplained, like the British pilots who crashed, had to give assurances of not being Russian before he could be welcome. Ghausud-din's request for support from the British had shrewdly commenced by linking Amanullah with Russia.

Kandahar, especially, feared a Russian alliance, so the arrival of the plane from Moscow did not relieve all Amanullah's tension that day.

February 8 was Friday, the holy day of the week when all the men
of Kandahar and a few veiled women went to the courtyard of the Friday Mosque to pray. Early that day the town crier, beating his drum,
went around the streets calling out that King Amanullah would speak
to his people after prayers.

They were all present. Ghulam Siddiq spoke first. He reminded them
of 1919 and the fight for independence, when standards had been raised
and men summoned to them to fight for the King, and there had been
two hundred to three hundred men under each standard. Now, ten
years later, Amanullah had been in Kandahar for almost a month and
got only promises.

Amanullah then said that if Bacha Sacao was still ruling in Kabul on
New Year's Day, he would lead any army to fight him and would perish
at its head if necessary.

A Farsiwan, a Shiah of Persian descent, spoke up saying that if men
of his community went off to fight, the Afghans would loot their homes.
An old man called out, "We poor people cannot help you. You must
ask those who have a taste for ladies' fashions!"

That poem of Yeats's would go:

> The best have no conviction, while the worst
> Are full of passionate intensity.

Amanullah, however, had passionate intensity. It burst. These days
he never moved without a pistol in his belt. He lifted his pistol and
pointed it toward the men who had upbraided him. His Minister of
War, Abdul Aziz, was standing beside him and saw the gesture in time
to strike his arm down.

The men in the mosque also had seen it. The listening audience became a chattering, crying, protesting mob. Men turned and went
through the gate as rapidly as the press of other men would let them.
Ghulam Siddiq called out to stop, but no one heard him. Then those
in the front turned back toward him and Amanullah. They stood still
and silent.

Amanullah told them that all his actions were unselfish and dictated
solely by love of his country. He said that Afghanistan was hedged in
by two powerful nations who would crush her unless she maintained
a united front. The men looked at him and said nothing, then turned
and, in an orderly fashion, walked away from him.

It was the beginning of Ramzan, the Moslem month during which no food or drink must pass the lips of the faithful from sunrise to sundown. Nerves and tempers were easily shattered; it was a period for doing as little as possible. Amanullah's grandfather had never observed Ramzan, calculating that a monarch was entitled to the same exemption as a traveler or a sick person.

But Amanullah was being very careful to observe all religious rituals; he could not afford to justify the appellation "kaffir." Souraya was never seen unveiled. He made a ceremony of going to the mosque every evening to pray, his Rolls-Royce standing outside the gates of the palace, while Kandaharis gathered to stare at it, and a guard of honor was drawn up on either side, until he came out wearing a smart military uniform and was driven off. One concession he refused to make to the orthodox: he never exchanged his uniform for the traditional robe and turban, and he never grew a beard. On the latter point the conspiracy against him would have ignored reality, anyway, for although he kept his mustache, a pronouncement by the tribes would say that he had shaved it off and resembled a butterfly.

While suffering from the demands of Ramzan, Amanullah was in a crisis that would not let him relax. He had only about fifteen hundred men under arms in Kandahar; yet their small number was not so disturbing because in any conflict in Afghanistan the power was held by the tribes. Every day he interviewed tribesmen who he hoped would fight for him. It was largely a matter of money, for their loyalties had been bought and sold before.

The telegraph line to Chaman was his only communication except for runners and mounted couriers from different parts of the country and the telephone lines as far as Mukur. There was no airplane in Kandahar; Amanullah was trying to get two from Junkers. Such news as came was not good; a mutiny in Mukur cost him the money kept there; there had been trouble near Farah. The Ghilzais, the tribe over which Sher Agha had most influence, kept sending word to Kandahar that they objected only to the kaffir King Amanullah and could not remain passive unless he was turned out but would promise for the present not to attack Kandahar. That word "kaffir" frightened the Kandaharis; they feared that from being applied only to Amanullah it might soon be applied to themselves, and even the sound of it was an assault. The only thing to do, Amanullah decided, was to move his government to Herat.

The world of which Amanullah was so unaware was very much aware of him. The London *Daily Express* published a cartoon, "Putting a Kick in It," in which Amanullah told an impassive tribesman, sitting with his rifle beside him, "Now I am going to make you a Western cocktail! First we take some Italian vermouth . . . then we put in a little French vermouth and some British whiskey . . . after that a spot of German lager and a toothful of Russian vodka . . . and complete it by a strong dash of Turkish kemal! Then shake . . . and you drink it." And the tribesman drinks and then kicks Amanullah out.

Only one Western newspaper, however, made the expensive effort to send a correspondent to see Amanullah in Kandahar, and that was an American newspaper which alarmed everyone by its interest: the Chicago *Tribune*, which proposed to send Larry Rue.

The comment of Sir A. Willert of the Northern Department, Foreign Office, was "The Chicago *Tribune* is not a particularly pleasant paper and it is sometimes anti-British. But it is not professionally anti-British like the Hearst press. It is, rather, blatantly pro-American. It is, moreover, almost the most powerful paper in the U.S."

Larry Rue arrived from Tehran on February 14, his plane almost mobbed on landing by the curious people of Kandahar, who were beaten back with a whip by an officer who escorted him to the palace. Rue and his pilot were given favored treatment. A Persian colonel accompanying them was treated with superficial politeness and told there was no need for Persian help.

Nur-us-Seraj, the little sister whom Amanullah had always cherished, was about to have her first baby and his apprehensions about her safety had led him to ask the British, through a wire to Chaman, to admit her to Karachi or Bombay for medical attention. Humphrys advised showing her every courtesy, "She is a charming girl." This was an opportunity to give Mahmud Tarzi also a transit visa, to balance the attention shown Bacha Sacao's emissaries to Nadir.

Now that he expected to reign from Herat, Amanullah decided to send his sister to Herat if he could do so by plane and on to Tashkent for her delivery. Abdul Wahab Tarzi, who had become Foreign Minister on Ghulam Siddiq's departure, asked Rue's pilot to carry Nur-us-Seraj to Herat; after all, he would have five idle days while Rue was getting his stories. The pilot had no extra fuel for such a trip. But there were a few hundred gallons of airplane gasoline in Kandahar, and Amanullah was willing to use these for his sister.

Rue's comment in his newspaper was: "Russia is not yet sufficiently intimate to permit the King's sister the use of its airplane which is of the same type as that used by the *Tribune*. Although this plane had been in the hangar for two days before our plane arrived, it was the *Tribune* plane which . . . made the special trip to Herat on a mission the King regarded as vital to the health and possibly the life of his sister."

Mahmud Tarzi and his wife accompanied Nur-us-Seraj. They went to the plane wearing European dress, Tarzi in a modern tweed suit. Both the ladies wore hats with heavy veils covering their faces. Tarzi chatted with Larry Rue in French about the advantages of living on the Riviera, in Paris, in Berlin, in Vienna. He said that he was going to consult a doctor in Tashkent about a stomach ailment.

They boarded the plane. And then both women lifted their veils and smiled farewell to the relatives who were seeing them off.

This first flight was aborted; after ten minutes it had to return because of an overheated motor. Amanullah, who knew nothing of machinery, and who had not eaten or drunk since sunrise, angrily sent word that the plane should have continued anyway, since it ran splendidly and that was all that was necessary. The second flight was successful, the plane was welcomed in Herat, where the Governor was a relative of Ulya Hazrat, and Amanullah gave the pilot and the mechanic five hundred dollars each.

But Nur-us-Seraj never got beyond Herat. Her baby, a boy, was delivered there by a local midwife.

Larry Rue, meanwhile, was making ten appointments for an interview with Amanullah and having each one broken. Once Amanullah was said to have a bad cold; once he was taking a bath. His greetings to Rue, like his salutations when the men glimpsed each other at a distance, were cordial. But he spoke with him only through Abdul Wahab Tarzi.

Amanullah's statements exonerated the British completely from guilt in the insurrection against him. The Russian Foreign Office man, Solovieff, had told Rue that the Russians also had men with the mullahs, and knew that Lawrence of Arabia had bribed them. Amanullah, speaking through Abdul Wahab, said that the mullahs had opposed him without being paid. He knew that Bacha Sacao had spoken with Humphrys at the gate of the Legation but believed that only the safety of the Legation was discussed. That is what he said to the reporter. He actually believed that his attempt to unite Persia, Turkey and Afghanistan in an alliance with Russia had provoked the British to oust him, but dared not say so.

The British were gratified when this news favorable to them appeared in the newspaper they had feared.

For five days Larry Rue studied Kandahar, bringing an American newcomer's surprise to such details as the custom of washing dishes in the drainage ditch, the slap in the face administered by a drill sergeant to a recruit whose hands crept up his sides, the sand in the rice, the bare feet in the cold weather.

He sent Amanullah, in the efficient American manner which was so alien to Afghanistan, a list of questions. These included a request for names of the tribes, subtribes, etc., supporting Amanullah, with the numbers of men for each. Such a specific inventory would have been impossible, considering the casual nature of the Afghan tribes, under any circumstances. Not receiving a reply, Larry Rue deduced that Amanullah did not know who supported him. Despite the defect of his reasoning, this deduction was true.

The Russians departed. Solovieff told Larry Rue that he considered the outcome of Amanullah's efforts mainly a question of how much money Amanullah was able to raise to subsidize the tribes.

Cruelly, the Russians took away the wireless, saying there was not enough traffic to justify it. Amanullah, who had thought it a gift to him, again was cut off.

In Russia the newspapers were advising Amanullah to save himself by dividing land among the peasants. Russians did not realize the difference in social structure between Tsarist Russia and Afghanistan, where large land-holdings were not a problem; they were unaware that certain Pathan tribes practiced a sort of communism by reapportioning their land every few years; only recently Humphrys had been surprised and pleased to learn from the gossip of the Italian Minister how little the Russian Ambassador knew of frontier geography and manners. Once Amanullah had told a visiting Indian Communist, M. N. Roy, that he himself was a revolutionary and a communist;[2] indeed he was revolutionary in a country where one could become so by uncovering women's faces, but what he took for communism was not any dialectic or social structure but an overall feeling that everyone should be happy and equal.

Amanullah quarreled with Abdul Karim, the Governor of Kandahar, who thereupon asked the British Consul secretly for permission to transit India to Persia or "to reside in India until present chaos subsides."

The people, seeing their governor also about to leave, as they thought, with Amanullah, realized how unprotected they would be. There was panic among the Hindus; the homes of the Farsiwans had been barricaded against reprisals ever since one of them made his rash statement in the mosque. Many Afghan officials were discovering in their families an illness that could be treated only in India.

Amanullah had a private fortune with him of 1,100,000 rupees, which he sent to India to be stored in a private serai in Chaman. His kitchen truck, from which food was to be prepared along the journey to Herat, already was at Girisk on the first stage. He announced that he was leaving as regents his mother, his brother Obeidullah, and his relative Abdul Aziz, the War Minister, all three having ties to Kandahar.

He bade Kandahar another farewell on February 22 in the mosque, saying that having no response from them, he was going to Herat for help; that Bacha Sacao was gaining strength every day and was ruining Kabul. He wept.

This time Amanullah had his people with him. They responded to his tears and his unhappiness, some with tears of their own. They began to talk, and they began to say things that had not been said before because he was the King.

They said, among other things, that the Governor and his brother, who was in charge of recruiting, had been the main instruments which impeded the response from Kandahar, that these two were really working against his interests. Amanullah slapped the brother's face.

Seeing the fruits of their reluctance in their own futures and the future of Afghanistan, the men of Kandahar were suddenly ready to make amends. They called out that they would not let Amanullah go, that they would stand firmly behind him and would see him again ruler of Afghanistan.

Amanullah remained. The money was brought back from Chaman, the kitchen truck summoned home, a message sent to Ghulam Siddiq in Herat. Abdul Aziz was appointed new Governor of Kandahar.

Two days later Amanullah and the men of Kandahar gave each other pledges in their most solemn fashion.

In Kandahar was a sacred relic, a mantle once worn by the Prophet Mohammed, a short knee-length cloak woven of camel's hair by a woman of his family. It was said that even the summer heat of Kandahar had caused no disintegration, that this cloak looked as it did in the Prophet's day. The legend was that after the Prophet's death his son-in-law Ali gave it to one of his companions, on whose death it was moved to a cave near Mecca. After many years a sheikh carried it off to Baghdad, and after many more years the sheikh's descendants transferred it to Bokhara. Eighty years later it was taken to Balkh, the ancient city near Mazar-i-Sharif, and thirty years later it was moved east to Faizabad in Badakhshan. Balkh and Badakhshan were not then part of Afghanistan. But toward the middle of the eighteenth century Ahmed Shah Abdali, the man who welded Afghanistan together, gained possession of them. The Prophet's mantle was given to him and he brought it to his own city where his own tomb still stood, Kandahar.

"This sacred relic has sanctified Kandahar and bestowed a special blessing on this center of Afghanistan," wrote the Kandahar newspaper. A small mosque had been built called the Khirqa Sharif, or Sacred Cloak, filled with candelabras and chandeliers, with the cloak reposing in a casket in the sanctuary. At times of special peril the casket was opened and the cloak was looked upon. Thereby the Kandaharis felt that Allah had strengthened their arms.

The cloak in its casket was carried from the Khirqa Sharif to the largest mosque in Kandahar, which on February 24 was crowded with most of the residents of Kandahar, including a great many veiled women. At one o'clock, with great solemnity, Amanullah opened the casket and the Prophet's cloak was exposed. He did not lift it up. The sayeds, the descendants of the man who wore it, were standing closest to Amanullah; so were the most revered mullahs; they looked upon it. For two hours the cloak was there in the open and even those who could only glimpse the casket from afar were shaken with religious awe.

Amanullah recited the profession of faith, "There is no God but Allah and Mohammed is His Prophet." This was the profession that some of his men, captured by the Ghilzais, had been made to recite to prove they were not kaffirs like him. A Koran was brought. Placing his hand on it, Amanullah took a vow to obey the religious laws of the Shariat. Some mullahs stepped up and, on the same Koran, took oaths that they would raise forces for him; others kept coming forward and taking the same oath. The ulema, the council of religious leaders, issued a proclamation that, since Amanullah had promised under oath to obey the laws of Shariat, anyone opposing him would be liable to be stigmatized as a rebel and would be worthy of death.

Animal sacrifice was reserved by the Moslems for very special and solemn occasions. This was such an occasion. Both sheep and cows had been brought to the mosque. Amanullah, even in the eleventh hour when he had snatched a triumph, continued to think beyond Islam and to contemplate other men's religion. He decreed that the cows should not be killed, to avoid offending the Hindus of Kandahar; so the throats only of the sheep were cut. The flesh hung on the mosque walls for a while, then was given to the poor to eat.

Islam always had unified Afghanistan. Now in the religious drama of this ceremony, Amanullah found the passionate intensity which the good men of Kandahar needed. Various men planted banners in the ground as a sign for those who wished to enlist. Soon each banner had a crowd beside it. Amanullah said he would march on Kabul as soon as possible, and the Hindus agreed to supply each stage on the road with a certain amount of grain.

Amanullah was hopeful again. He had another reason for optimism: Nadir was on his way.

Humphrys finally informed Ata-ul-Haq on February 20 that Great Britain was removing its Legation from Kabul.

As Humphrys had expected, good humor was not evident as Ata-ul-Haq demanded how the British would communicate with him and whether the Consul would remain in Kandahar. Humphrys' reply was that Ata-ul-Haq could still telegraph, and that the Consulate would be withdrawn simultaneously from Kandahar. The latter decision had been taken also to insure Ata-ul-Haq's good humor.

While the two men talked together, a heavy snow was falling. The Kabul airport had not been fit for landing for several days, and the outlook for the next days was not good. Humphrys told Ata-ul-Haq that on the final day of evacuation he would need eight planes; the surface of the airport was rapidly becoming dangerous and the British Legation could not function if its personnel fell below a certain minimum. He thanked Ata-ul-Haq for his great courtesy and pointed out that it would be unstatesmanlike to send him away in a bad humor.

Ata-ul-Haq agreed to eight planes, and then settled down to a conversation based upon his hope that the Legation would return soon. He said that Bacha Sacao's authority was gradually extending over the country and that every day fresh declarations of allegiance were being received from the outlying districts. He listed several persons who had sent their allegiance that day, but Humphrys was not impressed, particularly as one of those named was Ghaus-ud-din.

Then Ata-ul-Haq spoke the significant phrase, "the new king, whoever he may be." This king, he said, would not repeat the mistake of seeking assistance from foreign nations other than Britain. "Amanullah was at heart a friend of England," said Ata-ul-Haq, "and the only foreigners for whom he had respect were the British, but he was led astray by inexperienced ministers and greed. It was not so much Amanullah as Ghulam Siddiq who plunged the country into civil war. Afghans now look toward the British Empire to save them from anarchy."

Humphrys' comment later was, "These and many other flattering remarks were doubtless to a great extent inspired by a lively anticipation of good things to come, but remarkable friendliness of Afghans of all classes toward us at present is unquestionable."

During the next two days Humphrys burned all the Legation documents of which there were duplicates elsewhere, appointed servants to care for the Legation, locked ten motorcars in the garage, and "arranged for a regular supply of information." He also spoke to the Russians, offering seats in the British planes to safety. The G. of I. had decided a month earlier, "It would seem not merely common decency but policy for Humphrys to offer to come to [the Russians'] rescue. As far as we know, Russians in Air Force put no obstacles in the way of our airplanes landing in the first instance." The Russians declined, but they were touched.

The weather was clear on February 23 but a foot of snow remained on the airport. A plane landed but could not take off. The next morning Humphrys employed several hundred Afghans to come to the airport and walk on it; they treaded down the snow to a smooth surface almost like cement, and then they began with shovels to clear a track. The wind was blowing first from one direction and then from another.

But the eight planes managed to land and on February 25 they all took off for Peshawar. In the last plane to rise above the hills around Kabul sat His Majesty's Minister, Sir Francis Humphrys.

Since December 23 the Royal Air Force had conveyed 586 persons in 82 airplanes without a single mishap to passengers, flying over mountainous country in the depth of winter.

This was the world's first airlift.

It ended exactly seven years after the day when Humphrys first crossed the border into Afghanistan as Great Britain's first Minister, bringing a new era.

Nadir and his brothers arrived at Bombay aboard the *Kaisar-i-Hind* on February 23. Their official greeting was ordered in a telegram to the political department of Bombay:

". . . with all friendliness . . . the G. of I. much regret that their policy of non-intervention in Afghan affairs, circumstances of the time, and to some extent Nadir's own interests unfortunately preclude the facilities and courtesies which the G. of I. would otherwise have been pleased to show to so distinguished a visitor.

"They trust he will appreciate reasons why special facilities are not being offered and the motives underlying their desire that he should refrain from any sort of political activity while in India and proceed as expeditiously as possible to Afghanistan.

"During their stay in Bombay, party should be kept under careful unobtrusive surveillance . . . Baggage should be passed through Customs without questions. Please telegraph interview on board ship and subsequent movements."

While the *Kaisar-i-Hind* was climaxing its long voyage with the final miles into Bombay harbor, and all the other passengers were at the rail looking toward the famous arch known as "Gateway to India," Nadir was sequestered with the British official, Freke.

He was anxiously trying to learn from him a secret of the G. of I.; which of the Afghan claimants the British rulers of India really preferred.

"I am strongly pro-British," Nadir said, "and I am anxious to adopt a policy favored by the Government of India so long as it is consistent with an independent and strong Afghanistan.

"I am not definitely pledged to support Amanullah or anyone else."

Nadir said that Amanullah had ordered him to travel to Afghanistan by way of Russia, which was the route already taken by Amanullah's eldest son, Hidayatullah, who had been studying in France. But he, Nadir, preferred to travel by way of India.

In Bombay the three brothers stayed just long enough to have a large number of pamphlets printed. Carrying Nadir's signature, they began:

"In the name of God, the most Merciful and Compassionate,

"My dear tribesmen, sincere advice to my countrymen."

The pamphlets said that as a devoted servant of Afghanistan Nadir, and his brothers, had come for the service of "my country."

"Neither I nor any of my relatives have any desire for the throne of Afghanistan."

Then Nadir left for Peshawar by way of Delhi. In Bombay, however, he had another visit from Freke, who transmitted a verbal message from the G. of I., whose "one desire is identical with his own, the early restoration of an Afghanistan peaceful, united, independent, strong and friendly. As a patriotic and farsighted Afghan he will, they are sure, realize that his consummation would be imperiled, not advanced, if they allowed their sympathies with Afghanistan in its present misfortune to deflect them from the path of strict nonintervention even to the extent of tendering counsel. He may, however, rest assured that when peace is again restored to a united Afghanistan, proofs of their friendship will not be lacking."

Freke's private impression was "that Nadir has not ruled out the possibility of himself becoming candidate for the supreme power in Afghanistan."

Three men of significance in Afghanistan converged on Peshawar on the same day, February 25, from three directions by three modes of travel: Humphrys by plane from Kabul, Nadir by train from Bombay, and Ali Ahmed through Mohmand territory that was not so dangerous to him as some other, by his own feet into the administered part of India and for the rest of the way in a car sent by the sympathetic Political Agent.

CHAPTER 31

February 25, 1929, to March 24, 1929

Coincidence alone had put Nadir and Humphrys in the same place at the same time, but the Government of India, in view of the extraordinary publicity which would be focused on Peshawar, hesitated to permit Humphrys to have an interview with Nadir.

"Whether I see him or not," Humphrys protested, "Russian Embassy will take for granted that I have had an interview with him.

". . . Fate brings myself and Nadir Khan together in the same place and he and his brothers, who are my oldest and closest friends in Afghanistan, will . . . misunderstand the whole position if I decline to see him . . . Russia and a certain section of the India press will abuse me whatever I do, but to antagonize the most influential family in Afghanistan . . . seems to me to be the worst thing that could happen."

It had been more than five years since Humphrys had seen Nadir. He had not felt so warmly toward him then, had deprecated his predictable flattery of all things British while considering him a menace to British interests on the frontier. In official papers Nadir had been described once as "the villain of the piece." There had been reference also to "his undoubted abilities for intrigue," but with his return to Afghanistan as the *deus ex machina* to bring order out of chaos, such abilities seemed desirable in one who was now being called in British correspondence "exceptionally cultured for an Afghan" and "the best mind in Afghanistan."

Shah Mahmud, the brother of Nadir, who stayed at home, was touring the southern provinces on behalf of Bacha Sacao, but he had used Bacha Sacao's emissary to Nadir, Ahmed Shah, to send a message asking an Indian businessman, M. A. Hakim, to meet him in Afghanistan.

"Hakim professes ignorance as to the object of summons from Shah Mahmud. He is a British subject, a member of a firm of contractors and commission agents who do a large business in Kabul and has been forbidden to go by his firm . . . [He] is reported to have in his possession a considerable sum of money advanced to him by previous Afghan Government."

Nadir himself arrived in Peshawar on February 27 with Shah Wali and Hashim. They stayed at a borrowed bungalow.

"Many deputations have waited on them to press them to go to Kandahar to support Amanullah," the British reported, "and have been politely told to mind their own business."

Two emissaries from Amanullah were on their way to Peshawar for the same purpose for which the two emissaries from Bacha Sacao had passed through earlier that month: to fetch Nadir. Amanullah had written Nadir a succinct letter giving a summary of events and telling him, with no attempt at persuasion, in the matter-of-fact way any sovereign would write to any official, to come to Kandahar.

Before Amanullah's men arrived, Nadir called on Humphrys.

Nadir first pressed Humphrys to tell him whom the British Government would prefer to see on the Afghan throne, and particularly if Amanullah was acceptable.

"Afghans can set their minds at ease about the attitude of Great Britain toward their present troubles. We shall do nothing to interfere with their independence and we shall not take advantage of their helplessness."

Nadir begged Humphrys to advise him as an old friend what he should do. Humphrys advised him to convene a meeting and try to get the tribes to acknowledge one man as their king, whether Amanullah or anyone else.

Then, for one of many times, the British put to good use the statement in the House of Commons that Chamberlain had made by mistake. Humphrys quoted it to Nadir, saying that Great Britain would be ready to hold out the hand of friendship to the king who succeeded in establishing a settled government.

"Many doubts that had been working in my mind have been laid to rest," Nadir said. He outlined his future plans: after three days in Peshawar he and one brother would go to Jalalabad, while another brother would meet Shah Mahmud in the Southern Province. He ended by praising Britain's friendship, "Afghans will never forget all this when we succeed in setting our house in order," and then Nadir qualified this statement with the remark of every Afghan toward every enterprise: "Inshallah" ("God willing").

He said also that he did not intend to honor Amanullah's command.

A few days later Humphrys received a private telegram from Ata-ul-Haq asking him to send Nadir by airplane to Bacha Sacao in Kabul. In anticipation of this arrival Bacha Sacao gave orders for a triumphal arch to be erected at the airport as a greeting for Nadir. He was quite willing to yield part of his power to this man who seemed better able to use it, by making Nadir his Prime Minister and real chief of government. The bandit had a stronger sense of *noblesse oblige* than many born to *noblesse*.

Meanwhile Ali Ahmed, who was staying at Dean's Hotel, was making attempts to talk with the frontier tribes, but the day after his arrival a police guard was put on his quarters and no British tribesmen were permitted to see him. He drove out into the country occasionally but the British assured themselves that he "could hardly have found the opportunity to organize any conspiracy." Later they learned that he had secretly sent letters to the Afridis asking a thousand men from each section. He had a talk with Shah Wali and told someone afterward that he might go to Kashmir to live.

"I am in urgent need of money," Ali Ahmed said when he paid a call on Humphrys. "I cannot believe that the British Government would be so shortsighted as to refuse me financial help in my hour of need. I am a lifelong friend of the British Government and this is your opportunity, which will never come again. Once I am established on the throne, I will make it my first business to conclude an offensive and defensive alliance with Great Britain and to scotch all Bolshevist tendencies in Afghanistan."

Once more Humphrys made use of the inadvertent statement in the House of Commons. "Therefore you must put out of your head all hopes of financial help to enable you to gain the throne."

"The money might be paid secretly," Ali Ahmed suggested. Humphrys said he deprecated such a suggestion.

Then Ali Ahmed hinted that he would be obliged to go to Kandahar and support Amanullah if he could get no help from the British, although he loathed Amanullah and all his works.

Humphrys reminded him that during the tour of Europe, he had reproved him for being openly disloyal to Amanullah. "You are free to make your own decisions."

Ali Ahmed said he wished to stay a few days in Peshawar before deciding on his next move. Humphrys told him not to stay long.

A few days later Nadir inquired of the British whether Ali Ahmed was to be given any money, and whether he would be allowed to return to Afghanistan. The reply was that he would have to return, and that he was getting no money. That evening this message was sent: "Ali Ahmed had long interview this morning with Nadir Khan and his brothers. After 4 P.M. he was drunk." Ali Ahmed had suggested that one of them become Amir. Nadir insisted on first eliminating Bacha Sacao.

That was when Ali Ahmed sent his son, who had accompanied him on his flight to Peshawar, into Afghanistan to ask if Amanullah would take him back.

In a few days the Government of India had a new problem: "how it can best be brought home to Nadir and Ali Ahmed that they must move on, as they have outstayed their welcome."

Nadir left first. He and Shah Wali headed toward the Southern Province, while Hashim went toward Jalalabad. Nadir first stopped at Thal in British territory, where the Political Agent of the Kurram was his old acquaintance from Kabul, R. R. Maconachie. On March 7, preceding a social call on Mrs. Maconachie, Nadir asked Maconachie's advice "as a personal friend."

"The imminent danger," said Nadir, "is that Amanullah, while consolidating his position in the South-West and North, will fall more or less into the hands of the Russians and then, finding himself unable to regain control of Kabul and the Southern and Eastern Provinces, will attempt, as he did in 1919, to divert the opposition of these tribes for himself by proclaiming jehad against India. In such a fatal scheme he would be encouraged for their own ends by the Russians and it could only be defeated if Kabul and the Southern and Eastern Provinces were united under an arbitrator who could control them and prevent them from being misled to their own ruin.

"What is your opinion of this scheme?" asked Nadir.

"I have no authority," said Maconachie, "to speak officially regarding such matters."

"I quite understand this, but I am only talking to you as a former friend who has always treated me very frankly."

"The weak point," said Maconachie, "seems to me to be that any such disinterested arbitrator might be distrusted by the tribes, who might suspect him of bringing them under control merely as a preliminary to handing them over to somebody else. The suspicion was incurred by Ali Ahmed and seems to have been one of the reasons for his downfall."

"I agree with you in regard to Ali Ahmed," said Nadir, "and the danger which you mention is a real one.

"What impressions," continued Nadir, "have you gathered as to the probable attitude of the Southern and Eastern Provinces in regard to myself?"

"The tribesmen to whom I have spoken have given me to understand that these provinces would be ready to follow your lead and even to accept you as Amir, but they consider you to be ill, tired, and unwilling to make any claim to the throne."

"I have been very ill indeed," said Nadir, "but I am now much better. Originally I had no idea of claiming the throne for myself, but I may accept it if I am compelled."

Nadir then returned to the Russian menace, saying that although he had little inside information, he understood that so far the Russians had given Amanullah no help openly.

Shah Wali interrupted, "They have given him airplanes."

"But I have heard," said Nadir, "that money is being supplied from Russian sources through private persons and merchants in such a way as to conceal the real origin of these payments." Later Nadir told Maconachie's assistant his opinion that Russian internal economic and political difficulties would prevent her intervening openly even if she wished to do so.

"It is inconceivable," said Nadir, "that Bacha Sacao will remain in possession of Kabul, and I think it unlikely that the Southern and Eastern Provinces will accept Amanullah Khan again, especially so long as he is surrounded by his present advisers, Mahmud Tarzi, Ghulam Siddiq, Abdul Aziz, and the others, who were absolutely blind as to the inevitable consequences of the policy on which he embarked."

Maconachie reminded Nadir of the prophecy he had made in 1924, when they said good-bye, that before long they would see Afghanistan in ruins as a result of Amanullah's hasty reforms.

Suddenly Shah Wali asked a new question, "Why is Amanullah so popular with the Khilafat movement in India?"

"I don't know much about Khilafatists," Maconachie replied, "but it seems to me that anyone becomes a hero of theirs who has given the British trouble at any time. Nadir's own popularity with them is probably more apparent than real and mainly due to the trouble he gave us at Thal in 1919."

Nadir was amused by this. Turning to Shah Wali, he commented on Maconachie's habit of plain speaking. Then he said that Ali Ahmed was hoping to raise a force of Mohmands and Afridis from the British side of the line for an advance on Kabul and he asked Maconachie's opinion.

"Do you want my opinion from the British or from the Afghan standpoint?"

Nadir laughed again. "Years ago in Kabul you rubbed your opinion of such interference with your tribes into me, and I have not forgotten it. But I want to know what you think of it from the Afghan point of view."

"It seems to me essential that Afghans should work out their own salvation without assistance or interference from outside."

"That is what I told Ali Ahmed. But there is another objection to such a plan, that it would give the Russians an opening for intervention on the opposite frontier."

Maconachie did not respond: he was making a point of not discussing Russia. So Nadir said that the scheme was not likely to be successful anyway, as the Chief Commissioner had put sentries on Ali Ahmed's hotel room to keep people from coming to see him.

Late that night Shah Mahmud, who had been summoned from the other side of the border, arrived in Parachinar, bringing a letter from Bacha Sacao. Nadir, reading it, laughed heartily. One passage that amused him particularly was:

"I have done all this for you. It is very unlikely that I shall be selected as king by all the people. If you maintain friendly relations with me, and help me, I see no objection to your coming to Kabul where you will have no trouble with me."

Nadir asked Shah Mahmud the attitude of various tribes, whom he had seen while canvasing on a mission from Bacha Sacao. All were in favor of Nadir, was the reply, except some Ahmedzai Ghilzais, some men in Logar and some of the Shiahs.

"Nothing must be done which will make people think that we are hostile to Amanullah," said Nadir, "or which would disgrace us in the eyes of the public if we fail."

Shah Mahmud was delegated to gain the confidence of the people, carry them letters from Nadir and do nothing further while awaiting the outcome of Hashim's visit to the Eastern Provinces, since if they could obtain support of that province also, all four brothers could go together to Kabul. Shah Mahmud handed Nadir a small parcel of gold bricks.

Shah Mahmud left early the next morning, but not too early to receive visitors. One was the businessman, M. A. Hakim, who intended to accompany him into Afghanistan but was prevented by the British.

Two Khilafatists from Thal also visited him and asked for an assurance that Nadir and his brothers would make united efforts to restore Amanullah.

"My family does not want the throne for one of ourselves," said Shah Mahmud, "but desire to see a successor chosen by all of Afghanistan. The cause of the present rebellion was the fact that Amanullah has driven away all his true friends . . ."

The deputation asked if Bacha Sacao had given Shah Mahmud £400 to bring Nadir from Europe. He denied this.

They then demanded how it was that, when Shah Mahmud and other officers were in possession of Kabul arsenal, Bacha Sacao succeeded in gaining control of Kabul without serious opposition.

When the Army and the whole people became unhappy, said Shah Mahmud, he himself was compelled to submit. "My brothers and I have no special sympathy with Bacha Sacao."

The deputation requested emphatically that the brothers do everything in their power to assist Amanullah.

Nadir would have waited a day before entering Afghanistan, but a messenger whom he had sent to Khost returned with the news that tribesmen about to attack the provincial capital of Matun had decided to postpone their attack on hearing that Nadir was coming. It was essential, Nadir told Maconachie, that he get in touch with these men and take advantage of their attitude, which was more favorable than he ever expected.

On the afternoon of March 8 Nadir, accompanied by Shah Wali, crossed into his own country, which he had left in the spring of 1924 and had not seen since.

After his departure, a piece of paper was found in the room he had occupied, part of a letter from the eastern to the southern tribes, summoning them to a jirga. Shah Mahmud was soon trying to convoke this jirga at Gardez after the end of Ramzan but was finding it diffi-cult to satisfy the demands of the tribesmen that they would not even-tually be handed over to Amanullah and that the rifles they had looted would not be taken away.

"It seems likely," wired Maconachie, "that sooner than they wish the brothers may be obliged to show their hand."

Bacha Sacao would have been difficult to recognize as the bandit who had taken Kabul.

The British were about to publish their correspondence concerning the Afghan rebellion, and in editing the first draft they had changed the word "rebels" to "tribesmen," an acknowledgment of a new status due to success, and they had deleted all reference to Bacha Sacao's for-mer profession. His appearance had altered to suit his new status in a remarkably short time. Suppressing his old urge to hang himself with bullets, he always wore a smart military uniform and on his hands were something he had never known before, gloves. His beard was pruned to a regal configuration.

His followers all were having themselves photographed. Because the Prophet had forbidden the representation of the human figure, photography should have been one infidel invention to be particularly scorned. But vanity won over religion. They stood before the cameras, too awe-struck to smile, in their tattered clothes, carrying their rifles, in Afghan shoes turned up at the toes, their barefoot children solemnly seated at their feet, even the little girls too young to be in purdah.

Other photographs came into the hands of these new rulers of Kabul, photographs of the young, unmarried girls of the traditionally ruling clans.

Amanullah's father had been such an amateur of photography that there was an abundance of photographs not only of everything around the royal family but of everybody. People showed these photographs to Bacha Sacao, Sayed Hussein, and the others, for they knew that in the face of a young girl of noble family they were showing one thing that the bandits, while acquiring the palace and arsenal and all such paraphernalia, had not acquired.

Bacha Sacao was smitten by the features of a beautiful young grand-daughter of Abdul Quddus, named Binazeer. He had a wife who had followed him through all his campaigns of banditry, for which she was known as Bibi Sangeri or "The Lady of the Trenches." She was much admired for her bravery. But Bibi Sangeri did not fit into his new life, and he told Binazeer's family that he wanted her for his bride. Under the circumstances, they had to agree.

Bacha Sacao's bride-elect tried to kill herself. Then she submitted, but when Bacha Sacao looked into his bride's face on his wedding night, it was covered with soot. "Blacken one's face" was the Afghan expression for heaping dishonor, and she was thereby informing him what she thought of the marriage.

He was not angry with her; he was gentle and understanding. Soon she saw that she had a husband who respected her even to the extent of letting her make him into what he could become. It was she who showed Bacha Sacao how to put on the gloves. She taught him to issue orders in a controlled voice instead of bellowing. His leg muscles gradually became accustomed to sitting in a chair instead of squatting. No longer did he hurl a bone in the direction of a plate-glass window. She could not stop him from staging cockfights in the bathroom with the lapis lazuli tiles, but all over the world other wives were saying, "Take that mess into the bathroom."

All these lessons Bacha Sacao learned happily. They were leading him toward the world in which he had always longed to participate, and his teacher was a young, beautiful woman who finally had no fear of him. Years later, when his highborn bride had married someone else and had a family, her relatives would describe him as "a good husband" and their life together as "very happy."

Sayed Hussein saw a photograph of Aliah and commanded her hand in marriage. Her brothers, forewarned by the experience of Bacha Sacao's new in-laws, sent a reply: they were most deeply grateful for the great honor bestowed upon them, but their sister Aliah was not a single woman. She had been married without public announcement on December 31 to the former Amir Amanullah.

Bacha Sacao had changed the name of the official newspaper to conform to his own name, Habibullah. Now the *Habib-ul-Islam* announced the marriage of Aliah and Amanullah with a tirade against the wicked Amir, who, while depriving others of the pleasures of multiple marriage, took that pleasure for himself.

This newspaper was now publishing accounts of burglaries sometimes before they took place. Householders reading that they had been burglarized could make the account inaccurate by buying off the proper members of Bacha Sacao's court, who had not adapted as he had. Experienced brigands, they could guess the principal hiding-places of people's valuables, and when guessing failed, they tried torture.

The greatest zeal at torture and other ways of banditry was shown by the official who, before Bacha Sacao gave him this opportunity, had been a respectable citizen, the new Mayor of Kabul, his former employer Malik Mohsin, who had a private jail all his own. Malik Mohsin was copied to a degree by the ordinary soldiers who called themselves "independents" and snatched at passers-by in the street, demanding money as the price of not being shot.

Even in his improved state, Bacha Sacao saw the threat of reprisal as a perfectly normal instrument of state. Amanullah's trade agent and some other partisans in Peshawar were diminished in their function as pro-Amanullah, anti-Bacha Sacao propagandists because they had families in Kabul who could have suffered. The pilots in Kabul were unwilling at first to fly planes on the missions of dropping leaflets proclaiming the new régime, so their families were taken to the airport as visible hostages.

Yet he took his power in this regard more lightly than he might have. It was considered that under the circumstances, he kept Kabul more peaceful than anyone would have expected.

Bacha Sacao was fast outgrowing his old companions. Soon he was living in the palace on a high level and they were grasping in the streets for whatever they could clutch, alienated from one another.

Affairs of state were more difficult to learn than the social graces. A story would be told later that Bacha Sacao, on meeting diplomats of foreign countries, told them, "You are nice fellows, I am going to raise your salaries." That on meeting a Frenchman with a beard, he said, "I am glad to see there are religious men in France also."

He had, however, the approach to government which would be known in other countries as "grassroots."

"All government servants and members of the nation are . . . hereby informed that they should show good manners in their dealings in order to please the Almighty God," went one proclamation issued in Bacha Sacao's name. "It is necessary that all ministers and government servants should treat the said officials with due politeness." Such emphasis on politeness showed signs of coming from one who had experienced "the insolence of office," and was reminiscent of Amanullah's pronouncements. "We proclaim that the officers, petty officials, and even soldiers should purchase things on cash payments on reasonable price agreed to by parties. Our Royal Majesty thinks that members of the public are Moslem brethren of the civil and military officers and therefore the civil and military officers and soldiers have no right to inflict any injury on their brethren of the civil population . . . Government dues should be recovered with due regards to good manners and decency."

Wali, who had headed Amanullah's government as regent, had been one of three officials granted special permission in writing to accompany Inayatullah, having to sign promises they would not oppose Bacha Sacao. Wali remained behind in Kabul, however. Some blamed his illness, for which he was already planning to seek treatment in Europe; some said he was reluctant to leave his large family, and there were those who would say he remained because he was secretly in favor of Bacha Sacao.

In the first confusion of the capture of Kabul, no one had known where Wali was. Later Bacha Sacao invited him into his company and spoke to him with a respect that was later to cost Wali dearly. One day in February, in the sort of gathering that was now commonplace in Kabul, of the aristocratic men of the city together with those who had formerly been its scum, Bacha Sacao held out the fine rifle which Wali had given him through his gardener and publicly thanked Wali for the gift. That was the occasion of his remark that his morals as a bandit were higher than those of Amanullah's ministers. Wali was visibly embarrassed.

Bacha Sacao's deference toward Wali was often noted and questioned by those who did not realize that the two symbols of the establishment who had never broken faith with Bacha Sacao were Wali and the British Empire. He was good to the British also; when some soldiers entered the Legation garden and stole blankets and firewood, he sent for the caretaker to apologize with the comment that he had only good will toward the British and confidence in their neutrality.

A half brother of Amanullah and Inayatullah, the Kabir who had once, in his dissatisfaction at family arrangements, fled to India, now was a friend of Bacha Sacao with such enthusiasm that the rest of the family called him a disgrace. Bacha Sacao, however, was nostalgic for his old friends and was loyal to them. Before Humphrys left Kabul, Bacha sent him a request to free from the Peshawar prison four men who had been his accomplices in the Koh-i-Daman raids a year earlier, when he had still been only a bandit.

When the news of Ali Ahmed's defeat brought delight to Bacha Sacao, his messengers to Nadir were already on their way. With one rival out of the way and his position more secure, men asked themselves if Bacha Sacao would now be so agreeable to the entry of Nadir and his brothers on a scene which he dominated.

Bacha Sacao continued to look toward Nadir and sent him the letter by Shah Mahmud offering to give him "no trouble." Through Ata-ul-Haq he asked the British to send him in a plane, and he decorated the airport.

Nadir did not arrive. Days passed. He still did not arrive.

Then Bacha Sacao learned that Nadir had gone into the Southern Province, and that Shah Mahmud, his own representative in the Eastern Province, was working there for Nadir. And they were attempting to take by force the very thing that he had offered as a gift; he was not fit even to accept power from. Once again he had held out his hand to the establishment and been treated with contempt.

This would be the last such experience for Bacha Sacao. He told his men that they were free to go into the houses of Nadir's family and take whatever they wished. He gave an order to deport the family to Kohistan, but later relented and addressed a letter to them:

"On account of the injustice which they suffered at the hands of Amanullah I sympathized with Nadir Khan and his family and requested Nadir Khan to return to Afghanistan to take up an exalted position in the State. Contrary to my advice and expectation I regret that the attitude of Nadir Khan and his brother Shah Mahmud has been treacherous toward my royal favor. As far as possible you and your relatives in Kabul will be protected until a public declaration of his disloyalty is made by Nadir Khan. After such declaration has been made, any misfortune that may befall you should be laid at Nadir Khan's door. For the safety of your lives you should act as you think best."

Bacha Sacao sent men to the airport to tear down the arch of welcome for Nadir. And then, still angry, he sent other men to smash part of the monument that Amanullah had erected after the War of 1919 in honor of Nadir.

In Kandahar also Nadir did not arrive.

Amanullah considered this insubordination. But Nadir was making statements about peace and the election of an Amir, and unlike Bacha Sacao who had no illusions about his chances in an election, Amanullah considered that he would be that Amir. So Nadir's activities, though not under his control, appeared to him as beneficial.

Ali Ahmed's efforts, on the other hand, had been only disruptive. So Amanullah was not receptive to his request for an invitation to Kandahar. But Ali Ahmed was still the beloved nephew of Ulya Hazrat. Souraya also felt tenderly toward him. The two women did not like each other and under the pressure of life in Kandahar had quarreled so bitterly that Ulya Hazrat had moved into a relative's house. But they united on behalf of Ali Ahmed, and Amanullah finally sent word to Peshawar telling him to come on.

By the time Amanullah's message arrived, Ali Ahmed was even more of an embarrassment to the British. "It will become easier to deal with Ali Ahmed now that Nadir and his brothers have left . . ." G. of I. wired to Peshawar on March 8. Humphrys had left Peshawar and gone to Simla, having "completed my arrangements for intelligence."

"Government of India will be glad if you will take effective steps to make [Ali Ahmed] cross frontier. It should be pointed out to him that presence of a possible candidate to the throne and an ex-Amir is embarrassing to them and acquiescence in a longer stay might be construed as a breach of neutrality, and they must ask him to leave within two days in the direction of Afghanistan.

"Perhaps it might be as well for Deputy Commissioner to back up a letter to him from you with a verbal message which would leave Ali Ahmed in no doubt that we mean business."

On March 14 Ali Ahmed was still in Peshawar and again was given two days to leave. The time was extended to await Amanullah's message. Even that did not solve the problem of Ali Ahmed. Two weeks later he had got as far as Quetta, but the Agent there was writing, "He is very doubtful whether he will receive welcome at the hands of Amanullah, and says that if his son's report is unfavorable he will not cross the frontier. He wished to know whether in that event he would be allowed to cross frontier at Peshawar or reside in Kashmir. My reply was that I was certain Government would not agree to either proposal but that to satisfy him I would refer the matter for orders."

A message had just been transmitted from London: "We are adverse to permitting Ali Ahmed again in event of his failing to come to terms with Amanullah to transit frontier province, as he suggests, for Jalalabad. It seems unlikely that he would be able to go to Jalalabad and his destination would more likely be Mohmand country where he would probably be a cause of embarrassment to frontier administration by his efforts to involve British Mohmands in civil war, although he seems a spent force. It is also possible that again he would find plausible excuses for staying on in Peshawar and we might be reduced to undignified position of having by force to turn him out."

There in the frontier post of Quetta, Ali Ahmed made one last effort in the direction of the British Empire. "He discussed Afghan affairs at length, accused Amanullah of being strongly pro-Russian and suggested that the British Government should secretly support him with money against Amanullah as being a genuine friend of the British. This I said was out of the question and I advised him to accept the inevitable and either proceed to Kandahar or leave India either from a seaport or via Duzdap."

Ali Ahmed crossed the border, saying he would take as long as possible to reach Kandahar.

One claimant to the throne of Afghanistan was almost forgotten. This was Omar, the young man of slow speech and effeminate manner, offspring of former amirs, whose escape into Afghanistan had precipitated the deportation from India of many of his male relatives.

Except as a theme for propaganda, Omar had always been regarded by the British as so slight a threat that Peshawar had been advised, "If he can be tracked down, he can be told that all we would do to him would be to keep him out of harm's way until the storm has blown over." Shinwaris had been sheltering him in Afghanistan. Now they sent an offer to surrender him to the British under certain conditions: his allowance should not be reduced, he should not be punished for absconding, they must receive Rs15,000 for him, and the British must promise to return him to the Shinwaris if he was needed as a king.

The first two conditions were easy to accept, with the proviso that Omar must go temporarily to Burma; on the third count the British tried to reduce the price. But they refused to maintain Omar as a possible King of Afghanistan.

"The contingency of his being selected as King by the whole of Afghanistan is too remote to be included in the conditions," they said in

London, "and Government of India considered it would be open to misconstruction to do so."

In June, Omar would surrender on no conditions at all and would be sent to Burma.

On March 24 Humphrys summed up the situation: "If the tribes are unable to agree and if heavy fighting takes place without any side gaining an overwhelming advantage, I consider it probable that we shall be asked eventually to intervene to restore order and place a generally acceptable candidate on the throne. Unofficial suggestions that I should act as mediator were made to me before I left Kabul.

"Even if Nadir succeeds in inducing the tribes to agree without fighting to give their unanimous support to a single candidate, I think that the nominee would be unlikely to accept the throne without a guarantee of British support. Interesting developments are expected in the course of the next ten days. It is important that we should observe strict neutrality so long as it is practicable to do so."

The North-West Frontier Province already had reported, as a matter of little importance, "Chakmanni maliks have asked Political Agent Kurram for secret interview as they hear that Russians are coming to restore Amanullah and they wish to hand over country to the British. We have given the usual reply."

Amanullah's emissaries to Nadir in Peshawar had carried another message. It was for the British, but since these men were not received by any official higher than the Chief of Police of Quetta, they had no response. What they wanted was the secret importation to Amanullah of his armaments lying at Bombay and Karachi. The other part of their undelivered message was:

"Amanullah feels that the British Government have turned against him for reasons he does not understand. Please correct the misunderstanding."

CHAPTER 32

March 25, 1929, to April 18, 1929

Spring in Afghanistan was always restless. Through the rocky passes, flooding the roads and lanes, flowed the torrent of population that was the returning nomads. They traveled like an army. The men were heavily armed and at least one of them stayed awake every night outside the tents, his rifle on his knees, while dogs napped fitfully around him, ready to snarl to alertness at an unfamiliar sound.

Robbery was always a threat to a nomad. He was a trader, traversing India as far as Calcutta, bringing into Afghanistan the articles that were scarce there. The legend in both Afghanistan and India was that all nomads were rich, and although many had bank accounts in India, prospective robbers were correct when they guessed that most of a nomad's wealth was traveling with him.

Another constant threat was the antagonism of their seasonal neighbors. Afghans spent the winters as well as the springs and summers in their harsh land, enduring the cold and the ungiving earth, and then, when life was becoming easier, they saw these people sweep in from the easy land where there had been no winter, and they saw the newcomers' sheep and goats nibbling the green grass that was almost the only thing their rocky soil had to give. There had been fighting over the rights to graze, particularly in the Hazarajat, which was the westernmost spot to which a nomad was likely to penetrate. The Hazaras had a history of protesting with weapons the infringement of their land.

Already the battles between nomads and Hazaras had begun. Certain nomads had decided to settle in Afghanistan permanently, a step to which the Afghan Government was often urging them. Their Hazara neighbors drove them out; in reprisal the nomads attacked the Hazaras, with bloody results for all.

Most nomads were of the tribe of Ghilzais, the most numerous of those tribes that could be called Afghan. Ghilzais had controlled that part of the world in the mid-eighteenth century before Ahmed Shah Abdali of the Durranis, the ancestor of both Amanullah and Nadir, had conquered them and shaped a hodgepodge of tribes into a nation that he called Afghanistan. The Ghilzais never forgot that they once had ruled where now they roamed; they never accepted completely the dominion of the descendants of Ahmed Shah. Their spring arrival always added a new dimension to the political life of Afghanistan, bringing in thousands of shrewd fighting men fiercely opposed to the family in power.

This year the Ghilzais were moving to the Afghan highlands earlier than usual; some caravans had tried to get through even while the passes were blocked by snow. In London a British general was writing in a newspaper, "They will have the last word for Amanullah." The Ghilzais were bringing this year not only their numbers but an extra fierceness, for they had been listening to Sher Agha, who had been concentrating on them all his attention and his reputation as a holy man. Sher Agha and his agents had been telling them that Amanullah was a kaffir who should not reign.

The nomads would cross the route on which Amanullah would have to fight toward Kabul; he would have to move swiftly if he wished to avoid an encounter with the largest wave of migrating Ghilzais, who would probably be hostile. Still he delayed his departure from Kandahar; it was not so easy to raise an army.

And bad news attended his preparation. A messenger brought word of the murder in Herat of the Governor, who was his kinsman. Amanullah kept this news secret from the people of Kandahar. He assured himself and his intimates that one of his undoubted friends, Shuja-ud-Dowleh, was on his way through Russia to take charge at Herat. Amanullah did not know that Shuja-ud-Dowleh, leaving his post as Afghan Minister in London, had been seen off at the airport by detectives of Scotland Yard, the result of a dispute with his second-in-command over the ownership of several cases of lapis lazuli. At any rate, that would have been one of the things that a ruler of Afghanistan was accustomed to overlook. Amanullah saw in his approach the salvation of Herat, and this western city was traditionally the last stronghold of Afghan amirs;

remote from the center of government, it was the place to which, when power collapsed around them, they could retreat; several had done so in the past.

Another messenger reported the defeat by Bacha Sacao's troops of the Wardaks, a tribe farming peacefully southwest of Kabul, who were friendly to Amanullah. The commander of his troops in this attempt to regain his kingship was Abdul Ahad, who was a Ghilzai by birth but had lived among the Wardaks so long that he was one of them, who had been forgiven by Amanullah for supporting Nasrullah in 1919 and was one of his favorites and Minister of Interior.

First Amanullah fought with proclamations. The tribes of the east, those in Afghanistan and the British tribes living across the border, were being besieged by words. Those among them who could read were kept busy with communications from Amanullah, from Nadir, from Bacha Sacao.

Amanullah's proclamations were printed on gold manuscript with a blank space for the name of the recipient to be written in by his messenger. One of these spoke of "the people who had kindled the fire of mischief and wanted to carry out the intention of our enemies by making Afghanistan void of its pomp and power, wealth and materials," adding, "It was my wish to pull up Afghanistan and give it an honorable position in the world . . . You would have seen to what disgrace and shamefulness the boys and girls of Kabul have been subjected. And worst of all the deposits of the National Exchequer and the stores which have been collected by me and my ancestors for the defense of the sacred country of Afghanistan against 'Kufr' [infidels] and for the advancement of Islam are being wasted . . . I will now march on Kabul. My government has pardoned all your past misdeeds . . . and hopes that you will remove the past blemishes from Afghanistan's honor by means of your brave and dauntless swords. It hopes that you will not . . . make yourself questionable before God and the Holy Prophet."

Nadir was sending out this proclamation: "Be it known to you that in France I heard the dreadful news of Afghanistan. Though I was very ill at the time, I considered that service to Afghanistan was and is my primary duty and so with all haste I reached Peshawar . . . We will proceed to Kabul and after dethroning the tyrant robber who has usurped the Kabul throne will elect with the consent and unity of the tribes as king a man who is able to serve the Faith."

At the same time the Trade Agent in Peshawar, Abdul Hakim, who was loyal to Amanullah, was preparing this proclamation about Nadir and his brother Hashim:

"Both the dirty fellows are treacherous. [Nadir] is the man who murdered Amir Habibullah. Their family was expelled from Afghanistan by Amir Abdur Rahman as they were not faithful to the country, but they were recalled by the deceased Amir. They gave a clear proof of their treachery in taking the life of their master. They are faithful to the British as they were brought up by them during their stay in India. They are the enemies of Islam and they are trying to bring Afghanistan under British influence. The present revolution was also created by them at the instigation of the British.

"The ulema, who were paid and are being paid by the British Government, also helped them in this connection. They want to ruin Islam by putting Afghanistan under British influence as they have received a sum of 3,600,000 rupees from the British Government to carry on propaganda. So these treacherous people must not be allowed to stay any longer in Afghanistan. I was present in Peshawar when they made an agreement with the British Government. Anyone who helps them [Nadir and his brothers] is siding with the British."

Nadir made a point of showing to the British copies of all his letters to their tribesmen, as an assurance that he really did not intend to seek their help. He did this secretly, for the charge that the British were backing him, believed by many besides the Trade Agent, was damaging his prospects. His friend who delivered these letters assured the British official on the frontier that Nadir at present wanted no interference from outside tribes, but would welcome fifteen Wazir and fifteen Mahsud representatives to help select the new amir.

"He confirmed Nadir's hostility to Amanullah," reported the Agent. "He said that [Nadir] intended at a big meeting at Gardez three days after Id to denounce [Amanullah] as well as Bacha Sacao."

Nadir's plans did not advance according to schedule. When he and his brothers started toward the center of the Southern Province, they encountered enmity and had to withdraw.

"Reports from all sources indicate that the revulsion of feeling in favor of Amanullah is spreading both in Southern and Eastern provinces and among our own tribes," said the March 14 report of the North-West Frontier Province. "Nadir has been pressed by several of the Khost tribes to declare openly for Amanullah, failing which they would not help him; similarly at Lalpura . . ."

The Chaknawar mullah, the influential religious man whose friends included Abdul Wahid Shinwari alias Mr. Wade Australian, Amanullah's old enemy, had hoisted over his mosque a new flag with the inscription "Religious law shines brightly and all other codes of law are in vain." He had already proclaimed that the supporters of Amanullah would be visited by divine wrath; the flag indicated a distaste for all kings.

"Reaction in favor of Amanullah seems to be largely due to discontent with exactions of Bacha Sacao and to the general state of disorder prevailing under his regime," said the British report.

Some men in Bacha Sacao's army had sent Amanullah secret assurances of help. Bacha Sacao's supporters were bound to him largely through fear of what might happen to their homes; they were perturbed also by stories of vast amounts of munitions being sent to Amanullah from Russia. Bacha Sacao began to send troops to Ghazni, the most important way-station between Kabul and Kandahar, closer to Kabul. The Wardaks promised these troops safe-conduct through their territory, then ambushed them. "Bacha Sacao personally led a large force to avenge the treachery of the Wardaks," went the information which reached Sir Francis Humphrys in Simla one week after the event. "He returned to Kabul after burning some Wardak villages with twenty-eight Wardak prisoners and a quantity of cattle and loot . . . The heads of two Tagao leaders who were killed in fight near the Singing Sands have been exposed in Kabul bazaar. Sixty-eight Tagao prisoners were marched through the streets of Kabul with blackened faces."

On March 25 Amanullah at last moved from Kandahar. He camped for three days in Manzil Bagh, offering a final opportunity for men to join him; very few did.

In Kalat, Amanullah rejoined his troops who were camped under Inayatullah's command in a pleasant place with green fields and meadows and a running stream. His cars drove up at noon while they were putting up tents and drinking tea. The band played the national anthem, and in a relaxed mood he had a meal, rested, said his prayer, then walked to the riverbank and shot some ducks, foxes and jackals.

While he was doing all this, a thousand Hazaras, commanded by his teen-age brother Amin Jan, captured Mukur for him. Mukur was a dingy place consisting of a mud fort, a serai, and a few bazaars, but it was also the farthest point on the telephone line toward Kabul which Amanullah had been able to reach. Its capture was important. Abdul

Ahad, riding up with the intention of taking Mukur by force, was greeted with pleasure. The slant-eyed Hazaras, lowest on the Afghan social scale, misfits by being Shiah Moslems instead of Sunni Moslems, saw Amanullah's royal standard on the car in which Abdul Ahad was riding. Thinking that here was the King who had abolished slavery, they ran up and kissed the car.

Amanullah in his camp kept looking with field glasses toward Mukur. Two cars came toward him speeding. One was the car that the Hazaras had kissed, and when it stopped, the tribesman riding with Abdul Ahad leaped out, waved a sword, and cried in Pushtu, "We have captured Mukur and the enemy has been routed!" Amanullah did not know until the next day that it was the Hazaras who had done this.

More good news arrived, the return of a group of young Afghans who had gone to Turkey for training as military officers. They brought the news that Ghulam Nabi, the Minister to Russia, was headed for Mazar-i-Sharif, where Bacha Sacao's men had ousted his brother, the fat Abdul Aziz who was Governor there. They reported also that Shuja-ud-Dowleh had taken over in Herat.

Amanullah had been warned that some of the tribal leaders accompanying him were secretly raising parties to oppose him; he relayed the warning to his own advance troops but did not alter his attitude toward the suspected leaders; what he was undergoing was only one of the professional hazards of kingship. Abdul Ahad returned to Mukur, but first Amanullah cautioned him: "Do not consider that the enemy is incapable of striking another blow. They may, even tonight, make a surprise attack. If not tonight, at the first opportune moment." Abdul Ahad replied that he had placed guns and machine guns on the heights. "The rest lies in the hand of God." Amanullah's parting words to him were about the telephone service, which had been disrupted.

That evening Amanullah learned that the Hazaras had been his champions and he was touched. The telephone line was repaired, and he spoke with Abdul Ahad, sending grateful messages to the Hazaras.

On the following day, April 6, Amanullah made a ceremonial entry into Mukur. Along both sides of the road stood the troops from Kandahar and those sent from Herat. Drawn up to greet him were the Hazaras, but also, to his surprise, were the defeated troops of Bacha Sacao, who were carrying their arms.

After midday prayers, Amanullah entered a large durbar tent and first of all sent for the Hazaras, about three hundred of whom had served in the British Army in India. Many Hazaras, seeking work outside their cruel homeland the Hazarajat, were accustomed to go to India and enlist as soldiers; whenever the British protested to Afghanistan about interference with British tribesmen, they had to remember that they likewise interfered with Afghan tribesmen to the extent of putting them into their army; one regiment was called the Hazara Pioneers. Ten of the Hazaras present knew how to use a machine gun, and their leader was an especially gifted marksman who astounded British military circles whenever he appeared on a rifle range; they said that the fire of his rifle was the équivalent of Lewis Gun fire. The other Hazaras were farmers but they too brought their own rifles. Amanullah gave each man two rupees and his thanks.

Then he sent for Abdul Ahad and demanded why he had not taken away the weapons of Bacha Sacao's men after their surrender. Abdul Ahad said he was waiting for orders. "You are mistaken," said Amanullah. He had the men disarmed and arrested and ordered their colonel shot. A few of the men were from Kandahar; these he turned over to men from their own communities. Sixty-seven were from Tagao; he sent these home. The rest, who were Tajiks from Ghazni, he kept as hostages, telling them that if, when he reached Ghazni, their fellow Tajiks repented of their past actions and surrendered to him, they would be pardoned; if not, they would be killed.

Amanullah rested for three days and moved on. About a thousand additional Hazaras joined him; their leaders kissed his hands and were permitted to pitch their camps close to his. Another group came who had cause for gratitude to Amanullah, the Wazirs from British territory whom he had settled in Shahjui after the War of 1919 and who, by behaving so badly with their raids, had embarrassed him at the close of the Kabul conference into surrendering a piece of land to the British. Now the Shahjui Wazirs redeemed themselves; they kissed his hands and were loyal.

Messages to Amanullah from the maliks of the Wardaks had urged him to hasten, to establish himself before the nomad Ghilzais could come in numbers. He started north again and pitched camp at the end of the day.

That evening Amanullah went for a walk and noticed a house burning. He made inquiries and learned that some of the volunteers from Kandahar had set the house afire deliberately. At once he sent criers to go among all his troops proclaiming that he would not tolerate any repetition of this act. Summoning the owner of the house and hearing that the loss amounted to two hundred rupees, he gave five hundred rupees in compensation.

"We have come to overcome rebels, not to turn friends into rebels."

No one had seen Amanullah look truly content since his arrival in Kandahar. Now his face was almost happy. On the following morning he moved a little farther north and, having a large tent pitched close to the road, entertained five hundred persons at a breakfast of cold meat, bread and tea. Tribesmen from the area came with their drums to entertain.

In Kabul his adversary was still restricted by snow and cold. Here he was in spring. He was traversing the same road over which he had gone in the opposite direction three months earlier with such heartache and frustration. Again he had a small kingdom to rule and, if good fortune remained with him, he could hope to rule again in his large kingdom.

Sher Agha was on his way back to Afghanistan.

On April 19, with his rigid turban and unquestioning eyes, he reached Dera Ismail Khan, the city near the Afghan frontier from which he had organized the conspiracy against Amanullah. Thirty Afghan mullahs accompanied him like a court of avenging Magi. He held a meeting in the mosque, which was as crowded as if it had been Friday. Nomads in great numbers were passing through Dera Ismail Khan on their way to the Afghan grazing grounds. One group of nomad Ghilzais wished Amanullah well, remembering that he had tried to give them teachers to travel with them. These stayed aloof from Sher Agha, knowing what they would hear. All the others attended.

Sher Agha said that King Amanullah had brought the trouble on himself. Bacha Sacao was incapable of ruling. Sher Agha therefore was going to Afghanistan to avert further bloodshed.

Then he arranged for three mullahs to issue a proclamation against Amanullah, calling him not merely "kaffir," which means an unbeliever in Islam, but "zandig," meaning he had defamed Islam.

As far away as London, people knew one of the less openly expressed motives for Sher Agha's return. Gul Agha, his brother in Kabul, had quarreled with Bacha Sacao. The *Daily Express* put on its report from Karachi the sensational headline "Kabul Usurper in Peril, Deserted by his Chief Mullah." Investigating, the British sent a secret letter from

Peshawar: "It seems that Hazrat Gul Agha did have some disagreement with Bacha Sacao . . . It is not, however, believed that the estrangement is very serious. According to present information he is back in Kabul and although the families of Sardar Nadir and Shah Wali have taken refuge with him, is again on good terms with Bacha Sacao."

On April 10 Sher Agha, singleminded against Amanullah whatever his other purposes, left Dera Ismail Khan to join a caravan of nomad Ghilzais and cross with them into Afghanistan.

For all his good fortune, Amanullah was looking for more help, and he could call only on the tribesmen who lived in India. He wrote urgent letters asking them to join him in Ghazni; these he entrusted for surreptitious delivery to a petty official whom he disguised as a holy man. But in Waziristan the messenger sought aid, since Amanullah had impressed on him the need for haste, from a friend who had connections with the British, who were soon reading those letters. "The ex-King has certainly overstepped the mark and has initiated a deliberate attempt to subvert our tribes in his own interest," said the British. And the man with the letters suddenly found himself the object of much attention and hospitality. He stayed and stayed and stayed.

Nadir, for his part, had constantly assured the British that he would not seek the help of their tribes. Nonetheless, they adopted a rule: groups of tribesmen might not go into Afghanistan to fight for any claimant, but if an individual went, G. of I. would make no effort to stop him. G. of I. knew that the effort would be futile, anyway.

Nadir's messages were sent openly to Humphrys in Simla. He said that he hoped to conquer Bacha Sacao and set up a constitutional government with an elected king. Then he asked for money. In refusing, Humphrys added the polite advice, "If it was suspected that he was being helped by a foreign power [financial assistance] might indeed do harm to his cause . . . I personally send my best wishes to Nadir in his patriotic attempt."

Nadir was having some success at Gardez with the tribes, partly with the help of Ghaud-us-din, whose "undoubted abilities for intrigue" exceeded his, and Hashim felt strong enough to summon a jirga at Gardez which included an overnight stay for the tribesmen with Shah Mahmud and a greeting by Nadir himself two miles out of Gardez, accompanied by a band of musicians. The Ahmedzai Ghilzais received from the arsenal the rifles that Amanullah had taken from them after

the Khost Rebellion. After three days of entertainment by Nadir, Nadir's guests said that they would accept neither Bacha Sacao nor Amanullah as King but wanted Nadir.

Thereupon Nadir wrote to Bacha Sacao: "My dear brother Habibullah
Khan: I really appreciate your bravery. Your gallant deeds are worthy of
high praise . . . I write this to let you know that I am perfectly willing
to sacrifice my own life and the lives of my brothers and other family members for the sake of Islam, the welfare of my nation and country . . . You as well as myself have both been the servants of the State,
and a servant must not think of doing anything else but service to his
country. There is no doubt that considerable amount of State Treasury
has been wasted by your men, and therefore you may be working under
a belief that in revenge the royal family will destroy you and the people
of Koh-i-Daman. This is not true. No wise man should think like this
. . . You and your men will be granted complete pardon and honor
if either Amanullah or any other member of the royal family resumes
the throne. You should, however, see that the rifles and the State Treasury are properly protected. I have been forced by duty which a Moslem
brother owes to another Moslem to write these few lines to you. You
have power to act as you like."

Bacha Sacao's answer fell from the sky. Leaflets were dropped by airplane on all the inhabitants of Gardez:

"I must instruct you in regard to this rebel and his deep-dyed treachery." Bacha Sacao accused Nadir and his brothers of murdering Amir
Habibullah. "Then, when they joined Amanullah, since the wheel of
treachery does not always go forward, in a year or two the names and
traces of all of them vanished from Afghanistan, and so far from making the Islamic pilgrimage they made a pilgrimage to France. God save
us.

"Well, enough of this. When I, this lowly servant by the Grace of
God was honored by the title of servant of the faith of the Prophet of
God, I had not tasted the cup of these traitors' treachery and thought
that they had been unjustly wronged and were after all Moslems, and
as the Islamic Kingdom was—God be praised—now established, they
should be given work in the administration of government and return
from a foreign land to their own country. It was for this reason they had
official appointment and a large sum of money from the treasury was
given for the service of Islam to Nadir's brother Shah Mahmud who
had made promises and undertakings in the name of God and had given

me his allegiance and I sent for him so that he might come with honor.

"In contrast to my good will, Nadir, who through guzzling pork in Europe and following and imitating all the infidel races had blackened his brain and bones, instead of honestly following the path of Islam displays his treachery by himself going to the Southern Province and sending his brothers to the Eastern, where they go about concocting lies. But by the kindness of God the enticements of devils make no impression on the ears of the faithful . . . I . . . give orders to you pious Moslems that it is lawful to shed the blood of these traitors and any person who destroys them will be a ghazi and a well-wisher of Islam and will be honored as follows by the court of this Islamic Kingdom:

"Anyone who brings Nadir alive will receive a reward of Rs40,000 and anyone who brings his head will receive Rs30,000 in cash and a magazine rifle.

"For his three brothers alive Rs10,000 each or Rs30,000 in all, and anyone who brings the head of these or brings any one of them alive will receive Rs10,000 and a magazine rifle."

After this price was put on his head, Nadir increased his guard and began to spend each night in a different house.

On April 18 Nadir wrote to Maconachie that he was "going strong."

On that same day in London an official of the India Office was writing something similar about Amanullah:

"[Amanullah] seems to have relatively better chances than any other single candidate (though absolutely his chances may not be great) of re-establishing himself as ruler of Afghanistan. It is obvious that he alone as the possible candidate has certain assets, such as the moral support of other Moslem countries—Turkey and Persia (which is unlikely to try to fish in troubled waters) and he is also able to draw material assistance from Russian sources. Though even with these assets, he may not be able to re-establish his rule over the whole country, it seems at any rate probable that he will be able to maintain himself in Kandahar and Herat . . . If [Nadir's] program fails, it is probable, as Nadir predicts, that there will be a long period of civil war and that Afghanistan will be dismembered; there is little reason to suppose that in the event of such dismemberment Amanullah would fail to retain the southwestern half of the country marching with Baluchistan. In view of this probable event, it seems desirable to reduce to a minimum actions which, in their cumulative effect, might make it difficult for the G. of I. to live on terms with him."

The action against Amanullah which H.M.G. was reluctant to take was being urged by Sir Francis Humphrys, still the Minister of Afghanistan although he was in Simla and would soon leave for England and would never return to Afghanistan. As "the man on the spot" he had been consulted and heeded by both H.M.G. and G. of I. in forming their attitude toward Amanullah, and from the first he had declared unequivocally "Amanullah's chances are dead." He was obviously eager to dissociate his government from a loser. There had been times when he had needed strong persuasion in order to prevail. He had insisted, and won, on deflecting the mail bag intended for Amanullah to Bacha Sacao; he had insisted, and won, on transporting Bacha Sacao's emissaries to Nadir in R.A.F. planes. But he had wished to exclude Amanullah's emissaries to Nadir from India until it was too late to accomplish their mission, and here he had lost.

Now, on April 9, Humphrys wired: "It seems to me incongruous that Amanullah's agents should be allowed in future to and from India to purchase saddlery, bandoleers, lorries and petrol, and distribute proclamations to our tribes." Humphrys had just learned that a British Indian motor driver had been arrested in Kandahar on the charge of being a British spy, and that bail had been refused. Humphrys, who was receiving reports from many spies, protested, "A harmless British subject is imprisoned."

Amanullah's ardent admirer Abdul Hakim, the Trade Agent at Peshawar, was Humphrys' target; he wished him removed from British territory. The British did not yet know of Abdul Hakim's proclamation stating exactly how many rupees the British had spent to subvert Afghanistan; the accusations of which they had knowledge spoke vaguely of "enemies of Afghanistan," a phrase that G. of I. took personally but did not expect to impress the public.

"If Government of India prohibited purchases of all kind of supplies, it would give the appearance of a policy of pinpricks," was the opinion in London, "and action to prevent Amanullah's having any dealings with British India must have the effect of throwing him more than ever into the arms of Russia." And later: "Case of intrigue against our tribes on behalf of Trade Agent is clear enough, but I doubt wisdom of expelling him very much. Among large proportions of inhabitants of British territory and of tribes there is strong feeling in favor of Amanullah and of the Trade Agent's activities they are aware. To expel him would be regarded as a definite act of hostility to Amanullah which with material available for publication it would be difficult to justify."

A little earlier London had commented, "[Government of India] has hitherto shown the most scrupulous regard for neutrality, even to the discomposure of Humphrys on certain occasions . . . Humphrys' discounting of Amanullah's prospects of returning to power is not quite so convinced as it has previously been."

A few weeks later London would be saying of Amanullah not too happily, "His star has some appearance of being in the ascendant."

CHAPTER 33

April 19, 1929, to May 23, 1929

In Moscow the issues of the Afghan Rebellion would have seemed elementary to a fundamentalist Marxist. On one side was an absolute monarch. On the other side was the water-carrier's son, a classic symbol of the proletariat.

But the Soviets knew that nothing, except in their propaganda, was as simplistic as it seemed. The water-carrier's son had been brought to his eminence by the persons who, in the plays and operas of Russian Turkestan, were always shown as the villains: the mullahs. The Russians believed sincerely that he had been installed also by the British; they had intercepted many of the British documents on their way between London and Kabul, and in Humphrys' accurate predictions as to the trouble which would befall Amanullah they thought they detected not simple foresight but direction.

"Moscow was embarrassed at not knowing what line to take," would be written later by Georgei Agabekov, the former resident in Kabul of the Russian Secret Service, the O.G.P.U.[1] "It had tried to penetrate Amanullah's intentions with respect to the U.S.S.R. subsequent to his trip to Europe; also to ascertain the strength of the revolt of the southern tribes, its precise aims, what foreign backing it had; finally, to get information concerning the Water Boy, his program, whom and what he represented."

The O.G.P.U. could not answer these questions; its diplomatic courier service was disrupted by revolution in the areas through which the couriers would have to pass; there had been three O.G.P.U. residents in Kabul in four years, the first two having departed because of conflict with Ambassador Stark. The telegraph lines toward Russia were not working.

What the Russians learned about Bacha Sacao did not encourage them. The symbol of the proletariat had become a friend of their most deadly enemy among kings, the Amir of Bokhara whom they had driven into exile in Kabul. On fair days, according to the slight intelligence that got through, there were picnics in Paghman attended together by Bacha Sacao and the ex-Amir. To this association the Russians attributed the renewed vigor of the bands of stubborn Bokharans who had been harassing them along the Afghan frontier ever since they had gathered Bokhara into the Union of Soviet Socialist Republics.

Meanwhile Afghanistan was full of rumors of massive Russian aid to Amanullah in the form of munitions. Humphreys had even mentioned this aid in his proposal to keep Amanullah's agents from buying nonmilitary supplies in India, and H.M.G. had replied calmly that its intelligence did not verify these reports.

The airplanes which Amanullah hoped to receive from Russia did not arrive. They had been promised in December.

But Amanullah did get an airplane.

One of the Afghans whom he had sent to Russia to be trained as a pilot was a young man named Omar, who was appreciatively aware of how much he owed to Amanullah. Except for his energetic, tolerant King, Omar would never have been allowed to leave Afghanistan, would never have learned an exciting profession, and would have seen many doors close before him because his religion was that of the Shiah Moslems.

After Bacha Sacao became Amir Habibullah, he appointed Omar as special pilot to his Minister of War, Sayed Hussein, who gave a formal order to his unruly soldiers that they should not tease Omar. It went against Omar's grateful nature to fly against Amanullah, but once in the sky in the airplane, he was his own master. He was ordered to drop bombs on the home of the Wardak leader, Abdullah, called Lalacolonel or Elder Brother Colonel, the brother of Abdul Ahad who had succeeded in delaying Bacha Sacao's march to Ghazni. Three times Omar was told to bomb Lalacolonel's fort; the first time he threw the bombs in the river, the second time he dropped them on a nearby hill where they did no damage, and the third time they fell on an uninhabited place.

Omar was ordered next to bomb Amanullah's troops. This would have been easy, for Amanullah put a white cloth on a hillside as a beacon. He thought he could count on the sentiments of these fliers, so he had added in large letters an invitation to join him. Omar twisted the fuse of his bomb very tightly so that it would not explode, then dropped it at a sufficient distance to assure it would do no harm if it did explode. This trick worked three times.

After the third flight Bacha Sacao discovered the ineffectiveness of his bombing and deduced treachery. Omar would have been arrested except for the shortage of pilots in Kabul. Meanwhile he received an invitation to the home of Amanullah's Finance Minister, Mir Hashim, who knew from secret messages how desperately Amanullah wanted a plane. Showing Omar a bag full of gold coins, Mir Hashim said that these were all his if he would take a plane to Kandahar.

Omar refused the reward, accepting only one coin, which he kissed because it bore the insignia of Amanullah.

He was entrusted with one more mission for Bacha Sacao, to drop the leaflets offering a reward for Nadir and his brothers. Bacha Sacao had excellent military advice, which came from General Mahmud Sami, who had been Amanullah's old teacher and close friend and who was now directing the forces of his enemy. This advice told precisely how much aviation fuel was required for a specific air mission; his pilots always left the Kabul airport with the amount of gasoline that would take them to the target and back, not a drop in excess.

When Omar was airborne toward Nadir's camp, he revealed his plans to his observer, Sayed Mohammed, who had shared his other sabotaged missions and who now agreed to accompany him to Kandahar. He changed his course southward. The fuel in the tank was not sufficient to take them to Kandahar, so Omar flew at a very great height, which enabled him, after the gas tanks were empty, to glide down toward Kandahar, and in this way he arrived at the airport where so long a watch had been kept for a plane.

Omar was welcomed not only for his airplane but for the news he brought. Kabul was full of reports that Ghulam Nabi was approaching Mazar, that Nadir was threatening from Gardez, that Amin Jan was leading his Hazaras against Bacha Sacao. Kandahar now had some airplane fuel and Omar's first assignment as Amanullah's only pilot was to drop leaflets containing this news in the vicinity of Ghazni. This time he hit the target.

In 1924, when the Khost Rebellion had made Amanullah desperate for aircraft, he had bought, against the advice of the British, several old airplanes from an adventurer in India named Murphy. One of these planes, a DH9A built in 1918, was lying in sections in crates at Karachi. Amanullah now remembered Mr. Murphy's plane and telegraphed to the Afghan Consul at Karachi, who still took orders from him, to ship it to Chaman. It arrived there on April 28 and a flying officer from Kandahar, who had made his way overland from Russia to join Amanullah, was waiting to take delivery.

"It must be quite worthless now," commented the G. of I., but they forbade its importation nonetheless, and it remained at Chaman lying outside the compound of the Customs House along with four thousand bags of cement and several cases of machinery as a symbol of what Afghanistan had acquired—almost.

Once again Amanullah tried to get from Karachi the machine guns he had purchased in France; they had been there since November 24, when he could have taken them without challenge. Procrastination had lost them.

Ata-ul-Haq would soon be wiring on behalf of Bacha Sacao to Humphrys in Simla, asking him to detain the arms and ammunition purchased by the Afghan Government from Europe. In an attempt to learn what those arms consisted of, he added, "Your Excellency is further requested to kindly intimate to this ministry the amount of the arms and ammunition received at the Indian ports and the name of the Government from which purchased." He received no list, but confirmation of the prohibition of "the export to Afghanistan of consignments of munitions from whatever source and to whatever destinations."

"Reply is meant for Russian as well as Afghan consumption," Humphrys told London.

The Foreign Office had discussed the wisdom of lifting the arms embargo. "Amanullah, who is incidentally likely to prove for us the least friendly and most unreliable of all the present claimants to the throne, is the only person who will benefit. It would therefore be unneutral in fact, if not in theory or appearance," went the Foreign Office Minute of April 20.

And then, although Amanullah had earlier lost the favor of the British by seeming like a loser, the writer of this minute argued against him because he seemed like a winner. "If Amanullah is allowed to have his machine guns at this moment, when his star has some appearance of being in the ascendant, he will regard it as a rather obvious bid for his favors. Far from conciliating him, this is likely to give him an exaggerated idea of his importance to us and render him more difficult than ever if he ever regains power."

But Amanullah's star was not really in an ascendant. He approached Ghazni toward evening and from a nearby station where there was a telephone connection he tried to raise someone in the citadel. He could not. Two Hindu traders approached him complaining that their cars had been looted by Andar Ghilzai robbers a few miles away. Some friendly Andar Ghilzais in the camp told Amanullah that the robbers were led by a bandit hostile to him, Bacha Baz. The similarity to other events with another bandit was ominous, and so was the reminder that he had not moved soon enough to avoid the onsweep of the returning Ghilzais.

There was worse news: Ghazni was occupied by forces sympathetic to Bacha Sacao, many of them Ghilzais. Abdul Ahad had surrounded it and was attempting a siege.

Amanullah had not realized that he would have to fight for Ghazni. He had expected no more serious opposition until the outskirts of Kabul.

A small printing press traveled with his camp. Overnight he had a thousand pamphlets printed ordering the men of Ghazni to surrender their city, along with the pro-Bacha Sacao Governor, by two o'clock the next day. In the morning he signed these and gave them to two men to take in a car to Ghazni, but the gunfire from the citadel kept them off, and at two o'clock, the deadline, they were returning to Amanullah's camp with his ultimatum undelivered.

Nervousness was eroding the self-control that so far had restrained the professional bandits running Kabul. From all four directions enemies were expected: Amanullah from the south, Nadir from the east, the Hazaras from the west and Allah knew what from the north where there were such wild rumors about Russians. Bacha Sacao dismissed Hazaras from government jobs and then started to dismiss officials who shared the Hazaras' Shiah faith. Eventually he ceased to trust men with family connections in any of the tribes from which he expected attack, which included the Safis of Tagao through whom he had become part of the grand plan to dethrone Amanullah. Only Kohistanis from his own home ground seemed safe for responsibility.

Sayed Hussein, the old comrade-in-banditry now War Minister, was the force behind the panic and also acts of cruelty. He and Bacha Sacao's brother Hamidullah directed one party in Kabul, which favored ruthless measures because it could imagine no other; the moderate party was headed by Ata-ul-Haq and Sher Jan, who knew that there were other methods. "Sayed Hussein is making preparations for the defense of Kabul," was the intelligence that reached the British. "He is said to be completely out of touch with the other members of the Kabul Government and his troops are getting out of hand."

Two atrocities were witnessed by the German Minister, Baron Plessen. Once he saw a body with an arm and leg amputated. Once as he approached the Foreign Office, he saw on the street a victim drawn up for torture. Rushing inside the Foreign Office he demanded to see Ata-ul-Haq, whom he persuaded to go outside and stop the torture. While such things took place, he said, it was unthinkable that any civilized government should recognize Bacha Sacao.

A notable fugitive of the time was a religious judge who, in the days of Bacha Sacao's banditry, had issued at Amanullah's request a proclamation declaring Bacha Sacao an infidel and giving permission to any good Moslem to kill him. After the bandit's accession his life was not safe, and Bacha Sacao's men finally found him. His execution was accomplished by knives at the gate of the police station; he was sliced slowly to death while reciting verses from the Koran and while a member of the Russian Legation made a home movie of the event.

It was possible to live in Kabul, however, without seeing such things or having firsthand knowledge of them. Everyday life could be uneventful; it was not, however, comfortable. The cold and snow had been unusually cruel and were lasting overlong. Living was costly; everything in the bazaar was more expensive than in the previous year and had none of the variety of the old days; some shopkeepers remained open only because they would have been punished for closing. Soon Bacha Sacao introduced a fresh complication. He had been shocked in January to find in the State Treasury paper money, engraved bank notes which Amanullah had intended to introduce. In May he decided that he needed that paper money, so he brought it out and stamped his own name over Amanullah's, then he issued a proclamation that began by deploring "the great trouble and waste in carrying around the metal coins of the former government" and continued:

"The notes, which have been put into circulation, were printed at a large expense paid out of the State Treasury of the Moslems . . . In view of their printing expenses it would have been a loss to the State Treasury if they had been left uncirculated."

Bacha Sacao ordered Afghans to accept these notes; he said that cash would be kept in the Treasury as backing, a detail of high finance that could have come only from persons more informed on government than he. Kabul would have been suspicious in any case of the substitution of paper for metal. When a professional bandit commanded them to take the paper, they felt that being a king had not altered his profession.

Bacha Sacao and Sayed Hussein foresaw the difficulties that might come to them from Kabul's unhappiness. They forbade gatherings of more than a few persons at a time; occasionally men were arrested simply for whispering together. On May 6 a proclamation made their nervousness public: they put a cordon around Kabul, announcing that no one might enter or leave without a pass obtainable only from certain officials. Bacha Sacao expected a siege.

On April 20 Ghulam Nabi captured Mazar-i-Sharif for Amanullah. Bacha Sacao's men had moved toward Herat and they did not have the forces to maintain themselves at both places.

Amanullah did not hear of this at once. But he did have good news: the beloved little sister, Nur-us-Seraj, reached Kandahar again with her new son.

Another good friend, Abdul Hadi, was heading toward him. The former Minister to London, who had been received at the Court of St. James's, put on the tribal dress of an Afridi and with all his family mounted on nine horses, including his wife in a chaderi, four children, a young brother and some servants, left late one night before the cordon was drawn. As they passed the southeast corner of Kabul, a sentry called out a challenge. A servant called back that the malik was going to a wedding, and the sentry let them pass.

Abdul Hadi left his family with friends in Jalalabad, and continued alone toward India. He had a choice of dangers; instead of the Shinwaris on the road he chose the raging, flooding Kabul River, on which he rode a raft down to Dakka. The rest of the way to Peshawar he walked.

The Afridi attire was in rags at the end, and the British, whom he had often offended, were sorry for him. "Abdul Hadi must be classified as a prominent personage," they said, "and requested to move out of India after a reasonable breathing space." But he did not require a breathing space of them. He left at once on the train for Chaman, and before he crossed toward Kandahar he looked around Chaman with the eyes of one who might again be a refugee there with his King. He noticed the guest bungalow and chose it as a good place to break a journey.

Amanullah had been traveling by motor. Now, facing a hostile Ghazni, he felt an urge to be more mobile. He went everywhere on horseback. He adopted a strange costume; with his military uniform, now too large for him because he was losing weight rapidly, he wore a turban, obviously for comfort rather than from a wish to appear orthodox, for he gave the turban an unorthodox air by putting a green sunshade over it.

Amanullah was haggard and tense. Something in his disturbed nerves made his lips parched and cracked. His cheeks sagged; his face was lined; his voice emerged in hoarse whispers painfully.

In the distance he could hear the guns around Ghazni. Ghazni was an old, important city, once the capital of Mahmud of Ghazni. Its crown was a citadel high on a hill, from the foot of which bazaars grew like the roots of a tree. The greatest danger to his men in front of Ghazni was a large gun that Amanullah himself had bought in Italy, booming down from the citadel. For a while Abdul Ahad had held the caravan serais and a few outlying bazaars, but this gun drove him back.

Separated from Abdul Ahad's troops but in hearing of their rifle fire, Amanullah did not receive with graciousness a group of Andar Ghilzais who came to him, each bringing a horse as a gift. Coldly he asked why they had permitted their tribesmen to fight against him.

"Ignorant people exist among every community," said the Ghilzai leaders. "Our hold over the people depends on the tribesmen's fear of the Government. We ourselves have lost all prestige." They blamed the outbreak in Ghazni against Amanullah on two persons. One was the robber Bacha Baz. The other was "the Pir Sahib."

Sher Agha was this "Pir Sahib." He was advancing toward Amanullah with the Ghilzai caravans like an implacable angel of retribution, like Kismet. He was almost at Ghazni, moving among a cluster of small villages about thirty-two miles to the east. All the way through India and Afghanistan he had been telling Ghilzais to attack Amanullah; it was his preaching that had driven them toward Ghazni.

Now, in the nearby village of Band-i-Daulat, Sher Agha summoned a jirga of various Ghilzai clans and some other tribes and spoke of Amanullah.

The mullahs, prompted by Sher Agha, passed another in the long line of religious decrees against him. They went another step further by conferring upon his adversary the immunity that Islam traditionally gave to a rightful ruler. They said that since Bacha Sacao was occupying the capital and throne of the Islamic Kingdom of Afghanistan, he was the ruler in actual fact and to fight against him would be unlawful in the eyes of Allah.

Sher Agha would later boast of those two days of talking.

The first person to receive a letter from Sher Agha had been Bacha Sacao, to whom he said that he had dispatched parties to fight against Amanullah in both Kandahar and the Southern Province, and that he himself would soon visit Kabul. Bacha Sacao's brother Hamidullah also was receiving letters from Sher Agha at Ghazni, where he was in command.

Nadir was in correspondence with Sher Agha, and many tribal leaders were coming and going in the little villages east of Ghazni to confer with the famous religious leader. One of these was Ghaus-ud-din.

Nadir and his brothers attempted a thrust toward Kabul. They thought they were succeeding, as they pushed ahead with Ghaus-ud-din and his Ahmedzai Ghilzais leading the attack. Then Nadir suddenly became suspicious of Ghaus-ud-din. He saw something which convinced him that this man was treacherous, that he was enticing him forward only to fall upon his rear. Hastily he withdrew. So did his brothers. There was no longer an immediate hope of advancing to Kabul.

"Nadir has not ceased to take interest in the journey back to India, which he thinks he may still have to perform," wrote the Oriental attaché in Peshawar. The Government of India announced a policy in this event: no long stay in India and a special compartment on a train.

"Two hundred thousand Indian rupees given to me immediately will serve as key to whole situation," Nadir informed the Government of India through a message sent in code to his Peshawar friend, M. A. Hakim. "I was told by British statesmen in Europe that British Government wished to see a strong Afghanistan. If British Government really wish to see end of chaotic condition in Afghanistan and re-establishment of peace, it is time now to help. Amanullah reinstated on Kabul throne by sheer force of Russian gold will never be suitable neighbor for British India."

India's response was, "Hakim should be informed by Oriental Attaché verbally and in suitably courteous terms that Government have nothing to add to message to Nadir of April 30, and that Humphrys has left India."

A Shinwari wrote to the British Empire in the person of the Assistant Political Officer of Khyber: "I write to ask you . . . if you will be so good as to advise us of the best means of getting rid of the King of Kabul . . . My own tribe as well as the people of Khugiani, Surkhrod and Laghman have all promised their help and if you wish to march on Kabul, I am with you and promise to take you as far as you wish to go. Nobody will stand in your way . . . I have . . . received a letter . . . seeking our cooperation in the matter of selecting a Moslem king. Pending your advice in the matter, I am not replying to this letter, as once a man is elected, it will be difficult to enforce our own will afterward."

This got no reply at all.

Almost all that Amanullah knew now was concentrated in the area just south of Ghazni. His army was military in organization, but in character was amorphous and shapeless. Except for the men of his royal guard and the Hazaras who had served in the British Indian Army, few of his soldiers had received any real military training. Many groups were actually small private armies owing their loyalty to the tribal chief who led them. And the loyalty of some of these chiefs to Amanullah was tenuous. Without any clearly defined limitations to his camp, it was easy for people to come and go. One of the few certainties in Amanullah's situation was that not everyone around him was truly hoping for his success.

The distance between Amanullah's forces and the advance troops at Ghazni was close enough to make the firing at Ghazni painfully audible, but more than the day's march away. Abdul Ahad sent a messenger from Ghazni suggesting a particular spot where Amanullah's men might camp on their way to join him.

Amanullah's private secretary recognized the place; his village was in its vicinity, and he knew that it had innumerable defects as a camping ground. He would write later that he "realized it was through

personal enmity to himself that reports of its suitability had been furnished by Abdul Ahad in the hopes that the Kandahari troops would
ruin the place." The troops were already marching and he kept silent.

No roads led to the spot; the motorcars could not get across the
rocky terrain, so had to go by a roundabout way. Many streams intervened, which the men had to wade through while passing the large
guns from hand to hand. Reaching the camp site, they found that in
spite of all the inconvenient water on the way, there was no water
nearby for drinking or washing.

For food Amanullah had expected to supplement the inadequate
amount he brought with purchases from the nearby villages. Supply
officers went in search of that food; they had to retreat under rifle fire;
hostile Ghilzais had taken over those villages. There were many horses,
mules and donkeys to be fed, and Amanullah told his men to cut the
unripe corn for them and to let them loose in the fields; he knew that
this would make enemies of the owners of the fields, but hoped he could
make peace later with money.

While Amanullah and his troops were settling to a fitful sleep, about
three hundred of Bacha Sacao's men crept up with two big guns. At the
first light of dawn they started firing into the camp. Amanullah sent
parties to attack the guns from three sides; the rebels retreated, but it
was noon before there was a brief calm. Then other enemies appeared:
the two groups of Ghilzais, Andar and Suleiman Khel, had united just
as they promised at Sher Agha's jirga they would. There were thousands of them; all that saved Amanullah was the superiority of his big
guns over their rifles.

By that time it was nearly the hour for another dinner, following a
day of great exertion and tension and very little food. Amanullah gave
Rs20,000 to an important officer whom he instructed to visit the villages
personally to obtain supplies on payment, and to see that no villagers
were molested by the troops. Taking two hundred transport animals to
bring back the supplies, this officer acquired food in the nearby villages,
but as he moved farther away from the camp, he was attacked by
Ghilzais who seized fifty of his animals and killed two of the King's
guard escorting him. When he returned with almost no food, Amanullah
was hearing an intelligence report that the Ghilzais were planning another attack that night.

Amanullah ordered his troops to have an early dinner and prepare to
move on to another place where they would be surrounded by friendly

Hazara villages, where he planned to halt for a day before joining Abdul Ahad. In an attempt to confuse the waiting Ghilzais, he commanded that the move be silent. But it was Amanullah's men who were confused. So many of their transport animals had been captured that some soldiers had to load up their own riding ponies. A local man had been engaged to serve as guide; he disappeared. The striking of camp and departure were disorderly and noisy.

For the first two hours of the march moonlight showed the path. Then clouds covered the moon, and the troops lost their way. With the help of Amanullah's secretary who knew the territory, they reached the fort of a chieftain who was friendly to Amanullah. But the friendly chieftain urged them not to stay, but to move on to Ghazni. If Amanullah rested there, he said, the Ghilzais would consider that they had inflicted a defeat and their morale would be raised enormously; it was best to join Abdul Ahad without delay. He himself volunteered to act as guide; the weary troops entered Abdul Ahad's camp after sixteen hours of marching without sleep or food.

Hazaras lived in the villages that now were close; they came out happily and sold their food. Then groups of Hazara fighting men began to arrive: one party of a thousand then another of a thousand, a third of eight hundred, two more groups of two thousand each, and another of five hundred. They brought their own arms.

Rested from his long march, Amanullah looked at all the loyal, slant-eyed men and began to feel a little more confident.

Among the Soviet leadership there were two opinions as to what Russia should do in regard to the Afghan rebellion. The O.G.P.U., the secret police, wished to champion the symbol of the proletariat, Bacha Sacao. Since he sprang from the peasants, they said, he would advance the cause of the peasants, and through him they would be able slowly to make Afghanistan a Soviet state.

The Commissariat of Foreign Affairs had a different theory. Only the population of the north supported Bacha Sacao, said Foreign Affairs, and therefore in order to survive he would have to adopt an aggressive policy toward the Soviets with a view to extending his influence into Soviet Turkestan. Amanullah, on the other hand, was finding his support among the tribes of the south, and therefore could be expected to adopt a challenging attitude toward the British in India. Besides, Foreign Affairs pointed out, it was not likely that Bacha Sacao would remain in power very long.

Ghulam Siddiq had been in Moscow for nearly two months. With his brother Ghulam Nabi he had been pleading with Chicherin, the Commissar of Foreign Affairs who had been so flattered during Amanullah's visit to be called by name by him, and Karakhan, the deputy for Asia who had played tennis with him, to send help to Amanullah to put him back on the throne. Finally the Politburo, the supreme body in Russia, made a decision. It would adopt the course favored by the Commissariat of Foreign Affairs and would aid Amanullah.

For many hours one night Ghulam Siddiq and Ghulam Nabi discussed what form this aid should take. The Russians with whom they talked were Colonel K. M. Primakoff, a former military attaché in the Kabul Embassy, and the dictator of all Russia, Joseph Stalin.

"It was decided to form an expeditionary force of Red soldiers disguised as Afghans," reported Agabekov.[2] "That force should be led by Primakoff; it should secretly cross the frontier and march against Kabul. The nominal leader should be Ghulam Nabi, who had a certain influence in the north of Afghanistan."

About May 10 the Russians and Afghans moved. Early one morning planes flew from the Russian frontier town of Termez across the Amu Daria River which separated the two countries. The Afghan frontier post of Patagisar was alarmed. A frontier guard detachment turned out to see what was happening, and the aviators, who were flying low, turned machine guns downward and killed them all. "Immediately afterwards," said Agabekov, "the infantry, composed of the best units of Tashkent, quietly crossed the Amu Daria. The expeditionary force— about eight hundred—with a good many machine guns and some artillery, proceeded toward Mazar-i-Sharif. The Afghan Government [Bacha Sacao] forces which opposed them were at once wiped out by machine gun and artillery fire . . . Ghulam Nabi rounded up the native population and made them march with his Reds against the neighboring town of Tashkurgan . . . The two forces fought it out. At the end of six hours Bacha Sacao's warriors took to flight . . . Our men and Ghulam Nabi's Afghans occupied Tashkurgan without further fighting and prepared to go forward toward Khanabad."

The men of O.G.P.U. considered that their prestige, already shaky at that time, was endangered by Stalin's preference for advice other than their own. To assert themselves again they decided to send Agabekov to Kandahar to report on Amanullah's situation and prospects, to sound out the sentiment of the tribesmen, to see what role the British were playing. While in Kandahar, Agabekov would be expected also to organize an espionage system in that city to operate in India.

But Herat had fallen to Bacha Sacao on May 4. Without the knowledge of Shuja-ud-Dowleh or any other officials, fifteen mullahs had sent Bacha Sacao's advancing General an invitation to enter the city. The advance guard of the government men mutinied and, in an excess of religious passion, killed about a hundred of the Hazaras marching with them. Bacha Sacao's General rode into the city followed by seventy camels carrying treasure with which he established his rule so effectively that even the clever Russian secret service found the area around Herat, through which their way led to Kandahar, completely blocked.

However, O.G.P.U. had a special section which deciphered the telegrams of foreign diplomats, and these revealed universal disapproval of what was being done in Northern Afghanistan. Even the Persians and Turks, among whom O.G.P.U. had expected to find complete sympathy for Amanullah, were displeased. The invasion was being reported in European newspapers; everywhere was disapproval.

In many places the cause of dissatisfaction was the trait in human nature that casts every person or entity into a certain role and is offended if he does not play his role as expected. Here was a Communist state, Russia, and it was behaving in an un-Communist way by supporting a king. Even those who disliked Communism wanted it to stay in character.

Russia valued the world's opinion; she wanted the official recognition of other nations and extension of trade. Later Chicherin would say that Russia refused aid to Amanullah for fear of starting trouble with England; he never admitted the expeditionary force.[3]

Moscow, faced with the O.G.P.U. report, decided that the Afghan excursion had been a mistake. Stalin called back the planes and troops. Within three days the Russian aid to Ghulam Nabi had vanished from Afghanistan.

But Ghulam Nabi still had his Afghan forces; some were Afghans who, being residents of Russian Turkestan, might be called Russian. They still had arms and determination, and they pushed on, by way of the Gourband Valley and Bamiyan where the giant Buddhas brooded, toward Kabul.

The arrival of the Hazaras, so pleasing to Amanullah, turned many of the other tribes against him.

Afghanistan was still a nation in fragments; loyalty belonged not to the Central Government, an abstraction that entered one's life only to take away money and men, but to the tribe. For ten years Amanullah had been preaching unity. He had been preaching religious tolerance. Now the Afghan tribes were offended that he expected them to fight on equal rank with men whose eyes slanted, who had competed with them for grazing land, and who let their arms hang by their sides when they prayed instead of folding them across the waist like Sunnis.

Some leaders around Amanullah had always been suspect. Since coming close to Ghazni they had been sending messengers toward Bacha Sacao's men, and in turn had received Bacha Sacao's propaganda leaflets: "Amanullah and his colleagues have been cursed by God and his Prophet and God willing, they will never see a good day in this world or in the world to come." These leaflets began to circulate among Amanullah's own troops.

Rain began to pour down on Amanullah's troops; his enemy had shelter in the citadel. But Amanullah was successful for two days of fighting and then attempted a master stroke.

The citadel of Ghazni, although on a hill, was overlooked by a higher hill. A detachment of Amanullah's men stormed this hill; among them were the Shahjui Wazirs whose irresistible urge to take what belonged to others had caused Amanullah trouble ever since he gave them land in Afghanistan. These Wazirs, with some men from Herat, captured the higher hill. They were now in an admirable tactical position. With the big gun on the hill, they fired down on the citadel.

This looked like victory.

One of the gates of the citadel was opened. Men came out holding Korans on their heads as a sign of submission. Within the citadel there was a great spurt of writing among those who could write; Bacha Sacao's men were preparing formal certificates of surrender to Amanullah.

Then the Shahjui Wazirs looked down from their hilltop and saw on the lower slopes a village that tempted them. It looked prosperous. As victors they could not refrain from leaving their guns and going down to loot it. Some other tribesmen on the hill, seeing what the Wazirs were going to get, went down also. The hilltop was left undefended.

From another village nearby Bacha Sacao's supporters went to the hilltop, seized it, and turned the gun on the Wazirs looting the village below.

In a few moments victory had turned to defeat.

The Hazaras asked Amanullah if they might retake the hill. That night they marched out, but meanwhile Bacha Sacao's men had reinforced it; watching through field glasses, Amanullah saw that his Hazaras were wasting themselves in a hopeless attack, and he called them off.

A party of Wardaks arrived, saying they had defeated Bacha Sacao's forces on their way to Ghazni and forced them to take refuge in neighboring forts. And they had captured a prisoner who puzzled them.

The prisoner could speak Pushtu and another language known to some of the men around Amanullah, Russian. In Russian he explained that he was a Pole from Warsaw who had gone to Herat four years previously and had been put under arrest as a political suspect, and later sent to Kabul where he established his innocence and was set free: that he had a friend in the Southern Province at whose house he had learned Pushtu, and that he had joined Bacha Sacao's forces merely as a means of getting to his friend's house.

No one believed him. Yet that part of his story was true. He was a miller's apprentice who with two companions had been lured to Russia by stories of the "worker's paradise." Imprisoned there as spies, the three men escaped to Afghanistan, where, fearful of being returned to Russia, they told authorities they were Englishmen fleeing China. They had been in jail in Kabul at the same time as Stratil-Sauer, who spoke Russian with them; one man embraced Islam and adopted an Afghan name and settled to a happy life; the other two remained in prison, destitute, until Count Potocki, the only other Pole ever to visit Afghanistan, interceded for them with Amanullah.

Amanullah had been the target of several spying and assassination attempts. A man who entered his tent a few days earlier, apparently to give him a petition, was found to be carrying an ax; those around Amanullah overpowered and killed him. Now, following the Moslem law, Amanullah appointed a three-man court to sit judgment on the new prisoner: his Oxford-trained brother-in-law Abdul Wahab Tarzi, his brother-in-law Hassan Jan, and Souraya's uncle Adib Effendi. These men were in a battlefield; they had no access to the files in Kabul, which might not have told this Pole's story anyway. Besides, the man was carrying Indian money and gold, and they were suspicious of the British, from whose direction all this animosity against them was coming, and who had offended their sense of fairness by refusing arms. The court decided this was a British spy. Also, what they needed to hold together their scattering forces was a common enemy, and here was one.

Amanullah presented the prisoner to the troops, calling him a British spy. "The guns which are firing from Ghazni were given to the rebels by the British and I have observed through my glasses that the artillerymen are British . . . Know therefore that our fight is not with Bacha Sacao but with the British who are harassing us." The troops shouted indignantly and Amanullah, who did not believe what he had been saying, gave the man to them to be put to death.

Bacha Sacao sent planes which dropped bombs that were correctly aimed. One killed a leading standard-bearer of Amanullah's volunteers from Kandahar; this was a man of unsavory reputation whose eyes were forever red-ringed from his eating of hashish, but his loss demoralized his men. Then the Treasury was found to contain no silver, only British notes, and the Hazaras refused to accept these. The men who had hired their animals to transport demanded payment in cash; they had not been paid for several days, and they seized the bridles of their donkeys and began to lead them away.

Amanullah had come to suspect the loyalty of Abdul Ahad. From Hassan Jan, who directed his intelligence, he heard that Abdul Ahad intended to lure him to Ghazni and leave him at the mercy of Bacha Sacao's men. The plan as Hassan Jan described it resembled a prediction which Humphrys had made more than a month earlier: that the Ghilzais would entrap Amanullah.

Hassan Jan spoke secretly with Amanullah. He told him that even if he were to become King again, he would be King of a chaotic country whose wealth had been dissipated. He called the Afghans ignorant people who had not appreciated ten years of hard work.

Amanullah gathered his troops and announced that the road to Kandahar had been blocked, that he was returning to open it. At ten o'clock that night he began the march southward again; all the way he was constantly hearing bullets strike the road around him: fire from Ghilzais.

At Mukur he got word that Herat had fallen. Herat was a symbol and a touchstone. Afghan amirs traditionally felt that as long as they held Herat, equidistant from Mazar and Kandahar so that one could

maneuver from that focus, they were secure. Now if Amanullah were
defeated he had no place but Kandahar to go.

News reached him slowly. He heard that Ghulam Nabi was on the
march, but he did not know enough details to calm his unrest. The
truth would have heartened him had he known. Ghulam Nabi had arrived in Bamiyan and was pushing toward Kabul, and Bacha Sacao's
men opposing him were being wounded in such numbers that no more
casualites were brought into Kabul for fear of starting a panic but were
kept in Charikar. And Bacha Sacao was issuing more proclamations:
"Ghulam Nabi is a liar, a drunkard, a pederast and an infidel and never
says his prayers."

Abdul Ahad wished to leave a small force at Ghazni and press on to
Kabul through the friendly Wardak land. So did the young officers
trained in Turkey. Forever Afghans would wonder, if Amanullah had
followed this advice, what would have happened?

He had another piece of advice from Nadir, the assurance given
when Nadir declined to join him in Kandahar, that they were both
working for the same cause. Nadir offered him hope of returning.

In an instant Amanullah made his decision. He sent Hassan Jan to
Kandahar to arrange transportation secretly; even there he was unfortunate, for the Ghilzais had stolen some of his motors, including
the Rolls-Royce in which he had been driven through England in such
honor. A wire was sent to the Afghan Consul in Bombay, another who
still took orders from him, requesting a visa for Inayatullah to cross
India en route the Eastern Province to be Governor; the British refused,
saying that would break faith with Bacha Sacao, but Amanullah did not
wait for their reply.

During part of this agony he had made his decision among falling
flowers. It was Id, a religious holiday, which came that year on May
20. Omar had gone aloft to observe it by bombarding the troops with
blossoms.

Reaching Mohmand, Amanullah summoned the man in charge of the
telephone lines and told him to cut the line to the north toward Kalat
and Mukur and to give him a connection for Kandahar. He talked with
his family. His cousin Ali Ahmed had come to Mohmand at his request; for an hour and a half he talked with Ali Ahmed, telling him
all there was to tell about governing Kandahar, but not revealing his
own intentions. Ali Ahmed left. Amanullah ordered the telephone
line to Kandahar to be cut.

Hardly anyone was aware when, at two o'clock in the morning, Amanullah with the War Minister Abdul Aziz got into the Hispano-Suiza which the Ghilzais had left him and drove from Mohmand toward Kandahar. Eight miles north of Kandahar he saw sudden stabs of lights from the south. By his prearranged plan, his family and friends coming from Kandahar had turned their cars northward and made a beacon for him with their headlights. Awaiting him were three Mercedes-Benz buses and about eighteen cars and lorries, holding twenty-seven men, thirty-five women and children and thirty servants. Two of the women, Souraya and Inayatullah's wife Kawkab, were in their last month of pregnancy. His mother was with them.

When the party finally set forth, Amanullah was at the wheel of the car which the Republic of France had given him, and he was headed toward India. From time to time the party would stop while a man climbed on top a bus and with long clippers cut the telegraph wire. Communication was Amanullah's enemy now.

A proclamation had been concocted saying that Inayatullah was on his way to Ningrahar as Governor; this was shown to the Afghan official at the frontier, who had barely time to look at it and widen his eyes. Then Amanullah, driving over the road that had carried him in triumph eighteen months earlier, was out of Afghanistan and no one at all could say that he was its King.

His idealistic experiment in government, that had begun in the bloodshed of the Great War, had ended. There was bloodshed behind him still.

CHAPTER 34

May 22, 1929, to September 7, 1933

An hour after Amanullah left Mohmand on the evening of May 22, the telephone lineman who had cut the wire for him drove toward Kandahar. "When I arrived at the place where the road to Chaman joins the Kandahar-Ghazni road," he related, "I noticed from the rut of the King's car that he had gone toward Chaman instead of going toward Kandahar." The lineman reached Kandahar early in the morning and told there the news of Amanullah's flight.

At one o'clock on the afternoon of May 23, almost at the moment that Amanullah was crossing the frontier into India, Ali Ahmed proclaimed himself for the second time Amir of a portion of Afghanistan. On the following day he enjoyed the sound of Amir Ali Ahmed being named in the Khutba in the Kandahar mosque.

On the following Friday the Khutba was read in the name of Amir Habibullah, the bandit whose forces had taken Kandahar in the previous week with little opposition, and Ali Ahmed was hiding in the house of a poor Hazara. Discovered a few days later, he was taken to Kabul and paraded through the streets barefoot in chains.

Ali Ahmed remained in prison until July 9, when he was taken to the large gun on the cliff overlooking Kabul and tied to a cannon for his execution. First he kissed the gun to show that he died like a man and to give thanks for relief from suffering. When the news reached London, this comment appeared in the margin of an India Office Minute: "One gun at least brought down a big bird."

When Amanullah left Afghanistan, his champion Ghulam Nabi was fighting for him in Bamiyan, having come down from Russia. He was within striking distance of Kabul when he heard that Amanullah's departure had left him not only without support from the south but without a cause to fight for. He retired to Mazar-i-Sharif, pursued by Sayed Hussein whom he had almost overcome, and from there withdrew, without fighting, into Russia.

The Hazaras kept fighting for Amanullah. Amin Jan, the young Prince who had become their leader, convoked the Hazara chiefs and explained that they had no money, no communication, scant arms. The chiefs said they would provide their own money and arms and men, so they established in the Hazarajat a base from which they harassed Bacha Sacao so effectively that when they offered him terms, he accepted some, which included free passage into India for Amin Jan. On his journey eastward Amin Jan met Nadir, who advised him to leave the country confidently and await Nadir's triumph and the election he would hold for a new Amir. Never doubting that anyone but Amanullah would be elected Amir, Amin Jan departed. Others of Amanullah's friends were placing their hopes in this promised election; Ghulam Siddiq and Ghulam Nabi forgot Nadir's antagonism toward them and sent him money. He was their only hope.

Turkey and Persia seriously considered putting the stamp of legitimacy on Bacha Sacao by recognizing his government.[1] The British contemplated this also and pondered the advantage of doing it quickly in order to get ahead of Russia. They finally decided, "If we are prepared to show 'friendship'; i.e., give practical help, in the future, some little delay in recognition will soon be forgotten."

Bacha Sacao's problems at home, however, diminished his illusions about the security of his rule. He had extorted too much money from merchants, his followers had shown too few principles in regard to women; he had given too many important positions to old comrades, and even the men of his own Koh-i-Daman were grumbling because he had taken so many of their youths into his army, as they were the only people he trusted.

Early in July he called a conference of the Koh-i-Daman leaders, expecting to have their full support whatever their advice. They told him that he should come to terms with Nadir, whom they suggested inviting to Kabul. Bacha Sacao refused to listen.

"If the people are tired of helping me," he said, "God is still on my side."

But he was mistaken. Already he had been abandoned, if not by God, then by the man who had held himself out as the deputy and interpreter of God, Sher Agha.

On June 13 Bacha Sacao's most important General made a surprise attack on Nadir and was defeated. But Bacha Sacao lost more than the men and ammunition.

Sher Agha called a jirga and issued a proclamation making Bacha Sacao an infidel. His authority was the commandment of the Koran that no one should make an attack without first summoning his opponent to a conference; Bacha Sacao had omitted the conference. As with Amanullah earlier, an attack on Bacha Sacao was not only permissible but praiseworthy.

In Sher Agha's script it was time for Bacha Sacao, having served his purpose, to leave the scene.

As Amanullah had done, Bacha Sacao invited Sher Agha to Kabul for negotiations. Once more Sher Agha said no.

But Sher Agha's strength had been his power to kindle into blaze the emotions of the fierce Ghilzais. And the Ghilzais were planning to leave Afghanistan earlier than usual this year. "Suspect they have lost faith in Nadir and Sher Agha on one hand, and also in Bacha Sacao," reported the Baluchistan Intelligence Diary.

The Ghilzais, with the keen intelligences that had kept them moving across a continent, had contemplated Sher Agha's maneuvers and decided that Afghanistan's affairs were none of theirs.

To Nadir, as to Amanullah, the pressing need was for more men, and the only men available were on the British side of the frontier.

Nadir's approach to them was different from Amanullah's. Boldly he wrote to the British announcing what he had decided to do. They wrote back to him that he should not. But meanwhile men were going to him in Ali Khel and the British efforts to restrain them were half-hearted. "To threaten more precisely drastic action at this stage, to have such threats flouted, and then, in event of further rush to Nadir's standard, to find it inadvisable or impossible to translate threats into action, would in all probability merely serve to make matters ultimately worse," was the way G. of I. justified this tolerance in a wire to an official asking what he must do about his departing tribesmen.

Then Nadir gave them additional cause for inaction with the information that he was of a mind to leave Afghanistan, and would like British aid in rescuing his family from Kabul.

The friend to whom Nadir entrusted these negotiations was the cultivated Haji Mohammed Akbar who had been Amanullah's Consul in Bombay, where he won the admiration of Sir Denys Bray, the Foreign Secretary of the Government of India, for his knowledge of public affairs. Now he was sufficiently knowledgeable about the operations of the Government of India to know exactly which questions he could ask in Parachinar which would have to be referred to Delhi and thence to London. He asked those questions. Every time the British negotiator apologized for the delay, Haji Akbar inwardly smiled.

While these delay tactics were working, more than five thousand Wazirs joined Nadir in Ali Khel. He was joined also by a young protégé of Shah Wali named Mohay-ud-din who had been sending him messages from Bacha Sacao's intelligence service in Kabul, where he held a position. Now Nadir knew all Bacha Sacao's military secrets, and much more that a businessman in Peshawar, M. A. Hakim, had learned through the coded wireless messages that his agents were permitted to send from Kabul.

Shah Wali led the Wazirs to Kabul. His strategy was to capture the enemy's officers, and the leaderless troops fled in confusion. Soon he was facing the Arg, the palace from which Inayatullah had been forced. His own family were prisoners inside, but Nadir's wife managed to send him a message, that he should attack and never mind the consequences to them.

On October 12 Shah Wali's guns began to fire on the Arg. Being full of ammunition, it exploded. Bacha Sacao, Hamidullah and a few companions climbed through a hole in the Arg wall, each carrying a bag of gold. Bacha Sacao's luck with weather, at least, held; the moon was covered with clouds and he managed to escape.

On October 15 Nadir entered Kabul on a black horse, to martial music. He went to the Idgah Mosque where a crowd was waiting. Many cried out that he should be their King. He made a few gestures of protest, but the cries continued. Nadir bowed his head, then raised it and agreed.

On the following day, October 16, Nadir proclaimed himself King of Afghanistan. He took the name of an earlier conquering King, Nadir Shah.

The people of Kohistan threw flowers on Bacha Sacao when he came back into their hills. For a season he had brought them more glory than they had ever expected. He was *their* son of a bitch.

But soon Nadir and Shah Wali sent men to Kohistan to burn the villages. On promise of amnesty Bacha Sacao and his companions gave themselves up and were taken to the Arg in Kabul, where they were treated as guests.

A few days later Nadir announced publicly that he had pardoned Bacha Sacao but had received a petition from officials and tribal leaders asking him to "hand over these traitors so that we may be able to put them to death."

Bacha Sacao was taken with his friends to the Sherpur Airport where a gathering of tribesmen waited: Wazirs, Mahsuds, Mangals, Zadrans and Daurs. These were told: "Here is the Bacha. If you wish him to be pardoned, he can be, and if you wish him to be killed, it lies with you." The Wazirs said that they were unable to forgive him and the Jajis should decide his fate. The Jajis said that it was up to the Wazirs.

But these were men of action. Some Wazirs lifted their rifles; it had been raining and they slipped in the mud, but they could shoot straight. They shot at Bacha Sacao. Other rifles were fired. Hamidullah, Sher Jan and fourteen others lay dead.

For the next three days their bodies swung from wooden pillars for all to look at. Photographs were taken, which for four months afterwards could be enjoyed in Peshawar by anyone with six pennies.

The Water Carrier's Son had had his final encounter with the establishment.

Russia was again the first nation to recognize a government of independent Afghanistan. The British said, "If we hurry into recognition, it will be assumed evermore that we put Nadir on the throne and that, as Nadir himself is clever enough to know, would do him no good in the eyes of his countrymen or of the Soviet, whom it is in his (or any Afghan Government's) interest, as well as ours, to keep guessing."

Amanullah told the British when he reached India:

"I want to live in a remote place so that the Afghans will know that I am not near Afghanistan and then the bloodshed will cease. I would like to be a farmer in Italy." He said also:

"I have no intention of ever returning to Afghanistan . . . The revo-

lution took me completely by surprise. I have not deposited a penny in
foreign banks . . . All my capital consists of what I have with me, the
equivalent of about 400,000 British rupees, which I have to share with
my brother and retinue."

Since Amanullah had wrested his independence from Great Britain,
Great Britain felt no responsibility for him as it had done for
nineteenth-century royal refugees. When told he would have no help
beyond the passage to Europe, Amanullah "accepted the inevitable"
with dignity and courage. He said, "You must know that I was no
wastrel like the former Shah of Persia, that I worked night and day for
the welfare of my people and in my downfall at least I have the solace of
a clear conscience." Then he broke down and blurted out, "I am sorry
that I was not annihilated with all my family like the Tsar of Russia
Now I am destined to wander in foreign lands."

To the King of Italy, however, he was still the holder of the Collar
of the Annunziata and a "cousin." King Vittore Emanuele, who really
was "a good man," gave him refuge and a house on the Via Orazio
in Rome. Inayatullah had gone to Persia. Ulya Hazrat and her other
son went to Constantinople, as did Mahmud Tarzi. Amanullah and
Souraya settled with their family, which included a daughter born in
India, at the Villa Orazio.

"Nadir is absolutely determined not to let Amanullah back into Afghanistan," Shah Wali told the British Foreign Office when he arrived
in London as Minister.

By October 26, 1929, Amanullah was writing to Peshawar about
"Nadir's usurpation." He had been shocked that he was not summoned
back to the throne or at least made a candidate in the election that
Nadir had promised.

Soon he would realize the depth and tenacity of Nadir's hostility.
Wali was put on trial in Kabul, charged with having plotted the rebellion with Bacha Sacao. He admitted his contacts with the bandit but
maintained that he had acted with Amanullah's knowledge and on his
orders. Amanullah corroborated this in frantic wires to Kabul which
were never put into evidence. Wali was sentenced to eight years' imprisonment while Mahmud Sami, who was tried on the same charge
and presented no defense, was put to death. Within a few years Amanullah, as a public show of faith in his regent, would marry his daughter
Abedah to Wali's son.

In 1930 Amanullah had a letter printed in India and circulated privately in Afghanistan denying various slanders to the effect that he had carried great wealth from the country and that, during his trip, he had opened secret bank accounts in Europe. He also accused Nadir of deceit in forestalling competition by telling him, during the rebellion, "We are all working for the same cause."

Nadir's rebuttal came publicly in a newspaper article that condemned Amanullah in such detail that it even called by name the dancer Idan Bai, who had performed "naked" at the 1928 Jeshyn. "What material benefit accrued to the administration for persuading the Queen, her sisters and other females of the royal family to discard the veil, appear half-naked, cut their hair and wear European clothes? . . . There was no profit to the country from the ex-King's making the consent of bridegroom and bride necessary before the marriage . . . He created feelings of hatred and dissension in the nation by setting up a young party against the elders."

This was a prelude to the Great Assembly which Nadir summoned to ratify his accession. At Nadir's bidding, these 286 men declared that Amanullah's property in Afghanistan belonged to the Government and that he should not share its income or proceeds in any way. It made official the charge of absconding with Government money and valuables, and suggested that steps be taken to get these back. "Crown jewels" were mentioned, although Afghanistan had no crown jewels.

Even while the Assembly was meeting, the British Foreign Office was wiring to its ambassadors and ministers all over the world a special code word, "Zuravulior," to be used in telegrams dealing with Amanullah's movements on a proposed Haj to Mecca. The British never ceased to note where he was and what he was doing, and the British Minister in Kabul, who was now Maconachie, passed the information to Nadir.

Nadir had opened the schools again, but on a limited basis and only for boys. "We are not going to offend the mullahs by undertaking universal education until such time as the nation seems ready for it," he said.[2] The mullahs had one of their own, Sher Agha, as Minister of Justice; a murderer was handed over to his victim's next-of-kin for public execution, and a man who had drunk whiskey was flogged publicly in the bazaar by indignant mullahs.

Even so, Nadir was having trouble. The Ghilzais again were rebellious, and although he sent Sher Agha to talk with them, he mistrusted the loyalty of Sher Agha, to whom he attributed personal ambition for the throne. Sher Agha again wanted to leave the country for Mecca, and Nadir's deputies persuaded his elderly mother to refuse him the permission which religious law demanded. As Nadir became more secure, Sher Agha's power waned. Gul Agha was shunted off to be Minister in Cairo. Hashim, who was Prime Minister, overthrew many of Sher Agha's decisions and when finally the Government sent soldiers into Sher Agha's house to remove a fugitive to whom the Hazrat Sahib had given asylum, this was an indignity never to be lived down.

Some of Amanullah's officials became Nadir's. Faiz Muhammed, who had been his Minister of Education, was now more important as Foreign Minister. Sher Ahmed was Minister to Persia and two of the Charkhi brothers, Ghulam Siddiq and Ghulam Nabi, were ministers to Germany and Turkey respectively.

Nadir did not trust the Charkhi brothers, especially after Ghulam Nabi wrote him a letter accusing him of usurpation. When Ghulam Nabi left his post in Turkey for several weeks, the British as well as the Afghans exerted great efforts to find out where he was.

Then, in the summer of 1932, Ghulam Nabi sent a pledge of loyalty on behalf of his family and asked permission to return to Afghanistan with Ghulam Jilani. Warily Nadir gave permission, but in Kabul Ghulam Nabi was under surveillance.

On November 8 Nadir called Ghulam Nabi into his office and showed him evidence that purported to involve him in pro-Amanullah intrigue. Ghulam Nabi lost his temper. He let fly against Nadir all the antipathy of three years of resenting the fact that he instead of Amanullah was the King. Nadir turned to his equerry and ordered him to execute Ghulam Nabi at once. Then he walked out of the room and, before the door had finished closing, soldiers were beating Ghulam Nabi with their rifle butts. They beat him to death.

Showing the evidence to the Cabinet, the Assembly and the Upper House of the Parliament, Nadir got all three bodies to pronounce Ghulam Nabi guilty of high treason. But, as Maconachie pointed out to him, the sequence was wrong.

Such an autocratic act, commented the British, would have made Abdur Rahman more powerful than ever. "But Nadir tries to fly other colors." And in between there had been Amanullah.

The chain of violence reached to Berlin, where a brother of Nadir was murdered by one of the Afghan students there who were grateful to Amanullah. On September 7, 1933, in Kabul another young Afghan walked into the British Legation and shot dead the British garage superintendent and two Indian employees. In the aftermath of this, some of Amanullah's imprisoned friends were put to death. One was Ghulam Jilani. Another was Wali, who before being hanged asked Nadir to cancel the decree forbidding his children to be educated. This was denied.

The young man who shot up the British Legation had said, "It is rumored generally that the British have secretly acquired Afghanistan and are deceiving Afghans." This was suppressed and his act attributed to a desire for unlawful drink, free love and loose living.

The British were in a position that they had described a few years earlier when looking for the missing Ghulam Nabi:

"We did not feel justified in initiating enquiries for fear that we might thereby seem to betray an undue interest in the internal affairs of Afghanistan and lend color to a story that was spread at one time that H.M.G. had connived at downfall of Amanullah because he was an inconveniently progressive monarch," reported the Berlin Embassy, and the Foreign Office approved: "It is, as you say, very important that our interest should not be misunderstood or misrepresented."

CHAPTER 35

November 8, 1933, to the present

Amanullah and Souraya spent the rest of their lives telling stories of Afghanistan to their large family. They took six children to Rome and had two more children, to whom they taught Persian.

Through their friendship with the rulers of Italy, they kept a certain social position, which always recalled their royal past. But they sold the personal jewelry which they had brought from Afghanistan and still did not have enough money. Amanullah, who knew no occupation except ruling, worked off his excess energy by making chairs and tables.

He really did, as the British and Nadir feared, intrigue. At the end of 1933 he might have had his opportunity to return to Afghanistan as King. On November 8, the anniversary of Ghulam Nabi's death, Nadir went to Dilkusha Palace to award prizes to a class of students. One of these students was a son of a servant of Ghulam Nabi, who had been reared in his home. He had a pistol, which he fired three times into Nadir.

Nadir's death was kept secret for two hours while arrangements were made to proclaim his only son, Zahir, aged nineteen, as King. There had been no effective pro-Amanullah party in Kabul to seize advantage of this ultimate reach of tribal vengeance. The dynasty of Nadir still reigned in Afghanistan.

The other opportunity for Amanullah's restoration was the Second World War. His old friend from the First World War, von Hentig, tried in vain to get German support for him. After the war Amanullah saw that restoration was an illusion; he wrote to King Zahir pledging his allegiance. The Cabinet, hearing from the Afghan Ambassador in Rome that Amanullah was living in cruel poverty, voted him an allowance. His relatives in Afghanistan finally were permitted to visit him; he greeted them with, "How are the people of Afghanistan?" A man who paused on the threshold to wipe his shoes was told by Souraya, "Oh, don't wipe off the soil of Afghanistan!" One nephew, the son of Shah Wali, awoke in the night to find Amanullah standing by his bed, forehead wet with sweat, fists clenched, muttering in agony, "Why? Why? Why?"

The years passed. The children grew up. One daughter became a physician; when she went to England to study, Amanullah thought of Sir Francis Humphrys, decided the time had come for forgiveness there, and asked Lady Humphrys to look after her. Rahmatullah, who had been Crown Prince, took two doctorates and became the owner of two boys' schools; Ihsanullah became an engineer with United Nations.

Mahmud Tarzi died in Constantinople, which was now called Istanbul. His last years had been spent riding on public conveyances and making notes for articles which he never wrote.[1]

Inayatullah fell dead of a heart attack in his garden at Tehran while making a photograph.

Early in 1960 Amanullah went to a clinic in Switzerland to be treated for a liver ailment. There, on April 26, having lived thirty-seven years as Prince and King and thirty-one years as a poor exile, he died. With him at the end was the beloved little sister, Nur-us-Seraj, now a middle-aged woman. She heard his final words.

Amanullah's body was escorted by an Italian guard of honor to a plane which took it to Afghanistan. In Jalalabad it had been planned that his half brothers would carry the coffin to the grave. But tribesmen pushed them aside and insisted on carrying Amanullah themselves. Some were Sangu Khel Shinwaris. There, in the garden beside his father, his last request was fulfilled. He was buried in the soil of Afghanistan.

THE SPARK FROM THE ASHES

I went to Afghanistan in search of Amanullah's story in 1967. I flew into Kabul on a plane of Afghanistan's own airline, Ariana; an American woman beside me called my attention to the wide concrete road below, sweeping from Herat to Kandahar to Kabul, and told me that her son-in-law was with the American firm that had built part of it. (The Russians had built the other part.) She said that her daughter played a lot of bridge and would hardly know that she was not in the United States.

Amanullah was so slight a figure in the libraries of America that I knew little about him except the outlines of a dramatic plot. Hardly was I off the plane when I knew that getting the rest of the story of Amanullah would not be simple. When Afghans heard what I was going to write, they gave me a searching look and said, "Well, I hope you tell the truth." So many said it that I knew that the truth—at any rate, their truth—had never been told. A young man on the street, who rescued me from a haughty policeman, said, "When I heard that someone was going to write finally about Amanullah, you can't imagine how my heart leaped up."

It was the time of Jeshyn, the celebration of independence, which Amanullah had won for Afghanistan. Yet I did not hear Amanullah's name. I watched the fireworks, and the final bursts sent down little flags floating on parachutes. Some flags bore the face of King Zahir, some the face of his father King Nadir, whose blue mausoleum was illuminated in the distance, and those which evoked the greatest applause bore the rising sun symbol of Pushtunistan, the land that the British called Independent Territory and which the Afghans always thought should be theirs. But no flag carried the face of Amanullah. I wondered what response would erupt in that crowd if an Amanullah flag should unexpectedly float down.

Amanullah had been almost erased from the history books of Afghanistan, but in a land where only about one-tenth the population was literate, this did not matter much. On the tongues of men in the bazaars, among the tribesmen who had come from the mountain passes to see the wonders of Jeshyn, Amanullah was just as alive as any other figure of Afghan history. "Amanullah was our best King," an illiterate woman told me. Although most of the bazaar stalls displayed prominently a large photograph of King Zahir, many held also a small lithograph in gaudy colors that was a drawing of King Amanullah. In Jalalabad I paid several visits to his tomb, a half cylinder of cement to one side of the marble-lace marker beneath which his father was buried. A similar cylinder marked the burial place of Inayatullah. No name appeared on any tomb; it was explained to me that everyone already knew who was buried there. On each visit I saw a fresh flower lying on the tomb of Amanullah and another flower on the tomb of Amir Habibullah. Inayatullah was still overlooked. Once I went at twilight and men were praying there in the Moslem fashion, with palms upturned. They motioned to me to take off my shoes. These were men of the tribes that had thrown him out.

About the events surrounding Amanullah all Afghans held one theory: that the British had deliberately conspired to get rid of him. When I went to the India Office Library in London to study the documents of those days, I expected to see a letter: "Let's get rid of Amanullah."

I found nothing so simple. The archivist warned me that nothing was being released concerning "spying, anything detrimental to anyone, or anything offensive to the establishment." Actually I found many reports of spies, many peeks into the ways of spying, many documents that commenced with the intriguing phrase, "According to information received." As for repression of material detrimental to persons, that applied only to the British, not to any other nationalities.

The story that unfolded for me was more subtle and human than the one I had expected. I saw how the British could have undone Amanullah without realizing it, and later, when the Pentagon Papers concerning American involvement in Vietnam were made public, I saw similarities to the case of Vietnam President Ngo Dinh Diem. Amanullah's downfall appeared as part of the disintegration of the British Empire, a disintegration that was pathetically apparent in a letter from the British Legation in Kabul lamenting that if it rebuilt a house destroyed in the 1928–29 rebellion, it would not be able to replace two worn-out lorries.

When I discussed my research with a knowledgeable Afghan, he did not think that I had the whole story. He took for granted that no nation would reveal too much to its discredit. Tracing through the bones of my materials, he saw different interpretations of events. In the British prophecy that Amanullah's hasty reforms would mean his overthrow, he saw the proof that the British were engineering that overthrow. This was the conclusion drawn also by the Russian secret service from those same documents, which it saw earlier because it intercepted them. The memoirs of the Russian spymaster in Kabul, Georgei Agabekov, published in 1930, quoted specific documents which I recognized although they were not available for perusal until 1968. Besides, said my Afghan friends, none of the Afghans whom I named in the plot was capable of directing such a project without a mastermind from outside.

Lawrence of Arabia is still an enigma; the things we are asked to believe about him, if he had no role in Afghan affairs, are improbable, and at the time there was suspicion even within the British Government. Also, one whole group of people remain a blank to me: the ordinary British soldier and official. All that I read was written by graduates of Oxford or Cambridge who saw events on the grand scale. Very rarely, from some book, I had glimpses of the man from a London suburb or Brighton side street who was in India to do a job and did not care past the next hour. He too was significant.

So I began to see that my picture was not complete, but had its shadowy places, and that to some people the shadows would take shapes different from those which I saw.

In the spring of 1968, after reading the British documents, I returned to Afghanistan. It was a new country when seen with a knowledge of Amanullah's Afghanistan. I saw a flourishing Kabul University which had been only a phrase in a speech he made at Oxford. A journey which meant days in his time now meant hours. I even flew from Hartford, Connecticut by jet to Kabul with only one change of planes. There was a new constitution adopted in 1964. A new Intercontinental Hotel was being built.

Women in smart Western clothes chatted with me; on the other hand, women in chaderis surveyed me with eyes that seemed young and lustrous through rows of crocheting; one veiled woman carried a Pan-American World Airways seat bag.

I heard of an evening ten years earlier, during the régime of progressive Premier Daoud, Nadir's nephew, when the Queen and her female relatives had appeared at dinner unveiled, and the next morning there were policemen on the streets to shield from aggression any woman who wished to follow their example. That evening followed by thirty-one years the dramatic moment of Souraya's throwing off her veil.

The United States had assumed the role of the former British Empire as the force competing with the Soviet Union in Afghanistan. But the United States is not there on the frontier; while it has inherited the responsibility, the frontier quarrels have been inherited by Pakistan. At any rate, Afghanistan, less important in a round world than a flat one, has less bargaining power in a world whose military weapons can bypass buffer states. Among the men who diminished Afghanistan,

Christopher Columbus and Genghis Khan, may be named Robert Goddard, who invented rocketry.

Souraya died in Rome on April 21, 1968. Ulya Hazrat had died a few years earlier, having outlived Amanullah. Aliah, the cousin whom Amanullah had married during the rebellion, still lived in Kabul; he had sent her a divorce from Italy, but she never remarried.

Once more, for Souraya, the Italians gave the ceremonies of royalty. Again a plane flew a coffin to Kabul and a military flight took her to Jalalabad.

When Souraya's body arrived in Jalalabad, I was at the airport. So were dozens of tribesmen in turbans, of the same tribes that had been so scandalized by her actions that they helped send her into exile and poverty. As the hearse, with Koranic verses painted on the windshield and flowers in pockets on the fenders, moved away from the plane, hands went to turbans in a gesture of respect.

The grave for Souraya was made just outside the little pavilion which held Amanullah. The officials of Jalalabad had worried that some demonstration might mar the day; a mullah did speak up spontaneously, but he did it to praise her. No women were at the ceremony except her family, and at a Moslem funeral even this was unusual. But as the important people were moving away, along came a party of old-fashioned women in chaderis, their hands outstretched, eager to pray at the grave of one who had tried to free them from the chaderi.

In August 1968 Afghanistan celebrated the fiftieth anniversary of its independence; I had expected the observance in 1969, but it seems that Afghans, who procrastinate in many things, are forehanded in regard to anniversary.

One hot morning, in front of a grandstand filled with distinguished Afghan ladies wearing, for the only time that year, their native dress, and with diplomats wearing, not for the only time, white tie and tails, King Zahir of Afghanistan made a speech. And twice he spoke the name of Amanullah. This was a signal for others to speak of him. His photograph appeared in a Kabul newspaper. Amanullah's reign now officially existed. It had taken forty years.

At a reception given by the King, I photographed an elderly man wearing a turban and a withdrawn expression who might have been Sher Agha. This, I learned later, was Masum, Sher Agha's nephew who had conspired with him against Amanullah. The following year, back in the United States, I read of a movement of Afghan mullahs inveighing against short skirts for women. The story had a familiar sound. I saw that many of the forces that had opposed Amanullah had little to do with him but were, as a British official said of the migration of nomads, a force of nature beyond even the power of kings to halt.

The high point of Afghanistan's development, it seems to me, came in 1972. This was an epic year when two seasons without snow on the mountains produced severe famine causing several thousand deaths. By their own efforts, however, the Afghans overcame that crisis so well that 1972 ended with new self-confidence, and the fourth largest industry was tourism. A confident Afghanistan must have disturbed the Soviet Union. The next year a royal cousin, Daoud, prodded by left-wing young men, staged a coup, exiling the king and proclaiming a republic. In 1978 left-wing leaders staged their own coup. In late 1979 the Soviet Union invaded.

The tribal ferocity that had driven out Amanullah now arose to drive out the "atheist foreigners." The whole world knows of the great jihad, or holy war, how the Soviets were seen as ineffectual against a "ragtag band" of guerrillas. By October, 1991 there was no more Soviet Union.

The forces of nature kept moving. When I visited Kabul in late 1991, it looked exactly as it had looked on my first visit in 1966, but with added layers of dust. The Soviet occupation had left nothing good behind, but at least the buildings stood. No one admitted having ever been a Communist, except for the very top men, and they were wondering how long they could hold off the tribesmen. Not for long. Soon civil war renewed and the ultimate winners in Kabul were a force from the eastern tribal lands and Pakistan called the Taliban. But theirs is a victory insufficient to bring peace. They still fight violently against the unsubdued minority.

Afghan homes are still being burned. Kabul is a city of rubble. Art treasures of the Kabul Museum are scattered to the four winds; Afghanistan is a pariah, combative toward those who would help her, and Afghans are gripped by a tyranny that reaches into private life in a way the historic conquerors seldom dreamed of. The Taliban are largely the orphans of the rebellion against the Soviet Union Having no ties, these orphans were fair game for any one who would organize them, .and those who scooped them up were hard-line mullahs in Pakistan who taught them only to fight for their version of Islam, ignoring that Allah is compassionate and merciful.

As I write this at the beginning of the 21st Century, Afghan women are beaten if they appear on the streets not sheathed in a chaderi, and receive only rudimentary health care and are denied education. The Taliban way of life surpasses in rigidity even that of a remote tribal village, and often extends into sadism. Almost the only available recreation today in Kabul is watching thieves' hands being cut off.

Throughout the Western world the Taliban are denounced for sheltering the most famous of all terrorists, Osama bin Ladin, credited with the bombing of two American embassies in Africa and with the capacity for more destruction in other lands. This bogey-man of the West is one of the young men who nurtured their antagonisms during the war against the Soviets, often with weapons and skills provided by the people at whom they are now taking aim. Americans, once regarded as beneficent friends, have bombed the areas of Afghanistan where they thought terrorists were training.

Amanullah's reign began with the fire of hope and ambition. It ended in the flames of destruction. Today in 2000 fear of terrorism is abroad in the world. Many see it as fire from Afghanistan.

in the United States, I read of a movement of Afghan mullahs inveighing against short skirts for women. The story had a familiar sound. I saw that many of the forces that had opposed Amanullah had little to do with him but were, as a British official said of the migration of nomads, a force of nature beyond even the power of kings to halt.

The high point of Afghanistan's development, it seems to me, came in 1972. This was an epic year when two seasons without snow on the mountains produced severe famine causing several thousand deaths. By their own efforts, however, the Afghans overcame that crisis so well that 1972 ended with new self-confidence, and the fourth largest industry was tourism. A confident Afghanistan must have disturbed the Soviet Union. The next year a royal cousin, Daoud, prodded by left-wing young men, staged a coup, exiling the king and proclaiming a republic. In 1978 left-wing leaders staged their own coup. In late 1979 the Soviet Union invaded.

The tribal ferocity that had driven out Amanullah now arose to drive out the "atheist foreigners." The whole world knows of the great jihad, or holy war, how the Soviets were seen as ineffectual against a "ragtag band" of guerrillas. By October, 1991 there was no more Soviet Union.

The forces of nature kept moving. When I visited Kabul in late 1991, it looked exactly as it had looked on my first visit in 1966, but with added layers of dust. The Soviet occupation had left nothing good behind, but at least the buildings stood. No one admitted having ever been a Communist, except for the very top men, and they were wondering how long they could hold off the tribesmen. Not for long. Soon civil war renewed and the ultimate winners in Kabul were a force from the eastern tribal lands and Pakistan called the Taliban. But theirs is a victory insufficient to bring peace. They still fight violently against the unsubdued minority.

Afghan homes are still being burned. Kabul is a city of rubble. Art treasures of the Kabul Museum are scattered to the four winds; Afghanistan is a pariah, combative toward those who would help her, and Afghans are gripped by a tyranny that reaches into private life in a way the historic conquerors seldom dreamed of. The Taliban are largely the orphans of the rebellion against the Soviet Union Having no ties, these orphans were fair game for any one who would organize them, .and those who scooped them up were hard-line mullahs in Pakistan who taught them only to fight for their version of Islam, ignoring that Allah is compassionate and merciful.

As I write this at the beginning of the 21st Century, Afghan women are beaten if they appear on the streets not sheathed in a chaderi, and receive only rudimentary health care and are denied education. The Taliban way of life surpasses in rigidity even that of a remote tribal village, and often

CHAPTER NOTES

Unpublished Crown Copyright material in the India Office Library or India Office Records in this book appears by permission of the Controller of Her Majesty's Stationery Office. This is my main source. Other information comes from personal interviews and from the following published sources:

Chapter 2
1. Otto von Hentig, *Ten Months in Afghanistan*, translated by the British Foreign Office.
2. Edwin S. Montagu, *An Indian Diary*, pp. 370–71.
3. Sir Michael O'Dwyer, "The Mohammedans of India and India's Mohammedan Neighbors," in *Journal of the Royal Central Asian Society*, 1921, p. 194.

Chapter 3
1. Abdul Ghani, *A Review of the Political Situation in Central Asia*, p. 92.
2. Ibid., pp. 92 and 93.
3. A. C. Jewett, "An American Engineer in Afghanistan," edited by Marjorie Jewett Bell, p. 214.
4. Alfred Harald Brun, *Troublous Times*, p. 78.
5. *The Nation* of August 23, 1919, quoted in *The Inside Story of the Peace Conference* by Dr. E. J. Dillon.
6. Leonard Mosley, *The Glorious Fault*, p. 240.
7. David Schoenbrun, CBS correspondent, on NBC television "Tonight" show, relating interview with Ho.

Chapter 4
1. Abdul Ghani, op. cit., p. 104.

Chapter 5
1. Sigismund Waley, *Edwin Montagu*, p. 327.
2. General Sir Wilfred Malleson, *Journal of the Royal Central Asian Society*, Vol. IX, part 2, 1922, page 96, transcript of speech made January 24, 1922. Malleson admits exploiting the religious strife in Kandahar, not inciting it.
3. General Staff Branch, Army Headquarters, India, *The Third Afghan War, Official Account*, pp. 30, 31.

4. Lieutenant-General G. N. Molesworth, *Afghanistan, 1919*, p. 87.
5. Ibid., p. 77 and p. 80.
6. Ibid., p. 84.
7. General Staff Branch, op. cit., pp. 128–31.
8. Ibid., p. 61.

Chapter 6
1. Arnold Toynbee, *Experiences*, p. 192.
2. F. M. Bailey, *Mission to Tashkent*, p. 168.
3. Ibid., p. 143.
4. Ibid., p. 174.
5. Molesworth, op. cit., p. 90.
6. Bailey, op. cit., p. 69.
7. Waley, op. cit., p. 223.

Chapter 7
1. Bailey, op. cit., p. 194.
2. Malleson, op. cit.
3. Frank A. Martin, *Under the Absolute Amir*, p. 110.
4. Jawaharlal Nehru, *Toward Freedom*, p. 54.
5. Ibid., p. 55.

Chapter 8
1. Vartan Gregorian, *The Emergence of Modern Afghanistan*, pp. 172–73.
2. John Alfred Gray, *At the Court of the Amir*, p. 402.
3. Anna Louise Strong, New York *Herald-Tribune*, March 24, 1929.
4. Abdul Ghani, op. cit., p. 142.
5. Philip Knightley and Colin Simpson, *The Secret Lives of Lawrence of Arabia*, p. 64.
6. Kinross, *Ataturk*, p. 339.

Chapter 10
1. U.S.A., National Archives, Index 033.90H and Ohio Historical Society Library (papers of President Warren G. Harding) for material on American experiences of Afghan Mission and Princess Fatima Sultana.
2. St. Clair McKelway, *The Big Little Man From Brooklyn*, pp. 21–47, background on Weinberg.
3. Lowell Thomas, *Beyond Khyber Pass*, pp. 242–45.
4. Chattar Singh Samra, *India and Anglo-Soviet Relations*, p. 97.
5. Thomas, op. cit., p. 241.

Chapter 11
1. *Excelsior*, Paris, November 20, 1921.
2. Lowell Thomas, *Beyond Khyber Pass*. D. W. King, the American photographer replacement, wrote *Living East*.
3. Maurice Pernot, *En Asie Musulmane*, p. 27.

4. U.S.A., National Archives, State Department, report of December 1, 1922.
5. Georgei Agabekov, *O.G.P.U., the Russian Secret Terror,* p. 23.

Chapter 12
1. Max Beloff, *Imperial Sunset.*
2. Waley, op. cit., p. 264.
3. Lilian A. Starr, *Tales of Tirah and Lesser Tibet,* pp. 163–247.

Chapter 13
1. U.S.A., National Archives, Letter of Jeanne Van Coover to U.S. Consul in Calcutta, December 23, 1923.

Chapter 15
1. James Michener, *Caravans.*

Chapter 16
1. Andrée Viollis, *Tourmente sur l'Afghanistan,* p. 152.
2. Agabekov, op. cit., p. 158.
3. Earl of Birkenhead, *Halifax,* p. 229.
4. Agabekov, op. cit., p. 158.
5. Ibid., p. 54.

Chapter 18
1. Roland Wild, *Amanullah, Ex-King of Afghanistan,* pp. 96–98.
2. Birkenhead, op. cit., p. 247.
3. Ibid., p. 248.
4. Shah Wali, *Yaddashta-i-man.*

Chapter 19
1. U.S.A., National Archives, Letter of Jeanne Van Coover to Allen W. Dulles, December 26, 1923.
2. Ibid., State Department correspondence January 20, 1929.

Chapter 21
1. U.S.S.R., *Dokumenty Vneshnei Politiki* (Documents of Foreign Policy of U.S.S.R.), Vol. XI, pp. 302–7.
2. Ibid., pp. 386–89.
3. Agabekov, op. cit., p. 88.
4. Ibid., p. 89.

Chapter 22
1. Kinross, op. cit., p. 53.

Chapter 23
1. Ben James, *The Secret Kingdom,* p. 279.

Chapter 24
1. Wild, op. cit., p. 184 and p. 196.

Chapter 25
1. Wild, op. cit., p. 123.
2. Ibid., p. 178.

Chapter 27
1. Knightley and Simpson, op. cit., pp. 187–206.
2. Ibid., p. 176.
3. Ibid., pp. 115 ff.
4. David Garnett, ed., *The Letters of T. E. Lawrence,* p. 521, Letter 311, to Edward March, June 10, 1927.
5. Ibid., p. 600, Letter 355 to A. W. Lawrence, May 2, 1928.
6. Knightley and Simpson, op. cit., p. 263.
7. Garnett, op. cit., p. 614, Letter 362 to H. S. Ede, June 30, 1928.
8. Ibid., p. 615, Letter 363, to G. B. Shaw, July 19, 1928.
9. Ibid., p. 618, Letter 364, to E. M. Forster, August 6, 1928.
10. Ibid., p. 615, Letter 363, op. cit.

Chapter 28
1. Najibullah, "Afghanistan in Modern Times," p. 366.
2. Habibullah, *My Life From Brigand to King,* is the source of some material, pp. 2–5 and pp. 28–30.

Chapter 29
1. Louis Dupree, "Mahmud Tarzi, Forgotten Nationalist," p. 9.
2. Flora Armitage, *The Desert and the Stars,* pp. 258–63.
3. Wild, op. cit., pp. 244–46.

Chapter 30
1. Agabekov, op. cit., p. 159.
2. M. N. Roy in *The Radical Humanist,* June 27, 1954, p. 307.

Chapter 33
1. Agabekov, op. cit., p. 159.
2. Ibid., pp. 165–69.
3. Louis Fischer, *Men and Politics,* p. 144.

Chapter 34
1. Agabekov, op. cit., p. 169.
2. James, op. cit., p. 277.

Chapter 35
1. Dupree, op. cit., p. 12.

Abdul Ghani, Dr., A Review of the Political Situation in Central Asia; Lahore, 1921.

Abdur Rahman, The Life of Abdur Rahman, Amir of Afghanistan, edited by Mir Munshi, Sultan Mohammed Khan, 2 vols., London, John Murray, 1900.

Adamec, Ludwig W., Afghanistan 1900–1923, a Diplomatic History; Berkeley, Calif., University of California Press, 1967.

Agabekov, Georgei, O.G.P.U., the Russian Secret Terror; New York, Brentano, 1931.

Allworth, Edward, et al. Central Asia, a Century of Russian Rule; New York, Columbia University Press, 1967.

American Universities Field Staff, K. H. Silvert, ed., Expectant Peoples, Nationalism and Development; New York, Random House, 1963.

Armitage, Flora, The Desert and the Stars; New York, Henry Holt, 1955.

Auboyer, Jeannine, The Art of Afghanistan; Middlesex, Hamlyn House, 1968.

Bailey, Col. F. M., Mission to Tashkent; London, Jonathan Cape, 1946.

Beloff, Max, Imperial Sunset, Vol. 1, "Britain's Liberal Empire," 1897–1921; New York, Alfred A. Knopf, 1969.

Birkenhead, Earl of, Halifax, the Life of Lord Halifax; Boston, Houghton Mifflin, 1966.

Bonarjee, N. B., Under Two Masters; Calcutta, Oxford University Press, 1970.

Bowles, Chester, Promises to Keep; New York, Harper and Row, 1971.

——, A View from New Delhi; New Haven, Yale University Press, 1969.

Brun, Capt. Alfred Harald, Troublous Times, Experiences in Bolshevik Russia and Turkestan; London, Constable and Co., 1931.

Busch, Briton Cooper, Britain, India and the Arabs, 1914–21; Berkeley, Calif., University of California Press, 1971.

Caroe, Sir Olaf, The Pathans; London, Oxford University Press, 1958.

Castagné, Joseph, *Notes sur la Politique Extérieure de l'Afghanistan depuis 1919*; Paris, Librairie Orientale et Américaine, n.d.

Chirol, Sir Valentine, *India Old and New*; London, Macmillan, 1921.

Clifford, Mary L., *The Land and People of Afghanistan*; New York, 1962.

Coates, W. P. and Zelda K., *A History of Anglo-Soviet Relations*; London, Lawrence and Wishart and Pilot Press, 1945.

Copeland, Miles, *The Game of Nations*; New York, Simon and Schuster, 1969.

Curzon, George Nathanael, *Tales of Travel*; New York, George H. Doran, 1923.

Deacon, Richard, *A History of the British Secret Service*; New York, Taplinger, 1969.

Dillon, E. J., *The Inside Story of the Peace Conference*; New York, Harper, 1920.

Douglas, William O., *Strange Lands and Friendly People*; New York, Harper, 1951.

——, *West of Indus*; New York, Doubleday, 1958.

Dunbar, Janet, *Mrs. G.B.S., a Portrait*; New York, Harper and Row, 1963.

Dupree, Louis, *Mahmud Tarzi, Forgotten Nationalist*, in South Asia Series, Vol. VIII, No. 1, Afghanistan; American Universities Field Staff Reports Service; January 1964.

Edib, Halide, *Inside India*; New York, Macmillan, 1938.

Edwardes, Michael, *Glorious Sahibs*; New York, Taplinger, 1968.

——, *A History of India From Earliest Times to the Present Day*; New York, Farrar, Straus and Cudahy; 1961.

——, *The West in Asia*; New York, G. P. Putnam, 1967.

Etherton, Percy T., *In the Heart of Asia*; Boston, Houghton Mifflin, 1926.

Felix, Christopher (pseud.), *A Short Course in the Secret War*; New York, E. P. Dutton, 1963.

Fischer, Louis, *The Life of Lenin*; New York, Harper and Row, 1964.

——, *Men and Politics*; New York, Duell, 1941.

——, *Russia's Road From Peace to War*; New York, Harper and Row, 1969.

——, *The Soviet in World Affairs*, 2 vols., London, Cape, 1930.

Fletcher, Arnold, *Highway of Conquest*; Ithaca, N.Y., Cornell University Press, 1965.

Forbes, Archibald, *The Afghan Wars, 1839-40 and 1878-80*; London, Seeley, 1896.

Forbes, Rosita, *The Forbidden Road, Kabul to Samarkand;* New York, E. P. Dutton, 1937.

Fouchet, Maurice, *Notes sur l'Afghanistan;* Paris, Éditions Maison neuves Ferres, 1931.

Frankel, Charles, *High on Foggy Bottom: an Outsider's Inside View of Government;* New York, Harper and Row, 1969.

Fraser, Sir Andrew H. L., *Among Rajahs and Ryots;* Philadelphia, J. B. Lippincott, 1911.

Fraser-Tytler, Sir W. Kerr, *Afghanistan, a Study of Political Developments in Central and Southern Asia;* London, Oxford University Press, 1953.

Fredericks, Pierce G., *The Sepoy and the Cossack;* New York, World, 1971.

Furon, Raymond, *L'Afghanistan;* Paris, Librairie Scientifique Albert Blanchard, 1926.

Garnett, David, ed., *The Letters of T. E. Lawrence;* New York, Doubleday, 1938.

Grassmuck, George, et al., *Afghanistan, Some New Approaches;* Ann Arbor, Mich., University of Michigan, 1969.

Graves, Robert, and Liddell Hart, B. H., *T. E. Lawrence and His Biographers;* New York, Doubleday, 1963.

Gray, John A., *At the Court of the Amir;* London, Richard Bentley, 1895.

Gregorian, Vartan, *The Emergence of Modern Afghanistan;* Stanford, Calif., Stanford University Press, 1969.

Griffiths, John C., *Afghanistan;* New York, Frederick A. Praeger, 1967.

Gunther, John, *Inside Asia;* New York, Harper, 1938.

Habibullah, Amir, *My Life From Brigand to King;* London, Sampson, Low, Marston and Co., Ltd., 1936.

Hamidi, Hakim, *A Catalog of Modern Coins of Afghanistan;* Kabul, Ministry of Finance, 1967.

Hamilton, Angus, *Afghanistan;* London, William Heinemann, 1910.

Hedin, Sven, *My Life as an Explorer;* New York, Boni and Liveright, 1925.

von Hentig, Werner Otto, *Mein Leben eine Dienstreise;* Göttingen, 1963.

A Hindu Nationalist (pseud.), *The Gandhi-Moslem Conspiracy;* R. D. Ghanekar, Poona, 1941.

Hitti, Philip K., *Islam and the West;* Princeton, N.J., D. Van Nostrand, 1962.

Hunter, Edward, *The Past Present, a Year in Afghanistan;* London, Hodder and Stoughton, 1959.

Hyde, H. Montgomery, *Lord Reading;* New York, Farrar, Straus and Giroux, 1967.

Ikbal Ali Shah, *Afghanistan of the Afghans;* London, Diamond Press Ltd., 1928.

——, *Modern Afghanistan;* London, Sampson, Low, Marston and Co., Ltd., 1938.

——, *The Tragedy of Amanullah;* London, Alexander Ouseley, 1933.

——, *Westward to Mecca;* London, H. F. and G. Witherby, 1928.

India, Army Headquarters, General Staff Branch, *The Third Afghan War, Official Account;* Calcutta, Government of India, Central Publication Branch, 1926.

James, Ben, *The Secret Kingdom, an Afghan Journey;* New York, Reynal and Hitchcock, 1934.

Jewett, A. C., *An American Engineer in Afghanistan,* edited by Marjorie Jewett Bell; Minneapolis, University of Minnesota Press, 1948.

Jones, Thomas, *Whitehall Diary;* Vol. 1, 1916–25; London, Oxford University Press, 1969.

Judd, Denis, *The Victorian Empire;* New York, Frederick A. Praeger, 1970.

Katrak, Sorab K. H., *Through Amanullah's Afghanistan;* Karachi, D. N. Patel, 1929.

Kharas, K. J., Ghandi, R. D., and Saroff, K. D., *Pedalling Through the Afghan Wilds;* Bombay, Bhandari, 1935.

King, David Wooster, *Living East;* New York, Duffield, 1929.

King, Peter M., *Afghanistan: Cockpit in High Asia;* London, Geoffrey Bles, 1966.

Kinross, Baron, *Ataturk: a Biography of Mustapha Kemal;* New York, William Morrow, 1965.

Klass, Rosanne, *Land of the High Flags, a Travel Memoir of Afghanistan;* New York, Random House, 1964.

Knightley, Philip, and Simpson, Colin, *The Secret Lives of Lawrence of Arabia;* New York, McGraw Hill, 1970.

Lamb, Harold, *Babur, the Tiger;* New York, Doubleday, 1961.

Lawrence, A. W., ed., *T. E. Lawrence by His Friends;* New York, Doubleday Doran, 1937.

Liddell Hart, B. H., *Colonel Lawrence, the Man Behind the Legend;* New York, Dodd, Mead, 1934.

Lockhart, R. H. Bruce, *British Agent*; New York, G. P. Putnam, 1933.

Longford, Elizabeth, *Queen Victoria, Born to Succeed*; New York, Harper and Row, 1964.

MacLaine, Shirley, *"Don't Fall Off the Mountain,"* New York, W. W. Norton, 1970.

Macrory, Patrick, *The Fierce Pawns*; Philadelphia, Lippincott, 1966; published in England as *Signal Catastrophe, the Story of the Disastrous Retreat from Kabul, 1842.*

Maillart, Ella K., *Turkestan Solo*; London, William Heinemann, 1938.

Martin, Frank A., *Under the Absolute Amir*; London, Harper, 1907.

McKelway, St. Clair, *The Big Little Man From Brooklyn*; Boston, Houghton Mifflin, 1969.

Mele, Pietro Francesco, *Afghanistan*; Florence, La Nuova Italia, n.d.

Melia, Jean, *Visages Royaux de l'Orient*; Paris, Bibliothèque Charpentier, 1930.

Mohammed Ali, *The Afghans*; Kabul, privately printed, 1965.

———, *A Cultural History of Afghanistan*; Kabul, 1964.

———, *Progressive Afghanistan*; Kabul, 1964.

Molesworth, G. N., *Afghanistan 1919, an Account of Operations in the Third Afghan War*; Bombay, Asia Publishing House, 1962.

Montagu, Edwin S., *An Indian Diary*, edited by Venetia Montagu; London, William Heinemann, 1930.

Moraes, Frank, *Jawaharlal Nehru*; New York, Macmillan, 1956.

Morris, James, *Pax Britannica*; New York, Harcourt, Brace & World, 1968.

Mosley, Leonard, *The Glorious Fault; the Life of Lord Curzon*; New York, Harcourt, Brace and Co., 1960.

Moyi-ud-din, *Bohran va Najat-i-vatan*; Kabul, 1931.

Murphy, Dervla, *Full Tilt, Ireland to India with a Bicycle*; New York, E. P. Dutton, 1965.

Najibullah, "Afghanistan in Modern Times"; unpublished manuscript prepared for Princeton University, 1961.

Nehru, Jawaharlal, *Toward Freedom*; New York, John Day, 1941.

Nicholson, Harold George, *Curzon: the Last Phase*; Boston, Houghton Mifflin Co., 1934.

Payne, Robert, *The Life and Death of Mahatma Gandhi*; New York, E. P. Dutton, 1969.

Pazhwak, Abdur Rahman, *Afghanistan, Ancient Aryana*; London, 1958.

Pernot, Maurice, *En Asie Musulmane, l'Inquiétude de l'Orient;* Paris, Librairie Hachette, 1927.

Philby, Kim, *My Silent War;* New York, Grove Press, 1968.

Poullada, Leon, *The Pushtun Role in the Afghan Political System;* New York, Asia Society, Afghanistan Council, Occasional Paper 1, 1970.

Pratap, Mahendra, *My Life Story of 55 Years;* Delhi, Rajhans Press, 1947.

Rahimi, Nour M., editor, *Kabul Times Annual;* Kabul, Kabul Times Publishing Agency, 1967.

Rand, Christopher, *Mountains and Water;* New York, Oxford University Press, 1965.

——, *A Nostalgia for Camels;* Boston, Little Brown, 1957.

Rao, J. Sambasiva, *King Amanullah;* Madras, Asiatic Nation Builders Series, 1929.

Rishtya, Sayed Kassim, "Between Two Giants"; unpublished English translation, published in Russia as *Iu. V. Gankovskii, Afghanistan v. XIX veke,* Moscow, 1958.

Roberts, Field Marshal Earl (of Kandahar), *Forty Years in India;* London, Macmillan, 1921.

Ronaldshay, Earl of, *India, a Bird's-Eye View;* Boston, Houghton Mifflin, 1924.

Rose, Kenneth, *Superior Person, a Portrait of Curzon and His Circle in Late Victorian England;* New York, Weybright and Talley, 1969.

Samra, Chattar Singh, *India and Anglo-Soviet Relations;* Bombay, Asia Publishing House, 1959.

Scott, George B., *Afghan and Pathan, a Sketch;* London, Mitre Press, 1929.

Shah Wali, Marshal, *Yaddashta-i-man;* Kabul, 1959.

Shor, Jean Bowie, *After You, Marco Polo;* New York, McGraw Hill, 1955.

Sinclair, G., *Khyber Caravan;* New York, Farrar, 1936.

Speer, Albert, *Inside the Third Reich;* New York, Macmillan, 1970.

Starr, Lilian A., *Tales of Tirah and Little Tibet,* London, Hodder and Stoughton, 1923.

Stratil-Sauer, Gustav, *From Leipzig to Kabul; an Account of My Motorcycle Ride to Afghanistan and My Nine Months' Imprisonment in That Country;* London, Hutchinson, 1929.

Sulzburger, Cyrus L., *A Long Row of Candles, Memoirs and Diaries, 1935–1954;* New York, Macmillan, 1969.

Swinson, Arthur, *North-West Frontier;* New York, Frederick A. Praeger, 1967.

Sykes, Sir Percy, A *History of Afghanistan*, Vol. 2, London, Macmillan, 1940.

Tanzi, Gastone, *Viaggio in Afghanistan*; Milano, Casa Editrice, Maia, 1929.

Thomas, Lowell, *Beyond Khyber Pass*; New York, Century, 1925.

Thornton, Ernest and Annie, *Leaves From an Afghan Notebook*; London, John Murray, 1910.

Toynbee, Arnold, *Experiences*; London, Oxford University Press, 1969.

———, *A Study of History*, parts 1–4, abridged; New York, Oxford University Press, 1947.

Trinkler, Emil, *Through the Heart of Afghanistan*, translated by B. K. Featherstone; Boston, Houghton Mifflin, 1928.

U.S.A., Department of State documents, National Archives, Washington.

U.S.S.R., Ministry of Foreign Affairs, *Dokumenty Vneshnei Politiki S.S.S.R.*, Vol. IX, January 1–December 31, 1928.

Viollis, Andrée, *Tourmente sur l'Afghanistan*; Paris, 1930.

Walder, David, *The Chanak Affair*; New York, Macmillan, 1969.

Waley, Sir Sigismund David, *Edwin Montagu, a Memoir and an Account of His Visits to India*; New York, Asia Publishing House, 1964.

Watkins, Mary B., *Afghanistan, Land in Transition*; Princeton, N.J., D. Van Nostrand, 1963.

Wheeler, Geoffrey, *The Modern History of Soviet Central Asia*; New York, Frederick A. Praeger, 1964.

Wheeler, Stephen, *The Ameer Abdur Rahman*; London, Bliss, Sands and Foster, 1895.

Wilber, Donald N., *Afghanistan, Its People, Its Society, Its Culture*; New Haven, Human Relations Area Files Press, 1962.

Wild, Roland, *Amanullah, Ex-King of Afghanistan*; London, Hurst and Blackett, 1932.

Wilson, Lawrence, *The Incredible Kaiser, a Portrait of William II*; New York, A. S. Barnes, 1963.

Wolfe, Nancy Hatch, in collaboration with Ahmad Ali Kohzad, *A Historical Guide to Kabul*; Kabul, Afghan Tourist Organization, 1965.

Newspapers consulted:

U.S.A.
New York Times
New York Herald-Tribune

New York World
New York Post
Chicago Tribune
Washington Star
Washington Post

GREAT BRITAIN
London Times
Daily Mail
Daily Telegraph
Observer
Daily Express
Dispatch
Morning Post
Nottingham Post
Manchester Guardian
Irish Independent

AFGHANISTAN
Aman-i-Afghan
Tulu-i-Afghan
Ittihad-i-Mashriqi
Islah
Anis
Seraj-ul-Akhbar
Kabul Times

OTHER COUNTRIES
Pravda, Moscow, U.S.S.R.
Izvestia, Moscow, U.S.S.R.
Pioneer, Bombay
Civil and Military Gazette, Lahore
Zamindar, Lahore
Milap, Lahore
Kesari, Lahore
Chronicle, Bombay
Sarhad, Peshawar
Angar, Peshawar
El Ahram, Cairo
Milliett, Istanbul
La Tribuna, Rome
Indian National Herald
Excelsior, Paris
Gazette de Lausanne, Switzerland

OTHER PUBLICATIONS

Asia

Asie française, monthly bulletin of Comité de l'Asie Française

Central Asian Review of Central Asian Research Centre in association with St. Antony's College, Oxford

Foreign Affairs

Journal of Royal Central Asian Society

Literary Digest

National Geographic

New Yorker

Time

INDEX

Surnames were rare in Afghanistan; in some cases a name in parentheses refers to the family. Not all the enormous cast of characters are included. Amanullah's name in the index has generally been abbreviated to A.

Abdul Ahad, Minister of Interior, accompanies A. to Kandahar, 469–70; commands in battle for Ghazni, 537, 540–41; loses A.'s confidence, 565

Abdul Aziz (Charkhi), 100; is sent to govern Mazar-i-Sharif because of undoubted loyalty and faqir's prophecy, 427

Abdul Aziz, is sent by Bacha Sacao to escort Nadir home from France, 500–1

Abdul Ghani, Dr., is freed from prison on A.'s accession, 38; delegate to Rawalpindi Conference, 80; resigns as Director of Education, 143

Abdul Hakim, Trade Agent, Peshawar, excoriates Nadir, 537–38; Bacha Sacao tries to remove, 546

Abdul Hadi, editor of *Aman-i-Afghan*, 60; delegate at Mussoorie Conference, 119–21; envoy to Bokhara, 160–77; Minister to Britain, 191; British fear caustic comments of, 249; as Minister of Trade negotiates with Russia, 399; fears A. too hasty in reform, 399; is only official to read document given by Bacha Sacao to sign, 481; flees to Kandahar, 555–56

Abdul Hamid, Sultan of Turkey, 8, 208

Abdul Karim, son of ex-Amir Yakub, goes to Khost in 1924 to claim throne of Afghanistan, 265–67, 278–79; kills self in Burma, 282–85

Abdul Karim, Governor of Kandahar, quarrels with A., 512–13

Abdul Quddus, confers with A. on death of father, 34; Prime Minister, 38, 131; General in War of 1919, 47, 63; suggests A. as Caliph of Islam, 72; negotiates in Khost Rebellion, 268

Abdul Wahab (Tarzi), attends Oxford, 199; Foreign Minister at Kandahar, 510; member of battlefield court, 564

Abdul Wahid, Shinwari, alias Mr. Wade, Australian, "Camel King of Australia," offers services to British provided they do not aid A., 451–53; friend of Nadir, 452; linked with pretender, Omar, 460

Abdur Rahman, Amir, 1889–1901, 4, 125, 132–34, 181; fantasy on reception in England, 349

Abdur Rahman, Afghan envoy to India, 60; tries to make peace, 62–63

Abdur Rahman, Begtuti, Judge, arrested in mullah plot, 391, 393, 396

Abedah, daughter of Amanullah, 294; married to son of Wali, 574

Acheson, J. G., delegate at Kabul Conference, 146

Adam, J. H., head of Afghan Bureau, Central Intelligence Division, 96

Administrative procedure, 131–33, 400–1

Agabekov, Georgei, Russian intelligence Agent, leads Russians to Enver Pasha in Bokhara, 208; reports attitude and involvement of Russia in rebellion, 549, 561–62, 582

Agriculture, 260–1, 289, 293, 307

Ahmed Shah, cousin of Nadir, commands guard on night of Amir Habibullah's murder, 29; asks to leave country, 318; sent by Bacha Sacao to bring Nadir home, 500–1

Ahmed Shah Abdali, founder of Afghanistan, 350, 514

Ajab, fugitive in Ellis murder and kidnaping, 219–22, 224–26, 236–39, 243–47; folk hero on frontier, 487

Akbar, Haji, 399; delays British reaction to Nadir's call to British tribes, 572

Akhunzada, Mahmud, Mullah of Khanki Bazaar, intermediary in rescue of Molly Ellis, 225–27

Ali, son-in-law of Prophet, 112, 131

Ali Ahmed (Shahgassi), 279, 331, 382; prominent in Nasrullah's attempt to take throne, 32–33; Chief Delegate at Conference of Rawalpindi, 79, 81–95; marries sister of A., 94; disturbs A. by ambition and flamboyance, 302–4; asks British to neutralize Russia in rebellion against A., 314–15; accompanies A. abroad, 321; negotiates for A. with rebellious tribes, 448, 460, 461; becomes Amir in Jalalabad, 495–97; defeated and humiliated, 497–98, 518; attempts to conspire in Peshawar until British order him out, 521–22, 531; returns reluctantly to A., 532; Amir in Kandahar, captured, killed, 569

Aliah, daughter of Nasrullah, marries A., 462, 527; divorced, 584

Humphrys, Sir Francis (*cont'd*)
respect, 438; warns London of disaster
if Legation harmed, 449; argues with
A.'s men who burst into Legation
grounds, 450; arranges evacuation for
Inayatullah and family by British aircraft, 474; arranges evacuation of all
foreigners in Kabul by British in first
airlift, 449–50, 453, 492–94, 495,
515–18; departs Kabul himself, 516; is
noncommittal in talk in Peshawar
with Nadir who presses him to state
British preference for King, 519–21;
tells Ali Ahmed he must leave India,
521–22; receives Nadir's requests for
aid, 543; reports A.'s prospects as
hopeless, 504, 546–47, 565; leaves India, 546, 558
Humphrys, Lady, helpful at Legation during attack, 437–38, 441, 449–50; years
later in London helps A.'s daughter,
580
Hylan, John F., Mayor, New York, 170

Ihsanullah, son of Amanullah, 580
Inayatullah, half brother of Amanullah,
Amir Habibullah's heir, 8, 128; favors
Turks in Great War, 18; present at
scene of father's murder, 29; renounces
throne to Nasrullah, 33–34, 38; plays
secondary role in Amanullah's reign,
73, 129, 195, 262, 301–2, 404; favored in Tagao as King, 415, 442; de-
clines A.'s offer of throne, 423; accepts throne, 466; becomes King, 471;
besieged in Arg, flees to India in British plane and travels by train and car
to Kandahar, 473–75, 477–78, 483;
renounces throne in Kandahar, 485;
goes to India with A., 567; death, 580
India, permitted use of Army in Great
War by Afghan neutrality, 8–21; disturbed by agitation for independence,
41–44, 46, 54–56, 62, 136, 152, 161–
62, 186–87, 213; Indian Civil Service,
69–70; enthusiastic toward A. on visit,
323–26
Industry, 202, 204–5, 289, 293, 301,
307, 347, 354, 411
Ireland, Afghan sympathy for, 144–46,
148, 158; U.S. arms for, 172
Irwin, Lord, Viceroy of India, unable to
greet A., 324–25; predicts Russian neutrality, 491; deplores decision to send
mail bag to Kabul instead of Kanda-

har, 493; hopes for Nadir's success,
501
Islam, 2, 115–17, 133, 135–43
Italy, first country to make trade agreement with Afghanistan, temporarily
blocked by British, 167–68, 200; receives A., 309, 338–40; home of A. in
exile, 574, 579–80, 584

Jalalabad, scene of Habibullah's murder,
29–36, 79; attacked in War of 1919
and bombed from air, 61–64, 104; attacked by Shinwaris, 417–23; blown
up, 499
Jalianwalabagh, square in Amritsar, India, scene of massacre, 39, 42–44
James, Ben, U.S. writer, quoted, 396
Japan, approached by A., 37
Jehad, holy war, 11, 44–47, 50, 55, 62,
65, 71, 74, 112, 268, 270, 273
Jemal Pasha, Turkish Minister of Marine, 9; in Kabul, trains Army, 136,
160, 162, 261; suspected of intrigue
by British, 149–52, 155, 157–58; negotiates in Bokhara for Afghans, 259
Jirgas, 112, 193–95, 214, 223–24; Loe
Jirga of 1924, 257, 259, 263–65; Loe
Jirga of 1928, 383, 386–89; Loe Jirga
of 1930, 575
Justice, traditional, 23, 38, 102, 196–97,
236–38, 279, 288–90, 293, 342; qisas,
execution by family of victim, 342,
575; stoning to death, 280–81; applied to Europeans, 282; *see also*
Nizamnamas

Kabir, half brother of Amanullah, self-
exiled in father's reign, 128–29; inept
Minister of Health, 300; accepts Bacha
Sacao, 472, 480
Kabul, bombed in War of 1919, 64, 67,
104; attacked by Bacha Sacao, 422,
425–28, 435–42, 445–67, 471; captured by Bacha Sacao, 472–75; captured by tribes under Shah Wali, 572–
73
Kalinin, Mikhail, President, Russia, 360
Kandahar, 46; protests conscription, 210,
263–65; visited by A. for scrutiny of
government, 287–93, 369; A.'s capital
during rebellion, 454 ff.; falls to Bacha
Sacao, 569
Karakhan, Leo, Deputy Foreign Commissar, Russia, 77, 107; talks with A.,
363